PRAISE FOR

Daniel Patrick Moynihan

"His letters recorded the evolving intellectual adventure of a restless mind. . . . This whole collection has been put together with superb care. While writing this review, I've been cursing Weisman's introduction for its mastery in highlighting all the crucial points in Moynihan's life. It is hard to write anything about this book that doesn't repeat that fine essay. Weisman has also written superb contextual paragraphs between the letters, so even people unfamiliar with Moynihan's career will be able to follow along easily. . . . [Moynihan] remains an exemplar for those who find that their lives and views don't fit neatly into a partisan camp, a guiding model for hybrids past and future."

—David Brooks, *New York Times Book Review*

"[This book] will probably be read more widely and for longer, and certainly with greater pleasure, than any of the others on the Moynihan shelf. . . . Steven R. Weisman has sculpted a work of coherence and energy. . . . [The] tensions and crosscuttings make for a stimulating book, just as they made for an adventurous mind and an eventful life."

—*The New Yorker*

"Students of history, philosophy and literature will find it hard to resist Mr. Moynihan's endless musings and eyewitness accounts of pivotal moments in twentieth-century history, from the assassination of President John F. Kennedy to India's ascent as a nuclear power."

—*New York Times*

"[A] portrait of a brilliant man, who made mistakes and owned up to most of them, but didn't resist intellectual battle." —*Chicago Tribune*

"A current celebration of Sen. Daniel Patrick Moynihan's ebullient life as an academic, diplomat, White House advisor, author and, finally, as a senator, underscores the lack of wisdom, wit, civility and vision that prevails in the legislature today. Stand advised to do yourself a favor by acquiring the just-published, *Daniel Patrick Moynihan, A Portrait in Letters of an American Visionary*. It's an invaluable history lesson and bewitching as well." —*Forbes*

"This is an autobiography written in real time. It offers a portrait of an American civic original, with an exuberant personality and a vibrant mind, both an optimist and a skeptic, full of a passion for putting ideas into action. And while the book doubles as an intimate history of the second half of the 20th century, its primary impact on me was something more than nostalgia: it made realize how much we need more Moynihans in our politics." —The Daily Beast

"Elegantly edited. . . . George Will has already skimmed the cream of Moynihan quotes and, quite rightly, praised Moynihan's eloquence and brilliant insights. His accomplishments are well-known. That leaves me with the scraps. But what scraps!" —Politico

"'Everyone,' Moynihan liked to say, 'is entitled to his own opinion, but not to his own facts.' Now, thanks to Steven Weisman's meticulous editing . . . everybody is entitled to Moynihan's opinions."
—George F. Will, *New York Post*

"The book is a rich treasury of the thoughts, casual and profound, of an elected official who in many ways seemed straight out of the best tradition of our early nineteenth-century leaders." —*Buffalo News*

"Moynihan is a delight to read. He was a gifted writer, funny, wry, quick with an allusion and good with a phrase, even as he stoked his own legend and trumpeted his prescience." —*Washington Monthly*

Daniel Patrick Moynihan

THE PUBLISHER AND EDITORS OF

Daniel Patrick Moynihan,
A Portrait in Letters of an American Visionary

JOIN WITH THE MOYNIHAN FAMILY IN EXPRESSING GRATITUDE
TO THE MAXWELL SCHOOL OF SYRACUSE UNIVERSITY
FOR ITS SUPPORT OF THIS BOOK.

Daniel Patrick Moynihan

A PORTRAIT IN LETTERS
OF AN AMERICAN VISIONARY

EDITED WITH AN INTRODUCTION BY

Steven R. Weisman

PUBLICAFFAIRS
New York

PublicAffairs books are available at special discounts for bulk purchases in the
U.S. by corporations, institutions, and other organizations. For more
information, please contact the Special Markets Department at the Perseus
Books Group, 2300 Chestnut Street, Suite 200, Philadelphia, PA 19103, call
(800) 810-4145, ext. 5000, or e-mail special.markets@perseusbooks.com.

Book design by Timm Bryson

Library of Congress Cataloging-in-Publication Data
Moynihan, Daniel P. (Daniel Patrick), 1927–2003.
    Daniel Patrick Moynihan : a portrait in letters of an American visionary/
edited by Steven R. Weisman.—1st ed.
      p. cm.
    Includes index.
    ISBN 978-1-58648-801-7 (hardcover)
    1. Moynihan, Daniel P. (Daniel Patrick), 1927–2003—Correspondence. 2.
Statesmen—United States—Correspondence. 3. United States. Congress.
Senate—Correspondence. 4. United States—History—20th century. 5. United
States—Politics and government—20th century. I. Weisman, Steven R. II. Title.
III. Title: Portrait in letters.
    E840.8.M68A4 2010
    973.92092—dc22
    [B]
                              2010022134
ISBN 978-1-61039-217-4 (paperback)
ISBN 978-1-56848-920-5 (e-book)

CONTENTS

Photo insert between pages 346 and 347

INTRODUCTION BY STEVEN R. WEISMAN

Daniel Patrick Moynihan led a singularly American life, but it was a life unlike any other in modern America.

As a youth in New York, Pat Moynihan struggled with poverty in a family devastated by the disappearance of his father at the height of the Great Depression. Young Pat shined shoes, tended bar, worked the piers as a longshoreman, and stole rides by clinging spread-eagled to the back of the crosstown bus to get to high school in Harlem. He briefly attended City College of New York before joining the Navy as a teenager during World War II. He served as a gunnery officer, traveled the world, returned to complete an undergraduate degree from Tufts, and studied in London, where he sought to define himself at the age of twenty-three. He wandered almost accidentally into campaign politics in New York City. And he then rose to become perhaps the most influential public intellectual of his time.

Moynihan was a pathfinder in John F. Kennedy's New Frontier, a commander in Lyndon Johnson's War on Poverty and Great Society, and an enabler in many greater and lesser moments of Richard Nixon. He was a renowned professor at Harvard well before becoming a successful politician. He was an outspoken envoy and challenger of shibboleths and of anti-Semitism while serving as ambassador to India and the United Nations. In four terms in the Senate—working with (or against) Presidents Carter, Reagan, Bush, and Clinton—he made a decisive impact in the areas of welfare reform, public works, transportation projects, international law, congressional prerogatives in the cold war, and the challenge to the cult of secrecy in Washington. He achieved these goals while setting a standard of bipartisanship sorely missed today. Determined that a nation's public spaces should reflect the legacy of its ideals, he was instrumental in the effort to revive some of America's greatest urban environments, from the Custom House in Lower Manhattan to

1

Union Station and Pennsylvania Avenue in the nation's capital. The span of his history was such that upon Moynihan's retirement in 2000, President Clinton bestowed on him the Presidential Medal of Freedom—the very honor that Moynihan had himself recommended be established under President Kennedy.

Above all, Moynihan, who died in 2003, was the originator of powerful ideas that were also powerfully argued—ideas that actually helped transform how Americans think about their country, its internal fissures and its place in the world. He understood early on, based on his studies and his own experience, that the breakup of poor black families contributed to the spread of crime and unrest in the cities—and he was attacked as a racist by some who a generation later admitted that Moynihan had been right all along. He recognized that ethnic and nationalist identities were far more powerful than ideology, religion, or politics in tying cities and nations together—and splitting them apart. As early as 1979, he predicted the fall of the Soviet Union, saying it would crack up from economic stress and ethnic conflict. Less well known, Moynihan was an early champion of automobile safety in the 1950s and is the one who brought Ralph Nader to Washington, jolting General Motors and causing a national uproar in the 1960s.

"Everyone is entitled to his own opinion but not to his own facts," Moynihan famously said, in one of many comments that entered political lore and that, if applied, would make for a healthier national discourse today. There were many other memorable turns of phrase, each distinguished by its surface elegance and underlying thought. He deplored the tendency to wish away society's ills—"defining deviancy down," as he put it. Criticizing the misguided social engineering of antipoverty programs, he declared: "The role of social science lies not in the formation of social policy, but in the measurement of its results." "The iron law of emulation" was the phrase he used to describe how the bureaucracies of groups in conflict (like the United States vs. the Soviet Union) tend to become more and more like each other over time. "Tangle of pathology" was the way he summed up the tragedies of poor black families. "The time may have come when the issue of race could benefit from a period of 'benign neglect,'" he wrote to Nixon, advising him to lower the rhetorical temperature on race—and employing two words that haunted Moynihan for years. One of the most important axioms of Moynihan's career, from his book *Family and Nation*, based on the 1985 Godkin Lectures at Harvard, sums up a basic internal conflict of Moynihan's calling as a scholar and advocate—his belief that government policies can make a difference, combined with skepticism toward the limitations of government programs and bureaucracies. "The central conservative truth is that it is culture, not politics, that determines the success of society," Moynihan wrote. "The central liberal truth is that politics can change a culture and save it from itself."

Moynihan's ideas live because of this evocative, candid, pungent, and sometimes dangerously pellucid style, which he applied to the eighteen books that he wrote or edited, and in countless speeches, interviews, and essays.

Less well known, he brought that same style to the private letters and journals he wrote from his earliest years in public life. The purpose of this book is to bring that important part of Moynihan's life to light—to offer "a portrait in letters" of someone who turns out to have been a man of letters in every sense of the word. In this volume, Moynihan's ideas, achievements, and quarrels—and the sheer joy and outrage he derived from political combat—can be savored for the first time by the public beyond the circle of friends and acquaintances to whom he vouchsafed his inner thoughts in private correspondence. The ideas highlighted here, moreover, can be applied in new ways to the personalities and issues of today.

Not only did Moynihan write letters. He saved copies, voluminously so, of even the most trivial among them. More than 10,000 pages of letters, journals, and personal memoranda repose in the Library of Congress, to which Moynihan bequeathed all of his papers. Indeed, they are the largest single collection of personal papers that the Library possesses. The fact that Moynihan saved his letters demonstrates the importance he must have attached to them as his way of processing the events of his life and the evolution of his thinking. He no doubt intended them for historians, which is why he left them to the Library of Congress. That we have these letters also indicates that from his earliest years he possessed a distinctive sense of himself and his destined place in history.

I first met Pat Moynihan in the early 1970s, shortly after he left the Nixon White House staff to return to Harvard, and I followed his career closely after that as a correspondent, editor, and editorial writer for the *New York Times*. What I found in editing these letters is not so much a different Moynihan, but a Moynihan more passionate, intimate, vulnerable, combative, and perhaps more self-absorbed than the one seen by the public.

There are moments that almost take your breath away. His memorandum to himself, for example, following the JFK assassination—the news came at a meeting with some Kennedy loyalists in Georgetown—is unforgettable. "Oh no! Killed! No!" he writes. Then the "dead silent" scene later in the hallway outside the Cabinet room: "Someone said, 'It's over.'" There is an acutely ironic letter advising Robert Kennedy on where he might live in New York when running for the Senate in 1964 (Moynihan leans toward Long Island), foreshadowing Hillary Rodham Clinton's awkward house-hunting when she prepared to run to succeed Moynihan in the Senate. There is a painfully honest letter to Senator Ted Kennedy after Bobby's assassination in 1968 (though never sent), worrying about the racial divisions sowed by the campaign that had just been cut down. "I loved Bob," he writes to Ted, even while lamenting that RFK's drive for the black vote had alienated working-class whites. "Those are your people," he adds, referring to the whites. "They were Bob's people before he got religion, they have been abandoned, and our politics are very much the worst for it."

Because he was a Kennedy man, Moynihan's relationship with Johnson was uncomfortable. There is a striking letter from Moynihan to Johnson summarizing the findings of what later became known as the "Moynihan Report," about the importance of broken family structures among the poor. Johnson's labor secretary, W. Willard Wirtz, forwarded this letter to the president, describing it as "nine pages of dynamite about the Negro situation." Moynihan writes to LBJ: "You were born poor. You were brought up poor. Yet you came of age full of ambition, energy, and ability. Because your mother and father gave it to you. The richest inheritance any child can have is a stable, loving, disciplined family life." In this message, Moynihan seems to be clearly thinking about his own upbringing and yearning for what he never had himself.

Moynihan's communications with, and about, Nixon must surely be counted as among the richest literary trove of that toxic era of war protests and racial violence. Nixon, unfailingly gracious to the other Harvard professor (besides Henry Kissinger) on his team, called for the wide internal distribution of Moynihan's lengthy private memoranda, which backfired when someone leaked Moynihan's memo recommending a policy of less overheated rhetoric, or "benign neglect." Moynihan's letters include his searing analysis of race, the war and student radicals, and his pleas to the president to let the Vietnam War be Johnson's and not Nixon's war. Imploring Nixon not to reescalate the conflict after the failure of the Vietnam peace talks, Moynihan wrote at the end of 1972: "I know there is an authoritarian left in this country, and I fear it. . . . Only in the last few months have I begun to feel that the advantage was turning to us and that, while it would take all of the 70s and more, the manner and the principles of democratic republicanism would now prevail. I say to you that all this is risked if the war is resumed."

Some months later, in Nixon's second term, Moynihan wrote painfully from distant India, where he was ambassador, watching in agony as Watergate consumed the Nixon presidency. After defending Nixon's record to liberal friends—citing the importance of welfare reform, the environment, and aid to education—Moynihan suddenly must admit that he too readily accepted Nixon's defense that lower-level aides had carried out the break-in and cover-up. "Have I been a fool or a whore or both?" Moynihan writes his close friend Nathan Glazer. "Or perhaps something quite different: something perhaps to be forgiven."

Moynihan's letters as senator are more businesslike, but always revealing. Included here are his lengthy confidential pleas to the first President Bush not to go to war with Saddam Hussein, but to invoke sanctions instead. In the post–cold war world, Moynihan promoted the idea of a new global order based on international law, much to the irritation of his old conservative friends. Having foreseen the end of the Soviet Union, he became preoccupied by the intelligence establishment's failures in overestimating Soviet economic and military power. There are rich communications with both Hillary and Bill Clinton about health care and what reads in part like a vivid travelogue reporting to Clinton on his visit to the Balkans, which was plummeting into ethnic conflict. "What is to be done?" he asks in this letter. "Probably not a great deal." But in studying the future of such conflicts he tells Clinton: "I beseech you not to ask the CIA. It is brain dead and should be honorably interred."

Beyond presidents, Moynihan had an astonishing circle of correspondents. He wrote to famous intellectual friends like Glazer, Kissinger, George Kennan, Irving Kristol, John Kenneth Galbraith, Lionel Trilling, James Q. Wilson, and William F. Buckley Jr., challenging them in a friendly way about disagreements, defending his views, and recounting his frustrations. He wrote to journalists, columnists, and editors, often in indignation over a project overlooked or misunderstood. (Woe to any writer who abused the phrase "benign neglect" or called him a neoconservative!) He wrote to politicians, intellectuals, and authors (Alexander Solzhenitsyn, Saul Bellow, Eric Hoffer, and John Updike), famous people (Jacqueline Onassis, Woody Allen, Yoko Ono, the cartoonist Herblock). And of course he wrote to constituents, collectively and singly. He wrote limericks and doggerel, scurrilous and innocent. And he wrote candid memorandums to himself about his conversations with presidents and prime ministers, including his testy dealings with the Clintons over health care and welfare. You can see the tribal nature of his Democratic politics, his love of old-line party organizations and disdain for Democratic "reformers" in such letters as the one to the Tammany Hall boss Carmine De Sapio, then serving time in federal prison for corruption, inviting him to Harvard when he gets out. ("I never got to know you fellows very well. . . . But I never for a moment doubted my fondness for you all.") Moynihan wrote notes or letters to publishers, doctors, tailors, shopkeepers, and the caretakers of his upstate farm, asking about money, ailments, the holes in his socks, and the latest efforts to clear a stream near his farmhouse. And finally he wrote to the secretary of the navy asking to be buried in Arlington Cemetery.

In the age of emails, it is common to lament the lost art of letter-writing, but Moynihan's letter-writing seems almost self-consciously of the nineteenth century. He could be simultaneously profane and elegant, with a sense of history and of literary trivia. You can actually picture Pat in his office, or in the one-room schoolhouse on the grounds of his farm in upstate Delaware County—his favorite place to write—pounding on his Smith Corona and apologizing for the typing errors.

But the letters also feel utterly contemporary.

At one level, they provide a unique and wide window into the tumultuous politics, debates, and social upheavals—not to mention the major actors—of the second half the twentieth century. At another, they shine a light on the dramas and conflicts of our era at the second decade of the twenty-first century. They entertain us, of course, with his wit and sparkle, his foibles and feuds, his acerbic criticism and gift for flattery. But they also bear a lasting relevance, because they bring Moynihan's clarity, understanding, and farsightedness toward the intractable questions and cultural conflicts with which the nation struggles today. It is perhaps not unusual for academics to see and delineate the longer term implications of contemporary battles, as Moynihan did, on such enduring issues as climate change, health care, welfare, the federal budget, the uses and misuses of intelligence, national defense, global ethnic and sectarian conflict, race, and family strains. But for a politician to embrace this kind of long-term thinking is extraordinary. Moynihan's solutions did not always match his vision. Indeed he was tentative about some proposals because he understood the limits of what government can do. But he avoided bogus solutions for political gain, and he insisted that facts not be ignored, especially those relating to lingering poverty and social deprivation. By maintaining friendships with leading Republicans and Democrats, he also tried to transcend the corrosive partisanship of Washington. In that sense, ironically, he used his status as a kind of misfit in politics to become a uniquely successful and beloved politician.

Finally, by living out loud through his correspondence, Moynihan left behind his distinctive voice and vision in these pages. The result in this book is what one might think of as the memoirs Moynihan never wrote. If we need a Pat Moynihan today, in this volume, at least, we have him. How the book happened is a story itself.

My first encounter with Pat Moynihan was unpromising. In the early 1970s, I was a newly minted reporter for the *New York Times*, exiled to the night shift and sent off to hear him speak at the American Irish Historical Society, at its elegant Fifth Avenue townhouse. I had read a couple of Moynihan's books. I knew also that Moynihan had made a forgettable foray into New York politics years earlier when he ran for City Council president and lost to another Irish-American politician named Frank O'Connor. It turned out not to be Moynihan's best evening. Carefully reading from a text about obscure aspects of the Irish experience in America, he put his audience to sleep, and that included me and a *Daily News* reporter who kept addressing him as "doc." No doubt he was an unusual presence, peering down from the podium at the puzzled audience. But it was inconceivable that within a half decade he would be representing New York in the Senate.

I caught up with Moynihan again in the late 1970s as a *Times* correspondent in Washington. By then he was comfortably settled on Capitol Hill, a rangy and already graying presence with his droopy bow tie, elaborate courtesy, obscure allusions, and syncopated speaking style. He could be painfully formal one moment and hilariously sarcastic the next. His press briefings were inevitably like seminars. ("Class dismissed," he would say at the end.) He had one of the most brilliant staffs on Capitol Hill, including Tim Russert, famous for his uncanny popgun-like imitations of the senator and later responsible for inviting him on *Meet the Press* dozens of times.

After covering the White House during Reagan's first term, I became bureau chief in New Delhi. Through that adventure my relationship with Moynihan and his family deepened. Before we left, Pat, who had served as ambassador to India from 1973–1975, had my wife, Elisabeth Bumiller, and me to dinner at his townhouse on Capitol Hill with his wife, Elizabeth, and daughter Maura. The senator himself came late, but we had an uproarious evening of stories about India. "Is it true you were constantly sick in New

Delhi?" my wife asked him. "I was only sick *once!*" he replied. "It lasted two and a half years!"

The Moynihans introduced us to many friends in India, and these friends became our friends. We also frequently saw Liz and Maura, who visited almost every year. I remember Liz in India juggling her interests in archaeology and history in South Asia with part of her mind focused back on New York—and how Pat was going to raise funds or campaign in Dutchess County. Maura, who had fallen in love with India the moment her family arrived in 1973, became a scholar of Hindu and Buddhist culture, a fluent Hindi speaker, and an organizer for the "Festival of India" in Washington in 1985. Once, my wife came home for lunch and found Maura relaxing with an entourage of street musicians, dancers, and jugglers sitting on the floor of our living room.

In the late 1980s, before we went off to my next assignment, Elisabeth and I had drinks with Pat in Washington. There was a lot of speculation then about who the Democrats would choose as their vice presidential candidate. "Why isn't anybody mentioning *me?*" Pat demanded with an ironic smile. But as near as I can tell, he loved the Senate and always rebuffed suggestions that he run for national office.

After moving back to New York in the early 1990s, we visited the Moynihans at their upstate farm. From their white clapboard house, Pat guided me in the pale afternoon sunlight up a hillside, past a meadow and a stream to a wooded area with two big cedar trees next to a little one-room schoolhouse with wild roses growing in front. This was the nearly sacred hideaway that he used for writing and reading. Inside it was crammed with memorabilia, pictures, and maps. I remember him pointing on the map to the network of New York's watersheds—and barking out in staccato how the drainage systems of the Susquehanna, Mohawk, Hudson, and Delaware Rivers shaped George Washington's strategy in the Revolutionary War. To visit Pat in that tiny room at Pindars Corners was to experience the vast range of his intellect, curiosity, and heart.

Liz Moynihan persuaded her husband not to run for a fifth term in 2000 so they could enjoy his retirement together. Sadly, that was not to be for long. Following his death, Maura came up with the idea of a book of his private correspondence. The problem was that Pat's papers are spread through more than 3,000 boxes at the Library of Congress, where a team of specialists took years to catalog them.

When my friend Peter Osnos at PublicAffairs asked me if I might edit the letters and journals into a book, I was intrigued. I was leaving the *Times* after a career of writing and editing in New York, Washington, and overseas, moving to a new life at the Peterson Institute for International Economics, but I hesitated. I frankly feared the job would be overwhelming. Then Liz suggested that we ask for research help from the Maxwell School at Syracuse University, where Pat held his first teaching job after serving Governor W. Averell Harriman in New York—and his last teaching job as a visiting professor upon his retirement. The school's dean, Mitchel Wallerstein, who has since left to become president of Baruch College in New York City, generously agreed to fund the work of a dozen Syracuse students and graduates to go through the boxes and photograph the letters under my direction, which made it possible to produce this book.

To understand the arc of Pat Moynihan's life, it is important to know, first, that he came from a broken home of the kind he wrote about in the famous "Moynihan Report" in 1965 about poor minority families in the cities ("The Negro Family: The Case for National Action"). Moynihan's grandfather emigrated as a teenager to the United States from County Kerry in Ireland in the 1880s. His father, a journalist and advertising copy writer—and a drinker and gambler once beaten by gangsters to whom he owed money—walked away from the family in 1937, when Moynihan was ten. The father went on to acquire a new wife and family—never to see Pat again—though in the early 1950s Pat's brother, Michael, tracked him down in California, where he was a reporter for the San Jose *Mercury*. Pat's mother struggled through two more marriages, many jobs, and constant moves, mostly around the New York area. Moynihan's odd jobs helped the family make ends meet.

   The earliest personal papers in the Moynihan collection are the documents that deal most extensively with his family's particular "tangle of pathology." They are from a journal he kept when he was a graduate student at Tufts but living in London with a Fulbright grant at the London School of Economics. It was there that he struggled to write his doctoral dissertation from the fall of 1950 to the summer of 1953. The topic was the history of the International Labor Organization, or I.L.O., and he did not complete the dissertation until 1961.

   Moynihan humorously entitled his journal: "An Intellectual History of Our Times: Being a Descriptive Journal of Adventures and Meditations Having Occurred to the Author During a Grand Tour of Great Britain, Ireland and the Continent of Europe." You might therefore think that he intended even these writings to be made public some day. But they contain many private annotations about his family and his prodigious romantic and sex life, in part because he used the diary to recount his lengthy sessions with a psychoanalyst. The diary entries are fragmentary, but illuminating and often explicit—probably the most introspective writing that he produced. Many entries were private and should remain so. But other parts are extraordinarily revealing about who he was, and who he wanted to be. They tell us much about the evolution of a young and ambitious student trying to establish the identity that came to fruition in his later work.

To begin with are the troubled reflections about his father and mother, no doubt the psychological basis for his deep lifelong commitment to defining family stability as a key to a society's success.

"My relations are obviously those of divided allegiance," he wrote in that journal. "Apparently I loved the old man very much yet had to take sides. . . . I must think it out more clearly—I have from an early age been called upon to choose between mom and pop—choosing mom in spite of loving pop." At another point: "Both my mother and father—They let me down badly. The interesting thing is that I have almost no memory of dad—and no emotions—on the other hand I find thru the years this enormous emotional attachment to Father substitutes—of whom the least rejection was cause for untold agonies—the only answer is that I have repressed my feelings towards dad—Now then we have inductively established the emotions about the father, but have not as yet come up with them ourselves in the analysis. I'll try. . . ." And still another entry, reporting that he was making progress in his free-associating sessions with the psychiatrist: "As when I left Tuesday full of sudden and warm feeling for my father—we'd been talking about how much I liked him, I'd be going over old memories—all of them good. That night at Everyman I was literally overwhelmed by simple tender childish emotions. . . . I am getting somewhere I know it."

Moynihan's ambitions (lofty and otherwise) are clear. "If I can sit down and do this I shall not only greatly advance myself socially but I shall improve myself personally—I want to advance socially because only in so doing will I have a chance to do the work I want to do and that is important—In a sense I want to improve personally because only then will I really feel up to picking myself a wife—today I'm still out for delicious sex or a mother. . . . A wife and a job—simple enough."

But he did not seek merely to climb the rungs of society. He wanted to be witty, erudite, and charming like the people he met in the parlors and pubs of

London and the common rooms of Oxford and Cambridge. "I never like the first impression I make—maybe it will be a big obstacle for me," he wrote in 1950. And then later: "God I wish I were more entertaining. I am never up to sustaining a real conversation with anyone. I would like to be an English novel character—full of stories and odd bits of fascinating info."

He wanted to become. . . . *Daniel Patrick Moynihan!*

As two of his biographers, Godfrey Hodgson and Douglas Schoen, have shown, Moynihan discovered his political center in these years. It was defined by sympathy for the working class, the labor movement, and the British Labour Party—but revulsion toward Communism in unions, and also the kind he encountered in complacent upper-class drawing rooms, where anti-Americanism was rampant. He immensely enjoyed defending his country in public. "I was hot in my subject, knew it well and gave a damned good talk," he said of one of his appearances. "Figured I had my audience with me. First question from an anchor: Did I think Roos. [Roosevelt] started the war. . . . I fumed and fulminated . . . whilst they shot one asinine absurdity after another. Loved it tho—loved arguing for something bigger than myself which I thought was right."

London certainly posed its frustrations. ("The weather is shitty. I am not reading the great books and am not getting laid.") But he wandered its byways, studied its architecture, and took in its many charms, from debates at Parliament, where he found Churchill disappointing ("He is old now and apparently never was very quick") to a pageant-filled concert at Royal Festival Hall where the conductors Malcolm Sargent and Adrian Boult led symphonic works by Handel, Purcell, Elgar, and Vaughn Williams. The audience, Moynihan gushed, included the prime minister, the king, and the archbishop of Canterbury. "The great personalities everywhere . . . the wonderful aristocrats beplumed with medals and ribbons and sashes—very much a medal evening. . . . The English women utterly handsome . . . smacking of Empire, etc. . . . Midway, Sargent did a real thundering, booming, storming, stomping, stand up version of Rule Britannia and believe <u>that</u> crowd went wild!"

Moynihan also relished his travels in France, where he further developed his love of history, art, architecture—and the pleasures of food, drink, and female companionship. "Off to Blois and the great Chateau of the Orleans Regime," he wrote in one entry. "Pretty exciting—most of all the aile Gaston d'Orleans 1635 which is Mansart [the architect] at the greatest. So perfectly beloved it seemed to float. The Francois I wing was good with the Duc de

Guise death dramatized by the guard whose French I somehow managed to understand. Loved the monsignor of Henry II, Catherine of Medici his wife and Diane of Poitiers his mistress. . . . H everywhere even on the prie dieux at Chambord. Set out walking down to Tours but by the time the drivers began thumbing their nose at us we were getting disheartened when we [ran] . . . into an Auberge de Jeunesse at the Blois-les-Grouets. . . . Communist posters in German. . . . Trekked into the village for shopping—huge pork chops, butter, wine, bread, etc. and gorged. . . ." Another entry describes "the most perfect picnic ever by a wide rippling stream in soft green grass and hot sun. Wine bread and cheese and am I happy. . . ."

In London Moynihan seems to have acquired his distinctive British linguistic tics, such as "whilst," "of a sudden," and starting sentences with the word "mind." At times he had writer's block, distracted as he was by the partying, drinking, and serial romantic liaisons. (Mind, this was years before he met Liz.) He also struggled with doubts about whether he really was suited to be an academic, as opposed to someone more engaged in public life. Ultimately, of course, he found a way to incorporate both. He continued his love of teaching in numerous settings—at the university, as an advisor to presidents, as an envoy, and finally, as an elected official. "What bullshit I write—just reading Edmund Wilson—even his deliberately [fourth] rate characters talk better than I," he says in 1952. His friend Frank Fenton, later a steel industry executive, shares Moynihan's career doubts. "Frank thinks teaching is a mistake for me: I am not quite smart enough to get by without working and I simply do not like academic work. If I liked it I would long ago have done my thesis etc. etc. He's right, isn't he?"

Around Christmas time of 1952, as Moynihan began preparing to return to the United States, he revived the conversation about his livelihood with Fenton, with whom "once more with his great lucidity we discussed my career and my increasing distress with the idea of becoming a half-baked academic who's growing more and more bitter at being deprived of the fruits of the great wide world beyond and being increasingly unsatisfied with the bitter fruit of the withered vines of my ivory tower. I just do not have the stamina for a professor. I can't study like that and that's all there is to it."

Moynihan gave some thought to journalism, perhaps to writing books. One idea for a book appears to have come from a conversation in late 1952 with Theodore H. White, then a young writer for *Time* magazine ("wonderful guy—Boston Jew") who had covered the Communist revolution in China (and who later transformed political journalism with his "Making of the President" series and an article in *Life* magazine that described the brief Kennedy presidency as "Camelot"). They talk about how the Irish used politics to integrate themselves into American culture. "Good idea for a book," Moynihan wrote in his journal. A decade later, he was writing that very book (*Beyond the Melting Pot*) with Nat Glazer, to whom he had been introduced by Irving Kristol, then editor of the magazine *The Reporter*. It was to become a road map for much of his later work. ("I would be delighted to try to do the Irish essay for you," Moynihan later wrote Glazer in 1960, at the beginning of a wonderful lifelong friendship, which is brought to life in their correspondence.)

The decade of the 1950s, following Moynihan's time in England, is unfortunately little revealed by Moynihan's letters, however. In this period he fell into politics at the suggestion of a friend, first as a speechwriter in the successful mayoral campaign of Robert F. Wagner Jr. in 1953 and then as an aide to Averell Harriman, the wealthy patrician diplomat and cabinet member under Roosevelt and Truman, who was elected governor of New York in 1954 and who harbored presidential ambitions throughout the decade. While working for Harriman in Albany, Moynihan met Elizabeth Brennan, whom he soon married. The letters show deep affection for Wagner, who much later tried to recruit him to City Hall, and a friendship tinged by occasional difficulties with Harriman, whose single four-year term in Albany was plagued by political missteps. (Nelson Rockefeller defeated him in 1958.) In one letter, Moynihan says that after serving the imperious Harriman in the state capitol, Harriman continued to treat him as an "indentured" servant for years. It did not help their relations when Harriman's third wife, Pamela, campaigned for the liberal feminist Representative Bella Abzug and spread stories about Pat's drinking during the Democratic primary for Senate in 1976. (After Averell died, Pamela Harriman became a doyenne of the Democratic Party and an ambassador to France, but no friend of Pat's. Indeed he tried, as noted in a letter in this book, to blackball her from the Century Club: "It is depressing to say this, but I would find it difficult to enter the Century were there any prospect of this person being there.")

In 1961, Moynihan eventually finished his dissertation—"The U.S. and the I.L.O., 1889–1934"—and got his PhD from Tufts, just as he was also writing the Irish chapter for *Beyond the Melting Pot*. His letters from the 1960 presidential campaign, meanwhile, reflect his close ties to the Democratic kingpins in New York and his passion for Kennedy. Like the Kennedy enthusiast Arthur Schlesinger Jr. at Harvard, Moynihan disdained the liberal reformers of the university world who clung to the former Illinois governor Adlai Stevenson, who had lost twice to Dwight D. Eisenhower. ("Thus my argument comes to this: Kennedy can win," he wrote to a Tufts colleague.) But for Moynihan, Kennedy—the dashing Harvard-educated war hero, Pulitzer Prize–winning author, son of the business buccaneer and New Dealer Joe Kennedy, and grandson of the mayor of Boston—was the beau ideal of Irish Catholic Democratic politics. The letters also show although Moynihan loved teaching, he made strenuous efforts after the election to get a job in the Kennedy administration—followed by letters to colleagues explaining that he had not sought such a position but that the Kennedy team wanted him and, after all, duty called.

It was logical for the ambitious author of a dissertation about the I.L.O. to go to Kennedy's Labor Department. There he became a protégé of Labor Secretary Arthur J. Goldberg, later a Supreme Court justice and (like Moynihan) U.N. ambassador. (Moynihan edited a volume of Goldberg's papers in 1966.) But Pat was not about to let a policy job in the Labor Department restrict his reach. With brilliant bureaucratic ingenuity, he leveraged his power to become a policy maker on urban affairs, poverty, race, and federal architecture. (He also served as the labor secretary's representative on a presidential commission to plan for new office space in the nation's capital, from which post he launched a lifelong campaign to revitalize Pennsylvania Avenue.) How Moynihan came to the war on poverty is portrayed in the letters. He seized on a report by the Selective Service, about the weaknesses of draft-age youth, to write a report entitled "One Third of a Nation," which called attention to the general problems of health, unemployment, family structures, and "manpower conservation" in urban and rural America. His findings led to a role in drafting the anti-poverty program that Kennedy planned and Johnson continued.

It is clear from the letters that President Kennedy's murder shattered Moynihan. Everyone of a certain age knows exactly where he or she was when the news first flashed. Moynihan took the trouble to write that note about where he was to himself. But for him the event would also be enshrined in his famous conversation with the columnist Mary McGrory, then of the *Washington Star*, and a close friend and neighbor. She wrote about it in the newspaper. He went further, obtaining a transcript from radio station WTOP and keeping it in his files, as if he knew it would be recalled for the rest of his life: "I don't think there's any point in being Irish if you don't know the world is going to break your heart eventually. I guess we thought that we had a little more time . . . heavens, we'll laugh again, it's just that we'll never be young again."

Johnson's presidency was a testing time. Moynihan had become a semi-famous intellectual after the publication of *Melting Pot* and was writing memos, included in this book, about poverty, the African American family, and job training. The problem, however, lay with those around Johnson who thought Moynihan was getting too much publicity. For years, Moynihan sought to explain in letters that he never intended for the "Moynihan Report" to become a big story, and that it was Bill Moyers, LBJ's press secretary, who provided it to journalists. The furor predicted by Labor Secretary Wirtz forced the Johnson White House to disassociate itself from Moynihan, a bitter pill for many years. ("I am now known as a racist across the land," he wrote the civil rights leader Roy Wilkins.) To make matters worse, there was also a dispute over Moynihan's role in doing a first draft (later reworked by Richard Goodwin) for LBJ's important Howard University address in 1965 proclaiming the goal of achieving "not just equality as a right and a theory but equality as a fact and as a result." Moynihan later wrote to Johnson and others that despite what many thought, he never sought credit for the speech. "I was sorry that my name somehow got into the papers. . . ." Moynihan wrote LBJ. "I should tell you that I left for a U.N. conference in Yugoslavia three hours before you gave it. Someone told someone, but it wasn't me." One does not need Freud to come from the grave to recall the diary entry from his London years about Moynihan's "enormous attachment" to—and fear of rejection from—"father substitutes."

Notwithstanding LBJ's suspicions, Moynihan had never been close personally to JFK. He was much closer to Bobby Kennedy when, five years after Dallas, history cruelly repeated itself. In 1968, Moynihan campaigned for RFK in the Democratic presidential primary in California and stopped off at his hotel to wish him good luck before flying back to Cambridge. But the candidate was napping and so he never said goodbye. Then Bobby too was felled. Again and again in these letters, Moynihan recounts to the Kennedy clan, with a mixture of anguish and attempts to ingratiate himself, that he had missed this final opportunity to swear his fealty. You can feel how membership in that tribe was as demanding as it was rewarding. It was all the more painful for Moynihan, then, to see the Kennedys moving away from their white, working-class constituents who loved them. Sometimes he even felt that Bobby had abandoned that base, as he suggests in the draft of the letter to Ted, mentioned above. Other times he tried to convince people that Bobby actually was more aligned with Moynihan on domestic issues than many supposed—as when he writes Schlesinger, who was researching a biography of

RFK, that Bobby told someone else that a Moynihan article reflected his own views.

One of the themes of Moynihan's writings and letters was his disdain for social engineering measures. He explained in correspondence that in analyzing the problems of African American families, the solution lay not in social work but money and jobs. He thus derided the "community action programs" and "maximum feasible participation" of the poor in the War on Poverty, the theme of his book *Maximum Feasible Misunderstanding* in 1969. As a political scientist, Moynihan was skeptical about government-sponsored social work. As a party politician, he understood that establishing rival power bases of poverty bureaucrats in big cities would threaten local mayors and political organizations, producing conflict and paralysis. This is exactly what happened in the anti-poverty programs in New York City.

The cleverness of Moynihan was that he was able to take this prescient critique to a Republican administration, as illustrated in his letters. The idea of simply making sure that poor families had more money, and were not punished if the father left the family or got a job, was in many ways conservative, he argued all along. Thus while backing Kennedy and then Hubert Humphrey in 1968, Moynihan also quietly reached out to Nixon on the side, writing the Republican nominee from Harvard: "If you are ever in the Cambridge area, we should be enormously honored to have you as a luncheon speaker. . . . This is a forum which is not without advantages for you, but of course the greatest benefit would be to the faculty and graduate students here who would be fascinated to learn more of your views. . . ." What we also see in the letters is that later in the White House, Moynihan sold Nixon on the guaranteed annual income, which became the Family Assistance Program (FAP), as a Republican idea. "It will be the center piece in your domestic program—truly an historic proposal," Moynihan wrote the president in 1969. In another letter he told Nixon that his administration would be "moving away from a services strategy in dealing with the problems of social inequality, toward an income strategy." Translation: FAP would provide resources to the poor but not empower the liberal do-gooders distrusted by Nixon.

While working for Nixon, Moynihan tried to hang on to his Kennedy ties. Hence his letters to Ethel Kennedy, Robert's widow, and his attempts to convince Ted Kennedy of his closeness to Robert and of the genuine interest that Jackie Kennedy had in the Pennsylvania Avenue renewal project. He even asks Jackie to reach out to Teddy and tell him that Nixon was more supportive of Pennsylvania Avenue than Johnson had been.

He pleads also in these letters for Ted to support the FAP—painfully, without success. Kennedy tells Moynihan that the income floor for poor families was too low and that Massachusetts, New York, and other states would see their own federal welfare budgets cut. Liberal distrust and conservative concern about federal giveaways killed the plan in 1970, permanently reducing Moynihan's influence in Nixon's inner circle and hastening his departure. The Democratic opposition wounded him the most, however. A deeply hurt Moynihan urges Kennedy to stop abusing the phrase "benign neglect" by invoking it against Nixon. Ted Kennedy is polite but not especially warm in return. Much later in the 1980s and 1990s, Moynihan forged a closer working relationship with the last of the Kennedy brothers, and there is a warm letter of gratitude to Ted for standing with him against President Clinton's signing legislation ending welfare as an entitlement in 1996.

There was simply nothing more complicated in Moynihan's career than his relationship with Nixon. It is important to recall, first, how it was buffeted by the chaos of the times—the race riots in the cities, the campus rebellions, the poisonous distrust across generations, and between liberals and working-class conservatives. Much of it was fomented by hot rhetoric from the administration. From his early days as a Communist hunter, Nixon had been one of the most divisive figures of his era. In his letters you can feel Moynihan trying at times to appeal to Nixon's better angels, advising him to keep cool and embrace liberal reforms by following the example of the "Tory men and Whig measures" of the nineteenth-century British prime minister, Benjamin Disraeli. At other times Moynihan tries to mount the ramparts with Nixon and stoke his venom toward crime, black militants, student uprisings, and antiwar protests. Uneasy about the Nixon White House from the start, Liz Moynihan declined to move with the family to Washington. They remained in Cambridge. This was the period that turned many onetime liberals into conservatives—or neoconservatives, a term Moynihan detested. (He regarded it as a left-wing slur.) The letters repeatedly show Moynihan amazed and outraged that his liberal friends could not appreciate Nixon's support for the poor, not to mention health care reform, revenue sharing with the states, establishment of the Environmental Protection Agency, and federal aid to schools. After Nixon resigned from office in 1974, Moynihan kept up his correspondence, and Nixon generously returned Moynihan's loyalty. ("Keep swinging!" Nixon wrote Moynihan when he was an embattled envoy at the U.N. "Don't let that Irish temper of yours drive you into resigning. . . . After all if you could get along with me as long as you did, when I know you were disappointed in some of my decisions on the war as well as in the domestic area, you can get along with anybody!")

For me, Moynihan's letters in the era of Nixon and his successor, Gerald Ford, are among the most powerful documents of their time. It is in these writings that one sees Moynihan growing alienated from the liberal world and the ivory tower, but still feeling some solidarity with that world, trying to understand it, and yearning for its approval. His writing bristles with resentment toward those he viewed as pampered liberal elitists who lacked appreciation of the white, working-class families like his own, but still seeing universities as the great promoters of equality in American society. He cannot believe his eyes and ears as he sees the leftist hatred from campuses and former allies in the civil rights movement. His letters to civil rights leaders and fellow academics are painful, poignant, and sometimes blunt, as when he tells a member of Harvard's board that "you need a man with balls" as president to stand up to the protesters.

Letters to those friends usually described as neo-cons are among the liveliest and most honest in this book, starting with Nat Glazer, with whom Moynihan had earlier corresponded about the drinking and sexual traits of the Irish and Jews. Moynihan confesses in his letters that his best friends were always Jews, but that Jews disappointed him because of their antipathy toward Nixon. When the 1973 Yom Kippur War broke out, Moynihan noted acidly from India that the same Jewish critics of Nixon and the Vietnam War were suddenly asking him to help Israel, as in this letter to Lionel Trilling: "I watch with pity and terror the antics of those who helped destroy the American Presidency—and it has not needed much external help—demanding that we put an end to our military role in the world, now demanding the very opposite and in terms that could impose a fearful cost."

Parallel to Moynihan's relation with Nixon is his rivalry, not always friendly, with Kissinger, his fellow Harvard professor at the White House. Seeing Kissinger (however implausibly) as a kindred spirit, Moynihan tried to draw him into his concerns about ethnic conflicts at home and overseas. Once Moynihan lost influence after the failure of the Family Assistance Plan, Nixon and Kissinger asked him to serve as envoy at the United Nations. Moynihan demurred, returned to Harvard, and instead went later to India. (He agreed to the U.N. job under Ford.) Moynihan's mission in New Delhi: to improve relations with Prime Minister Indira Gandhi two years after they had hit bottom as a result of the American "tilt" to Pakistan during the Bangladesh war of independence in 1971. Moynihan is dazzled by Kissinger's brilliance in helping him negotiate a crucial financial agreement with India, and he writes cogent letters to Kissinger analyzing the Indian political scene, especially its Marxist leanings and interplay of caste and ethnic conflicts, all of which played into his lifelong interests.

Glazer and others have pointed out that throughout his career, Moynihan traversed from domestic ethnic concerns in *Melting Pot* to his analysis of ethnicity in totalitarian societies (like Russia) and democratic ones (like India). His internationalization of the topic of ethnicity culminated in his 1993 book, *Pandaemonium*, about the post–cold war eruption of sectarian wars across the globe. The letters and journals from India in 1973–1975 make up, in their entirety, a remarkable exploration of the Asian subcontinent, as Moynihan reflected on whether India's socialist economy, which kept it mired in poverty, was nonetheless essential to keeping its fractious society intact. (He was also a terrific travel writer, as the journal of his marvelous trip to a coronation in Bhutan demonstrates.) In a different vein, Moynihan also warned the State Department—with chilling prescience—not to rearm Pakistan lest it "start pushing around the Pushtoons and the Baluchi ... pretty soon there will be a full scale insurgency going, and in time the further partition of Pakistan." The current American and Pakistani war against the Taliban, which has its bases in the same Pushtun and Baluchi areas, is playing out exactly as he predicted.

Moynihan's aversion to the third world America-bashing he found in India led to his important 1975 article in *Commentary*, "The U.S. in Opposition," which called for the United States to push back. But it was when he tried to translate those ideas into policy as U.N. ambassador that Pat's difficulties with Kissinger crested. The problem arose as Moynihan waged a highly publicized campaign to defeat a General Assembly resolution equating Zionism with racism, stirring accusations that he was using the issue to pave the way for running for the Senate from New York. Moynihan responded by renouncing any interest in the Senate. Still he became convinced that Kissinger stood with the critics, and his suspicions were confirmed in January 1976 when the columnist James Reston wrote in the *New York Times* that both Ford and Kissinger deplored their ambassador's tactics "in private." Moynihan knew a telegraphed message when he saw one. In this book are three resignation letters from Moynihan prompted by Reston's piece: a formal one to Ford, a cold one to Kissinger, and a white-hot angry one to Dick Cheney, then the White

House chief of staff, making clear that he felt stabbed in the back. ("It wasn't working, and it won't work. . . . God knows I tried.")

Years later, Moynihan wrote to one of his successors at the U.N., Jeane Kirkpatrick, that contrary to what she had heard from Kissinger, he had never thought about using the U.N. envoy's post as a stepping-stone to the Senate. But of course he eventually was persuaded to run for the Senate in 1976, despite his earlier disavowal, squeaking by Bella Abzug in the Democratic primary, in large part because of support from Jewish voters who remembered the Zionism-is-racism fight. Kissinger wrote Moynihan denying that he had ever tried to oust him from the U.N., as Moynihan charged again in an interview with *Playboy* magazine after he got into the Senate. Moynihan then offered the former secretary of state "a measure of apology" but continued for years to suspect him of underhanded tactics.

Missing from the letters, unfortunately, are any communications from Moynihan during his turbulent 1976 Senate campaign. The reason is simple. His campaigns (then and always) were run quietly and efficiently by Liz Moynihan, while Pat raced across the state.

Once in the Senate, Moynihan's relations with presidents, and his correspondence with them and others, changed somewhat. Now Pat had a major political base, a constituency to represent, and a powerful and prestigious new megaphone at his disposal. No longer an intellectual dabbling in politics, he was a major politician himself. Suddenly media appearances and speeches (on Capitol Hill and at commencements and other forums) were the focus of attention, though his letters embellish details and behind-the-scenes maneuvering.

Moynihan's ties to President Jimmy Carter in this period were not especially warm. One letter shows Moynihan disagreeing with Carter over the senator's bill to ease the welfare cost burden on New York, which the White House argued was undercutting the larger cause of welfare reform long championed by Moynihan. Reagan, after ousting Carter in 1980, brought Moynihan back to his liberal roots in many ways. Though Moynihan voted for Reagan's tax cuts in 1981, he later told correspondents that he eventually understood Reagan's plan to be a cynical one of tax reductions so drastic they were intended to "starve the beast," i.e. leave no money left for vital domestic programs. The Iran-Contra episode in Reagan's second term led to a thorough breach with the administration and with some of his conservative friends, including Podhoretz, Kristol, and Buckley. He defends himself in letters against charges that his dispute with the administration over Nicaragua was undermining the crusade against Communism in the western hemisphere. The senator argued that he could not fail to challenge the Reagan administration over its misleading of the Senate Intelligence Committee in the mining of Nicaraguan harbors— and its refusal to submit its actions to international courts.

President George H. W. Bush, by contrast, was a good friend from the Nixon years whom Moynihan wanted to support any way he could. Moynihan had stayed with Bush in Beijing on the way back to the United States from India and—as Pat noted in his journal—Barbara Bush even did his laundry. The last throes of the cold war in Bush's term were a moment of exquisite significance for Moynihan—historically and personally—and for the politics of the American left, which he always felt had flirted irresponsibly with Communism, especially in the 1930s. Moynihan knew and debated with many of those intellectuals of what he called "the authoritarian left" in his note to Nixon, and so vindication at the end was sweet. Perhaps his most heartfelt expressions of joy are in his letters to his constituents, in which Moynihan cannot resist playing the professor, recalling the early debates about Communism and Socialism that he used to hear in Union Square. "I am now a man in his sixties; my first political memories are of New York City in the thirties," he wrote as he reminisced about those old rallies. "I'm going to ask you to be patient with me and let me walk you through some of those times and places." Equally penetrating are his thoughts expressed in memos to Senator George Mitchell, the senate majority leader, and memos to himself about his conversations with President Bush on the challenge posed by Iraq's invasion of Kuwait in 1990. Moynihan argued against a military response and favored economic sanctions instead. Bush tells Moynihan, according to Pat's memorandum: "I know you are committed the other way but wanted to talk with you anyway." The President then speaks of his concern over the coming loss of life. Moynihan responds: "Marines do not sign up for summer camp."

The Clinton era, coinciding with Moynihan's last term and greatest influence in the Senate, ironically produced more tensions than cooperation. These were spurred by a magazine article quoting an anonymous Clinton aide saying that the incoming White House, if necessary, would "roll over" Moynihan, who had just become Senate Finance Committee chair. Clinton was livid and apologetic, Moynihan records. But the wound didn't really heal. The letters record how both Pat and Liz Moynihan got their friend Senator Bob Kerrey of Nebraska to provide the crucial yes vote that led to approval of Clinton's budget in his first year. But there remained a fundamental disagreement between the senator and the White House on other priorities.

Moynihan records that he tried to convince both Hillary and Bill that they should set health care reform aside and push for welfare reform—to no avail. The Clintons were meanwhile irritated that on the eve of the president's big speech on health care, Moynihan appeared on *Meet the Press*, deriding the administration's "fantasy numbers" and declaring that there was "no health care crisis." They clearly viewed Moynihan as a gadfly scoring intellectual points without offering solutions. In a letter to Hillary in 1992, Moynihan called the breakup of families "the most important issue of social policy" facing the country but added, perhaps a bit self-importantly: "I picked up the early tremors, and have followed the subject for thirty years now. But haven't the faintest notion as to what, realistically, can be done."

On health care, the letters show Moynihan's somewhat pedantic side. The senator kept writing Hillary Clinton, urging that she consult William Baumol, a business professor at New York University, who had argued that rising health care costs were driven by factors beyond the government's ability to control. ("He has not heard from anyone, and still hopes he might.") Liz and Pat later got Hillary to meet with Professor Baumol at their apartment. But however interesting she may have found Baumol's analysis, Hillary obviously did not want to hear that little could be done to restrain costs. In the end, although Moynihan held hearings on health care and got the Finance panel to send a flawed bill to the floor, he wrote in his letters that he found the Clinton approach of elaborate cost controls and government regulation "coercive" and harmful to New York's teaching hospitals.

Moynihan remained bitter that Clinton supporters portrayed him years later as an obstacle to health care reform—note the angry letters to the *New York Times* for its article in 2000 endorsing that view. His irritation flared also in 1996, when he proudly and defiantly opposed the Republican-sponsored welfare "reform" that Clinton felt politically pressured to sign into law. That measure ended welfare as an entitlement, and Moynihan predicted that millions of children would soon be sleeping in the streets. He had memorably ridiculed Clinton's promise to "end welfare as we know it" as "boob bait for the Bubbas," a term he later said he regretted. But Moynihan did loyally stick with Clinton during the impeachment trials and other battles. And of course in 2000 he turned around and anointed Hillary as his successor in the Senate, without which she might not have won. Hillary responded that year by writing Pat: "If I had listened to you about health care in 1994, I would be far better off today—but more importantly—so would the nation's health care system."

The letters from these Senate years are replete with Pat's roving intellect and interests. He helped Bill Buckley with one of his spy novels. He tried to get into the *Guinness Book of World Records* for the longest word in the English language, just as he had earlier tried to get himself named for having written the biggest check in history (to India in 1974). He proudly persuaded the *Fontana Dictionary of Modern Thought* to run an entry by him on the definition of "ethnicity." He wrote about secrecy, "cop killer" bullets, human rights in the Soviet Union, and the science of acid rain. He wrote about his hard-luck upbringing, New York politics, and the need for government aid to parochial schools.

He wrote to the Vatican about its misuse of the word "liberal," to the *New Republic* about misusing the word "neoconservative," and to a Clinton cabinet member for incorrectly describing Social Security as an "entitlement" program. He wrote fundraising appeals and about his distaste for fundraising. He wrote sometimes self-indulgently about how few people appreciated his efforts to bring billions of dollars in aid to New York; that no one listened when he warned that someone might try to kill JFK's accused assassin; that no one understood earlier and better that minority families were breaking up under economic and social pressure; and that Communism was headed for collapse in the 1980s.

A powerfully-recurrent theme of Moynihan's letters and journals, finally, is his commitment to architecture and public and private spaces as the embodiment of American history and values. In his diary from the early 1950s, Moynihan recorded how he climbed to the top of the dome of St. Paul's Cathedral for its view of London. In a crypt at St. Paul's, its architect, Christopher Wren, is buried with the famous inscription, "Lector Si Monumentum Requiris, Circumspice," or, "Reader, if you seek his monument, look around." One could easily say the same (in Latin or English) for Moynihan's legacy in Washington and New York. In 1962, Moynihan wrote the "Guiding Principles for Federal Architecture," which remain in use by the General Services Administration. They call for architecture to reflect "the dignity, enterprise, vigor, and stability" of the national government and to embody "the finest contemporary American architectural thought" while eschewing "an official style." His subsequent efforts led to the renovation of Foley Square and the saving of the neoclassical Custom House in Lower Manhattan, the revitalization upstate of the Erie Canal, and the establishment of the Women's Rights museum and park at Seneca Falls. Hectoring letters to Governors

Cuomo and Pataki, and Mayors Koch, Dinkins, and Giuliani to get these projects under way attest to his persistence. The one unfinished project, of course, is the building of a new Penn Station in the beaux arts home of the old post office building on Eighth Avenue. When completed, it will deservedly be called Moynihan Station.

In Washington, Moynihan presided over the construction of the modernist Hirshhorn Museum, a part of the Smithsonian complex, and stopped the destruction of the old neoclassical Post Office, the beaux arts masterpiece that is Union Station, and the Pension Building, with its vaulted interior reminiscent of a Roman palace. All these projects had many champions, but without Moynihan's leadership they very likely would not have happened. It was a lifelong irony for Moynihan, as he tirelessly wrote in his letters, that he was attending a meeting in Georgetown on the Friday of November 22, 1963, to discuss plans for renovating Pennsylvania Avenue—then a squalid thoroughfare scarred by parking lots, pawn brokers, tourist traps, and sex shops a stone's throw from various nondescript government buildings. Their intention was to present their plans to President Kennedy upon his return from a political trip to Texas that weekend. After Kennedy's death, Jackie Kennedy asked LBJ to continue the project, but Moynihan wrote the architect Nathaniel Owings that Johnson seemed not to be following through. He pleaded with Owings not to abandon hope and wrote Jackie endlessly that he would persevere. The letters continued through the late 1980s, and when the project was just about completed, Jackie wrote Moynihan: "Twenty-five years is a long time to not give up on something. . . . I think that the completed Pennsylvania Avenue will be a monument to your dedication. I hope that Americans realize that. I will be forever grateful, dear Pat, for your messages to me all along the way, for the spirit you brought to something Jack cared about so deeply, and for this happy ending." Fittingly, a lovely plaza on the avenue has been named Daniel Patrick Moynihan Place in his honor.

In editing and preparing this book, I have often wondered whether these letters may also serve as a kind of monument to Moynihan, or at least a substitute for the autobiography he never got around to writing. My hope is that this legacy in letters, unlike any other in contemporary American history, reflects the plenitude of the man and his loyalties—without exaggerating his achievements or leaving out his foibles. It is fitting, in the end, that when Moynihan said farewell to his constituents and told them in his valedictory newsletter of his gratitude for the Presidential Medal of Freedom, he said it was a moment of joy and melancholy—in part because of the connection to the first president he served. He included in the newsletter a copy of the memorandum he had sent to President Kennedy in 1963, recommending that such a medal be established. Till the very end, Kennedy remained for Moynihan, as for many of his generation, the political leader who had pulled the sword from the stone.

Almost exactly forty years after that memorandum to JFK, Moynihan died and was buried in Arlington Cemetery, as he asked in one of the letters included in this book. His closing words in his last newsletter, written from the little schoolhouse in the woods, near a meadow and a stream in Pindars Corners, were: "So there it is. Outside the goldenrod mixed with blue aster is gleaming. And signaling time to go. And so again, Liz and I are ever grateful."

The country can be grateful, too.

A note on the text: Spelling errors, resulting from mistyping or other factors, have been corrected in the letters in this book.

CHAPTER ONE

"I Think We Are Going to Make History"

After a tour in the Navy and three years in graduate school, Daniel Patrick Moyni-han found himself in London on a Fulbright scholarship, studying at the London School of Economics while completing his dissertation on the International Labor Organization. The letters in this chapter trace his career concerns there to his time in the state capitol in Albany working for Governor Averell Harriman, and later at Syracuse University, and finally to his deepening interest in the campaign of Senator John F. Kennedy for the Democratic presidential nomination. In this period, he forms a partnership with his lifelong friend and coauthor Nathan Glazer, which in turn leads him into ethnicity as a scholarly subject. From there he serves President Kennedy first as an assistant to the secretary of labor and then as assistant secretary. The shattering event of Kennedy's assassination thrusts him into an uneasy rela-tionship with President Johnson, whom Moynihan suspected distrusted him as a Kennedy loyalist. Nevertheless, Moynihan pursues the explosive subjects of poverty, unemployment, and race, which came to define his career.

This first job application by Moynihan was submitted to the International Labor Organization in Geneva shortly after he arrived in London on a Fulbright to pre-pare his dissertation on the history of the I.L.O. It suggests that he was at least thinking about a career outside the academic world. The job did not materialize.

29 MARCH 1951

W. CALDWELL

HEAD OF PERSONNEL OFFICE

INTERNATIONAL LABOR OFFICE

GENEVA, SWITZERLAND

Dear Mr. Caldwell,

I am accompanying my application for the post of Member of Section in the Legal Division with a personal data sheet that should assist you in assessing my qualifications. For convenience I will here specifically refer to the categories enumerated in the Notice of Vacancy.

1. Nationality: United States of America
2. Age: 24
3. University Degree:
    Bachelor of Naval Science
    Bachelor of Arts (cum laude)
    Master of Arts
4. Technical qualifications: My best legal training is in the field of international law to which I have devoted much of three years of post-graduate training as well as five years of under graduate work. Having taught American Government, I have a good knowledge of American constitutional law and a fair knowledge of the subject as a whole. My general legal training has derived primarily from my studies of labor law which has been extensive, particularly since beginning work on my Ph. D. thesis "The United States and the International Labor Organization."
5. Languages: English is my native language. I have a good working knowledge of French, a fair reading ability in Spanish, and some German.

In closing I should like to point out that the position for which I am applying represents, for me, more than just a good job—it represents a career for which I have been preparing many years. The International Labor Organization is something I believe in; I want to work for it and with it. For my part I am certain that this is a job I can do and do well. I sincerely hope that I will be given the opportunity to do so.

While on his Fulbright, Moynihan became interested in Labour Party politics and met a number of left-wing intellectuals, giving rise to suspicion of Communist sym-

pathies by some in the armed forces. This letter to the commander of the "Office of Special Investigations" in the U.S. Air Force in London indicates his concern that suspicions of that he harbored Communist sympathies were not only misplaced— they could derail his career ambitions.

21 MAY 1953
COLONEL KIRBY M. GILLETTE
COMMANDING
OFFICE OF SPECIAL INVESTIGATIONS—U.K. DETACHMENT
UNITED STATES AIR FORCE
KEYSIGN HOUSE
421–429 OXFORD STREET
LONDON W.1

Dear Colonel Gillette:

I would like to thank you for the courtesy and understanding with which you received me on the 13th; throughout this unfortunate business you have been an unfailing source of reassurance and confidence without which I should be far more disturbed than I am. I deeply appreciate it and want you to know how grateful I am.

One thing remains. As you know, Captain Brown went over my "file" as you requested and afterwards pointed out to me a matter of such importance that I must bring it to your attention. When I was called in by Mr. Segal and told that I was suspected of communist sympathies, I was given to understand that this suspicion was based on two things: my having been seen reading the "Daily Worker" and having been seen at the Unity Theater. These of course are entirely circumstantial matters which of themselves indicate nothing whatever. Knowing of nothing else, I was appalled to think that so fantastic and potentially disastrous an allegation could rest on such meaningless trivia. It insults my intelligence to ask why I read the "Daily Worker." Besides, the Air Force buys it and posts it on our bulletin board, etc. That is why I came to you, explained my concern, and asked if there was not something else behind all this. If there was I wanted a complete and exhaustive investigation of every allegation made against me. If there was not, I wanted an apology. I repeated this request to Major Jaynes at some length, but I was not told of any other allegation. Now I understand, from Captain Brown, that there was another. An allegation of an entirely different order than the insignificant nonsense I was originally told about: some person or persons have alleged that during 1951 I made statements evidencing a sympathy with communism. This is not true. But it is an allegation of substance and importance which gave you every reason to pursue the matter. I feel everything is a lot clearer to me now, but I am also confirmed in my original impression that I was not given a full opportunity to defend myself for the simple reason that I was not told about the only meaningful and serious allegation that was made about me.

I consider this a matter of the highest importance. Things being how they are in the world, it is not possible for an organization such as yours to inform persons such as myself who are their accusers, what information is known about them, and so forth. I regret this, just as you regret it, but I also recognize that it is necessary and inevitable if you are properly to do your job. However, because of this it is doubly important that a person in my position be given every opportunity to defend himself by being told exactly what he is suspected of. Because this was not done originally, I would like now to make a statement which I request you to place in my "file."

During the first eight months of 1951 I was studying at the London School of Economics on a Fulbright Fellowship. Afterwards I was employed by the U.S. Air Force. I was not then nor have I ever been a communist sympathizer. During the year, as part of my activities with the American Students Association I spoke in defense of American foreign policy before local political organizations of the Labour or Conservative Parties. Late in January, in reply to an attack by Professor G.D.H. Cole, I wrote a letter defending American foreign policy to the "New Statesman & Nation" which received some attention. During the first half of the year I was continuously in the company of Mr. John E. Barry, a young but distinguished Member of the Oklahoma Bar. My tutor at L.S.E. was W. Pickles, Esq., a well known authority on European socialist thought. During the year I met and came to know Mr. Howard K. Smith, European Director of the Columbia Broadcasting System. These are men of competence and position who know me and know what were my political sympathies at that time. If any question exists, I ask that they be consulted. I do not know whether the person or persons who accused me did so out of maliciousness or out of stupidity, but they were wrong and I want it clearly established that they were wrong.

I am sorry to have troubled you yet again in this matter, but you have made it clear how concerned you are about this subject and I have not hesitated to do so. I wish once more to thank you, Major Jaynes and Captain Brown for your great consideration.

Following his defeat for reelection, Governor Averell Harriman gave his papers to Syracuse University and enlisted Moynihan to use them to write a history of his years as governor. The history was never published.

14 JANUARY 1959

Dear Governor:

You will be pleased and no doubt relieved to learn that in a scant week and a half I have so far mastered the rudiments of University bureaucracy as to have persuaded them to buy me a typewriter and find me a place to use it! This is the only visible sign of progress on our project to date, but I attach to it the greatest symbolic importance.

As Dean [Harlan] Cleveland [of the Maxwell School at Syracuse] has written, the papers have arrived in great quantity and reasonably good order. The Dean of Libraries, Wayne Yenawine, is really quite delighted with your generosity and is taking great pains with the rearrangements that the arrival of the papers entail. To begin with he moved 17,000 books down from the top floor, a sort of oversized attic, in order to provide a spacious and well defined area in which to house the collection. This room is now being entirely refurbished. It is to be repainted, equipped with fluorescent lights and air-conditioned in order to provide the necessary humidity control for sulphite paper as well as to make the area livable in the summer. All of this will take some time, and will delay us a bit, but I consider it absolutely essential if the Harriman papers are going to <u>invite</u> research in the years to come, rather than defy it, which is most often the case with such collections. The Dean is now in Washington looking for an archivist. If he is successful, I think we have the makings of an important research center. We certainly hope you will come up to see the arrangements when they are completed.

I have received 4-year reports from Civil Defense, Correction, Health, Insurance, Labor, Military and Naval Affairs, Public Service, Social Welfare and State Police. I don't really expect to get any more except from Jack Bingham who is editing a draft he finished a few weeks ago. The only thing I will really miss is an account from Dean [Paul] Appleby [of the Maxwell School]. I mean to write him about coming to Syracuse, etc., and indicate I hope to talk with him about the early years. However, if <u>you</u> were to ask him to put something on paper I am sure he would be happy and indeed pleased. His address for the rest of the winter is Kings Ranch Resort, Apache Junction, Arizona.

I would like to talk with you about our project now that I have some ideas about it. Perhaps you will have some time next week? I will call Mrs. McCray early next week to enquire. . . .

Margaret (Peggy) O'Donnell, a Moynihan family friend and executive assistant to the governor of Massachusetts, tried to help Moynihan after he was stopped and arrested at a police roadblock in the Berkshires. The police were looking for a bank robber who wore an Irish hat and tweed jacket. She tried to enlist a local Democratic notable, Bill Goggins Jr., for which Moynihan was grateful.

17 MARCH 1959

My dear Pagean,

A word only to tell you I am once again a free man and ever more your slave. The fact that I really did appear to know you and that you would refer me to Bill Goggins had an, if anything, alarmingly magical affect on the assembled constabulary of Pittsfield. They called chez Goggins only to find everyone out of town save a younger brother named Anthony. He very kindly and without hesitation agreed to come over and cash a check for me. However, before he had left the house I managed to get the money through some people at the Shaker settlement outside of town and was able to save him the trip. As I do not have his address, could I ask you the final favor of expressing to him my very sincere appreciation for his unhesitating courtesy. It was a fine thing to do.

On the other hand, you can keep Trooper White! There I was of a soft Saturday afternoon in March driving along a tiny country road in the Berkshires—<u>not</u> speeding—when I found myself entering a hamlet. From nowhere a trooper suddenly steps out into the road and orders me to halt. Which I did, only to find myself under arrest and being treated not like a speeder so much as an escaped criminal. Unhappily, and wouldn't you know, I did not have my automobile registration papers with me. However, I had official plates on my car (I am a lame duck Commissioner) and all manner of identification, in addition to my license. I urged the Trooper to call the New York State police who would identify me and while they could not at a distance guarantee that I was not driving a stolen car, could at least vouch for my character and verify the fact that I would be entitled to official license plates. I would have thought this was an elemental courtesy to be afforded an official of a neighbor state. If I turned out to be lying, well, so much the worse for me. But surely there was no harm in doing what I asked. Trooper White would have none of it, but rather took the attitude that my simple request made me even more suspicious and hauled me off to jail, having first suggested that the fact that I was using a safety belt when stopped was a sure indication that I was a professional speeder, if not indeed a fugitive from justice.

On arrival at Pittsfield I pleaded not guilty to the charge of speeding—on the grounds that the Trooper had not followed me one foot, but had only seen me coming down the road towards him, and then could only have watched me for two or three seconds, that being a twisty, country road. As you may know, I became something of the office expert and I know that no New York State Trooper would dare arrest a man for speeding on the basis of such wholly and utterly unreliable evidence. . . . The fact seems to be that there was an accident in the village some time ago and White was making a show for the local citizenry. Unfortunately I was the victim. When I got to the police station I found I was charged not with violating some specific speed limitation, which I would have argued, but rather with driving at an "unreasonable" speed. Or perhaps it was not driving at a "reasonable" speed. At all events it was the kind of charge in which my word against a police officers would not count for much, so I pleaded guilty and gave them $18.00.

Upon learning that I knew someone who knew Bill Goggins, Trooper White became quite solicitous, indeed anxious. I have nothing against him, but will not recommend him for preferment as he seemed to expect I might!

Once again, I am glad I found you. It is a source of great comfort to have friends in high places. I shall be in Boston before very long and will stop by to see you in all your glory.

The blessings of this day on you.

After publishing an article about auto safety in THE REPORTER, *Moynihan discussed with Henry Robbins, editor of Alfred A. Knopf, the possibility of writing a book on that subject and also a book about the Harriman administration in Albany.*

MAY 14, 1959

Dear Mr. Robbins:

I was afraid I would get a letter such as yours. The fact is I wrote <u>The Reporter</u> piece in an almost frantic effort to get the subject of traffic safety out of my system and so get on with my "real" work. Without ever intending or expecting to, I found myself getting more and more involved with this problem during the latter years of the Harriman administration and when I left the government it followed me. I then got the idea that stating what I knew in print would have the effect of turning the problem over to my successors, as it were. Instead I find myself more than ever involved: in a small way publicly, but primarily as a personal concern. I have received letters from first rate physicians throughout the nation actually pleading with me to write a book telling what we all know on the subject (through all the letters of the older men the theme keeps pounding: <u>The Jungle</u>). I have received all manner of publishing offers—although none from a firm of Knopf's stature and seriousness. But most of all, I suppose, I find myself beginning to react, much as have some of the doctors I wrote about, to the plain arrogant indifference in Detroit to what I had to say. Not a sound, not a shrug, has issued from the mid-West. I honestly believe I could get the article enacted as the 26th Amendment to the Constitution and the attitude at General Motors would be "Who reads law books?" . . .

(I came around to my present position only by way of the idea that this was, after all, a cultural problem; introducing the concept of safety, with its association of pain and loss would impair if not in fact destroy the personal and social symbolism of the American automobile which is as precious to those who manufacture them as to those who buy them. Hence their opposition. After all GM had averaged 24% net profit after taxes on its gross investment during the decade 1948–57. How could they be concerned about a few pennies for padded dashboards? I have since, however, come to modify that Idea.) . . .

I am utterly convinced traffic safety is an idea whose time has come. I would incline to think we were not ready for it as little as ten years ago—but there has since been a profound change of attitude, not unconnected, I should think, with the downgrading of the automobile as a status symbol. People don't put statues of the Virgin Mary on the dashboard of automobiles that represent worldly affluence and success to them. The public is deeply, if inarticulately, troubled. 1,400,000 people have died tawdry, painful, meaningless deaths. They were young mostly, and they are remembered. 5,000,000 people a year are seriously hurt. Tens of thousands of police, government officials and service organization members have been working on the problem with the greatest earnestness but now are beginning to realize they are not getting anywhere because, in a sense, they have been misled as to what is the problem.

I must not go on like this, however, as the point of my letter is to say that I simply could not consider doing such a book at the present time as I am committed to the University to finish the Harriman project within a year or so. If you feel you can wait, however, I would be interested in taking this up next. There would be one advantage in such a delay: a number of extremely interesting and significant research projects on this subject, the first of their kind, have just got underway, financed by the Federal Government. . . . On the other hand, if you get in now, you are sure to get in first. Let me say, however, that I am utterly convinced a book must be written and I have no hesitation to plead with you, as men like Horace Campbell have pleaded with me, to do something about it and will be pleased to do what I can to help.

It was characteristically good of Editor Bingham to mention my Harriman administration book. The working title is "Government in the Empire State." I hope to produce a volume somewhere in between Warren Moscow's Politics in the Empire State and V. O. Key's American State Politics: a description of the government process as it actually works in New York State, but related to some general propositions about State government as a national problem. The Governor has turned over the entire files of the Executive Chamber, including his personal papers, to Syracuse University for my exclusive use. Good or bad, I believe this will be the first descriptive account of State administration by someone who was part of it and subsequently had full access to its records. The Governor has put up the money for the project, but he has made it clear I am wholly on my own. He is much too big a man to have any interest in an apologia and may I say his performance has no especial need of one. On the other hand the record of the four years shows the desperate limitations of State government in our time. Either we should make it work or we should abolish it. I have not yet given any real thought to the problem of publication, but I should be most interested to talk with you about it, particularly as you published both Politics in the Empire State and American State Politics.

I get to New York regularly and, if you like, will let you know next time I am to be there. And again, thank you for your encouragement.

Moynihan's work on the Harriman book project went slowly. (It was never published.) Harriman also wrote Moynihan saying he thought his approach to auto safety was "too single-minded" and filled with "curious omissions and implications," including the failure to give Harriman more credit for being on top of the subject.

JUNE 23, 1959

My dear Governor,

. . . Our project has been moving along well. After six months of exasperating delay, I have finally got the Executive Chamber to provide me with a set of your press releases—all of which were kept behind, unbeknown to any of us. I have been doing a fair amount of traveling, gathering information and conducting interviews. I was in Washington last week for several long and most valuable discussions with Dean Appleby. He and Mrs. Appleby are in thriving health and spirits and send you their warm good wishes.

I can report a truly enormous response to the Reporter article on traffic safety. Thousands on thousands of reprints have been ordered, from all over the world. The insurance industry has sent copies to a mailing list of ten thousand executives. The Cornell people have sent two thousand to physicians and public health officials around the country. It is going into the Congressional Record and will be used as a discussion paper at a forthcoming meeting of the Council of Europe. All in all I think we have established the fact that the Harriman administration was "First" in the scientific approach to this problem, and I think you will find in years to come that it wins us a place in American history.

Politics are more discouraging. I find Rockefeller has completely neutralized our "liberals" leaving the opposition to the State Committee mentality whose entire notion of what's wrong with our Republican Governor is that he is "a radical and a spender." . . .

Moynihan shows increased interest in education issues, including the requirement of loyalty affidavits for teachers, in this letter to Helen Rowan, education specialist at the Carnegie Corporation.

OCTOBER 27, 1959

Dear Helen:

I was much taken by the account in yesterday's Times of the 54th Annual Report of the Carnegie Foundation for the Advancement of Teaching. I am dimly aware you and they are not the same, but I assume there is some sinister form of interlocking directorate which would enable you to obtain for me a copy and I should be grateful indeed were you to do so.

Throughout my four years in quandary one of the things I found most curious was the ease with which we obtained money for the education of children formally denoted as "uneducable," while I could not interest the most wild eyed, radical, give-a-way, spender in the notion of a program of special state aid to provide "enriched" programs for the smart kids. The fact is, I believe, that the only new education program begun in New York State under Harriman was a system of state aid for the education of morons. Had we not been relieved of our burdens, I am sure we should now be working on visual aids for idiots. I ought not to sound cruel, but the faintly distasteful fact behind this is that the allocation of resources in education, as elsewhere, reflects the political power of the interests concerned, and where the parents of backward children were organized parents of the bright ones were not. . . .

Finally, let me get to the real point of my letter which is to say that I am thinking of making an effort to test the constitutionality of the loyalty affidavit—not the oath, which is a lost cause—in the Defense Education Act. I think I can raise the money and make a case on the basis of the First Amendment. I wonder if somewhere along the line Carnegie has not sponsored some studies of this question which you might direct me to. I need grounds. I genuinely think that the present Court would be receptive to an argument that the constitutional government of the United States is not competent to inquire into the question of "belief." The Government has the right to determine in what way a citizen intends to act, and may properly require a citizen to state his intentions in this respect. However a man's beliefs cannot of themselves constitute any threat to the Republic. A Fortiori, as the lawyers say, in that belief cannot be demonstrated it ought not to be alleged. It is my thought that if a case could be got to the court the Judges themselves could think up reasons why the damn thing is unconstitutional. In the meantime I would like to know if Carnegie has had any thoughts on such subjects. . . .

Irving Kristol, editor of THE REPORTER, *introduced Moynihan to Nathan Glazer, and suggested they team up in writing the study of ethnicity that later became* BE- YOND THE MELTING POT. *Note the salutation, "My dear Glazer," which indicates that the two did not know each other well yet. Later letters are addressed to "Nat." (In his reply two days later, Glazer appended a postscript: "So it's Pat Moynihan? I am so parochial I didn't even know that Daniel might equal Pat!")*

APRIL 7, 1960

MR. NATHAN GLAZER

309 WEST 90 STREET

NEW YORK, NEW YORK

My dear Glazer,

. . . I am fascinated by your project. It happens at this very moment I am trying to explain in writing how the political appointments of the Harriman administration reflected the ethnic groups and dynamics of the New York City democratic party, with particular attention to the Irish-Italian-Jewish triangle, or triumvirate, if you will. All of this makes sense to me, or at least it seems to, but I am finding it difficult to state the process in terms that will be acceptable to political scientists reading a book about the government of New York State. A book put together by you on the whole subject would be a marvelous thing to read. I may be wrong, but my experience of fifteen months in a university suggests to me that such a book might also help considerably with the education of some of our political scientists.

I would be delighted to try to do the Irish essay for you. The subject has absorbed me for a number of years, for the usual complex of reasons. I grew up on a neighborhood so completely Irish I didn't really learn I <u>was</u> Irish until I joined the Navy. For a good while I was interested in the subject only as it provided an explanation for the things that were wrong with the way I was brought up, but time, a long visit to Kerry and a decade of Tammany politics, have given me a somewhat more detached view. I think. At all events it would be a subject on which I have a fair number of misconceptions.

This would be the problem in accepting your offer. I am not a sociologist and know nothing of the literature. This would present a genuine danger for you. Moreover, I am very weak on immigrant history. I will admit membership in the American Irish Historical Society, but you will not be surprised to learn this has little to do with history. In fact about the only thing I have to offer is a reasonably good knowledge of the Irish role in the current political-economical life of the city, and some doubtless distorted notions about the role of the Church in the life of the city. (I ought to say in candor that while I am reasonably strict in my observances, I am like Lord Melbourne, more a buttress of the church than a pillar, in that I support it from the outside.)

These are the shortcomings I know of and will admit to. There are others you will be quick to discern. But if you still want to talk about it I would be delighted for any opportunity to meet you. . . .

With many thanks for your kind offer and for a decade of good reading, I am,

Cordially,

Moynihan thanks Kristol for introducing him to Nathan Glazer.

MAY 3, 1960

My dear Irving,

I have just returned from a trip to New York undertaken for the curiously conjoint purpose of attending the Tammany dinner and talking with Nathan Glazer about his project on the nationalities of New York.

He has asked me—on your recommendation—to do the chapter on the Irish. For the usual jumble of reasons, this is an enormously important thing for me. I have agreed, perhaps too eagerly, certainly with too little thought to the other things I shall have to do before the year is out, but I couldn't turn it down. It is necessary, however, to write to you to tell you how truly grateful I am and at the same time to warn you of the risk you have taken! Yet I shall be doubly concerned, lest dishonor touch we 'Sons of City College' as the old refrain has it.

Glazer is a lovely man: and so damned smart. It will be a great experience working with him—and that is but the least of the things for which I thank you.

I trust your children are restored and plans for Europe are abuzzing.

Moynihan responds to an effort by Albert Imlah, dean of the Fletcher School and Moynihan's former professor, to rally academics behind Adlai Stevenson for president in 1960. His mention of Catholic resentment over what was done to "Al" by "that snot nose from Groton and Harvard" refers to Al Smith and Franklin Roosevelt.

JUNE 26, 1960

MR. ALBERT IMLAH

FLETCHER SCHOOL OF LAW & DIPLOMACY

MEDFORD 35, MASSACHUSETTS

Dear Dr. Imlah:

Any letter,* howsoever public, from a former professor commands a reply. The obligation is the greater if the reply is to be negative. I will therefore ask a moment of your time to explain why, as a member of the New York delegation to the Democratic National Convention I will not, at the outset, support Adlai Stevenson, despite the fact that I completely share your feelings as to his unique greatness as a leader of our party.

A word of personal history is necessary here. After finishing my second year at Fletcher I went to England on a Fulbright fellowship to the London School of Economics in the late summer of 1950. I remained in Europe for three years. These were bad years for America and particularly bad for an American in Europe. Not having the confidence in my own knowledge of our country to oppose with any vigor the European view of events, I watched the perils of the Korean war, the emergence of [Senator Joseph] McCarthy and

---

* The New York Times, June 15, 1960.

the debate over foreign policy through English and French eyes. It was, you know, a troubling sight.

Then Adlai Stevenson emerged from all the mess and, along with all of Europe, I was stirred by his vision, his understanding, and the great courage that underlay his high spirits. Then, I with the rest, was startled by his defeat. The last journey of my <u>wanderjahre</u> was to Berlin and Vienna to observe in the one what Russian tanks did to Europeans who believed in the doctrine of liberation and in the other to see what Cohn and Schine did to Americans who shared the same confidence in the pronouncements of their leaders. . . .

My eye opening had just begun. Personally I had a comparatively easy time of it. I managed to get to Albany with the Harriman administration and in time got to be Secretary to the Governor, the youngest person, I might say, ever to hold the post. After we went out in 1958 I was made secretary of the policy committee of the Democratic State Committee and have generally served as one of the organization eggheads, a lonely eminence but one not without rewards and which, in particular, provides an opportunity to keep in touch with the rank and file of this giant working class party. It is in this connection that I have been kept in a state of permanent dilation.

I found to my shock that it was not the Republicans who had rejected Adlai Stevenson, but the Democrats. The working class and the lower middle class in New York State—that is the only state I claim to know anything about, and in as far as my remarks extend, although I doubt things would be much different in, say, Massachusetts—had profoundly lost confidence in the principles of foreign policy, even of public and social policy which most liberals regard as essentially self-evident and substantially unquestioned. Stevenson had in fact attracted a significant vote from the professional and upper elements that normally vote Republican. But he lost Brooklyn and the Bronx in droves. The hard truth is that much of this resulted not from the attractions of Eisenhower but from plain hostility towards Stevenson and the Democratic national leadership. . . .

Now what is the point of all this, which you know well enough anyway? The point is that Jack Kennedy, who stands for everything Stevenson stands for, and is if anything a bit more decisive about it, produces just the opposite reaction among these people. They trust him, they like him, they agree with him. <u>They want him to win.</u> Again, I can't explain it fully. His being Irish and Catholic explain much of it, of course. The Democratic Party in New York is still Irish and Catholic and the memory of Al Smith is still cruelly alive. (So much of the ruthless attack on the institutions of the White Anglo-Saxon Protestant establishment, for Foreign Service officers, the Harvard professors, the Achesons which gave objectives to the McCarthy movement, was really a kind of hidden, belated revenge for what was done to "Al" by that snot nose from Groton and Harvard). But it is something more than that. Race and religion is not everything in politics. (I would say it was only about 99% in New York!) There is still something left over for things like public policy. In this fraction of the political mind open to reason, I think the realization has spread, particularly in the past two months, that the Republican administration has brought the country to deep trouble, not all of which was inevitable, some of which, perhaps, could have been prevented had Stevenson been elected. Our people are ready to vote for the Democratic national ticket again, but it is too much to ask them at the same time to vote for a man they have voted against twice previously. I think this may be the clue to so much of the enthusiasm about Kennedy in the minds of the right-wing Democrats: he represents on and to the old arguments and the old generation of leaders. Whatever it is, it is something to behold. Our delegation caucused in Albany last week; the feeling for Kennedy was intense. The Bronx delegation came up raging mad at a rumor that the Stevenson forces were going to block an endorsement of their man. If you consider that Roy Cohn, and his father Judge Cohn, are members in eminently good standing of the Bronx Democratic Organization, and that Kennedy only a few days prior to our caucus had made a foreign policy speech Cohn and Schine would have labeled "Communist" eight years ago, you can measure the curiosity of the event. The fact simply is that the Irish Catholics who run the New York organizations were joining the Democratic party again and it made everyone feel good.

Thus my argument comes to this: Kennedy can win. But it is a bit more than just that which concerns me. For seven years now I have been working more or less full-time in New York politics and with each year I have become more concerned with the increasingly rigid, irreconcilable opposition of the catholics to so much of liberal doctrine, particularly in foreign affairs.... Just as Lippmann urged in 1952 that only a Republican administration could continue the foreign policies of the Truman administration, I now suggest that only Kennedy can give Americans government based on the principles and programs of Adlai Stevenson. If Kennedy can't get it, I shall of course support Stevenson, but I don't think we'll reach that fourth ballot. As for the big one in November, I can report that right along our polls have shown Kennedy ahead of all the other candidates in the vote he would get against Nixon. For some time he was doing well enough, 51% as against 45% for Stevenson, but the poll taken week before last, he had risen to an astonishing 58% of the vote. Even if this is more or less out of the question, we still have the makings of victory. . . .

Moynihan reports to Theodore Sorensen, Kennedy's speechwriter and close aide, on progress lining up support for Kennedy in New York.

JUNE 27, 1960

Dear Ted:

. . . You would have been enormously heartened by the atmosphere of our caucus in Albany last Thursday. People, who between you and me, abhor as radical and visionary just about everything your boss stands for, were ready to shed blood on his behalf. By the curious magic of leadership they were joining the Democratic Party again after all these dreary years of McCarthyism, and the rest. It was a wonderful sight for us to see and a grand omen for Los Angeles.

Perhaps I will see you there. Count on 110 votes for Kennedy in New York.

Reporting to Nathan Glazer about the Democratic convention in Los Angeles, where Kennedy got the presidential nomination. Moynihan was a proud delegate from New York.

JULY 20, 1960

Dear Nat:

. . . Los Angeles was almost worth it. I got caught up running errands and writing second speeches for Harriman (nine drafts!) which kept me away from some of the traditional kinds of fun, but it did give me a chance to solidify my relations with the Kennedy staff, which will, I hope, turn out to be a useful thing to have done. I must say I came away much impressed by him and, perhaps particularly, by the kind of people he has around him. On my level you never get to know a big man really. I incline to think that no one ever gets to know really big men. On the other hand, I do know a bit about the kind of staffs the different kind of political leaders pick, and I can assure you everything I saw about the Kennedy crowd is flattering to their boss. They are tough, individual, straight and fiendishly free of the blind spots that give a pattern to reality for most of us. They made everyone else look not so much amateurish as antiquated. The era of the filibuster died in that town last week, but so equally did the era of the New Republic.

I think I got some good material for us. In an interesting way it was very much an Irish show. Apart from the South, which seemed so irrelevant, and apart from Adlai, who seemed so unreal, Kennedy plain dominated it, with his staff of O'Donnell and O'Brien plus brothers and sisters. His chief manager was Bailey of Conn., his chief allies Brown of California, Lawrence of Penn., Daley of Chicago, etc. These men ran the convention. On top of it, far the best speech was [Senator Eugene] McCarthy's tribute to the memory of A.E.S. [Adlai E. Stevenson].

The Jews were noticeably restless with the reports of Kennedy Sr.'s antisemitism. Either Stevenson or Johnson circulated a planted column of Drew Pearson reporting a captured German document in which some Nazi diplomat recounts a conversation in which Kennedy apparently said it was alright to kill Jews so long as it was not done in public. Ugh. True or not, it will be circulated in widening circles. . . .

Moynihan thanks Mayor Robert F. Wagner Jr., for whom he campaigned in 1953, for leading the New York delegation in Los Angeles.

JULY 20, 1960

Dear Mayor Wagner:

In the difficulties ahead it may be of some consolation, even some use to you to know how very much it meant to delegates such as myself to have you as our chairman at Los Angeles. It would not be too much to say that you gave us our dignity back—after too many years of being lumped in with the entourage of hoodlums and shysters that our leaders have surrounded themselves with in the knowledge, conscious or not, that the best way to keep people docile is to keep them ashamed of themselves.

For all I am an immigrant up here, I feel I can speak for many up-staters in saying I confidently expect and hope that this will not have been our last taste of liberty—or leadership.

Moynihan offers suggestions to Nathan Glazer about their book and thoughts about the presidential race.

AUGUST 15, 1960

Dear Nat,

A few random thoughts which might be worth recording:

. . . Have you thought of sending an expedition up to the Yale Center on Alcohol or whatever the exact title is? Over the years I have noted reports of theirs to the effect that the Irish have the most alcoholics, the Jews the fewest, etc. This would indicate they have done some good ethnic studies on alcohol use and possibly related matters. There is so little information of this sort— and anyway, attitudes to alcohol are surely of sufficient importance in themselves—that I would think we might be rewarded if we made a general approach. I mention this only because I will want to do this on my own in any event, but it occurs to me that you would find that Irish have the most, etc., and information on negroes et al. in between would also be of interest. As a respectable academic enterprise I should think they would want to help us. I have some friends among the alumni, the rich alumni that is, whom I am sure would put in a word for us if needed. . . .

The way we figure it up here, Jacqueline Kennedy's pregnancy is going to be the key to the election: the protestants can't help recognizing and approving it as an example of planned parenthood; the catholics will surely applaud the advent of a large family; the only opposition we've heard of came from Nixon himself who apparently figures he's been screwed out of the election.

Moynihan expresses concern to Glazer about conservative anti-Communist Catholic opposition to Kennedy. THE BROOKLYN TABLET *is the newspaper of the Brooklyn Catholic Archdiocese. McCarthy is Senator Joe McCarthy, the anti-Communist crusader censured by the Senate.*

SEPTEMBER 1, 1960

Dear Nat,

I am in a black mood myself, mostly brought on by you. A few months ago, thanks to you, I resumed my reading of the Brooklyn Tablet. Contrary to the impression one might have had from the Europe of the thirties, fascism is a limitlessly dreary avocation and the observation of its proponents is hardly more inspiriting. But in the process I have come to realize that the—the what? nihilism—of the Irish Catholic leadership in the country has gone so far now that we've decided not to agree with them about McCarthy, et al., that they are even going to cut Kennedy. The Tablet is filled with correspondence about how could he be a good katlik when he went to all those commie schools. Now today I read in the Times that the Jews are going to cut him because of his old man (good enough reason, granted, but don't hurt less for being justified). As you would say, these are things I knew anyway—from a month of trying to get Citizens for Kennedy off the ground in Syracuse—but I hate like hell seeing it proved for me in print. I think we are going under, but don't say I said so. . . .

You seemed to have written about everything I can think of. Your Commentary piece quite fascinating. Although the Irish and Scots developed distilling, I would incline to question whether the medieval celts had enough extra grain ever to distill any significant amount of liquor—we might thus find they are the current victims of their own product which they are only now able to hurt themselves with. (A friend and I have been exploring the possibility that the relatively declining death rate in automobile accidents, which we think we can show is accompanied by an increasing injury rate, is that the death susceptibles are being weeded out of the population. We have already killed about 2 million people in cars in only little more than one generation, so that this might be the case, or rather could be.) However, I <u>know</u>

the Irish drinking is connected with their sexual repression. You will, however, have to supply me with proof of this, as I wouldn't know what proof looks like in such matters. But one could make the case, could one not, if a people have preserved intact their religion and their drinking pattern from the old country, that there is a strong indication other patterns may be preserved as well.

Incidentally, do we think races are different? Do Chinamen incline to do things differently than Sicilians? Dogs do, don't they? Almost all the other breeds and species of animals have different characteristics. Are there not such differences among men, or are we essentially of the same stock and therefore of one breed. . . .

Two items of city lore before leaving you in haste to rally the registrants of the 15th Ward. The word "shikker" in your opening of the Commentary article. From way back in my childhood I recall dimly a street song which the Irish kids picked up from the children of the shopkeepers in our neighborhood. It went something like this, phonetically,

> *Shikker iss a goy*
> *Shikker iss a goy*
> *Shikker iss a trinken missa*
> *Vile eir iss a goy.*

[As] I recall it, it was a Yiddish drinking song intent on describing the goyim as drunks while jews drank! . . .

Do not despair. If Kennedy loses we will have a grand time proving how prejudice did it, which will make our book, or rather your book and my chapter, even more important. Asked why he gave all his musicals Irish names, George M. Cohan said "The Jews come anyway." This way we might sell some Catholic copies too.

More frustration conveyed to Glazer about Kennedy's political difficulties. "Editor P. of Commentary" is Norman Podhoretz, who wrote an article in COMMENTARY *saying there was little difference between Kennedy and Vice President Richard Nixon.*

SEPTEMBER 17, 1960

Dear Nat,

... Much disturbed about Editor P. of Commentary and his outrageous snot nose-ism about Kennedy and Nixon being much of a muchness with nothing to distinguish or recommend either to a cultivated political palate. Let them keep it up. Eight years of government by Normon Vincent Peale may sharpen his appetite if it does not improve his taste.

Outraged by Dr. Dennis Wrong's article on Liberal Hero Rockefeller. I have hardly ever read such hopelessly wrongheaded blather. Yet there is much to be learned from it. The facts as I understand them are that Rockefeller has not been a good Governor, or rather he has not been in any way a "liberal" one as we have come to associate the word. I know something about this subject and I assure you he has pretty much hewed to a very conservative Republican program, interspersed with speeches about the quest for excellence. Yet he remains the darling of the left of center Democrats. I think this gives us a clue to a momentous movement in American politics: the Liberals are discovering their class interest. For half a century people we call liberals have identified themselves with the class interests of the workers. As they have succeeded in their object, this has brought about a certain impairment of their own interests, while it has greatly expanded their numbers. Today many, perhaps most liberals, the likes of you and me, are penniless, but happily not witless. But we are vulnerable and we do need help from government for various things. Such as college education for our children. In the latter years we have been finding that initiative we have built up keeps the public housing programs rolling somewhat and the minimum wage levels rising, etc., but in the meantime damn little political support can be mastered for issues of interest to the Liberals as a class—again, higher education or health insurance. In the meantime our beloved workers are voting for Senator McCarthy who wants to make things even harder for us. The result is a considerable disenchantment with Tammany Hall and a marked interest for chaps who talk about the quest for excellence and seek it by sales taxes. (Dig Galbraith.) ...

Moynihan's "Impressions of the 1960 Convention" in Los Angeles.

First and last: Never again Los Angeles. The purpose of a national convention is to bring representatives of the state parties together; the effect of Los Angeles was [to] keep them apart.

The delegations were isolated, each in its own hotel, hours away from any other. (Distances are measured in automobile driving time.) There was little of the mingling and exchange of greetings and even, occasionally, ideas that take place in circumstances such as Chicago provides. Once the hotel switchboards broke down even the party leaders, who normally call back and forth across the country every day, seem to have lost touch with each other. It is well the delegates arrived overwhelmingly for Kennedy: If we had had to make up our minds on the spot, as say in 1952, we'd be there yet. . . .

The National Committee over-organized the distribution and tickets and the like, which is just as bad, and produces far worse tempers than the usual blowzy conspiracy that attends such matters. . . .

There was some talk about a Hollywood casting director hiring us as stand-ins for a musical about the Gay Nineties but the notion of any association with the arts, even at such a remove, was repugnant to our rank-and-file $100,000.00 a year New York City lawyers and the idea was dropped in favor of a general hijera to "Vegas."

New York would not have looked so much out of it had we been choosing anyone but Kennedy for the nominee. Kennedy does not represent a movement in the Democratic Party: He represents a new era in American political history. The Democratic Party entered that era when we nominated him. Although Mayor Wagner saved our dignity, nothing could save our importance in an age when New York style politics and politicians just don't matter anymore.

As Gore Vidal told the AP man, he was for Kennedy because Kennedy is an intellectual. What is an intellectual? "A man who deals with concrete problems and solves them." So much for the Bronx delegate who on nominating day gleefully confided to a colleague that "Jack is gonna disband da study group," meaning, presumedly, the National Advisory Council.

The question as to who is to be disbanded will be answered later.

Moynihan seeks help from Myer (Mike) Feldman, a top aide to JFK, in landing a job in the Kennedy administration. Sander Vanocur, a prominent television correspondent and a close friend from London, also lobbied the Kennedy team to bring Moynihan to Washington.

DECEMBER 23, 1960

Dear Mike,

Sandy Vanocur suggested I write you about coming to work for the administration. I admit I can't (daren't) wait to be asked.

I enclose a resume. As you will see, my experience and interests have been those of a general political executive. I have written in half a dozen fields, all substantially unrelated save that they involve problems of American government. This makes it difficult for me to choose any one job I would wish to be considered for over any other. The sole exception to this would relate to the International Labor Organization. My Ph. D. thesis is on the U.S. and the ILO; I know a fair amount about the subject, have spent considerable time in Geneva, and I am violently of the opinion that we have done a miserable job there, in a field that should be for us one of singular opportunity. I have also written with some success on the subject of highways and traffic safety, but here again I have been only offering a rather sharp generalist's reaction to the incompetence of specialists. Traffic safety, is, I fear, my avocation. I will send you my basic statement on the matter. In the meantime let me thank you and Frank Sieverts for allowing me to include a reference to it in Senator Kennedy's statement to the AAA. It has brought a most grateful reaction from the public health schools around the country with which I am in contact.

That's about all I can really say for myself. As you know, I feel very strongly about Senator Kennedy. I think we are going to make history in the next few years. I would like to be part of it, particularly part of the work of producing the new ideas and putting them on paper.

I was, of course, delighted by your appointment. I do hope that for all the overwork, and frenzy, and, of course, expectation, that you had the time to consider what a great moment had come to you—if only long enough to get it fixed in your memory, to be enjoyed at a later date!

Happy New Year indeed!

Seeking help from Mary McGrory, the columnist, who was close to the Kennedy inner circle.

ROOM 401, MAIN LIBRARY
MARCH 1, 1961

Dearest Mary Glorious,

   . . . As you will see from my resume, my experience is general—as I have tried to keep it. But this makes it most difficult to state precisely which job I want. I would have liked to work in transportation, but that is not to be, and the President's message yesterday said everything I have ever suggested in the field anyway. (I fancy I put them on to the ideas, but that is no matter.) My first love is international labor affairs and I have talked to Bill Wirtz about being a deputy to George Weaver, the Assistant Secretary-to-be for International Labor Affairs. I take it Wirtz liked the idea, but the job of director of Weaver's office has been abolished. It could, of course, be recreated, but such things do not happen easily in government.

   I should say I declined a more-or-less offer to be an assistant to [Luther] Hodges for speaking engagements and Congressional mail. If I go to Washington it must be to do something for this country, not for one of its politicians. I love politicians, but I have tired of working for their careers and prefer in that eventuality to stay here raising my family and writing books.

   But I bore you. I dare not risk your displeasure and will conclude hastily with the thought that only a person of the uttermost generosity such as yourself would think to do what you have done without ever being told that I happen to be an extremely useful and handy home carpenter, expert in installing insulated fire walls and such like conveniences for friends.

Explaining to Henry Robbins of Knopf why he must abandon the traffic safety book.

JULY 11, 1961

HENRY ROBBINS, ESQ.

ALFRED A. KNOPF, INC.

501 MADISON AVENUE

NEW YORK, NEW YORK

Dear Henry:

This is a hard letter to write. As you can see, I have been drafted. More exactly, some weeks ago, rather suddenly, I was asked by the Secretary and by the White House to take this job. I had not sought it—I didn't even know such a job existed—and had arranged my life in an entirely different direction. But suddenly there it was, and for many reasons I felt my responsibility was to do as requested.

This was not easy. I don't suppose it ever is easy to make an abrupt change of plans once you get to the point in life of really having some plans. It was of course exceeding painful with the University. But the worst for me was the thought of having to put off the traffic safety book. As you know, I have been planning it, and collecting material for it these last two years. I had just come to the point of writing it, and would have been done in twelve weeks time. . . .

And so—I feel I have let you down. I know I have done so. This is a more serious matter for me than you might suppose. I enclose a check for the advance I accepted so cheerfully two years ago. I have not given up my plans to write a book on this subject, and propose to use my present position to gather yet more information about it, but it is obvious that I cannot meet my deadline, and I must therefore leave it to you to do what you must.

Again, I feel awful about this. I would be more than willing to discuss it at whatever length you want. I am, as you can imagine, full of the subject. In particular, I should be delighted to turn over my materials to anyone you might suggest.

Moynihan supports the establishment of a civilian presidential decoration to his boss, Secretary Arthur J. Goldberg. He received the medal himself upon his retirement from the Senate in 2000.

JULY 18, 1961

MEMORANDUM TO THE SECRETARY

At the time you spoke to me about the cabinet inquiry, on the matter of civilian honors, Mr. Leslie had just completed a memorandum for you on the subject. He has shown it to me and asked that I send it on to you.

I think his proposal is eminently sensible. I would make one comment on it, and one further suggestion.

> 1. Would it not be both wise and proper to propose a revival of the wartime Presidential Medal for Merit, rather than to establish a brand new order? The ways of a democracy should be incremental!

I would suggest that the great value of the Medal for Merit is the rosette. I know one man who would wear it in swimming if he could manage. It is commonly mistaken for the Legion of Honor, but ça suffit; by the time 10,000 persons are wearing them it will in any event be recognized for itself. This, I feel, is important as I very much doubt we should have any success with alphabetical appendages to American names in the manner of the O.B.B. and the K.C.M.G. Even the Congressional M.C. Has not really caught on. It is the austere fashion of the republic to wear our monickers unadorned. Hence the essential role of the rosette.

> 2. I wonder if we might also propose to establish the Presidential Citation as a form of civilian decoration. Here again we have an existing form, used principally (if not exclusively) for military purposes until now, but clearly adaptable for civilian purposes—perhaps particularly for services in connection with the cold war.

If you agree that the Medal for Merit should be awarded on the recommendation of a non-partisan board (this could be argued) I would then suggest that the Presidential Citation be awarded solely on the initiative of the President. I would suggest that it should tend to be given in recognition of specific services and actions, while the Medal of Merit be given in recognition of long, continued performance of public service of the highest quality.

Do you want me to continue on this assignment? If you like this general approach, we can prepare a presentation for the Cabinet.

Moynihan's relationship with Averell Harriman, now assistant secretary of state in the Kennedy administration, continued to be plagued by irritants over the unpublished history of the Harriman administration in Albany and troubles getting his official portrait painted.

JANUARY 12, 1962

THE HONORABLE AVERELL HARRIMAN

ASSISTANT SECRETARY OF STATE

WASHINGTON 25, D. C.

Dear Governor:

I am really very sorry that we seem to have had a misunderstanding about the progress of my manuscript. When I spoke with you in Geneva I had finished the third draft of the first six chapters (some 100,000 words in all) but had not yet given it to a typist. Upon returning from Geneva I undertook to arrange this, but was at first appalled by the prices. Finally in early December I gave the manuscript to a handicapped woman who does such work around the Department. She will have it back to me on January 26th, which is somewhat later than originally scheduled and unfortunately, is the day I leave for Geneva. I will therefore get it to you the week I return, let us say Friday, February 16.

This manuscript includes the chapters on State finances which I said I was anxious to get to Dean Appleby. I gather you understood me to say that I had already sent them to him.

I gather from Clark that you feel I have not interviewed enough members of the Administration. Is there anyone in particular you think I ought to see? This can easily be arranged. I should say that there are a number of people I plan to talk with further in connection with some chapters yet to be finished—particularly on discrimination and housing.

A final point, you indicated to me that you felt the rather brief reference to the 1958 Buffalo Convention in my Commentary article was not accurate. Would it be possible for you to give me an hour of your time to go over those events? I have talked with many of those involved and the picture only grows more obscure.

It is now some two years that I have been holding $1900 contributed by members of your Administration towards the cost of a portrait for the Hall of Governors. There were a number of cabinet members among the subscribers, but on the whole the money came from persons down the line, including quite a few of the secretaries. I fear they are wondering if I did not abscond with the money. Do you think there is any chance that you will find the opportunity for a portrait in the next year? I would like to give the subscribers a progress report as I have done from time to time.

Advising Secretary of Labor Willard Wirtz on choosing recipients for the Medal of Freedom.

MARCH 11, 1963

MEMORANDUM TO THE SECRETARY

You may have noticed that on Washington's Birthday the President announced that arrangements had been made to award the Medal of Freedom once each year to a list of persons who have "contributed significantly to the quality of American life." Recommendations will come from an expanded Distinguished Civilian Service Awards Board, of which you are a member. The Board meets March 22 with the President. I will be there to answer any questions that come up about the Executive Order.

Hopefully, this marks the beginning of a Civil Honors system. (With any luck, it also marks the end of my Culture assignments.) I think you should know that from beginning to end, this project—one which dozens of committees and individuals have heretofore undertaken without success—was the work of the Department of Labor. I believe the President is quite clear on this point.

The President has indicated he would like Justice Frankfurter and Robert Lovett included on the July 4 list, but has also said he does not want this to be an exclusively octogenarian affair. Adlai Stevenson has written the President urging that Eleanor Roosevelt receive the first posthumous award. We are thinking of having the President propose to Churchill that he accept one on the first list. We do not expect that any nominations will be discussed at this first, preliminary meeting, but you might want to start thinking about persons from the labor field.

Finally, you might want to glance at the proposal as it was submitted to the President. Section II is a background paper, Section VI is a note on the British and French systems.

Moynihan invites Ralph Nader to Washington to work on auto safety.

MAY 16, 1963

Dear Ralph:

Thank you for your always fascinating reports on the Connecticut experience. I find myself working closely with Senator Ribicoff these days and mean to take it up with him very shortly.

A serious question. Would you be interested in coming to Washington to work on this subject?

Moynihan mischievously reports to Mary McGrory, in Rome, that President Kennedy himself wanted her back in Washington.

JUNE 27, 1963

Dear Mary:

It is just as we feared—you won't ever come back to us. I was about to write you last week to say how absolutely startlingly marvelous everything you have written has been, called the City Desk at the STAR for your address, and was told you were on your way home. Called tonight to learn when you had arrived, only to learn you had not yet left. However, lest you feel this has become a matter of concern to your friends I hasten to assure you otherwise.

In the last hours before leaving Washington the announcement of the Pope's coronation reached the White House, raising the question whether the

President ought to go to Rome after all. "Out of the question," spoke the Chief Executive, "I have to go to Rome in order to bring Mary back." (Honestly.)

Memorandum seeking support for donations to create a Cultural Center on the Potomac, a cause supported by "the President and Mrs. Kennedy." It became the Kennedy Center.

JULY 9, 1963

MEMORANDUM:

I am writing a limited number of persons in the Department of Labor to ask their special support of the campaign now under way to raise funds for the Cultural Center. As you know, this effort has the full and active support of the President and Mrs. Kennedy.

Congress has provided a splendid site for the Center, and, of course, Edward Stone has produced a striking and original design. It is now upon the citizens of Washington to help to build it.

It has become something of an international cliché—not less irritating for being so familiar—that the performing arts barely exist in the capital of the United States of America. This condition exists, in the first place, because there are really no adequate facilities for many activities. The creation of the National Cultural Center would dramatically reverse this situation. It would make all our lives more pleasant and more interesting, and would provide for our families, particularly our children, an important source of new ideas and wider experience.

I would like to ask you, as one of the executives of the Department, if you will not be as generous as the circumstances allow, in supporting the Cultural Center. I know the Secretary would be most appreciative.

Moynihan seeks medical advice from Dr. Janet Travell, Kennedy's personal physician.

JULY 17, 1963

Dear Dr. Travell:

I hesitate to trouble you with a personal problem but Jim Reynolds assures me you will not mind.

For some years—since Navy days generally—I have been troubled by a ruptured lumbar disc. This Spring I managed to fall off a dais (making room for the President!) and it has since got somewhat worse. I would have no trouble continuing in my present circumstances but I am somewhat anxious about the long-run prognosis which, I gather, to be somewhat gloomy in matters of this kind. I would like to talk to someone who knows something about the subject and could advise me as to what if anything I might do about it.

I understand there are several physicians out at Bethesda who are quite outstanding in the field. If this is so, do you suppose that you might arrange an appointment for me?

Seeking a refund from the Hotel Madison.

AUGUST 2, 1963
HOTEL MADISON
AT NORTH STATION
BOSTON 14, MASSACHUSETTS

Dear Sir:

I was a guest at the Hotel Madison on July 30, 1963. In checking my receipt I noticed that I was charged for telephone calls that I did not make. Would you mind checking your records to find the error and refunding the $1?

Apologizing to Frances Perkins, former labor secretary under President Franklin Roosevelt, for not being able to help her on her book about Governor Al Smith of New York.

SEPTEMBER 17, 1963

Dear Miss Perkins:

I can hardly begin this letter. It is much more a disappointment to me than it may be to you. However, it would be even worse to delay. I simply must tell you that after a summer of railroads, racial crisis, and the Alliance for Progress, I have come to realize that however much I may <u>hate</u> to think so, there is simply not time or energy left over from my job to work with you on the Al Smith book. I should greatly prefer to do that than anything else I can imagine, except serving the President in the present situation of the nation. <u>The</u> moment I leave this job you will hear from me. You have an absolutely marvelous book there, and it must be published.

Reaching out: Moynihan invites Theodore Sorensen to a dinner party for Norman Podhoretz and his wife, Midge Decter, both increasingly prominent conservative critics.

SEPTEMBER 17, 1963

Dear Ted:

For some time I have been suggesting to Norman Podhoretz, the editor of <u>Commentary</u>, that if he really does want to know how the world is run he must come to Washington to meet some of those who help run it. He has at length agreed and we are giving a small dinner for him and his wife Midge on Friday, October 4. You are the one person he has specifically asked be invited: it seems he has just written a colloquy between Podhoretz and Sorensen in which Sorensen wins. He is curious to learn why, as this rarely otherwise happens.

I said I would ask, but with no very great hope of success as you are not much given to these things. But, of course, we would be delighted if you could come.

Nathan Glazer and I share page 3 of the New York Times Book Review with you next Sunday. Tom Wicker is apparently most generous on the subject of Presidential decisions. Oscar Handlin decidedly less so with regard to our musings about the melting pot.

Cautioning Secretary Wirtz about moving too quickly to integrate schools in the North.

SEPTEMBER 30, 1963

MEMORANDUM FOR THE SECRETARY

For whatever it is worth, I am persuaded, and find others such as Phil Hauser completely agree, that it would be a serious mistake from the Negro point of view to integrate the Northern school system at this time. The present level of achievement and family support among most Negroes is so far behind that of most whites that any <u>artificial</u> effort to integrate the schools can only have the effect of consigning almost the entire Negro student body to the bottom of the class, with all the psychic injury that results.

Perhaps it is too late to change the direction of Negro efforts. Perhaps not. My understanding is that the preponderant view of Negro parents is that they would like better schools, not necessarily more integrated ones. If it were to turn out that my view is shared by others in the Administration who have some experience in this field, would it be sensible to start looking into possibilities of special Federal assistance for what would, in effect, be predominantly Negro schools?

An object might be to bring Negroes in elementary school up to performance levels where they can compete successfully in fully integrated <u>high schools</u>.

I doubt there will be much integration of elementary schools, anyway. The neighborhood patterns are too dominant. However, if too much Negro energy goes into an effort at artificial integration at this level, an opportunity for upgrading might well be missed.

As you know, I believe in quotas and a lot of other un-American devices. We have four centuries of exploitation to overcome and we will not do so by giving Negroes an equal opportunity with whites who are by now miles ahead.

Letter to W. Dale Brown, Otsego County agent of the State Agricultural Extension Service, requesting help in purchasing a vacation home.

OCTOBER 10, 1963

Dear Mr. Brown:

For some time I have been looking, without great success, for a farm in Delaware County that my family could use for vacations and an occasional weekend. I have assumed that somewhere I could find a house in good enough condition with a fair amount of acreage that had gone out of cultivation. I have particularly wanted a place on a dirt road with, generally speaking, as much isolation as possible.

Recently one of my colleagues in the Department of Agriculture suggested to me that the world's leading authorities on properties of this kind are in fact the local county agents—authorities I would add on this and many other matters! I am going to be in Otsego County over the weekend of October 18–21 and would very much like to look at anything you might know of. May I take the liberty of calling you in a few days to learn whether you have any thoughts on the subject.

Announcing to Mrs. Averell (Marie Norton Whitney) Harriman that an artist has been found to paint Averell's portrait.

OCTOBER 14, 1963

Dear Mrs. Harriman:

I have talked with Bill Walton, who much approves the thought that Marian Schlesinger might do the portrait of the Governor for the State Capitol. If you are still inclined toward the idea, perhaps you would speak with her about it. Alternately, I would be more than happy to do so.

As you recall, we have $1900. More could doubtless be raised now, for reasons not entirely creditable to the contributors, but of no necessary concern to the artist!

Reporting to his wife, Liz, on a trip to Geneva.

MONDAY, 8:00 A.M.

Dearest Liz,

I begin to realize that it is impossible for the likes of me ever to write regularly on an expedition such as this. There is simply not one moment of privacy at any hour of the day or night. Even though I have been getting up regularly at 6:00 A.M. (for some reason I simply cannot sleep on these trips) there are always the cables, the afternoon speech or the 8:00 breakfast meeting to get ready for. I am really quite bored with it all, and for the first time ever, rather wish my two week trip to Europe were at an end!

I find it odd to be saying this of an enterprise which has proved endlessly instructive, and about which I shall bore people for years to come! ...

My shopping has proved only modestly successful. I have bought for B-Bussy a quite lovely ceramic dove in one of the avant garde galleries in the vieux quartier. She will probably break it, although it is quite thick and seemingly durable, but if she gets it through the next year or so she will have a very handsome objet d'art.

I can't think what to bring Tim or John Boy. I am considering an enormous Swiss sled for the latter, but I don't think TWA will put up with it.

This will go on for some time. Today I hope to hear about getting to see the Butler papers at long last. They are very bureaucratic and timid about it all. Heaven help the American caught in the I.L.C., as is Harry Herrick's brother. Dinner with them tonight, also lunch with Betsy Johnston, whom I ran into Saturday while having a brief call on the Lubins who were passing through en route to Israel.

Am using Harriman's office, which brings the circle yet another turn.

I miss you so much. Have had some very nice meals and a number of good rambles through the old city which is always pleasing. I think maybe you should come along next time, but we will talk of that later.

Much love to you, Tim, Maura, John, Harry, and Tick Tock.

In this Memorandum to Secretary Wirtz, Moynihan offers recommendations about organized crime and recalls that he was in Albany during the infamous "Appalachian Meeting" of mafia leaders in 1957.

OCTOBER 22, 1963

MEMORANDUM FOR THE SECRETARY

As you know, for some years I have been interested in and in a small way involved with the problem of organized crime. Both as an academic and as a working government executive I have found myself continually running into the problem. I have come to regard it as one of the most significant, ominous, and least understood aspects of American society. As Assistant Secretary to Governor Harriman at the time of the Appalachian "convention" I was involved in that enquiry, and (although I should doubt he would recall it) I worked with the Attorney General on some aspects of the McClellan Committee hearings. At that time I first sensed that Robert Kennedy was the rare man who took this matter seriously, and not simply as an occasion for publicity or the pleasure of middle class umbrage. I wrote just that in a Reporter article "The Private Government of Crime" (which he may have read, as he has recently cited the title) and everything he has done since has added to my conviction that his being where he is provides an enormous—certainly unprecedented—opportunity to do something about this subject. . . .

I would offer the analogy that our effort to control organized crime today is about where our effort to counter the threat of Communist military aggression was in the late 1940's. We have awakened to the danger, and we have developed some basic containment measures. That is about all—at least that I know of. This would be about the equivalent point fifteen years ago when those responsible for national defense began to bring new kinds of thinking to bear on a subject that had until then been pretty much a preserve of the military. Men such as Herman Kahn, Thomas Schelling and Henry Kissinger began to work with the Pentagon, and the result, if I understand it, was an immensely creative cross-fertilization which has brought our defense policy to the present high level of sophistication and effectiveness.

I would suggest that something similar could be done with the subject of organized crime. Let me illustrate by means of five propositions which, to my mind, indicate the need for further enquiry of a kind that would not normally accompany even the most vigorous and intelligent processes of law enforcement.

1. <u>Organized crime is a phenomenon of prohibition</u>.

Americans have been singularly reluctant really to dig into the subject of what prohibition did to American society. I could argue that apart from the general impact of technology, it was the most profoundly disorganizing event, in the sense that psychologists use the term, since the Civil War. (Interestingly, we are still trying to cope with the aftermath of both events, and the Attorney General is the focus of that responsibility.) Prohibition was the final effort of fundamentalist Protestantism to impose an ethic on post-Protestant America. The result was disastrous on many counts, not least the extent to which it discredited the Protestant ethic. One specific result was the organization of bootlegging into criminal syndicates, which have never since ceased to exist, although in general a second generation leadership has now taken over. Typically, the principal activity of these syndicates has been to provide legally prohibited pleasures and outlets—gambling, prostitution, narcotics—to a community many of whose members do not at all share the ethical imperatives on which the statutory prohibitions were based. Of late there is much evidence that the syndicates are looking for new outlets for the capital they have amassed—a familiar enough event in the business world—and that this is causing many changes to take place, as the Attorney General has noted.

2. <u>Organized crime is an Italian phenomenon.</u>

Nothing is to be gained by trying to avoid this fact. At the same time it should be seen as one example of immigrant response to a new environment. The processes by which the Southern Italians have come to control organized crime are not in any fundamental way different from those by which, for example, the Jews came to dominate the clothing industry or the Irish, at one point, to control local politics in the North East. It results from a combination of the advantages and disadvantages which a particular immigrant group faces. The Eastern European Jews arrived in New York bringing with them a thousand years of experience of living in cities as merchants, combined with a similarly urban attitude that held there was nothing unmanly about operating a sewing machine: the result of these, and a number of other factors, was Seventh Avenue. The Irish arrived fresh from the political experiences of the O'Connell era, were fundamentally conservative and spoke English. The result was Ward 8. The Southern Italians, however, tended to be radical, and could not speak English, which kept them out of politics for a long while. They had no mercantile experience, and this kept them out of business. . . .

Thus organized crime stacks up as another of the post-immigration phenomena which Glazer and I have tried to describe in Beyond the Melting Pot. The fact of twenty million highly sensitive Italian Americans makes organized crime a different kind of problem than it would be were its members a wide cross section of the population.

3. Organized crime competes with organized politics.

The stereotype has it that corrupt political organizations produce organized crime. The evidence seems to be just the opposite: that "corrupt" political machines are the only social force capable of controlling organized crime, and that when the machines are broken, the syndicate takes over.

In New York, the defeat of Tammany by LaGuardia was followed by the entry of the syndicate into politics. LaGuardia proved, or at least gave ground for the suspicion, that a crusading, reform mayor on his own cannot touch the syndicate, and even in some ways comes to rely on it if he has broken completely with the indigenous urban political organization. In Chicago it should be noted that the political machine is a post prohibition event. . . .

It would seem to come down to a question of incentives and rewards. Because the incentives of "clean" government are so few and getting fewer, the ability of organized crime to destroy the party machines, or as the case of New York under De Sapio, to force the machine to do business with it, has been on the rise. It could just turn out that Reform has been an asset to organized crime.

4. It is not at all clear what the future holds.

Everything we "know" about society would lead us to presume that by now the combination of affluence, second and third generation complacency, and the prospect of security should be steadily diminishing the criminal element of Italian enterprise, but this does not appear to be happening. Perhaps this is not the case, but if it is, we are confronted with events different from any we have known. To wit: the self-stabilizing forces of American society, which for centuries have incorporated outside challenges, are now working. . . .

5. Organized crime is an almost wholly unexamined phenomenon.

As you know, after the 1958 election I spent several years at Syracuse University working with the Harriman papers. A good part of my time was directed to this subject. Nothing surprised me more than to learn that what I had come to regard as a major issue of American political science had been studied not at all. To my knowledge, the entire range of events of the Kefauver Hearings has not produced a single article in a scholarly American publication. The Academy of Political and Social Science has recently put out an inconsequential issue on the Annals of the subject, but it remains true that no American scholar of competence has yet undertaken a sustained enquiry on the subject of organized crime, with the possible exception of Professor Daniel Bell's Fortune articles, which are included in The End of Ideology.

The reasons for this are perhaps twofold. First, political science is still gripped by concern for the ideal, and is not attracted to the study of pathology, which organized crime is. Second, and more important, there are no data. No scholar in his right mind would try to investigate the subject on his own, and police intelligence files have understandably been closed.

This brings me to the proposal I would like to make. Several years ago, after my Reporter article appeared, I was asked to lecture on this subject at the Joint Center for Urban Studies of Harvard University and the Massachusetts Institute of Technology. To my surprise I found that one of the younger members of the Harvard faculty, James Quinn Wilson, was very much interested in this same subject, and had been thinking much along the lines I had. In this he was joined by his colleague Edward C. Banfield, one of the most distinguished members of the Harvard Department of Government. Since that time I have had occasion to talk to Wilson about bits and pieces of the subject and I find his interest if anything on the rise. As he has since become Director of the Joint Center for Urban Studies, he now has quite a range of resources to bring to bear on the question.

I would therefore like to suggest that it might be useful for the Attorney General to bring Professors Wilson and Banfield, and any others such as Professor Daniel Bell of Columbia who might be similarly disposed, down to Washington to talk over the question of whether it would be desirable for the Justice Department to establish a relationship with a small number of political scientists (as well perhaps as sociologists and economists) to undertake a joint study of the subject of organized crime. . . .

It may be the Attorney General is already doing this, in which event, my apologies for an interminable memorandum. But on the chance that he might not have, you might want to broach the subject with him, as it is, of course, a matter of great import to the future of the labor movement.

Resigning after the assassination of John F. Kennedy. Note incorrect date of November 21, 1963.

NOVEMBER 21, 1963
THE PRESIDENT
THE WHITE HOUSE
WASHINGTON, D.C.

Dear Mr. President,

As you assume the awesome responsibilities that have devolved upon you, I would like to offer my resignation as Assistant Secretary of Labor in order that you might in this respect, as in others, have the fullest freedom to organize the government in the best interests of the Administration and the Nation as you perceive them. I do so with the utmost assurance of my complete support and continued prayers.

Memorandum dictated to himself, describing his chaotic, terrible day after news of the assassination reached Washington. William Walton was an artist and Kennedy family friend. Charles Horsky was a prominent lawyer and White House adviser on national capital affairs.

NOVEMBER 22, 1963

Bill Walton, Charlie Horsky and I were just finishing lunch at Walton's house—in the grandest good mood with Walton leaving for the Russian tour that afternoon—I was talking about Brasilia and the phone rang. Oh no! Killed! No!. Horsky's office had phoned for him to return. We rushed upstairs. Television had some of it but the commercials continued. Bill began sobbing. Out of control. Horsky in a rage. Clint(?) Jackie's agent had said the President is dead. Walton knew this meant it was so. He dressed more or less and we went directly to the White House from Georgetown. On the way the radio reported that Albert Thomas had said he might be living.

We went directly to the President's office which was torn apart with new carpets being put down in his office and the cabinet room. As if a new President were to take office. No one about save Chuck Daly. McGeorge Bundy appeared. Icy. Ralph Dungan came in smoking a pipe, quizzical, as if unconcerned. Then Sorensen. The three together in the door of the hallway that leads to the Cabinet room area. Dead silent. Someone said "It's over." Bundy called for Secretary McNamara.

We still did not entirely believe it, with television not sure. But quickly enough one report added to another and the President was dead, as we watched in Dungan's office. Silence. Humphrey arrived. Dungan had by this point called Mary and laid his head on his desk for a bit. Humphrey and Dungan went to the adjoining room. Bill said he thought he would go home. I went with him. As we left the entrance to the West Wing the Flag was just being lowered. I pointed it out to him and he just about lost control. The photographers would not let us go alone as we hiked the long distance to the gate. Midway Walton straightened up and said let's walk out the way he would have expected us to, but he could not quite manage.

I put Walton in a taxi and went back to see Holborn if he were there. A guard asked for my identification but I asked him what difference it made.

And the thing is, Dungan had said, they will blame it on that 25 year old boy.

Memorandum for himself, recording that Mrs. Kennedy wanted a renewal of the drab and unsightly Pennsylvania Avenue to be carried out as a legacy of the Kennedy administration. He was to keep Mrs. Kennedy abreast of the progress for twenty-five years.

NOVEMBER 29, 1963

FOR THE RECORD:

Bill Walton called this morning, before leaving for his scheduled trip to Russia, to say he had spoken to Mrs. Kennedy about the Pennsylvania Avenue plans. She is completely behind them and will, he feels, be the greatest source of strength in years to come. She has given President Johnson a list of those projects left undone and which she feels were of great interest to President Kennedy. Pennsylvania Avenue is on this list. She feels that the National Cultural Center, the Stadium, and even LaFayette Square, had their origins in the Eisenhower Administration, but Pennsylvania Avenue is one of the Kennedy Administration entirely.

On Wednesday Walton showed the plans for Pennsylvania Avenue to the Kennedy family, including the Attorney General. They were all immensely impressed and particularly interested in the possibility that the National Square might become Kennedy Square.

Moynihan tells Mrs. Kennedy (still Mrs. Kennedy—much later it became Jackie) that he will carry on the Pennsylvania Avenue plan. His involvement arose from his role as the labor secretary's representative to the Ad Hoc Committee on Federal Office Space, empanelled by President Kennedy. Moynihan had written its "Guiding Principles for Federal Architecture" in 1962.

DECEMBER 2, 1963

Dear Mrs. Kennedy:

Before leaving for Russia, Bill Walton told me of his conversation with you about the Pennsylvania Avenue Plan (he and I and Fred Holborn are the Government members of the President's Council on Pennsylvania Avenue). We are, of course, immensely heartened by your interest. I believe that you, in turn, will be interested to read the comments of Ada Louise Huxtable, the architectural critic of the New York Times:

> The proposal for the Avenue emerged as one of the most impressive civic plans of modern times—grand in scope, sweeping in scale, awe-inspiring in its potentialities for greatness. As a concept it is worthy of Rome and Sixtus V; it has the clear possibility of providing one of the memorable landmarks of the 20th Century.

Following the assassination, a radio reporter from WTOP in Washington interviewed Moynihan. Mary McGrory also wrote about their conversation in the Washington Star. Moynihan obtained a transcript of the radio interview for his records, realizing its importance.

DECEMBER 5, 1963 [DATE OF TRANSCRIPT]

... WALKER: "Is there any meaning you can find in what has happened?"

MOYNIHAN: "I suppose the point that cuts deepest is the thought that there may not be. . . . You know the French author, Camus, when he came out at the end of his life, he said the world was absurd. A Christian couldn't think that, but the utter senselessness, the meaninglessness. . . .

"We all of us know down here that politics is a tough game. And I don't think there's any point in being Irish if you don't know that the world is going to break your heart eventually. I guess we thought that we had a little more time. So did he.

"This nation will never be the same after he has been President. We are a bigger, a stronger, a better nation. I think we know more about what it is we have to be. I think we know somewhat more about how to be it. It. . . . For some of us you'll say it won't be the same in other ways. Mary McGrory said to me that we'll never laugh again. And I said, 'Heavens. We'll laugh again. It's just that we'll never be young again."

WALKER: "Is the New Frontier leaderless?"

MOYNIHAN: "No sir! We have a leader. He is the President. If we learned anything from John F. Kennedy, we learned to serve the President. I think that the single, one thing that some of us are holding to, to keep our minds together, is that we will do exactly as the President wishes us to do in exactly what capacity he indicates."

WALKER: "Do you think the Johnson administration will continue the programs of the Kennedy administration?"

MOYNIHAN: "Well, I certainly believe with the deepest part of me that President Johnson will work for these programs with the fullest of his great ability. He helped formulate them. Here in the Department of Labor, I suppose we have worked with the President about as closely as any executive department. He's the Chairman of the President's Commission on Equal Employment Opportunities. We've had two years of working day and night with him and he's done a magnificent job. And I can't imagine his wanting to. . . . These are his policies as much as the administration's— as much as the former President's. And he has a reputation for accomplishment. That's why he's the leader of our party and why he's our President today."

WALKER: "Will the New Frontier still be able to realize its dreams?"

MOYNIHAN: "Oh, we're no good at answering questions like that today. You say dream. I think of the lines from *The Tempest*: 'We are such stuff as dreams are made of. . . . ' Well, you know that passage begins, 'Our revels now are ended.'"

Pat and Liz Moynihan, nearly inconsolable after Kennedy's death, and determined to buy a farm upstate, seek help from real estate brokers.

WASHINGTON, D.C. 20008
DECEMBER 9, 1963

Dear Sir:

I wish to purchase a farm in New York State for use as a summer and vacation home. I am looking for an isolated spot with a fair amount of acreage of an upland kind that has no longer any value for crop purposes. I would like something on a dirt road, in a location likely to remain permanently rural. I want a house in good condition structurally, but without modern improvements such as central heating.

I would particularly hope to find a house of Victorian design, but this is not essential. If you can send me photographs of anything you have, I will promptly return them.

Moynihan urges Theodore H. White, the journalist and author of THE MAKING OF THE PRESIDENT, 1960, *to write more about "the Negro" issue.*

JANUARY 23, 1964

Dear Teddy:

As you know, I thought your series on the Negro was brilliant. I very much hope you will not let go of this subject. I enclose a report, which we sent to the President on January 1, on the persons found unqualified for military service. The President accepted our recommendations, and we are moving with as much vigor as we can command to begin the testing of all 18-year-olds, with the object of learning which of them simply do not measure up.

As an entirely private matter, let me add that the majority of the Negroes in the nation fail the mental tests. But it is also interesting to note that in our survey of 2500 such persons, there was no significant difference between the unemployment rate, etc., of the Negroes as against the whites. At the bottom of the barrel a certain rough equality is at last achieved.

I learned yesterday that <u>Beyond the Melting Pot</u> has been chosen "among the leading contenders" for one of the National Book awards. I must rush out and apply for the Cosmos Club.

Urging Secretary Wirtz to recruit Negroes and women.

JANUARY 29, 1964

MEMORANDUM FOR THE SECRETARY

I learned that there are no Negroes or women members of the labor or management research committees associated with the Bureau of Labor Statistics. I hope to do something about this on both counts.

Reporting to Paul Mattern, the new cooperative extension agent in Delaware County, N.Y., that he had found a farm.

FEBRUARY 25, 1964

Dear Mr. Mattern:

We have been fortunate enough to find a farm in the town of Davenport, of the kind I wrote to you about earlier.

I will be taking possession late March, and plan to be there the first week of April. I hope at that time I might impose on you to look over the place with me and advise me on the best practices I should follow with regard to the maintenance of the fields, which I gather are in fair shape but need attention.

Moynihan expresses sympathy to Mayor Wagner about his wife's illness. Wagner decided not to seek reelection the following year.

FEBRUARY 29, 1964

Dear Mayor Wagner:

I had a good talk last evening with Dudley Morris. He is a first-rate man; if we ever get a poverty program going he ought to be part of it, and we will keep closely in touch.

I write for another reason. I took the occasion to ask about Mrs. Wagner, and for the first time learned how deeply ill she is. This fact must burden you to the exclusion of all thoughts and persons outside your own family, and I feel almost presumptuous to intrude even this much. It is mostly for one's own self that one writes at times such as this. I first met Mrs. Wagner in the 1953 campaign when I, as one of your speech writers, and she as "the candidate's wife" were equally awed and encouraged at the ease with which you would march before the still new and unfamiliar television cameras thirty seconds before air time, and somehow manage to make sense and even substance of the script we had thrown together for you. Through all the grimy battles of the decade since, she has added a touch of grace and a good woman's reserve, reminding us that the most important thing would be won or lost depending on how we handled our own selves, rather than how the voters reacted. She has our prayers, and every last bit of affection.

CHAPTER TWO

"Nine Pages of Dynamite"

Moynihan's service in the Johnson administration as it launched the War on Poverty brought him ever deeper into his preoccupation with the issue of poor black families. But in this period the political consequences of his actions hit him with full force, creating a new crisis for him personally and also renewing his determination to speak the truth as he saw it. Moynihan sought to support LBJ with his candid views on the challenges of poverty and race following enactment of historic civil rights legislation, and also to explain the sudden eruption of violence in American cities. He was proud of his involvement in writing a draft of an important Johnson speech advocating efforts to achieve great equality between the races. Meanwhile, he kept close to the Kennedy family, advising Robert Kennedy on his run for the New York Senate and pursuing the renewal of Pennsylvania Avenue as a project he knew had the support of JFK and Jacqueline Kennedy. The letters here also show Moynihan beginning to expand his interest in ethnicity to a global scale. By the end of 1965, he had resigned from the Johnson administration to make his first foray into elected politics—a failed run for City Council president in New York.

Moynihan asks Justice Goldberg to prod the White House to take an interest in raising architectural standards for the Pennsylvania Avenue redevelopment project. As labor secretary, Goldberg had assigned Moynihan to represent him on the Ad Hoc Committee on Federal Office Space.

MARCH 11, 1964

Dear Mr. Justice:

Here are the relevant extracts from the Report of the Ad Hoc Committee on Federal Office Space, plus some related comments from <u>Architectural Forum</u> and elsewhere. As you will see, the President really had little to say about this, although he was immensely interested. The problem was that nobody around him in the White House or in the Bureau of the Budget really gave a damn about this subject. It was simply never taken seriously.

To my knowledge, the guiding principles have never even been printed apart from the press release of the Committee Report. I have sometimes thought to take this subject up with Kermit Gordon. It seems to me a typical problem of communication of Presidential policy in an area where neither the politicians and the bureaucrats are really involved. For my part, I continue to be very much interested. I don't really know a great deal about architecture, but I do know that buildings such as the new Smithsonian and the new House Office Building are unmistakable signs of a civilization in decline. (I should very much like your comments on this subject.)

Senator Kennedy might also be interested in the citation which was presented to the President by the American Institute of Architects—the first such citation in the history of the AIA.

Moynihan enjoyed teasing Harry O'Donnell, a longtime Albany veteran and now press adviser to the foundering presidential campaign of Governor Nelson Rockefeller, who had just lost in an upset in the New Hampshire primary to former Senator Henry Cabot Lodge of Massachusetts, prompting Moynihan's joke that it cost him $850 a vote. ("Carmine would be appalled" is a reference to the Tammany Hall boss, Carmine De Sapio, who had been credited with forging the careers of Mayor Wagner, Governor Harriman, and President Kennedy.)

MARCH 12, 1964

Dear Mr. O'Donnell:

Owing to the New York Times account of the diligent use of ethnic appeals by the Rockefeller National Campaign Committee in the New Hampshire primary, I am constrained to bring to your attention a matter of more than passing seriousness to you and to me. An unnamed bigot in your organization has sent to me an anonymous letter which intends clearly: First, to malign a representative of an important American minority group, one whom people have given many brave soldiers and pianists to the world, by holding up his Christian name to ridicule. Second, this anonymous bigot clearly is undertaking to suggest that both the Attorney General and myself were reluctant to enter a Presbyterian Church, when in fact the bold stands of ecumenicism have made such an assertion a matter of grave concern, except where it can be forgiven under the rubric of invincible ignorance.

I am sure you will want this matter looked to promptly by the Minorities Committee. If you have not by now disbanded the Committee, that is.

All here in Washington much dismayed by the results. Rough calculation would indicate Rockefeller results factor out to about $850 per vote. Carmine would be appalled. Under the circumstances I feel it necessary to return my button.

Asking Secretary Wirtz to approve a trip to Europe to study poverty.

APRIL 10, 1964

MEMORANDUM FOR THE SECRETARY

. . . The more I have thought about the subject of poverty in America, the more I have come to think that the most revealing fact about the nature of our problem is that the Europeans seemed to have solved it.

The United States is clearly the first nation in history to attain a general standard of living that might properly be described as mass affluence. On the other hand, we may end up the last of the industrial democracies to retain within our borders something like mass poverty.

It is a question of values. The Europeans have been concerned, even, as in the case of the British, preoccupied with getting rid of poverty. Our preoccupation has been with opening up equal opportunity for prosperity. The two are not opposite sides of the same coin.

I am satisfied from the literature and the statistics that the Northern Europeans have pretty much got rid of poverty as it exists, say, in the black belt of Chicago or in Appalachia. However, poverty is something that you can smell more readily than you can quantify, and I would like to make a quick trip to Europe to check out my impression, and arrange for a systematic flow of information from OECD.

I would like to spend two or three days at OECD headquarters in Paris, a day or two in Hamburg, the rest in Liverpool, perhaps one day in London. If I left the weekend of April 25, I would be back about May 6 or 7. . . .

Memorandum to Secretary Wirtz about automation.

APRIL 16, 1964

MEMORANDUM FOR THE SECRETARY

I am disturbed about your remark that after three years in the Department you still don't feel you know any more about automation than when you arrived. Part of my distress is that I expect I could say the same.

Would it be possible for you to sit down with some of us one evening to talk over the question? Clearly, we are not doing our job by you. At the same time, I sense there may be some rather important divergence of views which you should at least be aware of. But mainly, I think we need a closer look at what it is you need from us.

A first outline of Moynihan's proposal that blacks (Negroes) need more than equal opportunities; they need more equal results.

APRIL 20, 1964

MEMORANDUM FOR THE SECRETARY

Has the time come to organize an inquiry into the subject of unequal treatment for the Negro?

Those responsible for public policy in America are being asked where they stand on this point. It seems to me, however, that the response, in general, is one of bewilderment and confusion at a wholly unfamiliar proposition. The subject is much in need of analytical and philosophical discussion, and we have not the accustomed leisure to reach a consensus.

American doctrine is centered on the proposition of equal opportunity: of equal protection of the laws. The social struggles of the past have characteristically centered on the question of whether this group or that was being denied equal treatment.

The Civil Rights Bill will mark the consummation of that effort as far as the Negro is concerned.

Now comes the proposition that the Negro is entitled to damages as to unequal favored treatment—in order to compensate for past unequal treatment of an opposite kind.

We could cope with such a proposition were it put in terms of the rights of a group of workers, or of bond holders—functional groups—but have no precedent for treating with an ethnic group. (Consider the difficulty encountered in justifying "benign" quotas in activities such as housing projects which are designed to achieve a balance of races.)

But we cannot avoid it. The Negroes are asking for unequal treatment. More seriously, it may be that without unequal treatment in the immediate future there is no way for them to achieve anything like equal status in the long run.

Whitney Young has spoken of a "Marshall Plan" for the Negro. This term may have a negative effect with some people. Would the analogy of infant industries be better?

In any event, do you think the President might under any circumstances, come out for some form of special treatment—as part of your plans for the coming Summer? Obviously this is filled with political peril, but I suspect we may have to face it anyway.

An early warning to Wirtz that welfare laws were producing "an entire subculture of dependency."

MAY 6, 1964

MEMORANDUM FOR THE SECRETARY

One of the things it seems to me has got to be said before long is that the greatest single danger facing the Negroes of America is that the whites are going to put them on welfare.

As Secretary of Labor, it seems to me you are precisely the person to sound this warning.

The conservative votes of most communities profess a great distaste for welfare, et al., but in actual fact—if you accept the line of analysis I try to develop in the St. Louis speech—it will be a good deal easier just to pension the Negroes off, as it were, than to accept the major and sometimes wrenching changes in our way of doing things that will be required if we are going to bring them in as full-fledged members of the larger community.

This process is already in evidence. Aid to Dependent Children goes up and up and up. Half the recipients are Negro. In New York today 17 percent of the city's Negroes receive public relief—an increase in numbers of 73 percent since 1957. Etc.

Nothing would be more terrible, if it should come to pass. We will have created an entire subculture of dependency, alienation, and despair. We have already done as much to whole sections of Appalachia, as I understand it, as also to the Indian reservations. It is in truth the way we cope with this kind of problem. As against giving the men proper jobs and a respectable place in their community and family. . . .

Moynihan tells Wirtz that he turned down an offer from Mayor Robert F. Wagner of New York to serve as city labor commissioner.

JUNE 2, 1964

MEMORANDUM FOR THE SECRETARY

Mayor Wagner has asked me to come up and be his Commissioner of Labor. In some circumstances I might seek such an opportunity, but I certainly would not consider leaving the administration at this time, for all the complex of reasons which you well understand. I will tell him so, and trouble you with the matter only to avoid any misunderstanding.

Moynihan's message to Mayor Wagner indicates that Wagner had discussed appointing Moynihan with President Johnson.

JUNE 10, 1964

Dear Mr. Mayor:

The White House has now reported to me your conversation with the President at the dinner for Prime Minister Eshkol. I suppose that must put an end to any question of my coming to work for you at the moment, but it does not in any way lessen the appreciation with which I responded to your offer.

You are, Sir, one of the great public leaders of our time, and to have been asked to serve in your administration is an honor I value more than I can readily express.

Moynihan seeks the help of Carmine De Sapio, the onetime Tammany Hall boss, in preparing an oral history of the Kennedy years for the Kennedy Library. By this time De Sapio had been ousted as Manhattan Democratic leader by party "reformers," including Mayor Wagner, who had turned against him.

JUNE 16, 1964

Dear Carmine:

We are making progress with the oral interviews for the Kennedy Library. Many prominent people are contributing personal recollections of events.

As Bob Kennedy wrote to you, your interview would be highly confidential. Some day, years ahead, historians and scholars will make use of it and will be able to place your role in true historical perspective. But you can set the date when and the conditions under which your memoir can be used.

We are learning a great deal of valuable information about the way President Kennedy won the Democratic Party nomination for President in 1960. You played an important part in making the New York State vote meaningful and no one knows better than you how it came about that 104 ½ of New York's 114 votes went to Kennedy on the first ballot. Your interview will put your point of view on the record and will give valuable help to the nomination. . . .

Moynihan asks his staff to assist Ralph Nader.

AUGUST 17, 1964

MEMORANDUM FOR MR. BRICKETT

Mr. Ralph Nader, who will be working for me for the next three months, would like to have the New York Times delivered to his office in room 2314. He would like the daily and Sunday papers.

Moynihan recommends that Attorney General Robert F. Kennedy select New York City Council President Paul R. Screvane, a party regular, as his campaign manager in the New York Senate race. Screvane later ran for mayor in 1965 and asked Moynihan to run on his ticket as City Council president.

AUGUST 18, 1964

MEMORANDUM FOR THE ATTORNEY GENERAL

Governor Harriman just called to ask me to the 6:00 p.m. meeting on Thursday, and in the process asked for any thoughts I had on a campaign manager.

I suggested Paul Screvane. He is an elected official of the City. By background a regular (a city employee, actually) but by election a reformer. He represents the Mayor and is heir-apparent. He is Italian.

Just as important, he is the most orderly and effective a man in a campaign headquarters that I have yet to see in New York. You fellows have high standards on these matters, but he might meet them.

The Governor asked that I send you this note, suggesting that you might want to think more about Screvane.

Moynihan suggests that Robert Kennedy establish his base outside of New York City. Kennedy chose Glen Cove, Long Island, where Liz Moynihan assisted in the campaign.

AUGUST 19, 1964

MEMORANDUM FOR THE ATTORNEY GENERAL

I wonder if you should not be prepared to suggest where you propose to live in New York after you are elected.

There is a sort of tradition that one Senator is from New York City, the other from upstate.

That being the case, you might want to pick a site with this in mind.

One possibility would be Long Island. It is not considered part of the City, and is a place where you will have a great following, as well as a good political organization.

Jim Mead, our last Senator save Lehman, came from Buffalo, but it is such a lousy place to live I fear it would look artificial for you to opt it.

A case could be made for Albany. It is the center of the State in terms of transportation routes. It is the Capital—but Rockefeller is there. It would symbolize your commitment to State issues. It is not a bad place to live.

Moynihan, in a memorandum to himself, records private comments made by Robert Kennedy expressing displeasure over FBI Director J. Edgar Hoover, who had sent him reports on JFK's sex life, perhaps as blackmail. His brother's activities were not known publicly at this time, which is probably why Moynihan made a note of it for his papers.

RFK TO DPM ____31 AUG 1964

(when state committee proved no help in handling hesitation of afl-cio to endorse rfk)

Of course I can't complain. If they were any good at these things I wouldn't be here today.

RFK to Joe Kraft.

J. Edgar Hoover was furious when the President called [Allen] Dulles before him to say they would be reappointed [as C.I.A. director]. All this the result of one of Neustadt's studies that said you are going to reappoint these guys eventually, might as well do it right off.

When the President was still alive Hoover continually sent RFK reports on his sex life—just to show they were watching.

RFK apparently became very bitter at hoover's quick shift of allegiance to President Johnson.

Moynihan urges Peace Corps Director R. Sargent Shriver, who was designated to run the War on Poverty, to focus on urban as well as rural poverty.

SEPTEMBER 9, 1964

Dear Sarge,

I grow preoccupied with the question of research on urban poverty. As you very likely have already made arrangements in the area, I will keep this letter short.

We know almost nothing about urban poverty except that it is not going away. (Did you notice that welfare rolls in New York City grew by 12.4% last year?) The poverty program is made up of a collection of ideas which seem to make sense, but hardly any have been subjected to anything like a systematic research and testing procedure. You will recall, for example, our reluctance about accepting the effectiveness of community action programs as an established fact.

Unless you are in a position to measure your results you will never be able to bring the program to a high level of efficiency, much less to prove it to Congress.

Should you not set up a group to consider what a research program on poverty, rural as well as urban, would look like?

Moynihan expresses concern to Wirtz that Kennedy was losing the Senate race to the incumbent, Senator Kenneth Keating.

OCTOBER 12, 1964

MEMORANDUM FOR THE SECRETARY

The basic argument for Robert Kennedy is that New York needs a Democratic voice in the Senate and a victory in the State.

Since the Second World War, out of all the elections that have been held, only four Democrats have been elected, a total of only seven times. (Lehman twice, Harriman once, Kennedy once, Levitt three times.)

This failure is showing. New York is by far the most liberal of the great industrial States, it is by far the largest source of financial support for liberal candidates around the nation, but it has no voice of its own in national affairs.

Robert Kennedy is a natural leader of the New York Democracy.

He did not seek the Senate nomination. It sought him. The best men in the Party in New York—John English, the Ed Costikyans—came to him and asked him to raise the banner of a resurgent Democratic Party based on the ideals of his brother and the leadership of President Johnson.

Nonetheless Robert Kennedy is losing.

He is losing primarily because the people of New York do not understand that Keating is not a liberal Senator. Keating is a passive, conservative Rochester lawyer who was promised a State judgeship in 1958 in return for leaving the House of Representatives to provide a conservative, upstate name on Rockefeller's slate. After the debacle of the Democratic convention, Keating won—beating Frank Hogan by a bare 130,000 votes, 450,000 behind Rockefeller.

Keating has consistently voted against Democratic programs in housing, education, medical care for the aged—in 1960, not of course this year—manpower training, etc. But the people of New York do not know this.

What Kennedy must have is a massive television spot campaign to get Keating's record over to the natural Democratic majority. This costs money.

If Kennedy wins, it will not be a moment too soon. New York is in trouble—economic trouble, ethnic trouble, government trouble. The Rockefeller administration is turning out to be the most corrupt and inadequate of the century. But there is no Democratic alternative without State leadership. With Kennedy elected Senator, we can look to a vigorous New York party that will take advantage of winning the legislature—which it will probably do for the first time since 1935 at this coming election—to reapportion the State so that the natural Democratic majority can make its voice known.

The alternative is a continued defunct party, and a dangerously unstable situation in our most important State. This summer New York had mass working class violence for practically the first time since the great strikes of the 1880's. Nothing short of the highest leadership can put this situation back into place in the time available to us.

Providing an update on the election to the distinguished Cambridge University historian, J. H. Plumb, whom Moynihan had met in England in the early 1950s.

OCTOBER 30, 1964

Dear Jack,

. . . The election, thank God, is all but over. I am off for a weekend stumping about central New York, after which a good week at the farm, shooting grouse and drinking Beausejour if all goes according to plan. It has been a miserable three months but not without interest. Immense ethnic strains throughout. One unlooked for by-product was that the New York Times made what I would regard as a major concession to the Glazer-Moynihan thesis and began running regular stories on what the Jewish vote, the Italian vote, the WASP vote, etc., was doing—these being categories they refused to recognize existed until this election. If I have the time this winter I would like to work on this whole question of ethnicity as a contemporary phenomenon. I think we can safely say we are beyond the point of having to establish that it exists—the question now is how come, and to what consequence. I wrote a longish piece this summer as a book review for Commentary—a staff product which Norman Podhoretz very much wanted reviewed—but then decided

not to publish most of it as my thoughts weren't clear enough by half. Now I
suspect I may return to the subject. . . .

Moynihan argues to Wirtz for federal aid to Catholic schools.

NOVEMBER 16, 1964

MEMORANDUM FOR THE SECRETARY

Nothing would be more misleading than to suggest that a proposal for Federal
aid to education that would in one way or another include Catholic schools
or Catholic school children would be greeted with general acceptance in the
nation. To the contrary, all hell will break loose among some groups. There is
no way to avoid it. On the other hand, there has been, I feel, a strong movement of opinion towards some accommodations in this area, and it is more
than likely that the votes could be found to enact one. That is all I suggest.

There have been four major developments over the past five years or so that
have tended in this direction.

First, the image—and the position—of the Catholic Church in America
has changed.

When the issue of Federal aid first snagged on the question of Church-
related schools in the 1940's, the Catholic Church was viewed with as much
alarm in liberal circles as in fundamentalist ones. Cardinal Spellman vs. Mrs.
Roosevelt. "McCarthyism," John C. Bennett, President of the Union Theological Seminary remarked recently, "was a special Roman Catholic temptation." Things have changed profoundly since then. Pope John, President
Kennedy, the Ecumenical Council have profoundly changed the image of
American Catholicism, and have given it new directions as well. Typically, the
Catholics seemed almost as immune to the recent revival of the radical right
as were the Southerners to McCarthyism. Dr. Bennett's remark continued:
"but the new Goldwaterism is a special Protestant temptation."

In some measure also, the persistence of the issue has generated some light
along with the heat. It can no longer be said that <u>no</u> American liberal is aware
the Catholic schools in Great Britain and Canada, for example, receive (for

the most part) regular public assistance. Institutions such as Walter Lippmann and the <u>New Republic</u> now favor aid to parochial schools.

Thus, there has been a lessening of liberal opposition.

2. <u>The Civil Rights movement has brought the American faiths into active collaboration for the first time in history</u>.

It would be difficult to overestimate the long-run effect of the intimate and organized relations between the various church bodies that sprung up in support of the Civil Rights Act. Nothing like it has ever happened before. The resulting sense of shared moral—and social—purpose has done a great deal to relieve the tensions between Catholics and Protestant bodies.

Last February the National Council of Churches held a carefully planned and prepared conference on Church and State. I understand that the leadership was quite amazed at the extent of delegate support for State aid to church schools.

3. <u>There is a growing interest in non-Catholic private schools</u>.

The inevitable uniformity and bureaucracy of the public school system has aroused considerable interest in the possibilities of private schools. Most of the interest involves Protestant and Jewish groups, but not a little is purely secular.

4. <u>It appears the deadlock cannot be broken without aid to private schools</u>.

This is now the general view, whether or not it would be affected by the present election, I could not say. What is certain is that many groups have abandoned the idea of general Federal aid altogether in favor of limited forms of categorical aid, and others such as the American Federation of Teachers in its recent statement, have come out for aid to church schools.

The AFL-CIO Executive Council is on record in support of inclusion of private schools in a Federal aid proposal. . . .

Moynihan asks Richard Goodwin, speechwriter for LBJ, to enlist the president in support of the Pennsylvania Avenue renewal project.

JANUARY 7, 1965

Dear Dick,

I hope you will not mind my pursuing with you the question of President Johnson's relation to the Pennsylvania Avenue project—in the light of your remarks about it at dinner some weeks ago, and his statement about the Potomac in the State of the Union.

Point number one of the Great Society is to rebuild the American city. The New York Times described the Pennsylvania Avenue Plan as "one of the most ambitious architectural plans ever prepared for a major part of a capital city." But it is more than that: it is a proposal to build the first modern downtown urban complex of the Twentieth Century.

If it were only a matter of making Washington more attractive, I don't think any of us would have clung to the subject with the wrongheadedness that will be evident in this letter.

The question is whether America will be the first to do something that must be done the world over.

It is, further, a most rare event for the City itself. . . .

Clearly, work on the plans to rebuild the Avenue began during the Kennedy Administration. However, the report was not finished during his Administration. It was to President Johnson that it was finally submitted, in May 1964, and it was he who called it a "bold and creative" plan and asked that it be "carefully examined and thoroughly studied" by the appropriate agencies of the Executive Branch. And it was he who, having received the reports of the government agencies, formally endorsed the plan during the Presidential campaign.

In a word, the report was made to President Johnson and endorsed by him. If the plan is now carried out, it will surely be regarded as one of his great achievements—unless of course history decides the whole thing was a bad idea, but that is another matter!

Seeking help from the Soil Conservation Service, in upstate New York, in building a pond on his farm, following the advice of Mattern, a Delaware County Agriculture official.

3100 MACOMB STREET, N.W.
WASHINGTON, D. C. 20008
FEBRUARY 25, 1965
PERSONAL AND UNOFFICIAL
GENTLEMEN:

I recently wrote Paul Mattern to ask his advice about building a pond on my farm in the Town of Davenport, Delaware County. He advised me that the Soil Conservation Service could give some assistance in pond design. I do not wish any cost-sharing, but do need technical advice, etc.

Mine is a working dairy farm, with a stream that slows down considerably in August, but does run year round. I would like to build the pond this summer. Could you advise me whether it would be possible to get on your technical assistance list this year?

Moynihan's memorandum to President Johnson, containing what Wirtz, in a cover letter, describes as "nine pages of dynamite about the Negro situation." It is a distillation (clearly for the personal consumption of LBJ) of the so-called Moynihan Report, published by the Labor Department Office of Policy Planning and Research, as "The Negro Family: The Case for National Action." The report indeed exploded politically, becoming known as the "Moynihan Report" and forever helping to define Moynihan's political identity.

MARCH 5, 1965

MEMORANDUM FOR THE PRESIDENT

The attached Memorandum is nine pages of dynamite about the Negro situation.

It was prepared by Pat Moynihan as a Memorandum to you from me.

I agree with Pat's analysis and concur in his recommendations.

But if this were to be a formal Memorandum it would have to be put in different form. I think you will want to get the full impact of Pat's more vigorous approach. So I am transmitting it this way. We can prepare something else later in the light of your reactions.

The key points in the Memorandum are these:

1. Negroes are now going to demand not just equal <u>opportunity</u> but equal <u>results</u>.
2. Most of them don't have enough education and background to achieve equal <u>results</u> even if they get equal <u>opportunity</u>.
3. The principal reason for this is the breakdown of the Negro family structure. This breakdown is getting worse, not better.
4. Federal policy should be built around the necessity to restore the structure of the Negro family.
5. Seven specific recommendations are made at the end of the Memorandum.

W. Willard Wirtz

MEMORANDUM FOR THE PRESIDENT

On every hand there are unmistakable signs that the civil rights movement is entering a second stage and a new crisis.

In the first stage Negro Americans fought for and won rights which are traditionally associated with <u>Liberty</u>:

- the right to vote
- the right to assemble and to petition
- the right to move about freely in public places
- the right to compete for jobs and other rewards of the market place.

In the second state of the civil rights movement the Negroes are clearly going to begin demanding rights that are associated with the democratic ideal of <u>Equality</u>:

- equally good education
- equally good housing
- equally good jobs.

These are, in effect, demands for <u>equal results from equal competition</u>.

America has never been comfortable with this type of demand. Movements for equality of <u>results</u> are often fiercely resisted: witness the initial hostility to the Populist movement, or to the Trade Union movement.

In the second stage of the civil rights movement, therefore, Negro organizations will lose much of their middle-class support. They in turn will become more bitter at what they already term "phoney liberals."

More seriously, the entire nation, Negroes included, will run smack into the fact that equal opportunity for Negroes does not produce equal results—because the Negroes today are a grievously injured people who in fair and equal competition will by and large lose out.

Many persons mistakenly compare discrimination against Negroes with past discrimination against other groups.

As if, for example, breaking down barriers to Negro apprentices in the buildings trades was like breaking down the quotas on Jewish students in medical schools a generation ago. It is not. Once the bars were down the Jewish lads swarmed in to the schools and were more than equal to the competition of their fellow students.

We have been in the business of breaking down job barriers to Negroes for four years now. We can no longer deny that our hardest task is not to create openings, but to fill them.

This problem is now compounded by a biological explosion. When you became Vice President one of every ten Americans was a Negro. Before 1972 the proportion will be one in eight.

In the next five years the Negro work force will expand 20 percent. Twice the rate of the whites.

Many of these young persons pouring into the labor force are simply not going to be prepared to compete.

There is one dramatic measure of their disabilities: 56 percent of the Negro youth called up for Selective Service fail the mental test. That is a test of ability at about the seventh-eighth grade level. 14 percent of whites fail it.

Little wonder 22 percent of Negro male teenagers are unemployed today.

How come?

Many explanations are put forward. In the Department of Labor, however, we feel that the master problem is that the Negro family structure is crumbling.

Somehow American national policy (quite the opposite is the case in Europe) has never given serious attention to the role of family structure in social problems. Yet everyone knows from personal experience how fundamental it is.

You were born poor. You were brought up poor. Yet you came of age full of ambition, energy, and ability. Because your mother and father gave it to you.

The richest inheritance any child can have is a stable, loving, disciplined family life.

A quarter of the Negro children born in America last year were illegitimate.

- 29 percent in Chicago
- 36 percent in Memphis
- 43 percent in Harlem

The white illegitimacy rate is 3 percent.

Almost one-fourth of nonwhite families are headed by women. 36 percent of Negro children are living in families with one or both parents missing.

56 percent of Negro youth sooner or later on, receive Aid to Families of Dependent Children payments provided by the Federal government. As against 8 percent of whites.

<u>Probably not much more than a third of Negro youth reach 18 having lived all their lives with both parents.</u>

Because many middle-class Negro families are doing very well indeed, these overall statistics probably conceal the degree of disorganization among the families of the Negro poor.

<u>Without exception every statistical measure of Negro family stability has gotten worse, not better, over the past fifteen years.</u>

The main reason for this is the systematic weakening of the position of the <u>Negro male</u>. This problem is as old as America and as new as the April unemployment rate.

- <u>Slavery</u>—destroyed the Negro family. Mammy was a respected figure. Sambo was jeered.
- <u>Reconstruction</u>—terrorized the Negro male by lynching, and humiliated him by segregation.
- <u>Urbanization</u>—poured families into slums where the family had no identity. The cabin in the cotton was at least a separate housing unit that defined the family. (Negroes are now more urban than whites.)
- <u>Unemployment</u>—undermined the role of the Negro man as the breadwinner. Last year 29 percent of Negro males in the work force were unemployed at one time or another—half of these for 15 weeks or more.

By contrast Negro women have always done and continue to do relatively well. There are, for example, more Negro women college graduates than male. In relative terms Negro women get better jobs, higher salaries, more prestige.

There is much evidence that these problems are beginning to feed on themselves—that matters are getting worse at an evermore rapid rate.

The Department of Labor has always felt unemployment was a key problem—and it was. Up until the last few years the number of broken Negro families, new welfare cases, and suchlike rose and fell with the Negro male unemployment rate as if they were connected by a chain. But in the past few years this connection seems to have been broken. Unemployment has dropped. But broken homes, illegitimacy, welfare dependency continue to rise.

Make no mistake. This is the problem that is making our cities ungovernable. It is the problem of poverty. It will not go away. By the middle of the 1980's seven of the ten largest cities in America will probably have Negro majorities.

The breakdown of the Negro family is the principal cause of all the problems of delinquency, crime, school dropouts, unemployment, and poverty which are bankrupting our cities, and could very easily lead to a kind of political anarchy unlike anything we have known.

- Last summer there were Negro riots in New York, Rochester, Jersey City, Elizabeth, Paterson, Dixmoor, and Philadelphia. Mostly made up of young Negro youth who know how bad off they are. There will be more.
- Last year the number of persons on welfare in New York City went up by one-eighth.
- In most of our cities about three-quarters of the crimes of murder, forcible rape, and aggravated assault are committed by Negroes. Given the childhood experience of most of these youth, psychologists state that their later behavior is entirely predictable.

The point is this: Most of the welfare assistance, the special education efforts, the community action programs which we are now doubling and redoubling are essentially the provision of surrogate family services. Society is trying to do for these young persons what in normal circumstances parents do for their children. Only these children have no parents.

We can go on providing this kind of welfare assistance forever. The evidence of a quarter-century is that it does not change anything.

- In 1940 there were a quarter-million AFDC children whose fathers were absent—i.e. had deserted them. In 1963 there were nearly 2 million. Two-thirds of the increase were Negroes.

<u>Or the Federal government can make an historic new departure. It can make the decision that an object of national policy is to bring the structure of the Negro family into line with that of the rest of our society.</u>
I am convinced that if this is done we will solve the Negro problem for once and all. It is the work of a half-century. More is the reason to begin now. More is the reason to define our program in terms of the dynamic factors which at present work against equality, but can work for it.

- Many people think the color problem is insoluble. Nonsense.
- A quarter-century ago Japanese Americans were subject to the worst kind of racial discrimination and mistreatment. All of which has practically disappeared before our eyes. The reason is that the Japanese (and the Chinese) have become a prosperous middle-class group. They now send twice as large a proportion of their children to college as do whites. Have twice as large a proportion of professional persons. Having solved the class problem, we solved the color problem. One of the reasons it was possible to do the former is that Japanese and Chinese have probably the most close knit family structure of any group in America.

How can this be done?
I am convinced that the first step must be to bring all the persons and agencies in the Government concerned with this problem to the point where they are aware of the problem of the Negro family, and agree that our basic strategy must be to strengthen it.

We have a tendency to rush off after solutions before really agreeing on what the problem is.

Once we agree on the problem, I believe we will find it relatively easy to come up with sound proposals for action. Of great importance, we will have an absolute measure of whether or not our efforts are producing any results.

This is not the least advantage of adopting a family structure strategy—we will not be able to tell ourselves that we have changed anything until we really have.

As a start I would suggest seven steps.

One. Appoint a working party to review every relevant program of the Federal government to determine whether it is helping to strengthen the Negro family or simply perpetuating its weaknesses. For example, we are practically the only industrial democracy in the world that does not have a system of family allowances for families with <u>fathers present</u>, but we have a vast Federal system to support families with <u>fathers absent</u>.

Two. Men must have jobs. We must not rest until every able-bodied Negro male is working. Even if we have to displace some females. (In the Department of Labor, after four years of successful effort to increase Negro employees, we found that in non-professional categories 80 percent were women!)

Three. Family housing must be provided. We must find ways to get emerging middle class Negro families into the suburbs, where the surroundings tend to reinforce the integrity of the family—just the opposite of the Negro ghetto.

Four. Negro youth must be given a greater opportunity to serve in the Armed Forces. This is the most important experience the Federal government can provide young Negro men. It is without question our shining opportunity. Negroes are now seriously under-represented in the Armed Forces. It should be the other way around. Just as an example, the Manpower Development and Training Program can take youth who volunteer but are rejected, and bring them up to military standards.

Five. Birth control. There is no way to control this problem unless we bring the Negro birthrate back into line with that of whites and cut down the rate of illegitimacy. There is much evidence that this can be done.

Six. More can be done about redesigning jobs that are now thought to be women's jobs and turning them into men's jobs. This is a great problem for the Negro male: his type of job is declining, while the jobs open to the Negro female are expanding.

Seven. Negro information center. There does not now exist anywhere in the Federal government a place where all of the relevant information about the situation of the Negro is brought together, correlated and made available to the many agencies that need it. This could be an important means of measuring our success or failure, and alerting ourselves to emerging problems. The Department of Labor could establish such a center, as could a number of other agencies now in existence or soon to be established.

Harry McPherson, President Johnson's close aide, became a Moynihan confidant and lifelong friend. Here Moynihan outlines a proposal for an international conference on ethnicity, an early indication of his interest in expanding his study of the subject to an international scale.

MARCH 12, 1965

MEMORANDUM FOR MR. MCPHERSON

I am writing you as Chairman of the Government Committee on Culture and Intellectual Exchange for the International Cooperation Year [ICY], on which you have asked me to serve as a member. I would like to raise the possibility of an international conference on Ethnicity in the Modern World. This could be an ICY project. In any event, the subject might be of interest to you on general grounds. . . .

The Sources of Twentieth Century Conflicts

Within months of its establishment the UN was caught up in the Cold War, and its proceedings have been pretty much dominated ever since by that aspect of international politics.

The point about the Cold War is that it has adopted for its definitions a mid-19th Century view which sees the world evolving around the issue of property relations. Communism, Socialism, Capitalism. Each of these is a 19th Century ideology. In the 20th Century the Communist cause was taken up by Russia, the United States remained Capitalist, while much of Europe and the new Nations opted for the socialist alternative (not the socialist compromise). Whatever the sources of conflict in the Cold War, the argument was allowed to settle into this framework. The American claim that the real issue is individual freedom has been obscured by the fact that all causes espouse freedom:

our opponents simply insist there can be no freedom under capitalism, while we argue there can be none under Communism.

I feel there is no question that the West starts out with the worst of any argument defined in these terms. There are, as Lincoln observed, too many poor people around. In any event, history has been rather conspicuously moving in quite another direction, so that more and more these particular terms of the Cold War are simply irrelevant to events.

The Nineteenth Century that gave birth to the ideologies of property, also brought forth the spirit—it has never quite been a system of thought—of what was then known as nationalism, and in our time should probably be seen under the more general heading of ethnicity. As the years pass, the phenomenon is turning out to be a far more enduring and mischievous source of conflict than any thing dreamed of in the philosophies of Karl Marx.

The troubles began in Ireland and Poland, and spread throughout Central Europe. World War I made ethnicity a world issue. There has been no peace since.

It is instructive to note that the Second World War, despite the Cold War that followed it, was in itself very much a war of conflicting nationalism, with the all-important addition of racism. From the attempted extermination of the Jews and other ethnic groups in Europe, to the effort to throw the white man out of Asia, World War II gave a grimly accurate forecast of things to come.

Since that time, despite what might be called the presumptions of the Cold War to be the prime source of conflict in the world, what have been the events that have actually disturbed the peace, or seriously threatened to do so?

Most have involved conflicts between ethnic groups, defined by nationality, color, religion or region.

> Hindu against Moslem in India.
> Jew against Arab in Palestine.
> Indonesia against Malay in Southeast Asia.
> French against North Africa in Algeria.
> White man against Black man in South Africa.
> East Indian against Negro in British Guiana.
> Chinese Communist against Russian Communist the world over.
> Greek Cypriot against Turkish Cypriot.
> Watusi against Bahutu in Burundi.
> Bhuddist against Catholic in Viet Nam. . . .

The American Experience

The fact, of course, is that neither has the United States escaped this near universal experience of our time. The single greatest failure of our nation at the present moment has been our inability to resolve the racial problem. This problem has been with us from the beginning of the Republic, but in the past decade has developed into open racial conflict. To date the terrorism which characterizes this type of conflict all over the world has been confined to white Americans; but this cannot last.

Clearly, the price we are paying in world prestige is enormous. I don't know how one measures these things, but I would speculate that the photographs of the Alabama State Police taken in Selma last Sunday cost us at least as much good will in the world as the Peace Corps won for us in the previous years. Indeed, they simply confirm a thesis widely put forth by the Communists to explain phenomena such as the Peace Corps: that America is filled with good and decent persons who want to do right, but that it is a rotten nation because it lives under a rotten system. ....

The point here is that the United States is increasingly known in the world for its failures in an area where, in fact, we have had our most distinctive success.

Perhaps it is time the world was given an opportunity to appreciate just how much of an achievement the American melting pot has been. If we have not solved the Negro problem, neither has any other nation in the world, except possibly Brazil. But we have at least produced a Negro leadership that is nothing if not a moral inspiration to the world, no less than to this nation, the response of organized religion in the United States to that leadership, and of the whole electorate at the last election is no less impressive. In the meantime, the United States has shown a fantastic capacity to absorb an incredible range of ethnic groups, allowing those who wished to do so to retain their identity, enabling those who so desired to assimilate completely and disappear, allowing others to keep some characteristics while dropping others, etc.

If this looked easy in the 19th Century, the world is beginning to find out it is damn hard. America has something to teach here. ....

The Ellis Island Conference on Ethnicity in the Modern World

It seems to me that a world conference on ethnicity might have very considerable intellectual interest around the world. I am not thinking of a conference of ethnic politicians or spokesmen. There are, God knows, enough of them, from Bandung to the NATO Council. Rather, I would think in terms of a gathering of scholars and intellectuals, from as many nations as possible, who are interested in the problem of ethnicity as a source of conflict, and perhaps particularly in the curious persistence of ethnicity in the modern world.

The conventional expectation has been that with the advance of technology, communications, transportation, et al., ethnic differences will tend to disappear. Hence all the wailing about the homogenization and standardization of modern life. But they don't. On the contrary, people seem to cling to such identities, as matters of great importance. In the United States successive immigration groups have quite transformed themselves in terms of customs, manners, and circumstances, but have never quite disbanded. In some cases their group consciousness has grown stronger, not weaker with the passing of time and events.

My hunch is that technology is behind this.

It is notorious that the great writers and artists of the Twentieth Century have been indifferent, if not actually hostile to the strivings and accomplishments of Twentieth Century industry and the politics that have accompanied it. The general reason for this is clear enough. No one will seriously question that an industrial society takes away, even as it gives. What it takes away is "the old intuitive life" as G. H. Bantock has put it, the fact of community, of relationship, of mutual awareness that overpowers anyone who gets to know a peasant people, or even for that matter their first or second generation progeny in an American city. C. P. Snow has described it as "the loss of significance in commonplace acts," the meaningfulness, and shared awareness of that meaning, of a full range of individual activities that are "not private but part of the social condition."

> And the loss, which begins to occur at the earliest stages of industrialization, is linked perversely not with a decrease of individuality, but an increase of it. The loss of significance, together with the increase of individuality, means that men have lost a support. The industrial workers of Schenectady are probably more individual than members of any preindustrial community: they have far more free choices; but the binding forces of sacred custom have left them, and they are more alone.

Typically, the political scientists and sociologists have made some considerable advances in measuring the "ethnic effect" in matters such as voting behavior, without ever really asking how come this has all kept on this way. The poets and novelists, however, have occasionally got very close to the subject.

John Wain seemed to me very near the mark in a recent comment on the Welshness of Dylan Thomas as a factor in his poetic style and purpose:

> The question has an importance that goes far beyond the mere problem of whether or not a poet was influenced by a minority tradition. As the world shrinks to a village, local traditions become increasingly more important. If there is no essential difference between Paris and New York, if Manchester is the same as Stuttgart, humanity founders in a desert of boredom in which the sudden discovery of local idiom, regional idiosyncrasy, the tan of life in one fold of the mountains rather than in another, comes as a desperately needed oasis. In the railway age, minority languages such as Irish or Welsh appeared to be doomed. Homogenization attracted the men of the time because they had not yet tasted its Dead Sea fruit. So that Matthew Arnold could speak admiringly of "the tone of the center." Now we are at that center, we can see the whole pitiful delusion of a "central" idiom for what it is. The search for local roots goes on more and more urgently, and every sensitive modern man has two polarities: one to the broad social and economic area that he lives in, with its attendant politics and mores; and the other to his native region.

There is more to ethnicity than simply the recognition and preservation of group differences. It has its attractions, occasionally, and it has its value. Perry Miller, for example, has proposed that religious liberty in America revives not so much from the enlightenment of Puritan divines, as from their inability to muster a majority made up of any one denomination in order to suppress the others.

(An interesting and almost unnoticed point in this connection is that the Civil Rights Act prohibits discrimination of various forms based on religion and national origin, as well as race. The latter is almost a traditional subject of legislation in the United States. The former provisions were absolutely brand new. I doubt there are many countries that have anything like such prohibitions. I have often thought the President might want sometime to draw attention to this aspect of what will always be one of his greatest legislative achievements.)

I feel all of this has some relevance to ICY because the State Department seems to have decided that the uses of technology should be the central theme of the year. The President's statement says "Let this be the year of science." Three main projects are proposed: disarmament, disease control, and a worldwide weather system.

This makes great sense: as we talk about cooperation, let us do something about it, something which everyone can understand. But I wonder whether we ought not take a small initiative in another direction—i.e. to explore some of the side effects of technology, and some of the troubles they can cause you. Also some of the byproducts which can be put to use.

The persistence of ethnicity is—I think—one of these. Glazer and I have argued, for example that Americans, Madison to the contrary, have always been much motivated by value judgments, as against economic interests, and the decision of so many persons to retain ethnic identities is an example of such value judgments in operation.

This is an interesting subject. There is much to be learned, and many examples to be pointed out that will respond to the advantages of the United States. Even perhaps some advantage from being the first to raise the subject. Whether such a conference could be held inside of nine months, even supposing it was a good idea, I cannot say, I just wanted to raise the possibility, and perhaps also to alert you to the dangers of putting people with electric typewriters on committees.

Moynihan shares with McPherson the difficulties of responding to new frustrations in the civil rights movement and among black leaders, and dealing with the changing political consciousness of young Americans.

MAY 20, 1965

MEMORANDUM FOR MR. MCPHERSON

The American Academy of Arts and Sciences is publishing an issue of <u>Daedalus</u> this Fall on the Negro American. Our object is to devise a strategy of reconciliation. We may just.

We met this past weekend to read and criticize our papers. As the subject of the Negro American and that of the racial and religious conflicts we have been talking about in connection with the ICY are much linked in my mind,

I had sent copies of our proposal to a number of the persons on hand for this meeting.

I was struck by the reaction. Almost without exception there was intense interest in the idea. More to the point, as the three-day meeting progressed, the relation of the two subjects, one to the other, seemed to grow more evident to a number of the persons present. In the end we were often talking simultaneously about both. (In particular, Talcott Parsons became steadily more interested, and in our final session spoke to this point at some length. There may be a more intelligent person in the United States than he, but that person is assuredly not a sociologist. Given Parsons' international reputation he may be a man to enlist in any enterprise we undertake.)

The point of this memo is to suggest a somewhat new way of looking at the general subject of ethnic, racial and religious issues in the world today.

The subject came to my mind in the course of discussing the "split" in the civil rights movement which many persons perceive, but none can quite explain: clearly SNCC and CORE are moving in a direction different from that of the NAACP or the Urban League, or rather elements in all four seem to be diverging, etc. Saunders Redding put it that SNCC "is leaving the civil rights movement." Whether this is so or not was discussed at length with no one much satisfied with our information or conclusions.

I suggested a different way of looking at it: not in terms of a "split" but rather in terms of the dualism of the movement.

This dualism is characteristic not only of the civil rights movement, but of American democracy itself. It has been with us from the beginning.

American democracy is founded on the twin ideals of liberty and equality. Our education and general mindset does not much distinguish between these two ideals, but the fact is that they are distinct. If they are joined together in our common understanding, they are not always joined in our basic documents. The Declaration of Independence, for example, begins with a proposition about equality, but the subject is not mentioned in the Constitution—until the 14th Amendment. (One of the reasons for this, surely, is that at the time the Constitution was adopted one American in five was a slave.)

Nor, over the years, have the two ideals enjoyed the same acceptance. Liberty has been the American middle-class ideal par excellence. It has enjoyed the utmost social prestige. Not so equality. Men who would carelessly give their lives for Liberty, are appalled by equality. And there is also an opposite style to be seen: men who are passionately devoted to equality, but on the whole troubled by liberty. Most importantly, the great movements for equality in our history—from Jacksonian Democracy through Populism to the Trade Union Movement—have invariably been met with fierce opposition.

The Civil Rights movement has this same duality. It is a movement for both liberty and equality. The March on Washington was for Jobs <u>and</u> Freedom. Until just now, the two components have been running along together without any great tension, but this phase is coming to an end.

Until now the great American middle class has seen the Negro movement largely in terms of a movement for liberty: for the right to vote, to assemble, to petition, etc. This is not really an issue in America. Any group that asserts its rights in this field, and can show that its rights are infringed upon, quickly receives the overwhelming support of the middle class and the legal institutions of the nation.

In the South, where the Negro demands have been almost exclusively directed to the issue of liberty, the White middle class has increasingly allied with them in a political coalition <u>against</u> the white lower classes. Atlanta is a striking example of this political development.

But in the North the Negroes have liberty. What they want there is equality, which they do not have. Here, unfortunately, our ways of thinking are ill-equipped to cope. <u>The New York Times</u> which is unflinching in support of the demand for the right to vote—liberty—is thunderstruck by the demand for special assistance, benign quotas, etc.—equality.

We are not going to escape this confrontation. We must therefore learn more about it. Why and how people demand equality is not something we know much about, or are much equipped to deal with.

The connection of all this with international affairs is rather direct in my mind. If I sense the course of recent world events, it is that more and more the <u>tiers monde</u> is demanding—not liberty, they have liberty—but equality. Being nonwhite is not enough. As Sartre says in his introduction to Fanon's book, <u>The Wretched of the Earth</u>, "Not so very long ago, the earth numbered two thousand million inhabitants: five hundred million men, and one thousand five hundred million natives. The former had the Word; the others had the use of it." We have given the "natives" liberty, but not equality, and they therefore do not yet regard the score as settled. (Lincoln freed the slaves, but did not give them equality. Therefore we are still struggling with the issue.)

I sometimes have the feeling that part of the mutual uncomprehension that is so evident in the encounter of Americans with that world is that we are talking liberty and they are talking equality.

That is why our success in dealing with the demands of the Negro American revolution can be the <u>bona fide</u> achievement with which we should strive to establish our true role in the Twentieth Century.

It is in this sense that Talcott Parsons said to us at the end of our meeting that it was clear to him that the Negro American has an historic role as the bearer of equality: both in reasserting its value in American life, but also with regard to the American role in world affairs.

It seems to me that if there was one thing for which Lyndon Johnson was put on earth, it is to make it possible for this to happen.

This may involve a considerable reshaping of our image of ourselves. Are we in fact a young nation: Or are we not the oldest constitutional <u>democracy</u> in the world? Are we a revolutionary people, or to the contrary a miracle of stability. (I believe you will find that of the one hundred fourteen members of the United Nations, all I believe but nine either did not exist in 1914 or have had their form of government changed by force at least once since that time.)

We may also need to revise some of our ideas about what comes easy and what comes hard in the world. We have mostly been brought up (at least we C.C.N.Y. men were brought up) to think of revolution as the great achievement. I wonder if the great challenge of our time will not be turning things upside down, but rather keeping them steady. The revolutions are over. The colonial peoples are liberated.

The supreme challenge of our age will be the quest for political stability: an elusive and ill-understood condition that we are hardly yet interested in as a political condition.

The issue of our time will be how to attain equality with liberty, pluralism with unity, national purpose with local initiative. These are things not easily come by, but probably more in evidence in the United States than any nation on earth. Anyway, any enormous nation.

Is this not the true cultural and intellectual mission of the United States in the world?

I very much fear that most of our cultural enterprises have their origin in the rather pathetic effort to prove to the Europeans that we have a soul. And a genteel, middle-class soul at that. Balls. What we have to say to the world about how to live with one another is much the most important fact of our lives, and in ways of theirs.

That this should not be clear to the world is hardly a matter for wonder. But it troubles me that it does not seem to be clear to us either. I have been sick to see our students and intellectuals give up so quickly in Viet Nam. I am convinced it is not because they are so naive about life under the Viet Cong. It is just that they have so little faith in America's ability to say anything meaningful to any Asian people. They don't think we're good enough.

I do.

I think a specific theme in American policy in the world should be that liberty and equality are in fact hard things to put together, that we probably know as much about how to do it as any, but that no one knows much. Religious, ethnic and racial tensions are at the heart of so much of the demand for equality. They are legitimate demands. They must be accommodated. But it is damn hard.

The legitimacy of our claim to a world role in this area will be the success or failure of our Negro revolution at home.

It has always seemed interesting to me that never in the long history of the American republic have we occupied the role of what Lewis Feuer calls "the nation of conscience" for the intellectuals of the world. As for example, England was in the 18th Century, France after the Revolution, Russia in the 1920's and 1930's. I genuinely believe that we may yet have such a role, as the course of history makes the American experience more and more relevant to the "felt necessities" of the time. I don't know that the government can do much to bring this about, but surely it is possible to make better known abroad what we are doing at home to earn that position.

Johnson's speech at Howard University calling for "equality of results" as well as "equality of opportunity" was a seminal moment in his presidency. Here Moynihan tells Wirtz of the request from Hayes Redmon, a White House staff aide, for a draft. Moynihan was proud of his role in drafting the speech, but also stung by efforts among some around LBJ to disassociate Moynihan from it because of the furor over the Moynihan Report. As a senator, Moynihan rummaged through his own papers to find proof to skeptics that he had prepared the first draft of the speech, but he also had to assure LBJ that he was not trying to claim undue credit.

JUNE 1, 1965

MEMORANDUM FOR THE SECRETARY

Hayes Redmon called me yesterday to say Bill Moyers had talked with the President about the Negro family thesis for his address to Howard University this coming Friday, and would I do a draft. This morning Dick Goodwin called to say the draft should be an effort to go beyond the current demands of any civil rights group; that we should say whatever we think should be said, and they would decide what can be. I enclose the somewhat hurried result, which we sent over this afternoon.

Telling Richard Goodwin, LBJ's chief speechwriter, about the Howard University speech.

JUNE 3, 1965

MEMORANDUM FOR MR. GOODWIN

It might be useful for the President to note that he is speaking at the citadel of the affluent Negro America. That for the graduates he is addressing, there are already more jobs than there are graduates. That not all their problems are resolved by any means, but that the outlines of the main solutions are already evident, and the next decade will surely see them in operation.

What the President is concerned about is the two-thirds of Negro Americans who have not made it, for whom opportunities and jobs and new horizons are not opening, for whom they are in many ways closing.

(At the same time he might want to address himself to the apparent concern of many young Negro graduates that they are being sought after for window dressing. They are not.)

Making sure that Wirtz knew of Moynihan's hand in the speech.

JUNE 4, 1965

MEMORANDUM FOR THE SECRETARY

Dick Goodwin and I worked all last night on the President's speech, which he will deliver at Howard in about an hour. So far everyone has been most enthusiastic, notably Roy Wilkins and Whitney Young, to whom it was read by Dick.

He sent a copy over to you for comments by noon today, but I explained you were in the middle west, and that you had sent the proposition to Moyers in the first place.

It is a grand speech, and could be a major event. I enclose the latest telephone message from Goodwin's office.

Moynihan offers some details about himself to Paul R. Screvane, who was running as mayor to succeed Wagner. Screvane later invited Moynihan to run for City Council president on his ticket in the Democratic Party primary.

JULY 8, 1965

Dear Paul:

Here are the brief annals of the Moynihans. There are more details, but none particularly significant save perhaps that after graduating from Benjamin Franklin High School I went to work on the piers, much as you drove a truck. I am one of the considerable number of young men who owe a lot to World War II.

I am by profession a professor of political science, and have served on a number of faculties, most recently as Director of the New York State Government Research Project at Syracuse University between the time Harriman went out and Kennedy came in.

Moynihan resigns from the Johnson administration to run for City Council president, telling the president that he will have fulfilled the legendary saying of House Speaker Sam Rayburn that government officials should have "at least once run for sheriff."

Earlier, Moynihan's name had been suggested by Averell Harriman, Robert Kennedy, and other Democrats as a mayoral candidate. When this was reported in the Times, *Moynihan lost the chance of any further assignment in the Johnson administration. Unprepared to run for mayor, he accepted Screvane's offer to join his ticket.*

JULY 18, 1965

Dear Mr. President:

With a reluctance that I know you will understand, I should like to ask your leave to relinquish my post as Assistant United States Secretary of Labor.

Over the past week a number of prominent New York citizens, persons I know to represent the central liberal tradition of the Democratic Party, have come to me and asked if I would offer my name for President of the City Council of New York. In other circumstances I would almost certainly have preferred to remain at my work here in Washington: In the present one I feel the responsibility to accept.

This will bring to a close more than four years in which I had the privilege to serve first President Kennedy, then yourself. They have been among the most creative and eventful years of our nation's history. Nothing will equal them in my life.

If fortune favors us, you will have in the nation's greatest city an administration committed to the leadership of Lyndon B. Johnson. If not, in whatever public service may later come my way, I will at least fit Mr. Sam's prescription of having "just once run for sheriff."

Responding to Robert W. Dowling, a wealthy real estate developer, who had evidently expressed support after Moynihan lost for City Council president.

22 OCTOBER 1965

Dear Bob:

Good God, you are magnificent! To have done what you did for us, and then to write me such a letter two days later o'er reaches my understanding of how far a great heart and an indomitable constitution can take a man.

I hope I was not too much a disappointment. I had said to Paul that I could not help him get nominated, but that I could help him get elected. We shall never know. But it was an entirely worthy undertaking, and we came out of it like men. Whatever doubts may afflict me these days, I do know that I was on the side Robert Dowling chose, and that is honor and company enough for me.

My only keen disappointment came election night: as I stepped before the cameras to congratulate Mr. O'Conner it came to me that here was the perfect occasion for Wilde's response to Niagara: "Speaking of the election returns," I was about to say, "I am reminded of Oscar Wilde's observation that Niagara Falls would be more impressive if it flowed the other way." Alas the red eye had gone out, and the scene had shifted to the Summit.

Lamenting to Gunnar Myrdal, the Swedish economist (and later Nobel Peace Prize–recipient) whose 1944 book, AN AMERICAN DILEMMA: THE NEGRO PROBLEM AND MODERN DEMOCRACY, *was a seminal event in the civil rights movement, that his report on the Negro family has destroyed his reputation.*

DECEMBER 5, 1965

Dear Dr. Myrdal,

You are immensely kind to have written at all: and uncannily so to [have] done so at this time.

When we last met, at Berkeley in February, I was just finishing my short report on the Negro Family. My purpose, as will be evident enough to you, was to persuade the administration that the Negro revolution was hardly begun, far less coming to a close, and to describe the problem in terms that would seize the attention of the President and his aides. I did so, and the result was the President's speech at Howard University in June, surely the most advanced civil rights position ever taken by an American chief executive. Word of the report gradually leaked out, but the reception was golden. Then came Watts, I suppose, and a whole series of second thoughts in a movement that does not know which way to turn. The result is that by the time the White House Conference met I had been anathematized as a racist, a fascist, an authoritarian, a bourgeois and so across the spectrum of epithets. Not everyone thinks this, of course, but so violent are the emotions of the movement that no one save Kenneth Clark has dared speak up for me. You will thus better understand how much I appreciated your letter. . . .

Thanking the theologian Reinhold Niebuhr for his support over the Moynihan Report controversy.

DECEMBER 9, 1965

Dear Dr. Neibuhr,

I have known many kindnesses in my life, and have been helped when I much needed it by many good men. No one, however, has ever offered me more understanding when I so terribly needed to be understood.

I am utterly grateful for your letter.

I am prepared to believe that we will prevail. I have found that the white world, which understands so little and cares so little about the Negro, can nonetheless sense the horror of the life in the slums in the terms I was using, which is why I used them. Certainly the President does. I was raised in such slums; I think I know what it is like; I am hurt right now, but I am not defeated.

Your intervention has enormously strengthened me. All I ask is that you not grow too much concerned or troubled. . . .

With my kindest regards to Mrs. Niebuhr, I am

Most sincerely,

CHAPTER THREE

"We Were Going to Change This Country"

*The late 1960s plunged the United States into a frightening period of racial vio-
lence, antiwar protests, and political assassinations. While disagreeing with Robert
Kennedy as Kennedy moved to the left, at least rhetorically, Moynihan campaigned
for him in California and tried and failed to say goodbye before returning home
to Harvard. Kennedy's murder after winning the California primary shattered
Moynihan's political bearings, and although he campaigned for Vice President Hubert Humphrey as the Democratic presidential nominee, he also began to reach out
to the campaign of the Republican nominee, former Vice President Richard Nixon,
a move that shocked some of his old friends like Harry McPherson. The letters attest
to Moynihan's growing alienation from some of his old allies in the civil rights
movement—and their alienation from him, which helped pave the way for his
move toward Nixon. Moynihan was proud that some of these old associates came
to his defense. But his skepticism of liberal orthodoxy was solidified with his book,
MAXIMUM FEASIBLE MISUNDERSTANDING, which excoriated what he felt was a
misbegotten effort to establish "community action" programs rather than simply
improve the incomes of the poor. Amid the anguish of this period came fame, including a TIME magazine cover on Moynihan. In the background was Moynihan's
growing conviction that although the Vietnam War was well intended, it was not
succeeding and it was also sowing irreparable divisions in the United States. It
was only a short step from this disenchantment to the idea that Nixon could unite
the country, end the war, and address the issue of poverty in a real way. Moynihan
joined Nixon at the White House and began writing him memoranda even before
his inauguration.*

The Moynihan Report continued to provoke criticism of its author years after its dissemination in 1965. Here Moynihan explains his situation to Roy Wilkins, head of the National Association for the Advancement of Colored People (NAACP). THE CRISIS *is the NAACP's magazine and CORE is the Congress of Racial Equality, a civil rights group.*

JANUARY 12, 1966

Dear Mr. Wilkins,

... The fact remains, of course, that I am now known as a racist across the land. The fact that an obscure white member of CORE said so in <u>The Nation</u> would not have established that fact. That young Dr. Payton picked it up and persuaded the Protestant Council of New York to say so, would not have established that fact. That James Farmer said so in the <u>Amsterdam News</u> would not necessarily have established that fact. But that <u>The Crisis</u> said so settles it.

I will admit to feeling misused. I am not a particularly aggressive man (you and I have been together in at least half a dozen meetings at the Labor Department and The White House, but I rather doubt you would recognize me if we met again) nonetheless, I am not a person without reputation. I have served in the subcabinet of two Presidents. In 1964 the book I wrote with Nathan Glazer received the Anisfield-Wolf Award in Race Relations. In 1965 I received the Arthur S. Fleming Award as "an architect of the nation's effort to eradicate poverty." In the summer of that year I was [the New York County Democratic leader] Ray Jones's candidate for President of the New York City Council. It is no great secret that I became concerned about whether and how our civil rights movement would turn from the problems of the South to those of the North. I wrote a report after speaking with some of the most distinguished scholars in the nation. Men such as C. Eric Lincoln, Kenneth Clark, Whitney Young, and G. Franklin Williams have publically attested to the accuracy and importance of the report. Its relation to the President's speech at Howard University is well known. Nonetheless, when an all but anonymous member of CORE decides I am a racist, the editor of the official organ of the NAACP prints his article, or rather, reprints it.

The shame of it all is that none of the people who started this thing have anything against me particularly. Dr. Payton said to me at the White House Conference meeting that he was of course attacking the President, but that for "strategical" reasons he felt it best to name me. . . .

My point is this: It is now about six months since the report became public and I was identified with it. In that time not a single civil rights agency has got in touch with me about any aspect of it. It seems to me very clear that a telephone call from James Farmer, or Dr. Payton, or James Ivy would have answered many questions, or at least raised some. It seems to me quite clear that communications are not very good here (unless there was some special reason for not wanting to talk to me, which I do not know of). I offer you the thought that in the future the movement will want to be in touch with persons such as myself as it becomes more and more involved in problems which we think about and write about, and maybe even know something about. The kind of knowledge which sociologists and political economists have about social issues is probably going to be as relevant to your work in the future as was that of constitutional lawyers in the past.

In the social sciences, no more than at law, one man's opinion is not necessarily as good as another's. For The Crisis to publish an article by an obscure psychologist which declares that the data in a report prepared in the Department of Labor and drawn upon by the President of the United States are invalid . . . that way lies folly.

I am sure you have thought about all this much more deeply than I, but I wanted this letter to be something more than yet another cri de coeur.

Seeking a sympathetic ear from Gunnar Myrdal, the Swedish economist and author of AN AMERICAN DILEMMA: THE NEGRO PROBLEM AND MODERN DEMOCRACY, *published in 1944.*

JANUARY 14, 1966

Dear Dr. Myrdal,

As I know how carefully, and hopefully, you follow these matters, I would hope to impose on your work from time to time just to keep you posted on the progress of our studies of the Negro family.

The organized Negro reaction to the report has about—I hope!—run its course. It ended with a two part blast from James Farmer of CORE just as he was on the point of leaving to become head of a foundation that will deal with just the problems the report talks about. Or some at least. All this is familiar enough: Frazier went through it, Kardiner got it, I hardly belong in such company and could hardly expect to be exempted.

The important point is that I find a very considerable amount of research going on about the country which fits well into the hypothesis that lower class family structure has become a principal negative influence in the Negro situation at this present moment. As you will quickly perceive, my methodology or rather my analytical concept, is taken wholly from your principle of cumulation. You might recall in Appendix 3 listing "stability in family relations" as one of the variables which affects the Negro plane of living both in its own right and through its secondary effects on the other variables.

My great hope for all this was a system of family allowances of negative income tax. I fear that may be lost however, through a combination of Negro hostility and the expenses of the war in Vietnam.

Even so, I continue to get an important response from White America. LIFE magazine, for example, devoted an article to the subject in a year-end issue on Cities. This idea <u>reaches</u> middle class Americans: they see the claims of family as legitimate. Somehow, claims made in the name of abstractions such as unemployment do not excite us.

You might just be interested to read one of the several Negro attacks on my report. This is by a young sociologist, minister who has just become director of the Commission on Religion and Race of the National Council of Churches. As I think will be evident enough to you, he had not read my report before attacking it, nor had he very much read yours!

Moynihan was stung by an article in HARPER'S *by William Shannon that asserted that Robert Kennedy had maneuvered Moynihan and Frank O'Connor, the New York City Council president, into running on different slates in the 1965 New York City mayoral primary, presumably to have an ally on each slate. Moynihan's effusive reference here to Mayor John V. Lindsay of New York is clearly sarcastic. This letter elicited a response from Kennedy that he was "outraged at Shannon's article" and wrote a heated letter of protest that was toned down by an aide. Enclosing copies of*

both versions of the letter, Kennedy said: "I thought you would be interested in how the political processes are calming down my wild spirits."

18 JANUARY 1966

Dear Bob,

I was troubled, as perhaps you were, by the passage in Bill Shannon's article in <u>Harper's</u> which states that you deliberately maneuvered Frank O'Connor and me on to opposing slates in the primary in order that you would have a man in City Hall whichever ticket won. As far as I am aware, nothing of the sort happened, and I would want you to know that I have no such impression. Alas, I should have wished you to be more Machiavellian, not less!

As your putative protégé, however, let me report that it appears I am going up to Harvard. I am being offered the directorship of the Joint Center for Urban Studies of Harvard-M.I.T., a professorship in the Graduate School of Education, membership on the faculty of the Graduate School of Public Administrations and, of deepest interest to me, Dick Neustadt would like me to be one of the group that gets the Kennedy Institute going. I had rather hoped to settle in New York, but nothing came up save an oblique approach from our brave, handsome, dashing, gallant, new young Mayor [John V. Lindsay], but things are not yet that bad. . . .

Defending himself to Oscar Handlin, the distinguished Harvard sociologist.

FEBRUARY 1, 1966
PROFESSOR OSCAR HANDLIN
DEPARTMENT OF HISTORY
HARVARD UNIVERSITY
CAMBRIDGE, MASSACHUSETTS

Dear Oscar:

A few weeks ago, having learned that the NAACP journal <u>The Crisis</u> had reprinted the Nation article calling my report on the Negro Family a racist tract, I wrote Ashley Montagu telling him how badly I felt about it all, particularly as it might somehow reflect on the Anisfield-Wolf award. He wrote back cheerfully to assure me that my tormentors were as nothing to some he had known, and asked if I would not send a copy of the report to his three colleagues.

I do so in the thought that you might also be wondering about it all. I guess my present mood is defiance: the report went to the White House on May 4th, 1965. One month later, on June 4th, President Johnson gave his speech at Howard University, surely the most advanced commitment to the cause of Negro equality any American President has ever made. Having written the report and the first draft of the speech, I don't much feel like apologizing to anyone. But I do want you to have the document for your own purposes.

P.S. I should add that Roy Wilkins has written me a very kind letter disassociating himself from the article reprinted in <u>The Crisis</u>.

Among those who sympathized with Moynihan was the renowned theologian Reinhold Niebuhr, whose wife sent a letter to the magazine CHRISTIANITY & CRISIS *over its attack on the Moynihan Report. She said the article "is more than acutely embarrassing for Reinhold and me"—so much so that it had "made Reinhold so sick at heart that his health has suffered" and that he "is not up to anything." As a result, she and her husband would not attend an anniversary dinner for the magazine.*

FEBRUARY 23, 1966

Dear Mrs. Niebuhr,

You will understand how upset I was by your letter. I am appalled that I should be the reason for such a decision by Reinhold Niebuhr. Yet you will also understand how very much it means to me that you and he should feel the way you do: the whole affair has become a nightmare of misunderstanding, and misinterpretation, and misstatement.

I have not read Dr. Spike's article, but I suppose I must. I have been keeping absolutely silent about the report: I have never said a word in public about him or Dr. Paton. Indeed I find myself in that most suspect of all postures: looking bewildered, and asking "What have I done?"

I know the President has been disappointed in the way things have gone. One of the ironies is that while many of the Negro leaders such as King, and Wilkins, and Young would like to see something done in this direction, the white liberal allies seem determined that nothing shall. Curiouser and Curiouser.

Please try to tell Dr. Niebuhr how much his action has meant to me—little as I would have wanted anything of the sort to happen.

Reaching out to John Rawls, the Harvard philosophy professor and author of articles (later a book) on theories of justice.

MARCH 14, 1966
PROFESSOR JOHN RAWLS
DEPARTMENT OF PHILOSOPHY
HARVARD UNIVERSITY
CAMBRIDGE, MASS.

Dear John Rawls,

... It may be, as you say, that philosophical abstractions at times seem unhelpful to persons caught up in great movements. I would urge, however, that this is not such a moment, certainly not in civil rights. It is a time of intense ambiguity; the unjust laws which, as it were, landed Martin Luther King in the Birmingham jail have been by and large struck down. How then to turn a protest movement against situations rather than statutes? The seizure of the tenement in Chicago provides a good instance: you may have noticed that King was excoriated by a Negro Federal judge.

But no more of this. I write only to ask you if there is anyone you would like to have on the panel to comment on your paper. Someone whose opinions are sufficiently like or unlike your own as to help with your exposition. Don't bother to write me if no such person comes to mind. In that case I will try to get some activists who have, as it were, been there. I am also trying to get one paper on what you might call survey data of who gets involved in this kind of thing. ...

Ralph Nader's 1965 book, UNSAFE AT ANY SPEED, *attacked the auto industry for its safety record. News stories reported that General Motors had tried to discredit Nader by tapping his phones and even hiring prostitutes to entrap him. The allegations were to be the focus of congressional hearings, and Moynihan was determined to stand up for Nader, here in a letter to former White House colleague, Harry McPherson. (Nader later sued General Motors and settled the case for $425,000.)*

MARCH 14, 1966

HONORABLE HARRY C. MCPHERSON

THE WHITE HOUSE

WASHINGTON, D. C.

Dear Harry,

I rather assume that as Counsel to the President you have been keeping an eye on the troubles brewing between General Motors and the U.S. Senate over Ralph Nader. The F.B.I. is now investigating, and Senator Ribicoff has scheduled hearings for March 22nd.

You should know that I brought Nader to Washington, and that he was on the Department of Labor policy planning staff (as a "consultant") until about the time I left. His book was written at this time. He did a long report on traffic safety and represented me around the government on this issue. He and I have associated for some years: automobile design happens to be another of my compulsions. I am sure GM knows of his relationship to the administration and I wanted to be certain that the administration did.

Averell Harriman, while serving at the State Department, was said to be a critic of escalating the Vietnam War. Here Moynihan shares his skepticism and reminds him that his portrait for the State Capitol was still not finished.

MARCH 18, 1966

Dear Governor,

How grand to hear (from Hildy) that you are getting a bit of rest after—what, five years? She writes also to say that you are to speak at the New York County Dinner and wish to know what suggestions I might have.

It seems to me you have two courses, one of which I would urge on you, although it may not fit your objectives.

I think you should make a foreign policy speech, or rather a Viet Nam speech. It is not just, or even mostly that there would be a general interest in what you say. The important point is that there would be a very real interest within the New York Democratic Party where, to a degree that might surprise you, the dominant opinion of the liberal-left groups is utterly opposed to the President and the administration. You may have noticed that in the contest over who would be the Reform candidate to run against [Representative Leonard] Farbstein, the various contenders outdid one another in denouncing our policy in Viet Nam. In the Mayoralty primary contest this summer the Ryan forces were openly against the Administration on Viet Nam and got that vote—by which they beat Screvane, and the rest of us. Which was their object. (To be sure they might have beat us anyway, but having done so, it was proclaimed a victory for the anti-Viet Nam forces. The subsequent defeat of Beame only rounded out the ideology.)

I listened with considerable care to the President's speech at the Freedom House dinner (I have just become a Trustee thereof, for reasons that escape me.) It was not a success. The scene was not propitious. Inside the main ball room of the Waldorf Astoria Hotel were rather more than a thousand aging liberals, Jewish for the most part, anti-Communist from their European encounters, but hardly enamored of war in Asia. Outside were three to four thousand persons chanting things like "Hey, hey, LBJ: How many kids did you kill today." All this could have been surmounted save that the President's speech (which was largely written by Harry McPherson, who is a dear and close friend) was utterly lacking in any suggestion of the desperate ambiguity of our present position in the Far East. The audience would have been entirely prepared to accept the President's view of what must be done, if only he had indicated his awareness of how awful that necessity is.

I can imagine that such talk makes no sense to you, but I wish to urge on you the thought that the President's enemies in the Party are active, almost exultant, while those who support him are inert, either out of prudence, stupidity, or indifference, or combinations thereof.

Thus I would suggest that you, who stands as a symbol of what it has meant to be unswerving in the face of the insolent self assurance of the left, ought to make a deep and candid speech about Viet Nam. . . .

On a personal note, I am going to Harvard to be Director of the Joint Center for Urban Studies of Harvard University and the Massachusetts Institute of Technology, Professor of Education and Politics at the Graduate School of Education, member of the Graduate Faculty of Public Administration and a member of the Kennedy Institute of Government. Which is a mouthful, considering the salary. In the meantime, I continue to pay printing bills from the primary, and somehow protect that $1900 which we garnered for your portrait lo these many years ago!

Moynihan again stands up for Ralph Nader, this time to Robert Kennedy. Kennedy wrote back that he was "not aware that Ralph Nader had worked with you" or that "you were an expert" on auto safety, adding playfully: "You were a busy little figure weren't you?"

24 MARCH 1966

Dear Bob,

You have been doing a magnificent job on traffic safety, and I hope you somehow manage to see it through. As you may know, I brought Ralph Nader to Washington to work with me on the policy planning staff of the Department of Labor. We were moving along fine when parties unknown decided I should run for Mayor of New York!

During the 1960 campaign I wrote a number of statements on this subject for President Kennedy, who was the first chief executive to say anything intelligent on the subject. ("Traffic accidents constitute one of the greatest, perhaps the greatest, of the Nation's <u>public health</u> problems.") I had hoped we could get some action in reformulating the problem in these terms, but you will recall that you appointed a Los Angeles Cadillac dealer Under Secretary of Commerce for Transportation, and nothing whatever happened. Ralph Dungan tried to get me to be his deputy, but I was vetoed by the bureaucracy. . . .

Again defending Ralph Nader and the cause of auto safety, here to Henry Ford II, head of the Ford Motor Company.

MAY 14, 1966

Dear Mr. Ford,

I write first to congratulate you on your speech to the National Association of Purchasing Agents, and secondly to enclose the testimony on automobile safety which I recently gave before the House Committee on Interstate and Foreign Commerce.

As you will see, my testimony is critical of some statements you have made, but I hope you will see that I in no way intended to cast any doubt on your own personal integrity, but only on the great trouble the automobile industry seems to have in getting it clear what your critics are talking about. I have been concerned with this problem for about a decade now—as secretary to Governor Harriman in New York I was chairman of the Traffic Safety Policy Committee and began to run into the questions of vehicle design and such like at that time. After we left office I wrote a long article for The Reporter entitled "Epidemic on the Highways" in which I argued that what we had here was a public health problem that was by and large not being attended to. One, but only one of the problems was that of vehicle design. I wrote, however that it was the kind of problem that was going to lead directly to the dreariest kind of government regulation unless the industry came to its senses.

You would perhaps understand some of the recent events better if you had been in my position at that time and in the years since. I made a serious effort to get to various automobile executives in order to explain my views and to suggest to them that they must act in their own interests. For example, I wrote you a long letter pleading that you might take the leadership here. I was treated like a crack pot.

In 1961 I went to Washington with President Kennedy. (I was Assistant Secretary of Labor for Policy Planning and Research). I had written statements on this subject for President Kennedy during the campaign and seriously hoped to get something done. I was utterly frustrated. The industry dominated everything. In the end I concluded that government regulation was inevitable, and brought Ralph Nader down to be a member of the policy planning staff and work up a plan.

Government regulation is now, of course, inevitable. But war is not. The problem of traffic safety is much greater than just that of vehicle design—as you correctly point out in your address. But somehow, some communication between the industry and the academic-intellectual community must begin. I am going to Cambridge in July where I will become director of the Joint Center for Urban Studies of M.I.T. and Harvard. If this proposition interests you, I would be willing to be of what service I can in organizing or participating in such an effort. I am sure you will understand that I have other things to do, and am not seeking such an assignment, but only that I would be willing to explore its possibilities, as they say.

A final word which I hope you will not find offensive. There is no need for you to answer this letter if you do not wish to (nor any need for your staff to show it to you if they so conclude) but this time I would hope to hear from you personally, or not at all.

Irving Kristol founded a new magazine, THE PUBLIC INTEREST, *in 1965. Moynihan served as a member of the publication committee. The article by the sociologist James Coleman was a seminal study of educational opportunity.*

AUGUST 22, 1966
DR. IRVING KRISTOL
THE PUBLIC INTEREST
BASIC BOOKS, INC.
404 PARK AVENUE SOUTH
NEW YORK, NEW YORK

Dear Irving:

As a member of the publication committee, and a not infrequent contributor, I am not perhaps the most objective person to call on for an assessment of the impact of The Public Interest during its first year. On the other hand I have for those reasons followed the subject much more closely than would normally be the case. I would like then to report one general impression and cite one specific instance.

Since coming to Cambridge I have been immensely impressed with how widely we are read. I think it is not to be doubted that we are getting through to the audience we had in mind. Hardly a day passes but I find myself talking to or corresponding with someone who mentions an article in The Public Interest: frequently something I've written, but more often the work of other writers, or of the tone of the magazine itself. We seem to come through as liberals in whose judgment other persons have confidence. . . .

As an item, let me cite our forthcoming article by James Coleman about his report "Equality of Educational Opportunity." This, as you know, was perhaps the most extensive social science research project in history. It was directed to an area of intense interest and emotion in American life: the consignment of Negro youth to segregated, inferior schools. Commissioned by the Civil Rights Act of 1964, everyone knew what the study would find. As Coleman said in an interview with Southern Education Report last winter: "the study will show the differences in the quality of schools that the average Negro child and the average white child are exposed to. You know yourself that the difference is really going to be striking. And even though everybody knows there is a lot of difference between suburban and inner-city schools, once the statistics are there in black and white, they will have a lot more impact." Of course, the report found nothing of the sort. The quality of schools attended by Negroes turned out to be hardly different, and in places superior to those provided whites. But more importantly, it turned out the quality of the schools couldn't explain the enormous differences in pupil achievement anyway: the differences come from family background and peer group influence.

Potentially, this report could transform American education and lead us away from what could be a disastrous course of events we seem embarked on. Logically pursued, the data constitute the most powerful argument yet made for integration. However, the findings are simply too powerful and too unorthodox for the standard communications media or the traditional bureaucracies to handle. The Office of Education released the report in terms of its having shown that schools in America were still segregated, and the press from the New York Times down reported that fact and little else.

The whole thing might have disappeared from sight—perhaps that exaggerates, but it might have taken a lot longer coming to the surface—were it not that we got hold of Jim Coleman and asked him to do an article before he left for a year in Europe. I believe it is fair to say that another publication might not have had access to the essentially covert information as to what was really in the report, and in any event Coleman probably would not have stopped everything to write something as requested. So far as he was concerned—and he made this clear to me—the readership of The Public Interest was exactly the one he wished to reach, feeling they would understand the complexities of the information he came up with, and that they would be in a position to influence the national response. . . .

Moynihan shares thoughts and frustrations with Harry McPherson, at the White House, on civil rights, race, and poverty, as well as the meaning—more than a year later—of LBJ's speech at Howard University.

SEPTEMBER II, 1966
THE HONORABLE HARRY C. MCPHERSON
SPECIAL COUNSEL TO THE PRESIDENT
THE WHITE HOUSE
WASHINGTON, D. C.

Dear Harry,

I have been thinking of a number of the things that came up the other evening, and conclude it may be well to spell out some of the things I said in more detail inasmuch as they seem to fit in with your present thinking more than I would have thought. If you and the President tend at this point to think that the thesis of the Howard University speech was and remains a sound one, then probably I should be more in touch with you than I have been. I had assumed the subject was closed, but I did not in the least blame the administration for having closed it. I think it fair to say that I took my lumps with as much dignity as one can muster whilst being anathematized by the likes of C. Sumner Stone and Stokely Carmichael. I plan to write a piece for Norman Podhoretz this winter in which I will argue that the President was badly let down by the white liberal community which panicked at the thought that it might have to pursue for a moment a line of thought unpopular with the Negro militants, leaving the administration in a hopelessly exposed position from which it had to withdraw. And, of course, I am writing a book on the subject itself, hoping at least to set the record straight and possibly to keep the issue alive until in one form or another it can be again raised in terms of public policy. However, our conversation last Monday leads me to think that it may not be entirely dropped, which prompts me at this point to write you in terms I have not done, and which I would not have done.

It is necessary to distinguish between the <u>thesis</u> of the Howard speech, and its <u>strategy</u>, an exercise of some subtlety inasmuch as both involved the question of family. The thesis of the speech was that the family was a good point—was far and away the best point—at which to measure the net, cumulative plus or minus impact of outside forces on the Negro community. All the abstractions of employment, housing, income, discrimination, education, et al. come together here, and on balance, in a rough sense things get better or worse. As you will recall my bet was as follows: inasmuch as it was clear that a Negro middle class is coming along—look out the window—but yet the overall national statistics concerning family stability were still worsening somewhat, it was probable that conditions within the Negro lower class were getting considerably worse. The civil rights movement has been immensely successful in creating a national consensus about upholding the legal rights of Negroes in the South, but there was no certainty whatever that an equivalent consensus could be reached concerning the problems of class in the North. Barring massive action on these problems, it was likely that the existing civil rights consensus would begin to crumble as lower class urban Negroes grew more restless, violent and demanding, but in terms that could not evoke general agreement on a response. Hence the need for a master stroke of Presidential initiative that would leapfrog the usual processes of slowly accumulating agreement, in the manner of Medicare, and in two or three years move the country ahead two or three decades. You will recall that in the Spring of 1965 we had the money and the votes to think in such terms.

The strategy of the speech was another matter altogether, withal it concerned the same subject. The strategy was that by couching the issue in terms of family—in the first instance—white America could be brought to see the tired old issues of employment, housing, discrimination and such in terms of much greater urgency than they ever evoke on their own. Moreover, family as an issue raised the possibility of enlisting the support of conservative groups for quite radical social programs. For example, most liberal Democrats such as us have little contact and less sympathy for the intense moralisms of conservative Catholic and Protestant religion, but examined more closely a good deal of this emerges as simply a clumsy effort to maintain standards of family stability that most of us would regard as eminently sane. Of the greatest importance, the strategy of family welfare provided a means whereby a pro-Negro would have immediate and direct benefits for the vast number of working class whites who were certain to grow more and more resentful at the attentions and favors that Washington seemed to be showering on Negroes. A family allowance, for example, would benefit 30 percent of the American people in one stroke, including that vast population of white workers who have to hustle to bring home $80 a week themselves.

Now then: the strategy of the speech turned out to be faulty. Not that we did not attract conservatives. On the contrary there is abundant evidence that these <u>were</u> terms in which otherwise unsympathetic persons could be brought to see the great disadvantages under which Negroes live. I would cite, for example, the repeated references to the Negro Family report in <u>Life</u> magazine. I have had lunch with the editors on several occasions and without exception have found them fully aware of what the President was saying and, given the evidence, which was quite new to them, fully prepared to support him. The strategy failed because we underestimated (or in my case did not even anticipate) the savage reaction of the Federal bureaucracy in H.E.W. and Labor, and to some extent O.E.O., and the even wilder resentment on the part of what might be called the Civil Rights left. I was not even aware of the role of the bureaucracy until late last fall, but I am satisfied [Harvard sociologist Lee] Rainwater is accurate in his report that within weeks of the Howard speech the Welfare Administration types had gone outside the government to tell persons in the civil rights movement that the report was inaccurate, insulting, misleading and dangerous to the interests of the movement. The older civil rights leaders were willing enough and in some cases even anxious to pursue the Howard thesis, but could not take the heat from the younger militants who are, after all, rivals as well as colleagues. And no help whatever came from white liberals. When the administration gave the staff assignments for the conferences that followed to civil servants who had been active in attacking the thesis, while no role whatever was given to any of those who had worked with me in developing it (much less a role for me as such), and when a traditional civil rights bill was sent up to the new session of Congress, the Howard initiative was dead. Let me be clear: I think the civil rights bill was a good one and an important one, and I think the report put together for the White House conference in June was filled with important and useful proposals, but in general (the education section being an honored exception) the ideas behind them belong to the pre-Howard era, they reflect the traditional, conventional wisdom of the 1940's and 1950's. Like a good many ideas of that period it is long past time we adopted them, but it is not to be imagined they represent any new departures in social thought or policy.

It may still be possible to salvage something from the strategy of the Howard speech. A White House conference on family welfare, for example. But obviously one can no longer address oneself to the subject of the Negro family as such. On the other hand, I would think it makes sense for you to keep in touch with the thesis. The fact is that in the course of the past year a number of important pieces of evidence have come to light which suggest most powerfully that the President's thesis was not wrong, but rather that he was more right than any of us might have thought. . . .

The point of this letter, which is already overly long, is to suggest that you probably ought to keep in touch with this line of thinking. I believe for example that you cannot understand the nature of the rioting this summer without these facts—although here as elsewhere I need hardly remind you that I could be grossly mistaken. (If you will examine the opening passages of the Negro Family report you will find the statement:

> There is no very satisfactory way, at present, to measure social pathology within an ethnic, or religious, or geographical community. Data are few and uncertain, and conclusions drawn from them, including the conclusions that follow, are subject to the grossest error. Nonetheless, the opportunities, no less than the dangers, of the present moment, demand that an assessment be made.

At the same time, if it is a fact that these and a half dozen similar studies have not been brought to your attention I will urge on you that this is the most natural thing in the world. As far as the Federal bureaucracy is concerned this is an unmentionable subject, a fact which pleases some more than others, but impresses one and all alike. I will forebear to expand on what the view within the bureaucracy is as to what happened to me and to the persons who worked with me, but if my head were sticking on a pike at the South West Gate to the White House grounds the impression would hardly be greater. E.g. the official release on the Coleman study was written in one day of furious activity—following a month in which the bureaucracy gazed at the results in horror—by a dear friend of mine who works for John Gardner. She knew perfectly well what the report uncovered, but was determined to protect her boss and yours and as a result the word "family" does not even appear in the 54 page summary which was released to the press.

I believe that at this point if you want to keep in touch with this kind of development you will have to make special arrangements to do so. This means either getting yourself someone in the Bureau of the Budget, perhaps who would regularly send you material and stimulate research. Or, alternatively, seeing that the government finances a systematic study of the subject at a university such as Harvard which can be depended on not to get caught up in the ideology of it all. (You may have noticed that the one common characteristic that united all of those who attacked me was their detestation of the war in Viet Nam. Unfortunately this issue is one that connects with a whole range of other ideology.) Remember that the United States government is the most powerful research organization in the world. It can find out anything it wants to find out.

Moynihan worried that the War on Poverty, headed by Sargent Shriver, was foundering because the money was being spent on elites in the field rather than on the poor themselves. His concerns led him later to support a "negative income tax" that would send money directly to poor families.

OCTOBER 31, 1966
MR. SARGENT SHRIVER
DIRECTOR
OFFICE OF ECONOMIC OPPORTUNITY
1200 19TH STREET N.W.
WASHINGTON, D.C.

Dear Sarge:

I have been perhaps unnecessarily concerned not to trouble you with this matter and the next since leaving Washington. It was never my impression that you lacked either advice or things to do with your time! However, I do somehow feel the need to write to say that I am very anxious about the way the Poverty Program seems to be heading for the breakers. I am not reporting my impression, but rather what seems to be the increasing assumption on all fronts.

Just this morning I am told it is impossible to get anyone worthwhile to come to work in the Poverty Programs hereabouts, that the local office is filled with snippy Smith girls just out of college, et cetera, et cetera. I very much doubt either of these things is true, but they are rapidly becoming one of those things "everyone knows," and they can do the program no good.

As you may know, I am Chairman of a Seminar on the Poverty Program for the American Academy of Arts and Sciences. We work pretty hard at the business, and may even get some good done before the year is out. I don't think there is much possible work we can do to help you—what people say about intellectuals by and large turns out to be so—at least this is my impression, but we certainly would want to try, at least I would. Is there anything we can do? . . .

Frank O'Connor, a Queens politician who had defeated Moynihan for the job of New York City Council president in 1965, lost badly to Governor Nelson Rockefeller in 1966.

DECEMBER 30, 1966
HONORABLE FRANK O'CONNOR
PRESIDENT
THE CITY COUNCIL
CITY HALL
NEW YORK, NEW YORK

Dear Frank:

Not at the end of this year, but at the outset of the new one, I want to write to tell you that for all the disappointments of the campaign, you nonetheless carried our banners with honor and integrity, and left the party more than able to be proud of itself, and perhaps a bit more willing to begin doing the things we have to do to win. One of the things I had hoped to do in New York City politics was to try to enable some of the leaders of the working class, lower-middle class party to better understand the new group of educated liberals and vice versa: neither side has distinguished itself for empathy, and by and large the reformers have shown atrocious manners. But that was not to be, and the job is left to you: approaching from an opposite direction perhaps, but with the same intent. Keep at it: so much is at stake.

With my kindest regards to Mrs. O'Connor, I remain,

Most faithfully,

Moynihan asks for help from Robert Kennedy's press spokesman, Frank Mankiewicz, in getting some of his papers returned.

MARCH 14, 1967
MR. FRANK MANKIEWICZ
OFFICE OF SENATOR ROBERT KENNEDY
SENATE OFFICE BUILDING
WASHINGTON, D.C.

Dear Frank:

I wonder if I could ask you to help on a dumb problem which I should have known was inevitable. As you may know, Senator Kennedy sent me up to New York in 1962 to "do" for Mr. Morgenthau. I did, and on return began collecting a file on Governor Rockefeller in anticipation of his being the 1964 Republican candidate. President Kennedy knew about this, and wanted it done. I had worked out the strategy that had led Rockefeller to pledge that he would never no more raise taxes, for example, so we set to work documenting with considerable care the ways in which taxes were raised, etc. etc. Occasionally we would send a report to the White House.

I took these files—some four file drawers in all—with me when I left Washington. Last spring I got in touch with John Burns and offered them to him for use in the 1967 gubernatorial campaigns. As you will imagine, there was nothing on hand for John to use when he took over the State Committee. He accepted naturally enough, and the papers were turned over to him last May, accompanied by the usual pledges to return them. Alas, however, they appear to have fallen into the hands of Bill Haddad. Last January John asked Haddad to send them back to me, but of course nothing has been done.

Could you ask someone in your New York office to help? These papers belong to me, I suppose, but of course I plan to deposit them with the Kennedy Library. They are a small but not uninteresting part of the political history of the administration. Moreover, there are a number of quite personal items mixed in with the more routine research material that I would not want to see circulated. I turned them over to the party because I felt they were needed—and they were, as the outcome of the election would suggest. Nobody likes to clean up after a debacle—a point I know something about personally—but I do feel that someone ought to get them back to me—not for me, but for the Kennedy Library.

Clarifying his views on race, poverty, and ethnicity to Jason Epstein, vice president of Random House, Moynihan suggests that blacks possess a much broader set of as-pirations than many analysts believe. Moynihan had been working with Epstein on a book about the Moynihan Report, emphasizing his concerns about the need for job and income assistance for blacks. The book idea was shelved when Moynihan later joined the Nixon White House.

MARCH 23, 1967

MR. JASON EPSTEIN

VICE-PRESIDENT

RANDOM HOUSE, INC.

457 MADISON AVENUE

NEW YORK, NEW YORK 10022

Dear Jason:

You and I do not disagree, and I wonder that you keep seeming to think so rather. I have only one major difference with you, or rather the likes of you, about which I have written at some length in our manuscript. I do honestly believe that upper middle class Jews, whatever the precise economic status of their parents, have great difficulty comprehending the viability of a kind of routine working class ethnic oriented life. The alternative for Negroes is not to remain as they are or to become middle class. There is an intermediate op-tion which I swear to you most of them are seeking: to become mailmen and teamsters, army sergeants, nurses, waitresses, local politicians, Dodger fans. It is a perfectly good enough life, and I wonder if we are not making it harder for them to get there by insisting that they won't like it in advance.

Your idea of folk schools is a damn good one. How can we manage to get them run by the Baptist church?

I have just this moment got hold of the cornerstone of my statistical argu-ment: a special survey of the poverty population done for O.E.O. by the Census in February 1966, and just this moment tabulated. Almost exactly as I would have forecast, there turn out to be just under 5 million poor Negro children—more than half the Negro children. There are 2,395,000 poor Negro children living in central cities, vs. 1,905,000 whites. Of these 1,209,000 Negro children live in female-headed families, as against 723,000 whites. Etc., etc. I was right.

Greetings of this day.

Moynihan had concerns, expressed here to Harry McPherson, about mobilizing specialists at Harvard and M.I.T. to help build urban infrastructure in Vietnam.

MARCH 29, 1967
HONORABLE HARRY C. MCPHERSON
THE WHITE HOUSE
WASHINGTON D.C.

Dear Harry:

Monday afternoon Bob Culbertson, who is Associate Director of the A.I.D. mission to Vietnam, accompanied by H. Charles Ladenheim, chief of the Revolutionary Development (1) group at the Department of State in Washington, came to see us to ask if the Joint Center would be willing to enter a contract with A.I.D. for a back-to-back operation in Saigon with the Vietnamese government. Culbertson described the Saigon situation in some detail, the essence of which being a population growth from .5 million to 3 million in a very short period, during which the usual resources of the countryside have not always been available. He seemed to feel with some heat that living conditions are so bad for most of the cities' inhabitants that we are very much in danger of finding that by the time we have won over the countryside, we will have lost the cities. Which would be a curiously American thing, I suppose. In any event a combination of national and local government ministries is settling up a "Greater Saigon Urban Planning Office." They would like us to put together an American cadre which would work with opposite numbers in the Vietnamese operation. This would be quite similar to the work the Joint Center carried out in Venezuela over the past five years, save that in that case we were building a new city rather than trying to keep up with the growth of an old one. (The Calcutta experience, of course, provides some guidelines to this kind of work.)

This proposition came to us without any advance warning, and I am a bit off balance. To go to Saigon, taking the name of Harvard and M.I.T. with us, could hardly be thought a casual affair, much less a short term one. The university communities will want to know a lot more, both about the extent of U.S. and Vietnamese government backing, and the willingness of American urban planning types to become involved. (In Venezuela the core of our personnel were from Harvard or M.I.T., but two thirds of the total were recruited from around the nation, and for that matter the world.) Could I ask your advice on how I ought to proceed? I gather you are much involved in these matters now. . . .

Moynihan grew increasingly concerned about not offending the Johnson White House, though his disenchantment was clearly growing, as he indicates to Harry McPherson and Bill Moyers.

AUGUST 8, 1967

Dear Harry,

I called Bill Moyers this afternoon and learned in passing that you and Joe Califano felt there was a suggestion in my Newsday article that if President Kennedy were alive we would not be in our present difficulty.

Several interpretations of this occur to me. One is that you are all more than normally sensitive on this point—in a way that I would not be—and that you really are disturbed. If this is so, let me ask that you accept my apologies, and perhaps also that you tender them to the President, as I certainly intended nothing of the sort. Nor do I think anything of the sort. Indeed, I thought I went out of my way to cite the failure of the 1962 Welfare Amendments as an example of our refusing to confront reality.

Best,

Note for Bill Moyers:

I hope you won't mind my sending this note. It is in the family. If an apology is in order, I feel I ought to offer one.

I may have misled you in my remark about Edinburgh. I recall that you studied there, but do not recollect that the doctrine of the forgiveness of sin was ever very prominent in that branch of Celtic theology!

Praising the Republicans to Representative Melvin Laird, a powerful member of the House leadership.

14 AUGUST 1967
HONORABLE MELVIN P. LAIRD
MEMBER OF CONGRESS
HOUSE OFFICE BUILDING
WASHINGTON, D.C.

Dear Congressman Laird:

I would not be more in agreement with you as to the pointlessness—and at this moment, with respect to the Democrats—the arrogance of the debate over who really recognizes these problems. The English say that no man is a hero to his butler, and I say that neither is any political party to a man who has served it. One of the impressive developments of the past few years has been the intellectual cutting edge of the criticism you fellows have been leveling against us, and that is all to the good.

I would be honored to take part in any kind of exchange you suggest. Let me make a suggestion: I am a member of the Institute of Politics which has been established here in Cambridge in memory of President Kennedy. (Congressman Ford was one of our guests last year.) How would it be if you and some of your colleagues came up for a long evening discussion, or perhaps a day of discussion some time this fall? We would be honored, and you would find it pleasant, and even possibly of use. I have not talked about this with Dick Neustadt, but he is the most agreeable of men, as I am sure you know.

TIME *magazine put Moynihan on its cover for an article about the crisis in the cities, for which he was grateful in a message to Hedley Donovan, the editor.*

AUGUST 16, 1967

MR. HEDLEY DONOVAN

EDITOR-IN-CHIEF

TIME MAGAZINE

TIME & LIFE BUILDING

ROCKEFELLER CENTER

NEW YORK, NEW YORK 10020

Dear Hedley Donovan:

I learn that you were trying out for Managing Editor on that issue of Time in which I appeared. I write to tell you how much we at the Joint Center are in your debt. I don't exactly know what that means, but it does have a meaning, and beyond that of fund raising!

For my own part, a mild ambivalence has emerged as I learn more about the peculiar genus of international voyeur that collects autographed covers of Time Magazine, only a portion of whom, alas, sends stamps to accompany the cover! . . .

Nathaniel Owings, the architect and founder of Skidmore Owings and Merrill, was chairman and Moynihan vice chairman of the Temporary Commission on Pennsylvania Avenue. Both were frustrated about the pace of the project.

AUGUST 25, 1967

Dear Nat,

I am afraid we lose again. As is his practice, Congressman [Wayne] Aspinall [chair of the House Interior Committee] adjourned his committee yesterday noon for the remainder of the year. I learned that he was going to do this early yesterday morning, but there was nothing to be done.

The White House report is about as follows (all from Harry McPherson who told me about Aspinall in the morning, and with whom I rode down the avenue in the afternoon). After you spoke with him, he took the bill up with the President. The President wants the bill, but obviously it is not on the top of the list. A letter was drafted in Interior for the President to send to Aspinall, but he had just written him about the California redwoods and did not feel he wanted to write another letter. Instead he directed Barefoot Sanders, the new legislative aide, to see Aspinall. Sanders did this, and was told by Aspinall that he was personally for the bill, but would not report it out without Saylor's acquiescence. This of course is a way of saying he was not for it—inasmuch as Saylor's views are unchanged. In any event Saylor fell ill at about this point—about two weeks ago, as I judge—and went home to Pennsylvania. And that was the end of it.

I don't know where we are, Nat. No one is against us particularly, but neither is anyone really for us. Moreover, it begins to appear that maybe there really are some people seriously against us. . . .

Harry McPherson is an old friend and I was as blunt with him as I could be. Is the problem, I asked, that this is regarded as a Kennedy project. He replied with some force that this is not so. I accept this partially. As I see it the problem is as follows, in a descending order of importance:

1. No matter what you say, Pennsylvania Avenue is a project for spending money. The Administration does not want to spend a dime. Not even in response to the worst outbreak of racial violence in history. A fortiori not to play City Beautiful.
2. No one in Washington really knows or cares much about this sort of thing. It is women's work. Lady Bird and Mary Bountiful. (Incidentally, can it be as I gather from Galston, that we are still not in the Beautification Plan.
3. It is a Kennedy project.
4. X factor. Something you and I do not know about. Somebody who doesn't like you, etc. etc. (I don't think I am sufficiently associated with the undertaking any longer to bear on anybody's judgment, although this is possible. You should know that when we set out to get the bill again in earnest this summer I wrote to McPherson saying that if I was any obstacle he could have my resignation immediately, as I certainly did not want to get in the way.) . . .

Well, there we are. I gather you are going to ask the Commission members to dig up some money for us for the coming year. This would be in line with the kind of thing McPherson proposes. Whether you will get it or not, I cannot say.

I can imagine this news will depress you somewhat, particularly after a camping trip. (Where do you get your energy!) You have not much taken me in your counsel in this matter since I left Washington, and I don't know how much free advice you want. Let me give it, however, for what it is worth.

Your options are at least three fold.

1. Resign. You have a perfect right to resign. (I would go with you.) You could say you have been at this for five long years, and that while everyone has been nice to you, the fact is that no one has ever done anything. In five years you have never seen the President, etc. etc. Moreover the Democratic leadership of the House has done nothing for you, etc. etc. America doesn't want to do anything about its cities, etc. Lincoln in the civil war kept on building the Capitol dome, but we don't seem to have a Lincoln. Or simply resign quietly and be done with it.

2. Demand that the administration get you the bill. Insist on seeing the President. Say if you do not you will resign. Demand that Aspinall's son be fired, as it were, or that he deliver on his deal. Raise hell, say you are not going to let the city of Washington be lost because you can't make people listen. Get a Presidential endorsement, picture with the new model, etc.

3. Wait out the present domestic stalemate and go on with the job of putting the project together by bits and pieces. Keep prodding, get out some good brochures. Build a little more of a clacque in Washington, etc. Hopefully the day will come when the war is over, and we have the energy to move on with something like this. There are all kinds of action looking things you could do: eg. Get more persons appointed to the commission.

It seems to me you have no alternative, but to choose the latter option, or some other that may occur to you. In any event, them's my thoughts. . . .

Moynihan's growing disappointment in the Johnson administration is expressed here to former Labor Secretary and Supreme Court Justice Arthur J. Goldberg, now ambassador at the United Nations.

25 AUGUST 1967
HIS EXCELLENCY ARTHUR J. GOLDBERG
UNITED STATES MISSION TO THE UNITED NATIONS
799 UNITED NATIONS PLAZA
NEW YORK, N.Y.

Dear Ambassador:

What a very generous note, in a not especially pleasant time. Somehow nothing works. I wrote that article that appears in the <u>Washington Post</u> because Bill Moyers asked and urged me to do so, and in just the terms that finally appeared. The response from the White House? That it was a tasteless thing to suggest that if President Kennedy were alive we would have no problems. However, one thing the past two years have taught me was how to live without being popular. Actually, the mail on the <u>Post</u> article has been extraordinarily favorable. The nation wants leadership. They want an administration that will be seen and candid and try to explain as much as can be explained. Instead, we are getting utterly transparent evasions and pieties. . . .

Moynihan charged that many critics of the Moynihan Report, including Kenneth G. Neigh of the United Presbyterian Church, had never read it.

OCTOBER 3, 1967
MR. KENNETH G. NEIGH
BOARD OF NATIONAL MISSIONS OF THE UNITED PRESBYTERIAN CHURCH
475 RIVERSIDE DRIVE
NEW YORK, NEW YORK 10027

Dear Ken:

I suppose I was a bit harsh in Washington last August, but I was going through a moment of rather intense annoyance with the world, which you somewhat triggered. The point being that you said you were thinking to write me a letter about my work in Rochester. The point is that I would never have been involved in Rochester at all if someone at the National Council of Churches had not gleefully reported to Saul Alinsky that Kodak had now gone and hired that racist bastard Moynihan as the latest of their atrocities.

The point is a very simple one, Ken. There are certain public controversies in which reputations are attacked, during which it becomes extremely important for the civilized community to maintain a solid front in the face of character assassinations. All liberals found it easy enough to see this point when Senator McCarthy was abroad. Very few until very recently have recognized that the Paytons are cut of the same cloth and do the same damage. You say had you read my report and Payton's beforehand you might have averted the controversy. My question is why were you silent afterwards? The only man in your group who resisted the latter day McCarthyism is Reinhold Neibuhr, a fact not surprising to you or me. It is just not enough to feel good; the question is what you do.

An exactly similar case is taking place now with Professor James Coleman, whose report on the "Equality of Educational Opportunity" is being labeled as racism by civil servants in Washington, while the pious stand by clucking and saying nothing. If he were labeled a communist, they would come screaming to the fore. I would urge anyone concerned with the moral niceties of the subject to read Stephen Spender's essay in R. H. S. Crossman's study, The God That Failed.

Moynihan felt that auto executives including James M. Roche, executive vice president of General Motors, continued to hold his views on auto safety against him.

SATURDAY, OCTOBER 21, 1967
MR. JAMES M. ROCHE
EXECUTIVE VICE PRESIDENT
GENERAL MOTORS CORPORATION
GENERAL MOTORS BUILDING
DETROIT 2, MICHIGAN

Dear Mr. Roche:

I had not expected to be back at you so soon, but it would seem I am having General Motors trouble again.

This morning a friend of a quarter century's standing, who is now assistant general counsel to one of the largest and most respected business firms in the nation, called me in a state of some perplexity. As with many such firms, there is a large Negro population in the Northern city in which their headquarters are located, and of late my friend has been much involved in efforts to provide employment opportunities for Negroes in private enterprises, including the one with which he is associated. In the course of these efforts he has come in touch with the Plans for Progress group that operates out of Washington. You may recall that this voluntary organization of business with government contracts was set up under President Kennedy, and in early years was one of President Johnson's major interests. It would seem that they are having an annual meeting, or some such affair in the near future, and a number of persons have suggested that I be asked to speak. However, a representative of General Motors, who is somehow involved in the hierarchy, has objected. . . .

I am sure I don't need to tell you that the prospect of not receiving a speaking invitation is one I can endure with equanimity. Like most persons involved in urban affairs I am already much over-committed: I receive upwards of twenty invitations a week, and can accept only a tiny fraction. If I thought the General Motors man was simply looking out for my welfare, I would not mind, but you and I know that this is not so. . . .

I am sure you deplore this as much as I do, and as a political scientist I am supposed to know how little a person in your position can really do to control such matters. But I think you should realize that these things are going on, and that they surely do your firm no credit. After all, in what way have I offended? As a government official and as a social scientist I worked in collaboration with a group of other such persons to devise what we hoped would be a better approach to a serious problem of public health. I have never made a penny out of traffic safety. I have never, so far as I am aware, been in any way abusive to persons in the automobile industry. I have not even been very much publicly associated with the traffic safety legislation. Why should I be so treated?

A final point, which I offer as nothing more than a statement of fact. As the person responsible for bringing Ralph Nader to the Department of Labor, and as his immediate supervisor during that period, it is more than possible that I will be called by him as a character witness in his forthcoming suit against General Motors. What on earth am I supposed to say if asked whether my own experience would suggest that your company is in the practice of making trouble for its critics?

Please don't think of this as an angry letter, as it is not. But I am disturbed, and I do think you should know of these events. . . .

Moynihan found it increasingly difficult to defend LBJ against the Left and also criticize the Vietnam War, as he tells Harry McPherson in the White House.

NOVEMBER 8, 1967
HONORABLE HARRY C. MCPHERSON, JR.
SPECIAL COUNSEL TO THE PRESIDENT
THE WHITE HOUSE
WASHINGTON, D.C.

Dear Harry:

... I am not sorry we had our conversation yesterday morning. I gather I have now made clear what I meant when I wrote last summer. I do think you all have great difficulty sympathizing with the obligation of persons in our position here to say what we think. This is not an option, Harry, it is as near as possible to the central fact of the vows we take when we enter this cloister. Please remember—I know it won't make any difference, but I'll say it anyway—that I went before the Americans for Democratic Action and told them that we must face the fact that liberals have been in charge of American foreign and domestic policy for the last six years, including the present one; that getting out of Viet Nam is not so much a problem of meaning well as finding a way; and that Lyndon Johnson was going to be re-elected next year. If you think that made me any friends, you should have been present. I said it because I think it. It would have been easier and more advantageous to me to declaim that Lyndon Johnson is a Fascist, racist, imperialist, paranoid beast. I did not because I do not think it to be so, indeed because I think it to be an outrageous calumny. But, Harry, you must expect me to say what I think, even when it is not agreeable, and I would hope you would grant that I have not gone out of my way to say disagreeable things.

Even as he prepared to support the Democratic ticket in 1968, Moynihan wrote to Richard Nixon, then campaigning for the Republican presidential nomination.

DECEMBER 20, 1967
RICHARD M. NIXON, ESQ.
MUDGE, STERN, BALDWIN AND TODD
20 BROAD STREET
NEW YORK, NEW YORK

Dear Mr. Nixon:

I was much interested—as I am sure many others were—in Bob Semple's report this morning of some views of yours on the subject of urban poverty. The idea of a national job census is an extremely useful one. You are perhaps aware that the 1960 Census simply missed 10% of the Negro population altogether and probably missed upwards of 30% of Negro males age 20–29. This is a subject the Joint Center is most interested in, and it is very encouraging to find a person of your distinction similarly interested.

If by chance there is a text of your remarks, I would be most interested to read them, and would appreciate having a copy.

But the principal purpose of my note is to say that if you are ever in the Cambridge area, we should be enormously honored to have you as a luncheon speaker at the Joint Center. This is a forum which is not without advantages for you, but of course the greatest benefit would be to the faculty and graduate students here who would be fascinated to learn more of your views, and who might help you to develop them further through their questions.

Still Moynihan remained a supporter of Robert Kennedy, as he tells his wife.

JANUARY 9, 1968
MRS. ROBERT F. KENNEDY
HICKORY HILL
1147 CHAINE BRIDGE ROAD
MCLEAN, VIRGINIA

Dear Ethel:

. . . I have sort of a thing against writing fan letters to politicians, but you might just do me the favor of telling your husband he really was quite brilliant on the Joey Bishop Show last Friday. It was quite the most lucid statement of our situation I have heard yet, and I do hope he is proud of his performance. There is so little for anyone to be proud of any more.

While teaching and writing at Harvard, Moynihan tried to broker an employment and job-training deal in Rochester, N.Y., between William S. Vaughn, president of Eastman Kodak, and the militant grassroots civil rights group FIGHT (Freedom-Integration-God-Honor-Today), which was established after the riots in Rochester in 1964.

FEBRUARY 2, 1968
MR. WILLIAM S. VAUGHN
PRESIDENT
EASTMAN KODAK COMPANY

Dear Mr. Vaughn:

... The essential fact is this. In June, 1967 the FIGHT organization in effect saved the reputation of the Kodak Company by withdrawing a written agreement which, from their point of view, required the company to do something specific for and with them. They did not have to withdraw this agreement. Lesser men, with less vision, might very well have clung to it, insisting on its validity and demanding compliance through endless months and years of squabbling vilification, and worse. It may be noted that in such an exchange they had nothing whatever to lose, and Kodak had a great deal to lose.

More than half a year has now passed, and if one were to ask what has FIGHT received in turn from Kodak, I fear the answer would have to be: Nothing. This is why I write. I write because I am concerned that you and your colleagues at the top of the Kodak Company be fully aware of the nature of the agreement you reached with FIGHT last June, at least as I perceive it, and as I believe it to be perceived on their part. You did not enter a contractual relationship. You entered a gentleman's agreement. The terms were essentially as follows: FIGHT gave up a specific claim on Kodak which they could enforce, in return for a generalized claim which they could not. (I am sure you understand that I am aware of how weak the FIGHT organization was getting to be at that point, how divided the Negro community was, and all the usual complexities. The fact remained that the power and entitlement—from the point of view of public opinion—to damage Kodak <u>did</u> exist. I would expect never to hear this fact questioned by a Kodak official.) What was the nature of the generalized claim which FIGHT obtained with respect to Kodak? Very simply, it was a claim for a tangible, public success. How, what, where, are details. But by now FIGHT ought to have had an important success to show for its willingness last June to give up a near impregnable position of stalemated hostility in return for an exposed position of friendly cooperation. . . .

I do not feel that Kodak understands that hell or high water, cost what it will, and ridiculous as it may be, Kodak has to provide a success for FIGHT. FIGHT has to have something it can show for last June's agreement. Some one thing it can point to. It still does not have any such thing, and until it does I would feel that Kodak has not discharged a debt of honor. . . .

George W. Ball, a reputed "dove" on Vietnam in the Johnson administration, became United Nations ambassador after the resignation of Arthur Goldberg, who had his own disputes with the White House over the war. Moynihan was sympathetic to both.

APRIL 29, 1968

HONORABLE GEORGE W. BALL

3100 35TH STREET N.W.

WASHINGTON, D.C. 20016

Dear George:

Having sat with Arthur over the weekend in which he agreed to leave the Court at the President's behest, and having helped with his statement accepting the United Nations appointment, you can imagine my fury with the way he was dismissed. On the other hand, he was planning to leave, and it had to happen eventually. This is a note simply to say that the misery is mitigated only by your willingness to take up where he left off. If I can be of help, you have only to ask.

Moynihan thanks Johnson for supporting the establishment of an academic center to honor Woodrow Wilson.

APRIL 29, 1968
THE PRESIDENT
THE WHITE HOUSE

Dear Mr. President:

As Vice Chairman of your Commission and the member who had the responsibility for handling the Woodrow Wilson Memorial proposal, I write to express my deepest appreciation for your having included this proposal in your District of Columbia message. After many long conversations with Doug Cater, I feel I am perhaps especially alive to your concern with education, and the hope that your years in the Presidency will be first of all remembered for your achievements in this field. The establishment of a Center for Scholars as a memorial to Woodrow Wilson may well be the crowning achievement of that record.

It will be built. And there is every hope that it will turn out to be, as our Report proposes, "an institution that the 22nd century will regard as having influenced the 21st." One recalls that of the four things Jefferson asked to be remembered for on his tomb, one was the founding of the University of Virginia. The founding of the Woodrow Wilson Center for Scholars in Washington may turn out to mean as much to you. It is a proposal for which the nation and the world will be in your debt.

Moynihan reminds Robert Kennedy of his support as RFK's race reached its climactic phase in California.

MAY 21, 1968
HONORABLE ROBERT F. KENNEDY

Dear Bob:

. . . I am just back from three days in California speaking for you in Los Angeles, Santa Barbara and Berkeley. It was tough, but interesting. I found

McCarthy sentiment widespread but not, I thought, very deep. On the other hand, I fear we are in an almost hopeless situation at the universities. But conversely, a rally on the steps of Sproul Hall at Berkeley went very well indeed, or so most people seem to think.

Raymond Price, special assistant to Richard Nixon in his election campaign, wrote to Moynihan praising his article about race in COMMENTARY *and adding: "I don't expect to win you away from loyalty either to the Democratic party or to Robert Kennedy. But I do think there's a great kinship of aim and approach here between Mr. Nixon and yourself—and I hope that, even as the campaign develops, it won't be lost sight of." Moynihan's reply:*

MAY 23, 1968
MR. RAYMOND K. PRICE, JR.
SPECIAL ASSISTANT
NIXON FOR PRESIDENT COMMITTEE

Dear Mr. Price:

What a hell of a nice letter, and what a generous thing to have done! Much as I think you do, at this particular time especially, I value such efforts to find common agreement enormously.

Do have the kindness to thank Mr. Nixon for that mention in Dispatches. Certainly it was a most impressive document. I wonder if it would be possible to trouble you for a copy of his recent statement on crime which evinced considerable interest hereabouts?

We are indeed near Cooperstown, namely in West Davenport, about fifteen miles away. Should you ever be in the area—obviously you will not be this year—do by all means come down for a bi-partisan meeting of talking and drinking.

Moynihan thanks Saul Alinsky, the grassroots Chicago organizer, for his support on the same day that Robert Kennedy was shot after winning the California primary.

DICTATED JUNE 5, 1968

MR. SAUL D. ALINSKY

Dear Saul:

... I do very much appreciate that you spent your time defending me, but in all truth I think I would be better off if you attacked me! Can you manage that? I would be willing to provide remuneration!

I don't really feel funny today. I have been out on the coast campaigning for the Senator. I only hope some of those intellectual bastards who were so snobby about him are having some second thoughts.

I can't sell you a part of the Joint Center, but I can give you part. How would you like to spend a month or so here as a Visiting Associate? We will set you up and provide you everything you need, including interesting audiences. Anything of this sort that we could work out would be an honor for the Center and the universities.

After the assassinations of Kennedy and the Reverend Martin Luther King Jr., Moynihan tells their widows that he wanted to dedicate two scholarly books to them.

MRS. ROBERT F. KENNEDY

HICKORY HILL

1147 CHAINE BRIDGE ROAD

MCLEAN, VIRGINIA

Dearest Ethel:

I am writing on behalf of a group of some two dozen members and associates of the American Academy of Arts and Sciences who, for the past two years have met regularly as a seminar on race and poverty. Next winter we will be publishing two volumes, the first on conceptual problems in the study of poverty, the second on the origins of the Federal anti-poverty program. ...

As chairman of the group, I have been asked to write to say that we would like to dedicate the two volumes jointly to Martin Luther King, Jr., and to Robert F. Kennedy. Most members of the seminar knew Bob, many worked with him, all were stricken by his death. Like the <u>jongleur de Notre Dame</u>, all we can offer in his honor are the things we write, but with your permission, we should consider it a great privilege to do that.

I never did see you during the campaign, nor for that matter Bob. I was out in California for some time, but naturally was sent where he was not. That last week I really began to feel us picking up. We were going to change this country.

You have our love as he has our prayers.

Moynihan's anguished letter to Senator Edward M. (Ted) Kennedy—discussing painful issues of race, class, and politics—was drafted in response to a request from the surviving brother on June 14 for Moynihan's thoughts about "a permanent living memorial that can be established for Bob." A cover note addressed "Dear Dave," apparently David Burke, a legislative aide, suggests that it should be passed on only if he wanted. A subsequent letter from Moynihan to Ted Kennedy indicates that this was a draft that was never sent.

JULY 25, 1968

Dear Ted,

I have been much aware of not having replied to your letter concerning a memorial to Bob, and write as much to say that to you as to offer any real advice. I gather from the Times that plans are already taking shape, and in about the form I would have anticipated. These are sufficiently divergent from the direction of my thoughts as to make me hesitate to trouble you with minority opinions that are neither yours nor those of persons on whom you most rely. On the other hand, you did ask me. Perhaps the best thing to do is to proceed tentatively, with the understanding that I do not expect any particular reaction, certainly not a positive one from you.

My difficulty comes to this. Over the past several years I have found myself less and less in agreement with Bob on what you might call strategies of social change. I tried to express this to him once by saying that he was in danger of becoming the Jay Lovestone of the Left. You know Lovestone, né Linsky as I recall, the hardline, uncompromising head of the Communist party of the U.S.A. who defected in the thirties, and switched over to being George Meany's hard line, uncompromising anti-Communist. A man who can be de-

scribed as having been something of a political disaster at all states of his career. (That being so very much the case Frank Mankiewicz counseled against
making the remark, but Bob was kindly, if a little annoyed!) What I was trying
to say and in elaborating did so, was that having been a very model Boston
Irish Catholic in his youth, at rather a low period in the history of that tribe,
he had acquired a kind of insensitivity to the nuances of social ideas, so that
having swung over to the cause of social change he was constantly on the
verge of calling for social upheaval. More and more, or so it seemed to me, he
was being used by an all too familiar upper middle class radical whose fondest
hopes are to bring about the war of all the lower orders against all the lower
orders. Starting of course with the massacre of all those crypto-fascist geno-
cidal Irish cops by a righteously outraged lumpen-proletariat.

I loved Bob. And as I saw this happening, or thought I did, I became all
the more upset as I was sure they would let him down in the end, as they did.
I had got to know him in the mid-1950's when he was in Washington and I
was working for Harriman in New York. At that time his standards of political
innovation extended as far and no further than Charlie Buckley, and in terms
of who he could count on when he needed them, or rather when Jack did, he
was right. I was a member of the New York delegation in 1960, and the people
who surrounded Bob when he later went to New York were precisely the ones
who were against us—who held him and his brother and the whole tradition
in the party that they represented in contempt. And where were those people
when he needed them this year?

I feel especially bitter about this. In the spring, after he had announced
Norman Podhoretz asked me to write an article in Commentary on the campaign and the Democratic choices. I had voted for McCarthy at A.D.A., as
who would not have, but had no doubts that we should nominate, or try to
nominate Bob, and said so. I wrote a good article—Mac Bundy said it was
the best one written for Bob—in about as strategically a located forum as you
could find. (Perhaps you saw it: I sent you a copy.) And I cannot describe the
hostility of the mail that came in from the liberal/left. In a sackfull, only <u>one</u>
letter suggesting that Bob Kennedy might after all be a kind and compassionate man. They went back to dismissing him as a ruthless machine politician the moment it was in their interest to do so. I realize I am becoming
anthropomorphic about "They," but if you have lived with that mindset as
long as I have, you might bend that way too! In May I came out here to the
Coast to campaign for him. I was sent mostly to campuses and to suburban
gatherings. Again that acid contempt.

This is probably more than you want to read, and is already more than I intended to write. What I wish to say comes to this. I would hate to see a memorial to Bob fashioned in the image of whatever is the current vogue in upper middle class models of social change on behalf of whatever segment of the lower orders that are currently most in favor in the salons of Central Park West. Community action, neighborhood corporations, black, green, yellow power, peril, or whatever. Bob Kennedy as a political man descended from a tradition of stable, working class urban politics. It is the only element, so far as I can see, in the political system that ever did anything for him or for his family. That tradition is very much isolated now, and very much in trouble. It no longer fully understands what is going on, save to be clear that no one in power or fashion any longer is much interested in its problems. It seems to me that a Memorial for Bob must in some way include this group. In a word, the people of South Boston and Dorchester ought to be as much in our minds as those of Roxbury or Bedford-Stuyvesant, or whatever. Those are your people, they were Bob's people before he got religion, they have been abandoned, and our politics are very much the worst for it. No one is much interested in them, no one admires much less likes them, no one tries to help them break out of the sour and self defeating attitudes which they have acquired, much as Negroes are said to internalize the negative images they perceive that they have in the larger society.

I have one thought of possible interest. The great social issue of this moment is the effort to find a place in the cities for the Negroes who are the newest migrants. This is much complicated by resistance and hostility from older migrant groups who have remained in the ranks of the working and lower middle classes. They feel they made it on their own, expect Negroes to do so as well, etc. etc. They are relating to their understanding of that incredible, still difficult to conceive gathering in of the nations that produced the American people. Trouble is we know very little about it, and still do not understand it. Just possibly, if we did know more we could handle our present situation better. In any event, the process of learning more could provide an opportunity to train a generation of desperately needed social science researchers and activists now seeking to bring about for the blacks something of the social change and mobility that obviously (though painfully and slowly) came to the Irish, et al. The Kennedy family is perhaps the supreme symbol of ethnic success in America. Would not a center, associated with a University, devoted to the permanent study of this phenomena, and associated with the training of young persons drawn from the groups involved, be an interesting memorial. I need hardly tell you that this question of racial, ethnic, and religious hostilities and accommodations is steadily, as the Twentieth Century makes its bloody way through history, turning out to be <u>the</u> question in just about every part of the world. So there is nothing parochial in this proposal.

In any event, I feel we ought somehow to learn more about it. Returning from the funeral I found myself in a much deeper depression that I had imagined. Wanting nothing whatever to do with the present, I sat down and wrote a small book about the past—the community action programs that Bob so helped to get started. As you will see if you care to glance through the manuscript (I am sending you a copy today) it suggests we fouled that up for lack of appreciating the complexity of ethnic and racial relations in large cities. I don't know if it is a good book, but in the manner of the jongleur de Notre Dame it seemed the one thing I could do in his honor.

Nothing will approach your eulogy.

As he did for Mrs. Robert Kennedy, Moynihan asked Mrs. Martin Luther King Jr. about dedicating the planned books to King and Kennedy. Mrs. King replied saying she would be "most pleased" about that honor.

12 AUGUST 1968
MRS. MARTIN LUTHER KING, JR.

Dear Mrs. King:

I am writing on behalf of a group of some two dozen members and associates of the American Academy of Arts and Sciences, who, for the past two years have met regularly as a seminar on race and poverty. . . .

As chairman of the group, I have been asked to write to say that we would like to dedicate the two volumes jointly to Martin Luther King, Jr., and to Robert F. Kennedy. Many of us knew and worked with Dr. King; all were stricken by his death. As with so many Americans, now that they are gone we realize even more the leadership and inspiration they provided. We should be most grateful if we could have your permission, then, to make such a dedication.

We have never met, but I did know and deeply admired your husband. He asked me to come down to speak to a gathering he held in Miami Beach just before Washington's birthday. He was cordial and welcoming as always, but I also felt he seemed tired, as if with a sense of foreboding. But you have thought of all this too often, and I must not interpose myself.

Moynihan communicated his concern to McPherson about the faltering campaign of Vice President Hubert Humphrey. His suggestion that a Nixon administration "would be genuinely interested in our views" prompted an incredulous McPherson to reply: "My God, consider that sentence. . . . Do you know Nixon? Do you know who will run the government for him?"

24 SEPTEMBER 1968
HONORABLE HARRY C. MCPHERSON, JR.

Dear Harry:

. . . I write promptly to tell you that I have come out for Humphrey in the way it seemed to me would be most useful. Bill Moyers asked me to write a piece for his Sunday syndicate in a series he is doing on "Agenda for the Next President." I wrote as intelligent a statement as I could manage based in part on our last conversation, and up in the beginning stated explicitly that I supported and would vote for Hubert Humphrey. It seems to me people pay more attention to such statements when they are embedded in an otherwise neutral set of reflections on the complexity of things. I wrote a piece for Bill's syndicate a year ago and it got tremendous circulation.

I am disturbed by your obvious pessimism on the campaign and its obvious outcome, but I suppose everyone shares it. Let me say, however, that I do think one small part of the problem is that there are a great many people like me who in all realism could only expect that a Humphrey victory will mean that the persons who have so assiduously kept us out of influence in these recent years will be continued in power. On the other hand, we have every reason to think a Nixon administration would be genuinely interested in our views. I say this quite seriously. As you know, in these recent years I have been distressed not to have any influence on anybody down there because I feel I was more accurate than those whose advice was being taken, and nothing has caused me to change that judgment. . . .

To McPherson, Moynihan dismisses concerns that he might join a Nixon administration.

3 OCTOBER 1968
HONORABLE HARRY C. MCPHERSON, JR.
SPECIAL COUNSEL TO THE PRESIDENT
THE WHITE HOUSE
WASHINGTON, D.C.

Dear Harry:

Perhaps you saw the enclosed. Have no fear that I will accept the job. I have life tenure at Harvard University and make twice as much money as a cabinet officer with no particular effort, and have four-month vacations besides!

On the other hand, you overreacted to my point that "Nixon . . . would be genuinely interested in our views." He <u>will</u> be interested, probably conspicuously so. But then, I doubt he will do anything about them. This is quite a different thing. All I am saying is that it will be for many persons in academia a more pleasant atmosphere than the sour sterility of the recent period.

But why do you consider the election lost? Why don't you fellows get out there and fight?

On the eve of the 1968 election, Moynihan supports Humphrey but reaches out again to Nixon.

24 OCTOBER 1968

Dear Mr. Nixon:

I was greatly impressed by your radio address on the subject of employment. It seems we are finally beginning to see that employment is the key to social stability, a fact which you made clear and explicit.

You hardly need letters from Democrats to tell you this. In truth, I am writing with something else in mind: the apparent intention of the Business Council to press for a 5.5 per cent unemployment rate as an anti-inflation measure. (Perhaps you saw the story in Monday's <u>Times</u>. Ralph Lazarus presented the proposal to a meeting at Hot Springs, and it was accepted without apparent dissent.) Although you are hardly to be held responsible for the views of the Business Council, the assumption that its members would have some influence in an administration headed by you prompts me to send this brief but troubled letter.

I understand and accept as fully legitimate the concern of businessmen about inflation at this moment. Yet I feel that <u>they</u> do not understand what such an unemployment rate would do to the urban Negro social structure, only just now, and very tentatively recovering from the battering sustained during a decade of savagely high unemployment rates that commenced in 1954. A rate of 5.5 per cent for the work force generally, means 11 per cent for Negro males, and 35 per cent for Negro teenagers. It means more broken families, more welfare recipients, more persons sent to prison . . . more of all the problems you will be trying to resolve.

I speak not in hyperbole. In the past several years I believe I have been able to tease out, as the mathematicians say, the relations between unemployment and various forms of social pathology. If you like, after November (assuming everything goes well for you!) I should be happy to show this material to whomever of your advisers might be interested. The point is quickly enough made, and thereafter they can make such use of it as they choose. . . .

A last attempt to get LBJ to support the Pennsylvania Avenue project.

26 NOVEMBER 1968

THE PRESIDENT

Dear Mr. President:

At Harry McPherson's suggestion I am writing to suggest that in your final message to the Congress you might want to make some reference to the progress, such as it has been, of the Pennsylvania Avenue plan. . . .

A cycle of sorts is ending for me as well in this matter.... Arthur Goldberg and I thought up the idea in the Labor Department back in 1961. We set up, with no legal foundation whatever, something we chose to call the "President's Council on Pennsylvania Avenue" with Nat Owings as chairman and the Labor Department as <u>de facto</u> sponsor. President Kennedy was good natured about it all—we managed to get our other work done as well—but not really much interested until the plan began to take shape. At that point, the spring of 1963, he became very interested indeed, feeling as he did that all administrations are transient and soon over, and that great public architecture is often the most important memorial left behind. As he left for Dallas he instructed us to prepare a meeting to show the plan to the Congressional leaders. Bill Walton, Charlie Horsky and I were doing just that when the White House switchboard rang on November 22nd. It is my understanding, although I could be quite wrong, that the Pennsylvania Avenue effort was one of the several items which Mrs. Onassis suggested to you President Kennedy would most have wished to see carried forward....

I have always been treated with the greatest courtesy. On the other hand, I feel that neither I nor Nat Owings (although he would want to speak for himself) ever succeeded in making this a matter of genuine interest and satisfaction for your people. Somehow, curiously, the opportunity to influence public design, which should be one of the great rewards of office normally shows up as simply the demand of yet another importunate pressure group.... As I assume there will be no formal occasion on which former members of your subcabinet will have an opportunity to make their official farewells, I wonder if I might take this informal one. It was a great honor serving you, in a time of historic progress. I feel history will surely establish this....

Outlining to President-elect Richard Nixon how he might serve him at the White House in a new structure of domestic affairs advisers. His initial title became assistant to the president for urban affairs.

DECEMBER 8, 1968

MEMORANDUM FOR THE PRESIDENT ELECT

In an accompanying memo I describe a possible interim arrangement for bringing about a measure of policy coordination in domestic affairs comparable to the NSC arrangement.

This would involve me serving as executive secretary of the Economic Opportunity Council, with Secretary Finch as Chairman.

This would provide me a staff and considerable leverage in the government. However it could only work if my position as Special Assistant to the President for Domestic Affairs were genuinely comparable to that of the Special Assistant for National Security Affairs.

The Special Assistant must be the President's man. He must have automatic access to the President. He must be free to tell the President things no one else will tell him, especially as to how the departments are working. The departments must know this, which they will quickly enough if it is the case. He must be free for Presidential assignments in any and every direction.

The Special Assistant must be responsible for preparing the major Presidential papers on domestic affairs. He need not actually write them, but it must be his task to assemble the major proposals and options for presentation to the President, and thereafter to see that the President's decisions are set forth accurately in the relevant state papers.

After thinking about it at some length—I hate titles—I feel also that the appendage "for Domestic Affairs" really is necessary if I am to do for you the job I believe must and think can be done.

Undated Memorandum to President-elect Nixon, advising him on the makeup of Negro—or black—leadership with whom he will meet.

FROM: DANIEL P. MOYNIHAN

MEMORANDUM FOR THE PRESIDENT-ELECT

You are meeting at 2:00 p.m. with a group of "moderate" Negroes, a term which has, however, quite a different meaning today than even five years ago.

They are considerably more militant and, in a sense, aggressive on the issue of racial consciousness than ever in the past.

(Incidentally, you may want as a general policy to use the term "black" rather than Negro. A close question.)

I expect, however, you will find the group to be friendly and well enough disposed toward the new Administration. (I spoke at some length with Roy Wilkins at the time you were talking to me about my job. He urged me to take it.) As you know there is much apprehension in some parts of the Negro community. Your task force on Urban Affairs reported, for example, a widespread rumor that the new Administration plans to build a system of concentration camps for blacks. As I mentioned at the meeting of the Cabinet-designate, there is a pervasive preoccupation with genocide. However, there is at present no solid black political front. General political attitudes would seem to divide into three categories, corresponding to three social groupings.

First, militant, politicized, middle class youth, of the kind who organized sit ins five years ago and are seizing University buildings today. It would be hard to exaggerate their bitterness or race consciousness.

Second, a fairly large, moderate—but politicized—middle and lower middle class group, still deeply Southern in much of its life style. These make up the N.A.A.C.P. national membership of 450,000 persons, and that of the Improved Benevolent and Protective Order of Elks, which has the same number of members distributed in 2600 lodges throughout the world. By contrast there are today perhaps 35 (sic) members of the Student Nonviolent Coordinating Committee, while at the height of its activity there were probably not more than 150.

Third, a large, disorganized urban lower class. This "community" began forming about a quarter century ago, and is in deep and growing trouble today. As Kenneth Clark states in the Brookings Institution's new book Agenda for the Nation, "Pathology is rampant in the Northern urban ghettos." Increasingly this pathology has become semi-politicized, taking the form of aggression against "white" institutions, as in various types of crime, and exploitation of "white" institutions through the welfare system, the poverty program, etc.

It would appear that the most important development of the 1960's would be the different experiences of these three general groups. One has the impression that this has led to different political attitudes.

The first group, the militant middle class youth, have become a privileged class in America. They are everywhere deferred to, catered to. And they seem determined by their own outrageousness to make up for three centuries of the humiliation of their forbears. There is nothing that can be done about them.

The second group have benefited enormously from the economic expansion and civil rights measures of the 1960's. For the most part they only needed an equal opportunity to improve their lot, and when one came they did just that. Economic progress has been striking. In 1967, 37 percent of nonwhite families outside the South had incomes of $8,000 or over, the latter being roughly the median national income. This was an increase of 4 percentage points in one year. In the North Central states, Negro family income as a percentage of white income reached 78 percent in 1967. Last year the unemployment rate for nonwhite married men was about 3.3 percent, probably the lowest point in recent history.

The third group have seen a similar rise in living standards and economic opportunities, but for reasons that simply are not understood, there has been a wholly inconsistent increase in all the indices of social pathology—crime, dependency, family stability, etc. It is this fact that preoccupies the first group of young militants, and increasingly disturbs and puzzles the stable group. . . .

I believe today's group will be looking for some indication from you that the new Administration will continue the commitment of the national government to improve the situation of the black poor, both urban and rural. But I believe they will also respond to an indication that you are aware that the black middle class has problems of its own, and legitimate claims on this society. Certainly the idea of black ownership should appeal greatly to them.

Alan Rabinowitz, a colleague at Harvard, wrote a humorous poem "The Knight Before Nixon," about Moynihan's joining the Nixon White House. The reply:

DECEMBER 28, 1968

Dear Alan,

> *Eschewing his past of striving and greed,*
> *Rabinowitz calls for an elitist creed*
> *Of mystic abstractions so subtle and dense*
> *As to claim exemption from making much sense.*

But Moynihan, seasoned in battles of yore,
Rides forth once again to the blood & the gore.
Firm of demeanor yet gentle, inclined,
He asks simply that you be so kind,
To accept his best wishes
For the life of the mind.

Moynihan's thoughts about American divisions on the eve of the Nixon presidency.

3 JANUARY 1969

To: The President Elect

Before the storm breaks, as it were, on the 20th, I would like to send in a few extended comments on some of the longer range issues that face you, but will tend, I should imagine, to get lost in the daily succession of crises.

I would like to speak first of the theme "Forward Together."

This appeal was much in evidence in your very fine acceptance speech at Miami, and during the campaign the logic of events, and your own sure sense of them, brought it forward ever more insistently. In the end it was <u>the</u> theme of the campaign and, in the aftermath of victory, it stands as the most explicit mandate you have from the American people. I would hope it might be the theme of your administration as well.

It has fallen to you to assume the governance of a deeply divided country. And to do so with a divided government. Other Presidents—Franklin Roosevelt, for example—have taken office in moments of crisis, but the crises were so widely perceived as in a sense to unite the country and to create a great outpouring of support for the President as the man who would have to deal with the common danger. Neither Lincoln nor Wilson, the two predecessors whose situations most resembled yours, in terms of the popular vote and the state of then current political questions, had any such fortune. No one would now doubt that they proved to be two of our greatest leaders, nor yet that their administrations achieved great things. But, alas, at what cost to themselves.

A divided nation makes terrible demands on the President. It would seem important to try to anticipate some of them, at least, and to ponder whether there is not some common element in each that might give a measure of coherence and unity to the President's own responses and, by a process of diffusion, to provide a guide for the administration as a whole.

I believe there is such a common element. In one form or another all of the major domestic problems facing you derive from the erosion of the authority of the institutions of American society. This is a mysterious process of which the most that can be said is that once it starts it tends not to stop.

It can be stopped: the English, for example, managed to halt and even reverse the process in the period, roughly, 1820–40. But more commonly, those in power neglect the problem at first and misunderstand it later; concessions come too late and are too little; the failure of concessions leads to equally unavailing attempts at repression; and so events spiral downward toward instability. The process is little understood. (Neither is the opposite and almost completely ignored phenomenon: some societies—Mexico in the 1920's— seem almost suddenly to become stabilized after periods of prolonged and seemingly hopeless chaos.) All we know is that the sense of institutions being legitimate—especially the institutions of government—is the glue that holds societies together. When it weakens, things come unstuck.

The North Vietnamese see this clearly enough. Hence the effort through the subtleties of seating arrangements to establish the NLF as an independent regime, and the Saigon government as a puppet one. In contrast, Americans, until presently at least, have not been nearly so concerned with such matters. American society has been so stable for so long that the prospect of instability has had no very great meaning for us. (As I count, there are but nine members of the United Nations that both existed as independent nations in 1914 and have not had their form of government changed by invasion or revolution since.) Moreover we retain a tradition of revolutionary rhetoric that gives an advantage to those who challenge authority rather than those who uphold it. Too little heed is given the experience of the 20th Century in which it has been the authority of <u>democratic</u> institutions that has been challenged by totalitarians of the left and the right.

Even the term "authority" has acquired for many a sinister cast, largely one suspects from its association with the term "authoritarian." Yet it remains the case that relationships based on authority are consensual ones: that is to say they are based on common agreement to behave in certain ways. It is said that freedom lives in the interstices of authority: when the structure collapses, freedom disappears, and society is governed by relationships based on power.

Increasing numbers of Americans seem of late to have sensed this, and to have become actively concerned about the drift of events. Your election was in a sense the first major consequence of that mounting concern. Your administration represents the first significant opportunity to change the direction in which events move.

Your task, then, is clear: to restore the authority of American institutions. Not, certainly, under that name, but with a clear sense that what is at issue is the continued acceptance by the great mass of the people of the legitimacy and efficacy of the present arrangements of American society, and of our processes for changing those arrangements.

For that purpose the theme "Forward Together" responds not only to the deepest need of the moment, but also, increasingly, to a clearly perceived need, as the facts of disunity more and more impress themselves on the nation's consciousness.

What has been pulling us apart? One wishes one knew. Yet there are a number of near and long term developments that can be discerned and surely contribute significantly to what is going on.

Of the near term events, the two most conspicuous are the Negro revolution and the war in Vietnam. Although seemingly unrelated, they have much in common as to origins, and even more as to the process by which they have brought on mounting levels of disunity. The French philosopher Georges Bernanos once wrote: "There are no more corrupting lies than problems poorly stated." I, at least, feel that this goes to the heart of much of the present turmoil of race relations and foreign policy. In a word, those in power have allowed domestic dislocations that accompany successful social change to be interpreted as irrefutable evidence that the society refuses to change; they have permitted foreign policy failures arising from mistaken judgments to be taken as incontrovertible proof that the society has gone mad as well.

The fact is that with respect to Negro Americans we have seen incredible progress since, roughly, the Brown vs. Board of Education decision of 1956 and President Eisenhower's subsequent decision to send Federal troops to Little Rock, thus commencing the Second Reconstruction. Nowhere in history is there to be encountered an effort to bring a suppressed people into the mainstream of society comparable to the public and private initiatives on behalf of Negro Americans in recent years. As I would like to discuss in a later memorandum, the results have been dramatic. Yet it was only after that effort had begun, and had been underway for some time, that it became possible to see the true horror of the situation white America had forced on black America and the deep disabilities that came about in consequence. The first to see this, of course, were the blacks themselves. The result on the part of many was a revulsion against white society that has only just begun to run its course. Large numbers of middle class, educated blacks, especially young ones, have come to see American society as hateful and illegitimate, lacking any true claim on their allegiance. Well they might. The problem is not that one group in the population is beginning to react to centuries of barbarism by another group. The problem is that this cultural reaction among black militants is accompanied by the existence of a large, disorganized urban lower class which, like such groups everywhere, is unstable and essentially violent. This fact of lower class violence has nothing to do with race. It is purely a matter of social class. But since Watts, the media of public opinion—the press, television, the Presidency itself—have combined to insist that race _is_ the issue. As a result, middle class blacks caught up in a cultural revolution have been able, in effect, to back up their demands. This has led to a predictable white counter-reaction. And so on. In the process, we have almost deliberately obscured the extraordinary progress, and commitment to progress, which the nation as a whole has made, which white America has not abandoned, and which increasingly black America is learning to make use of.

To the contrary, it has been the failures of policy that have seemed ever more prominent. The essence of the Negro problem in America at this time is that despite great national commitments, and great progress, a large mass of the black population remains poor, disorganized, and discriminated against. These facts are increasingly interpreted as proof that the national commitment is flawed, if not indeed fraudulent, that the society is irredeemably "racist," etc. This interpretation is made by middle class blacks and whites for whom, outwardly at least, society would seem to have treated very well, but the continued existence of black poverty makes their argument hard to assail. Moreover, increasingly that argument is directed not to particulars, but to fundamental questions as to the legitimacy of American society.

Vietnam has been a domestic disaster of the same proportion, and for much the same reason. As best I can discern, the war was begun with the very highest of motives at the behest of men such as McNamara, Bundy, and Rusk in a fairly consistent pursuit of the post war American policy of opposing Communist expansion and simultaneously encouraging political democracy and economic development in the nations on the Communist perimeter, and elsewhere. At the risk of seeming cynical, I would argue that the war in Vietnam has become a disastrous mistake because we have lost it. I quite accept Henry

Kissinger's splendid formulation that a conventional army loses if it does not win, the opposite being the case for a guerilla force. We have not been able to win. Had the large scale fighting by American forces been over by mid-1967 (which is my impression of what Bundy anticipated in mid-1965), had the children of the middle class accordingly continued to enjoy draft exemption, had there been no inflation, no surtax, no Tet offensive, then I very much fear there would be abroad at this point at most a modicum of moral outrage.

But this is not what happened. The war has not gone well, and increasingly in an almost primitive reaction—to which modern societies are as much exposed as any Stone Age clan—it has been judged that this is because the Gods are against it. In modern parlance this means that the evil military industrial complex has embarked on a racist colonialist adventure. (I have heard the head of S.N.C.C. state that we were in Vietnam "for the rice supplies.") But the essential point is that we have been losing a war, and this more than any single thing erodes the authority of a government, however stable, just, well intentioned, or whatever. I would imagine that the desire not to be the first President to "lose" a war has been much in President Johnson's mind over the past years, and explains some of his conduct. But the fact is that he could not win, and the all important accompanying fact is that the semi-violent domestic protest that arose in consequence forced him to resign. In a sense he was the first American President to be toppled by a mob. No matter that it was a mob of college professors, millionaires, flower children, and Radcliffe girls. It was a mob that by early 1968 had effectively <u>physically</u> separated the Presidency from the people. (You may recall that seeking to attend the funeral of Cardinal Spellman, Johnson slipped in the back door of St. Patrick's Cathedral like a medieval felon seeking sanctuary.) As with the case of the most militant blacks, success for the anti-war protestors has seemed only to confirm their detestation of society as it now exists. Increasingly they declare the society to be illegitimate, while men such as William Sloane Coffin, Jr., the chaplain at Yale, openly espouse violence as the necessary route of moral regeneration.

The <u>successful</u> extremism of the black militants and the anti-war protestors—by and large they have had their way—has now clearly begun to arouse fears and thoughts of extreme actions by other groups. George Wallace, a fourth rate regional demagogue, won 13 percent of the national vote and at one point in the campaign probably had the sympathy of a quarter of the electorate, largely in the working class. Among Jews—I draw your attention to this—there is a rising concern, in some quarters approaching alarm, over black anti-semitism. They foresee Negro political power driving them from civil service jobs, as in the New York City school system. They see anti-semitism becoming an "accepted" political posture. With special dread, they see a not distant future when the political leaders of the country might have to weigh the competing claims of ten million black voters who had become passionately pro-Arab as against one or two million pro-Israel Jewish voters. In the meantime we must await the reaction of the Armed Forces, and the veterans of Vietnam to whatever settlement you get there. No officer corps ever lost a war, and this one surely would have no difficulty finding symbols of those at home who betrayed it. All in all there are good reasons to expect a busy eight years in the White House.

There is a longer term development contributing to the present chaos which bears mentioning. Since about 1840 the cultural elite in America have pretty generally rejected the values and activities of the larger society. It has been said of America that the culture will not approve that which the polity strives to provide. For a brief period, associated with the Depression, World War II, and the Cold War there was something of a truce in this protracted struggle. That, I fear, is now over. The leading cultural figures are going—have gone— into opposition once again. This time they take with them a vastly more numerous following of educated, middle class persons, especially young ones, who share their feelings and who do not need the "straight" world. It is their pleasure to cause trouble, to be against. And they are hell bent for a good time. President Johnson took all this personally, but I have the impression that you will make no such mistake!

It is, of course, easier to describe these situations than to suggest what is to be done about them. However, a certain number of general postures do seem to follow from the theme "Bring Us Together." I would list five.

First, the single most important task is to maintain the rate of economic expansion. If a serious economic recession were to come along to compound the controversies of race, Vietnam, and cultural alienation, the nation could indeed approach instability. It would be my judgment that the great prosperity of the 1960's is the primary reason we have been able to weather this much internal dissension. The lot of Negroes has steadily improved, and so has that of most everyone else. Black demands for a greater share have thus been less threatening. The war has been costly, but largely has been paid for through annual fiscal increments and recent deficits. Consumption has been affected not at all. If this situation were to reverse itself, your ability to meet Black needs, the tolerance of the rest of the society for your efforts, the general willingness to see military efforts proceed, would all be grievously diminished.

Second, it would seem most important to de-escalate the rhetoric of crisis about the internal state of the society in general, and in particular about those problems—e.g., crime, de facto segregation, low educational achievement—which government has relatively little power to influence in the present state of knowledge and available resources. This does not mean reducing efforts. Not at all. But it does mean trying to create some equivalence between what government can do about certain problems and how much attention it draws to them. For this purpose the theme you struck in presenting your cabinet on television seems perfect: yours is an administration of men with wide ranging interests and competence whose first concern is the effective delivery of government services. There is a risk here of being accused of caring less than your predecessors, but even that will do no great harm if you can simultaneously demonstrate that you do more. It is out of such perceptions that the authority of government is enhanced.

It would seem likely that a powerful approach to this issue will be to stress the needs and aspirations of groups such as Mexican-Americans, Puerto Ricans, American Indians and others which have also been excluded and exploited by the larger society. This, of course, is something you would want to do in any event.

Third, the Negro lower class must be dissolved. This is the work of a generation, but it is time it began to be understood as a clear national goal. By lower class I mean the low income, marginally employed, poorly educated, disorganized slum dwellers who have piled up in our central cities over the past quarter century. I would estimate they make up almost one half the total Negro population. They are not going to become capitalists, nor even middle class functionaries. But it is fully reasonable to conceive of them being transformed into a stable working class population: Truck drivers, mail carriers, assembly line workers: people with dignity, purpose, and in the United States a very good standard of living indeed. Common justice, and common sense, demands that this be done. It is the existence of this lower class, with its high rates of crime, dependency, and general disorderliness that causes nearby whites (that is to say working class whites, the liberals are all in the suburbs) to fear Negroes and to seek by various ways to avoid and constrain them. It is this group that black extremists use to threaten white society with the prospect of mass arson and pillage. It is also this group that terrorizes and plunders the stable elements of the Negro community—trapped by white prejudice in the slums, and forced to live cheek by jowl with a murderous slum population. Take the urban lower class out of the picture and the Negro cultural revolution becomes an exciting and constructive development.

Fourth, it would seem devoutly to be wished that you not become personally identified with the war in Vietnam. You have available to you far more competent advice than mine in this area, and I am sure you will wish to proceed in terms of the foreign policy interests of the nation in broader terms, but I do urge that every effort be made to avoid the ugly physical harassment and savage personal attacks that brought President Johnson's administration to an end. The dignity of the Presidency as the symbolic head of state as well as of functioning leader of the government must be restored. Alas, it is in the power of the middle class mob to prevent this. I would far rather see it concentrate, as _faute de mieux_ it now seems to be doing, on attacking liberal college presidents as "racist pigs."

I fear the blunt truth is that ending the draft would be the single most important step you could take in this direction. The children of the upper middle class will not be conscripted. In any event, the present system does cast a pall of anxiety and uncertainty over the lives of that quarter of the young male population which does in fact require four to eight to ten years of college work to prepare for careers which almost all agree are socially desirable, even necessary.

Fifth, it would seem important to stress those things Americans share in common, rather than those things that distinguish them one from the other. Thus the war on poverty defined a large portion of the population as somehow living apart from the rest. I would seek programs that stress problems and circumstances that all share, and especially problems which working people share with the poor. Too frequently of late the liberal upper middle class has proposed to solve problems of those at the bottom at the expense, or seeming expense, of those in between.

Obviously the theme "Forward Together" is essential here, and there are other symbols at hand of which I would think the approaching 200th anniversary of the founding of the Republic is perhaps the most powerful. In the final months of your second term you will preside over the anniversary ceremonies of July 4, 1976. It would seem an incomparable opportunity to begin now to define the goals you would hope to see achieved by that time, trying to make them truly national goals to which all may subscribe, and from which as many as possible will benefit.

Hopefully our 200th anniversary will see the nation somewhat more united than were those thirteen colonies!

On the "urban crisis" and the future of liberalism.

JANUARY 9, 1969
TO: THE PRESIDENT

In the months ahead I will be harassing you with details of the "urban crisis." Whatever the urgency of the matters I bring before you, I will be doing so in an essentially optimistic posture, which is to say that I will routinely assume that our problems are manageable if only we will manage them. This is the only position possible for government. Yet, of course, it does not necessarily reflect reality. It may be that our problems are not manageable, or that we are not capable of summoning the effort required to respond effectively. It seems to me important that you know that there are responsible persons who are very near to just that conclusion. (To be sure, twenty years ago in many scientific/academic circles it was taken as settled that the world would shortly blow itself up, yet we are still here.)

I had thought to summarize the views of the apocalyptic school, ranging in style as it does from the detached competence of Lewis Mumford who for forty years had foretold the approach of "Necropolis," the City of the Dead, all the way to the more hysterical members of the New Left who assume that the only thing that can save this civilization is for it to be destroyed. However, I have just come upon a document that states the case much more effectively than I might, being a summary of the views of a group of careful men who recently met to discuss the state of New York City. I am associated with a quarterly journal, <u>The Public Interest</u>, which is devoting a special issue to New York. On December 17 we assembled a group of city officials and similarly informed persons for a day-long session at the Century Club. (I could not be present owing to my new assignment.) Paul Weaver, a young assistant professor of government at Harvard, attended as a kind of rapporteur. Later he summarized his impression of the meeting in terms that seem to me persuasive, and as he himself put it, "not a little chilling."

His central point—an immensely disturbing one—is that the social system of American and British democracy that grew up in the 18th and 19th century was able to be exceedingly permissive with regard to public matters precisely because it could depend on its citizens to be quite disciplined with respect to private ones. He speaks of "private sub-systems of authority," such as the family, church, and local community, and political party, which regulated behavior, instilled motivation, etc., in such a way as to make it unnecessary for the State to intervene in order to protect "the public interest." More and more it would appear these subsystems are breaking down in the immense city of New York. If this should continue, democracy would break down.

To be sure, New York City is not America, etc. Yet my discussions with District officials would suggest that things are not that different in Washington. Throughout the nation, in general, trends are in the New York direction. (You may have noted that Lindsay's next budget provides for 1.3 million persons being on welfare by June 1970.)

What this comes to is the realization that much of what is now termed "the crisis of the cities" is more a moral and cultural crisis than a material one. Indeed it is frequently the former that produces the latter. Weaver, for example, refers to the "growing rate of building abandonment" in New York. It would seem impossible that land in New York City could become valueless, but this is true in the worst slums. Whole "zones of abandonment" are growing up in Brooklyn, with owners literally leaving their vandalized properties behind, much as slum dwellers abandon junked automobiles on city streets.

Clearly material programs are a necessary condition of reversing the trend of events, but they are not sufficient in themselves. Somehow the country must come to understand the nature of its "urban crisis." This is the highest task of leadership.

The key problem is that of late the rhetoric of "realistic liberalism" in its more narrow political sense, has become increasingly hostile to those subsystems. As a result, "The thoroughly liberal society ... cannot know what makes it work."

Here is Weaver's summary of the day's discussion:

1. The social fabric of New York City is coming to pieces. It isn't just "strained" and it isn't just "frayed;" but like a sheet of rotten canvas, it is beginning to rip, and it won't be too long until even a moderate force will be capable of leaving it in shreds and tatters. No doubt I'm being too apocalyptic. Still, consider some of the evidence. Among a large and growing lower class, self-reliance, self-discipline, and industry are waning; a radical disproportion is arising between reality and expectations concerning job, living standard, and so on; unemployment is high but a lively demand

for unskilled labor remains unmet; illegitimacy is increasing; families are more and more matrifocal and atomized; crime and disorder are sharply on the rise. There is, in short, a progressive disorganization of society, a growing pattern of frustration and mistrust. This, I take it, is one of the reasons for the high and growing rate of building abandonment; the immediate area surrounding the lot is such as to render the value of the land nil, even for the potential resident owner. This general pathology, moreover, appears to be infecting the Puerto Rican community as well as the Negro. (It is a stirring, if generally unrecognized demonstration of the power of our welfare machine.) A large segment of the population is becoming incompetent and destructive. Growing parasitism, both legal and illegal, is the result; so, also, is violence.

2. Something comparable is happening in the political arena. New York used to be the very model of moderate, materialistic, incremental Madisonian politics. Only the goo-goos challenged the whole system, but not out of self-interest, and rarely intemperately. Otherwise, participation was limited to the pursuit of limited self-interest; live-and-let-live logrolling was both fact and value; and conflict was avoided as much as possible. But today, there is the "spirit of confrontation," in which self-interest and a desire to change the system are merged in groups which depend for their existence on pursuing a "conflict" strategy. The result is that, to the extent this pattern exists, political executives are less free to determine the mix of (partly inconsistent) values and interests which best defines the public interest; public tranquility is unsettled; and political cohesion is threatened. The consequence is to increase the tension between responsibility and responsiveness in government. Thus, Lindsay orders a "no-arrest" policy at precisely the point when law and order are manifestly in decay; it "cools" the city "off" in the short run but may heat it up in the long run. The general problem is whether representative government can maintain a country or city which is divided against itself and which discounts its long-term interest so heavily.

3. Are we then witnessing the ultimate, destructive working out of the telos of liberal thought? The viability of liberal thought rested

on the ability of the country which adopted it to be largely self-regulating, self-maintaining, and self-improving. As long as the typical individual was formed and directed in socially useful ways by the more or less autonomous operations of private subsystems of authority, a government which permitted great freedom and engaged largely in the negative and peripheral activity of the umpire was possible. It was also possible for citizen and statesman to live with a rhetoric which denied the existence, functions, and basis of those private subsystems. Being traditional, those subsystems were (on the rhetoric's terms) "irrational;" being particularistic, they were not "universal;" constituting and maintaining differences among men, they fostered "inequality;" and forming character and directing energy as they did, they were "authoritarian." The thoroughly liberal society, in short, cannot know what makes it work. Now, in parts of New York City, those subsystems are absolutely breaking down. At the same time, the rhetoric is getting an ever stronger and more blinding grip on "informed" opinion as well as on partisan opinion. The rhetoric leads to policies which actually hasten the dissolution of the subsystems.

That the society is breaking down means that the liberal state will no longer do. It must, on pain of anarchy or civil war, be replaced by a regime which explicitly recognizes the necessity of the subsystems and which is prepared to create substitutes for those subsystems when they break down. Our problem is that informed opinion is moving in precisely the opposite direction.

4. All of which is to say that we are moving from Locke to Hobbes. This does not mean we need the Leviathan because the war of all against all is still confined to one segment of the population. There are plenty of public spirited and peaceful people around. But their opinions need to be changed, and the resources of their government increased, or at least centralized.

CHAPTER FOUR

"Welfare Is a Bankrupt and Destructive System"

Moynihan's memoranda to Nixon and his staff at the White House were widely distributed internally at the president's request. Nixon told his chief of staff H. R. Haldeman that they should be read, not as final policy papers, but as "the kind of incisive and stimulating analysis which I think should constantly be brought to the attention of policymakers." Nixon's high regard for his aide led Moynihan to speak with increasing candor about a wide variety of subjects, from welfare to student turmoil and finally to the war in Vietnam. In the first year, Moynihan also successfully lobbied Nixon to support a guaranteed income for poor families, regardless of whether the father was absent or working. He argued that this "income strategy" to poverty was perfectly aligned with Republican Party principles not to engage in social welfare programs that were simply a way of employing middle class bureaucrats. While Nixon endorsed what became known as the Family Assistance Plan (FAP), it continued to be opposed within the administration by conservatives, particularly Arthur Burns, later chairman of the Federal Reserve. In his letters, Moynihan appealed to those outside the White House to appreciate that Nixon was struggling to find a new and more successful approach to dealing with poverty. He waged an internal campaign to persuade Nixon that he was the moderate of the White House, and to get others in the White House to moderate their rhetoric that had become hostile to protesters and dissenters. This was a period for Moynihan to find a political grouping with which he could identify, but the efforts were not always successful.

Before taking office, President-elect Nixon sent a memorandum dated January 15, 1969, to his top aide, H. R. Haldeman, indicating that a Moynihan memorandum of January 9 "and others like it" should be "made available to the research team and to the Cabinet members who are on the Urban Affairs Council." Though the wide distribution of these communications reflect Nixon's high regard for Moynihan, it paved the way for embarrassing leaks, particularly of the "benign neglect" memo of January 16, 1970.

Moynihan writes to the President-elect about the upcoming inaugural address.

JANUARY 13, 1969

MEMORANDUM FOR THE PRESIDENT

You asked for thoughts concerning your Inaugural Address.

I have only a small number, and they will be thoroughly familiar to you. This, however, seems to me a matter of interest in itself. Although it is possible, even necessary, to be considerably concerned about the internal unity and coherence of American society at this time, it is not less true that there is a surprising convergence of views among thoughtful persons as to just what the next moves ought to be. That at least is my reading of events such as our weekend gathering of the professoriate where near unanimity was to be had on an amazing range of issues from a group of congenital troublemakers. The plea is for a reordering of priorities, put also for reassurance that certain basic national commitments will continue in force.

First to the matter of commitments. There are three groups which, by and large, were not important to your candidacy, but which can prove immensely important to your Presidency. These are the black poor, the white working class, and the educated youth.

The Black Poor desperately need to be reassured that you have no intention of turning away from the great goals of the civil rights acts of 1959, 1964 and 1965, the goals of a free and open society in which equality and opportunity for blacks increasingly has the outcome of equality of achievement as well. It would be difficult to overstate the present anxiety. Although opinion surveys repeatedly show blacks, at all social class levels, to be exceptionally optimistic persons, they are afraid of the new administration. I repeat the statement of your urban affairs task force: The rumor is widespread that the new government is planning to build concentration camps.

You, of course, have just the opposite intentions. I would urge you to state them in the simple, direct eloquence which you repeatedly bring to such declarations.

The White Working Class almost voted for Wallace out of fear that its newly acquired, precarious, and at best relative prosperity was going to be sacrificed by upper middle class whites in the cause of lower class blacks. They must be reassured that this is precisely what you propose <u>not</u> to do, that to the contrary nothing is now more clear than that we move forward together, or not at all.

Educated Youth having been given so much by this society now asks even more of it: it asks that society provide not only wealth and opportunity but also meaning in life. It is not clear how much the political institutions of society can provide in such matters, but the demand is nonetheless made. You have frequently made clear that you understand both these matters: that you wholly welcome a generation that wants to live big lives, infused with large and honorable purpose. Yet you fear the day when all things are political and you would hope they might come to share that concern. But fearing that does not in any sense mean that you fear protest, or controversy, or reassessment. To the contrary it is to just such issues and such forms that the nation must turn, men of our years no less than of theirs. . . .

Finally, almost on a personal note, I would urge some reference to "post war priorities." The Mayors with whom you visited just before Christmas were immensely impressed and heartened by your statement that if you had $50 billion to give them that day you would do so, but that you simply didn't, and wouldn't until the war in Viet Nam is over. They understood the reality you face, and so I believe would the nation. But it seems to me immensely important to state now, at the outset of an immensely promising era, that this is what your priority will be once events make it possible for you to set your own. I deeply believe it will help enormously to tide you over the months and maybe even years ahead when you will still be bound by the priorities of your predecessor.

Recommending that the lights go back on at the White House.

JANUARY 15, 1969
TO: THE PRESIDENT-ELECT
FROM: DANIEL P. MOYNIHAN

MEMORANDUM

Early in his administration President Johnson announced he was saving money by turning off lights in the White House. Some $3000 to $5000 a month was later said to be involved. Which may or may not be so. In any event in the process of turning off lights <u>inside</u> the flood lights that illuminate the exterior were also, largely, turned off. (Obviously, these would account for only a portion of the "savings.") As a result at a time when the most unassuming New England village floodlights its First Presbyterian Church as a matter of course, and most of the public buildings of Washington are brilliantly lit at night, the White House appears to be in permanent mourning.

Whatever the considerations that prompted the move, it seems to me to have been undignified, reflecting at very least a low estimate of the intelligence and taste of the American people. I would like to suggest that on the first day of your administration you direct that the exterior lights of the White House be turned on again.

I would think there is no need to say anything about it: If asked, Mr. Ziegler can simply say you remembered the White House illuminated at night, liked it that way, and assumed visitors and residents of the capital did so as well.

It may be some new installations would be required.

Moynihan was concerned that a newspaper column by Mary McGrory would leave Nixon with the impression that he would quit and go public with his disagreements. Nixon's reply at the bottom: "Pat—Mary wants us to worry about what she writes—it just gives me a laugh! RN."

JANUARY 27, 1969

FOR THE PRESIDENT

I think you will want to read today's column by Mary McGrory. As you will see it is altogether friendly, but she does comment on what has become one of the favorite guessing games around Washington, namely how long Henry Kissinger and I will be here. As Mary suggests, the betting in my case is six months. Alas she does go on to suggest that if I were to leave I might "document" my "disenchantment."

I think I had better say two things on this subject.

First, I have no intention of leaving until my two years are up. Mind, the black extremists could eventually raise such a ruckus that I would be of no value to you and would have to leave, but that would be your decision. It will of course be easier if I could get, as Martin Luther King used to say, "a few victories." But easy or hard, I mean to stay.

Second, regardless of what happens I wish to offer my solemn commitment that I will not in any circumstances write anything political about my experiences in the White House.

Moynihan takes note of the rise in welfare rolls in New York City and elsewhere.

JANUARY 31, 1969

FOR THE PRESIDENT

Like the girl and the book about crocodiles, I fear that I may end up telling you more about welfare in New York City than you want to know. The situation in New York City has been developing for quite some time. Three years ago, John Lindsay asked me to serve on a poverty task force which he had assembled just prior to his inauguration. At that time indications of trouble were sufficiently clear that I said to him and the group, that it seemed to me that there was a serious and inexplicable problem of family structure growing up in New York City, as well as in some of the other northern cities, and that this could become a major problem for him. I must report that he and the rest of the group dismissed the idea as ridiculous, charging that the 400,000 plus number of welfare recipients then on the rolls was simply a mark of the incompetence of the Wagner administration, all of which will soon be a thing of the past. As you know, there are now a million persons on welfare and the current budget estimates provide for 1.3 million by June 30, 1970. Estimates are that one out of every eight New Yorkers, over one million people, will receive public assistance in 1969, at a total cost of two billion dollars.

What I sensed would happen has happened, but three years and much writing later I still don't really feel like I know any more about Why.

You may recall that report on Negro family structure which I wrote in the winter of 1964. I set out to write it in order to document a basic thesis of mine that male employment controls family structure. From which it would follow that if we wished to affect the various social problems, such as welfare dependency, which are brought about by a weak family structure, the master strategy would be full employment of adult males. I was able to show an almost perfect correlation between the non-white male unemployment rate and the number of new AFDC cases throughout the 1950's. However, in the 1960's this correlation suddenly ceased. Unemployment rates started going down and the number of non-AFDC cases started going up. All I can really tell you four years later is that this new non-relation has continued. ...

B. NON-EXPLANATIONS

There is no really conclusive evidence in favor of any explanation of New York's experience, but a number of hypotheses can be rejected. In the following material, I draw primarily on a study just done by Professor Lawrence Podell for a New York state legislative committee.

1. Immigration. The rise in New York welfare costs is not due to immigration from Puerto Rico and the South. The New York data indicate that new arrivals account for only a few percent of the cases recently added to welfare rolls in the city.

2. Medicaid Publicity. There was a large mass media campaign designed to persuade the poor to sign up for Medicaid, and this took place throughout New York state. But nowhere else was there a rise in welfare comparable to that in the city itself.

3. The Welfare Rights Movement. Although it is widely claimed that the poor were organized by the poverty program or by the Welfare Rights Movement and thereupon come to demand their fair entitlement to welfare previously been denied them, a comparison of neighborhoods where organizing efforts did take place and those where it did not, fails to show any significant difference. ...

D. TWO UNDERLYING CAUSES

1. It is increasingly clear that the amount of money a low skilled male family head can earn in a city such as New York is just not enough to maintain a family at what are now expected standards of living. The City Workers Family Budget, compiled during the autumn of 1966 set the average needs of families in urban areas as a whole at $9,191. For the New York-Northeastern area the

estimated need was $10,195. But in that year the Population Health Survey of the Center for Research of the City University of New York estimated the median income of male-headed families in the city of New York as $7,136. For non-white families with a male head the estimate was $5,333, half the "required amount." And for Puerto Ricans it was $4,366, less than half. For whatever reason, during this period the number of male-headed families in New York City declined, and the number of female-headed families increased. Incredibly, the income in male-headed non-white families appears to have decreased from $5,566 in 1964 to $5,333 in 1966. During this time the relative attractions of being on welfare obviously increased. In a competent study, it was shown that under a Lindsay incentive plan, whereby female-headed families being supported by welfare could be encouraged to obtain extra income by being permitted to retain all of their earnings up to a certain point, and a portion thereafter, the welfare payments and wages combined could be permitted to reach $4900 a year for a family of four. This would be a weekly income of $94.23, as against an estimated $90.01 of factory earnings for that period after deductions from $110.95 gross earnings.

A probable further influence is the curious "mix" of employment opportunities in New York which increasingly favor not just white collar as against blue collar workers, but also, relatively, women as against men.

2. Beyond this there is the serious possibility that the mere fact of being on welfare in any form breaks up male-headed families where they exist. In another study, Podell found that most of the families, in a sample he gathered, came on the welfare rolls before the wives were separated from the husbands.

PROPOSAL FOR PRESIDENTIAL ACTION

I believe the time has come for a President to state what increasingly is understood: that welfare as we know it is a bankrupt and destructive system. It destroyed the American Indian. It is destroying the lower class Negro and Puerto Rican, while the telltale signs of matriarchy, family break-up, and general social miasma are showing up in Appalachia as well.

A majority of Negro youth are supported by AFDC at some time or another before reaching eighteen.

It is also necessary to state that no one really understands why and how all this has happened. (I fear the welfare bureaucracy of the Federal establishment are much responsible for this. They have not wanted to know. Recently John Gardner told me that towards the end of his period in office he had become convinced that the bureaucracy was, in effect, lying to him in its constant

underestimate of future welfare costs, and very near to insubordinate in its refusal to give him information about subjects such as illegitimacy.) These are
subjects social scientists are perfectly capable of investigating if they are given
this opportunity. So far they have not been, save for a very few studies such as
Podell's.

I BELIEVE THE SINGLE MOST DRAMATIC MOVE YOU COULD MAKE
WOULD BE TO SEND A MESSAGE TO CONGRESS CALLING FOR NATIONAL
MINIMUM STANDARDS IN WELFARE. THIS SHOULD BE ACCOMPANIED BY
THE APPOINTMENT OF A NATIONAL COMMISSION TO FIND OUT WHAT IS
GOING ON. CERTAIN MINIMUM FEDERAL REQUIREMENTS FOR STATE PAR-
TICIPATION SHOULD BE PROPOSED, PRINCIPALLY THAT ALL STATES
ADOPT THE AFDC-U PROGRAM, INSTITUTED IN 1961, WHICH ENABLES
FAMILIES WITH AN UNEMPLOYED MALE HEAD TO RECEIVE BENEFITS.

The advantages of a national minimum standard, of perhaps $30, with fed-
eral sharing up to perhaps $70 (these were the recommendations of your wel-
fare task force) are as follows:

1. It will give money to women and children who desperately need it,
   mostly in the South. Mississippi provides $8.50 per month to
   support a child.
2. It will give financial relief to large cities that are now providing
   decent enough welfare payments, but at great costs to their
   taxpayers.
3. It will help the Negro poor. Half the children on AFDC at
   present are black.
4. It will be received by the white middle and working class as a
   measure that will impede northward migration. I have some
   doubts whether it actually will, but it will be taken as such, and
   that is a plus. i.e., that is a good reason for Northern congressmen
   to support such a measure.

The proposal for a welfare commission would have to be fitted with Dr.
Burns' recommendation to you on the future of the Income Maintenance
Commission which President Johnson announced two years ago, appointed
a year ago, and which has a year yet to run. Frankly, my opinion is that the
commission is dominated by a type of economist who persistently misses the
point about the interaction of income flows and social change. On the other
hand, I tend to think that none of us knows much about the subject.

F. <u>APOLOGIES</u>

I wish I could tell you that a real tough enquiry into the New York City mess would produce much political or societal benefits. I doubt it. It would mostly give the Welfare Rights Movement a chance to create martyrs. The fact is the more one knows about welfare the more horrible it becomes: but not because of cheating, rather because the system destroys those who receive it, and corrupts those who dispense it. . . .

I leave you with the thought that the Pennsylvania Society for the Promotion of Public Economy called for "a radical change in the present mode of administering charitable assistance (and a new arrangement of public relief on the grounds that) present methods create and prolong dependence"—in 1817.

How do you wish me to proceed?

Moynihan sought the help of journalists, including James (Scotty) Reston of the NEW YORK TIMES, *in insuring that the press gave Nixon credit for supporting programs for the poor.*

FEB. 19, 1969

Dear Scotty:

I think I need your help, and from our last conversation feel at least somewhat free to ask for it.

The President's message on the future of the poverty program has been received with fairly routine views, left and right about equally unhappy, but almost no one has grasped the central point. At our lunch we discussed the problems the program will face as successive waves of large and small scandals sneak in the press in the months ahead. Far more seriously, we are also heading for a succession of research reports which will argue that the various specific undertakings have failed. The most consequential of these will be a large, and, as best I can tell, assailable study of Head Start by the Westinghouse Learning Corporation. It will report, bluntly, that Head Start does not work. It does nothing for the education achievement, attitudes, motivation, or whatever of poor children.

I have been expecting this. The study is only the biggest and best to date, but earlier ones have pointed in this direction. What I fear however, is a reaction of frustration, even disgust in Congress. The program has been so oversold. Now it turns out that even it does not work. What in God's name can work? Etc. Etc. This will be accompanied, of course, by endless cries of sabotage, racism, cruelty to children, and methodological inadequacies from the true believers.

The President's message tried to telegraph the punch (I have marked the paragraphs) and to ensure one and all that they need have no fear of failure in a frankly experimental undertaking. He then made—to me—an extraordinary commitment to "the first five years of life." But it is a commitment I fear no one much is going to be interested in unless we take the view that we have learned something of value when we find that Head Start "doesn't work."

The general reaction, I fear, will be ideological and utterly defeating. What I am asking is that the TIMES really try to be careful in reporting these issues in the next few months. I would be less than candid if I did not say that complex problems are not always depicted as such in the press. Obviously I will be available to anyone who wishes to talk to me.

Moynihan was a careful observer of the condition of American Jews.

MARCH 10, 1969

FOR THE PRESIDENT

I think you will find interesting and disturbing, the lead article in the current issue of <u>Commentary</u> entitled "Is American Jewry in Crisis?" The author is a staff member of the American Jewish Committee. His article reflects a widely held view among New York Jews that the White Anglo-Saxon Protestants have determined to sacrifice them to the blacks in order to get social peace at home. The tone of the article can be got from two sentences in the penultimate paragraph: "In New York our remaining years in the civil service, and above all in the schools, are not many: if policy does not drive us out, terrorism will. (It has started.)"

The fear that black militancy will also take the form of anti-Israel influence on American foreign policy is also widespread, and not without a measure of justification. Thus, a group of black militants have won control of the student newspapers of Wayne State University in Detroit and have been printing long articles in praise of Arab terrorists.

Moynihan's first warnings about the political cost of the Vietnam War.

MARCH 11, 1969

FOR THE PRESIDENT

I am hesitant about straying so far from my field, but a larger sense of responsibility prompts two comments about ABM [Anti-Ballistic Missile].

First, it is depressingly clear that your budget situation is going to be painfully difficult for almost all of your first term. You will <u>not</u> be able to give the Mayors the money they need, much less the minorities, et al. ABM is not an expensive weapons system, but it is being depicted as such, and will be blamed for the "failure" to solve the "urban crisis."

Second, it would also appear the Vietnam war will drag on. So far, it is not "your" war. But if you should make a "hawkish" move on ABM, I fear your enemies will be able to make it "your" war, as there is clearly a strong association between these issues in public opinion of the moment. Conversely, a "dovish" move on ABM might very well buy you the time you need to get out of those swamps.

Moynihan expresses concerns about making money available for domestic programs.

MARCH 14, 1969

FOR THE PRESIDENT

Henry Kissinger briefed us this morning, stating that the modified ABM system you are to propose will cost $800 million to $1 billion in FY 1970. The Johnson budget called for an expenditure of $1.8 billion.

After Henry left I proposed that you state in your press conference that your move will free $1 billion for needed, even urgent domestic programs.

(Hunger?) I think there was general agreement in the staff that this was a potentially highly effective point. Dr. Burns dissented on grounds that the Johnson budget had to be cut.

I would argue just the opposite. At this moment when you are giving the Pentagon part at least of what it wants, and doing so in a highly charged atmosphere—this is the moment to say you are willing to spend money for education, health, poverty or whatever, and to hell with the details.

In a White House obsessed with leaks to the news media, Moynihan had advice to give Nixon. The Family Security System was later called the Family Assistance Plan.

APRIL 11, 1969

FOR THE PRESIDENT

Secretary Finch called today to say that the press seems to be getting hold of the general outline of the Family Security System and that we have to expect that the story will break fairly soon.

This, I think was inevitable. Putting the plan together, especially estimating costs and benefits, has required that a large number of career persons be brought in on the planning, and the result almost always is a gradual seepage. This development does, however, argue for doing it sooner rather than later.

I have always felt that if you decide to adopt the plan you should announce it soon after Congress returns. It will be the center piece in your domestic program—truly an historic proposal. You should put it on the desks of Congress and force them right off to begin discussing your program rather than new Kennedy-McGovern issues such as hunger, or old Johnson programs such as the Job Corps.

Certainly you will want to wait until the anti-inflation message of your budget cuts sinks in. But there are two publics as it were, for that message. One the business which will approve your move, likely as not, but is not likely to give you much public praise for having the courage to make it. In the meantime, however, the consumers of the government services being cut back (from Johnson's projection) will be howling.

All the more, then, is the case for sending up a truly momentous domestic proposal shortly thereafter. This case is further strengthened by the fact that despite its enormous implications, the Family Security System will not cost a great deal—\$1.6 billion per year in its minimum form—that part which eliminates the AFDC program—and up to \$3.4 billion in the form that includes the "adult" social security programs, a training program and a large food program. None can be expected to take effect until FY 1971, and possibly FY 1972. . . .

Moynihan weighs in about the nature of the "military industrial complex," which President Eisenhower, in his farewell address in January 1961, warned was wielding too much influence.

APRIL 15, 1969

FOR THE PRESIDENT

It may be I am all wrong about your making some kind of statement concerning the "military-industrial complex," in connection with a memorial to President Eisenhower. Certainly I have not found a simple way to state the case, which usually suggests to me that the case may not be very strong. . . .

Even so, here, as promised, is an effort. I begin with three premises.

First, that President Eisenhower was right in warning that the creation of a permanent defense capability had profoundly affected American society.

> "This conjunction of an immense military establishment and a large arms industry is new in the American experience. The total influence— economic, political, even spiritual—is felt in every city, every State house, every office of the Federal government." [January 17, 1961]

I agree with his warning: "We should take nothing for granted." This changed situation has indeed acquired extraordinary—if not, as he puts it, "unwarranted"—influence "in the councils of government." I believe it could indeed "endanger our liberties or democratic processes."

I suppose I am especially sensitive to this because I think I saw it happen to a group of men—the liberal intellectuals of the Kennedy and Johnson administrations—who assumed themselves to be all but immune to any such influences. I think I saw it—in the form of mistaken and over-reaching military advice—destroy Lyndon Johnson.

Second, I have seen what President Eisenhower only warned against as a possibility transmuted into a received truth by a large and enormously influential portion of the American population—the elite intellectuals and a large portion of the liberal, middle-class—such that <u>the legitimate and indefensible role of the military is being threatened</u>.

This is the irony of the present situation. Generally speaking, President Eisenhower's warning has been ignored by the military and governmental institutions to which, in a sense, he directed it. But the intellectuals—conservative, liberal and radical—have taken up the issue with a fervor. Thus writes <u>Time</u>:

> Economist Arthur F. Burns, now a senior White House Aide, has argued that the complex "has been affecting profoundly the character of our society as well as the thrust and contours of economic activity." The effects, according to Burns, have been mostly negative: promoting excess governmental spending, stoking inflation, diverting resources from civilian needs, warping college curriculums, luring professors from teaching into research and breeding a class of civilian managers and scientists whose sole orientation is toward the government.

The problem here is twofold. Unless I am mistaken, America has "lost" its first war: Four years, $65 billion, and 212,022 casualties have not enabled the most powerful nation on earth to overcome the resistance of a vastly outgunned, out-numbered enemy. My impression is that by and large the military advice given the President about this war has been mediocre at best. I have a distinct sense we are still fighting in Korea, just as the national guard and the police forces over here are still preparing to put down the 1965 riot in Watts. In any event, it is too much not to suppose that someone will be blamed, and that for many the someone will be the military.

Unfortunately, on the left, this failure has exposed the military to an unexampled display of viciousness. The one thing that appears to unite the students at Harvard and elsewhere in the Ivy League is their detestation of the R.O.T.C. and all it "stands for." It is, of course, at the heart of the Harvard crisis.

This is no small matter. The elite intelligentsia of the country are turning against the country—in science, in politics, in the fundaments of patriotism. How can we not pay for this?

What President Pusey of Harvard said about the R.O.T.C. is this: "I think it's terribly important that R.O.T.C. be kept here. I personally feel it's terribly important for the United States of America that college people go into the military. I do think the government in Washington remains our government. And the military arm of that government remains our arm." At least I think he said that. The passage is taken from a leaflet distributed in the Harvard Yard on Friday last as evidence of his complicity in the military industrial complex, and his utter unfitness for the Presidency of Harvard!

Note also that elements of the military are beginning to contribute to this theme. Thus General Shoup writes in the lead article of <u>The Atlantic:</u> "America has become a militaristic and aggressive nation." Ours, he says, has become a "militaristic culture."

Dare we expect that there will be no reaction from the right? No officer corps ever lost a war. Always it is betrayed. Why should the American officer corps be different? Especially given the elemental dishonesty and outrageousness of so much of the provocation from the left.

<u>Third,</u> I fear the nation is going to be in for a bitter disappointment when the Vietnam war is "over." We have been promised a "peace-and-growth-dividend" of $22 billion soon after the cease fire, and fiscal ease from thereon. As best I read the figures, there will be nothing of the kind. To maintain our 1965 military posture will require budget expenditures of $69 billion at least, while wise men predict we will not even return to that base. Some of this is unavoidable. But in the view of senior career men in the Bureau of the Budget it will also reflect the fundamental weakness of the institution of the Presidency when faced by demands from the military.

The danger, obviously, is twofold. A failure to divert a significant proportion of current military expenditure to domestic uses in the aftermath of the Vietnam war will not only disappoint those groups that might expect something in the way of increased social services, decreased taxes, or whatever, but will only serve to confirm the reality of radical charge that America has indeed become a militarist culture. . . .

Nixon's reply to Moynihan's suggestion that the government change its practice of identifying races was: "Good idea."

APRIL 14, 1969

FOR THE PRESIDENT

I keep trying to think of ways for you to establish a posture with respect to civil rights issues that is both admirable in its own right, and somehow more than an incremental extension of the programs of the past four Presidents. (Five, if you want to give Roosevelt credit for the few things he did.) I think I have one.

I do not believe this is a racist country. But it was. And there are many only half perceived carryovers of earlier attitudes still embedded in our every day routines.

One of these is the practice of the U.S. Government to classify its citizens as "White," or "Nonwhite." White is normal. Not to be white is not to be normal. That is the only possible interpretation. Once you begin to think of it, the present practice is outrageous.

What if you were to issue a directive that henceforth population statistics would be divided into four categories, by continent or origin? E.G. American (i.e. Indians), European, African, Oriental. Some other scheme might prove more attractive if we were to think harder. Does this interest you?

Daniel P. Moynihan

_____ Yes

_____ Premature

Moynihan mulls the growing discontent of the white working class.

MAY 17, 1969

FOR THE PRESIDENT

I think you are entirely right to have been disturbed by Pete Hamill's article: "The Revolt of the White Lower Middle Class." To be frank, I would have sent it to you myself, save that it seemed to me this is just what you were talking about during the campaign. "The Forgotten Americans."

> A new voice is being heard in America today. It is a voice that has been silent too long. It is a voice of people who have not taken to the streets

before, who have not indulged in violence, who have not broken the
law. ******* These forgotten Americans finally have become angry—

They have not really found a voice in American politics, but they are indeed
angry. And have reason to be.

You ask "What is our answer." To which I suppose my first reaction would
be to ask "What is their question?" . . .

What is the question? It is this: How is the great mass of white working
people to regain a sense of positive advantage from the operation of American
government, and retain a steady loyalty to the processes of American society,
at a time when those above and below them in the social hierarchy seem simultaneously to be robbing the system blind and contemptuously dismissing
all its rules.

This comes to two issues, one relatively simple, the other immensely complex. First, how to enable that working class to see what it <u>is</u> getting out of
government, and even, perhaps, to provide it more. That is not hard. Far more
difficult, however, is the question of how to reconcile the group to the astonishing onset of <u>role reversal</u> by other groups—black welfare mothers, white
students, et al.—which has shocked and disoriented almost everyone, but most
especially <u>this</u> group which places unusual emphasis on the importance of
people behaving "like they should."

I <u>think</u> the first point is relatively simple. We must cease definite social problems
in such a way as to separate blacks (and to a degree Hispanic Americans) from
the rest of the society. Much of the legislation of the 1960's did this, even, as
in the case of the Poverty Program, when it was specifically designed not to.

I believe you have already laid the foundation for this by moving away from
a <u>services strategy</u> in dealing with the problems of social inequality, toward
an <u>income strategy</u>.

A service strategy is just that: it provides services to people who need
them, typically above and beyond those that other persons receive. Some services seem to work well—the Agriculture Extension Service, job training, family planning are examples. Others seem to be marginal or worse.
Compensatory education, for example—Head Start, Title I of the Elementary
and Secondary Education Act of 1965—seems to produce very few results,
despite large investments.

The problem with a services strategy is two fold. Performance is spotty,
but more importantly, in the present time the service dispensing groups in

the society—teachers, welfare workers, urban planners, nutrition experts, etc. etc.—are preoccupied with the black problem and almost at times seem to resent hearing that there are whites who are in difficulty or marginally so. Hamill is right about this. The upper middle class is color blind to the point of being seemingly unable to see that there are <u>any</u> deserving whites around save those who dispense services to the black poor. (Also the white upper middle class of New York seems to have come to the conclusion that the City is turning black. It isn't. Negroes make up about 15 percent of the population, and the proportion is only barely increasing. This is true of the country as a whole.) Other whites are perceived as enemies of the black—the prototype villain being the building trade unionist.

Thus a services strategy tends not only to exclude working class whites, but also to set up a great many middle class whites (and blacks) in the <u>resentment business.</u> They earn very good livings making the black poor feel put upon, when they are, which is often the case, and also when they are not. . . .

I once described the services strategy as one of feeding the sparrows by feeding the horses. An <u>income strategy</u> is something quite different. It begins with the assumption that what the poor and near poor lack most is money. It seeks to provide adequate incomes for all, so that as much as possible everyone purchases services in a single market. Thus the government does not seem to be playing favorites, by providing sumptuous special services for one group—public housing, welfare, compensatory education—while ignoring the needs of others who are only marginally better off.

* Your <u>tax reform proposals</u>, which would exempt 5 million persons in poor families from income taxation was the first step in constructing an income strategy.
* Your <u>hunger program</u>, which will provide food stamps, a form of currency, to all persons below certain income levels with the wherewithal to purchase an adequate diet, was the second step in constructing an income strategy.
* <u>The Family Security System</u>, which would aid the working poor (sixty percent of whom are white) as well as the wholly dependent poor, and do so as one system of income maintenance, would be the third step in an income strategy.
* <u>Revenue sharing</u> with state and local governments, which if large enough could begin to ease the ferocious burden of regressive sales

taxes and the like on Hamill's urban working class, would be the
fourth step in an income strategy.
  * <u>Manpower training</u> on the level and with the organizational
    structure now being proposed by the Labor Department would be
    the final step—for now at least—in an income strategy.

Taken together, these measures have the making of a social revolution
which preserves the fabric of American society, rather than tearing it to shreds.
At long last the people-in-between would begin benefitting from the efforts
of government to redress the long-standing and fully documented grievances
of the people at the bottom.

But there is another problem.

I have been trying to find a way to explain to myself, and to you, the seemingly inexplicable behavior of white suburban upper class college students
and, to a lesser degree, of the black urban poor.

Thanks to a conversation with Erik Erikson (who is surely the most significant psychiatrist since Freud) I believe I have an answer.

What has been going on is a pervasive and quite unprecedented onset of
<u>role reversal</u>. The process of "socialization" is one whereby the infant and then
the growing child is gradually taught to perform certain roles that are appropriate to his age, sex, and to a greater or lesser degree his class and caste (in
the case of certain minorities.) These roles are not performed in a vacuum.
Rather, they relate to other roles. In the case of youth, to that of adults. In the
case of blacks, typically to that of whites. Typically these have been hierarchical
roles, with one person being superior and the other inferior. These roles have
had "authority." They have been occupied. In Erikson's formulation, this authority gradually forms as childhood moral standards are acquired, and these
gradually transmute into ethical standards in youth.

(The child is taught what he "must" do and "must not" do, the youth learns
what he "ought" to do). For reasons difficult to understand, young persons are
suddenly reversing these roles. Of a sudden <u>they</u> are the superior ones, and
are treating their elders as inferiors. They do so, moreover, with a moralistic
harshness that is a caricature of the adult world. They become in effect super-
moralistic, treating adults as children who do not know what they are doing
really, and certainly cannot fool their all powerful, all knowing guardians. They
turn on adults in a caricature of adults. (The hippies are more premoralistic,

but it comes to much the same thing in attitudes towards those previously presumed to be in authority). . . .

I am pretty sure that nothing can prove more disastrous than for those whose roles have been reversed to insist that things be turned upside down once again, so that the upstart students or blacks, or whomever are relegated to an appropriate subordination. No. That won't work. But neither will it work for the society to go on submitting to the dictation of usurping mobs claiming a moral superiority which has no basis either in experience or in understanding.

But in the meantime, the "white lower middle class" is likely to become increasingly estranged itself. Hamill, I think, is right. Things could go very badly indeed. I have little to offer save the formula of my long memorandum of March 19. We must dissolve the black urban lower class, turning it into a "black lower middle class" in its own right, and simultaneously seek the ethical and political formulations that will restore legitimacy to our society in the eyees of its elite youth.

I don't have to say again that the one indispensable step to doing that is to get us out of Vietnam, and on this you have my prayers and respect.

Moynihan finds he has to campaign for the Family Assistance Plan with Nixon himself.

JUNE 6, 1969

MEMORANDUM FOR THE PRESIDENT

I am asked to comment on Paul McCracken's memorandum concerning a "Possible Resolution of the Welfare Reform Controversy."

I agree with almost everything he says. Clearly, the two major proposals before you have much in common. Clearly we are moving toward a general income support program. Clearly there are a good many technical details concerning the Family Security System which one would like to know more about. It is, after all, the first major change in social welfare policy since the Elizabethan Poor Laws, and is likely to reverberate through the society for generations—much as the Poor Laws have done.

However, I feel the issue before you at this point is not technical, but political. This Congress is almost certainly going to begin the discussion of a major change in our welfare system. The 1970's will almost certainly see such a change instituted. The changes will profoundly influence American society for at least the remainder of the century.

<u>It is open to you to dominate and direct this social transformation.</u>

The matter comes to this. Income maintenance proposals are springing up everywhere. The Urban League, the Urban Coalition, the various welfare professional groups, the welfare reform groups, the children's aid groups, the Chamber of Commerce, the AFL-CIO. Everyone is getting into this business. Not least, in September, <u>President Johnson's</u> Commission on Income Maintenance will be coming in with a $1.5 million report that will propose a system very much like Family Security, but somewhat broader.

Just as clearly, Congress is ready to begin this discussion. From the most conservative to the most liberal ranks, an amazing number of members agree that AFDC must go.

Thus I would argue that if you move now, you will dominate the discussion. Congress will be discussing <u>your</u> proposal. It hardly matters what final form it takes, or how many times we change our position in the process. The end result—if you wish it to be—will be <u>your</u> change. . . .

Therefore I am doubly interested in seeing you go up now with a genuinely new, unmistakably Nixon, unmistakably needed program, which would attract the attention of the world, far less the United States. We can afford the Family Security System. Once you have asked for it, you can resist the pressures endlessly to add marginal funds to already doubtful programs.

This way, in 1972 we will have a record of solid, unprecedented accomplishment in a vital area of social policy, and not just an explanation as to how complicated it all was.

More reflections on the antiwar protests and challenges to authority throughout the country on university campuses.

AUGUST 19, 1969

MEMORANDUM FOR THE PRESIDENT

Autumn now approaches, and with it—such being the singular capacity of American life to compress the social change of generations into demi-decades—the season of student unrest, disorder, and turmoil.

You have been trying to keep the Federal government out of the now recurrent campus upheavals, and have been altogether correct in wishing to do so. Moreover, it appears we have been successful in heading off any seriously repressive legislation, although this will remain a continuing threat. . . .

But beyond the simple issue of campus violence—simple in the sense that almost everyone will agree that students should not club the dean, but neither should they be prevented by bayonets from doing so—the far more complex question of the relationship of the American polity to the newest generation of middle class youth awaits you. You because, as President, you are the embodiment of that polity. It is, in a sense, entrusted to the President that he be concerned with these profound matters of continuity and change. You also because so long as the Vietnam war continues student protest constitutes an immediate and direct threat to the day-to-day effectiveness of the national government, quite apart from any long range concerns.

I would expect there will be considerable anti-war protest in the coming academic year. (Thus plans are now afoot for a nationwide series of campus strikes: one day in October, two in November, three in December, and so through the year.) I am not sure what you can do about all this, except of course to end the war, which is precisely your desire and intent. But to do so successfully imposes restraints on what you can say in public: so great that I would imagine there can not be much successful dialogue between the students and the Administration on this issue per se. Until the war is over, or its gradual subsidence becomes manifest to even the most skeptical, any American president will face more or less bitter opposition from the now radical children of the Republican middle class. (With the scion of an occasional Democratic lawyer thrown in!)

On the other hand, there is one step you can take, and which I would urge you to consider: you could make your proposed reforms of the draft a national political issue. It would be nigh impossible to overestimate the influence of the present system on the consciences of college youth. The sequence goes something as follows. Intensely committed to social progress at home and peace abroad, they detest the war and do everything possible to avoid serving in it by avoiding or evading the draft. It is possible to do this because they are more or less affluent, privileged, and well connected young persons who can get into college, until recently could go on to the shelter of graduate school, and even now can find exempted positions in education, public service, etc. But this does not end the war. All it does is ensure that the children of the poor, the black, and such, are drafted to take the place of the white middle class youth who has bought his deferment just as surely as did any merchant's son during the Civil War. Hence those very persons the college youth most wishes to see served by society are sent off to be killed and wounded because those higher in the social hierarchy have refused to do their duty. All this exaggerates, but only a very little bit. The inevitable result is a generation of college youth afflicted by intense and persistent emotional crises. At very least they can prove their manhood by roughing up the administration. But the true demand on them is to transform (i.e., overthrow) the system that put them in this pickle in the first place. . . .

At the great risk of using a term of clinical psychiatry to describe a crisis in the culture I would offer the thought that American society is becoming more and more schizophrenic. Two opposite and increasingly equal tendencies, often as not united in individuals, are splitting the nation. Norman Podhoretz, editor of <u>Commentary</u>, cites as illustration the fact that just about the two leading box office attractions of 1968 were <u>The Graduate</u> and <u>The Green Berets</u>. This is in ways a continuance of the old "pale face red skin" dichotomy of American culture, but it has now reached massive proportions. To a degree that no one could have anticipated even three or four years ago, the educated elite of the American middle classes have come to <u>detest</u> their society, and their detestation is rapidly diffusing to youth in general.

The effects of this profound movement of opinion will be with us for generations. It will, for example, drastically limit the role which the United States can play in world affairs—in contrast with the past three decades or so during which the national government has been really extraordinarily free to do what it thought best. There will be indirect effects. The movement of the American youth away from business will almost surely affect business. If it continues, I would imagine it almost certain, for example, that by the year 2000 the Japanese will have a higher per capita income than do the Americans. In one way or another, we are involved in a change of cultural dimensions that will be pervasive in its consequences. . . .

The trouble is they are on to something. Really. The something, in essence, is the collapse of religious vision in almost all parts of the Western world combined with the rise of genuine technological terror in the form of the weapons of modern warfare. The result is a situation which no sensitive—read sensible—person can or should endure. After twenty-five one learns, I suppose, to live with things one shouldn't have to live with. But before that, especially to persons of good education, fine intelligence, and comfortable means, the circumstance is to one degree or another intolerable. The result is a "desperate ethical yearning" in the young—make no mistake, a religious yearning—which they seem to share the world around, which they recognize in one another, and which truly does set them apart from, and very much against the rest of us.

I believe as President you <u>can</u> do something about this ethical yearning. You can acknowledge it. You can make clear that you know what's going on out there. (If, that is, you come to share this analysis of what <u>is</u> going on.) The ways of doing so are many, and more subtle than otherwise. But I could imagine quite extraordinary consequences if you should try to do so in a more or less systematic way, just as I can foresee all manner of misfortune if someone doesn't try. . . .

Following are letters from this period showing that Moynihan had other things on his mind besides ruminating about issues for Nixon.

To Bernard Briggs, a neighbor who sometimes did work on his farm.

APRIL 16, 1969

Dear Bub:

I am down here in the White House basement thinking of the farm, and realizing spring is probably finally getting there. That being the case, I wonder if you would take care to give the lawn a couple of mowings this Spring. Last year we never quite caught up once it got out of hand. We have a new lawn-mower in the stable, which I think you will find in good working order.

I do hope all goes well with the family and the farming. See you soon.

Staying in touch with Ethel Kennedy, widow of Robert Kennedy.

MAY 14, 1969

Dearest Ethel:

Time somehow stumbles along faster than it would seem here in the White House basement. I have been in Washington four months, with hardly a day passing that I have not thought to call or write in the hopes of seeing you. And of course I have not until now done so. Maxima culpa, indeed.

Do you ever get out to lunch? Or could I stop by for a drink? I would so like to see you.

Moynihan's mother, Margaret, was in the hospital.

JULY 1, 1969

MARGARET MOYNIHAN

METROPOLITAN HOSPITAL

1901 FIRST AVENUE

NEW YORK, NEW YORK

HAVE BEEN SO WORRIED AND AM NOW SO RELIEVED TO KNOW THAT YOU ARE THROUGH THE WORST. DO TRY TO REGAIN YOUR SPIRITS. HOPE TO SEE YOU SOON.

MUCH LOVE

PAT

Moynihan was not too busy to bring décor to the attention of H. R. Haldeman, the White House chief of staff.

JULY 30, 1969

FOR H. R. HALDEMAN

The lady decorators of the new White House Mess came by this morning to show me their color schemes, et al.

I was appalled.

I told them as nicely but firmly as I could that this was to be a naval officers' mess. It was not to be Schrafft's-in-the-Basement. It was not to be the fantasia of a southern California fairy. It was not to be an extension of the erotic longings of middle-aged corporation wives whose husbands had acquired interests elsewhere, but maintained the domestic accounts in guilty abundance.

I told them that there happened to be a fairly distinctive design tradition in these matters, and that they would do well to fly up to Boston to look at the wardroom of the U.S.S. Constitution. In any event, I said that if we were to have a new room (news to me) the Smithsonian should be brought in to consult on what paintings and scrimshaw they could provide. I know they would be honored to do this, and will contact them if you like.

Sorry to bother you, but they bothered me.

CHAPTER FIVE

"The Erosion of Authority Will Continue"

After his first six months in the Nixon White House, Moynihan wrote increasingly alarmed memoranda about social and political conditions and his concern that Vice President Spiro Agnew's divisive rhetoric was feeding the unrest. Alert to changing trends, however, he urged Nixon to embrace the growing feminist movement and to pattern himself after the British nineteenth-century reformer, Benjamin Disraeli, and his "Tory men with Liberal principles" who sought to strengthen democratic institutions. The letters indicate that Moynihan felt a certain loyalty to Nixon but saw his role as a kind of truth-teller because of his roots outside the Nixon inner circle, who was therefore able to see, for example, that the country was losing patience with the administration's failure to end the war in Vietnam. Though Moynihan reviled much of the alienated youth that was protesting, he called on the White House to take the problem seriously lest it grow too powerful to overcome. He warned against the dangers of prosecuting the so-called Chicago Seven, the antiwar protesters from the Democratic Convention in 1968 who were on trial in that city. His realization that Nixon could not affect race issues by talking about them himself was conveyed in the memo recommending that Nixon cease talking about race. But his use of the phrase "benign neglect" for that course of action blew up when the memorandum leaked to the public, no doubt a consequence of Nixon having asked for his messages to be widely distributed within the White House. Moynihan's personal anguish became palpable when his own house came under threat of violence by protesters at Harvard. Nixon's decision to send troops

*into Cambodia in the spring of 1970 deepened the student turmoil, and Moynihan
drafted a letter to resign. But Nixon persuaded him to stay on because of the Family
Assistance Plan (FAP).*

Highlighting the issue of "female equality" in the 1970s.

AUGUST 20, 1969

MEMORANDUM FOR THE PRESIDENT

Predicting the future is never an especially productive enterprise in politics.
But when seemingly unmistakable signs of an emergent political force begin
to appear on every hand, and yet are somehow ignored, it is worth the slight
risk to one's reputation to try to point them out.

I will predict, then, that female equality will be a major cultural/political
force of the 1970's.

The signs are everywhere. As is often the case, it is among young people
on the left that the inclination has assumed the proportions of a movement.
The student left of the moment has been mostly reported in terms of its fondness for Eldridge Cleaver and Chairman Mao. Almost unnoticed, but very
prominent in the deliberations and literature of an organization such as SDS,
is the subject of "Women's Liberation." It would appear, for example, that the
split of the SDS at its Chicago convention in June was in part at least precipitated by the Black Panthers' insensitivity to the subject. The theretofore dominant faction of SDS, playing up its ties with the militant blacks, gave the
floor to the Panthers, who proceeded to address the group in terms of "male
chauvinism," and proved a disaster for their backers. (In the thought that your
reading need not always be humorless, I attach an account of the event from
<u>The Old Mole</u>, the Cambridge underground journal.) The convention ended
up pretty much in the hands of the Maoist Progressive Labor faction, for
which the exploitation of blacks is regarded as no different from, or worse
than, the whole regime of bourgeois exploitation, including most prominently,
the exploitation of women. . . .

I do not wish to burden you with details. The essential fact is that we have educated women for equality in America, but have not really given it to them. Not at all. Inequality is so great that the dominant group either doesn't notice it, or assumes the dominated group likes it that way. (An old story!) Did you happen to note, for example, Erik Erikson's comment that there were no women present at our meeting of educators. He might well have commented on the general absence of women from higher education in America. It is considered too important for them. <u>They</u> teach kindergarten. (Which, I might add, may indeed be too important for them!) I would bet there are proportionately more women in the Marine Corps than on most University faculties. Thus higher education subtly perpetuates the notion that women have equal rights, but not really equal potentialities, etc.

I am no great fancier of India or Ceylon. But consider the apparent ease with which those countries have accepted female heads of state. Consider how odd the idea of a lady President would be to us. I repeat: male dominance is so deeply a part of American life that males don't even notice it.

I would suggest you could take advantage of this. In your appointments (as you have begun to do), but perhaps especially in your pronouncements. This is a subject ripe for creative political leadership and initiative.

Much commentary in the press in the early Nixon years focused on Moynihan's comparison of the president to Prime Minister Benjamin Disraeli, the Conservative British statesman, as a proponent of reform—or, "Tory men and Whig measures." The allusion was adopted as "Tory men with Liberal principles," enlarging and reforming democracy. Moynihan suggests that Nixon read the 1966 biography of Disraeli by Robert Blake. This memorandum suggests that Moynihan consciously promoted the idea to the press as part of a "theory" of understanding Nixon.

AUGUST 21, 1969

MEMORANDUM FOR THE PRESIDENT

You may have missed this column by Alan Otten of the <u>Wall Street Journal.</u>

It is the best of the series we have "produced," all of which turn on the theme "It is Tory men with Liberal principles who have enlarged democracy."

The quote must by now be in twenty columns. The point is that journalists need an explanation, a theory of what is going on in order to make sense of the swarm of events. They were utterly confused about the New Federalism: "How could Nixon ... etc"? until we gave them such a theory. But as any psychologist will tell you, you have to have some idea of what a chair looks like before you can perceive one.

I am working on a more general "theory" of the administration, that is to say, description of how and why what you have been doing fits together and makes sense <u>as a whole.</u> Because increasingly it does.

Moynihan was alert very early to the prospect of climate change resulting from the "greenhouse effect" from carbon emissions.

SEPTEMBER 17, 1969

FOR JOHN EHRLICHMAN

As with so many of the more interesting environmental questions, we really don't have very satisfactory measurements of the carbon dioxide problem. On the other hand, this very clearly <u>is</u> a problem, and, perhaps most particularly, is one that can seize the imagination of persons normally indifferent to projects of apocalyptic change.

The process is a simple one. Carbon dioxide in the atmosphere has the effect of a pane of glass in a greenhouse. The CO_2 content is normally in a stable cycle, but recently man has begun to introduce instability through the burning of fossil fuels. At the turn of the century several persons raised the question whether this would change the temperature of the atmosphere. Over the years the hypothesis has been refined, and more evidence has come along to support it. It is now pretty clearly agreed that the CO_2 content will rise 25% by 2000. This could increase the average temperature near the earth's surface by 7 degrees Fahrenheit. This in turn could raise the level of the sea by 10 feet. Goodbye New York. Goodbye Washington, for that matter. We have no data on Seattle.

It is entirely possible that there will be countervailing effects. For example, an increase of dust in the atmosphere would tend to lower temperatures, and might offset the CO_2 effect. Similarly, it is possible to conceive fairly mammoth man-made efforts to countervail the CO_2 rise (e. g., stop burning fossil fuels).

In any event, I would think this is a subject that the Administration ought to get involved with. . . .

Moynihan expressing alarm to Haldeman that the White House was oblivious to American sentiments on the war. Around this time, Moynihan's influence was headed into eclipse as his Family Assistance Plan proposal ran into opposition among conservatives in Congress and within the Nixon White House. His job title was shifted from assistant to the president for urban affairs to counselor to the president. Though this change elevated Moynihan to the status of a member of the cabinet, it was also seen as a sign among some that he was being marginalized.

OCTOBER 1, 1969

<u>PERSONAL</u>

MEMORANDUM FOR H. R. HALDEMAN

As you know, and have been unfailingly sensitive to, it is difficult for me to offer political advice to the President, or more particularly to his aides. I have been an active Democrat, and if they allow me (which alas I doubt) I will be one again.

But for the moment I am doing something I happen to know something about: serving a President of the United States. This normally should involve giving one's opinion on political matters. Normally, however, I do not. There are exceptions.

One exception occurred last Friday morning when I tried to state as clearly and openly as I could my feeling that the war in Vietnam is a political disaster which the President is <u>not</u> responsible for, and which in no circumstances should he allow himself to be labeled with.

I was surprised at two reactions in the room. First, there seemed a number of people who quite clearly feel the American public is behind the war. Still. Second, there were at least a few persons who seem to think the war is some kind of Presidential prerogative which we must not allow college boys or effeminate professors to infringe.

God have mercy on us if this mood prevails. . . .

The "Vietnam Moratorium Day" was a large protest calling for a general strike against the Vietnam War on October 15, 1969. It was seen as a cause of concern in the Nixon White House.

OCTOBER 16, 1969

MEMORANDUM FOR THE PRESIDENT

Bob Haldeman has sent word that you would like to have from me, today, such thoughts as I may have on how we might respond to yesterday's Moratorium, and especially how we might move its younger leaders in the direction of your efforts to bring about peace in Vietnam, rather than allowing them to be taken over by the extreme elements in the "peace movement."

This seems to me exactly the question to ask. I would offer at the outset two general observations.

1. <u>The Moratorium was a success</u>. It was not perhaps as big as some may have anticipated—"substantial but not enormous," in David Brinkley's words—but in style and content it was everything the organizers could have hoped for. The young white middle class crowds were sweet tempered and considerate: at times even radiant. (Really. The only term by which to describe the march past the White House is joyous.) The movement lost no friends. It gained, I should think, a fair number of recruits and a great deal of prestige.

2. <u>The New Mobilization Committee demonstration of November 13–15 is likely to be enormous.</u>

The NMC is made up of old line peace organizations—Women's Strike for Peace, SANE, and such—plus religious groups, primarily Methodist, United Church of Christ, and Quaker. The leadership is tough and experienced. (They ran the 1967 march on the Pentagon.) Negotiations are now underway between the Moratorium group and the NMC, whereby the young people will support the November demonstration. They hope to have a million people in Washington, and one would have to bet they might just. Yesterday's was the biggest peace demonstration in history: November's is likely to be bigger.

There is not much you can do about this. Or at least not much I can think of. The course of events in the near term is pretty much set. It would, I think, have been possible to make friends of the Moratorium as it were. (Kennedy did just that to the 1963 March of Jobs and Freedom which began as an open effort to force him to do something about employment and civil rights.) But that course was not chosen, and for the moment the most we can hope to do is to keep matters from getting worse than would otherwise be the case. . . .

That, at all events, is my view. Here are four proposals.

1. <u>Stop the red baiting</u>. The Vice President's press conference Tuesday morning was a blunder of the first order. The Moratorium leaders feel that they had avoided any personal attacks on you, or for that matter on the administration. My impression is that this is the case: their appeals were very general, and not anti-administration. Suddenly, on the eve of the demonstration the Vice President makes a clumsy and transparent attempt to link them up with Pham Van Dong. They regard it as an "unconscionable" attack upon their patriotism. They also, I suspect, privately know that it was just about the best thing that happened to them. The middle class, academic, intellectual world will now be solidly with them. . . .

2. <u>Take special measures to avoid or minimize violence on November 13–15.</u> We, of course, cannot control this outcome, but we can influence it. A good deal of learning has taken place in the past few years, and police forces are much more skillful at handling demonstrations such as yesterday's. The Washington police were superb. . . .

3. <u>Consider spending a day on a college campus talking with students about the war, your efforts to bring about peace, and the administration's views in general.</u> This is a tricky question, I know, but a case can be made for visiting a campus somewhere, and spending some time in relaxed, informal, open discussion. There are risks, but there are also opportunities. The big danger is that we will come to be thought indifferent to public opinion. . . .

4. <u>The White House Staff probably ought to have some personal contact with the Moratorium leaders.</u> Part at least of the difficulties involved here is that the players don't know one another, and not unnaturally suspect the worst. Sam Brown, for one proposes to be in that headquarters until the war in Vietnam is over. (A cease fire will not do.) This could be some time. In the interval the domestic equivalent of a hot line should be established. . . .

Moynihan was increasingly concerned about the alienation of the younger generation spurred by the Vietnam War.

NOVEMBER 13, 1969

MEMORANDUM FOR THE PRESIDENT

Last night Teddy White related to me your hopes for reviving the Eisenhower-Nixon majority. This seems to me altogether a worthy goal, and a perfectly feasible one. But I fear we may be jeopardizing that outcome by certain present postures which are now in no way central to any of your other goals or policies.

The Eisenhower-Nixon majority was broadbased. (Ike got 20% of the black vote in 1952 and twice that in 1956.) But its bedrock consisted of the business and professional class of the nation. These provided the brains, the money, the élan.

Clearly your overall policies are ideal for mobilizing that group once again. Your fixed intention to get us out of that war in Asia; to put the economy back in balance; to restore the authority of public institutions; to achieve social progress with social stability—all are precisely the goals of that group.

I think, however, you could lose much of it—needlessly—if <u>their children</u> begin to take personally your necessary, proper and essentially impersonal opposition to their own effort to make foreign policy in the streets.

It must be remembered that to an extraordinary degree the demonstrators are an elite group.

* I would hazard that half their parents are Republicans.
* I would not be surprised if those parents contributed half the funds spent by either major party in the 1968 election.
* Note, for example, that much of the money behind this weekend's demonstration comes from General Motors and Singer Sewing Machine fortunes. (The Ole Mole, the radical journal in Cambridge, is financed by the granddaughter of Merrill, Lynch, Pierce, Fenner and Smith. There is no end to such examples.)

As with most such groups, they really are kind of arrogant. . . . They can also be wonderful. Maureen Finch who took part in the Moratorium worked for me this summer, and was superb. I gather that Mel Laird's son who also took part is equally an attractive young man.

And in the mass they are powerful. One of the least understood phenomenon of the time is the way in which the radical children of the upper middle classes have influenced their parents. That is why Time Magazine, Life,

Newsweek, NBC, CBS, the New York Times and the media in general will take their side against anybody whatsoever: the Democratic Party, the Pentagon, Mayor Daley. Or, if it should ever come to it . . . you. . . .

I sometimes like these kids. More often I detest their ignorant, chiliastic, almost insolent self confidence. But I think it extremely important for the administration not to allow itself to become an object of their incredible powers of derision, destruction, and disdain.

Moynihan wanted to keep a record of Nixon's offer to appoint him ambassador to the United Nations in 1969. He later accepted the appointment by President Ford in 1975.

FROM: DANIEL P. MOYNIHAN

SUBJECT: REPORT FOR THE PRESIDENT'S FILE ON HIS MEETING WITH ME ON TUESDAY, NOV. 17, AT 4 P.M.

MEMORANDUM FOR: JOHN H. BROWN III

I met with the President on November 17 at 4 p.m. to discuss his offer to me of the position of United States Ambassador to the United Nations. I had previously indicated that I would accept this position and at that time confirmed my acceptance. We talked at some length about the U.N. and the President's desire to somehow turn it into a more active organization.

On the following Friday, November 20, the <u>Boston Globe</u> reported that I would take the U.N. job. I was at a Time, Inc. housing conference in Acapulco when this happened. On the same day a key vote in the Senate Finance Committee cast by Senator Harris with Senator McCarthy's proxy, more or less killed family assistance. I returned to the United States Sunday feeling badly about both these things. On Monday night I determined that I really ought not to go to the United Nations. Tuesday morning I wrote the President a letter to this effect. On Wednesday, Mr. Haldeman asked me if my decision was irrevocable. I explained that it was and he accepted it. On Friday, November 27, this was announced to the Press.

The news that a search-and-destroy retaliatory attack turned into a massacre of more than three hundred civilians at My Lai, in Vietnam, inflamed the anti-war movement—prompting Moynihan to caution Nixon on how to respond.

NOVEMBER 25, 1969

MEMORANDUM FOR THE PRESIDENT

... Many times over I have stated, in public, that Vietnam is the war of liberal anti-communism. I have done this largely because as it has become obvious that we cannot "win" the war, and that those who persist in prosecuting it are likely to "lose" at home, there has been a considerable effort by liberal politicians to disengage. This has taken the form of suggesting that it is really a war of <u>conservative</u> anti-communism, of the Barry Goldwater variety. (In personal terms this comes down to whether it is Johnson's war or Nixon's war. I fear to say that altogether too many people in your administration, because they happen to be conservative anti-communists, would like to convert it to Nixon's war, and in recent weeks have pretty much succeeded in doing so.)

I persist in stating otherwise partly because I think the facts should be kept straight, but mostly because I have genuinely feared this tendency in liberalism which it seems to me has been blind to many of the probable consequences.

One of those consequences has now come to light.

It is clear that something hideous happened at Mylai. (Or Song My. The name appears not yet settled.) The abhorrent thing occurred.

I would doubt the war effort can ever now be the same. Nor the position of the military. Look, if you will, at the pictures in <u>Time</u> this week. As a father of sons about the age of those lying dead in that Vietnam ditch, I shuddered when I came to that page. How could it be that there could be such a thing to be looked at?

I fear the answer of too many Americans will simply be that this is a hideous, corrupt society. If I may strain your patience, this is why I began talking to liberals about this two and one-half, three years ago. (It is why I campaigned for Robert Kennedy, who had been the leading gung-ho Green Beret shoot 'em up in Washington in the early 1960's, but who gradually came to see what a disastrous mistake we had all made.) I believe sinners understand sin. It seemed to me inevitable that in moving in there in our Messianic way to save those peasants from International Communism we would end up, as young [Paul] Meadlo—he was only 20 then, and is minus a foot today—emptying four clips of an M-15 into a huddle of women, children, and babies. . . .

I repeat. By and large the groups that led us into the war will <u>not</u> now try to understand it, but rather will seek to blame it on others. Some of the forces which inherited the war will—incredibly!—try to be defensive, and act as if nothing happened.

You must be different. You must try to lead the nation in the quest for understanding. (The troops were worn out. They had taken too many casualties. Their Lieutenant looks and sounds like a Southern psychotic. It is not the American character that came out at Mylai. It is what war can do to that or any character. I joined the Navy in 1944 at age 17, and am proud of it. I later served as a gunnery officer on a ship at sea. I have seen what the mere proximity to violence does to certain personalities.)

I don't know with whom you take counsel on matters this serious, but I would hope you might turn to them now. I think it would be a grave error for the Presidency to be silent while the Army and the press pass judgment on these haunted young men.

For it is America that is being judged. . . .

Moynihan felt that the Family Assistance Plan was being undermined by Republicans despite Nixon's support.

DECEMBER 15, 1969

MEMORANDUM FOR THE PRESIDENT

. . . You will recall that your first message to the Congress on a substantive domestic issue concerned the poverty legislation. To the great surprise of almost all concerned, you proposed that the OEO [Office of Economic Opportunity] continue. (A sign on the elevators at OEO headquarters had said "This building will self-destruct on January 20.")

After your message went up I met with a series of Congressional groups, explaining what you wanted, and insisting that you meant it. Republicans and Democrats alike as much as accused me of lying.

Now you have delivered. You saved the poverty program. No one else could have done it.

Unfortunately, lack of loyalty to your program (and the ability to count) in the House Republican leadership has enabled too many people to claim that you really were against it all along, and in fact "lost" the vote last Friday. (This is the theory of the "hidden agenda," namely that the positions you take publicly are not in fact your real positions. It is widely propagated by your opponents—Republicans and Democrats alike.) Don Rumsfeld's brilliant management of the bill did much to dispel this charge, but it lingers.

This being the case, I would suggest that some effort be made by members of the administration to point to the fact that the first thing you promised this year was to fight for the continuation of the poverty program, that that is what you did, and that you won.

Though Senator George McGovern, the liberal South Dakota Democrat, was a vehement critic of Nixon's conduct of the Vietnam War, Moynihan worked with him on programs to combat hunger. McGovern ran against Nixon in 1972 as the Democratic presidential candidate.

JANUARY 5, 1970

Dear George:

It was splendidly—and characteristically—generous of you to issue that statement on the Administration's efforts this past year to overcome the problem of hunger. I think you are right. It has been perhaps our most important accomplishment, in the sense of things actually done as against merely proposed. (Even so, there is still that food stamp bill to get enacted!)

What has gratified me, and I expect you also, is that the subject has not become partisan. There has been an atmosphere of accusation, even denunciation on the fringes of the subject, but those with the ability and responsibility to act have kept their heads, and I think we can all be proud of the result.

My best to you in the coming year.

The famous memo recommending to Nixon that the corrosive issue of race "could benefit from a period of 'benign neglect'"—leaked shortly thereafter to the NEW

YORK TIMES—*created a furious controversy that dogged Moynihan for the rest of his career. His reference to the reception for the Black Panthers at the home of Leonard Bernstein prompted a letter from Mrs. Bernstein to Moynihan on March 9, which he saved, noting that "the only concern at the above-mentioned meeting was civil liberties." Moynihan repeatedly explained that the phrase "benign neglect" applied to rhetoric about the issue, not policies. Many years later, he wrote that he came up with the phrase, though at the time he thought he might have borrowed it from somewhere.*

JANUARY 16, 1970

MEMORANDUM FOR THE PRESIDENT

As the new year begins it occurs to me that you might find useful a general assessment of the position of Negroes at the end of the first year of your administration, and of the decade in which their position has been <u>the</u> central domestic political issue.

In quantitative terms, which are reliable, the American Negro is making extraordinary progress. In political terms, somewhat less reliable, this would also appear to be true. In each case, however, there would <u>seem</u> to be countercurrents that pose a serious threat to the welfare of the blacks, and the stability of the society, white and black.

1. <u>Employment and Income</u>.

The 1960's saw the great breakthrough for blacks. A third (32%) of all families of Negro and other races earned $8000 or more in 1968 compared, in constant dollars, with 15% in 1960.

The South is still a problem. Slightly more than half (52%) of the Negro population lived in the South in 1969. <u>There</u>, only 19% of families of Negro and other races earned over $8000.

<u>Young Negro families are achieving income parity with young white families.</u> Outside the South, young husband-wife Negro families have 99% the income of whites! For families headed by a male age 25 to 34 the proportion was 87 percent. Thus it may be this ancient gap is finally closing.

Income reflects employment, and this changed dramatically in the 1960's. Blacks continued to have twice the unemployment rates of whites, but these were down for both groups. In 1969 the rate for married men of Negro and other races was only 2.5 percent. Teenagers, on the other hand, continued their appalling rates: 24.4 percent in 1969.

Black occupations improved dramatically. The number of professional and technical employees doubled in the period 1960–68. This was two and a half times the increase for whites. In 1969 Negro and other races provide 10 percent of the other-than-college teachers. This is roughly their proportion of the population. (11 percent.)

2. Education.

In 1968, 19 percent of Negro children three and four years old were enrolled in school, compared to 15 percent of white children. Forty-five percent of Negroes 18 and 19 years old were in school, almost the equal of the white proportion of 51 percent. Negro college enrollment rose 85 percent between 1964 and 1968, by which time there were 434,000 Negro college students. (The total full time university population of Great Britain is 200,000.)

Educational achievement should not be exaggerated. Only 16% of Negro high school seniors have verbal test scores at or above grade level. But blacks are staying in school.

3. Female Headed Families.

This problem does not get better, it gets worse. In 1969 the proportion of husband-wife families of Negro and other races declined once again, this time to 68.7 percent. The illegitimacy ratio rose once again, this time to 29.4 percent of all live births. (The white ratio rose more sharply, but was still only 4.9 percent.)

Increasingly, the problem of Negro poverty is the problem of the female headed family. In 1968, 56 percent of Negro families with income under $3000 were female headed. In 1968, for the first time, the number of poor Negro children in female headed families (2,241,000) was greater than the number in male headed families (1,947,000).

4. Social Pathology.

The incidence of anti-social behavior among young black males continues to be extraordinarily high. Apart from white racial attitudes, this is the biggest problem black Americans face, and in part it helps shape white racial attitudes. Black Americans injure one another. Because blacks live in de facto segregated neighborhoods, and go to de facto segregated [schools], the socially stable elements of the black population cannot escape the socially pathological ones. Routinely their children get caught up in the anti-social patterns of the others.

You are familiar with the problem of crime. Let me draw your attention to another phenomenon, exactly parallel, and originating in exactly the same social circumstances. Fire. Unless I mistake the trends, we are heading for a genuinely serious fire problem in American cities. In New York, for example, between 1956 and 1969 the over-all fire alarm rate more than tripled, from 69,000 alarms to 240,000. These alarms are concentrated in slum neighborhoods, primarily black.... In 1968 one slum area had an alarm rate per square mile thirteen times that of the city as a whole. In another the number of alarms has, on average, increased 44 percent per year for seven years.

Many of these fires are the result of population density. But a great many are more or less deliberately set. (Thus on Monday welfare protestors set two fires in the New York State Capitol.) Fires are in fact a "leading indicator" of social pathology for a neighborhood. They come first. Crime, and the rest, follows. The psychiatric interpretation of fire-setting is complex, but it relates to the types of personalities which slums produce. (A point of possible interest. Fires in the black slums peak in July and August. The urban riots of 1964–1968 could be thought of as epidemic conditions of an endemic situation.)

5. Social Alienation.

With no real evidence, I would nonetheless suggest that a great deal of the crime, the fire setting, the rampant school violence, and other such phenomenon in the black community have become quasi-politicized. Hatred—revenge—against whites is now an acceptable excuse for doing what might have been done anyway. This is bad news for any society, especially when it takes the form which the Black Panthers seem to have adopted.

This social alienation among the black lower classes is matched, and probably enhanced, by a virulent form of anti-white feeling among portions of the large and prospering black middle class. It would be difficult to overestimate the degree to which young well educated blacks detest white America.

6. The Nixon Administration.

As you have candidly acknowledged, the relation of the administration to the black population is a problem. I think it ought also to be acknowledged that we are a long way from solving it. During the past year intense efforts have been made by the administration to develop programs that will be of help to the blacks. I dare say, as much or more time and attention goes into this effort in this administration than any in history. But little has come of it. There has been a great deal of political ineptness in some Departments, and you have been the loser.

I don't know what you can do about this. Perhaps nothing. But I do have four suggestions.

First. Sometime early in the year I would gather together the administration officials who are most involved with these matters and talk out the subject a bit. There really is a need for a more coherent administration approach to a number of issues. (Which I can list for you, if you like.)

Second. The time may have come when the issue of race could benefit from a period of "benign neglect." The subject has been too much talked about. The forum has been too much taken over to hysterics, paranoids, and boodlers on all sides. We may need a period in which Negro progress continues and racial rhetoric fades. The administration can help bring this about by paying close attention to such progress—as we are doing—while seeking to avoid situations in which extremists of either race are given opportunities for martyrdom, heroics, histrionics or whatever. Greater attention to Indians, Mexican Americans and Puerto Ricans would be useful. A tendency to ignore provocations from groups such as the Black Panthers might also be useful. (The Panthers were apparently almost defunct until the Chicago police raided one of their headquarters and transformed them into culture heroes for the white—and black—middle class. You perhaps did not note on the society page of yesterday's Times that Mrs. Leonard Bernstein gave a cocktail party on Wednesday to raise money for the Panthers. Mrs. W. Vincent Astor was among the guests. Mrs. Peter Duchin, "the rich blond wife of the orchestra leader" was thrilled. "I've never met a Panther," she said. "This is a first for me.")

Third. We really ought to be getting on with research on crime. We just don't know enough. It is a year now since the administration came to office committed to doing something about crime in the streets. But frankly, in that year I don't see that we have advanced either our understanding of the problem, or that of the public at large. (This of course may only reveal my ignorance of what is going on.)

At the risk of indiscretion, may I put it that lawyers are not professionally well equipped to do much to prevent crime. Lawyers are not managers, and they are not researchers. The logistics, the ecology, the strategy and tactics of reducing the incidence of certain types of behavior in large urban populations simply are not things lawyers think about often.

We are never going to "learn" about crime in a laboratory sense. But we almost certainly could profit from limited, carefully done studies. I don't think these will be done unless you express a personal interest.

Fourth. There is a silent black majority as well as a white one. It is mostly working class, as against lower middle class. It is politically moderate (on issues other than racial equality) and shares most of the concerns of its white counterpart. This group has been generally ignored by the government, and the media. The more recognition we can give to it, the better off we shall all be. (I would take it, for example, that Ambassador Holland is a natural leader of this segment of the black community. There are others like him.)

A Georgia resident sent $5 to Moynihan to get a haircut and complained about Nixon policies destroying "the white people of the south."

JANUARY 30, 1970

Dear Mr. Smith:

It is not every day one receives such an interesting letter, and with a check enclosed!

It would not be appropriate for me to use the money for personal adornment or otherwise, but I do mean to add it to my annual contribution to the National Association for the Advancement of Colored People, and I do thank you for your generosity.

Moynihan valued the advice of David Riesman, the Harvard sociologist, when he and Nathan Glazer revised BEYOND THE MELTING POT.

FEBRUARY 2, 1970

Dear Dave:

First, let me tell you how extremely grateful both Nat and I are for your endlessly informative, helpful and generous comments on the new version of the Melting Pot. I confess to have a tendency to underestimate the intellectual force of Catholicism in New York. I would only argue that this involves a fairly small group of people and is, as it were, somewhat secret knowledge at this time. Surely its presence is hardly at all felt on the New York literary-political scene. Commonweal persists, but follows rather than leads the Left. Fitzpatrick works away but his books are not in fashion—compare their vogue to those written in the Columbia School of Social Work for example. Ilych is mostly in Mexico. Harrington is lapsed. And so it goes. Still you are right.

I am glad to see that you accept the thesis of social aggrandizement through social compassion. It has been bothering me for a long while and I felt the time had come to speak up. The trouble is I never know whether such things are true or even sort of true.

Finally, let me tell you how pleased I am to see that you agree, indeed have for years been working on the issue of verbal violence. I don't know whether Nat left it in the final version, but I wrote a section describing the reversal of roles in New York City during the 1960's in which whites were placed in the situation that blacks had suffered in the South. i.e., that would be the subject of constant vilification, and could not answer back. I went through a little bit of that myself and know the mood that follows. One only can suppose that it is a much more general mood now that the pattern of attack is so much more general.

Somehow I cling to the faith that saying these things helps people recognize what is going on and has some effect on what goes on thereafter. Do you? . . .

Moynihan's concerns about domestic terrorism, expressed to Haldeman, were fueled by violent activities of the Black Panthers and student radical groups. In March 1970, a group of young radicals belonging to the Weathermen (later the Weather Underground) and led by Cathy Wilkerson accidentally blew up a townhouse in Greenwich Village in New York City. In August 1969, the pregnant actress Sharon Tate (who was married to Roman Polanski at the time) and others were murdered in their home in Los Angeles. A family of hippies and criminals led by Charles Manson who were living on a commune at a ranch in Topanga Canyon were convicted of the murders. The SNCC refers to the Student Non-Violent Coordinating Committee, a civil rights group whose members later became increasingly militant.

MARCH 12, 1970

MEMORANDUM FOR MR. H. R. HALDEMAN

For about a year now I have been keeping a file and thinking to send you a memo on the subject of terrorism. The time has come.

It seems to me that we have simply got to assume that in the near future there will be terrorist attacks on the national government, including members of the Cabinet, the Vice President, and the President himself. We do not know this. It is not knowable. But we have to act as if it were going to happen, much as the military in peace has to act on the presumption that it might at any moment be at war.

In a legitimate sense, the war has already begun. The level of political violence has been escalating steadily for the past two to three months. In the last week bombs have been exploding up and down the Eastern seaboard. So far only the terrorists appear to have been killed. But that has to be regarded essentially as part of the learning process. We have to assume, for example, that the Mad Dog faction of the Weathermen will in time learn to make anti-personnel bombs, as they evidently were trying to do in Miss Wilkerson's house on West 11th Street in New York City last weekend. We have to assume that the SNCC organizers will learn to transport bombs, as evidently Featherstone and Payne were doing on Monday night. We have to assume those folks blowing up corporation headquarters in New York City will turn to blowing up corporation heads. In the meantime, today, schools and offices all over Washington are receiving bomb threats.

Political violence is not new to the nation. We are alone among the "stable" democracies in the number of presidents we have had assassinated. Our early labor history was singularly violent. And into our time whites have ruled over blacks in the South with the threat and the use of violence. (Think what you will of the Black Panthers. They still haven't blown up any children in church.) But I do believe the present situation is different. What we are facing is the onset of nihilism in the United States. The characteristics of the phenomenon are well enough known [from] 19th Century European experience, especially in Russia. The three most important points are that nihilists are almost entirely drawn from the educated, even upper classes. They are extremely idealistic, seeing themselves as agents of the purist charity. They are violent in the most extreme ways. There is perhaps a fourth point. Nihilist movements typically have led to political regimes of the most oppressive and reactionary qualities, be they of the Left or Right. (e.g., the Bolsheviks in large measure reaped the nihilist harvest.) . . .

There is also an element of psychopathology in all this. Just how much I don't know—wouldn't know how to know—but consider that at the last convention of the Weathermen Charles Manson's photograph was everywhere. He and his band of psychotics were the cultural heroes of the occasion. Consider Bernadine Dohrn, interorganizational secretary of SDS for 1968–69 addressing the conference, rhapsodizing to the Convention on the murders in Los Angeles.

"Dig it, first they killed those pigs, then they ate dinner in the same room with them, then they even shoved a fork into a victim's stomach! Wild!!" (Liberation News Service, Guardina, January 10, 1970.)

II

It would be impossible to say just why all this is breaking out at this moment, but it is pretty clear that certain events have contributed to the rush of events.

* The trial of the Chicago Seven was a terrible setback to the cause of social stability. Even Life magazine headed its editorial "Justice in Chicago: an ominous farce." Authority was made to look foolish, incompetent, impotent, corrupt. (Of all the people who buy judgeships in Chicago, how could we have chosen Hoffman?) Every possible opportunity was given the defendants to undermine the legitimacy of the most fragile of all institutions in a democracy, the courts, and they used every opportunity. And why shouldn't they have done, with a jerk like Hoffman on the bench, trying a case under that miserable law.) At the time of the sentencing, Rennie Davis declared "We're going to turn the sons and daughters of the ruling classes in this country into Viet Cong." He meant it. And at very least, it can be said he turned some of them into a mob that burns branch offices of the Bank of America.

* Police encounters with the Black Panthers, and the unprotesting way in which we have allowed to be assumed that all this is directed by the Justice Department has greatly abetted the idea in left circles that it is the Federal government and not the nihilists who are being violent.

* The general presumption that we have allowed to develop that we are rolling back on civil rights, etc., however untrue, does both encourage and in a curious way legitimate violent attacks on government. (Lamar, S.C., legitimates . . . what?)

III

I think we have to respond to this in some systematic way. It simply won't do to add the extra guard detail here or there, or to pay for a few more informers, etc. At least central issues have to be considered.

First, we must take a thorough look at the question of the security of the President. Times simply have changed.

Second, someone really ought to look into the question of just who is in charge of our intelligence in these areas. Really, dealing with the old Stalinist Communist Party was child's play compared to dealing with the Weathermen.

The Communist Party was a hierarchical, rational organization. We are dealing with diffuse, decentralized, irrational, even psychotic groups.

Third, we ought to ask ourselves how the government can act in such a way as to minimize the spread of the present mood and tactics of the Left. This is not easily done, but I think it can be. It is a subject that will respond to thought.

Seven radical anti-war protesters who helped disrupt the Democratic Convention in Chicago in 1968 were later charged with conspiracy and inciting to riot in 1969. The explosive trial became a cause célèbre for the antiwar movement. Protesters' anger focused on the heavy-handed tactics of Judge Julius Hoffman, who at one point ordered Bobby Seale, a Black Panther defendant, bound and gagged in the courtroom to prevent him from interrupting the proceedings. The defendants— including the yippie leader Abbie Hoffman (no relation to the judge), Jerry Rubin, and Tom Hayden—taunted and assailed the judge throughout the trial. Bobby Seale was later tried separately. The proceedings led to acquittals of most charges in 1970 and a reversal of most of the remaining convictions in 1972. Moynihan plainly worried that whatever the merits, charging these dissenters was backfiring and Judge Hoffman's tactics were a political disaster.

APRIL 3, 1970

CONFIDENTIAL

MEMORANDUM FOR THE PRESIDENT

John Ehrlichman stopped by this afternoon to report he had talked with you about the assignment of Judge Hoffman to the new conspiracy trial in Chicago. I had raised the matter with him at lunch, telling him how desperately depressed I was.

I believe the disservice being done you in incalculable. The kookiest left wing nihilist <u>might</u> have predicted that the Federal government would move against the Weatherman, using the same miserable statute employed against the Chicago 7. Such a person, given the notoriously weak grasp of reality of upper middle class radicals, <u>might</u> have predicted that the Assistant Attorney General of the United States would declare it to be the intention of the administration to wipe out the leadership of the Weatherman. But no one, no matter how kooky, no matter how deranged, would have dared predict Julius Hoffman would be assigned the trial.

We have played right into their hands. They will win, we will lose. The courts will lose. The erosion of authority will continue, the legitimacy of American institution will be weakened, the polarization of the society increased. . . .

I may seem a bit overwrought, but I strongly feel that we are at a moment of crisis, and I would like to talk with you about it. Surely there is something we can learn from our experiences with the Black Panthers and the "Chicago 7." But are we?

Nixon's expansion of the Vietnam War, including his intervention in Cambodia in 1970, ignited protests across the country. The deaths of four students at Kent State University in Ohio, shot by National Guardsmen, became a milestone that turned many Americans against the administration and the war, but that also caused conservatives alarmed by the protests to rally around the White House. At Yale, a protest against the war and the trial of Black Panthers in New Haven led the university president, Kingman Brewster, to sympathize with their cause as he tried to calm the campus.

MAY 6, 1970
<u>CONFIDENTIAL</u>

MEMORANDUM FOR THE PRESIDENT

. . . The culture is becoming politicized.

The culture is now centered in the Universities. Traditionally these have been politically neutral. (If the faculty has been liberal, the administrators and trustees have been conservative. Etc.) But a number of events (as I see them) have combined to politicize them. <u>First</u>, universities have grown enormously in size and number. Five hundred thousand faculty members, seven million students. Roughly the size of the C.I.O. unions. <u>Second</u>, the Vietnam war and the Negro revolution brought intense emotional issues to the campus, which engaged the allegiance of students of otherwise widely differing politics and life styles. <u>Third</u>, a combination of cultural movements has produced a younger generation of middle class students very much more willing than any in our past to take to the streets in the traditional style of working class turbulence. (Although students have also acted this way before.)

From the onset of the Vietnam war to the end of the Johnson Administration there was a mounting demand from students and faculty that the universities become political actors, primarily matters with respect to Vietnam, but also with respect to matters such as racial equality. With rare exceptions university administrators resisted these demands (agreeing, as they should have, to increasing black enrollments and things like that, but not to becoming political actors). Sometimes they won; sometimes they lost. But until recently when they have lost it has simply meant that they fell in battle. Another man replaced them, pledged to defend the same principles.

The fundamental change that took place over this winter is that the administrators have now in very large numbers joined the faculty and students. They have accepted the politicization of the universities, which is to say the culture. Thus the 39 university and college Presidents who wrote you on Monday did not ask that you exempt their students from the draft, or help with their money troubles, or whatever. They demanded that you change American foreign policy in Southeast Asia.

It would seem to me that two general events of the past year have led to this result. The first is simply that the pressure got too great for the administrators to withstand. Too many good men were going under. The destruction of Nathan Pusey—an honest and courageous man—by the students and faculty of Harvard, the one institution that was thought invulnerable to such attacks, was I think a general signal that the time for resistance was nearing an end. There was of course nothing we could do about this. Unfortunately, we are exclusively responsible for the second factor in the collapse of the administrators, namely that we began to attack the university community including the administrators. First under the generic heading of "effete intellectual snobs," and latterly by name. Fleming must go. Brewster must go. Etc.

Yale was the turning point. Kingman Brewster is not much for lost causes. Still, he was resisting the "fanatically argued" demand that the university associate itself with the Black Panthers. (That being the description by a Yale professor of the debates that went on last week.) The pressure was mounting. He was bending. But not breaking. Then of a sudden the Vice President attacked him. In a flash he joined the students; Yale went on strike; and a new era began in American politics.

The deaths of four students at Kent State University simply precipitated what was going to happen anyway. Or so would be my analysis. . . .

I don't know what counsel I would offer you at this moment, but I do feel you ought at least to know how I interpret the events of the past months. Moreover, there is one specific issue that I think you should deal with, namely the posture of the Administration with respect to Federal interference in university affairs.

It seems to me that with respect to this critical matter you have done exactly what is right—both in terms of what is good for the university, and what is good for the Presidency. Unfortunately, at almost every turn your position has been undermined or subverted by the Vice President. As a result you have been either made to look weak, or to look duplicitous. (Even the most sophisticated university administrators—this at least is my experience—simply cannot believe that the Vice President's speeches are not cleared in advance.) Either way, the Presidency has been weakened. . . .

What to do?

First, I think it important to realize that you can't do much. Great damage has been done and will not easily be undone.

Second, I would hope you might stick to your clearly stated position— hands off university affairs. You are on record to this effect from March 1969, and you restated the exact position in March of this year. This is a record which I think you should point to.

Finally, I would hope it were possible to insist that all members of the Administration adhere to your position.

This might do some good. I think you would be amazed at the number of persons who really see the Vice President's speeches as an attempt by you to take over the nation's universities. (Just as "everyone knows" that you have commissioned the Rand Corporation to study what should be done if student/radical disorders become such that you are forced to cancel the 1972 Presidential elections.)

But to repeat: we should not expect much peace for some time to come. There are people around here who no more understand the explosive nature of the ideas they have been tossing around than did those kids on 12th Street in Greenwich Village understand how to make nitroglycerin from dynamite.

※

Moynihan grew more and more concerned that the Kent State killings and other protests were driving the country apart. He was also concerned that inflammatory speeches by Vice President Spiro T. Agnew were aggravating the climate.

MAY 7, 1970

CONFIDENTIAL

MEMORANDUM FOR THE PRESIDENT

The most important two things to do in your press conference tomorrow are: First, to make clear to the students that you are not out to punish them. Second, to make clear to the nation that you have not been "captured" by the military.

I am getting old and cynical, and certainly I have been fed up with the liberal left a lot longer than most, but I am frankly surprised at the universality and vehemence of these beliefs. You don't need details, but I will offer one. This morning in a delegation from Grinnell College a middle aged lady put it to me: "I am an Iowa Republican. I voted for Goldwater. I am terrified at what you are doing to the country."

Ergo: you must try to restore confidence and calm.

1. Students.

I doubt anybody around here quite understands how menacing the administration has seemed to students and faculties alike.

* The Vice President has gone around denouncing students, calling for the resignation of college presidents, in the manner of Joe McCarthy, and generally giving the administration the reputation for harassment and oppression. The Attorney General has, often unfairly, been similarly identified.
* In your Cambodian address you seemed to associate the enemy in Indochina with your political opposition on campus. "Here in the United States, great universities are being systematically destroyed. The remark next day about "bums" (which was perfectly understandable to me—you were sending men into battle, you were tired, you were annoyed) added to the impression. The statement given out in your name after the deaths at Kent State University confirmed it. The Monday statement, which I know you wrote, and which in other circumstances would have been

perfectly appropriate, seemed to blame the deaths on the students. It was widely interpreted as a sign that you approved what the National Guard had done. Signs everywhere on campuses assert that you ordered the action. (I know you can take this kind of memo. I wished I could be sure that I could if I were in your shoes.)

I would therefore make very clear that you are only opposed to violence, and that only because it destroys the freedom of the university. You believe in dissent. But you fear the impulse to oppression that will grow still greater unless dissent is peaceful. You do not want the Federal government interfering in colleges and universities. You have repeatedly said just that, and that is the position of the administration.

As for those kids at Kent State University, the action of the National Guard is utterly to be deplored, as any military officer, any experienced soldier will agree. The men involved can be forgiven. They were untrained and panicky. But their action cannot be condoned and must not be repeated. The governors of the states must assume their responsibility to see that this is not repeated. Next time it will not do to blame it on a private. The officers of the guard—militarily and politically must be held responsible. By the public and by the Federal government.

I would retract the statement about "bums." You could make perfectly clear that you were talking about persons such as those that burned the life work of Professor Srinivas at the Center for Advanced Studies in the Behavioral Sciences at Palo Alto, to whom you had just written. (Letter attached.) Or who had tried to burn the Yale Law Library. But you appreciate that it was understood to apply to all who protest the war in Vietnam and you intended nothing of the sort. . . .

The protests by Students for a Democratic Society (SDS) at Harvard after the Cambodian intervention affected Moynihan and his family personally. Reports that SDS planned to "trash" the Moynihan house prompted Liz and the children to leave. The protest petered out.

MAY 9, 1970

CONFIDENTIAL

MEMORANDUM FOR THE PRESIDENT

Yesterday in Cambridge the SDS announced that my house would be burned during the night. The University asked my family to "evacuate" and they, in effect, went into hiding. Six Divinity students guarded the house, and nothing finally happened. I don't know what will come tomorrow.

Even so, I'm sticking here. I am choosing the interests of the administration over the interests of my children. But this would be the act of a fool if I did not feel free to tell you exactly what I think, and to feel that you at least were hearing me out.

As you know, I think you were superb last night. What you said was masterful and truthful. But allow me to call attention to three additional items from the morning press.

* Vice President Agnew in a speech text described the protesters as "choleric young intellectuals and tired, embittered elders" and for good measure denounced the Chairman of the Senate Foreign Relations Committee.
* (AP)—"Clark R. Mollenhoff, special counsel to President Nixon, Friday night characterized those causing college disorders as 'thugs and outlaws.'"
* (Washington Post.) "A Small Business Administration press release said yesterday that 'when the Democrats ousted Senator (Ralph) Yarborough, they repudiated their own dismal record and delivered a knockout blow to the bloated monarchs of one party rule in Texas.'
  - "The release printed by government employees on SBA equipment, contained excerpts from a speech SBA administrator Hilary Sandoval, Jr. will make tonight in El Paso.
  - "It is a violation of federal law for civil service employees to engage in partisan political activities.
  - "An SBA official said last night that 'somebody goofed'."

I don't think you can afford this. It makes you look duplicitous. You take the high road, your aides take the low road. You talk of political sacrifice, they capitalize on it. Etc.

If you are willing to pursue a high risk foreign policy—as you feel you must, and I do not contest your judgment—it seems absolutely necessary that you call a halt to the vulgar partisanship (e.g. Sandoval) and hysterical demagoguery (e.g. Agnew) of people theoretically on your team.

Young men on the White House staff have been meeting all day with groups of protestors. Maybe they saw three hundred. How many millions hear Huntley-Brinkley describe the Vice President's remarks, or read of Mollenhoff.

This is the kind of thing that forced Bob Finch this morning to allow that the Vice President's remarks surely contributed to the atmosphere that led to the killings at Kent State.

<u>Should you not consider the possibility of something like a national government?</u> You talked of this just after the election when there was an air of national crisis. We are once again in such a situation. I think you need a broader political base. At very least, you need to call off attacks on groups whose support, or at least acquiescence, you need.

Moynihan's young staff, some of them Democrats, grew increasingly uncomfortable as antiwar protests mounted. Some of them resigned themselves. This letter of resignation to Nixon was not sent, and it contained several phrases and words that were crossed out and are unreadable. A separate toned-down draft is in the files dated May 13, but neither was it sent.

MAY 12, 1970

Dear Mr. President:

With a regret that I am sure will only deepen with time, I must ask to resign.

I should first make clear that I am not leaving directly because of any act of yours with respect either to foreign or domestic policy.

I leave because of a seeming inexorably mounting condition of American life which I feel must be addressed, but which cannot be openly engaged by a member of the cabinet, especially one who is also, and in essence, a member of the White House staff. The extremes of left and right have joined in a dance of death. They are dancing around the institution of the Presidency, as around every other institution of order and reason in American society: The courts, the universities, the places of public assembly, and, not least, the streets themselves. . . .

The left and right extremes have entered a symbiotic relationship which I believe they understand full well, but which those of us attached to the traditions of the American polity seem not to understand. Worse, of late, too many of us young and old, seem willing to exploit this changed condition for short term, narrow, shallow purposes. The extremists of the left and right need each other, complement each other, strengthen each other. With each day they grow stronger. The left speaks with ever greater confidence and expectation of The Repression. The right obliges with ever more suggestive gestures, and where it is within its power, actual events. I do not of course refer to organized political movements, but nonetheless to clearly recognizable tendencies that have ever more pronounced constituencies and demands. Such persons on the left look forward to something like fascism; their counterparts on the right are not unwilling to oblige. To repeat, they need, and complement, and strengthen one another.

What is at issue is the quality, and ultimately the survival of the American democracy. The drift of events must be resisted, and in time reversed. But this is not something easily done from within government while the war in Vietnam persists. . . .

My views on the war are well known to you, and have been from the outset of my service to you. That you have determined to seek peace by different means has never to my knowledge in any way [altered] our relationship. Yet I conclude the time has come to leave, and to do what I must on my own and elsewhere.

Even as anti-Nixon fervor surrounded him, Moynihan continued to apprise Jacqueline Kennedy Onassis of his devotion to her late husband and his efforts to renew Pennsylvania Avenue. From Athens, Mrs. Onassis (she had married the shipping magnate Aristotle Onassis in 1968) replied by handwritten note that she was "so touched" by the letter, adding: "I often wondered what had happened to all the hopes for Pennsylvania Avenue—I decided they had just fizzled away. . . . If anyone can make them materialize—it will be you. . . . Thank you, dear Pat."

MAY 29, 1970

Dear Jackie:

Today, of course, is President Kennedy's birthday. On behalf of President Nixon I went over to Arlington Cemetery this morning and laid a wreath. On the way back to the White House it suddenly came to me that I was going to spend most of the day working on a Presidential Message to Congress on the redevelopment of Pennsylvania Avenue. This was precisely the subject on which Bill Walton, Charlie Horsky and I were working when the news came from Dallas. He had left instructions that he wanted the plans ready to show to a group of Congressmen when he returned.

I have understood that this was one of a very few items on a list of things you felt he would have wanted finished, which you left with President Johnson. Anyway, I have stayed with it these many years. With any luck before the fortnight is out we will have a formal Presidential proposal and a bill.

If all goes well, I will send you copies. For the moment, greetings. We think of you often.

Moynihan continually pushed for the Family Assistance Plan, but opposition from both Republicans and Democrats were impossible to overcome. In a separate letter to Haldeman, Ehrlichman, and Labor Secretary George Shultz, Moynihan said "This is the NIXON administration. We need a NIXON program." But the Nixon administration abandoned the proposal as the 1972 election approached.

JULY 1, 1970

MEMORANDUM FOR THE PRESIDENT

I fear the chances are now less than even that Family Assistance will be passed this year, and if not this year, not this decade.

The problem lies in the Senate Finance Committee. Our people report that Senator Curtis is obviously out to kill the bill, that no Republican is resisting him, and that increasingly the Democrats see an opportunity to deny you this epic victory, and that at the same time blame you for the defeat.

The bill can be saved, but at this point only you can save it by working on the Republican Senators.

CHAPTER SIX

"... a President They Trust and Admire"

Moynihan concludes his two years of service in the Nixon White House and returns to Harvard. In his final months, however, he again pleads with the president to moderate his tone and battle for the center of American politics. In this period, Moynihan begins to see the awakening of conservatism as a respectable intellectual alternative to the bankruptcy of liberal intellectuals and to find common cause with others who have come to be called neoconservatives—even though that is a term he would never accept for himself. In these letters, Moynihan begins to see the emergence of an "adversary culture" with which he can no longer identify. After declining Nixon's offer to become United Nations ambassador, Moynihan accepts appointment as the public member of the U.S. delegation, a parttime job he held while at Harvard. In that capacity he pointedly disagreed with the Nixon administration's "tilt" toward Pakistan, which was heading toward military conflict with India over the creation of Bangladesh. Two years later, after his reelection, Nixon appointed Moynihan ambassador to India, and India accepted him as someone known to be sympathetic to its concerns. Nixon's reelection, meanwhile, is seen by Moynihan in these letters as a triumph that could heal the wounds of his first term—though he writes of his concerns about the possibility of Nixon's reescalation of the war in Vietnam in late 1972 and early 1973.

Nixon's embattled press secretary, Ron Ziegler, developed a warm and sometimes teasing relationship with Moynihan. Moynihan's professed shock that Ziegler arrived

on foot at a Washington dinner elicited this response from the press secretary: "First of all, let's get one thing straight. When you've been in as many Presidential motorcades as Ziegler has, the thrill is definitely gone."

JULY 9, 1970

MEMORANDUM FOR RON ZIEGLER

At about 1932 hours last evening I was arriving at the NWPC [National Women's Press Club] dinner in the Presidential motorcade. I was accompanied by my hostesses Kay Graham, who is a publisher of the <u>Washington Post</u>, and Meg Greenfield, a member of their editorial staff. We were exiting from Rock Creek Park, preparatory to the 240 yard leg northwest followed by descent to the hotel rear entrance when, well let me put it this way, Ron, we were all surprised to see you standing on the corner, apparently walking to the reception.

Despite her gay and sometimes seemingly artless charm, Kay Graham is a tough, seasoned observer of the Washington scene, and it was not hard to see that some observations were going through her mind. I quickly made light of it all, saying something to the effect that "I see Ron has a night off." I added the usual kind of remark about how hard you work, and how I just don't see how anybody can do it all. (And, honestly, Ron, I don't.) But Kay would know that I would have sensed her observation and would try to distract her. I frankly fear that my intervention did not succeed.

I know that appearances mean little to you, Ron, and that many of the supposed perquisites of White House office seem more like burdens or even unnecessary expenditures to someone whose life has been so much lived in the more easy going atmosphere of the Far West. Yet this just isn't the way the game is played here in Washington. People—and especially the Press, who are after all people just like everyone else—expect to see you in an official White House car, <u>with the President.</u> (I would be less than candid if I did not say that more than a few persons noted that I <u>was</u> in the motorcade, and enquired in that sort of casual, nonchalant way of the Washington Press corps as to whether my duties might not be shifting.)

You and I, Ron, have had a good many straight-from-the-shoulder conversations, so I don't think you will mind this short note. It will be clear that I am thinking about your future. And believe me, Ron, you have one. But you have got to keep ever in mind the rule that <u>appearances count.</u>

The National Urban Coalition, an alliance of civic leaders supporting more aid to cities, ran an article in its journal criticizing Moynihan. He objected to John W. Gardner, former secretary of Health, Education, and Welfare and chairman of the group.

JULY 17, 1970

Dear John:

I am writing to you to express considerable disappointment in the article in the current issue of <u>City</u>, published by the National Urban Coalition, which states in so many words that I have given the President "seriously misleading" data concerning the economic and social conditions of Negroes.

Whatever else is to be said I think—I hope!—you will agree that I have standards about public service. I do not give the President of the United States misleading statistics. ...

I want you seriously to know, and Heiskell and Eberle also, that I regard my honor as having been impugned.

In worrying about the dangers of political instability and extremism, Moynihan tried to get Haldeman, Ehrlichman, and others at the White House to develop a coherent, conservative approach to governing with the help of conservative intellectuals.

JULY 24, 1970
<u>PERSONAL & CONFIDENTIAL</u>

MEMORANDUM FOR
JOHN D. EHRLICHMAN
H. R. HALDEMAN

Over last weekend I found myself thinking about our brief discussion of the difficulty the administration seems to have in linking up with competent, respected conservative thinkers. I had not the time, as they say, to write a brief memorandum, and so I send you this, as I felt both of you were interested in the subject. You should be: the Presidency is at stake.

You will recall my saying that I thought the President was ill-served by a sequence of administrative acts whereby the liberals of the country, having first been brought to the point of frenzied fear and detestation of us, are then empanelled, in various guises, as formal Boards of Enquiry to pass judgment on the administration record.

Having just read the [Alexander] Heard report, I am ever more persuaded of this view. I await the report of the Commission on Campus Disorders where, as John Roche writes me, we will learn that the killings were caused by "racism, poverty, and war." The Heard report fundamentally asserts that the administration has failed, and should be replaced. The Commission report will get as close to that as Scranton will allow. The premises on which this conclusion will be based are, to my mind, intellectually disgraceful. The problem is that no one, especially no one outside the administration, is willing to demonstrate this. There are any number of persons who believe it. Our task should be to give them some reason for saying it.

You may further recall my impression of Republicans, after living among them as an interested and sympathetic observer for almost two years, as a group you have almost no confidence that any serious thinker could be with you on any issue of consequence. Economists, perhaps, but few others. To a Republican a serious thinker is a liberal Democrat or a left wing anti-democrat. I said finally that this reminded me somewhat of the situation of the English Catholics in the mid-nineteenth century. It was a demoralized church in the sense that none of the bishops really felt himself the social or intellectual equal of the Anglican establishment. They assumed the Protestants had won the theological battles, and for their part were resigned to tending to the equally undemanding religious needs of the Duke of Norfolk on the one hand, and the Liverpool Irish on the other. From time to time, however, men of great and acknowledged intellectual powers would convert to Catholicism and ask to be put to work. The bishops were at a loss to think what to do with them, and for the most part simply avoided the issue. What none knew was that they were at the beginning, not the end of a process. Triumphant Protestantism had just about run out of intellectual and spiritual authority. England was becoming dechurched. In the Century that was to follow English Catholics were, by contrast, to be an intellectual and spiritual force of considerable consequence. I have, as I say, a somewhat similar feeling about this moment with respect to political ideology. In the best universities the best men are increasingly appalled by the authoritarian tendencies of the left. The inadequacies of traditional liberalism are equally unmistakable, while, not least important, the credulity, even the vulgarity of the supposed intellectual and social elite of the country has led increasing numbers of men and women of no especial political persuasion to realize that something is wrong somewhere.

These persons are the President's natural allies. They can be of help to him, and to the country. But I do not see them brought into our counsels. Mostly, if I am right, because of a sense of inadequacy hereabouts. Better stick with Kate Smith and the Silent Majority. They aren't very smart, but then neither are we.

As I say, I feel this is wrong, and that something of importance is at issue. Moral authority and political power.

Pragmatism is a noble political tradition. It is vulnerable, however, to a form of oversight which can be calamitous. The pragmatic mind in politics tends to underestimate, even to be unaware of, the importance of moral authority. In a nation such as ours, and especially at a time such as this, moral authority is a form of political power. For many groups within the society it is the most important form of power.

A consequence of this is that individuals and groups struggle for moral authority. This struggle can assume surpassingly complex and involute forms, but it is at bottom pretty much an affair of tooth and claw. Those who ignore it, do so at their peril.

For some years now the struggle for moral authority has centered on two issues: the war in Vietnam and the blacks. In the course of this a subtle change has occurred. Originally the struggle was directed to control of the government. Increasingly, however, some of the most important players—the educated young, the upper class left, the more ambitious blacks—have become, in effect, anti-government.

Thus it was inevitable that an element in our Commission on Campus Unrest should wish to place the moral authority of the Presidency on trial. The killings at Kent State and Jackson State fused the issues of the war and the blacks and the emerging one of youth as a social class. If it can be established that Richard Nixon's finger was on the trigger there will be a corresponding transfer of moral authority away from the Presidency. . . .

Why am I troubling you about all this?

Two reasons.

The first is that I sense that in a number of ways the administration is beginning to feel that things began to go wrong for us last Fall, and that some reanalysis is in order. This suggests it may be useful to restate some of my ear-lier views about our general situation. Second, I would like to offer some thoughts for the future.

The erosion of authority of American government.

As best I can tell, I got my job in the Nixon administration as the result of a speech given in 1967 to the board of Americans for Democratic Action in which I proposed that American politics were approaching instability, and that liberals who understood this should seek out and make alliances with their conservative equivalents in order to preserve democratic institutions from the looming forces of the authoritarian left and right. It seemed to me the three-way split in the election made the argument even more compelling. I took the President's offer of a job to me as an indication that he shared this view, or at least appreciated it enough to be willing to have someone around with such opinions. . . .

My contribution to lowering the voices occurred early on, and took the form primarily of a series of Presidential statements and messages in which he made clear that he would not dismantle the Great Society. The Poverty Program was to stay; Model Cities was to keep on; Head Start was to con-tinue, etc., etc. This was, I think, setting a tone. The campaign rhetoric was left behind; thoughtful and accepting statements were issued to the effect that for all their faults the innovations of the previous administration would not be scrapped. I repeat that this is a rhetorical stance (as well, of course, as a substantive one). One of the great inventions of democracy has been the prac-tice of parties returned to power accepting the changes that had occurred while they were in opposition. Thus Eisenhower and Dulles accepted the for-eign policy of Truman and Marshall. This was a fundamental act that deter-mined the stability of American Foreign Policy after World War II. It seemed to me that if Nixon were to do the same in domestic affairs, a similar stabi-lizing effect would occur. By and large I think this did occur. After six months in office there was a distinct sense of returning to social peace, while the Office of the Presidency was clearly on the mend. (Let me say here that Paul Mc-Cracken asserted the same continuity in economic policy—and this has been acknowledged by Democratic economists such as Arthur Okun.)

My second task was more subtle. I wanted to put together a set of govern-mental themes by which the administration would be known and understood. (It seemed to me especially urgent to do this as the fiscal and monetary situ-ation of the moment would require us to act almost as caricatures of classic Republicans worrying about the value of money, rising unemployment, cutting the budget, etc.) I am, I hope, sufficiently professional about political ideas to have had some feeling for what could be done, and by and large we did it. Those Urban Affairs Council meetings might have seemed chaotic and ill staffed to some, but in about four months I would dare to argue that we gave an intellectual raison d'être to the Nixon administration. (With powerful assists, of course, from other parts of the White House.) What I would hope to persuade you of is that I was trying to put together something more than a random collection of programs. I was looking for programs based on Republican ideas or precedents, or barring that, which would make sense to Republicans. Allow me a few examples.

a. <u>The Principle of Policy Oriented Government.</u> As best I can read the Eisenhower administration, it was always striving for orderliness in government, but could never find a conceptual tool for achieving it. Government is too complex. In the end they settled for an appearance of more order by attempting less government. (In the process storing up some of the domestic disasters of the 1960's.) We came forward with the idea of policy as against program oriented government. The cybernetic idea of policy <u>does</u> provide a conceptual tool to achieve the Eisenhower goal. It is, moreover, an <u>advanced</u> idea. Accordingly, among other things, it would attract the notice of persons who are serious about government.

The first task of the UAC was to formulate a national urban policy. By late February I had produced a draft. I published it in <u>The Public Interest</u>, and devoted a book to it (<u>Toward a National Urban Policy,</u> Basic Books, 1969). More recently I published a paper on the principle of policy, also in <u>The Public Interest.</u> I have had quite a reasonable response to all this from the political science world. <u>The problem is no response whatever, from Republicans, other than the President, George Shultz, and a few men around the White House such as yourselves.</u>

b. <u>The Principle of Reform.</u> If there was one idea waiting to be picked up when we came in it was that modern government isn't working. You recall I sent the President an article by Peter Drucker which declares that the only things modern governments seem able to do [are] to wage war and inflate the currency. All else fails. Hence we began a whole series of measures directed to the issue of enabling government actually to achieve the goals it proclaims. This continuity with something extra. President Nixon would not only keep Head Start, he would try to see that compensatory education actually did some compensating. (The National Institute of Education, etc.) Some reform ideas came forward naturally, as in the case of Selective Service. Others were there for the taking, as in the case of Revenue Sharing which was one of Mel Laird's many creative ideas as a Congressman.

Before long it was clear to me that we had made a record here. A year ago I sent a note to Haldeman on the theme of a Reform Administration, and this was the <u>subject of a detailed Presidential Message to Congress in October.</u>

But what then? Nothing. As best I can tell, no one in the administration took any heed of the President's message.

c. <u>The Principle of Future Planning.</u> <u>I will not linger on this one as the experience has been rather too painful.</u> Briefly, on July 13, 1969 the President announced the formation of a National Goals Research Staff, to begin the systematic exploration of future options. In the announcement and the press briefing, I went to considerable pains to point out that only two Presidents in our past history had attempted anything of this kind: Herbert Hoover and Dwight Eisenhower. i.e., it was a <u>Republican</u> idea. <u>However, from the outset the White House has treated it as some crazy socialist scheme.</u> In the recent report we did move the President's idea of a National Growth Policy a few feet forward, and we did not add too much to our emerging reputation for ideological pettiness. But to repeat, it was and is a Republican idea that Republicans seem instantly suspicious of. (And to think I spent a month wading through Recent Social Trends—the Hoover product—in the simple minded expectation that I could persuade these new Republicans otherwise.)

d. <u>The Principle of the Income Strategy.</u> Of all the domestic issues inherited by the President those of poverty and race were the most complex. The previous administrations had approached them with a bewildering range of service programs, many of which were profoundly flawed, and none of which was particularly effective. A break with the past was in order, and there existed a brilliant <u>Republican</u> alternative: the Family Assistance Plan.

Does anyone around here understand that this is a Republican idea? (Milton Friedman's.) And that it is just about the best social idea of the second half of the Twentieth Century. Allow me to put it that <u>this</u> Democrat does, and so does my neighbor and friend John Kenneth Galbraith.

> This idea unquestionably belongs to the Republicans. The guaranteed income, in a variant called the negative income tax, was first influentially broached by Professor Milton Friedman of the University of Chicago, a man of highly independent mind, is not reliably wrong or even conservative. Liberal economists, most notably James Tobin, who was one

of President Kennedy's economic advisers, have improved the idea. But it was President Nixon who proposed it to Congress. Though the rate suggested—$1600 for a family of four—is derisory, the political authorship of the idea is not in doubt.*

I am beginning to sound contentious and I don't want to overdo. It would not be fair to say that no Republicans have recognized FAP (along with abolition of income taxation on the poor, and the provisions of our proposed Manpower Act of 1970—remember the Principle of Policy) as a creative Republican contribution of social policy. To the contrary, as I said in a recent speech to the Urban Coalition, support for the measure has come almost exclusively from corporation presidents. They get it. The question, as the President once asked me, is why doesn't the Cabinet? Why doesn't the Republican side of the Senate? Why doesn't the Republican National Committee?

There is a point to this endless essay.

I genuinely feel that the failure within the administration to grasp the intellectual coherence of the administration's program has led to a great deal of the most serious kind of trouble. The administration took office and did brilliantly for six months. The initiative was all with us. Then, inevitably a counterattack began. Significantly it did not come from the Democratic party, the leaders of which could readily enough see that we were turning out to be as good or better than they on their own ground of program formulation. The attack came, rather, from the Peace Movement and the Civil Rights Movement. In both cases what they challenged was the moral authority of the administration. In both cases (despite some mildly disgraceful hanky panky with Southern racists) there were perfectly good answers which the administration could have given, but which it did not. Nor did anybody on our behalf.

The result was the disastrous sequence that began more or less with the Vice President's speech at Des Moines and continued until the end of June, 1969. Attacked, we attacked back. We began to raise our voices. Mistakes began to engender mistakes. All along there was one repeated phenomenon: we acted in such ways as to increase the moral authority of our opponents and to diminish our own. We tried to invoke the moral authority of the silent majority: the plain, good Americans who still Believe in God, and in America, and are proud to display the flag. The problem with this strategy is that

---

* Galbraith, John Kenneth, "Who Needs the Democrats," Harper's, July 1970.

it positioned the President on the side of one group of Americans, against another. We may not see it that way, but the other group did and does. Against the students, against the universities, against the journalists and commentators, against thoughtful opinion in general. Thus thoughtful opinion was relieved of any responsibility to take the President's programs seriously. . . .

What is to be done?

This first thing to be clear is that our own power to influence events is limited. America has developed, in Lionel Trilling's phrase, "an adversary culture." I wrote of this in a memorandum to the President of January 3, 1969. . . .

The "culture" is more in opposition now than perhaps at any time in history. The President will have to live with it permanently, I should think. We can't change this. As Richard Hofstadter recently observed, some really surprising event—equivalent to the Russian-German Non-Aggression Pact of 1939 is going to have to happen to change the minds of the present generation. But in the meantime it is within our power to make matters worse. We have shown that we can do so. I would argue that in such circumstances the first [rule] of patriotism is the willingness not to worsen things, even when the provocation is outrageous, even when there may appear to be a short term advantage to be gained.

This is not just the measure of patriotism, it is the measure of prudence as well. I would hope the events of the past winter will have demonstrated how extraordinarily weak we are. When attacked, nobody defends us. On a good day Senator Dole and David Lawrence. No one in the Congress, certainly no "liberal" Republican helps us. No one writes articles for us, much less books, or plays, or folk songs.

Nor are we very good at defending ourselves. Here permit me a sympathetic word about the Vice President. He alone of administration spokesmen has sought to take up some of the intellectual issues of the time and to argue the conservative case. But it has been a disaster for the President. Many things the Vice President says are true, at least I would think so. But there does not now exist a spectrum of opinion in which his views are seen to be located in a particular point, a bit to the left of this reasonable person, a bit to the left of that one. Opinion is so concentrated on the liberal left that Agnew's mildly conservative positions are easily portrayed as the voice of Radical Right. The Vice President has greatly contributed to this by attacking individuals by name. It might be argued that some had it coming to them—although the attacks on Flemming and Harriman were inexcusable—but the main point is that the attacks enabled the opposition to the administration to ignore anything of substance he said, and to depict even his most reasoned statements as the frenzied precursors of Fascist Repression. Never mind that anyone so fortunate to be attacked by the Vice President becomes an instant culture hero. The fact is that in the contest for moral authority, they win.

To repeat, this unequal condition will persist. Every consideration from patriotism to prudence suggests that we should accordingly be very careful about whom we pick fights with, because nine times in ten it is we who will end up both with the bloody nose, <u>and</u> the reputation for having hideously assaulted an innocent victim.

<u>At the same time, however, I would argue that we should begin devoting a much greater effort to expounding the administration's program and philosophy at a level of intellectual competence and concern.</u> A great deal of our problem with the press, for example, is that the ideological equipment they picked up in college five to twenty-five years ago is simply obsolete. Only a few of them sense this, and those who do naturally resist the idea. There is no alternative save to bring them in and go over the material and explain that we are perfectly aware of what they think, but that we think differently because as we see it the world has changed, and recent liberalism has not kept up with those changes. A post liberal critique is necessary and we are trying to evolve one: not because we don't know enough, but because we know too much to be content with the wisdom of the 1940's. Etc. <u>I have spent eighteen months in this building pouring gin into various newspapermen, and I can attest that it is possible to get them to consider the possibility that what I say might be true. But I can't do it anymore. It needs to be done by real Republicans.</u>

<u>Simultaneously, I believe the President has got to begin associating himself with academics and intellectuals</u> who are capable to understanding what he is up to, and able also to expand his own understanding on the basis of their special competencies. There are such persons. There are hundreds of them. The problem, to return to my opening theme, is that it seems impossible for a Republican activist really to believe this.

Let me put it this way. The Vice President has assembled an advisory group of writers and professors. I have a rough idea of the panel and I would not hesitate to state that for sheer intellectual distinction is head and shoulders above anything any Democratic candidate for President is likely to assemble for similar purposes.

A point to note about the Vice President's group is that (I would bet) most of its members are Democrats. The particular issues with which we must be concerned cross party lines. We should be willing to go wherever substantive support can be found. (After all, you keep me around.) . . .

Envoi

I have troubled you with all this because I am conscious that my time here-abouts is fast running out. I feel deeply about this matter. I don't yet feel others feel deeply enough. By which I mean, I feel that much of the trouble we are now somewhat unceremoniously trying to dig our way out of could have been averted had we kept in mind the precariousness of the President's—any President's—position in America at this moment. I restate it now in the thought that if anything is to be done there would still be time for me to be of some possible help.

Another chapter in Moynihan's twenty-five-year campaign to renew downtown Washington, particularly, Pennsylvania Avenue, and to keep Jacqueline Kennedy Onassis aware of his progress. Here he asks her to inform Senator Edward Kennedy of Nixon's help.

SEPTEMBER 8, 1970

Dear Jackie:

I know you will be pleased to learn that our Pennsylvania Avenue efforts continue, and even possibly brighten. Today the President and I took a one-hour tour of the area, after which he issued the enclosed statement in support of a bill to create a Federal City Bicentennial Development Corporation. This bill was drafted by us, but in those complex ways that they have, the principal Congressmen involved demanded that they be allowed to introduce the legislation as their own. The President said it mattered not at all to him, so long as the bill got passed. President Nixon really has been most supportive of this enterprise. He knows what it meant to President Kennedy and what it means to you. If I may say the contrast is refreshing.

I wonder if you might sometime mention this to Ted. For years I lobbied Bob on the subject. He was always very friendly, but I had the feeling that he only believed about half of what I was telling him about President Kennedy's involvement and that he generally regarded the whole matter as a harmless eccentricity on my part. I have not even tried to get through to Ted, who probably has his doubts about me these days anyway! It would help a bit if you did so. The problem of an enterprise of this kind is that while almost everybody is willing to <u>see</u> it happen, almost nobody is willing to make serious sacrifices to <u>make</u> it happen.

For that matter, you might even wish to send a note to the President as well.

Moynihan had tough advice for Francis Burr, a Boston attorney and senior fellow of the Harvard Corporation, about the search for a successor to the beleaguered outgoing Harvard president, Nathan Pusey, at a time of antiwar protests at the university.

DRAFT/MOYNIHAN/24 SEP 70
FRANCIS BURR, HARVARD UNIVERSITY (SENIOR FELLOW)

Dear Mr. Burr:

This is an unsolicited and almost certainly unnecessary letter. I don't want to appear emotional, but I am moved nonetheless by something very like emotion.

It happens I was at dinner the other evening in the home of a Washington journalist whose daughter is a graduate of Radcliffe and whose prospective son-in-law a graduate of Harvard. He comes from an old Harvard family, and old partners to my little tale are solid, upper middle-class and upper-class Americans, as you well know. The point of my tale is simple. These young people with absurd ferocity and unyielding intensity went on for four hours describing Harvard University under Nathan Pusey as a kind of Nazi death camp. Its evil was relieved only to the degree that it was representative of the whole of American society. I could hardly believe myself as the privileged young people described the regime of such a superb and liberal man as Nathan Pusey and _____, as oppressive, brutal and evil. They described their own lives in terms of near heroic endurance. (The young man repeatedly referred to his own experience as having been beaten insensible by the police. Only at the end of the evening did I learn that these were the Paris police.)

And most importantly of all, as the evening went by I found my willingness to resist their arguments steadily diminishing. I had not the strength. It was simply too much.

The minds of these young people were largely formed at Harvard, in an atmosphere that we somehow created that made legitimate their intense forms of behavior. I believe an element of our faculty has been largely responsible for this, but from out or within it has happened. I write simply to say that unless the next President of Harvard is a man who simply will not suffer the lying and deceiving intellectual outrages of the radical left, you're going to end up with a university in which the decent men simply do not try to serve their function of teaching and learning. It is simply too much. I would almost plead with you to try to understand the position of so many of your faculty, perhaps especially your Social Scientists. We were in surprising numbers born to working-class families. And surprisingly few of us went to Harvard. (You may have noted a footnote in the report of the Wilson Committee on <u>The University and the City</u> that noted that none of the eleven members President Pusey has appointed was in fact a Harvard man.) We are immensely proud of teaching at Harvard, but at the same time there is a limit to our endurance in the face of what is practically a form of class arrogance on the part of the children of the upper class who in this generation insist that we know nothing of the life of the poor much as their grandparents would have made clear we knew nothing of the well-to-do.

I think I speak for more persons than just myself when I say that nothing is more dispiriting for persons such as us than to observe the behavior of frightened patricians faced with the demands of these young people. It is our acceptability, and in many ways our careers, that are to be sacrificed. Up against the wall, a CCNY man has almost the first instinct of an old Porcellian when first faced by the nihilist threats of a billionaire's daughter. I assure there are a great many otherwise extremely attractive folks who are in this respect old Porcellians at heart. I plead with you not to deliver the university into the hands of one such. Perhaps I betray our own class, but you need a man with balls for this job. And brains.

Henry Kissinger, the national security adviser, was increasingly becoming a celebrity and seen about town with beautiful women.

NOVEMBER 5, 1970

MEMORANDUM FOR DR. HENRY KISSINGER

If I am the more photogenic, why is it that you get all the movie stars?

Moynihan decided to turn down Nixon's offer to appoint him ambassador to the United Nations.

NOVEMBER 24, 1970

<u>PERSONAL</u>

Dear Mr. President:

After a weekend of torment I have concluded that I must not go to the United Nations. My reasons are varied, but conclusive.

I fear my family simply could not take the strain. I have been away for two years. They have expected to resume a normal life; the prospect of not doing so has been a profound shock. For me to go forward with our plans nonetheless would be an act of callousness or worse.

What is more, I am penniless. When I came down here I had assets of some $60,000. These are now gone. Bills mount. It would be a grave mistake to suppose I could somehow manage the UN ambassadorship in such financial condition.

It is also clear to me that neither Bill Rogers nor Henry Kissinger really wants a change at the UN. They would have every reason not to. It would be foolish of me not to see this, and foolhardy to ignore it. In Secretary Rogers' case, the fact that the move leaked makes it doubly difficult for him. Ambassador Yost has been done a disservice for which, ultimately, I am responsible.

Finally, I am deeply depressed by the decision of the liberal Democrats to kill Family Assistance. I had hoped your administration would teach them something about the bases of political and social stability. I fear it has not, and now will not. I conclude I had best leave government and start writing again.

I would hope to stay where I am until Family Assistance is finally disposed of. Although I then return to Harvard I shall continue to be at your service for anything you might want that I might be able to provide.

It would be beyond me just at this moment to express adequately my respect for what you have done, my gratitude for the way I have been treated, and the extent of my wishes for your success.

Moynihan wanted Nixon to know that a new book by Edward Jay Epstein had a different take on the killings of black militants by the police.

DECEMBER 2, 1970

CONFIDENTIAL

MEMORANDUM FOR THE PRESIDENT

We talked yesterday about the situation with students, youth, universities and such like. You will recall my saying that what we most need is a period of calm and reassurance, and that the prospect for such a period would seem to be very good.

I would doubt that any of us fully realizes the degree to which young persons, intellectuals, and liberal persons generally have come to feel the country is in the grip of dark and sinister forces that are moving us toward some terrible fate. There is a kind of mass paranoia out there: a phenomenon not at all unusual in history, and as with early occurrences linked to certain genuine historical events. Thus I would imagine that the first hard political memory of most of the "youth" of the present time is the assassination of Kennedy.

(I have a ten-year-old boy of a basically serene and untroubled nature. But for some years now the one cloud in his existence is that he expects I will be killed, as was President Kennedy, Robert Kennedy, Dr. King, men he knows I worked with. Just yesterday the <u>New York Times</u> reviewed two books on the Kennedy assassination. The new editor of the book review made clear that he for one is not yet satisfied that we have been given the truth about the event. This is a pervasive attitude—and fear.)

Almost simultaneously with the advent of your Administration, a series of events occurred which significantly increased the level of fear. The most important of these was the trial of the Chicago Seven, an event of great visual and psychological power. Then a year later came the killing of two Black Panthers in a raid by the Chicago police, whereupon immediately the notion of a national conspiracy to "genocide" the Panthers took shape and was given great currency and respectability by the major news media. (Perhaps especially by the Times.) Then came Cambodia and the deaths at Kent and Jackson State. Six months ago middle-class youth—and their middle-class parents— were near to panic.

For whatever reason—I suspect the emotions were too intense to be sustained for long—the panic has ebbed. The campuses are quiet, and so are things generally. Here again, genuine events are involved. The fall elections, for example, were so utterly "normal" as to shake anyone's belief that apocalypse was nigh. No Panthers have been killed in eighteen months. The trials in New Haven and New York have been manifestly fair and open. There have been no urban riots. The war is closing down.

Simultaneously, and as importantly, voices of reasonableness and sanity are being raised with increasing clarity and insistence. A major event of this kind has just occurred. For the past six months a young friend of mine, Edward Jay Epstein, who is a graduate student at Harvard, has been writing a story for The New Yorker about the "plot" to "genocide" the Panthers. As best I can tell he was given the assignment in the expectation that he would demonstrate the existence of such a plot. (He is the author of Inquest, a devastating account of the way the Warren Commission did not do its job.)

They did not reckon on their man. Epstein went out and carefully, doggedly traced down the facts. The facts are roughly as follows. The white leftist lawyer (Garry) who first announced that the police had murdered twenty-eight Panthers—which "fact" was immediately accepted as gospel— when asked could only provide the names of twenty dead persons. Of these, ten were killed by other Panthers, other black militants, or other civilians. Of the remaining ten who were killed by police, all but two were killed by officers who had already been wounded. More than half the deaths occurred while Ramsey Clark was Attorney General.

The story is devastating. (Not least because in most of the cases the Black Panther account published in their own newspaper substantially agrees with the police account. They brag about killing pigs.) In the end one realizes that the charge of "genocide" was a vulgar, transparent, and almost certainly cynical fabrication. Which was instantly accepted as truth by the most respectable men and institutions of the nation. . . .

I would predict this will be a major intellectual event. Keep in mind that The New Yorker, while still by and large the most influential and respected journal of its kind in the country, has become increasingly radical. The word "repression" regularly appears in their commentary. They greeted your inauguration with a series of articles about the Department of Justice which depicted Ramsey Clark as a saint and John Mitchell as an evil and dangerous man, more or less avowedly intent on the destruction of civil rights and civil liberties in America. . . .

My point is this. Things are getting better. Probably the best thing for us to do is to do nothing. (Not that it matters, but that is what I really intended by the term "benign neglect." It seemed to me the young were getting ever more panicky about the Panther situation while the Justice Department was adding to the panic by acting as if it was really up to something.) This is a battle the Epsteins can win on their own.

And I would add, perhaps once too often, that here is yet another example of the Administration being supported on a fundamental issue of social stability—does the Department of Justice commit political murders—by a man you might suppose would be against us. Typically, when Epstein inquired of the Department of Justice whether or not the Attorney General had ever actually declared the Panthers to be a threat to national security, he got no answer. His suspicion was that the AG had said nothing of the sort, that the Times had just made it up. I talked to Dick Moore this morning, who shares that impression, and will get in touch with Epstein. But he was at first assumed to be an enemy. We need friends. . . .

Seeking help from Senator Ted Kennedy on the Pennsylvania Avenue development project.

DECEMBER 3, 1970

Dear Ted:

I am, of course, finishing up my two years and about to depart Washington. One of the things I leave behind not just from this Administration, but from the last one, and the one before that, is the question of Pennsylvania Avenue. This of course was one of the very important legacies left us by President Kennedy, and some of us have tried to see it through to completion. President Nixon has been completely supportive, but of late a new kind of opposition has been arising from the social welfare end of the spectrum, and I fear we are getting in trouble once more. The enclosed article will give you a sense of what I mean.

Could I stop by and see you about this? I really feel your help is essential here, but frankly I really don't know if it interests you. I'm afraid it did not interest Bob, although he was always endlessly patient with me on the subject. Jackie cares a good deal, but she of course is not in the Senate.

Moynihan warns Nixon about the reaction provoked by the arrest of two Catholic anti-war activists by the F.B.I. under its director, J. Edgar Hoover.

DECEMBER 7, 1970
FROM: DANIEL P. MOYNIHAN
SUBJECT: THE BERRIGAN BROTHERS

MEMORANDUM FOR THE PRESIDENT

On several occasions you have jokingly asked me about my religious affiliations, and I have been correspondingly irreverent in my responses. The time, however, is at hand to acknowledge that I am indeed a practicing Catholic, and have been involved in Church work more or less regularly over the years.

I report this because I feel I ought also to report my impression that within Catholic circles there has been a troubled, even angry reaction to Mr. Hoover's attack on Father Philip Berrigan and Father Daniel Berrigan. I fear this anger extends to you for the simplistic reason that outside the small circle of persons who know something about Washington, it is assumed Mr. Hoover, and all such officials, speak for the President.

I know Dan Berrigan, and would have to say to you that I am not especially sympathetic with either his politics or his theology. Nor, probably, are most Catholics. But the fact is that he is an ordained priest, as is his brother, and we are wont to put much store in such matters. It is hard for us to believe that the two of them, while in prison, are plotting, in any operational sense, to blow up the country. Which is what Hoover's charge came to. It seems not only absurd, but unfair. After all, they are Federal prisoners. Surely we can keep an eye on them.

It may be you know all about this. But if you do not, I would be happy to talk to the Attorney General to see if somehow we can't find out what Hoover is up to. (This is becoming an issue in Congress.)

By the by, in this week's TIME, Hoover is both needlessly insulting to a dead man, Martin Luther King, but outrageously and unforgivably so to ten million Puerto Ricans and Mexicans.

> "You never have to bother about a President being shot by Puerto Ricans or Mexicans. They don't shoot very straight. But if they come at you with a knife, beware."

I would estimate his interview will cost you between half a million votes in Florida, Texas, California, Illinois and New York in 1972.

Moynihan's closing tribute to Nixon at his farewell reception prompted many to ask for a transcript. Here, he sends one to Robert Hampton, chairman of the Civil Service Commission.

JANUARY 1, 1971

Dear Bob:

On this, my last day as a member of the Cabinet, I write simply to say how much I have enjoyed our association sharing as we have done, the honor of serving the President.

I spoke at some length about all this at our gathering in the East Room December 21st. It was only some days later, however, that I saw a transcript of my remarks and realized that the essence of what I wanted to say was to be found in a few closing sentences, which were not part of my prepared text.

> I am of those who believe that America is the hope of the world, and that for that time given him the President is the hope of America. Serve him well. Pray for his success. Understand how much depends on you. Try to understand what he has given of himself.
>
> This is something those of us who have worked in this building with him know in a way that perhaps only that experience can teach. To have

seen him late into the night and through the night and into the morning, struggling with the most awful complexities, the most demanding
and irresolvable conflicts, doing so because he cared, trying to compre-
hend what is right, and trying to make other men see it, above all, caring
working hoping for this country that he has made greater already and
which he will make greater still. Serve him well. Pray for his success.
Understand how much depends on you.

And now, good-bye, it really has been good to know you.

There it is. Good luck. I hope we might keep in touch.

*Another reminder to Jackie Onassis about progress on Pennsylvania Avenue. His
letter prompted this response regarding his request for her to enlist Senator Kennedy:
"As you know, I talked to Teddy last year and I am more than willing to call him
again, if you think that is a good idea."*

FEBRUARY 11, 1971
MRS. ARISTOTLE ONASSIS
1040 FIFTH AVENUE
NEW YORK, NEW YORK 20433

Dear Jackie:

You might like to have a copy of the President's first "Special Message" to
the 92nd Congress in which he lists a number of legislative matters left over
from the 91st on which he asks action. Among these (Page 6) is the Federal
City Bicentennial Development Corporation. This is, of course, the final piece
in the Pennsylvania Avenue puzzle. You will recall I wrote you about it last
year.

If we can just get a little enthusiasm, I am sure the bill will pass. The President is now on record favorably. There is no problem in the Senate. All we
really need do is get through the House. If this is done, President Kennedy's
great plans will finally be completed. If it is not, I fear that while many good
things will have been done, the really great achievement will have escaped us.

The problem is that so few people see such an effort in terms of its importance to—what? our morale? our sense of ourselves? You know what I mean.

Even Ted, when I spoke to him about this in December, said something about "priorities having changed," etc. I truly think he is mistaken here. I cannot imagine a time in our history when doing something magnificent to the national capital ought to have greater priority. Anyway, we are still at it and would, of course, appreciate any help you might give.

I am back in frosty Cambridge. Perhaps we shall see one another if you come up for the Board meeting of the Institute of Politics.

For years after serving in the Johnson administration, Moynihan remained troubled over his strained relations with those who believed he had caused problems for the president because of the Moynihan Report, or had tried improperly to claim credit for Johnson's important speech at Howard University vowing to achieve "equality as a fact and as a result" for blacks. Moynihan wanted Johnson to know that he was proud of serving him, and Johnson replied to this letter ("Dear Pat") saying: "I know, of course, that you were active in my administration, and I heard many comments during that time regarding your numerous fine contributions. And I have followed your career since, through the press and the remarks of mutual friends." Johnson sent along the picture Moynihan requested, saying "I am glad you asked," and signing his letter: "Sincerely, L.B.J."

23 MARCH 1971

Dear Mr. President:

After returning to Cambridge, I delivered myself of some thoughts on "The Presidency and the Press," which I think might just interest you. The "reviews" have been mixed on all sides. George Reedy thinks it's pretty awful (as I gather). Hubert writes to say he thinks it is very good indeed. And so it goes. I would, of course, greatly value any reaction you might have.

I write, however, mostly as a pretext to raise quite a different matter. Just after it was announced I would be going back to Washington to work for President Nixon, Harry McPherson told me of a conversation with you in which you asked, "Would he have worked for us?" I wanted to write at the time to say that I <u>had</u> worked for you. I felt, however, that you would have too many things on your mind and that in my new circumstances it might be inappropriate. I know, of course, of the difficulties you faced with respect to some of us who had been working for President Kennedy, but it seems to me it should be clear that the overwhelming majority of us had no hesitation whatever in staying on with you. It was miraculous how you picked us—and the nation—up and set us to work on tasks we could never have expected, and probably did not deserve. In my case, for example, within weeks of the assassination you had me working with Shriver on the poverty task force: certainly one of the most rewarding experiences of my life. As Assistant Secretary of Labor, I went back to my regular duties when the bill was sent to Congress but kept close to that subject for the rest of my stay in Washington and, of course, worked closely with Moyers on the material that led up to your historic speech at Howard University in June 1965. (I was sorry that my name somehow got into the papers in connection with that, but I should tell you that I left for a U. N. conference in Yugoslavia three hours before you gave it. Someone told someone, but it wasn't me. I was over the Atlantic.) . . .

One other regret. I never got a picture of you. Do you still have any on hand? I never got one from President Kennedy either. Like most of us, I have too much assumed that things would work out, and there would be plenty of time.

Moynihan privately deplored the inflammatory speeches denouncing anti-Nixon protesters by Vice President Spiro T. Agnew. Agnew later resigned in Nixon's second term amid corruption charges.

25 MAY 1971

Dear Mr. Vice President:

. . . May I presume on your patience to make a general point which responds not only to my sense of obligation for the many courtesies which you showed me whilst we were fellow—if hardly equal!—members of the cabinet, but also to some general observations of a Democrat sojourning among a strange and wondrous tribe whose customs never failed to rouse the utmost wonder.

It comes to this. There has been a considerable shift in the nature of American society which has been reflected in its politics. In crude terms we have moved out of an early industrializing era into what is very like a post-industrial society. The bases for political power in these different societies are themselves different. Power in an industrializing society gravitates toward a business elite, which is to say those groups and interests associated with that process. This was the Republican era. Power in a post-industrial society gravitates toward a scientific and intellectual elite. This has produced a Democratic era. Just as the overwhelming proportion of industrialists were Republican, and supported their party, so the vast proportion of intellectuals and scientists of the present time are Democratic, unless indeed they have forsaken center politics altogether and associated themselves with various portions on the Left.

The media reflect this intellectual/scientific orientation, albeit in a sometimes dimly understood fashion. (The one remark of mine that aroused the utmost fury was the suggestion that the press was now being influenced by the "adversary culture." Thank the Lord for Robert L. Bartley of the <u>Wall Street Journal</u> who sensed that if any of the <u>journalistes enrages</u> would trouble to read a few passages of Lionel Trilling and Richard Hofstadter they will learn "that what Mr. Trilling calls 'the adversary culture' and what Mr. Hofstadter calls 'the avant-garde' is not really a matter of SDS kiddies but of figures like Melville and Powe and Whitman and D. H. Lawrence. Mr. Moynihan was too sensible actually to put the press in such company, but it's not necessarily a disgrace to have one's attitudes shaped by it.") The corollary to this assertion is that there is a corresponding dearth of such support for the Republican party.

It comes to this. You are hopelessly outnumbered. After all, you <u>are</u> in a controversy, and the outcome will in considerable measure be determined by how strong a case will be made for your thesis, and how strong will be the opposition to it. Battle analogues are not misleading here. How many troops have you? How many have your opponents?

The answer is that you are utterly outgunned. For me this is both an inductive and a deductive conclusion. Theoretically it ought to be so, and the evidence builds to the same conclusion. How shall I put this? There is no point being cute: let me out with it. There is simply nobody willing to help you who <u>can</u> help you. The kind of controversy you have been engaged in is a very specialized form of dialectic, half political theory, half content analysis, half literary criticism, with a sum at once lesser and greater than the parts. It is not an art easily acquired. It is learned through discipline and application, and requires a certain predisposition that might as well be called talent. You have such a predisposition. At least that would be my view: I have told a dozen colleagues here at Harvard that as a judge of intellectual horseflesh I do not know your equal in American politics today, which is not to say that I agree with you about many things, but simply that your judgment about who to have to lunch to talk about the world is in my view pretty damn good. But there are not half a dozen other Republicans who are in any way so disposed and so equipped. You are alone. You have no troops. No one carries on your argument, no one elaborates it, no one initiates comparable and parallel arguments. No journal of any intellectual status is open to your point of view. No one, as it were, receives you. Observe your colleagues in the Cabinet. How many take up your cause?

This is not to say that over on the Democratic side of things there is not a considerable amount of agreement with many of the things you say. But they will not allow you to say it. I recall early on a column by Kermit Lansner, editor of Newsweek, which with some foresight exclaimed: "I wish Spiro Agnew would get off my side." I don't have to tell you what has been the nature of the reaction since.

Unfair? To be sure. But as President Kennedy used to say, "Life is unfair." My point would be this. You cannot win the argument you are now engaged in. Frankly, the longer you pursue it, I expect the more you will lose. . . .

If you were to ask my advice it would be this. Cease attacking. Begin talking about the complex problems we must now face as we phase out of a war we have not won. Obviously you need not be explicit on the last point, but just as obviously it is the case. A great deal of charity and forgiveness is going to be required on all our parts to come through this experience whole. You really can help in this, and I know you would want to do so.

In returning to Harvard, Moynihan wanted to teach in the government department, not the graduate school of education, where his appointment had been earlier. Encountering resistance in the government department over his supposed lack of academic credentials, Moynihan enlisted his friends at Harvard—Nathan Glazer and, here, James Q. Wilson—to help and used an offer from Cornell as leverage. He also negotiated with various Harvard potentates, including the president Derek Bok. In the end, Moynihan secured a tenured appointment in the government department.

JUNE 3, 1971

Dear Jim,

As I am likely to have departed for Europe before you return, I write to say that I did decide to remain at Harvard, despite a quite glittering scene that was depicted, if not precisely displayed, for me at Ithaca. Liz was rather for going: money, mostly. It really would have put an end to that issue for good and all. Not just salary and public schools and such, but just as importantly, the permanent provision for secretaries, research assistants, travel, and such. As I contemplate my prospects for next Fall, I realize I made too light of that, and to think of twenty one more years of the same is depressing. Still, the question always was that of leaving Cambridge, which at no point have I wanted to do.

In early Spring I went to seen John Dunlop [dean of the Faculty of Arts and Sciences] to report that the offer was in process, and to say that I wanted to stay at Harvard, but not at the Graduate School of Education. I confined myself to saying simply that I was a political scientist of sorts and wanted to teach government, and that I wanted also to teach undergraduates. . . . His tone was that everything could be worked out. My question was whether I could be made a member of one of the regular departments, presumedly Government, or in some way given a "chair" in Arts and Sciences. . . . (On May 3, at his recommendation, I was made a member of the Faculty of Arts and Sciences, during tenure as Prof of Education and Urban Politics. In late May the story of the Cornell offer broke with a big front page Crimson account. I had not heard from John, did not know of the A & S appointment, etc. He was in Washington, out of touch. I thereupon called Bok and said I was waiting for word back, and that as I understood it the question was whether the University wanted to and would be able to raise the $600,000 to give me a chair in the yard. He was a bit puzzled, although very warm. He would take it up with the Corporation that was meeting Monday. (This was a Saturday.) The Corporation apparently took the view that something should be done. John returned, and came over for a drink. He felt I may have misunderstood him, that everything was all set. What is all set, asked I. Don't worry, said he.

I trouble you with this because you now become involved. On the evening of my meeting with John at the faculty club, the Department of Government at a regular meeting voted to invite me to give courses, supervise theses, and such like things in said Department. This occurred at Nat Glazer's initiative, who spoke to Sam Huntington about me and Cornell, and explained that I wanted to stay but wanted to teach in my regular field. The vote was unanimous, and apparently friendly enough. (Although of this more later.) In late May when John came over to Francis Avenue, I explained that what I was asking for was to be made a member of the Department of Government, if they would have me, and if not, some equivalent. Said he, this could be arranged and would be. . . . Very well, said I, I accept this offer and will decline that of Cornell. . . .

The problem is with the Government Department. I went over to see Sam after getting his nice note, and asked what would be my chances of getting into the Department proper. He was candid, as one would expect and desire. There would be opposition on grounds of scholarly competence. He mentioned the name of one senior member who had so indicated, and noted that some junior members had made similar sounds. I asked what if new money were made available for such a chair. He indicated that that would surely ease matters, and we left it at that.

If you have read this far, you will doubtless have been confirmed in your judgment that I ought never to consider sitting down at the bargaining table with Atheistic communists, much less Heathen Chinese. I have nothing in writing; there are no funds; the Department may not want me even if there were. I would plead only that I knew the chance I was taking. I propose to act as if it is all going to work out fine. . . . If you never raise the subject in my presence, I will understand. . . .

After leaving the White House, Moynihan served as a member of the United States delegation to the United Nations General Assembly under the UN ambassador, George H. W. Bush. Here Moynihan discusses the State Department's instruction that he raise the subject of Jews in the Soviet Union in responding to Syrian and Hungarian criticism of racial policies in the United States. When Moynihan was himself UN ambassador in 1975–1976, he again tangled with the State Department.

NOVEMBER 9, 1971

MEMORANDUM FOR AMBASSADOR BUSH

I fear I must express my almost angry disappointment at the instruction we received from the Department of State on November 1 to raise the subject of Soviet Jewry in our reply to attacks on the racial policies of the United States made that day by Syria and Hungary.

This has made the United States to appear dishonest with respect to our own racial problems, and has spoiled the opportunity for the United States to make a serious intervention on the subject of Soviet Jewry that might have helped Soviet Jews. What was shaping up as a positive contribution by us on both agenda items, that of the Elimination of all forms of Racial Discrimination and Nazism and Racial Intolerance has, instead, fizzled out in the same dreary pissing match with the totalitarians.

I believe the honor of the United States has been diminished. I did not accept the President's appointment to this Mission in order to be associated with such an event. . . .

This is intolerable. I care as much about the Soviet Jews as the next American, but the interests of the United States come first. But to suggest, as we did, that these two situations are comparable is intellectually scandalous and morally despicable. . . .

I hesitate to trouble you at such length about this matter, but I feel strongly that we must bring a measure of intellectual competence to bear on these issues. It is a disgrace to have American interests of the most fundamental kind discounted and damaged through the exercise of a sophomoric cold war diplomacy.

It is incomprehensible to me that a State Department that would take the nation into a hopeless and disastrous war in Asia in defense of abstract principles about democracy is not able—or in some perverse way—not willing—to summon the intellectual competence to defend democracy in a United Nations debate.

Moynihan was friendly with George H. W. Bush, who supported the Family Assistance Plan when he was a Texas congressman.

20 JANUARY 1972
AMBASSADOR GEORGE BUSH
U.S. MISSION TO THE UNITED NATIONS
799 UNITED NATIONS PLAZA
NEW YORK, NEW YORK 10017

Dear George:

... Somehow, someday, I will contrive to express to you my true appreciation for your patience and generosity throughout the 26th General Assembly. It was an honor to serve under you, and the most delightful pleasure getting to know Barbara.

Moynihan was irritated when anyone, including Senator Ted Kennedy, used the words "benign neglect" to batter the Nixon administration, which he says is a "bum rap" for him. His attempt to get Kennedy to support H.R. 1, the legislation that would create the Family Assistance Program, was rebuffed. Kennedy wrote back to Moynihan, "I will agree that, for you, 'benign neglect' is a bum rap" but that the term "aptly describes the tenor of official administration attitudes on race relations." He said H.R. 1 would be "a significant step backward from current law in terms of work incentives" and that it would threaten high welfare benefit levels in Massachusetts and other big states.

PERSONAL
JANUARY 23, 1972

Dear Ted,

Good news. After three years of negotiations GSA has arranged to swap part of Miller Field on Staten Island for the Willard Hotel. From the outset this has been the key to getting the space for "National Square" which in turn is the key to the Pennsylvania Avenue plan. ...

On a personal note, I was hurt that you choose to bring up that "benign neglect" thing in your Press Club speech. It was a bum rap. All that I intended by the term, and all the President understood was that I felt he should not get involved in the Black Panther hysteria of the time. I felt they would do themselves in by their own extremism. Which they did. Much as have the white extremists. In my view, which could be wrong, but it is my field, there is no better formula for social instability than to divide a society between two ascribed characteristics that are seen as opposite. Protestant-Catholic in Northern Ireland is a classic instance.

But that is aside the point. It was a bum rap. Everyone knew so at the time. The Washington Post ran two editorials saying so. I served Jack and worked for Bob over the years in terms that entitle me to expect more loyalty from you, especially as you know something about bum raps yourself.

Also, is H.R. 1 really that bad? It is a guaranteed income, and not a small one. A third of the population of Mississippi, a third of the black population of the nation would receive income supplements under it. It is, again in my view, too large a thing for one party to expect to do on its own and get all the credit. Has to be bipartisan. You may recall our having lunch in 1967. I raised with you the possibility of proposing a rather modest family allowance. If you recall, your reaction was that the cost was so enormous you didn't dare. There are some things that have to be done in concert.

Moynihan's response to Kennedy's reply to the letter above.

25 FEBRUARY 1972
SENATOR EDWARD M. KENNEDY
UNITED STATES SENATE
WASHINGTON, D.C.

Dear Ted,

I share many of your reservations about H.R. 1, especially with respect to the marginal rate of taxation, which was raised by Ways and Means. But I think more of its possibilities. It <u>is</u> a guaranteed income. Its immediate impact will be considerable. In the coming fiscal year it would provide payments to 25.5 million persons: 29.2 percent of the population of Mississippi, 33.7 percent of Puerto Rico, 20.4 percent of West Virginia. There are significant state savings on current welfare involved, thanks in large measure to an agreement Senator Percy got from the White House and to which Senator Long has agreed. Beyond that there are true benefits for Northern states. Massachusetts, for example, would move from 418,000 recipients under present legislation to 536,000.

The opportunity to <u>adjust</u> the program will come with every congress: the opportunity to <u>enact</u> it may not come again for a very long time....

My concern here is not about either party, but about the Presidency. I have had enough politics in my time and mean to remain a professor. But I would hope to be a useful one. An aspect of that usefulness, it seems to me, is to be honest with some one like you who might well be President one day. That is a burden for you. It means you won't get much honest counsel, apart from a rare Dave Burke. I happen to believe we are too hard on our presidents, too eager to break them. I recall almost with bitterness my days in your brother's administration. Much of the press, most of the intellectuals, were poisonous about him, at least in the beginning, and even worse about Bob. In October 1961 Reston wrote that among thinking persons the new regime was being described as "the third Eisenhower administration." He declared that intellectuals were "disenchanted by the absence of new policies, the preoccupation with political results, the compromises over education and the techniques of appointing conservatives to put over liberal policies and liberals to carry out conservative policies." Few seem to want to recall this, but by November 1963, the administration was near to demoralization: all with whom I was in touch had concluded we would have to wait until after the 1964 election to get anywhere with Congress. I have the impression Nixon has made the same judgment, and of course Johnson decided not even to wait.

That is why I would hope there could be at least a good debate on H.R. 1.... The issue is whether the center will hold. At the end of the 91st Congress Meg Greenfield, in a Washington <u>Post</u> editorial, wrote, with respect to FAP, "There has been meanmindedness on the right and showboating on the left and mostly apathetic silence in between." It is the in between that concerns me. The men of the center in the Democratic party have not troubled to learn the facts about this issue. In the meantime, Talmadge gets <u>his</u> legislation, and Harris gets his headlines. Not good enough....

In any event, I would ask you would drop that phrase of mine from your charges against the administration, especially as you know I will not answer back. There is an issue of personal standards here, and I hope you will see it as I do. You have speech writers enough! let them think up their own phrases!

On Pennsylvania Avenue, could you bring yourself to call Jack Brooks of the Government Operations Committee to indicate your interest—if you feel this way—in exchanging the Willard Hotel site for government-owned land on Staten Island. This, evidently, is our hang up. Brooks is just slow about these matters, and Benenson, the owner, is pressing me. (As you know, the Pennsylvania legislation has twice passed the Senate unanimously.)

You may have seen Ada Louise Huxtable's long piece in the <u>Times</u> on the F.B.I. building in which she describes the Pennsylvania Avenue plan as "a noble failure." Her view is that only the government buildings have been built, and not even the right government buildings. (Bob was much of the opinion that the F.B.I. building did <u>not</u> belong on Pennsylvania Avenue, but even in 1962 it was too late to change it.) She misses the kind of development we need the Willard for. I have written a friendly response for the Op-Ed page saying we are still much alive. . . .

Moynihan, in asking former President Johnson for an autographed text of the Howard University speech, again is concerned that Johnson may have thought that Moynihan was trying improperly to claim partial authorship of it.

8 MARCH 1972
THE HONORABLE LYNDON B. JOHNSON
L.B.J. RANCH
JOHNSON CITY, TEXAS

Dear President Johnson:

I am so pleased you found my memorandum on civil rights helpful and to learn that you plan to make use of it in your forthcoming addresses.

Thank you for inviting me to the Symposium to be held in April. To be frank, I was surprised not to have been asked to the opening of the library. I am one of the few political scientists to have served in your subcabinet, and over the years I expect to spend a fair amount of time down there.

While I have you, could I ask the favor of your autographing the enclosed text of the Howard University speech? It is not only a great event in your life, but one in mine as well. I left for a United Nations conference in Yugoslavia just an hour before you were scheduled to speak, and only when I got to Rome (where the event was front-page news) did I learn that you had indeed used the text we had prepared the night before. I was away three weeks and returned to rather a different Washington. Somehow word had got to the press that I had helped draft the speech. As best I can reconstruct, the leak came from the White House and was meant to be a friendly act. But you were distressed, as you had every right to be. At this time the question arose of my succeeding Harry McPherson as assistant secretary of state for cultural affairs. You turned down the proposal in terms that made me feel I had best leave Washington, which I did a few weeks after returning.

Keeping Jackie Onassis informed on "the Pennsylvania Avenue saga," Moynihan got this response on May 5, 1972: "What can I say to you about all you have done? You are the one who realized with all your heart how much President Kennedy's vision of Pennsylvania Avenue meant to him.... I hope you know that his children and I will always be grateful for what you have accomplished. Thank you for everything—and more than I can say." Moynihan then sent a copy of this letter to Senator Kennedy saying: "I am sure you would want to see how much this remains in her mind."

25 APRIL 1972
MRS. ARISTOTLE ONASSIS
1040 FIFTH AVENUE
NEW YORK, NEW YORK 20433

Dear Jackie:

Even the weariest river winds somewhere safe to sea, or something like that. Whatever the best image, the Pennsylvania Avenue saga is coming to a close. The last issue is the establishment of a development corporation to rebuild the area just to the north. Hearings were held 13 and 14 April, and the prospects look reasonably good.

I enclose my testimony and a—hopelessly mutilated—article on the <u>Times</u> Op-ed page. I was disturbed that Ada Louise Huxtable pronounced the plan "moving toward noble failure," and did my little bit to resist.

With considerable asperity, Moynihan tells Kenneth B. Clark, the pioneering African American sociologist, that he continued to believe that environmental— not genetic—factors were the cause of children's underachievement in schools.

12 JUNE 1972

DR. KENNETH B. CLARK

SEVENTEEN PINECREST DRIVE

HASTING-ON-HUDSON, NEW YORK 10706

Dear Ken:

I was hurt—why shouldn't I use that word—by reports of that briefing you took part in on Friday. Have you read our book? Every page fairly screams for the need for integration—as a moral issue and a practical benefit. Who could possibly want to turn the work of David Cohen and Tom Pettigrew and me, damn it, into separatist doctrine or whatever.

Must you attack us? You know we won't attack you. Is it fair?

Fair or not, is it wise? I simply cannot understand the business of linking up persons such as David Armor with Jensen, et. al. We are <u>environmentalists</u>. Almost the first person Jensen attacked—mind you, in gentlemanly terms that command my respect—was <u>me</u>. If I recall his phrase, I am an "extreme environmentalist." So be it. I happen to believe some environments are more powerful than others, and that the school probably is one of the less powerful. But all this I only learned from Kenneth Clark. What possible advantage can there be to the things you and I both value for you to associate yourself with such charges?

Moynihan lobbied Arthur M. Schlesinger Jr. on his view of Robert Kennedy for Schlesinger's forthcoming biography.

13 JULY 1972
PROFESSOR ARTHUR SCHLESINGER, JR.
GRADUATE CENTER
CITY UNIVERSITY OF NEW YORK
33 WEST 42ND STREET
NEW YORK, NEW YORK 10036

Dear Arthur:

When you last gave me lunch at The Century Club you remarked that you were at work, or soon would be, on a biography of Bob Kennedy. Or was it his papers? Either way, the subject most needs <u>your</u> intelligence and standards.

I have what may be a small item of interest. If you recall that last campaign, you wrote a short piece supporting him in the <u>New Republic</u>. Shortly thereafter I did a long piece for <u>Commentary</u>, which was running a series "dedicated to exploring the alternatives open to the responsible liberal voter in 1968." I sent galleys out to Frank Mankiewicz who later told me Bob had seen and very much liked the article, but I assume this was merely Frank being nice. ("The candidate has seen your memo.") I never saw Bob during the campaign. I went up and down California; but always, logically, in places he was not. In the last days I had to return East to give some commencement addresses and went round to say goodbye at the Fairmont, but he was asleep; so I said goodbye to Fred Dutton and Dick Goodwin instead, and that was the end of it so far as I knew. But of a sudden last winter Mike Forrestal volunteered that he had also been in to see Bob at the Fairmont, urging him to take some position or other on Vietnam and badgering him somewhat for not putting forth a general statement of principles. "Teasingly" is the word Mike uses. Whereupon Bob replied, "You're lazy, Forrestal. I highly recommend you read the article in <u>Commentary</u> by Pat Moynihan. This will give you an idea what I think." I enclose a copy. The story interests me in ways you will understand, but I dare to think there is somewhat of a significance. I had reached the point where I disagreed with just about everything Bob's staff put him up to. I felt he was leaving the Catholic working class without which the Democratic party (and the Kennedy's) would be nothing. A base on which to build, but not to abandon. Bob's legacy is being maintained in his staff's image, as best I can tell. . . .

It may just be you would want to know this, and so now my tale is done. . . .

*Moynihan believed that Nixon deserved better understanding and cooperation from
the university community, as he tells Clark Kerr, former president of the University
of California system and, in 1972, chairman of the Carnegie Commission on Higher
Education.*

13 JULY 1972

DR. CLARK KERR

CHAIRMAN

CARNEGIE COMMISSION ON HIGHER EDUCATION

1947 CENTER STREET

BERKELEY, CALIFORNIA 94704

Dear Clark:

... If, as would seem likely, the Administration is returned to office, I would
hope some efforts would be made to establish better relations with the university
world. I cannot approve what has gone on the past four years: on either side.
Perhaps if Richard Nixon is re-elected and it is finally over—no more chance
to beat him, no more chance for him to beat—some persons might grow more
sensible. I grow contemptuous of the leaders of higher education who seek to
secure the good opinion of their undergraduates by vulgar attacks on the President of the United States. I mean vulgar. Not a trace of elegance. But then they
would have to be vulgar if they were to make any impression on the minds of
the best educated generation in the history of the Nation. I went to the Harvard Commencement this year. (I have finally found a role for myself at that
ancient institution. At Commencement they require a number of large faculty
members to be on hand to sort of collapse in the aisles when the undergraduates rush the dais.) The student orations were so bad that for a fleeting instant
I thought one young man (a third-year law student) had contrived a stunning
parody. But no. He meant it. Why, I wondered as I walked away, does anyone
bother with children so insufferably stupid? Then a thought came to me which,
as with most my thoughts, derived from a comment by David Riesman who
several years back observed that if they keep it up all the people they come to
Harvard to get to know (whether they are aware of this or not) will avoid them.
My impression of our graduating class this year was of persons who had apparently scarcely had an adult conversation in their full four years. ...

Asking James (Scotty) Reston of the TIMES *not to misuse the term "benign neglect."*

AUGUST 1, 1972

Dear Scotty,

This may seem to you an improper request: if so, treat it as such.

I write to ask that the Times either cease to use the term "benign neglect," or else use it in the sense in which I intended it, and in which the President understood it.

As you would imagine, for me personally it has been a damn tough bullet to chew. I have spent most of my life until now working for racial equality; I will spend the rest of it with that miserable epithet hung round my neck. It has, for example, become near impossible to teach, the one thing I do best and ought to do most. For practical purposes the campuses are forbidden me, and it is because of that term.

That I feel for myself will be obvious, and I hope will seem natural. But I would hope also that you would know that I would not write for myself. I knew well enough when I went down with Nixon that the personal risk was enormous. Naturally I hoped to survive. Well I didn't and that's that. But I did not dream that I would become the vehicle of a gross distortion of government policy on the most vital issue that faces the American republic. But that is what has happened, and the Times has much to do with this. . . .

Letter to the imprisoned former Tammany Hall chieftain, Carmine De Sapio, who had just been denied parole while serving a sentence for a conspiracy and bribery conviction. De Sapio, though reviled by party "reformers," had been a major power in the New York Democratic Party and a key player in securing John Kennedy's nomination.

6 SEPTEMBER 1972
MR. CARMINE G. DE SAPIO
UNITED STATES PRISON FACILITY
ALLENDALE, PENNSYLVANIA

Dear Carmine:

It seems absurd for someone else to speak of disappointment at the Parole Board decision in view of what must be your own response. Still, I hope you will forgive my intruding to say that I am only one—I feel sure of this—of many persons who have known and respected you who look forward to your being free again, and would have hoped it might be sooner. Still, it is not that much longer in any event. . . .

I have been thinking of those Harriman days in connection with a small book I am finishing, and the more I do, the more I wish we had got to know each other better. I was terribly junior, I admit; but I had a certain sense of the opposing sides in the conflict that was even then shaping up. I was raised on Eleventh Avenue (in George Washington Plunkitt's old district, taken from him by the McManae), and yet grew up to know the crowd on the other side of town. I never got to know you fellows very well. It takes time with regulars. But I never for a moment doubted my fondness for you all.

I do hope your health is good. You have much to look forward to, as I am sure you realize. If you are ever around Boston, you should know you have a friend on the Harvard faculty.

Moynihan's letter to Alvin von Auw, assistant vice president of AT&T (American Telephone & Telegraph Co.), indicates his enduring money problems.

OCTOBER 1972
MR. ALVIN VON AUW
ASSISTANT VICE PRESIDENT
AMERICAN TELEPHONE & TELEGRAPH COMPANY
195 BROADWAY
NEW YORK, NEW YORK 10007

Dear Al:

I had a fine time yesterday at Princeton. I don't think there were more than a half dozen people in the room who both understood and were interested in what I was saying (nor am I sure that Robert D. Lilley was among them) but there were some (trust Bell Labs!) and I have no trouble settling for that.

One problem is that I was obliged to discuss an issue which is at once extremely complex, and as yet unsettled in my own mind. As you will see from the enclosed, Mr. Davidson did <u>not</u> want to hear about urban affairs, and was confident that the "Generation Gap" was "one of my talks." I fear it is nothing of the kind, and I was obliged to put a fair amount of work into the effort, albeit that it was worth it to me.

This, however, raises the question of money, which you discussed in your letter of September 23. In a word, I never speak to a commercial group for less than $1000, and rarely for that. We are in a market in this respect, and I maximize my position as best I can. As would you. Last week, for example, the folks at Dupont paid me $2500 for a private dinner with the executive committee, and a lecture to a management group such as I addressed yesterday. From my point of view, I take the highest bidders here in order that I can speak for nothing to academic and political groups. Hence I would feel that any future <u>speaking</u> engagements for Bell should be at the rate of $1000, although the two so far scheduled are subject to whatever terms you feel appropriate, inasmuch as I made no understanding in advance. . . .

Letter to Saul Bellow, the novelist who was a professor at the University of Chicago, after Chicago had asked Moynihan to join its faculty.

4 OCTOBER 1972
PROFESSOR SAUL BELLOW
1126 EAST 59TH STREET
CHICAGO, ILLINOIS 60632

Dear Saul Bellow:

What a fine honor to be invited to the University of Chicago! I don't ex-actly see how I could decently accept, given my situation here at Harvard; but let me go on about this for a moment.

I returned two years ago January, having completed the two years I had agreed to spend in Washington and which my leave allowed. It was probably a mistake to come back. The President had asked me to go to the United Na-tions and remain in the Cabinet, which would at least have been something to do. Here I found nothing. Politics, penis envy, and (to my mind) legitimate suspicions about some of my work combined so as to exclude me from any-thing I would have wished to be involved with. Cornell offered me their Sen-ior Chair, and I was about to accept when Harvard countered with a somewhat complex offer that involved my moving to "the Yard." I agreed to remain on those terms and feel I am bound by the agreement unless and until it becomes clear that it has not worked out.

It was a great honor to have you at our Commencement last year, even if it had to be shared with Yale. (I am sure you know that Benjamin Franklin was the first man to pull that off.) As a CCNY man I follow these competi-tions with the fascination and awe once reserved for the Notre Dame football team.

Moynihan's congratulatory letter to Nixon upon his sweeping reelection victory bears no hint of the troubles ahead.

10 NOVEMBER 1972

Dear Mr. President:

How very much I have hoped this moment would come to you, and it has done! It has come, also, to the American people. They have found in you a President they trust and admire. There is no one thing we needed more.

And now there is to be peace, and four years of what I know will be stunning achievement. I was glancing the other evening at the first memorandum I ever sent you—in the Hotel Pierre days. It began by noting that your Presidency would conclude on the 200th anniversary of the Republic: an unequaled opportunity to recapture and perhaps to redefine the meaning and the prospect of the American experience.

God guide you in that.

Moynihan had to apply for a leave from Harvard to serve as ambassador to India under Nixon.

13 DECEMBER 1972
DR. DEREK C. BOK
PRESIDENT
HARVARD UNIVERSITY

Dear Mr. President:

As you know, President Nixon has announced his intention to nominate me as United States Ambassador to India. I am accordingly applying to you for a two year leave of absence from my duties here at Harvard, to commence at the end of the current term. This comes unexpectedly to me, and I am not a little aware of the awkwardness of asking to go away after having been back only two years. However, as I have indicated to you, I propose to waive the sabbatical year I was to take in 1973–74 and hope this really will be the last of my travels. I did not in any way seek this assignment—or any other assignment—but I feel, as I am sure you do, that there are things which, if asked, one must do.

A month before the 1972 election, Kissinger announced in Washington that the negotiations to end the war in Vietnam had succeeded and that "peace is at hand." But the negotiations broke down at the end of the year, and Nixon resumed bombing North Vietnam to get the Hanoi government back to the talks. Moynihan, on the eve of his departure for his assignment in India, was alarmed. In response to this

letter, Nixon wrote Moynihan after the signing of a peace agreement in January
1973: "I must say first how good it is to have in this Administration friends close
enough and patriots loyal enough to speak from the heart at testing times, as you
have done now and so often before." Nixon concluded: "I can only trust that results
make the best explanations and actions the best reassurances for Congress, the coun-
try and concerned friends like yourself. I believe that the settlement we achieved is
one all Americans can be proud of—and increasingly so as we gain the perspective
of history. The coming of peace with honor opens up bright new opportunities for
South and Southeast Asia, and underscores my feeling that at such a promising time
there is no one I would rather be sending to New Delhi than you."

DECEMBER 28, 1972

Dear Mr. President:

... May I ask leave to express my enormous disquiet at the breakdown of
the Paris talks. In ten years of war I have not been so concerned as I have been
these past ten days. It comes to this: The country had understood the war was
over. If it now starts again, it will be a new war, and this time one unmistakably
of our making. The damage to our sense of ourselves could be—I am serious—irreparable.

It is because I have so admired your own concern with just this issue—our
long range sense of ourselves—that I have never spoken a word of criticism
of your policies. I asked to leave the Cabinet after Cambodia, but when you
asked me not to as it would be "misunderstood," I did not because indeed you
were right. I may have objected to the tactic, but I fully approved your strategy
of emerging from the experience with our sense of honor and purpose and
competence intact.

It is just this which I now feel is jeopardized. I share this view with many
of your strong supporters. A while back the Evening Star ran a very pleasant
editorial about my going to India. I called Newby Noyes to thank him. He
was away at the time and returned my call after the bombing had resumed.
This was all he could talk about. He said they had had it at the Star. They
were turning against the administration on the issue of the war. I urged him
to write you a personal letter before he did this publicly, and he agreed. But
those are his views and I have not talked to anyone who does not share them.

My concern can be put succinctly. I am an intellectual, as you are. I care
about ideas and know their power, as you do. I am a <u>hard</u> anti-Marxist, anti-

totalitarian. I was formed intellectually in the late 30's at the City College of New York in the company of such as Irving Kristol. I <u>know</u> there is an authoritarian left in this country, and I fear it. (I used to plead with friends in the Johnson White House to take this seriously. They couldn't. They thought the left was something Oveta Culp Hobby had dreamed up to keep down Social Security costs. They found out.) I watched the power and influence of this tendency, fueled by the war, grow and grow through the 1960s, acquiring ever more complacent supporters in the style of the Popular Front. (Hence my Address to the Freshman Class at Harvard which I published in the current issue of Commentary, and which I sent to you.) Only in the last few months have I begun to feel that the advantage was turning to us and that, while it would take all of the 70s and more, the manner and the principles of democratic republicanism would now prevail.

I say to you that all this is risked if the war is resumed. All the very worst positions will be retroactively legitimated. The most wrong people will be judged to have been most right. We will decline to an ideological condition approaching that of the sub-continent to which you are sending me. We will lose the respect of our allies, and our self respect. Strong statements: but I believe them.

I also believe that you will not let this happen. I know you want peace, and you deserve it to be <u>your</u> peace. Not, of course, altogether your terms. You have never sought that. But terms you decide and <u>by the nature of your intervention at this time</u> are known to have decided.

But in God's name: Soon.

CHAPTER SEVEN

"Something Perhaps to Be Forgiven"

Moynihan served as ambassador to India from early 1973 to early 1975. The challenge was considerable. Though India was officially neutral in the cold war and a leader of the "nonaligned" movement of nations, it was seen in Washington as, in fact, on the side of the Soviet Union. Prime Minister Indira Gandhi was a harsh critic of the Vietnam War and still angry that the United States had "tilted" toward Pakistan in the war with India that led to the independence of Bangladesh in 1971. Moynihan did succeed in improving relations during his time in New Delhi, culminating in a visit by Kissinger in 1974, and he grew from being a mere analyst to an accomplished diplomat.

But the service in India also pulled Moynihan back toward what he viewed as the tragedy of Nixon's downfall in the wake of the Watergate scandal. In his letters and diaries from India, Moynihan admits that he does not spend more than a couple hours a day doing the official chores of an ambassador. On the other hand, he is extremely busy writing—diaries, letters, and communications to his embassy staff. Watergate appalls him. Like many Americans at the time, he goes from thinking that Nixon was undercut by scheming aides to thinking that Nixon brought about his own downfall, but in the end was cheated of a prize he deserved and a presidency that he had begun to master on the world stage. In one crucial respect, India brought two aspects of Moynihan more deeply into focus. In India he confirmed his distaste for parlor left-wing intellectuals, especially the British-trained sort he had earlier encountered in London and now found surrounding Prime Minister Indira

Gandhi. He thus took up the cause of combating anti-Americanism and Communism in the developing world that flowed in the wake of Nixon's ouster.

The letters here are interspersed with Moynihan's diary entries and memoranda to himself.

John Kenneth Galbraith, Moynihan's close friend (and neighbor in Cambridge), had served as ambassador to India in the early 1960s under President Kennedy and wrote a memoir entitled AMBASSADOR'S JOURNAL. *Galbraith's wife, Kitty, was in India when the Moynihans arrived.*

FEBRUARY 21, 1973
HONORABLE JOHN KENNETH GALBRAITH
CHALET BERGSONNE
GSTAAD, SWITZERLAND

Dear Ken:

Not even <u>Ambassador's Journal</u> prepared me for everything in this new life. Certainly it gave no warning that Kitty Galbraith would be waiting when we got off the airplane at five o'clock Tuesday morning. It was a delight for Liz and me, but genuinely reassuring to Maura and John, who were otherwise a bit shaken by it all. Alas, it was only for the day, but a very important day in our lives. Liz and I are genuinely grateful. Kitty reports that she will be back in October, en route to Australia where you are lecturing. I trust this next visit will include Himself.

Letter to Dr. Nicholas Holowach, his ophthalmologist.

FEBRUARY 26, 1973
DR. NICHOLAS HOLOWACH
5 WEST STREET
ONEONTA, NEW YORK

Dear Nick:

From distant New Delhi may I bespeak your help. Age and whiskey caught up with me a month or so ago. Or whatever it was, my eyes have suddenly changed and the glasses you had fitted me with no longer work. I saw better without them than with and while not particularly uncomfortable, realized that something had to be done. On my last round in Washington I spent a day at Walter Reed Hospital where an obviously fine doctor put me through the refraction drill and gave me a new prescription. I have had this filled here in India but with no very reassuring results. I can see well enough near at hand when I have my glasses on, but everything goes blooey when I take them off. In other words, from having been able to see pretty well without glasses and not very well with them a week ago, I now find myself sort of able to see with glasses and not able at all without them. This exaggerates, but I am in a land of hyperbole. In any event, I wonder if you would have Mr. Bannon make up a set of near and distance glasses for me and mail them out here. At this point I will know whether the prescription is right or not.

If you don't trust the mails, why don't the two of you get on Pan American and bring them? Quickly, though, as it will be 115 in the shade any day now.

A month after arriving in India, Moynihan outlines his first impressions in these excerpts of a personal letter to Nixon.

MARCH 21, 1973

Dear Mr. President:

The first thing to say is that I have been very well treated. The Indians have made much of my appointment, and probably expect too much from it. But this would be natural. There is a near obsession here with things American. Nothing I have encountered elsewhere in the world equals it. . . . We have in truth all but vanished from India. Our buildings are half empty, our programs mostly closed or closing down. And yet to read the press one could think we were the only other nation in the world; you the only other Head of State. A quarter of almost any front page is devoted to the United States. When there is no news, they make up some. . . .

I sense this obsession with America, and its presumed higher standard, in the Prime Minister [Indira Gandhi]. The negative side comes forth more readily; but the preoccupation is also there. She cannot open her mouth without talking about or alluding to the United States. . . . In her case, ambivalence is overlaid with Brahmin hauteur and that peculiar amalgam of fear and disdain which the upper-class British Left acquired for America during the 1930s. She is primarily a political animal, and the carry-over of this leftist, "anti-colonial" political culture into present day India is such that anti-American remarks become an all-purpose means of affirming one's loyalty to the socialist and egalitarian principles of the Indian Constitution, a kind of a loyalty oath which wealthy Brahmins doubtless find it politic to subscribe to from time to time. . . .

And then there is the residue of the demi-raj. To begin with, Indians are clearly influenced by the Buddhist view which holds that "gratitude, if it exists, should be felt by he who gives and not he who receives, since the latter has been the cause of good action, which to the full advantage of the former, will inevitably by the iron law of Karma bring its own reward." (Karma involves one's next incarnation.) This is not a professor's notion: it can be read in Kipling. Nor are we ourselves free of such attitudes. We have had to pass "Good Samaritan" laws to protect doctors against the ingratitude of injured persons they encounter on the highway. You have heard me discourse on the peculiar corruption of welfare which enables middle-class professionals to acquire great virtue in their own eyes, and not unreasonable salaries, by "helping" the poor. . . .

The Indians have such good brains: if only they didn't have such bad ideas. They are committed to a socialism that cannot work. With each successive failure of the economy, they respond so as to hasten the next cluster of failures. (Thus in response to the current drought, they are nationalizing the grain trade, throwing out of work some 500,000 grain traders—possibly 2,500,000, no one really knows—who, whatever else, have evolved over 5000 years a system for moving food around.) The heart of the problem is discipline, or, if you will, incentives. They will not accept the discipline of the free market, although they have a potentially superb entrepreneurial class. . . .

What can the American role be? We wish India to succeed. This was the first point you made to me when you called to ask me to come here. How can we help? I confess to few ideas, save that we must not give the impression of trying to tell them what is best. All that is past. The Indians least of all wish it to return. American business could play a great role in economic development here, and I shall press that at every level save that which would be perceived as ideological. But at best it will be a slow process. . . .

The Nixon administration unraveled under the pressure of Watergate just as Moynihan settled in. Here he writes the president, from a regional meeting of ambassadors in Iran, that he had long been concerned about the potentially destructive behavior of Nixon's aides. The White House letters offer hints of this in the form of Moynihan's advice to lower the rhetorical temperature.

APRIL 22, 1973
UNITED STATES EMBASSY
TEHRAN, IRAN

Dear Mr. President,

It is Easter Sunday here in Tehran, where for some non-reason we have gathered for a Chiefs-of-Mission Conference. At Mass this morning we prayed for you, as is our custom, although I should have thought the Shah had a prior territorial claim on our devotions. In any event, I have been thinking of you almost continuously this past week.

I wonder, now, how well I served you. From almost my first day in the White House I sensed that the greatest danger you faced would be from the kind of misjudgments and misdeeds of which disclosure now is mounting. I never bluntly said so. I hinted, I alluded, I inferred, I groused even, but I never straight out said what I thought, which was that such things were going on, and would go on, and would come to grief. The closest I came was in the letter I sent you a few weeks after leaving, and even there I invoked the less than awesome authority of business men's talk about things in the administration that troubled them. For things undone, I ask—what?—forgiveness, I suppose.

But I write not for this purpose, nor to declare my own unshaken loyalty, and not at all to strengthen you, for you seem to find resolve in crisis. I write, rather, with a simple thought, which is that it has not really been evil that has brought on the present shame, but innocence. What struck me most, and alarmed me most, about the almost always decent men who came to Washington with you, or in your train, was how little they knew of government, and especially of the standards of personal behavior required of men in power. They had acquired in their youth, or as was sometimes the case, in long years excluded from national affairs, an oppositional frame of mind which much too easily assumed that squalid behavior was common rather than rare in Washington, and they were all too ready to judge what would be required of them by reference to what they thought others did, rather than what they knew ought to be done. There was a failing of education and imagination. As a teacher in an elite school I live with it daily from the opposite political perspective: The government is fascist; what then is wrong with <u>us</u> blowing up a building. But this is innocence not evil. I believe that, and I believe it of those of my former colleagues who have now got themselves and you in such trouble. It is in any event a thought, and I offer it.

I have no way of knowing what you are thinking, or what you will do. But if you think there would be any use in my returning to the White House, you have only to ask.

Moynihan regarded WHO'S WHO *as an outstanding research tool. In this letter to Kenneth Petchenik, publisher at Marquis Who's Who, Inc., he offers new data for his personal entry.*

APRIL 30, 1973

Dear Mr. Petchenik:

... Before responding to your letter, may I, as a somewhat harassed Ambassador, ask a favor of you. For some years now I have been trying to get my <u>Who's Who</u> entry straightened out, but with no very great success. About twice a year, or thereabouts, I have sent in revisions—additions, really—but not much ever gets added. Thus, the one government appointment I am rather proud of is that I was, for two years, a member of the Cabinet. I would really like to see that recorded, and would not want President Nixon to think I am concealing the fact! Similarly, I have some nineteen honorary degrees, but so far have only been able to persuade your editors to include that from St. Louis University. I am indeed proud of my St. Louis diploma, but won't want to appear to be slighting those other institutions!

I have found a Saturday afternoon, and have done my best to bring the entry up to date. The things I would like added, or whatever, are designated according to the print-out line number on the entry form you have sent me.

I should much appreciate it if you would see that this new data is entered—or as much as in your judgment is appropriate—and that the same material be made available to Who's Who in the World, which also sends me a somewhat different entry at this time. (I enclose both.)

If I were pressed to state something—anything!—concerning Who's Who which I considered less than wholly admirable, I think it would refer not to the difficulty of getting changes made—this is fully understandable to me, at all events—but rather the number of times one is likely to be asked to submit changes. Thus, just this morning as I resolved to my secretary that I would come back and do my duty to your great director, she informed me that yet another print-out had arrived, requesting my changes. Thus in the month of April I have received from you three print-outs—two identical, one somewhat different—each asking to be revised.

But this matters nothing whatever. Yours is the incomparable directory. I recall years ago reading a statement by Raymond Chandler that in the course of a day a writer might look at his dictionary on occasion, consult a thesaurus once or twice, but would turn to Who's Who at least half a dozen times. It is true! And not only of the writer. In my life I have worked at different tasks. Like Chandler, I have sat with my typewriter (and Who's Who) for long months of writing, concentrating on a single subject. At other times I have taught in a great university. I have served in state and national government in a variety of capacities, including that of a member of the Cabinet and Counselor to the President in the White House. Wheresoever I have gone, two books have gone with me: Who's Who in America, and the Statistical Abstract of the United States. My debt to your splendid organization is deep and will endure. . . .

Professor P. N. Dhar, secretary to Prime Minister Indira Gandhi, was a key inter-mediary who helped Moynihan develop a close relationship with India. But many irritants continually arose. Here, Moynihan assails threats to expel a young Amer-ican consulate officer in Calcutta, A. Peter Burleigh, for allegedly fomenting civil disturbances in the northeast. Burleigh remained and went on to a distinguished diplomatic career, culminating in service as ambassador to Sri Lanka, deputy am-bassador to the United Nations, and chargé d'affaires in India.

MAY 4, 1973

<u>PERSONAL</u>

Dear Professor Dhar:

On April 20 you called to my attention the possibility that Mr. A. Peter Burleigh, an officer of the American Consulate General staff in Calcutta, has been associated with civil disturbances in the course of his travels in north-eastern India. Earlier you had mentioned that such things are not unknown, and I had asked to be told the names of any persons that might be involved in deliberate efforts of the kind you described.

I have now talked with Burleigh, and have gone over his activities since he arrived here some nine months ago. As you will see from the attached vita and itinerary, he is a young man with a considerable interest in South Asia and South Asian languages. This is his first tour of duty in India. In the nor-mal course of events he has been visiting each of the states in the Calcutta area which is open to Americans and has made six trips outside that city since arriving here last July. As I gather, he has still to visit Orissa, after which his initial touring will be over. Shortly after he had visited Hazaribagh, I gather there was a communal disturbance there; and, of course, there has been trouble in Gangtok, which he visited last February. Something also as I gather came up in Assam last fall. . . .

I apologize for our relative ineptness in these matters. Mr. Burleigh is noth-ing more nor less than meets the eye: a rather young, intelligent, and enthu-siastic Foreign Service officer. To my certain knowledge, he has not in any way been involved in making trouble in India. The difficulty in denying this with any credibility is that the person issuing the denial has to be able at least to conceive the possibility of the charge being true. But surely you cannot imagine that I could take seriously the thought that a 31-year-old Foreign Service officer, nine months in India, can move in on an Indian city and turn it into a civic volcano in the course of forty-eight hours, most of which he spends with local officials and members of the Congress Party. I don't think there is even such a person in fiction, and we know what the fiction about foreign agents is like these days. The other problem is that the newspaper <u>Patriot</u> seems addicted to such stories. Five days after you spoke to me, a similar tale appeared under the heading "Sinister Moves to Create Trouble in Kashmir Valley." Therein I learned that:

> A "revealing" coincidence between the unannounced visits of American "diplomats, officials and writers" to Kashmir valley during the off-season for tourists and the menacing appearance of communal tension has substantiated popular suspicions about foreign complicity in a reactionary bid to start disturbances in this sensitive border State.

Who then should turn up among these sinister visitors? None other than "Mr. Chester Bowles, former American Ambassador in India accompanied by his secretary and some family members." The evidence of conspiracy consisted largely of the fact that there was no evidence. To wit:

> These persons stayed in different hotels and houseboats. Their carefully staggered sojourn provided them with apparently suspicion-free opportunities to meet local people. Several closed-door meetings are learnt to have taken place between now-identified local RSS men and the visiting "diplomats, writers, and officials."

I fear the Prime Minister might be distressed by this <u>Patriot</u> story, as Ambassador and Mrs. Bowles are devoted to her. But you will understand that it is difficult for us here in the Embassy to strike an appropriate note of incredulity mixed with tolerance. I was rather pleased then to learn of the editorial in the April 28 issue of <u>The New Republic</u> of Ranchi, Bihar under the caption "The Scapegoat Bunters." I attach the text. <u>The New Republic</u> is not, as I understand it, especially friendly to the United States, but the editorial clearly recognizes that there are limits to the ludicrousness of suggesting that Americans are so powerful that the mere appearance of a junior Foreign Service officer can turn peaceable valleys into communal holocausts. . . .

Moynihan shares his anguish with Nathan Glazer over the crisis caused by
Watergate and the Nixon operatives' break-in of the office of Daniel Ellsberg's
psychiatrist.

MAY 25, 1973

Dear Nat:

. . . I have been thinking of little but Watergate, and thinking of just the
question you put: " . . . Is Watergate a difference in the quantity of political
skullduggery, promoted into the disaster it is by a special relation to press or
media, or a difference in real quality, which reflects some basic moral and political failing both of Nixon and those of us who saw him in the mainstream
of American politics, rather than as some cunning aberration?" You say you
wouldn't know how to answer that question if anyone asked, and neither
would I. Thirty years of reading and forty of going to Catholic churches leave
me with almost no preparation even for putting the question; much less answering it. Have I been a fool or a whore or both? Or perhaps something
quite different; something perhaps to be forgiven.

Let me reconstruct. I left Washington for India in quite a good mood. One
recalled Watergate, if at all, as an event that had <u>preceded</u> the campaign. The
campaign itself had been a routine exercise: Republican moralism, Democratic
hysteria. Voter indifference. Nothing notably nasty occurred; the outcome was
never in doubt; and was decisive. The Democrats were taken over by a minority coalition, and that was that. I had looked, with others, for some relaxation after the campaign. None came, but then Colson left, and this was cause
for something near rejoicing among those in the White House who were and
are decent, honorable, competent public men.

I think these men knew little or nothing of Watergate. And yet what cring-
ing animals this makes of us all. "I Knew Nothing." It makes us not only animals, but liars. Not worse, different. Of course they knew. There is a sense in
which we all "knew." Not in the sense that anybody ever, for example, told them
anything, or indeed let them in on anything. Neither had I been when I was in
the White House. I <u>like</u> to think the Ehrichmans assumed I wouldn't go along,
but I expect it was simply that I wasn't trusted. Yet when the 1972 campaign

came round I wanted nothing to do with the administration. I knew. I would not join Democrats for Nixon. In a day of blunt telephone calls in October I flat refused to sign that New York Times ad which Paul Weaver was getting up. (There is a man betrayed!) The names were of the first rank: Irving Kristol, Oscar Handlin, Ed Shils, as I recall. You will recall there were about six Harvard names. (The publication of the ad produced a petition of some 2,000 students protesting.) Len Garment put it to me that my not signing simply would not be understood. I said so be it. He called up the next morning after the deadline had passed, all good humor again: "You didn't know I could be a bully."

(Jim Wilson showed considerably more style than I. He did not even let the argument be put to him that declining to sign that ad would foreclose future favor. The President was just then appointing him head of a new drug abuse council: an important job both to the President and to JQW. He told the White House when he was called about that ad that he might be willing to sign, but that if he did he would of course refuse that Presidential appointment and any future Presidential appointment, as his name was not for sale. The poor flacks pulled back instantly.)

Anyway, I made no speeches, signed no statements, took no positions. I did do an interview with Nixon for LIFE, but that was minimal. Yet neither did I protest. I wanted no part of that administration, yet I did not break with it. Next, I voted for it—privately, to be sure, but I did vote for it. Finally, I returned to it.

What do you call such a person? A Moynihan, I suppose. A term suggestive of moral and political failing. Yet what is it? Two things, somewhat opposed.

First, the moral failing of being more concerned with deviations from one's own general position than with positions flatly and openly opposed. This is the classic condition of the true believer, and one of which we have been more than a little contemptuous. And yet has it not been our condition also? Have we made a passion of pragmatism? Whatever the case, we spent much of the 1960s appalled at the decline of intellectual and even moral standards on the liberal/left. We saw this as a phenomenon of ideology, when in fact it was increasingly a function of what American government was becoming. When a conservative government came in and seemed sensitive to the fooleries of its predecessors, we were too grateful by half, and altogether too willing to supply arguments. We were willing to be used.

Our political failings were rather different. We recognized the movement of electoral weight in a conservative direction. Recognized without necessarily approving. (You, Norman, Me, Jim Wilson: which of us would not have hoped for Humphrey or Jackson as a 1972 candidate we could and would have supported. As it was all any of us did was to refuse to sign ads for Nixon.)

But while we saw the voters drifting to the right, we did not remind ourselves sufficiently of what we knew, namely that, if anything, there was a movement of political competence to the left. We <u>knew</u> this. Over and again Norman would tell me that the administration would someday be ruined by its seeming relentless insistence on incurring the hostility of <u>men who simply outclassed it</u>. I recall having lunch with him just after My Lai. When the news had broken, I had immediately sent the President a memo pleading with him to move fast in response to the moral disaster it had to imply for the nation and the armed force. I was musing to Norman that it was a bad break coming just as it did when the President seemed to be having some success with his peace moves. "Bad break my ass," said Norman. "You think it is a bad break that this one story broke. Good God, there are fifty men—five thousand and fifty men—out there digging for stories such as My Lai, and everyone of them is five times smarter than anyone who would even consider working as a flack for the Nixon administration." I agreed. I kept trying to tell people in the administration that a fundamental fact of their dialectical and rhetorical position was that they were permanently outclassed, and would have to respond to this fact by devising simple, workaday policies that above all did not rely on their own cleverness either at exposition, or execution. <u>They</u> never followed this. An understandable failing: what was I saying but they were not smart enough to follow what it was I was saying?

Watergate was one logical result of their blindness. To think they could pull it off, and if they did, to think they would know how to use the information! So equally the break-in at Ellsberg's psychiatrist. If the President had wanted Ehrlichman or Krogh to find out what they could about Ellsberg— not an outrageous suggestion, Nixon had every reason to wonder who the fellow was—it would not have been that hard to go about the task in a simple way. They could have called me, and I would have said, "Well, I met him at Nat Glazer's for dinner one night. You might ask Glazer what kind of fellow he is." Etc. But Ehrlichman was not intelligent enough to do this, nor Krogh sufficiently experienced, and so they disgraced the Presidency.

All right. But why did we not have the political sense to see that sooner or later this would happen? We know the world. We surely saw that the men of the Nixon administration who, in Elliot Richardson's words to the Senate Judiciary Committee, "betrayed" us by their "shoddy standard of morals" are not "normal" men. They are so straight they are deviant. Ehrlichman, for one, always seemed to me a clinical case. Buttoned up to the point of bursting. And if we could have seen this coming, we could have taken the great prudential precaution of being out of the way when it hit. I would not worry myself about your own position. (Thank God for your <u>New Leader</u> article with Dan.) But still, there is a general truth in your statement that "the people we have been fighting all along now seem to win." Accordingly, Norman loses, I lose, Irving loses ... and so down a not inconsiderable list.

I feel I myself had a lot to do with this. In a sense I introduced the Nixon administration to you all, and did so on much too favorable terms. Or rather, I never made clear, later, how much I had soured.

It began in the fall of 1969, with the first big peace demonstrations of the new administration. There were two. One not especially attractive; the other very much so. This latter was run by the young people—Brown and the like—who had been associated with the McCarthy campaign. The administration made an effort to cooperate: a new government approach to all that misery was in the making. But Mitchell, in the end, would have none of it. The demonstrators had marshals; the administration had people in touch with them. Most of my staff was enlisted for this latter role: Dick Blumenthal, Checker Finn, and such like. They did a first-rate job, but Mitchell got carried away: "It looks like the Russian Revolution," was his famous summation, gazing down from the Attorney General's offices. At one point he became convinced that Blumenthal was in cahoots with the demonstrators and had him removed from his post. Dick was certain he was going to be fired, and I was pretty sure an attempt would be made. I told him on the Monday morning that followed simply to do nothing and we would let Mitchell find out that there were limits to his power: if Blumenthal went, so would I have done, and in the end nothing happened. But the administration commenced to change rapidly. In part they were frightened. But another part of their minds told them that the demonstrators were losing public sympathy, and that to take an opposed stand would in the end produce the 1972 election results, which I suppose it did. <u>Both</u> results. At this point I was very much a part of things in the White House, arguing at morning staff meetings both for a tough-minded view of the peace movement, but also for and between people any democratic administration might be concerned with, and those it ought to be proud of. I didn't get very far, although I think I had had some influence in organizing the original response.

By October I was on my way out. Burns was leaving for the Federal Reserve. Haldeman and Ehrlichman—much more the latter—moved in to take over. All with the President's approval, to be sure. On the day it was announced that Bryce Harlow and I would be elevated to Counselors to the President and Members of the Cabinet (a small bit of treachery—I had agreed to succeed Burns in that role, but had not been told Harlow could be "elevated" also) a fascinating thing occurred. Jim Keough was then head of the speech writing staff, a purposely variegated group: Pat Buchanan, Bill Safire, Ray Price. A range from Right to Liberal. And all pretty good men. They cared about ideas and were careful about them. Either they were having a staff meeting that day the news broke, or assembled for one. The dismay was unanimous. "The balloon men," said one, "have taken over." Half the men there were distrustful (at very least) of my politics, the other half by Burns'. But this was nothing to them compared with the fact that domestic policy direction was now to be run by Ehrlichman and his small group whose campaign job—literally—had been to arrange the "balloon drop" at the end of each Nixon rally. The President very simply turned his domestic policy over to men without the intellectual or temperamental capacity to handle it. We had set things off on a sufficiently sensible course—Burns and McCracken and myself—and there were men such as Shultz with ideas of their own—such that things kept going, but intellectually it was downhill from there on, and with that so much else came. It was more innocence than evil. But oh the banality of evil.

I dropped out. Maybe I should have left on the spot, but I was excited about Family Assistance and some other things, and certainly had no complaint with the way I had been treated on policy issues. I opted for sticking with the initiatives I had begun, and leaving everything else to the new Domestic Council, which succeeded my Urban Affairs Council, and took my people with it. I stopped going to morning staff meetings in the Roosevelt Room and pretty much opted out of all the operational goings on of the White House.

The atmosphere began to worsen. Not for me. Personally it was pleasant. (Thus when Bob Finch had to leave HEW, I was the White House candidate to succeed him. He quite understandably felt it would look awful, and so Elliot Richardson was sent.) But the kind of upper and lower class nihilism of which we spoke so often in those days was mounting, and with it alarm and a kind of political vengeance in the White House. I grew enormously concerned about the Black Panthers. Mitchell and Ehrlichman either didn't understand what was being said about the government assassinations, or didn't care. Awful either way. I used to have assistant attorneys general over to grill them on just what we knew about New Haven, etc. (I remember asking one tough Texan whether the Panthers would get a fair trial. "A lot fairer trial than they gave that buddy of theirs," was the reply.) I felt Mitchell was almost hoping for confrontation. Probably I exaggerate, but there it is. It is in this context that I wrote my "benign neglect" memo which, if you will recall, basically assured the President that things were not going badly. Incomes had suddenly equalized for young couples outside the south; that there was a "silent black majority" also; we should keep things going on, getting better, and not fall into the Panther trap of accepting the charge that they were getting worse. (If only I could have known then that by 1973 Bobby Seale would be running for Mayor of Oakland!) The memo was clearly directed against Mitchell, and to the best of my knowledge the President accepted it as such. He scribbled comments all over it—favorable, save for one note: re the "silent black majority" he wrote: "No, this is Garment's view, it is a minority." But he did accept that there was such a group and it should be encouraged and facilitated. He sent the memo, with his comments to the entire cabinet. I found this out and called Haldeman immediately to say such things should not be distributed, that they would leak. Haldeman sent a young man around who picked up the annotated copies, but replaced them with "unmarked" xeroxes.

It leaked, of course, and suddenly the New York Times had me branded a reactionary. You will imagine the response inside the administration and especially the White House. The real reactionaries—and there were some—delighted at my disgrace, Mitchell feeling more powerful than ever, while the moderates and liberals were once more confirmed in their conviction that no matter what you did the New York Times would make the worst of it.

Then came Cambodia, and by now there was little give left. I recall the midmorning when a shaken Bud Krogh opened my door in the White House basement to say there had just been shooting at a place called Kent State. Did I know where it was, or what we should say? He had come to me out of a kind of memory that I had been the one pleading a different line about such things at the beginning of the school year. I sat down and wrote a compassionate—I thought—and certainly placatory statement for the President. Bud took it upstairs. I should have gone with him, for just the opposite kind of pronouncement was issued, and things were all the worse for it. After that I grew even more distant. I asked the President if I could resign. He asked me to wait a bit to help on FAP, which I did. What kind of morality is that? Well, in part it was the morality of not wanting to have the President of the US feel he cannot trust to the good will of even one Harvard professor other than Henry.

But what kind of politics? Note the good sense of Art Klebanoff. He left the third afternoon for Cambodia, and made the front page of the New York Times doing so. Politics is not just prudence, but in the absence of prudence, failure is not to be forgiven. It is deserved and a mark of inadequacy. (I saw Henry in Paris last Saturday. He made much the same point.) The President was not ungrateful for my hanging on. To the contrary. Shortly he offered me the UN. I turned it down. But then got caught up in the school desegregation effort. I have told you, have I not, of those committees we set up in each southern state, the meetings in the White House chaired by Shultz. Then to culminate it the President flew to New Orleans to meet with the whole group and tell them the South had decided to change. Within three weeks, as Jim Coleman put it, more change occurred in the school system of the United States than had occurred in the preceding century. In a flash the dual school system of the South disappeared. On the way back from New Orleans I told the President I would after all go to the UN. I was truly proud of him—and a little self proud also, I guess. (The Times had pictured him in New Orleans talking to two White Motorcycle cops wearing riot helmets.) But by the end of the year I had come to my senses about staying. Oh, but I was still proud enough of his moves on desegregation, and grateful for the real efforts he made for FAP at the end there, that I gave my farewell speech to the Cabinet. I suppose it will be held against me the rest of my life at a place like Harvard.

And yet. . . . Once home I began to get letters from the people who had been present. They are remarkable documents in a way. One man after another wrote how genuinely moved he had been that someone had said something nice about RN. Dwight Chapin wrote an extraordinary letter: there he was, he said, way over his head, and he knew it, trying to cope with things he didn't understand and wasn't up to, and doing it for a profoundly decent man whom he'd known and worked for for a decade and in all that decade I was the first person ever to say anything personal and kind about that man in public.

They betrayed us. But there is a sense in which they were also betrayed. Nothing they did could win the approval of those people and especially those papers now destroying them. The feeling was mutual, to be sure. (After the 1972 election Punch Sulzberger's sister described him as defending the paper's opposition to Nixon: "What am I to do with a President who wants to put me in jail?") No give either way. Government needs a little sympathy. It needs a lot of understanding. More than any one thing that is what you have been saying these past four years—not least in your excellent New Society and Commentary pieces. Nixon's didn't get much.

Gradually—I think this is the case—it didn't deserve much either. You recall the first letter I sent the President after leaving the White House: Pleading with him to see that the administration was not living up to Presidential standards in its concern for civil liberties. Not civil rights. They were doing more there than almost anyone would have expected. But civil liberties. I put it that this view had come to me forceably from businessmen with whom I had been meeting. (Always there was that slightly corrupting need to reassure Nixon that you are all right, really.) The letter was obviously directed to Mitchell. But what did they do? They sent it to Stans at the Commerce Department to see if he was picking up any such reaction from the business community. Whence it leaked to Time. Furor in the White House. Colson suggested I had leaked it. But Haldeman found out this was not so. In the meantime I had half a dozen calls saying the letter was the most brilliant thing I had done for the administration. It was not. What the calls were saying was that that cause was getting steadily weaker.

But I didn't know that. Not finally. And you certainly didn't and neither did Norman or Irving. Much less Beichman or Ross. And so down the slippery slope. They were not berserk. They merely let themselves get involved step by step into something that got out of control, whereupon they tried to cover up and thereupon came catastrophe. They were not evil so much as innocent: they believed what they told one another about the degraded standards of behavior in Washington. Much as do the elite leftists of Cambridge. And so they measured what would be permitted in their behavior by what they thought to be normal to the behavior of others. Well, they have found out otherwise, and we are all in trouble for it.

On a personal level, the trouble of someone like me is more or less irrevocable. I shall stick it out here for lack of any place to go, but with no great expectations. (On the other hand I shall feel freer to say exactly what I think.) For your part, I would not worry at all.

You will be one of the few surviving members of the band, and there will be work aplenty.

Love to Lochi [Mrs. Glazer]. New Delhi awaits you.

The following letter and many thereafter refer to the principal achievement of his time in New Delhi, an agreement involving settlement of a huge debt of Indian rupees in return for the United States' shipment of food grains under the P.L. 480 program, starting in 1954. To pay for the emergency food aid, India deposited rupees in its central bank, but these reserves—which climbed to more than $3 billion worth by the 1970s—were not available to the United States to spend anywhere but in India and were a source of political concern in New Delhi. The State Department's initial position was to waive interest payments and write off a third of the debt. Moynihan, meeting with Nixon and Kissinger, eventually got clearance to negotiate an agreement in which two-thirds would be written off.

In this letter, Moynihan provides an update on India to Kenneth Rush, deputy secretary of state, and his concern that the rupee deal may not be achieved. In discussing India's closeness to the Soviet Union and to Communists, Moynihan refers to a limerick once cited by President Kennedy:

> *There was a young lady of Niger*
> *Who smiled as she rode on a tiger;*
> *They returned from the ride*
> *With the lady inside,*
> *And the smile on the face of the tiger.*

MAY 25, 1973
PERSONAL-EYES ONLY

Dear Ken:

... Things poke along here. The Indians seem to have settled into a sort of acceptance of the fact that we do not <u>mean</u> them any harm, but that our near necessary attachments to Iran and to China mean an inevitable attachment to Pakistan also which may once again—as it has in the past—<u>do</u> them harm. For my part, I am no good at lying, and so my general message is to urge them to improve their relations with the Persians and the Chinese, pleading their proximity and our increasing remoteness.

I am a little sad at all this. As I remarked to Henry, I assume we fought the Vietnam War to save India from going Communist, or becoming Finlandized, as is the more proximate probability. I have heard two Presidents go on at some length about "dominoes." Clearly India is the biggest domino of all. As well as the only one that could be described as a democracy apart, perhaps, from Singapore. And so the final tragic irony of Vietnam is that because the Indians opposed our involvement in that war designed to maintain her independence we have quite abandoned our commitment to it. Which is not to say we desire to see India go under: merely that we will do almost nothing to help prevent this.

The test case, in my view, has been the handling of my rupee instructions. I haven't seen them, but it is obvious how they will come out. Two billion dollars or something thereabouts. We are approaching it as <u>rentiers</u>, who do not give a damn about anything but a modest income in a useless old age. Imagine asking Indians of the 21st Century to continue paying for the surplus food Eisenhower, Kennedy, and Johnson provided their grandparents and great grandparents. My own grandfather, when he had a certain amount of ale in him, would speak of men who "had the soul of a butler." <u>That</u>, if you will, is what I fear in America. The war took too much out of us.

This may sound ill-natured, but I am actually in good enough spirits. I came out here not because I wanted to but because the President asked me. Just as in 1969 I went to Washington and served in his cabinet. I can put up with whatever "the system" cranks out, but I propose to keep in mind what I think to be <u>the interests of the President</u>, and to keep them distinct in my own mind from <u>the interests of The Thing</u>. Mind, I am hardly flawless in perceiving what the interests of either are, but I am closer to events here, and for my own peace of mind have to think it possible I may be right and Washington wrong.

Thus it is clear to me that the interests of this President, the only one you and I are going to be working for (I can't imagine any future one hiring us), is to bring off a symbolic rapprochement with India to offset the impact of 1970. A generous rupee settlement would do this at near zero cost to the Administration. (A few mild protests in Congress, perhaps, but when has that deterred this Administration!) But apparently this is not to happen, and so be it. Similarly, the policy of The Thing should be to pursue the long-run interests of the United States. Here again a quick and "generous" rupee settlement is in order. (The word generous is a bit deceptive. This is, after all,

Monopoly money.) India owes the United States $3.3 billion in <u>real</u> money. Dollars. India is repaying faithfully ($116 million this year!). How long it will succeed in doing this I do not know. But surely we should do everything possible to ease the political burden on the government of keeping up payments. One such thing would be to get us out of the business of owning 20% or 50% or whatever of the Indian currency. If The Thing can't see this, well so be it. When the real debts are repudiated in the 1980s, I shall write a short piece for the <u>Times</u> Op Ed page saying I told you so.

In the meantime, I expect India will be at some pains to keep up appearances with the United States. We remain the most powerful economy in the world, and, for various reasons, the one in the best position to be of help to India. (Curiously, this is <u>not</u> the case with the Soviets who are short of the same things India is short of, etc.) . . . Let me sum up what seems to me the new situation. India perceives that the large and long-run geopolitical interests of the United States have second order consequences which will recurrently be detrimental to her. She cannot change this. Nor in a sense "can" we. Accordingly, the long-run political interests of India lie in solidifying its relations with the Soviet Union, without falling under external Soviet domination, or internal Communist control. This of course requires a degree of calibration which not many governments succeed at.

One recalls President Kennedy's limerick about the Lady from Niger. Already, Communists are everywhere in the Indian government, holding some of the most important posts for the long run, as for example the Education Ministry. Hence our diplomacy must be directed to preventing this latter development. In the meantime, the short-term economic interests of India require increasingly close and correct relations with the American economy. They hope this needful relationship will diminish with time, but it may not. Accordingly India will seek to minimize its political differences with the United States. For its part the United States should (and probably will) cooperate in this process in order to retain some political influence for the purpose of minimizing Indian dependence on Russia.

I should be interested if you very much disagree with this analysis. You might try it on Bill when he returns from South America. I have not presumed to trouble him with my musings on the subcontinent, but you may think it useful to do so now.

I can imagine your own feelings at this time, especially for John Mitchell who was and is your friend. There are men I held in some respect who seem also to have come to grief, and there is none of us—assuredly not I—who cannot conceive the process of self-deception that could lead to such tragedy. We were, as Elliot told the Senate Judiciary Committee, "betrayed." But is one not responsible for allowing himself to <u>be</u> betrayed. And therefore how shall it be said that we served the Republic?

Although Kissinger was in charge of foreign policy at the White House, Moynihan continued to keep close ties with Secretary of State William Rogers.

JUNE 1, 1973
<u>PERSONAL</u>

Dear Bill:

It is June. We last talked in February, and it occurs to me you might not object to an occasional note.

Not that there is much to report. My arrival here aroused considerable expectations, but as months have gone by and nothing has happened, a certain sourness returns. Partly, perhaps, as a result of my combined entreaties and threats, the government, and notably the Prime Minister, have (British usage—so soon!) pretty much abandoned the President-baiting which so upset us just before I left. But they sense no real friendship from the United States, and this I think they are right. I have spent most of my adult life in government and recognize an institutional posture when I encounter one. The institutional posture of the American government is that India is <u>de facto</u> an unfriendly power. It comes through in every cable.

I don't see the cure for this, given the present constellation of forces, but I do rather enjoy the irony. I assume we fought the Vietnam war to keep India from going communist. I have heard two Presidents go on at some length about dominoes. Which is the biggest domino of all? India obviously: the second most populous nation on earth, equal in numbers to South America and Africa combined: the great prize of Asia. But India did not support that war, and so we ended it not caring what happened to India. Indeed, taking a certain perverse pleasure, even, in those signs that India might be on that slippery slope. We conceal this from ourselves by the doctrine that India is a Power. It is nothing of the kind. To the contrary, it is near internal chaos—as it has been for years, and likely as not will be until it ceases to be a democracy. We might then find a totalitarian nuclear nation of a billion persons fundamentally hostile to <u>our</u> existence. In the meantime, after ten years of savage confrontation with the Congress over Vietnam, every time the slightest suggestion is made for improving things out here a bit, someone from Washington tells me it would upset some committee chairman.

As you know, I never thought much good was going to come of that war. I shall not ever forget the shock of that cabinet meeting at which you announced the Cambodian "incursion." I thereafter asked the President if I might resign. He said of course I could, but would I stay on long enough to help with the welfare legislation. Which I did, and so the point got lost, but it more than once comes back to me from the perspective of New Delhi.

I can sense how difficult things must be for you just now: as they are for all of us. I saw Henry in Paris two weeks ago, and he was much distressed. But then, the Vietnamese talks seem to have gone well.

I hope you are not leaving the Department. You stand for things that make a difference always, and make all the difference there is just now.

In his journal, Moynihan described a visit with Nixon before returning to India, as the Watergate scandal destroys many of his old colleagues in the cabinet and the White House.

JUNE 28, 1973

It has got to be the worst day of his life. His former Counsel has at just about this moment completed three, dry, devastating days of testimony in a hearing room in which the whole nation sat. He had stated that he and the President and half a dozen others had participated in a whole sequence of crime. At very least the President is guilty, in Dean's version, of misprision. Save that Dean's testimony should be shattered, the only thing that will save him from impeachment is the fear that so much damage has been done that the Republic dares not risk form. And risks its honor instead. Surely, the worst day in the history of the Presidency.

And yet he evidently means to get through it. We drift onto India. He makes his distinction between hardware and software in foreign affairs. I am tough on hardware: rupees, arms, and such. Soft on software: words, gestures, tributes. This is again what he told me in February. I am to bargain hard. I put my case that the moral nightmare of serving in India is that you can get so fed up at some "fucking Kasmiri Brahmin" that you don't care about or even welcome events which end in the death of swollen bellied children thousands of miles from the persons and light years from the thoughts of the self same Brahmins who won't miss a drink or a meal or an evening out in the process. "What is the Indian word for ducking?" "I don't know, but there must be a lot of them, because they do a lot of it."

That kind of morning.

Are the Russians undermining us in India? If I see any signs of it, I am to tell him, and he will talk to Brezhnev. He speaks as if a truce had been negotiated, and that he would want to know of violations. He is explicitly proud of the friendship treaty, adding "Henry did it." Until now the Soviets had wanted a bilateral treaty with the third party references. It would merely have dismantled our alliances, and roused the Chinese.

"Invite the Russian Ambassador to dinner."

He remembers to reassure me on Pakistan. "We would be mad to start up a huge military organization there." Henry mentions the rupee terms. I try to get in the point of keeping India non-nuclear, but they are off on a ramble about Brezhnev's carousing at Blair House. He had had dinner with him six nights running. Never had dinner with anybody other than his family six nights in a row. Obviously like him. They need sixty days to bring off a coalition government in Cambodia. Sihanouk (sp), the Lon Nol government, and the Khmers. It can only be done with Chinese intervention, and in Peking.

I mention my visit with Laird. "I know you will want to throw me out of the room, but Laird suggests we revive FAP." I only intended that he must be sick of the subject; he took it as suggesting he was not in favor, perhaps had never been in favor of the bill. He assures me otherwise. "I am for FAP."

"Do me one favor?" "Um?" "Turn that God damn right side up." As good a way as any to bring down the curtain. Leaving, he mumbles about not letting my colleagues get me down. O.K., I guess. He slaps me on the back of the neck. It hurts.

Henry and I go over our agreements. We will settle rupees at $1 billion, opening at $1.5. We will not quite follow the President's wishes on software. I make my point here: he *had* told me to be a Harvard professor. I will stay low. I need to give a press conference, my first. I will wait until his return from Peking. I will have to let it be known the rupee negotiations have started. ...

I had made my case on wheat. Butz [Agriculture Secretary Earl Butz] should be told that we give the matter special priority. My point had not been that subtle: Whatever they say, the Indians will not want to spend half their foreign exchange to make up a four months deficit in food. They will therefore tend to do the weak thing, putting off the decision until it is too late to make it, i.e. until shipping time will be greater than the time to the Fall harvest. If at this point they can claim that they tried to buy wheat but the American government somehow prevents its sale or export, they will have achieved their maximum goal: not to spend their reserves and not to take the blame. They don't have to have thought all this out in order to be following this strategy. Kissinger got it immediately. I don't think anyone else in Washington did. He had the attention to detail, and to precedence, of a Tammany boss. I traded something of value to him when I forewent my press conference. On the Peking trip he of a sudden asked, how I would get there. "Go to Hong Kong and take a train," I speculated. No, no. They would send a plane for me. Again, a trade. <u>He</u> is not going to fail. (And why should he?) ("If my shop had acted the way theirs did. If yours had . . .") Ruin, he sums up. Disaster. His foreign policy will now collapse. It absolutely depended on a strong regime in the United States, and Watergate has brought the regime down. It is a pity about the President. "All he ever wanted was respectability." . . .

Journal entry discussing his negotiating instructions.

JULY 10, 1973

What about it! My rupee instructions have arrived. They are everything I hoped for, and more. Henry kept his word which doesn't surprise me, but then went beyond it. The agreement was I would be instructed to ask for $1.5 billion, and when this became impossible would report failure and await his intercession to bring it down to $1 billion. A fair enough arrangement: he has the power, only he can break impasses. I expected a long painful couple of weeks waiting for him to come to my rescue. Instead, the fall back position is tacked on as a last paragraph of the instructions.

As the Indians know what we absolutely must have—I explained Friday to P.N. Dhar that a statute would be required to go under $1 billion—there is really not much to negotiate about. The proposal is extraordinarily generous. We turn over something like $6.5 billion in real or realizable assets in return for a $1 billion rupee account held at no interest. With normal use and current inflation it shouldn't last a dozen years. After which—or beginning with—the nightmare is over!

Curious, there is not I think another person alive who has just that relationship at this time with the Secretary of State, the Secretary of the Treasury, the Director of the Office of Management and Budget, the National Security Advisor to the President and the President such as to get such a package approved. It marks the first time in the current political era in which the President and the White House have rejected an interagency proposal concerning India on grounds that it was not generous enough. If only the Indians have the courage to see this and move quickly to an agreement, we can begin to turn things around. My negotiating team, which Howard Houston will head, thinks they will not.

Journal entry reflecting on the heat, sickness of India, the travails of Nixon, and Indian politics. It irritated Moynihan that Mrs. Gandhi surrounded herself with British-educated leftists (Etonians) in denial about the onset of famine. (He once told a group of Indians: "Food growing is the first thing you do when you come down out of the trees. The question is, how come the United States can grow food and you can't?") In this entry his wrath seems directed at the left in both India and the United States.

JULY 12, 1973

Ours is the summer of our discontent. I am sick. The Prime Minister is sick. On the first occasion I have asked to see her since coming. Now the Voice of America reports the President is sick. Pneumonia. Maybe.

Delhi is unendurable. They have mucked up their power stations so there is no air conditioning, which makes buildings designed for it near to unlivable. Government is at a stop. They need to buy ten percent of our wheat crop and still having not made a move. Yesterday, for the first time, to my noting, the word famine appeared in the press. In the meantime, the Etonians in the cabinet are traipsing about the Soviet bloc clucking class solidarity. . . .

It is poor Nixon now, is it not! Pneumonia. Mitchell [Attorney General John Mitchell] is behaving very much as I knew him, and not without his own dignity. He has that contempt of the half educated for the fancy. He showed it when he was up, and he is showing it now he is down. Years ago— it all seems—I was lamenting some performance or other to Garment [White House counsel Leonard Garment]. The Attorney General would not share our compassion for some unsettled group or other. Will government never teach him anything, I asked. No, said Garment, when they carry him out of here he will still be puffing on his pipe and looking distastefully on the batch of us. Well they damn sure carried him out: but he did not change.

It seems again and again to come back to Kennedy's remark after the first television debate: "No class." They did not have it, and now never will. As Henry said, the only thing he ever wanted to be was respectable. Now, pneumonia. Colson [White House aide Charles Colson] has evidently told the Detroit News that their insecurity led to madness. Irving Kristol's point! "That insecurity began to breed a form of paranoia. We over-reacted to the attacks against us and to a lot of things." It will be some while before I discover an excuse for him, and yet an explanation is in order. He is a bully, and presumedly therefore abnormally fearful of pain. But there is something else, and it has somewhere to do with the Weimar experience. The taunting class superiority of their enemies. . . . This made the Oxbridge Stalinism of the 1930s so difficult to deal with. Revolutionaries looking down their noses at you. The United States as the socially inferior class enemy. The carry over to Congress party hauteur is at times near total.

Journal entry describing his first meeting with Prime Minister Gandhi. Anti-American sentiment led to the United States turning over AID House, the building that housed its foreign aid program, to India.

JULY 17, 1973

My first private meeting with the Prime Minister. As successful as any such meetings are going to be now for a very long while. I gave Dhar a proposed agenda two weeks ago with no difficulty, but not the least effort on her part to be anything but correct. I began by telling of Henry's suggestion that she send an emissary over for a periodic tour d'horizon; an arrangement we had with the British, the Chinese, and the Soviets. I would assume that any other chief of government in the world would automatically and perhaps enthusi-

astically accept such an invitation. The Prime Minister explained that if someone were to go it would raise questions in Delhi as to why. I outlined our proposal on P.L. 480 rupees. Our holdings, preserve and prospective come to
$6.04 billion. We would settle for $1 billion. She said take it up with the Minister of Finance. I presented an Aide Memoire on the occasion of the end
after twenty one years of the American technical assistance program. We had
helped bring about the green revolution, eradicate malaria, build thirty three
colleges and universities. India had asked that the program be terminated. We
would also turn over the AID staff house, a complete high rise apartment
complex built for the technicians. She thanked me for the apartment buildings. I said I would give a party on the occasion of the transfer and hoped she
might come. She didn't say.

Then to food. They have been following, step by step, the pattern I foresaw,
putting off purchasing, looking to us somehow to come up with something.

They meet with American bureaucrats and ask if everything isn't terribly
complicated, and the bureaucrats of course agree. Yesterday I sent Henry a
cable asking if we couldn't get a public assurance that the grain would be there
if India wished to buy. He replied immediately that this would be our first
political priority, but the economic situation is now too uncertain. Fair enough.
I confine myself to saying that the President is concerned that India get what
she needs. For the first time she asked what might be done. In the circumstances all I could say was that my advice would be that they should have
bought what they needed three months ago. This is a lesson they had best be
encouraged to chew on for a long time. They will need to if they are going to
be able to swallow it.

Note to Kissinger about his conversation with Mrs. Gandhi.

JULY 17, 1973
PERSONAL

Dear Henry,

I met this morning with Mrs. Gandhi and put to her your suggestion that
she might send someone over periodically for a <u>tour d'horizon</u> of the sort you
have been having with the British. This was the first of five matters I raised

with her, and she had had a fortnight's notice of my intent. Even so, she was evasive, explaining that if someone were to go, all manner of questions would be raised as to Why. I allowed that the meetings you now have, while not "secret," nonetheless took place with no public notice of which I was aware. We left it at that.

It is not the suspicion around here that bothers me: it is the way suspicion blinds them to their own interest. But I see no alternative to a waiting game. We are not, in that sense, in any hurry. . . .

Journal entry as Moynihan grows increasingly concerned about famine.

JULY 19, 1973

The starving time appears to be at hand. The words begin to appear in the press. "Famine deaths' in Orissa" is the lead story of the Hindustan Times. Kerala, which in normal times must have food imports at this season, is on half rations from the central government and growing desperate. All schools have closed.

And so it is also America time once again. Kissinger has been extraordinary in getting me what I asked. A cable last night reported that after talking with [Agriculture Secretary Earl] Butz it was evident that the Indians could buy three to four million tons of grain if they moved immediately. We would see that it was exported. I asked first thing to see Dhar who said come up immediately. I gave him my news. Together we dictated a cable to their Washington embassy: buy. I talked, beyond my knowledge, of helping with freight and shipping. In the afternoon an hour with Kewal Singh who was forthcoming, even grateful. Odd. Or perhaps not odd. I make clear that we are not giving them anything, merely offering to help them buy with hard cash at inflated prices. I expect they are as responsive as if we <u>were</u> giving it to them. . . .

Journal entry reflecting Moynihan's growing anxiety that he will be tarnished by Watergate.

AUGUST 8, 1973

... A particular kind of Watergate sickness has got to me. I wonder each day what if any reputation I shall have left when I go home. Will mere association—and it was more than mere—with the administration be a form of disgrace not ever to be overcome. I have assumed so, and I think this will be the case. . . . There is more than just self pity to this. A man must know his powers if he is to be at all serious in using them. Thus I suppose I know as much—and possibly more—about black problems as they involve the Federal government than any white man alive, but I am silenced on the subject. I took a bad fall with "benign neglect," and now must stay apart permanently from this issue. It is a considerable waste, for I am really pretty good on the subject, and care as much or more than most people. I was raised with black kids on the streets of New York, working with them shining shoes, playing with them, and <u>fighting</u> with them. I know what Norman Podhoretz knows and seemingly no other white affluent liberal either knows or can be brought to understand, which is that blacks first enter the world of a white working class kid not as victims but as aggressors. If you do not know this you can never understand the politics of this issue, nor see the necessary failure of an idealistic politics dependent exclusively on the image of victim. So it is a waste for me to be permanently barred from discussing the subject. And it is not fair. But that is what JFK said of life, and what in the end he proved. My question has been does this now extend to <u>all</u> public matters. What would I do with my life if I were thus disbarred. Perhaps I shall find out. Perhaps not. . . .

Journal entry from Alleppey, a community of backwater canals south of Cochin, on the Arabian Sea in South India, where he traveled with his son, John. In Cochin, Moynihan was fascinated by the Jewish, Dutch, and Portuguese influences, and in Alleppey he went to snake boat races.

AUGUST 11, 1973

<u>ALLEPPEY</u>

The Snake boat races, for which I and the Governor are the chief guests are a spanking good time. Why have I never gone to such affairs. I assume it is because when I was eleven my mother gave my 75¢ to see the Yankees,

DiMaggio homered, Gehrig went hitless, and it rained in the seventh inning. She gave me another 75¢ and the same thing happened again. And there was no getting over it. This is about my first sports event since. The boats seat a hundred rowers with scarcely six inches of freeboard but grand towering sterns. They cover the mile in about four minutes; in the stretch the stroke gets up to 104 a minute, as I counted. I counted at least well enough to pick the winner in the final heat and win ten rupees from a sporting admiral. Governor Wanchoo, a Kashmiri Brahmin and old ICS hand, kept his enthusiasm in bounds, especially as his wife kept finding occasion to note that he still couldn't understand Malawali. Mind he has only just arrived, and his wife isn't even going to try. The crews tank up on toddy before and after their runs and look splendidly polynesian. The crowds are cheerful and the sport is general. Good for Alleppey. Nehru came here twenty one years ago and donated a cup, which is the race I bet on. Good for him too.

Journal entry from New Delhi describing the festivities of Indian Independence Day at the Red Fort, where the diplomatic corps assembled to hear Mrs. Gandhi speak. He refers here to Sir Edwin Lutyens, the British architect who designed the presidential palace and other government buildings in New Delhi.

AUGUST 15, 1973
INDEPENDENCE DAY

... The city is <u>en fete</u> sort of. Arches have been put up here and there and signs proclaim the curious ideological mix of Indian politics. LONG LIVE DEMOCRACY, SOCIALISM, AND SECULARISM. HOARDERS, BLACK MARKETERS, AND FOOD ADULTERERS ARE ENEMIEES OF THE PEOPLE. The streets are empty save for school children getting lined up and a few opposition groups holding up their own placards: "Long Live our Freedom. We Don't Want Speeches. Give us Cheaper Food." ...

There is a convention here of "Freedom Fighters," which seems to be a kind of pension oriented veterans organization. They were given seats of honor at the morning speech, and invited in the afternoon to the reception at the President's residence, once the Viceroy's Palace and now the Rashtrapati Bhavan. They float about amidst the medals and portfolios in frail Gandhi caps evoking for an American an almost physical encounter with gentleness, corresponding to and completing the setting of Lutyens's vast moghul gardens, all spit and polish and power, which look out through the occasional gateway on the billowing Hertfordshire meadows which secretly surround the Palace grounds, in the midst of the blasted North Indian plain, concealed alike from rulers and ruled. Even the British had their secrets.

Letter to Father Andrew Greeley, the author, sociologist, and Catholic activist, about India's experience with ethnic pluralism.

AUGUST 30, 1973

Dear Andy:

Yes, yes, come to India. Come to work and we'll pay most of your way. We've just initiated a series of guest speakers on the general-but-provocative topic of "Modern Society and Traditional Government." Nat Glazer started it last week, and Norman Podhoretz brings Act II in a few days. It's a multidisciplinary approach to the question of whether government helps or retards changes in the society, is helped or retarded by them. Like all such chicken-and-egg questions, we won't resolve it, but we'll at least stimulate some thinking in this land, which tends too often to see government as the root of all goodness and progress.

Ethnic pluralism in the United States, government efforts to cope with it, and their success or failure would be of considerable interest, and no one is better qualified to assay that one than you. In India it's known as "communalism," and it is both rampant and little discussed, partly because the government has made the subject taboo. . . .

Draft of a letter to President Nixon, recounting the political impact of a recent visit to India by the Soviet leader, Leonid Brezhnev, with whom Nixon was negotiating a détente.

[SEPTEMBER 1973]

Dear Mr. President,

As you know, Brezhnev has been here all week. On Tuesday he addressed a monster rally (at mammoth length) from atop the Red fort. (No play on words intended.) Those fortunate enough to attend were handed copies of his latest work OUR Course: Peace and Socialism. I thought you would like a copy as it consists almost wholly of speeches given on his last visit with you!

I count his trip something of a plus. Russia is the only great or near great power which the Indian government feels is concerned about and protective of Indian interests. To have the leader of that nation come down here to state forcefully and in public—on television—that detente with the United States is the greatest single force for peace in the world, and get the Prime Minister to say so in a communique is ... one of those "historic posts" you occasionally call attention to.

At the same time, the Indians, as best we can tell, kept their distance in military and diplomatic matters generally. No bases; no collective security pacts. As for the "massive aid" which today's papers announce, we will believe it when we see it. And I, for one, would welcome it if it appeared. If I have any opinion about this country at all, it is that it has been a moderate economic failure, but a distinct political success. There is a relation between these two seemingly contradictory conditions. Political success—the continuation and the strengthening of a viable, resilient, democratic political order has been achieved by adherence to ideals of social justice and modes of social control which simply make for very slow economic growth. There is a sense in which India, not wholly unwitting, has taken vows of poverty. As a Catholic this kind of thing may be easier for me to understand than for you, a Quaker. (Just as I find the renunciation of violence a difficult notion to feel.) There is a cost to the things which we, for example, are good at doing. God in heaven knows it shows. Well, it is a cost which for varying reasons Indians do not want to pay. For one thing, they fear the strains it would put on their social fabric, and [they] put their first priority on national unity and independence. And there are matters of concern also for which there is no better term than spiritual. ...

As for us, our problem out here—if indeed it is a problem—is that the most active and least ideological minds in Indian politics are coming to the conclusion that the United States just isn't any longer interested in this part of the world. No matter what it says. You would know my view: that this is true, and that it was a predictable consequence of our overcommitment—

everywhere—in the 1960s. The Nixon Doctrine contained, in my view, precisely the right combination of acceptance and assertion: acceptance that there is a point beyond which we will not go: assertion that there are points behind which we will not withdraw. I don't know if we have quite worked out the equivalent formulas for economic and political involvement with societies such as India. Or for that matter, with India as such. With the population of Africa and South America combined, it really is a case by itself. . . .

Journal entry from Kyoto, Japan, where Moynihan reflects on a speech delivered by Norman Podhoretz, the editor of COMMENTARY.

OCTOBER 5, 1973
KYOTO

Podhoretz is at the height of his form. He <u>has it</u>. He knows what has been going on in America since 1932 when Edmund Wilson, becoming Marxist, exulting in the Depression, pronounced that "We now have a chance to take our country away from the businessmen who took it from us." A score from Walden time, now to be settled, because the normal sources of strength of the republic had been shaken. A fantasy of power. So the 1960s. The radicalization of the intellectual community was not a response to a new perception of evils of bourgeois society, but a response to a new fantasy of power. . . .

The issues of "poverty," "war," "racism" were manipulated by intellectuals to establish their new politics. <u>He is right</u>. The main political values of the American intellectual community are anti democratic or non democratic. <u>I think he is right</u>. The armies of youth of the 1960s were commanded. <u>He is right</u>. . . .

Journal entry noting the beginning of war in the Middle East, as Egypt and Syria attacked Israel on Yom Kippur, the holiest day of the Jewish calendar. Moynihan was concerned about Israel and also about Jews who had assailed Nixon over Vietnam but who were now seeking U.S. help for Israel. He wonders if Nixon will support Israel as Johnson did in the 1967 war, and he notes the unfairness of anti-Israel sentiments in India.

War in West Asia, Porter King has begun briefing us and it suddenly comes home that the Israelis are massively out gunned. They had fewer than four hundred planes to start and have lost a quarter of them in three days fighting. The Egyptians are across the canal, and Russian missiles will keep them there. The sheer logistics of it are ineluctable. Jordan will come in, evidently the Iraqis—much stronger than I had supposed—will come across, the Russians will keep supplying what has to be had, and Israel will be defeated. Not destroyed, merely shown to be a very small country surrounded by large ones which mean to be revenged for things of the past which cannot now change. . . .

History's revenge. I assume the majority of the Israeli cabinet is Russian and was Marxist. Almost my only friends in the United States are Jews, and I care for them as for no other people, but I detest their messianic radicalism. As does Podhoretz. They brought it to the United States like cholera, and it is now everywhere that matters. And it always turns out this way. All power to the Soviets, and then see what happens to the nice guys. . . .

In the United States one would have to forecast a decline in Jewish influence, now unparalleled. The source of that influence is readily described. Jewish brains, incomparably the best in this age (or any age maybe) pitted only against Chinese and Japanese, and then mostly in the sciences, are overwhelmingly on the left, which is where intelligence has the most influence. (Consider Milton Friedman, a man with twice the class of most of his opposites. President Nixon does not know his name. Even his dearest friend Arthur Burns will have nothing to do with his policies.) Jewish money similarly, and perhaps more importantly, is also on the left side of the spectrum, where a given amount of money has incomparably greater leverage than on the right side by the mere relativity of things. (Recall Gene McCarthy: liberal money in politics comes from Jewish millionaires; campaign finance reform ought to have been a scheme devised in Houston.) Now these brains and this money must increasingly align with the American Presidency for only there, and possibly not even there, can protection for Israel be had. . . .

Here for fifty years Jews have provided the majority of American communists—or so Nat Glazer judges—and the preponderant influence on the left generally. Now they are preventing a Republican President from opening up relations with the Soviet Union because it does not allow Jews to emigrate to Israel, where the same community—not three percent of the population—

asks the United States to confront the solid disapproval or active military hostility of ninety five percent of mankind. Too much. As Mobil of California already perceived in asking its credit card holders to consider the desirability of a more balanced position in the Middle East. Even Nixon had his limits. At one point in 1969 he told Haldeman: "I have seen every black and every Jew in this town. Is there not a Catholic in Washington, D.C." I winced, but even at the time knew he was right. He demanded to see some Catholics, and he ought to have done. It was strange. Blacks and Jews had voted overwhelmingly against him in a close election; inevitably, they would do so again. There were no blacks, and few Jews around him. And yet blacks and Jews flowed into his office as Irish Catholic County Chairmen might have done in Roosevelt's first term. Such were the presumptions of importance and urgency in those years. This must now recede. . . .

Note to Nathan Glazer, expressing concern about Israel.

OCTOBER 11, 1973
<u>PERSONAL AND UNOFFICIAL</u>

Dear Nat:

I have been thinking of you repeatedly these past three days, and recalling those tense days of 1967 when you were staying with us, glued to the radio and terribly worried right to the end. I fear this time it is I who am probably the most worried. From this perspective it is so clear almost the whole world has turned on Israel. The imbalance seems to me ominous in the utmost degree. I write only to tell you you are in my thoughts.

Excerpt of a letter to Patrick Buchanan, President Nixon's speechwriter and political adviser, disagreeing with Buchanan's attack on foundations, particularly the Ford Foundation. Moynihan maintained a friendship with McGeorge (Mac) Bundy, former White House national security adviser under Kennedy and now president of the Ford Foundation, which funded many programs in India.

Dear Pat:

I was in Washington week before last and caught a glimpse of you on Educational Television. I need hardly say you seemed to hold up your side very well indeed; even if it was distressing to learn how few persons have actually read Larry O'Brien's campaign manual!

I am moved to write by your comments about the Ford Foundation: not to take issue, for the foundations can doubtless hold their own in any serious discourse on what I believe, as you believe, to be a serious subject. Rather, I would like simply to relate some history which you probably don't know, and which could well influence your overall judgment. You and I hold differing views concerning a mammoth range of unimportant matters, but I hope and believe we do agree on certain central concerns such as the integrity of public debate, and I know without bothering to ask that if there are facts that might affect your view of a matter, you would want to know them. . . .

What I am about to say is that the Ford Foundation, far from being hostile to the Administration was, at least in my experience of those early years, rather exceptionally supportive of it. I don't say this is the case with foundations generally, or rather with all foundations. The head of one of the more prominent ones has taken to providing me a press clipping service concerning the daily disasters of the Administration, a task to which he brings a feline energy not infrequently to be encountered among social activists educated at Groton, Harvard, and Emmanuel College, Cambridge. How, he asks with great solicitousness, do we "ex-liberals" feel now? I mention this only because you can smell these things and must know this to be, and for some time to have been, a mindset encountered in such places in New York. All the more then is it important to know that this was not in any encounter of mine the case with Mac Bundy and Ford. . . .

Let me, however, go beyond facts to comment on a problem that interests us both, which is that of establishing a viable conservative intellectual and political tradition in the United States. In a widely cited essay in 1948 Lionel Trilling declared that liberal ideas were wholly ascendent in the United States, that no conservative ideas were any longer in general circulation. As a liberal this bothered Trilling, and he asked whether it were not possible to generate forces internal to the liberal tradition which would nonetheless put liberal ideas under some pressure, lest they turn flabby and soft. The same issue came to preoccupy me as the 1960s passed. I took to saying as much in speeches to the Americans for Democratic Action and suchlike groups, a point Mel Laird did not fail to note. . . .

The ideas I kept pressing on the President were, to the best of my understanding, <u>conservative</u> ideas.

All this went forward with some success: others, of course contributed as well. But after awhile I began to see that most of the Administration just wasn't comfortable. I remember Bryce Harlow explaining that the first year of the Eisenhower Administration no Presidential program was sent to the Congress mostly because the Republican leaders would not have known what to do with it. They never <u>introduced</u> legislation; they only <u>opposed</u> legislation. Sixteen years later it was much the same thing: disbelief that any idea <u>could</u> be conservative. In medieval England a man accused of a crime who could prove himself literate was automatically assumed to be a priest and could opt for trial under Canon Law. So also this latest Republican Administration: to have a serious program idea was proof of liberalism. . . . I fear I fully share Norman Podhoretz's view that just as the experience of Stalin destroyed the reputation of socialism—it was too hard to explain that they were different—so Watergate will destroy the reputation of conservatism. You probably will not accept this, and I urge you not to. Moreover I note that, twenty years after Stalin's death, socialism is coming out of the closet once more. But I trust Podhoretz's sense of political culture. The kinds of thing you are trying to do are now made vastly more difficult. Carry on. After all, men like Irving Howe have devoted their lives to saying socialism <u>is</u> different from what the Soviets produced and his life is by no means a failure. But don't expect it to be easy. . . .

Let me conclude on a note which will seem even more personal, but which derives from little more than friendly tribal feelings. You, to the best of my knowledge, are a poor Irishman well into a career of writing speeches for conservative millionaires and their proteges. I am probably an even poorer one and even further along in a career that has mostly consisted of writing speeches for liberal millionaires and <u>their</u> proteges. I have got some good meals out of it but damn little else. If one of those Arabs the New Delhi constables are constantly protecting me from should succeed one day, I will leave Liz and the kids $10,000 in World War II life insurance, plus a mother and a mother-in-law. So I suspect would you. In the meantime, as I read from this morning's press file, investment bankers serving on the Yale Corporation and the board of the Ford Foundation will go on being appointed Under Secretaries of State. Think about it. . . .

Journal entry on a pleasant but unproductive meeting with Mrs. Gandhi.

THURSDAY
OCTOBER 18, 1973

A pleasant meeting with the Prime Minister. I convey the President's appreciation for the easy Indian response to Prime Minister [Zulfikar Ali] Bhutto's [of Pakistan] visit, (nod, smile) and commence my first serious effort to make contact with her. Dr. Kissinger had asked me to return to the United States. It was a difficult decision, as no matter what one did it was the wrong thing. In the end the President had let me off the hook by saying he was himself of two minds, and so I returned to India. Nod. Smile. Our relations clearly were improving: I was sure that in twenty years they would be much better. I was concerned however, that they were improving in proportion that they were diminishing We could have the most equable relations on the same basis that each of us has with Ecuador, which is to say scarcely any relations. That is why I was grateful for what I had taken to be her personal intervention to restore the flow of American scholars to India, however diminished it might be. Nod. Smile. I had been distressed just yesterday to receive a letter reporting that after fifty two years, the Rockefeller Foundation was closing its offices in India. Nod smile. I hoped for more closer economic relations, but I could see that they pose insuperable problems for the Democratic political system of India. Nod. Smile. And yet I had even so returned, for I was certain more could be done, and convinced that for our governments to do less would in an important sense fail our peoples. Nod smile. Comment that there are problems with persons travelling in places such as Orissa, causing troubles. Whereupon it is my turn to nod, smile, and go. . . .

Journal entry in which Moynihan tries to see Nixon's problems through his eyes.

OCTOBER 27, 1973

. . . What must dominate his thought is the incongruity. How would it go. He didn't do that much, and I paid scarcely any attention to it. I won 49 of 50 states, and if everything known now was known then, I would have won 40 anyway, AND THEY ARE TRYING TO STEAL THE ELECTION FROM ME AGAIN! They did it once. And I did not complain. But AGAIN!

And it doesn't matter that he can still perform <u>so well</u>. And for THEM! The Yom Kippur war was handled at least as well—better?—than the Cuban Missile crisis. It was learned behavior, one would have to think. He would not panic, he would not back down, he would match force with force, but not much more—in one week one billion dollars in arms were airlifted to Israel, the largest such movement in history, force at one remove—he would be affected by the universal hostility—in this instance world opinion. And in the end the Soviets backed down! . . .

Though sympathetic to Nixon, Moynihan tells Elliot Richardson of his support after Richardson resigned as Attorney General rather than obey Nixon's order to fire the special Watergate prosecutor, Archibald Cox.

OCTOBER 30, 1973
<u>PERSONAL</u>

Dear Elliot:

I have thought continuously of you these past days: so much as no longer to hesitate to intrude.

I am proud for you beyond reason: and in that pride reaffirmed in my sense of the honor and the indomitable virtue of the Republic. Words too large for any but the largest circumstance, but scarce large enough for the events you have been through, and which you have surmounted with a shining honor that will set a standard for public men and women so long as the meaning of freedom is understood.

Journal entry expressing concern that U.S. Naval maneuvers related to the Middle East war will be seen as hostile to India. The U.S.S. ENTERPRISE, *a nuclear-powered aircraft carrier, had steamed toward India in the Bay of Bengal during the Bangladesh War, provoking outrage in New Delhi and charges that it was mining*

the harbors of the Bangladeshi port city of Chittagong. As Moynihan notes, the charge was false. But now the ENTERPRISE *was involved again in the Arabian Sea near India, stoking India's paranoia.*

NOVEMBER 1, 1973

The U.S. military is magnificent except when it is not. In the late evening of Wednesday October 24, eight days ago, The President received a message from Moscow proposing a joint expeditionary force be sent to the middle east. The soviets were prepared to move within hours. It would have been—what?—the first expeditionary force in Russian history. OR something such. Certainly the first such leap in the cold war. And with it god knows what. The Joint Chiefs stayed up all night; the President ordered an Alert. Two million men climbed into flight jackets. The Russians backed down. Close. Superb. . . .

On Monday the Pentagon announced a U.S. Carrier Task Force was transiting the Strait of Malacca headed for the Indian Ocean. It was noted this would put the ships closer to the Mediterranean. (One week closer. Five weeks away.) It was noted the Soviets had increased the number of their ships in the Mediterranean. We read about it in the Newspapers. Gawd! The Enterprise again.

Tuesday: news black out. Slip of a lip Sinks a ship. Indian press getting ready to defend sacred Indian seas. Ceylon frantic. Bangladesh wakes up briefly to be alarmed. Malaysia and Indonesia state official regrets. But where are the damn things. This Embassy was never once told the sailing plan or location of the Enterprise, as I learned when the Prime Minister last spring allowed as how it had been mining Chittagong harbor. (It was never within 900 miles.) The leap of the Enterprise was a classic military blunder. Trying something which had worked fifty years earlier. It was expected to have <u>some</u> effect. Just what, and on whom, no one ever got clear. I can be thankful for it, as it so worsened relations [with] India as to have made it impossible for them not to improve during my tenure. Even so. I begin sending snotty cables asking how am I to persuade the natives to panic and the Nabobs to sign unequal treaties if I don't know where the bloody ships are. I.e. <u>which</u> natives, which nabobs do we propose to oppress. No reply. Probable lesson: don't be smart alecky when Admirals are at war games.

Wednesday. The Pentagon announces the task forces' operation is "totally without relation to the Soviets in the Mediterranean." It seems "It was there and it was available and it had been alerted and therefore the task force was gathered and was steaming together. It was in the vicinity. We do like to be in the Indian Ocean from time to time." You do, do you? I doubt it. But in any event <u>where</u> are the ships. Fortunately, the New York Times arrives by wireless. John W. Finney tells us they are headed for the Persian Gulf. SE-CRET cables from Honolulu tell us they are just sort of cruising around, don't you know.

Thursday. [Gen. Brent] Scowcroft hears my plea, and wires that they are of course headed for the Arabian sea, to stand off the Gulf or something of the sort. I wire CINCPAC in what I hope is for them unaccustomed language saying I will not be lied to, that I am perfectly capable of defending American policy, and enjoy doing so, but in no circumstances am I going to tell the government of India things that are not so. . . .

Journal entry on the transfer of the building that housed the U.S. international aid program being transferred to India.

NOVEMBER 4, 1973

The A.I.D. Staff House opened today as the Qutab Hotel, named for the Qutab Minar nearby, complete with Williamsburg dining room, Paul Revere bar, and India's first and only bowling alley. The Patriot awards credit to the Prime Minister for having moved swiftly to allot the buildings to the Ministry of Tourism after the U.S. decided to "surrender" them. We learned of the opening Thursday night from a civil servant George Isaac had brought round for drinks. Typically, I had not been invited, nor any of us. Which is not rudeness, but religion. It is one's duty to feed Brahmins. No obligation is returned. I let it be known in South Block that I thought this typical of the way Indians had responded to twenty years of American help, and the way they would respond to any further help if there were to be any. An invitation arrived by hand Friday afternoon. The Maharajah who is the Socialist minister of Tourism called Saturday morning. [Deputy Chief of Mission David T.] Schneider's arrived by courier Saturday afternoon. He went. The Complete career officer. But not without noting that ten years ago we would have invited ourselves, and sent teams of USIS photographers to record this latest benefaction. . . .

Moynihan often quoted Lionel Trilling, the Columbia University professor, as say-
ing that liberals, but not conservatives, embraced intellectual ideas. This letter to
Trilling refers, however, to Moynihan's concerns about Jewish attitudes toward
Nixon.

NOVEMBER 7, 1973
<u>PERSONAL</u>

Dear Lionel:

... I am immensely depressed with respect to the Middle East, the fragility
of Israel's situation seems so evident. I perhaps ought not to say more in a letter. I called Norman last evening but learned he is there, which seems to me
a good thing, as he was near beside himself sitting in New York. I watch with
pity and terror the antics of those who helped destroy the American Presidency—and it has not needed much external help—demanding that we put
an end to our military role in the world, now demanding the very opposite
and in terms that could impose a fearful cost. I think it no exaggeration that
Europe went neutral last week. It has got back its senses, but is one ever quite
the same after such an experience. A matter I leave to Lionel Trilling.

Journal entry hailing the Middle East cease-fire.

NOVEMBER 11, 1973

Triumph for Kissinger. Cease fire in the Middle East on terms no one
could have imagined. Diplomatic relations with Egypt. President Sadat for
an advocate. Scarcely to be believed, save that he is scarcely to be believed.
Somewhere Metternich remarks that he is the only man in Europe who
<u>thinks</u>. So also Henry a century and a half later. A massive ego and a pervading
fear combine somehow to inform him as to what it is that moves other persons, and then to pose alternatives that lead them of their own accord to move
as he desires. In the early years on Washington with the anti Vietnam, anti

Nixon liberals constantly at him, he never argued: he asked their help in maintaining his position against the reactionaries, against—"the worst side of Richard Nixon's character," to cite the Attorney General once again. When a few construction workers on Wall Street threw a punch or two at anti Cambodian marchers, Colson, quick to spot, brought some of them down to the White House along, as I recall, with [Labor Secretary] Peter Brennan [former construction worker union leader]. Right off Henry was telling the professors that if people keep taking to the streets it is <u>them</u> not <u>us</u> who will prevail. Power to the people means power to the hard hats and red necks. Mildly treacherous perhaps—what with the President thirty feet away probably accepting a hard hat from said delegation—but he survived to be the only reason anyone would want Nixon in office another day. ...

Journal entry expressing appreciation for the foreign service and disdain for the elite volunteers in Peace Corps.

NOVEMBER 19, 1973

The American Foreign Service is in the main tough minded, professional, detached. What is the Spanish? "With the great and powerful always a little patience." They bear with pretty much whatever comes in politics; taught by the world that America is no bad place and its politicians better far than most. I have yet to meet one with 1960s disease. They were spared as the military was spared, prudentially consigned to the saltmines of Dacca and Djibouti and—their special horror—Wagadugu (sp?) [reference to Oagadougou, the capital of Burkina Faso]. Radiation free, their gonads in serviceable condition, they confront their ruined country with a certain constructive compassion. <u>Have</u> you ever lived in Wagadugu? Think of them as a sperm bank and be thankful.

But not for their hangers on and those hung on them. Sad folk I fear. Our Acting Consul General, Charles McCaskill, a survivor from Athens and Nicosia, had been in for a buffet with the Ambassador. Three times as many as I had any notion were here, and twice as dim as one supposed. No escapees here; pockmarked all; balls dead. They finished school in the 1960s and now can only apologize for their country, which if they did well could be worth doing, but they don't seem to do anything well. ...

Coda: the Peace Corps. Never, ever, such a rip off by the upper middle classes. Fortunes spent to send Amherst boys for an interesting learning experience in Venezuela. Paid for courtesy [of] men equally young pumping gas on the New Jersey Turnpike. In India, on top of the dollar costs, we spend in local currency, which is to say we take out of the Indian economy, some 110,000 rupees per year per volunteer.

This is the average annual income of more than a hundred farm laborers.... And what do we have to show for it? If we closed down the Peace Corps today it would have vanished all together from the Indian memory in five years. Indeed it had already done. We had some 1300 volunteers here after Mrs. Gandhi visited Washington in 1966 and asked for them. Half spent their time smoking pot in Ahmenabad. We are at this moment down to zero volunteers in the field. Some thirty are in training, but none is at work. Who has noticed? ...

Excerpts on the tenth anniversary of President Kennedy's assassination.

NOVEMBER 22, 1973

Ten years. Not a short time: a sort of lifetime since the defining event of that "new generation of Americans—born in this century, tempered by war, disciplined by a hard and bitter peace, proud of our ancient heritage to which the 'torch' was passed...." Very little has gone well for us: almost nothing as we would have wished. Not all bad. The high school rhetoric has been knocked out of us: no more torches. Yet no more dreams and not much courage either. Had he lived we would mostly by now be half ashamed and half angry at the too great submission of our own persons to his persona. A wholly dangerous: an infantile thing. But the assassination destroyed any possibility of succession, of transfer. We were immunized instantly to a dependency that could have become our defining failure. Nor has it been any great succession of disappointments for those of us who understood then what had happened. It was all over for us; if you once knew that, what followed was tolerable enough.

Except some times when the ghost is abroad. As yesterday, in Bombay, a world away. A journalists lunch; some of the style of yesteryear. A company he might have known. Khushwant Singh, editor of the Illustrated Weekly of

India had produced an enormous Annual Issue with profiles of each of the States, where in it is reported—by a Gujuriti—that the natives of the Andaman Islands "flee at the sight of a human being." I come into the room with this—he had missed it—and things start very well. Much laughing. No elaboration required. Drinks. Whereupon Ajit Bhattacharjea, resident editor of the Times of India reports he has been reading me this morning. Kennedy. Ten years tomorrow. Did I remember. Yes, I remembered. You said "Mary McGrory said that we would never laugh again." I said, "Heavens, Mary, we'll laugh again. It's just that we'll never be young again." They knew this. Here. In Bombay. Half a world away.

At night, dinner at the Taj Mahal. Brandy with Charles Correa [the architect] and his wife in the Apollo room, talking of architecture. Did you ever, he asks, hear the remark "I don't suppose there is any point in being Irish if you don't know the world will break your heart eventually." Good God, said Liz, he's the one who said it. Two days after Kennedy died, ten years ago tomorrow. Correa did not know. He had read the line ten years ago in Time. It had stayed with him not as a matter concerning John F. Kennedy, but rather as defining the condition of the architect: and how you live afterwards. In Bombay half a world away. My God. We did indeed have a moment.

Excerpt from a journal entry recounting a state dinner in honor of the Soviet leader Leonid Brezhnev, hosted by Prime Minister Indira Gandhi.

TUESDAY

NOVEMBER 27, 1973

Mrs. Gandhi's dinner for Brezhnev was in its way a sincere, even touching, event. They are both of them hard, survivalist politicians. Yet that is not all that they started out to be, nor is it all they remain. They are socialists. Both. The dinner speeches as reported by the press could scarcely have been given on any other occasion. They declared themselves fellow socialists: pursuing different paths toward a common goal, the just and property-less society. They spoke of one another's first five year plans, of their opposition to colonialism, of the meaning to a young girl of the October Revolution, of the pride of a great northern power in seeing the emergence of a socialist and independent neighbor from the dark Colonial night of the past.

This is who she is: what she was made. She is, intellectually, more than any one thing a product of upper class England during the Popular Front days of the late 1930s. To read Orwell's papers is to simply know what she thinks about abstractions such as the Soviet Union, capitalism, imperialism—peripherally on the very edge of things, the United States.... Like most politicians I have known, she has only a limited stock of substantive ideas, and uses them repeatedly, to a point that would embarrass or bore, let us say, a professor. They are a kind of autonomic issues system which operates without thought, whilst they are absorbed with far more primitive, even unconscious calculations.... American aid in the 1960s went overwhelmingly—some 90 percent—to the public sector. We financed the creation of Indian socialism, providing the central government money for public enterprises, and payrolls, it could never raise by taxation. Before we came along socialism in India consisted of the ownership of the British railways. We built the secretariats, bankrolled the Plans. But she does not know this. She knows that the Russians built the Bokharo Steel Plant after we refused. (On grounds, evidently, that the public sector could not operate one.) We were dead right, and dead wrong. The mill has been a building for a decade, and may indeed someday produce some steel at maybe three times the price it can be got from Japan. But we are disastrously wrong if we think the Prime Minister of India either knows or cares about such things. ...

Excerpt of a letter to Peter H. Davison, director of the Atlantic Monthly Press, reflecting ongoing money concerns.

NOVEMBER 29, 1973
PERSONAL AND CONFIDENTIAL

Dear Peter:

Nothing could please me more than to have you for an editor. Candidly and, of course, privately, the arrangements with Random House just aren't very happy. Mostly because there are no arrangements. I don't make any greater demands than most authors, but, for example, with <u>Coping</u> bound and delivered to friends in the United States at least a month ago, you would have thought the might send me a copy. Etc. And I was crushed to learn that there was to be no index. But these are small things. I have published one book a year for six years now, and while I have no complaints whatever about the way the books have been produced, the way they have been handled seems to me not particularly impressive. In any event, I have had no real help from an editor. And I need that. On the other hand the question arises whether I will ever write anything again. I sometimes think it would be best if I did not. Still something should come out of this Indian interlude and I would be delighted to talk with you as soon as we get back, or before. Mind, in the end, I suppose money will make the decision for me. Not that there ever is any. I got five thousand from Random House for <u>Coping</u> which is about what it cost to get the manuscript typed. . . .

Journal entry describing the word received from the Egyptian ambassador of a possible attempt on Moynihan's life by the Palestine Liberation Organization (PLO). Moynihan was informed that President Anwar Sadat of Egypt had instructed the ambassador to warn him of the plot.

DECEMBER 15, 1973

. . . Telephone. The Egyptian ambassador wishes urgently to see me. The very model of a British ambassador. Thank God I had been to his place for a farewell party. Martini? Bloody Mary? Thank you, no. You wished to see me, my dear colleague? Yes: [he has] received a most urgent and secret message from Cairo that the Palestinians mean somehow to disrupt the Geneva conference due to open Tuesday, and are likely to try either to kidnap or murder me. He is dead serious, and obviously knows all too well what he is talking about. There seemed no alternative but to cable Scowcroft that something may be afoot.

Damn. Tomorrow was to be our first interesting Sunday since coming to Delhi: Ruth Jhabvala's husband, a Mutiny buff, is to take us on a tour of Old Delhi, where they live. Dead Man in the Market Place. Is that not [Dom] Moraes [writer and poet from Goa]? And yet curiously I shall be least expected in Old Delhi tomorrow, and accordingly, in theory, safest. . . .

Journal entry on his visit to "old Delhi," the old part of India's capital city, which surrounds the Red Fort. Despite the report of a possible attempt on his life, and concerns about their son, Moynihan visits the area with C.H.S. (Cyrus) Jhabvala, known as Jhab, the architect and husband of the novelist Ruth Prawer Jhabvala.

DECEMBER 16, 1973
SUNDAY

There are aspects to this absurd job which are not preferred. One <u>ought</u> to live prepared to die. If only those nuns had been able to explain it better. It is, after all, going to happen. Knowing that is supposed to be the difference between us and other things that wiggle. In any event, I opted for the tour of Old Delhi, troubled only that John wanted to come and did. Hand grenades are indiscriminate. He is surely as sunny and untroubled as ever a boy could or should be—yet early in his life, after the assassination of the President, he began to think that his father, too, would be shot. It was the first event of his life, and it happened to a father. In government.

Cyrus Jhabvala is a Munity Buff. They live in the Civil Lines, about where the British mounted the final assault at Kashmere Gate, which brought an end to the Mutiny and moghul India. He knows the area as an archeologist might, with a special interest in architecture, pointing to this remnant of a Swiss hotel, that set of bungalows built for the Durbar of 1910, a sudden European <u>glacis</u> jutting from a Mogul rampart. In the midst of the wild confusion of the old city, a Queen Anne Church. St. James. Scarcely out of place: in about the relation to the world surrounding it that the original would have had in London. It is winter suddenly. One alley swarming, all black and grey and the white of smoke and steam is directly from [Gustave] Doré. The Mutiny Memorial at the top of the ridge has a new plaque which states that it is henceforth to be known as the Martyrs Memorial, in honor of the vanquished rather than the victors. No country so neglects its good things.

The Memorial, and Ashoka's pillar nearby are the only two sites, only square meters of ground, in all of India that not only appear to be, but are deserted. The British graveyard is abandoned but not, as it were, empty. John notes that half the private soldiers and even some of the Sgt. Majors have Irish names. Some of the latter have wives as well. The canal had opened. The memsahib had appeared and old India was vanquished more surely than

Col. Nicholson ever did. His grave, untended, has small piles of the exploding cannon balls used in the assault. Jhabvala tells us that about half those fired did not explode, were picked up at the foot of the walls by neutral parties and promptly sold back to the British. Poverty has never been far. Ruth Jhabvala is the quietest and most expressive possible of people. At lunch she recalls D. H. Lawrence on Ceylon: "The world before the flood." And Old Delhi: the world before the Day of Judgment? . . .

CHAPTER EIGHT

"The Indians Have the Bomb"

Moynihan's second year in India was no less eventful than his first, coinciding with Nixon's final departure from office, India's explosion of a nuclear bomb, Moynihan's counsel to Washington that it react cautiously to the newest member of the nuclear club, and finally Kissinger's visit to India, the culmination of efforts to improve relations between Washington and New Delhi. This section concludes with Moynihan's return from India, his article in COMMENTARY *assailing third world dictatorships, his acceptance of the post of U.N. ambassador and his stormy time there, followed by his resignation.*

Excerpt of a journal entry reflecting on the future of the C.I.A. in India.

JANUARY 7, 1974

CIA is not dead, but dying, I should think. Killed by Howard Hunt. [E. Howard Hunt, one of the Watergate burglars.] Too much white shoe fun in an unfunny world. They have just mercilessly fouled up in Thailand: with a student government which had denounced the new American ambassador as a CIA agent before he even arrived last month, some clown dreams up a letter to the Prime Minister offering a cease fire from the Communist insurgents in the North. Object psych warfare. Make insurgents give up because they think it is all over. Alas, the illiterate youth who was given the letter to mail registered it with the home address of the agent who had given it to him. Result, black wreaths hung on the Embassy gates, apologies, silences. . . .

They are pretty good here. The station chief, who is declared to the government of India, is a Dryden scholar (Ph.D. Cornell, 1940), a sensitive and superbly prudent and patient man. I would rely on him more than anyone in the Embassy save [David] Schneider [Moynihan's Number Two at the embassy]. And yet in a year of trying to get them to <u>think</u> about Indian Communism for me, they have not been able to do so. . . . Indian counter intelligence is, as would be expected, vastly greater and clumsier. (Mail is opened routinely, and resealed with government issue glue of approximately the color and texture of shoe leather. Liz is keeping a note from Mrs. Onassis, written on the teeniest paper and sealed with babies breath. Then resealed in the Delhi Central Post Office.) . . .

Journal entry about going to church in New Delhi on Ash Wednesday.

FEBRUARY 14, 1974
ASH WEDNESDAY

I am becoming a princeling. Ad interim, I should hope. I overslept; missed 7:30 Mass. Not in the least overcome by the enormity of it all, I entered my limousine at ten minutes of nine and directed the faithful Kumar to take me to the Papal Nuncio, to whom I explained the object of the unexpected pleasure of my call. Ceremony is ever the inconvenience of the exalted, and the chapel had to be prepared before the ashes were administered and I abjured to remember man is dust, but what a long way from Holy Cross Church on Tenth Avenue. The Irish priests never made us feel the Church was ours, such that we could make claims on it. At age twelve I would have accepted hellfire in preference to presenting myself at the Rectory and saying I had overslept. . . . It is an experience, church in India. One <u>is</u> a prince. Treated like one; expected to act like one. Received at the church door, ushered to the front pew. No nonsense about hanging back. I find that forty years in the back corners of brick gothic horrors have left me, inter alia, with no <u>knowledge</u> of when to stand and when to kneel. One does what those in front do. And yet now, in the front pew, I learn what a grand thing it can be not to care what those behind are doing. . . .

Letter to the editors of the Guinness Book of World Records. The query was the idea of the Moynihans' son John. It worked. An item and a picture of the check was published.

FEBRUARY 25, 1974

GENTLEMEN:

I have the honor to report that a new record exists for the greatest amount paid by a single check in the history of banking. On February 18, 1974, I presented to the Government of India a check for Rs. 16,640,000,000. At the current exchange rate, this is the dollar equivalent of $2,046,700,000.

The Government of the United States did this for reasons of important public policy, but my role in the matter was not unaffected by the prospect of entering the Guinness Book of World Records and thereby winning the permanent regard of my 14 year old son who at times appears to read nothing else.

I enclose a photostat of the check in order that you should have no doubt of the matter.

Excerpts of a message to Lawrence Eagleburger, career diplomat and close aide to Kissinger, with recommendations to him and Kissinger's speechwriter, Mark Palmer, on what Kissinger should plan to say when he visits India later in the year.

MARCH 1974 [UNDATED CABLE]

. . . What has India ever done for the United States? Secretary Rusk once put this question to Ambassador Bowles in the presence of the Chief Executive. "It has survived," said Bowles. No mean virtue a decade ago, and rather a more conspicuous one a decade later. This is about what we have to report to you from New Delhi. The place goes on. Against all reason. It is much, repeat as you folk say, much more a close run thing than even our weekly reports of random calamity would suggest. There having been no general collapse, despite repeated predictions in the early years, we have come rather to suppose there cannot be one, to assume that India will always muddle through. This, at minimum, is an inductive error. Any place can collapse, and sooner or later all seemingly do. I am inclined to think sooner rather than later for this place. But in terms of a decade. . . .

It is no longer possible to believe that the aid programs of the 1960s are workable. It costs too much to give India money. For one thing they hate you for it; for another we do not have the economic or political resources to mount a significant aid program.

This does not mean we can afford to have no aid program at all. The Secretary surely will bring out with him the $75 million we have coming to us for next fiscal year. To do less will be taken by Indians and by the rest of the world as a deliberately hostile act. We would be squandering a reputation which we earned at great cost over a quarter century. Perhaps we shouldn't have started. But we did. And now, at a certain level of decent provision, we must continue. . . .

The fundamental cause of the economic crisis approaching India is the stupendous increase in oil prices which followed the Yom Kippur war, and the sympathetic increases in the prices of other commodities. India's terms of trade have deteriorated disastrously in the past four months. Some prices were going up anyway, as for example wheat which has gone from less than $3 a bushel the week I arrived here to more than $6 this week. Even so, last summer we were sending home fairly bullish accounts of the Indian economy, to the extent at least of saying that in their inimitably self obstructive way they were likely somehow nonetheless to cope. Now we think otherwise. There is not the least prospect of the recent price rises for Indian imports receding in any significant degree. . . .

For a moment there I thought the trebling of oil prices, with its devastating implications for such things as food production, would shock the Indian Third World mentality such as the Molotov-Ribbentrop Pact of 1940 shocked the European and American left. It didn't. Or hasn't. In part it is a tactical problem. At a time when half the members of NATO are running around signing treaties of perpetual friendship with Sheikdoms they hadn't heard of five years ago, why should India forsake the very allegiances which have been the essence of its foreign policy and its principal claim to world influence for virtually the whole span of its national existence? . . .

What then? A fairly straight course is indicated. The Secretary should come to Delhi—from Moscow—asserting that the world is a far better place after detente, that India has an even more important place in this new world, that the United States welcomes this development and likes to suppose it had something to do with bringing it about, and accordingly all the more looks forward to working with India in the great adventure of giving concrete and institutional form to that for which India has worked all these years.

Praise for India. Praise for its leader. Praise for great future. I would say nothing publicly about aid (Brezhnev didn't). It is something we take for granted, at a very modest level, as a member of the consortium and a regular participant in its activities. Nothing more. . . .

Telegram to Elwood R. Quesada, chairman of the Pennsylvania Avenue Corporation, expressing concern that plans for a Woodrow Wilson International Center for Scholars—another project for which Moynihan pushed throughout his career—called only for it to occupy three floors of a new building on the avenue. The center now occupies a mezzanine and most of the floors of a special wing of the Ronald Reagan Building and International Trade Center.

MARCH 18, 1974

ELWOOD R. QUESADA

CHAIRMAN

PENNSYLVANIA AVENUE CORPORATION

CARE OF WHITE HOUSE

WASHINGTON

Dear Pete:

Jim Billington has just informed me by cable that the overall plan to be approved by your board on March eighteen provides only that the Wilson Center be given three floors of an eleven story building on Market Square opposite the archives. This came as a blow to Billington, and I am sure also to Dave Packard who is being of the greatest help to us in commencing the fund raising for a proper Woodrow Wilson International Center for Scholars, repeat, as they say in State Departmentese, Center. . . .

We might speak of the larger issues involved. The Woodrow Wilson Center is to be the first of its kind. A living memorial, not a statue. As Nat used to say he was the first president not to ride a horse, and there was no alternative to a live memorial. A Center for scholars for our one scholar president. The presidential commission which made this recommendation took a chance, in the sense that it was willing to forego the glory of a vast pylon or the distinction of taking over Hains Point, as I believe was the plan for the Roosevelt Memorial.... Make no little plans gentlemen. We have not worked twelve years to consign the twenty eighth president of the United States to three floors.

Journal entry in which Moynihan discusses resigning with his trusted deputy chief of mission, David Schneider, because he has not been informed of U.S. plans for a base on the island of Diego Garcia in the Indian Ocean, which India perceived as a hostile step.

MARCH 21, 1974

By breakfast I had decided to resign and told Schneider when I came across the street. Step by step since the cable that reached us in Islamabad informing us that "Joe" Alsop had broken the story, Diego Garcia has become the central fact of diplomacy here. The military has systematically lied to us; the rest of the government has been wholly unresponsive to anything we have asked. The problem is that two antithetical explanations are possible. Kissinger may be involved in a complex set of moves with the Soviets of which only he and two or three people know about and which inter alia relies on the egregiousness of our handling of Diego Garcia to help win the move. Alternatively, it is plain blundering military incompetence, with no design whatever save the stone age cupidity of the Joint Chiefs of Staff. Eight thousand miles distant I am somehow supposed to decide which. And if either, should one be silent. Well, as a matter of fact, Yes if it is possibility one. No, if two.

By afternoon I settled for a back channel cable to K: I had become steadily more disturbed. I felt the Pentagon pronouncements on Diego to sound more and more like latter day Gulf of Tonkin resolutions. The Navy was deliberately creating a zone of conflict. They send ships. We send ships. They send more ships. We send more ships. They send more ships. We don't have more ships. Ergo the Congress must build some. This was the Vietnam mentality. Worse, it is the post Vietnam mentality which seems intent on concealing all serious information from the civilian side of government. ...

And why hurt Kissinger who is all we have. It wouldn't hurt him exactly— too inconsequential—but it would be a day's difficulty. When I don't know. Mrs. Gandhi thinks the Indian Ocean floor is crawling with American submarines. It is not. The Polaris and Poseiden missiles won't reach worthwhile targets from here. But the Trident would. I have to assume that is what they are really thinking about. But that assumes they can think. I am not sure of that.

So here I am. Having all but been thrown out of India for defending Diego Garcia, I am about to resign in protest against it. Pathetic. In any event the biggest question in my mind is that Maura wants to finish high school here.

Journal entry expressing concern about the C.I.A. being blamed for much that goes wrong in India.

MARCH 22, 1974

... Violence spreads in India. It begins to look as if we are going to be drawn into it. I gather it is a reflexive response out here: all the career men say so. The Communists are after Burleigh again, and this is spreading. ...

What makes <u>me</u> a bit cynical is that they never name a <u>real</u> C.I.A. agent. They know who they are. There is official collaboration enough; and expect a good deal of unofficial collaboration no one has felt it necessary to trouble me about. It cannot be pure chance—the mathematics are against it—that all the accusations of CIA activity are false; all the individuals fingered are innocent. They must have the same relation with the Russians. ...

I am getting the worst of it. The Secretary of State is letting his good friend Ambassador Kaul know that he is if anything amused at my discomfiture under the attacks occasioned by my publicly defending American policy, whilst simultaneously suggesting my standing at home be declining inasmuch as I privately protest American policy. Worst of both worlds. Ow. I cable Kissinger, "Fair enough. But where's my I D money. Image needs refurbishing." ...

Journal entry, again focused on blaming of two diplomats—Peter Burleigh and Paul Kreisberg—for violence in Bihar, the state in northeast India. Mrs. Gandhi's secretary, P. N. Dhar, is plainly worried that the violence will spread. The Bihar uprising was led by Jayaprakash Narayan, and spread in 1975, after Moynihan left, prompting Mrs. Gandhi to declare an "emergency" and suspend democracy.

MARCH 23, 1974
SATURDAY

The newspapers are about as bad as they get. Just as I gather the Bihar riots have been. They seem to have quieted [it] through mass arrests and something like mass killing, but now comes the question who is to be blamed and evidently it is to be us. The Communist papers are screaming Burleigh and Kreisberg. . . .

At noon I went to see P.N. Dhar. . . . Dhar knows how bad it is, but fears his days are numbered. . . .

He hadn't slept all night. They are that worried. He asked me as a political scientist what I thought would happen. I said political scientists don't know about such things, but clearly he had a middle class revolt on his hand, which is to say university students. Something such happened to us in the 60s. . . . I asked him if he would say to the Prime Minister for me that whatever else happens, I hope the Congtess Party won't take the easy way of blaming foreign agitators for India's troubles. He in turn advised me not to take the press so seriously, when it was obvious I was being set up. . . .

Message to the internal staff of the U.S. embassy in New Delhi, reflecting on the messages they send to the U.S. State Department in Washington.

NEW DELHI 4121
MARCH 26, 1974
SUBJECT: IN WHICH GOOD REPORTING MAKES BAD POLICY

1. This Embassy has recently received a number of letters and cables commending us for "superb" reporting.

2. On behalf of the career officers who did this work, I should like to express the Embassy's appreciation for the gracious and far from perfunctory tone of these messages. It was no more than the due of our career officers but that kind of recognition is not routinely forthcoming from any organization, the Department of State included, and for that matter the other institutions who evidently conveyed their own appreciation to the Department. We have the best Embassy in Asia and it shows.

3. As one who, like the rest of you, has only read and admired the reporting, I have begun nonetheless to wonder just how prudent it is to try to be tough-minded about things out here and to report our thinking in straight out terms. I begin to think we are going to win all the awards and lose all the prizes in this game, using the latter term in the sense Tom Schelling would employ.

4. The American Embassy in New Delhi has not had a good reputation with those in Washington who must think of many things, not just a few things. In the 1960s it became a symbol of clientism. There was no doubt truth to this, although the reality has been exaggerated. My general impression has been that our involvement in India during the 1960s was rather the obverse of our involvement in Vietnam. Both were redemptive, protestant sorts of things designed to "save" lesser peoples from misguided beliefs or incipient sins. Both hugely exaggerated the American capacity to influence events in distant and unhospitable climes; both were distorted by almost childish notions of time spans—everything had to be done quickly before nap time—both disastrously underestimated the willingness of the American people, who had not really been consulted in either enterprise, to continue unquestioned support of an expensive and unexplained policy. Mind, if anything, the clientism in the Embassy in Saigon was a considerably worse case than anything that broke out around here. The Americans in New Delhi may have got involved in devaluing the currency, but they never presumed to advise on the murder of the Chief of State. Still, it was bad enough. Relations with the American Embassy in Islamabad were particularly scandalous.

5. In recent years there has been an effort in New Delhi to combine informed and, where appropriate, sympathetic reporting of Indian events and views with quite detached judgments as to what are the American interests involved. (These interests need not at all conflict with Indian interests. To the contrary, the proper pursuit of the diplomatist is to seek out situations in which interests coincide.) The result has been the kind of reporting you got under Ambassador Keating. I have sought to continue and perhaps even to improve on this practice.

6. To repeat, however, I begin to wonder whether our effort has not been, to use one of the Department's favorite terms, counterproductive. No one is to blame, nor am I blaming anyone. If this were so I would settle for vengeance in my memoires and maintain for the present the most equable of countenances. I raise the matter because I believe there is an institutional problem here which fair-minded men at home if not too much harassed by other things, can address themselves to. . . .

Excerpt of a journal entry of Moynihan's visit to the White House as the Nixon presidency continues to be paralyzed by Watergate.

APRIL 12, 1974

. . . Steve Bull spots us and suggests I wait around and say hello to the President who is leaving for Key Biscayne. Of a sudden I have agreed, although last time I left without asking to see him, intending not ever to do so again. The White House gets to you. Men feel good in it. Everyone laughs, even now. Preening around that Presence, taking something from the air. Ziegler comes out. I congratulate him on the splendid job he has been doing for the President. He says he expects to get into the Guinness Book of Records: from 68 percent approval to Impeachment in 12 months.

No longer all laughs. Bull was cleaning his desk and found our exchange on nonattendance at the Inauguration, his lines on John Dean and the safe. What a dream world, he thinks. Not months ago. He has done nothing, is in no danger, in no fear, but he is already $15,000 in debt from lawyer's fees for his various court appearances in connection with the tapes, and there is more to come. Some weeks back his secretary Beverley died at her desk of a stroke. The F.B.I. investigated the possibility that he had murdered her.

We sat in the cabinet room talking of it all. I got off on Erving Goffman's theories of the tiny tilt that leads from normal to paranoid perception, recount the way the rumor got started that the 1972 elections were to be cancelled. When the White House denied it, the "underground press" took it for truth, for why else would it have been denied. Stupid of me, but what does one say. Bull seemed not to mind. He is much younger than I and tolerant.

The Departure is lively. Everything is lively at the White House and helicopters help. The President, wife and daughters, preceded by a trickle of doc-

tors and sometime generals, debouch onto the South Lawn ten minutes be-
hind schedule. They had been waiting for the Cox's who were then turning
up the drive. He greets me. I am looking splendid. Am I turning Hindu? No,
I have always been partial to meditation. I have been reading about the splendid things you have been doing. Thank you, Mrs. Eisenhower. Mr. President,
I hope to see Mrs. Gandhi on my return, may I give her your good regards.
By all means, give her my love. Then, turning back, having turned, he said,
"You know, your way," and stuck out his tongue, faced turned upward as a
child to someone in authority. It was just past three o'clock on the afternoon
of Good Friday.

God have mercy. Regression. I didn't do so well by him. He ends up able
to see only a cynical side of me: not a side that sees Mrs. Gandhi as far more
a stable democratic leader than he. Than he is now. They have wrecked him.
Several theys.

No one notices. The copter lifts off. Bull says what he would never in past
have said: that there are no first rate minds left in the place, that the Zieglers
can't do it.

Excerpt of a journal entry with Moynihan's reflecting that aid to India only makes
them ungrateful and resentful.

APRIL 27, 1974

... The more we do for them, the more they will hate us. Can one not accept this? It is a democracy. Democracies behave that way. We had better do
so, else there will be no AID. ...

What is it? In part at least a more or less common response as to the right-
ness or wrongness of a given argument and the evidence adduced therefore.
You have heard about Harvard men? Well, we are C.C.N.Y. men. ... Why
do I describe myself as a C.C.N.Y. man: I with five degrees from Tufts. Not
simply because I started at CCNY and left for the Navy which sent me to
Tufts. It is because I belonged at CCNY. Glazer almost went to Harvard.
Anybody could in those days. I wonder would it have changed him. I doubt
it. He belonged at CCNY. And yet Tufts was good and generous to me
throughout; the Aid principle.

Letter to SCM Corporation, makers of typewriters.

MAY 2, 1974
SCM CORPORATION
P.O. BOX 671
ENGLEWOOD, NEW JERSEY 07631

Gentlemen:

    ... It is 8:25 on a hot May morning here in New Delhi. The day began well enough, but for the past 25 minutes I have been trying to change the ribbon on your Electra SS model. It almost can't be done. You may recall that for some mysterious reason you replaced the normal metal pin which holds the ribbon reel to the revolving plate with a splayed plastic business which bends out of shape after the first one or two ribbon changes and thereafter defies efforts to make it do its simple task. After twenty minutes, I succeeded in snapping off the tops with a scissors: the first time in forty years at a typewriter that I have been forced to mutilate one. Next, of course, came the business of trying to attach the ribbon to the empty spool, with the usual cuticle abuse and the invariable smudging of hands, towels, typewriter, and what else in sight. Really: the machine is almost a century old now. If no one can devise a way of attaching the ribbon, surely there is no need to regress with respect to the spool.

India jolted the world and posed a major new diplomatic challenge by conducting a nuclear test on May 18, 1974, while Moynihan was visiting England. His journal entry:

MAY 18, 1974
SATURDAY
WESTHORPE, SUFFOLK

The telephone rang at 5:30. The code room at the embassy. A plain, pleasant, young man's voice. There was a message for me. He could say nothing on phone: "It is so tender." I went in.

The Indians have the bomb.

Kewal Singh called [David] Schneider [deputy chief of mission] in at ten o'clock to tell him the Indians had carried out a peaceful nuclear explosion two hours earlier. It had been an implosion device at a depth of over one hundred meters below ground. The Indian Atomic Energy Commission had carried out the experiment in order to keep India abreast of the technology concerning peaceful uses of nuclear energy for such purposes as mining and earth moving. Schneider replied that he believed this news would be received with considerable shock in Washington, as the U.S. held it was not possible to distinguish between explosions for peaceful as against military purposes. Singh said India was absolutely opposed to military uses.

The Department proposed to issue a statement that the U.S. "deeply regrets" the development, while noting India's reaffirmation of its commitment not to use nuclear energy for military purposes, we nonetheless considered this an "unfortunate step." I cabled my approval and was off to Cambridge with John [Moynihan]. Plumb greeted me with the Embassy telephone number. "Flash" from Damascus had come the Kissingerian command. There was to be no statement. If asked the spokesman might reply: "The United States has always been against nuclear proliferation for the adverse impact it will have on world stability. That remains our position." Ever independent minded, I endorsed this view also, and was off to Westhorpe in [J. H.] Plumb's Jaguar, with the welcome additional company of Bill Noblet.

I am no good at such moments. I accept the most extraordinary transforming events as if they had been going to happen all along, and in that sense mark no change in the order of things. Four pints of beer with cheese and pickle sandwiches at The Bell beyond Newmarket, a nap, and an hours' walk through Jack's park, iridescent with the bright, gemlike flame of bluebells, and I began to think. More precisely, this unusual event occurred in St. Margaret's Westhorpe, to which Plumb's Old Rectory was attached when the priesthood married in the 17th Century. Comfortable and cold I was inside—the first visitor I should think in a month or two—contemplating a large sign board on which some 18th Century squires had caused to be inscribed The Apostle's Creed when it came to me that yet another new era had begun. The third, I should think, or is it the fourth, of a lifetime.

From the journal entry after the explosion.

MAY 23, 1974

I got off what is probably the most important cable I have sent today after a day of mumbling about it and putting it off. Paul Kreisberg [of the U.S. embassy] didn't at all approve my first draft, which argued more strongly that it was the bomb that won China its place in the Oval Office. I toned it down because he knows more about it than I do. In any event I had nothing really to say except that it has happened and there is nothing we can do to make it unhappen. What we must do is begin to think about India and pay attention to it in some constructive way. Not to make India happy, but to make ourselves secure. The transparent effort to frighten the bureaucracy by citing the Secretaries is ... well, transparent. ...

Excerpts of Moynihan's cable after the nuclear bomb, cautioning against aggravation of relations with India.

23 MAY 74

... For some years now thoughtful persons in foreign affairs have concerned themselves with "The Nth country problem," wondering what might be done to prevent the proliferation of nuclear weapons. India has now supplied the answer which Dr. Kissinger anticipated many years ago. Nothing will be done. There are measures which by a certain definition would succeed. The United States could blow up any nation which exploded a nuclear device. The United States could make such a massive commitment of its own wealth to increasing the wealth of the pre-nuclear nations such that they might rest content to stay that way. But it won't and they probably wouldn't. ...

The capitalist press seems to have got onto the idea that the bomb was set off to raise Indian morale in a period of domestic depression and crisis. To some extent that was undoubtedly the Government's intention; in any case it seems to have had that effect. The initial reaction here was what may be described as jubilation tinged with some of the less agreeable traits often ascribed to Indians. Any country would be proud of the accomplishment, particularly a nation that is fond of thinking of itself as the leader of the third world, and any government seeking to reinstate a measure of national progress in an otherwise dismal situation might be expected to consider such a step. . . .

Thanks to the Secretary, the United States reaction so far has been less costly than it probably was going to be. The statement first proposed by the Department of State, while mild, was not mild enough. Within moments, however, the Secretary weighed in from Damascus to say there was not to be any Department statement and that, if queried, the Department spokesman was to make a "low-key REPEAT low-key response." It is well that we have chosen this posture. Under the duress of economic failures the Government of India has been slowly moving toward more moderate economic policies and toward better relations with the US. There is near panic among those of the left, whether Communist or Congress, about this change. Even the Soviets are worried, as our intelligence makes clear. . . .

Excerpt of a letter to Norman Podhoretz.

MAY 30, 1974
PERSONAL AND CONFIDENTIAL

Dear Norman:
. . . We are off to the coronation at Bhutan. From what I learned of that Kingdom and what I know of the rest of the world, I might not return.

I must record a lead from <u>The London Sun Telegraph</u> a fortnight ago: "On Thursday, Prime Minister Indira Gandhi, looking her radiant best, threw 20,000 Trade Union leaders into prison." I am reliably informed that it was this painful duty, plus the upcoming even more explosive concern which prevented her accepting Harvard University's most recent request that she give the commencement address and receive a citation for services to peace and freedom.

No kidding, destroy this letter. Remember you were once Soldier of the Week.

*Bhutan—the tiny, isolated Himalayan Buddhist kingdom—held a coronation of
its new king, Jigme Dorji Wangchuk, who had acceded to the throne at the age
of seventeen in 1972 but was not crowned formally until June 2, 1974. From
Calcutta, the Moynihans fly to the town of Bagdogra to get ready for an overland
trip through the mountains. The other guests on the jaunt include the Russian
deputy chief of mission, Boldyrev, and the Chinese ambassador, Ma Mu-Ming.*

MAY 31, 1974

First to Bagdogra by India Airways. Same crush, same steamy wait on the
tarmac. God what have we done? When suddenly we are out of the plane,
and into—onto?—what is obviously going to be a great romp. The Bhutanese
take over. They are magnificent! Smiling, bowing, knowing what to do, not a
scintilla of servility. We are guests to a coronation! . . . Our schedules show a
sequence of buffet lunches and dinners with various hosts, culminating with
a formal sit down dinner given by the King. . . . Clever people these Bhutanese.
An Indian journalist has written of their "deceptively somnolent polity." Pat
Ward's cars are lined up waiting for us; light blue Australian Fords, complete
with the ambassadorial flag. Off we go, a little bit high.

At the last coronation, in 1952, only two outsiders, the crown prince of
Nepal and the Indian political agent for Sikkim and Bhutan made what was
apparently a nine day journey from Gangtok by horse. This is to be a very different event and a different assertion. A large press corps went up yesterday.
There are thirteen countries in our caravan, and a considerable number of UN
officials. The reign of old Druk Gyalpo, Jigme Dorji Wangchuk was seismic
in its Bhutanese way. He was evidently a most special man: full of modernizing notions and yet close to reality and people. The former was not so very
difficult in the sense that almost anything a twentieth century person might
think would have been mighty modern in the Bhutan of his time. Everything
came—everything that <u>did</u> come—four or five centuries late here. Jigme Dorji
was only the third king, the monarchy having been established in 1907 by a
British political agent, Claude White, who had, to that degree, a modernizing
passion of his own. Previously, back into the encroaching mists, governance
was divided between a spiritual, Bhuddist ruler, and a secular ruler and there
was little by way of government. . . .

The trip across North Bengal is pleasant enough. This is Naxalite country, not far from the village of [Naxalbari] by which the movement was named. [Naxalites are Maoist insurgents.] Trains are derailed here and there: possibly the strike, more likely the students. Tea gardens and day labor; the shacks along the roads are made of boards, making one think the place is as poor as West Virginia. There seem to be mountains in every direction, but at one turn our driver sings out "Druk!," and there, presumedly, is Bhutan, rising like the Rockies from the Colorado plain. It is, as a small, nice archway proclaims, through which we enter the border town of Phuntsholing, whence up the mountain a bit to the first rest house. . . .

We are met in the lobby by a host of <u>young gentlemen</u> and a few young ladies, there to attend us. It seems everyone in school in Bhutan took off a month ago and has been practicing ever since for these six days to come. They dress in a kilt like robe with knee socks and six foot long scarves thrown over their left shoulder, which heightens the Scottish effect. . . .

Describing the trip through the mountains to Thimpu, the Bhutanese capital.

JUNE 1, 1974

SATURDAY

PHUNTSHOLING TO THIMPU

The trip to Thimpu is 179 kilometers. Up, up, up, Down, down, down, twist, twist, twist. Scarcely ten years ago it was seven days journey with tigers a sort of threat, snakes certain, and leeches constant. The Indians have done a brilliant job: there cannot anywhere be a more difficult terrain. The effect is splendid: about a third of the time looking far down to an ice blue torrent, another third looking up at a surely inaccessible peak, with a third sandwiched in a tiny layer of light, enclosed by fog above and fog below. . . .

As with India, there are some old things here, but not many. It is the <u>people</u> who are old, not the buildings. After a period we reach the interior valleys, tiny things, a kilometer wide if that, but delightful. The farm houses are three and four stories in the Alpine manner—to use up as little land as possible, I assume. But for every house occupied, there is a ruin next or nearby it, solid mud walls which Stein [Joseph Stein, architect] says last centuries, abandoned, the drivers will say to small pox or, variously, cholera, although I should think the older ones are simply the burned mileposts of one Penlop marching into another's valley. Monastaries peek out, high on the hillsides. As we approach the Thimpu valley we sight the great castle—dzong—which controls it. They are not really castles, rather, fortified monasteries, looking very Tibetan.

Thimpu is brand new, or, if one likes, instant ancient. The old king chose it for his capital, in the Asian style of moving these things about, and commenced the construction of shopping centers and government buildings, most of which aged quickly and mercifully. The golf course and the playground with up to date giant toys defy antiquing, but the rest looks normal. It is much too much spread out for a European taste, but this is their style, the villages being the same way. . . .

Our rooms are splendid. Too much so. I fear AID may have lent more money to the Oboroi hotel chain than is conducive to Ambassadorial virtue. Chivas Regal, Gilbey's gin, and better brandy than I can afford in New Delhi. I am deep in a calculation as to how one might combine all three in the quickest possible manner, when Tshering allows that if we like we could go down to the stupa—stortan in their usage—erected to the memory of the late king and present a white scarf as is their custom. I replied there was no religion in the United States and began thinking about whether to risk the ice. . . .

On the coronation itself.

JUNE 2, 1974
MONDAY

Up at 5:30 to robe and prepare for the coronation, commencing, as evidently all our events will, with forming up the caravan, led by a jeep and a great red guidon. . . .

The entry of the ambassadors and their ladies is a merry event and it is clear we are to have a merry time. A merry <u>medieval</u> time, for we are at court. Specifically, we are <u>in</u> a court—a courtyard—lined on three sides with pavillions set up for dignitaries of descending rank, and facing the lama's redoubt on the side of which is hung the world's largest <u>thanka,</u> an embroidered depiction of the Bhudda, say, forty feet high and thirty feet wide. The music has begun. It seems at first to have no form, rather no rhythm, but this slowly impresses itself. There are high pitched little trumpet affairs and the deep long horns resting on the ground and blown from a standing position. These go seeming independent ways, but every so often—fifteen beats after having noticed it you begin to wait for it—are brought together by a deep base drum: booooooooooo-ooo-ooo-mmmmmmmmmm. As the court fills with dancers and musicians, each improvising in some wholly disregarding way, it slowly emerges that in fact everything moves to the rhythm of the band/orchestra stationed on the walls. . . .

The real King arrives: rather matter of fact, pacing across the courtyard to a slightly raised platform facing two priests opposite him, whose backs are to the thanka. This is to be the Ceremonial Drink, prepared very much as at High Mass, only more expeditiously. One would think there is plenty of time for ritual here in the hills, but they seem rather inclined to get on with it. In a matter of minutes a silver dipper is brought across the court to His Majesty, who however, merely touches it. The thought that in Bhutan even the King won't drink the water is no more than suppressed, when he turns and disappears into the entrance way at his back. The ambassadors are asked to follow. . . .

Into the throne room, the previous episode somewhat undigested. The king is on a platform with a small table set before him with a bowl of fruit and various holy objects, his back to the outside wall of the palace. The most important guests are ranged against the wall to his right and left. The corps is seated on a double row of benches perpendicular to him on his left. Family is similarly seated on the opposite side of the small room. In between two rows of red robed monks face one another, with the high lama officiating in front of the King.

The ceremony is simple and nowhere is the King crowned. I am not sure it is a coronation ceremony at all, but simply a succession of Bhuddist sutras, each following the presentation of some object. The chants are deep and heavy and slow—the term "dzong" is onomatopoeic almost. The first impression is of a record running down on an old windup victrola, but—again—the slower rhythm finally asserts itself and is pleasing and devout. The King remains aloof, almost bored, which is obviously a manner, or the manner: I shall never know. He is extraordinarily handsome. The young man's eyes could have a touch of fright as they dart about the room, the head rarely moving. . . . It is now the guests' turn. We are each served butter tea. Then rice put in the butter tea. Then more butter tea. More rice. Tea. Rice. Tea. Rice. Nine times if I recall. Toward the end only the motion of serving is made. Then each of us is given an envelope with money. 18 Nu. Next, an envelope with pan leaves.

Then in succession an orange, an apple, a banana, a peach, a cherry, a plum, a nut and so down the list of fruits in the King's bowl. . . .

Diary entry back in New Delhi, observing romantic liaisons at the embassy.

JUNE 15, 1974

The Marines are letting me down, and worrying me. Just about every one is shacked up with a nineteen-year-old secretary and I don't have a <u>military organization</u> here any more. The Gunnery Sergeant is being sent home and if I have to install a brig in the Marine House I am going to get that platoon shaped up. They don't seem to know how they got the way they are and they are not in the least proud of it. The point is not that they have women, but that the American manner of the moment is that two people, regardless of circumstance, <u>move in</u>. Set up house! It was sure in hell not like that in the Old Navy. . . .

Excerpt of diary entry recording visit to Washington, starting with meetings on Capitol Hill and ending up at the State Department with Secretary Kissinger as the Watergate scandal reaches a culmination. They agree that Kissinger will visit India in October.

JULY 17, 1974
A TOUR OF THE NATION'S CAPITAL

EIGHT O'CLOCK.

The Capitol Hill Club, where Peter Frelinghuysen awaits on behalf of the SOS Club and the Chowder and Marching Society, two groups of Republican Congressmen who meet for breakfast and have speakers. . . .

George Bush saw me arrive and asked me next door afterwards. What a cost it has been to such as him: chairman of the Republican party through Watergate, the Democratic millionaire [Lloyd Bentsen] who beat him for Senate in Texas—accusing him of supporting Family Assistance which he had done—curiously now being mentioned for President. Of course they are all millionaires, I suppose. This one has class. Real class and his own. He is nice to me, although if I had taken that UN job I suspect he would have been spared the Republican National Committee. He is near to complaining about the President however. . . .

TEN O'CLOCK

People come and go around Henry Kissinger: [Lawrence] Eagleburger, with [Helmut] Sonnenfeldt and [Winston] Lord, stays. He half dropped dead on [Defense Secretary Melvin] Laird; he may yet do on HK; but he stays. In consequence of which has no time. . . .

12:30

The Secretary asks to see me privately for a moment, leaving [Assistant Secretary of State Roy] Atherton in the foyer. Grace of Favour, I assume. He is embattled now with [James] Schlesinger. All moments in Washington are, I suppose, strange, but this one trebly so. Two middle European Jews. (JS was bar mitzvahed. You may be sure Podhoretz knew.) . . . He must feel a little better with the President. Let them oust him, he states, and he would advise anyone running for office in 1976 to run as a candidate of the far right. This of course is an old tactic with him: Stick with me or our mutual enemy on the right will get us both. But he left Hitler's Germany. He has a right to think such things. . . .

ONE FIFTEEN O'CLOCK

Lunch with [Chairman of the Federal Reserve] Arthur Burns in that funny Greek temple building of the Federal Reserve, a kind of miniature Delphi with the Treasuries of Athens and Thebes and Corinth ranged along the sides of the central hall: Boston, New York, Philadelphia, each District in turn. . . . Puzzled by the language in the transcripts. I grow epatant, as in the past with him. Repressed homosexuality; sense of deprivation—a castration sense. He does not disagree. He is not Viennese for nothing. That is why the President preferred those smooth bottomed young men! . . .

SIX O'CLOCK

The Secretary again. He is late, which is natural, and I am horsing around his outer office which is compulsive. The night secretary, the kind of twenty eight year old blond who arranges place cards in the Department of State, asks if I would not take a seat in the waiting room across the hall as the Secretary prefers it that way. It occurs to me to ask if she has the rag on, but in the old tradition of my new craft I defer to expediency and withdraw a discrete interval. So that's it, eh? Waiting room. Time I got the hell out of this. . . .

We agree on the second half of October [for Kissinger's visit]. We agree to fight the Long Amendment [which would restrict aid to India because of its nuclear program] on the Senate side. He is agreeable to [Kentucky Senator] Marlow Cook's putting in a sense of the congress resolution on nuclear proliferation, but it may not extend to a Comprehensive Test Ban. . . . He thinks the Prime Minister of India hates us. He is right. I will not be around when the food is shipped or is not shipped. . . .

I ask what to say to her on my return. I am to say four things.

1. That we hope India will be restrained in its comments on nuclear matters as we have been in ours.
2. That this is a general problem, that general proliferation is as much our problem as hers—more hers, perhaps—but a general problem. He wants to talk about it with her, talk about a nondiscriminatory international regime.
3. I am to point out to her the threat to India which a nuclear Pakistan would constitute. India which was preeminent in South Asia would be returned to parity with its great enemy.
4. It will be tough to move things forward if we are made the whipping boy.

So be it. . . .

Memorandum of conversation with Dhar, the close aide to Mrs. Gandhi, who remained one of Moynihan's most important intermediaries and sounding boards for his attempts to improve India-U.S. relations.

AUGUST 3, 1974

MEMORANDUM OF CONVERSATION

P. N. Dhar came to Saturday lunch. We got right to drinking and to business.

The question, I said, was: "What do we want to do with each other." He agreed. I began.

The Indians had not put me to any use, and time was running out. I was something special by way of an envoy, and had been meant to be. In the past we had sent men of great distinction, but not men at the height of their careers. Some such as Cooper and Galbraith became persons of importance because of having been Ambassador to India.

Others, such as Keating, became Ambassador to India because of having been persons of importance. I was the exception, arriving at precisely the moment of my greatest influence at home. . . .

Watergate was then a cloud no bigger than a man's hand. It had since enveloped the President. I could no longer reach him on any matter of substance, and no longer tried. But even before this happened to <u>him</u>, it was clear that the Indians were not doing anything with <u>me</u>. I was working two hours a day, on government business, and otherwise living much as I would do in Cambridge. . . .

In the meantime, the relation between our two countries had eased into that condition which [the diplomat] L.K. Jha had foreseen. There scarcely was any. Such as there was sufficiently cordial, even amiable. The days of acrimony and bickering had passed, but this had been succeeded, at best, by an irresolute latency, readily overlooked, and more readily misinterpreted. Men of consequence in the American government paid it no heed. In the main we had come to the judgment that to the extent India had any important external relation, it was with the Soviet Union, that this was an arrangement of convenience mostly and ideology partly which suited them both. . . .

There was one exception, and this was the Secretary of State. As best I could tell, he thought of India frequently. I did not know why. I had come to assume it was because the Chinese prodded him to see if by establishing a relation out here, India might be distanced, somewhat, <u>from</u> the Soviets. I did not know this to be the case, and I would never would. I knew, as everyone knew, that the Chinese were constantly asking that we look out for their ally Pakistan. . . .

I said there were two areas in which we could cooperate and in which each of us had the strongest [interest] in doing so. These were nuclear proliferation and economic aid and exchange. I said I would not dare predict what [would] happen. . . .

I expected that for a long time our countries were destined to remain in the grip of stereotypes about one another. Americans would see 600,000,000 ingrates. Indians would see the white imperialist enemy.

At the word white Dhar leapt from his chair at the luncheon table and came over to me. I don't think he noticed that his sandaled foot was stepping on my bare foot. "Color," he said. "Do you know what color means to us." He insisted Indians were the most color conscious people on earth. I could not follow and I was a little alarmed. He was saying that nowhere does whiteness matter more than in India. But that Indians are not white? Nothing was clear. . . .

Journal entry about the arrest of an Indian naval officer accused of spying for the United States, leading Moynihan to conclude that the U.S. should simply pull all C.I.A. operations out of India, since they learn little anyway.

AUGUST 6, 1974

TUESDAY

Grimsley arrived first to report the Indians have arrested a naval officer who has been providing us useless information about the Russians. We do not work against the Indians. We work with them. But evidently we cannot resist a Lieutenant Commander who comes up at a dinner dance and tells some spook he would like to get on the payroll. He has told all. Three Americans must depart immediately. And so now I have a CIA source in jail in Bombay, an ex-CIA informer on bail in Delhi (they let Drobot out), and two poor kids in jail as spies in Calcutta, the judge there having announced he will try them under the Official Secrets Act and in camera. . . . What may I ask is a man to do with the rest of a day that begins in such manner? I content myself with a long letter to Eagleburger saying that Kissinger must pull the C.I.A. out of India. It is a devastating liability while it remains. . . . Unquestionably we would get better and cheaper information. The alternative is to remain on the front page of the Indian press for yet another decade, with a quarter of the charges true and three quarters believed to be true by the most sophisticated and best informed people in government.

Pat Moynihan, less than one year old, with his maternal grandfather, Judge Harry W. Phipps, who was a stable presence throughout his childhood. (Courtesy the Moynihan family)

John Moynihan shown with his children—Mike, Pat, and Ellen— in New York on the occasion of Pat's first communion. This is the only picture that exists of Pat and his father, who abandoned the family when Pat was ten. (Courtesy the Moynihan family)

Brother Michael, woman unknown, Pat, and his future brother-in-law, Red, (above) at Moynihan's Bar, in Hell's Kitchen, New York (right). (Courtesy the Moynihan family)

Ensign Moynihan on the USS Quirinus, 1945. (Courtesy the Moynihan family)

Moynihan in London while on his Fulbright Scholarship at the London School of Economics, 1950–1953. (Credit: John Barry)

Pat Moynihan having tea with Eleanor Roosevelt in Hyde Park, New York. (Courtesy the FDR Library)

Pat Moynihan stands in the back row as President John F. Kennedy signs a bill. (Credit: Photograph by Abbie Rowe, White House)

"We'll never be young again": Leaving the White House in tears with William Walton, artist and close friend of John and Jackie Kennedy. They first learned of Kennedy's shooting and death at Walton's house in Georgetown. They then went to the White House, where Kennedy's death was confirmed on television. Walton almost collapsed. Here, Moynihan is taking him home. (Credit: Arthur Ellis/The Washington Post via Getty Images)

With Lyndon Johnson, for whom Moynihan helped draft the Commencement address that Johnson delivered to Howard University on race in 1965. (Courtesy the Lyndon Baines Johnson Library & Museum)

Pat Moynihan in his first year at Harvard University in 1967, after leaving the Johnson Administration. (Credit: Ted Polumbaum/Newseum Collection)

As a special assistant for Urban Affairs, Moynihan took President Nixon on a tour of Pennsylvania Avenue to interest him in the redevelopment project started under Kennedy. (Courtesy the Nixon Presidential Library & Museum)

Early morning staff meeting at the White House. From left: Moynihan, William Colby, John Ehrlichman, Ron Ziegler, Arthur Burns, and Henry Kissinger are also pictured here. (Courtesy the Nixon Presidential Library & Museum)

President Gerald Ford meets with Moynihan, Nathan Glazer, and Orlando Patterson in the Oval Office. (Credit: David Hume Kennerly)

The Moynihans in Cambridge: (from left) Tim, Maura, Mr. Dooley, Liz, John, and Pat. (All photos on this page are courtesy the Library of Congress, Prints & Photographs Division, LOOK magazine photograph collection, LOOK–Job 69–5323)

And Derrymore: Liz and Pat on the back porch of the farmhouse.

Grouse-hunting with Maura. He was not a great shot; the grouse were hardly ever in danger.

The Moynihans arrive at the U.S. Ambassadorial residence, Roosevelt House, in New Delhi, on February 19, 1973. (Credit: R. N. Khanna)

Ambassador Moynihan takes part in an archery contest at the coronation of the King of Bhutan, Thimphu, 1974. (Credit: AP Photo)

In 1975, Moynihan became U.S. ambassador to the United Nations during which time the "Zionism is Racism" Resolutions passed under Secretary-General Kurt Waldheim (middle). Kissinger (far left) was Secretary of State. (Credit: UN Photo/Michos Tzovaras)

In 1991, Moynihan and Israeli president and former UN Ambassador, Chaim Herzog, reunited at the UN to see the Resolution overturned. (Credit: UN Photo)

Liz and Pat Moynihan flying back to NYC on November 2, 1976, after voting in Pindars Corners, knowing that he is likely to become the next senator of New York. (Courtesy the Moynihan family)

Moynihan and his daughter, Maura, at the Senate Book Party for Pandaemonium. *At each book party, the Senator would say, "This book is sure to sell in the hundreds," and he was usually right. (Credit: Lynn Keith)*

Senator Moynihan at work in his office in the Russell Building. (Credit: Diana Walker)

Urban architecture was an abiding passion: The senator on Manhattan's West Side, 1988. (Credit: Harry Benson)

Jacqueline Onassis honors Pat Moynihan at the Municipal Arts Society in 1992. They collaborated on the renovation of Pennsylvania Avenue and other historic preservation projects in New York and Washington. (Credit: Steven Tucker)

A photo composite that hung on several Democratic walls, including Moynihan's: "The Four Horsemen of the Apocalypse"—the Democrats who came together and made a joint statement on Northern Ireland—Hugh Carey, Tip O'Neill, Ted Kennedy, and Pat Moynihan. (Courtesy the Moynihan family; Credit: Unaltered version, The Granger Collection, NY)

At work in the School House, Derrymore, in the early 1990s. (Credit: David Hume Kennerly)

*At the Prudential Building in Buffalo, NY. Moynihan promised to establish his regional Senate office there if the building was saved from demolition, and he kept that promise. (Credit: Joe Traver/*Buffalo Courier-Express*)*

Moynihan never lost his deep concern for the well-being of poor families and especially children. (Credit: Diana Walker)

With His Holiness the Fourteenth Dalai Lama, old friends from India, 1994. (Courtesy the Moynihan family)

In 2000, Moynihan retired from the Senate undefeated after twenty-four years and received the Medal of Freedom from President Clinton. (Courtesy the White House)

Daniel Patrick Moynihan, March 16, 1927–March 26, 2003. (Credit: Tom Holowach)

Journal entry including the news that Nixon is resigning.

AUGUST 8, 1974
THURSDAY

The day began on a solemn note. Before leaving Washington I had peti-
tioned Ambassador Kaul to permit the export to Bangladesh of Mr. Donald
Born's Model A Ford. Mr. Born, founder of the Delhi Antique Car Society,
came upon said Model A Ford in reduced circumstances in a part of town
not normally frequented by members of the diplomatic corps. With his own
hands he restored said vehicle to running condition, but on departing for
Washington was forbidden to bring it with him in consequence of EXPORT
TRADE CONTROL PUBLIC NOTICE NO. 13-ETC(PN)/72 published in Part I, Sec-
tion I of The Gazette of India Extraordinary, dated the 6th of June 1972,
which banned with immediate effect "the export of Vintage Cars i.e. motor
cars of 1940 and earlier models as well as parts and components thereof." Mr.
Born having now been posted to Dacca, and needing such consolation as a
Model A Ford can provide, I had hoped an exception might be made. Mr.
Born now informs me that he has taken the matter up with the Commerce
Secretary, and that he is sorry to report that this cannot be done. He suggests
however that I might wish to take it up with the Foreign Secretary.

Inasmuch as said Foreign Secretary had asked to see me tomorrow, I decided I would do just that. What else is the Indian Civil Service for? Last
week we received an urgent telephone call from one of the Foreign Secretary's
Joint Secretaries telling us that the Kashmir negotiations were at a critical
stage and would be greatly abetted if the U.S. Consul would issue a visa—
theretofore denied—to a certain Muslim lady involved in marital sorrows of
an unstated nature. We issued the visa in 48 hours. Now, Sir, I envisaged myself saying, upright, straightforward, Now, Sir, what about the Model A Ford?
Such is the stuff of statecraft. . . .

*Hearing the news about Nixon's resignation, Moynihan summoned the embassy
staff to the movie theater and spoke. Following are excerpts of the transcript:*

AUGUST 9, 1974.

GOOD MORNING.

We have assumed that many of you have heard the President's message that was given just a few hours ago in Washington, but if many others of you have not, we thought that as a country team it would be useful if we heard it together and heard what he had to say. Afterwards, I will speak for a few moments. . . .

[TAPE]

That was the President's farewell address, if you will, to the American people. I thought I would say just a few words sharing some of my thoughts on this occasion. It's not a happy occasion and yet, neither is it a depressing one. If ever there was a demonstration that ours is a Government of laws and not of men—we have seen this in the last fifteen months in our country, and it is never any loss to remind ourselves how few such governments there are, or ever indeed have been. Yet, there is no mistaking another fact which is that this President Nixon is the third President in a row to be destroyed in office. President Kennedy was destroyed by an assassin's hand, President Johnson by the hands of his enemies in a sense, President Nixon by his own hand, and disparate as may be the origins of the personal tragedies involved, the national experience has not been that different. And there is, I think (we can see these as personal tragedies) there is an institutional dimension with which we, who are in Government, whose concern is with such institutions, who are part of them, ought to be concerned and can usefully consider. . . .

There are, if you like, two kinds of political regimes—those whose crimes you read about in the history books, and those whose crimes you read about in the newspapers. Ours is of the latter, less common kind. The corrective mechanisms of the system which seemed to be in good working order, the strong and moral men of the present administration, the Leonard Garments, the Elliot Richardsons, the Raymond K. Prices (Mr. Price, I'm sure, wrote the speech you just heard) are coming to be valued for the integrity they sustained in murky times. Strong and ethical men in other institutions, the Congress, the courts, the press, are seen for what they mean. Dignity is acquiring meaning, not least with respect to those who for the moment keep silent, for there is noise enough. . . .

It is with this general sense that I would add just a few comments on the President's speech. It was said, many of you will recall, of James the First that nothing so became his life as the manner of his leaving it. And, I think that the President has done well by us in that regard. He leaves office with a clean decision in the sense that there need be no legacy of bitterness. He has admitted that his judgments on occasion were wrong—clearly wrong and possibly, they went well beyond what might, in a simple description be entailed by the term 'a wrong judgment.' But in any event, the Congress has been left in no doubt with respect to the nature of the acts. They were impeachable acts. They were subsumed under the headings of "high crimes and misdemeanors." The President acknowledged this. That in the jury of his peers that would be so held, and so there need be no question of anybody being railroaded, or an election being stolen, or of a man being destroyed unbetimes. He asks that he leave in these terms. He says that he thanks those who supported him, and to those who could not, he leaves without bitterness. I think, we are in ways fortunate in what, we have been spared what could have been a most divisive and, bitter, of experiences—a prolonged debate on impeachment and a vote thereon. We have been spared the sense of the spectacle of a President holding to his office long past the point of the public's wishing him to do so.

We have been introduced to a new and troubling phenomena—not [that] of a President resigning from Office in the oldest, in fact, constitutional system in the world. This has never happened to us, and to have in a sense, the third comparable event in a row is to suggest the onset of difficulties with the stability of a system which can't be very reassuring, and yet, there is no political system proof against crisis. The question is, how well crises are surmounted, and I think on balance, we could say very well indeed, in this situation. . . .

Journal entry on the new vice president.

AUGUST 21, 1974
WEDNESDAY
AURANGABAD

The President has chosen Nelson Rockefeller. The record to date is brilliant. The whole Vietnam image of a Presidency that could not be moved by public opinion and was preoccupied with the use of military force against "social revolutionaries" could vanish in a year or so of this atmosphere. I fear America may come to be loved again. . . .

*Rapturous journal entry admiring the Ajanta Caves (misidentified here as the El-
lora Caves), an archeological site of giant structures carved out of rock near Aurangabad, northeast of Bombay.*

AUGUST 22, 1974
THURSDAY

The Ellora caves are among the diminishing number of places so different
from any other place, so little expected, and so awesome as to leave the visitor
changed. Nothing in Hellenism, too homosexual, nothing in Christianity, too
repressed, nothing now, too confused, approaches this Buddhist statement of
Woman. Not female, not feminine. Neither words nor remembered forms
connect the experience with anything earlier.

How could a celibate priesthood live without that which they had made
more desirable than any people before or since?

The Deccan Plateau: in Delhi people keep telling you about it, but somehow nothing registered. How could <u>South</u> from Delhi be kinder. But it is.
Cool, fresh, green. After three years of drought. The real India, I suppose. . . .
Happily by the time of the day I begin to be possessed with such thoughts, it
is time for a drink. . . .

*Moynihan frequently lamented his modest economic situation, as here in a letter to
John M. Thomas, assistant secretary of state for administration.*

SEPTEMBER 4, 1974

Dear Dr. Thomas:

You are most generous to ask about out-of-pocket expenses for representation. Knowing how long changes take, I would not expect myself to be a
beneficiary of any increase in the allowance for India, and will accordingly
not hesitate to tell you that it is a problem. . . . My representation allowance
is $6,000.00. This is to represent the United States in India, a country with

the population of Africa and South America combined. I estimate my out-of-pocket costs at roughly $20,000.00 additional. This is not as much as I could spend, it is simply all that I have, beyond a few Treasury notes which a man approaching fifty needs for burial expenses. I tell you no tale of woe, as I have lived a life I chose for myself, but I am penniless as a result. . . .

There is nothing I need tell you about why I contrive to spend as much as I do. I have a book publisher in New York whose expense account is exactly four times mine, and he runs short. I would, however, note three things. First, my "pay" was cut ten percent between the time I left Washington and the time I arrived in New Delhi, through the second of our devaluations. Businessmen out there got an automatic adjustment. Second, the Indian inflation, while not awful, is bad enough—roughly 26 percent last year. This must be a world-wide problem, and a brutal one in some capitals. Ambassadors do not get post allowances. . . .

But then, you see, I am an Ambassador, and I pay for the privilege. The United States is worse. There I am no one. But a solitary dinner on July 5 in New York City—I was alone and most restaurants were closed—cost me $36. I have still not got over it. I estimate it costs in the neighborhood of $100 a day in the United States beyond the—what is it—$25????? allowance. As I was staying at Ambassador Scali's July 5, I got $12 that day. One could get some back for taxis and things like that, but if you are thinking about things like that, you aren't thinking about your job. . . .

I ask no quarter for myself, but do hope you would think of the problem of the career ambassador. It is a hell of a thing to have your wife be nice to people she hates for thirty years, only at last to get to Ouagadougou and then find you must go broke to stay there.

Journal entry with more reflections on the C.I.A.

SEPTEMBER 5, 1974

. . . Early in my call on Dhar [Mrs. Gandhi's secretary] he asked if I knew a Mr. ******? I knew of him. Would I mind if Mr. ****** dropped in whilst we were chatting? I would not. Whereupon he went to the red phone on his desk and in due time the director of Indian intelligence appeared. He had learned

I was to be in the building. Having heard so many pleasant things about me he had dared to hope I would not be too much inconvenienced if he were to stop by just for the briefest chat. He had been wondering if Mr. Colby [C.I.A. Director William Colby] would consider a visit to India. The two services worked together so well, and on so many important matters. The training Indians had received in the United States was of such quality. The Director of C.I.A. would be so welcome. Under wraps, of course. Frontier? Oh, yes. They had picked up the trail. Toronto. Bonn. What is one to do? I returned to the Embassy and wrote [Lawrence] Eagleburger [of the State Department] that my proposal that we pull C.I.A. out of here was "inoperative." They want us. Possibly they even want more of us. . . .

The U.S. security cooperation with Pakistan, dating from the earliest days of the cold war, was a major irritant in relations between Washington and New Delhi. Tensions boiled over during the India-Pakistan war in which Indian military intervention helped East Pakistan secede and the United States "tilted" toward Pakistan, as a leaked memo put it. Here Moynihan drafts a cable the State Department, warning that military assistance to Pakistan will damage U.S.-India relations, though the cable was not sent, no doubt in part because of its coarse language. By calling Pakistan an acronym he is referring to its name devised by its founders as an agglomeration of Punjab, Afghania, Kashmir, Sindh and Baluchistan. His reference to "Pushtoons" and "Baluchi" are to the country's two western provinces, bordering on Pakistan, Baluchistan and the Northwest Frontier, populated by Pushtuns.

SEPTEMBER 11, 1974
DRAFT
ACTION SECSTATE
CONFIDENTIAL NEW DELHI
TAGS: MARR, PK
SUBJECT: ON THE DECISION TO REARM PAKISTAN

1. In the main I have decided to give up writing cables and to write a book instead. However the decision to rearm Pakistan is so fateful as to require some notice, however perfunctory.

2. A number of things are to be said about this decision of which the first and obvious is that it is unnecessary. It is no doubt this quality which has made it seem so compelling, but even so, historians will generally record it among the non rational of the American government in this era, and will speculate with wild inaccuracy as to just what dementia led to it. The answer of course is self evident. Pakistan is the last Asian country willing to kiss our ass in public. . . .

3. On the substantive point, however, it is to be noted that the decision was unnecessary. Pakistan has today virtually unlimited access to the arms, and increasingly has oil money to pay. (Some historians will, of course, conclude we did it for the cash to be had and nothing more.) Only last week, on September six, Prime Minister [Zulfikar Ali] Bhutto, observing the anniversary of the glorious Pakistani victory in the 1965 war against India, declared that "the possibility of another conflict cannot be ruled out" but noted that Pakistan had more than recouped its military losses suffered in 1971. . . .

4. Those who are not aware of the glorious victory of 1965 should visit India. Rather as mogul fortresses and mosques are to be encountered throughout the subcontinent, eloquent reminders of the great conquests of Akbar and Shah Jahan, so in most Indian squares one will see displayed a somewhat rusty Patton tank. This shows how far the armored columns of 1965 penetrated into hind.

5. A second point about the decision to rearm Pakistan is that historians will also surely note it opened the closing chapter in the history of that dubious nation state, the very name of which is an acronym. The main point about Pakistan in this regard is that its quarter century of dependence on American arms prevented its leaders from developing the political skills necessary to survive as a multi-national state. They depended instead on parade ground bravura, and in consequence they were clobbered by the Hindus every time they . . . started something. With the new supply of American arms Islamabad will start pushing around the Pushtoons and the Baluchi. This will play right into the Indian hands. Pretty soon there will be a full scale insurgency going, and in time the further partition of Pakistan. . . .

6. The prime minister of Pakistan visited Bangladesh in June and spoke of the "shameful repression and unspeakable crimes" of Pakistan's actions there in 1971, but "worse than crimes, they were blunders." There is not the least evidence that Pakistan has learned anything from this dreadful experience. . . .

7. The third, and far the most important fact, is that the decision to rearm Pakistan will quite devastate Indo-American relations. In ordinary circumstances this would not much matter, but with India having become a nuclear

power it will make impossible any serious negotiations to bring India into an international regime bent on controlling proliferation. The decision to rearm Pakistan marks the death knell of the nonproliferation treaty, and the failure of a decade of American diplomacy. . . . In no time nuclear weapons will be in the middle east. All because the Pakistanis kiss ass so well. I recall an Arab saying: "women for duty: boys for pleasure." And there is, of course, a boy lurking in every American man.

8. The Indians will react because they will see the decision to rearm Pakistan as part of a resumed American effort to surround India militarily. The first move was, of course, Diego Garcia. It would be difficult to exaggerate the impression our behavior in this matter has made on New Delhi. . . .

9. The likelihood is that the decision to rearm Pakistan will consolidate the Indo-Soviet alliance, with the Russians, for example, establishing the bases in the Indian Ocean which we have said they already have and hence, by orderly balance of power principles, are "entitled" to have. But one should not rule out Sino-Indian entente. . . .

10. This is all rather sad. When the Indians exploded their first nuclear device last May one could sense the relief of some harassed officers. "Thank god, India has a bomb," they seemed to say. "Now we can send some tanks to Pakistan and won't have to think about all that for another six months." This was not, however, the reaction of one of the senior officers of the department with whom I discussed this matter. A man of rare quality and incomparable experience combined with an almost penitential preference for truth telling, he remarked that the Indian explosion meant "thinking about the unthinkable." After a pause, he continued: "we must now treat India as an equal." . . .

Excerpt of a journal entry reporting that the University of Chicago is wooing Moynihan but that he will go back to Harvard, with mixed feelings.

OCTOBER 6, 1974
SUNDAY

The Committee on Social Thought at Chicago has asked me to come there. [Saul] Bellow, [Edward] Shils, [William] Kruskal. None better. And

God knows a better salary. Harvard is turning shabby without turning genteel. Never should have let in people like me. But I have moved too much and report to Chairman [James Q.] Wilson that I shall be reporting for duty February 1. In truth I have already left India. Two days in Cambridge has done it. It is a ravaged place. The students hate the likes of me, and it is a struggle, and a costly one, not to hate back. But it has been costly to the point where I haven't the energy to go anywhere else, so I shall return here. My only pleasure is that there is now a great deal of street crime. <u>Privately</u> the undergraduates are learning what we pigs have tried to tell them about the uses of order, as against their beloved disorder. Nothing like a little rape to teach the children of the rich what it means to be poor. But, damn, they are <u>so</u> young, and while they mean harm, they see this as an honorable role, and of course it is. . . .

Traveling with Kissinger in India, preceded by disturbing accusations attributed to Mrs. Gandhi that the U.S. was requiring India to "beg" for food assistance.

OCTOBER 24, 1974

We require India to beg. "They are using the word in regard to our country. The word is not used with regard to any other country, but only with regard to India."

The door from the forward cabin opens. The Secretary of State. Cable in hand. "The bitch!" What is an ambassador to say? What I say is "She will piss on your grave, Henry. There is nothing to be done about her. We come and we go: she remains." The door closes. Disaster.

The Secretary of State all grim. In five minutes it opens again. "I know what I will say at the airport. I will say "Beggars can't be choosers." It's going to be all right after all. . . .

He is superb at the airport. A dozen arrival statements had been written. Instead he spoke three paragraphs of his own. "The two greatest democracies in the world have rediscovered their common purposes and have exchanged ideas on an ever increasing range of topics." . . .

Excerpt of a journal entry expressing awe at Kissinger's performance in India and other details of the long-planned visit.

OCTOBER 28, 1974
MONDAY

Three hours sleep is fine by him; not by me. The Patriot [newspaper] greets us with a long front page story about how I am contemptuous of Kissinger behind his back, badmouth him, disavow his policies, and predict his imminent demise. If he has one rule with his staff it is to show him bad news immediately, and he must have seen this by the time I arrive but neither mentions it or shows any concern. What is this? Nancy [Mrs. Kissinger]? She has made an enormous difference to him. Where once his odd moment of relaxation was chewing off the finger joints of Assistant Secretaries, he now takes a break every so often to mumble around like any husband asking where his wife's boots are. Did she leave them in the plane? The guest house in Moscow? Can they be mailed?

Off to the meetings.

At noon he met with the Prime Minister, alone save for a few moments when P.N. Dhar was there. This is what it's all about. What exactly went on I shall never know, but evidently it went well enough. . . .

She began saying she assumed he wished to talk about the nuclear explosion. He said yes, he wanted to talk about the bomb. India had one now . . . its interest is now to see that others do not get one.

Turning to CIA he said that the United States supported the Congress Party. (A fact she must know, in the past having taken our money. He would know that she would know that he would know this.) Then, if I surmise correctly, that peculiar exchange that can only occur among the elect. He did not disavow any hostile intentions. He merely stated that he had not taken any hostile acts. There were no operations authorized against India, he said. He chaired the committee that gives such authorizations. He had not done so. If she found any American misbehaving, she had only to send him a personal letter. (For which read: lest there be any mistake as to who [could] turn it off and who could turn it on. . . .)

Dinner at Roosevelt House [the ambassador's residence at the U.S. Embassy]. A success, I should think. Liz puts people at round tables so they can talk, and the Secretary was clearly talking. Girilal Jain [editor of *The Times* of India] before sitting down had told him his address was the most important statement ever made about the Subcontinent by an outsider. Jain is curious in only saying what he believes. Kissinger seems to be able to distinguish in such matters and is impressed. Jain thereupon says he must give a press conference.

The toasts were mellifluous toasts.

But he is bored. Why is it, he asks, back at the Palace, that there was so little to talk about? In Peking the days and nights are never long enough.

More on Kissinger's visit to India, though Kissinger confesses to Moynihan that he is not sure how long he can last in the new Ford administration. Kissinger was under increasing attack from conservatives (led by Ronald Reagan, who later ran against Ford in 1976) for his policy of détente with the Soviet Union.

OCTOBER 29, 1974

... On the ride back from the meetings he allowed himself genuinely impressed by the way Indian ministers endure. I had mentioned that the four so far had clocked some 65 years as members of the cabinet. He doesn't think he will. When he went to Washington, he said, he simply didn't believe it when people said they wanted to get out. Now he understood. Every time you appear to have a great success and are congratulated, <u>you</u> know it is the beginning of a new problem. Now in the United States the atmosphere is so poisonous one knew that one slip would mean no mercy. You have to bat 1000. But you are up against players who are Big League also. ...

Clearly, as of one o'clock Tuesday October 29, 1974, Indian diplomacy has not persuaded the Secretary of State that it continues to be worth our while to be the only major country in the world that does not sell arms in South Asia. Indian diplomacy has not tried to do so. Indian diplomacy seems solely concerned to get him to admit that the United States in the past has behaved badly. You have got to admire the <u>chutzpah.</u> A nation half in rags which cannot feed itself. I do admire it. Their grandchildren will see they did not yield

simply because circumstances were humiliating. But it is no way to impress
Henry Kissinger. . . .

*Moynihan was frequently felled by giardia, dysentery, bacterial infections, and other
demoralizing digestive ailments in India. Here he manages to get out of bed to do
a postmortem on Kissinger with Indian journalists.*

NOVEMBER 2, 1974

A howling night of bacillary. Just when the visit was over and the living
looked good. Up til dawn. Sleep all day. Schedule ruined. Energy at about
thirty percent normal. Rather, thirty percent subnormal. We are all sick here,
all the time. I have been sick for two years, and it has begun to get to me.

Our talk is mostly of sickness, of miscarriages, of hepatitis, of abortions
following hepatitis. Delhi is the one capital in the world in which health facilities are judged by the Department to have deteriorated over the past
decade. In the course of the past year twenty percent of our people have been
put in the hospital, which means an eight bed affair in the British compound,
which is always overbooked. We are going to bootleg a hospital of our own in
the course of redoing some of the apartments in our compound. Curiously,
the civilians take this in an accepting or at least resigned spirit. It is the military who find it outrageous. . . .

I got out of bed long enough to speak to Girilal Jain's Saturday luncheon
club. Journalists mostly. They seemed well satisfied with the visit, although
the bitching about the 1950s and 1960s somehow never stops. . . .

*Letter to Eric Hoffer, the former longshoreman who became a revered author of
books about the working class, about Moynihan's own working-class background.*

NOVEMBER 6, 1974

Dear Eric Hoffer:

So much of what you have written has about it the quality of revelation. Nothing has meant more to me than the passage in your article in <u>The New York Times Magazine</u> of October 20 in which you write "Marx never did a day's work in his life...." How can it be that in all these years of wondering what was wrong with that man, this one elemental fact never occurred to me. I shall never think of him in the same way again. And it is about time.

Let me explain a bit. I was raised, rough you might say, on the West Side of New York. After the usual run of kid jobs, at age 16 I went to work on the North River piers. It was the middle of the war and a person my age could get work—something unheard of in the years before. I spent a year at it: eleven hours a day, six days a week on Pier 48; ten hours on Sunday at Pier 50. Most of us were delirious with that much overtime. Again something unheard of through the years that preceded. About ¾'s of the way through, with the number of gangs doubled and tripled, they ran short of checkers and, being able to read, they made me one. Whereupon I found myself with a pencil in my hand and whatever else may be said of my life since, I have never let go. I joined the Navy when I was 17 and that was the end of the piers. But I have more than once said to myself that I haven't really done a day's work since. Not a <u>real</u> day's work. This I think has been one of the sources of my immense regard for all that you have written. You know what it means, and almost none of the others do.

Brief journal entry from the South Indian beach resort of Kovalam, reflecting on his limited successes as ambassador.

NOVEMBER 13, 1974

... Had I come to Kovalam [in South India] two years ago and not left since, I doubt anything much would have been made of it at this end. In any event, that noble Gladstonite, the Honorable Chester Bowles [former ambassador to India] used to come here for a month at a time. I shall have six days and I shall enjoy them. I shall have for company Graham Greene, *A Sort of Life*, Solzhenitsyn, *The Gulag Archipelago*, Edward Shils *The Intellectuals and the Powers*, Fogel and Engerman, *Time on the Cross*, James Q. Wilson *Political Organizations*, Gertrude Himmelfarb *On Liberty and Liberalism*—her great book at last on Mills—and W. R. Rodgers' *Irish Literary Portraits*. Two late comers to a guest list long in the making. *Data Analysis for Politics and Policy* by Edward R. Tufte, a Princeton political scientist of formidable mathematical repute, who sent me a copy inscribed: "To Pat Moynihan, Whose influence of years ago fills Chapter 1." . . . Also [William] Buckley's *United Nations Journal*. I had not thanked him because I had not read it: as I have never read Galbraith. . . . The book shall be read.

Also of the party: six bottles Soave, 1 bottle Campari, 1 bottle brandy. Kovalam beer is good. Indian gin is good enough. . . .

Done then. A mission not without success. I will not be remembered. It has been my object not to be remembered. . . .

Journal entry expressing exasperation that the C.I.A. director, William Colby, has admitted to the press that the agency provides "discreet help" to political figures in other countries.

NOVEMBER 27, 1974
WEDNESDAY

. . . Incredibly—criminally!—Colby has given an interview with U.S. News and World Report in which, evidently, he asserts our continued right to interfere with other nations' politics. "A little discreet help to a few friends of the U.S. or a little help to a few people espousing a certain policy or programme in a foreign country" as the Express reports it. What can he think he is doing? . . . Is there <u>nothing</u> to which bureaucracy will not lead a man. Even a good man such as Colby. . . .

Traveling to Ajmer, a lakeside city in the desert state of Rajasthan, but the trip to this exotic place prompts Moynihan to reflect on the biography of the man who has emerged as the leader of the opposition to Mrs. Gandhi, Jayaprakash (known as

J. P.) Narayan. In 1975, after Moynihan departed, the spreading uprising led by Narayan prompted Mrs. Gandhi to crack down in the so-called "Emergency."

NOVEMBER 28, 1974
THURSDAY

... Reading Shils on "Asian Intellectuals." Of whom Jayaprakash Narayan is surely one. It has all come, not suddenly, but steadily, step by step, stage by stage. A year ago Indira Gandhi both ruled and reigned in India for the fullest spectrum of reasons, of which the single most salient was that there was no one who could rule in her stead. . . . Now there is another person. It is all very Hindu. We scarcely knew of him, although he was the one private Indian to meet Kissinger in 1971, when he asked for aid for the Bangladesh refugees. He belonged to no party, made no pronouncements, never left Bihar. He was a social worker. He had no money, no evident ambitions, no seeming complaints. Yet all this which is negative to us, in the sense that such a person appears to recede in the scheme of things, was positive to the Indian mind. He retained his influence <u>because he had renounced it</u>. As he had renounced other things. At his marriage, before Gandhi, he renounced sexual union. Nehru had wished to bring him into the first Indian government: he declined. He was briefly active in the Socialist party, and dropped that. With all of which he acquired merit. Last March the Bihar students asked him to lead their movement which followed on that of the Gujarati students that ended in the dissolution of the Gujarat Assembly.

It was hard to think he would get as far as he has got, and hard to think he will get any further. . . . His principle issue is that the Congress is corrupt, which it is. But he does not seem interested in the systemic nature of the corruption, nor has he any notion of how to get rid of it save by doing without political parties. Which means what? . . .

He started protests in the Gandhian manner. Rousing a town, stirring up the authorities, producing a confrontation, a certain amount of violence. Then stop. Move on. Start again. By early fall he was speaking to crowds of hundreds of thousands. He began to taunt the Prime Minister, calling her the "Queen of Delhi," suggesting her writ ran no further, that she was no longer Empress of India. She began to react, and then to overreact. On November 4 he staged a huge rally in Patna. The police charged. He was knocked down, the people around him clubbed. It was nothing brutal.... But it was enough. The Government of India had struck down Gandhi's disciple. ...

Excerpt of a journal entry in which Moynihan ponders but rejects the offer from Washington to become Librarian of Congress.

NOVEMBER 29, 1974

FRIDAY

NEW DELHI

The Librarianship of Congress is evidently all but set. [Senate Republican leader] Hugh Scott writes to say he has informed the White House that he supports my "candidacy." [Senate Majority Leader] Mansfield and [James] Cannon [White House assistant] are on board, as is [Speaker of the House] Carl Albert.

This was worth finding out. Now I must cable [Donald] Rumsfeld [White House chief of staff] telling him I don't want the job. I only realized this when I found out who had to approve. Not that there is one of them I don't respect. But I don't want to have to live conditional on their approval. Better to live with no very great reputation in academe. I have turned down the kindest of offers to join the Committee on Social Thought at Chicago, writing [Edward] Levi [president of the University of Chicago] that while Shils and Bellow and Kruskal don't know this, I am not their equal. Were I to settle among them they would find it out, and while they would never in the least way suggest that they had come to realize this, I would know they had and that would make it a waste for everyone. I have had a singular difficulty in these matters. ...

Moynihan tries different conversational gambits at his dinner with Mrs. Gandhi. The Ajanta caves refer to structures cut out of the rock, with interior paintings, in western India. Moynihan had visited them and feared they were being destroyed.

DECEMBER 5, 1974

At five o'clock P.N. Dhar calls. We will be at dinner tonight. He is much concerned that the opportunity not be wasted. The Department has sent two pages of instructions as to what I am to say. If cables such as that were leaked, the Foreign Service would be in trouble. The cable is FOR AMBASSADOR FROM SECRETARY, and he has added a few touches from Peking. The Chinese are still willing to make up. He had a successful visit: a fact being sufficiently insisted on in the cable traffic this week as to make clear he did not. [Deputy Chief of Mission David] Schneider and I map a campaign for total victory between the pineapple juice and the cardamom seeds.

Total defeat followed. For one thing she wasn't on hand for the pineapple juice. Parliament had been in total turmoil all day. A vast sit-in was scheduled for the day to follow. But I tried opening as planned with the Ajanta caves.

I had heard that day from [Indian art expert] Stella Kramrisch. She quite agreed. Especially about the strong light of the arc lamps which the chowkidars [security guards] knock against the murals like New York City garbage men bouncing ash cans on the sidewalks. "If the present state of affairs is allowed to continue the paintings will no doubt be non existent as works of art in the foreseeable future." Was it not possible, I suggested, to close the caves for a year or two, and to appoint a committee of Indian scientists to consider the matter of preservation? She had thought of that and had written, but "they" had replied it couldn't be done.

Very well try food. The food was delicious. As this would be our last month in India we were searching out Indian cuisines we hadn't tried yet. Last month in India.

She was not surprised I liked the fish. It was a specialty of the House. . . .

Very well, try the PRC [Peoples Republic of China]. The Secretary [Kissinger] wished her to know that the Chinese remain well disposed toward better relations despite a certain irritability over [Indian state of] Sikkim. They were especially pleased by his report of the warm reception he had had in New Delhi and of the continued improvement of Indo American relations. Was he now? Yes, and further I had come upon some interesting statistics which Professor Dhar would find especially intriguing. We had been recalculating GNP. We were now publishing a series which showed Indian and Chinese per capita GNP as very close: $185 as against $202. This was most interesting, was it not? India had been depicted as well behind China. We now felt this was not so. Was this not interesting? Silence. . . .

Over coffee she spoke of her youth when she had pleurisy, of an English-
man who lived in a tree nearby, of a Jesuit who was in fact a woman, of an
American lady who was a writer and her husband who specialized in high altitude farming. Of the size of the people of Tonga, of the importance of the
women's market place association in Nigeria. Some talk of saris. Finally, what
did we think of the French proposal for a consumer producer oil conference.
India did not want to get caught in between. I was in mid reply when Dhar
looked at his watch.

"I tried," I said to him as we left.

*Letter to P. N. Dhar, Prime Minister Gandhi's secretary, explaining the political
difficulty of obtaining approval in Congress for assistance to India.*

DECEMBER 20, 1974

My dear "P.N.,"

You asked if I would note down some of the Thoughts on Leaving India
which I was tossing about to such a late hour on Monday evening. . . .

I put it to you the other evening that it was a continuing mystery to me
that Indians were not more clear about the most elemental of geopolitical re-
alities, namely that of the other three massive powers in the world, two—the
two with which India shares the Asian land mass—are institutionally committed to a change in the Indian regime, whereas only the third, the United
States, sees its interests to lie in the success and continuance of the present
Indian regime.

As you must know, there was a time when US support to the Indian regime
was quite concrete. That was a long time past and nothing of the sort has existed since 1962. Nevertheless we still support the Congress Party in more
general ways as any careful examination of our policies would demonstrate.
Not in the sense that we oppose other democratic parties. We do not. In the
most generalized sense, we wish them well also. But we recognize that the
Congress Party has been and continues to be the government of the Republic
of India.

A consequence of this is that the United States has never sought any <u>in-
ternal</u> political influence in India in return for external aid. The success of an

independent, democratic India is all that we have ever hoped for. That, for us, constitutes achievement of a foreign policy objective. For example, I hear much confused talk about our opposition to Indian socialism. Good Lord. In the 1960s we financed Indian socialism. We put up the money and the food which gave your planners something to plan with. We knew we were doing it. We desired to do it. What we did not desire was that planning should falter once the heavy flow of American resources ceased. . . .

My surmise was that the way things are going, you are not going to get such assistance from the United States. First of all, you won't ask for it. But if you want it, you have to make a reasonable case. Not in any craven, or sub-servient way. But as one democracy to another. For the United States is a democracy, too. We are a nation of working people. My mother and my mother-in-law, an example, are both in their sixties. They both earn their liv-ing—one in a hospital, one in a restaurant—at tasks many Indians would con-sider utterly demeaning, even disgraceful. But these women are not disgraced. To the contrary, they can take pride in their work and in their independence, and American society acknowledges this. These ladies pay taxes to provide foreign assistance, and they simply will not do so unless they feel there is a legitimate need. . . . I have roamed the corridors of the United States Capitol on this issue, and I assure you the fundamental problem is that Congress feels India does not want American assistance, and resents ever having accepted any. . . .

Excerpt of a journal entry recounting his farewell press conference in India.

DECEMBER 22, 1974

It is not quite two years I have been in India; somewhat more than two that I have, in effect, been the American Ambassador. . . . I am leaving now to return to teaching, whence I came. It is perhaps time I said something here. Or, as some may think, time I had something to say.

To the former point there can be no very great dispute. I have not over-burdened either the Indian or American public with commentary or advice. I have spoken in public only four times in two years, and two of these occa-sions took place a fortnight ago. I have not until this moment given a press conference. As between two, and in each case, democratic governments, quiet diplomacy is ordained as much by ethical as by prudential principles. The diplomat has no right to try—and will fail should he in fact try—to pressure government. His task, rather, is to tell (in his view) the government he represents what policy should be, and to tell to the government to which he is accredited what policy is. . . .

Having established that I would expect to say little in public while an Ambassador, what of the second matter? Have I anything to say?

Yes. I do. It is appropriate, perhaps, to speak of the matter as I leave India, for it had everything to do with my coming here in the first place. I came here thinking that liberty was losing in the world. I leave thinking that liberty may well be lost. This has been the effect of these two years on my thoughts.

Two years ago, as it happens, I was offered in effect a choice of ambassadorships. I could have the United Nations, or I could go to India. . . . In any event, not for the first, but for the second time, I was asked to be United States Ambassador to the United Nations, and for the second time I declined. That corpse had already begun to decompose. If I am sorry for such language, I am sorry even more for the events which make it appropriate. The spirit of liberty had seeped out of that institution. . . .

I chose instead to go to India, for there, as I felt, and as I do feel, liberty resides. A democracy. One of few. One of three left in Asia. Three and a half, perhaps. But what a Democracy! The world's most populous. In ways, perhaps, the world's most popular. In that regard how very different, I thought, from my own democracy.

One can't be wrong in everything, and I was not wrong in coming to India, for here liberty does indeed reside. But here, as in so much of the world that remains to it, liberty displays an uneasy presence. An endangered species. A threatened environment. That Indian democracy should have to struggle to maintain itself is the natural condition of its being. All democracies have this struggle. What troubles me so is to find it struggling to maintain its reputation in the world. . . .

The heart has gone out of it; is going out of it. We no longer believe that liberty will prevail. Not here. Not, I suspect, much longer in Western Europe. Not, I fear, very much longer in the United States. . . . Both the United States and India have far closer and more cooperative relations with the totalitarian powers of the world than we have with one another. Indeed, it is from one another that increasingly we are isolated. It is the American practice to pay but little attention to India, and the Indian policy to see that little attention is paid. . . . Liberty is losing. . . .

As he was leaving India, Moynihan became drawn into his earlier battles by Kenneth B. Clark, president of the Metropolitan Applied Research Center and a prominent black sociologist with whom he had earlier worked. Clark took a swipe at Moynihan in an advertising blurb for a book by two welfare rights activists, prompting Moynihan to write Clark on November 5, 1974, saying he found the blurb "unprofessional and unfriendly" and adding: "Good Lord, Ken. What have I ever been but a friend of yours?" Moynihan also noted in that letter that he had often recommended funding for Clark's research center. Clark responded with a letter on November 20, 1974, defending his comments as professional and his right to his opinions. He added that it was his "personal belief that your famous 'benign neglect' memorandum was one of the most disturbing and dangerous publicly stated positions in an incredibly regressive Nixon administration." Finally, Clark acidly told Moynihan that he never asked him for help in funding and that "you are, of course, free to use your influence to withhold funds from any organization or person who does not share your views." Moynihan's response:

DECEMBER 24, 1974

Dear Kenneth:

Heavens. You must be very bitter at life to write such a letter as that. I feel worse than I did.

I can remember how upset you were when Adam Powell was taking over MFY [Mobilization For Youth, an anti-poverty program]. At the time I had never known any such experience, but even so I did not wonder at your distress. Since then you have been savagely attacked from so many sides that I do not wonder at all at your feelings. I would only say that I have been too. Both of us are academics who have wandered into public policy areas. We have been men of goodwill and decent intention. You must know that about me. I certainly know it about you. But we have been attacked with a particular ferocity, possibly because we are outsiders. I don't know. I only know that three years ago I walked out of a public meeting where you were being denounced in the most intemperate tones, and found myself thinking that we had more of the same experience than any two persons I know. Not long before I left the White House in 1970, Whitney Young called on me and said as much.

As for that memorandum of mine, I do think it is a loss to see hostility where none exists. All I intended to say and all I was understood to say was that we were getting too far away from the principles of the Civil Rights Act, seeing one another too much in terms of racial and ethnic categories, and not as individuals. At the time the <u>Washington Post</u> ran two long editorials pointing out what was the argument, and substantially agreeing with it. As I think you, too, would agree in substance.

How could you ever think I could oppose support for MARC. It is a splendid institution, and you should be proud of it.

Merry Christmas.

Letter to Donald Rumsfeld, a top assistant to President Ford, as he leaves India, urging him not to succumb to the paranoia of the Nixon White House.

JANUARY 2, 1975
<u>CONFIDENTIAL</u>

Dear Don:

I do indeed look forward to seeing you and the President in January. I come away from India with at least a few things to report in Washington. . . . For the moment I will take advantage of the invitation and your letter of December 13: "If you have any thoughts between now and then, know that we value them." You may or may not value this one, but I have been so miserable about the recent CIA "disclosures" that I have to write someone. You may just remember a letter I wrote the President in early 1971, a few months after I left the White House. I was struck in my first few weeks "out" by the degree to which plain Republican businessmen shared my view that the Administration was not sensitive to issues of civil liberties, and did not understand how concerned the public was about this. . . .

My concern now is that the Ford Administration should not fall victim of the aftermath of this incredible calamity. You are very different people and are immune, as best any outsider can tell, to the paranoid temptations that destroyed your predecessors. However, I find myself writhing out here in India as I read <u>The Stars and Stripes</u> and the ten-day-old <u>New York Times</u>. Every day there is a new story about some appalling federal intrusion on the civil liberties of the citizenry. If it is not the Internal Revenue Service, it is the Pentagon. The list goes on and on. I expect that there is no more than five percent or ten percent truth in most of the charges, and that a very great many are in fact false.

Yet they are not rebutted. . . .

Excerpt of a journal entry describing the flight from Hong Kong to Beijing to stay with the head of the U.S. mission, George H. W. Bush, and his wife, Barbara.

JANUARY 10, 1975

. . . George and Barbara Bush greet us at the airport, and I do believe we are welcome, an impression I cannot often have conveyed in New Delhi. She in mink; he in tennis glow. They are quintessential gentle folk, who have lived most of their lives in oilfields, political conventions, and now Red China; a triumph of good manners and good digestion. It could have been an altogether unruffled life. From Bones [Skull and Bones] down to Brown Bros. [the investment banking firm] and back, as it were, to New Canaan.

He chose instead to do for himself what had already been done for him, with the ups and downs that takes. Put everything he had into Zapata Oil— off shore drilling. Won. Sold out at a fifth what the stock was worth a year later. Ran for a House seat in Texas. Won. Then ran for the Senate. Lost. (Lloyd Bentsen making a particular point of his having voted for FAP.) Then I turned down the U.N. job for the final time. Whereupon the job went to him, which is a win. Damn good Ambassador. Win again. Republican National Chairman. Win yet again. Watergate. Lose. Big. Almost Vice President. Biggest win/lose so far. China. Small win. As Holmes said of Roosevelt, an absolutely first rate temperament, and a wife who will take anything but bad manners.

He is having Kissinger trouble, as who would not in Peking, but compounded in his case by the evident suspicion of the Secretary of State that just possibly a successor is being groomed. Or such is the impression Bush has, not without some merriment. He is finished with Nixon, to whom God knows he was loyal. Says that if he received a call from him today he is not sure he would take it. . . .

Normally Barbara cooks. I have arrived, in the ambassadorial manner, with a suitcase of laundry to be done, it being the genuine accomplishment of the Foreign Buildings Office, or whomsoever, that anywhere in the world [from] an American Ambassador's residence can [be] produced clean underwear in twenty four hour's time, with places like Tokyo getting it down to about twenty four minutes. But this is no Ambassador's residence. The employees do the laundry for the head of the Liaison Office and his wife. If my shirts are to be done, Barbara Bush will do them.

Journal excerpt: After stopping in Hawaii, Moynihan flies to New York City, jetting across upstate New York. Delhi is a town near his farm with a name and history that fascinated him.

JANUARY 20, 1975

. . . The great plane begins its descent at Buffalo, and we glide toward Boston in a direct line across the Finger Lakes. It is a kind of luminescent dark with the snow still in the woods on the tops of the hills set off as calligraphy against the soft background. Canandaigua. Geneva. Ithaca. Hamilton. Cooperstown. And to starboard beloved Delhi, whose green memories sustained many a bleak and sun blasted day in far Hind. Pronounced <u>Del-high</u>. It seems there was a Judge Foot who was majority leader of State Senate in the late eighteenth century, when the legislature was still at Kingston. The Western tier of counties up the Mohawk had been marked off at the river's edge, but pretty much left to extend indefinitely to the West, no one being quite certain how far indefinitely would prove to be, and few having heard of California. The time came when the county seats were much too far away for those who had crossed the Catskills and began settling the upwaters of the Susquehanna, which rises in Lake Otsego, pouring out through Cazenovia much as the Rhone debouches through Geneva from Lake Leman. A new set of counties was needed, and Foot set about fashioning them with the authority that had earned him the sobriquet "Great Mogul." When it was all over, the County of Delaware had been created, with its seat at a tiny hamlet on the West Branch. From what youthful stirrings we will never know, but the westward movement seized the Majority Leader himself. He left the Senate and moved to said hamlet, where the citizenry overwhelmed by the presence of the Great Mogul in their midst, renamed the County Seat Delhi in honor of the ancestral home of these men whose wont it was to redesign the world about them. . . .

Journal excerpt: Taking delight in being back in New York City, Moynihan discusses plans to write an important article for Norman Podhoretz for his magazine COMMENTARY *about standing up to totalitarian governments.*

JANUARY 22, 1975
WEDNESDAY
NEW YORK CITY

Podhoretz is enthusiastic about The Revolution of the Second International, which we agree should refer to the British Revolution. He has beautifully edited a twelve thousand word article to lead the March issue. I propose the title "The United States in Opposition."

You have to be away a long time and in a hard place to know once more how much you love what you left. This chunk of New York is precious to me as no place else. It is a bit of a way from 42nd Street and 11th Avenue and to 43rd Street and Fifth where we sit over bloody marys done in the Century manner—but not that long a way if you don't try too hard. And oh the women on the streets are beautiful, and the water sweet, and the beef red and rich, and the life worth living. . . .

Journal entry expressing amazement that Americans seem more interested in his stop in China than his tour in India.

JANUARY 23, 1975

WEDNESDAY

After two years in India, I stopped five days in China on my way home, and that is all anyone wants to talk about. I have written a "Letter from Peking" for the New Yorker, which Bob Bingham likes and even wants longer. Should have stayed the full week.

Excerpt of a journal entry describing his visit with President Ford to report on India and why he turned down the Library of Congress job. The Moynihans disliked the box-like design of Roosevelt House, their home at the U.S. embassy. The architect, Edward Durrell Stone, designed many such "boxes," including the Kennedy Center in Washington.

JANUARY 27, 1975

MONDAY

WASHINGTON

. . . My appointment with the President is for 11:30. Dave Broder [the *Washington Post* reporter] is in the West Lobby by way of greeting almost. Some people don't change yet seem somehow always renewed. . . . The West Lobby, by contrast, is unrecognizable, which has something to do with my mood, for it has looked like it does for four years now, and more, really. But my sense is that of leaving Washington, and my memory those of things that were there when I was first there. The Lobby was bigger under Kennedy, with a huge round table somehow that somehow incorporated buffalo horns in its design serving as a coat rack in the middle of the room, and beat up sofas against the walls. It smelled of tobacco spit and was presided over by unobtrusively omniscient black porters, as I think they were known, for they kept the President's gates. Now it is all gold carpet and Winslow Homer, a blond receptionist and Marine sergeant. Still, the tension is gone from a year ago. . . .

Gerry Ford is President now. It comes over a man: really: if you have been around during the changeover, you can sense it. He would have to be judged the easiest of the four I have known in that room, which is not the best news, but then consider what became of the others who were not easy. For reasons history will someday unravel, my farewell call on the President of the United States as his Ambassador to India begins with a discussion of the architecture of Roosevelt House [the ambassador's residence], as seemingly all discussions of American life in India must begin, I tell my Disraeli story. (Mr. Kremlin in Sybil, described as a man distinguished for ignorance, as had but one idea and that was wrong. Such it seems to me, to encapsulate the architecture of Edward Durrell Stone. Etc.) The Secretary of State discoursed on air conditioning arrangements of the Chancery.

I was following with accounts of cleaning the duck pond [in the embassy], when I came to my senses and said: "Mr. President, we have learned to deal with Communism in the World. We are now going to have to learn to deal with Socialism." I can't imagine he had the least idea what I was talking about, but it got Kissinger on to the subject of my cables—entirely generous, as he always has been—and the President on to the subject of India. He asked if it was breaking up, as it was said to be when he was last there, years ago. I replied that it was presumption to say such a thing to the President of the United States, but it was simply the fact that democracy is not the least effective form of government, that the Indians had in fact done a brilliant job putting together a multi-lingual state; that if I had to choose I would bet on India being intact in the year 2000 ahead of Russia or China. I said they had achieved this in part through the political use of centralized planning: a steel mill for this fellow's district, an irrigation system for that state. The President said such arrangements were not unknown in the United States. I said, yes, but the consequences were worse in India. . . .

Even so, I took it out on the President a little bit. Told him he had obviously made a mistake with the pardon of Nixon, even if I would have done the same. (This defines something of the personality. You find yourself saying to him: "Now, if I were President. . . ." Which you didn't find yourself saying to his predecessors.) He agreed, but said it had to be done sooner or later, and better sooner. I said he had restored honor to the Presidency, and no service to the Republic could be greater. I said the State of the Union had been a fine message, even if it left out Rumsfeld's Family Assistance Plan. I then started to berate him again, sneaking over, I suppose, to the question of arms. Was he going to be destroyed by military policy in Asia as Johnson had been, and in ways Nixon had been? In his first press conference as President, on August 28, the first question addressed to him had concerned Diego Garcia. He had answered: "The Soviet Union already has three major naval operating bases in the Indian Ocean. . . . "That was not true. They had nothing that could be described in those terms. The Indians wondered why he said they did. The Russians surely wondered also. He must not let the admirals do this to him, the military do this to him. The Presidency is at stake. Presidents are destroyed. I did not see any admirals destroyed. . . .

He then said it was his hope I might be interested to be Librarian of Congress. I said I would be—in any circumstances save those in which I found myself, for I had or was soon to have three children in college, had dependents, had some debt, and was penniless. He asked Rumsfeld, who was note taker for the forty minutes, what the job paid, and that settled the matter for him. He said the pay should be higher but there was no way he could promise it, and left it that somehow I was the aggrieved party. I got up to go, saying "Mr. President, we cannot go on dealing only with the dictatorships in the world." Rumsfeld took me to lunch in the mess, but I had nothing more to say.

As he had with Kenneth Clark, Moynihan also tangled with Robert C. Wood, president of the University of Massachusetts and former secretary of Housing and Urban Development. Wood had written in the journal DAEDALUS *that Moynihan had belonged to the group of sociologists arguing that genetics were a factor in the culture of poverty among blacks. Moynihan objected, and Wood wrote back that he was "perfectly prepared to believe" that Moynihan was not part of this school of thought, but that he believed Moynihan's writings had contributed to "an emerging new conservatism" and dismantling social programs under Nixon. Moynihan's reply:*

MARCH 3, 1975

Dear Bob,

If you withdraw, as you do, the suggestion that I have in any way been associated with the notion of genetic differences between races, then there is nothing in your article that offends me. The notion that I think the lower class is the root of all evil strikes me as bizarre, but it is not offensive. But the other matter is offensive, and is untrue, and we had best leave it that I am sorry this has happened.

Citing his COMMENTARY *article, "The United States in Opposition," Moynihan urges Rumsfeld to take the lead in making this approach U.S. policy.*

MARCH 17, 1975
THE HONORABLE DONALD RUMSFELD
ASSISTANT TO THE PRESIDENT
WHITE HOUSE
WASHINGTON, D. C. 20500

Dear Don,
    ... In all my scribbling, of which you will attest there has been considerable, I have not ever had a response such as the one I am getting to this article. Hundreds of letters.... All say one thing. Yes, we <u>should</u> "go into opposition," raise hell, state our case, present alternatives, stop apologizing for a merely imperfect democracy. The message is unmistakable. People are tired of our being ashamed of ourselves. (And Lord knows we are that.) There is indeed a new isolationism, but there is also an alternative. If, in a systematic way we started to send our people into international forums to make a vigorous and sustained case for our views in the world—and, if we had views—I think we might all be surprised at the rallying of spirits that might follow. I don't think this is a case the President can successfully make merely by exhortation. It has to be demonstrated. If we were to start making our case, the first effect might be that the American people might once more come to realize that we have one.
    I would not be so far out of channels save that Henry [Kissinger] called before leaving for the Middle East to say he thought the piece "spectacularly good." I say that even if he did leave me off his list for the next Secretary of State.

Moynihan conveys his concerns to Rumsfeld about the impending fall of Cambodia and the spread of Communism. Subsequently Rumsfeld wrote Moynihan: "Dear Pat: South East Asia. Ugh!" A postscript added, "Do what Henry and the President asked you to. We need you"—evidently to become ambassador to the United Nations.

MARCH 18, 1975
THE HONORABLE DONALD RUMSFELD
ASSISTANT TO THE PRESIDENT
WHITE HOUSE
WASHINGTON, D. C. 20500

Dear Don,

... When I paid my farewell call on the President I had meant to suggest he should prepare himself and the nation for the fall of Cambodia. I had just been at Pearl Harbor and had sat through the briefings put on there for Carl Maw, who was just returning from the area. If the military have learned anything about South East Asia, it is the logistics of the place, and it was clear from what they told the Under Secretary that Cambodia would go under by early-to-late spring, with South Vietnam possibly not far behind. The admirals hoped for a special appropriation from the Congress. I said to Maw privately that obviously the situation was lost, for there would be no such appropriation....

Thailand is three-quarters lost anyway. Malaysia, and for that matter Singapore, will be no problem to neutralize. In any event, the Big Domino <u>always</u> has been India. If we pay just a little heed to that place, it should be possible to bring them at least partially around to our side of things. The Prime Minister is increasingly dependent on a Communist Party alliance, but it is a Moscow party, and will be with her against Chinese pressure. In 1962, the last time the Chinese showed themselves on the Himalayan slopes, Nehru all but applied for Statehood. Remember India is an intact democracy, has the third largest army in the world, and leaves not the least doubt that if pressed it will fight. I am not trying to start a war, but merely saying that just possibly we are not without resources out there....

Excerpt of a letter to President Richard W. Lyman of Stanford University, following the protests at Stanford over Moynihan's commencement speech ("Can the System Work") earlier that summer.

JULY 3, 1975
PRESIDENT RICHARD W. LYMAN
STANFORD UNIVERSITY

Dear Dick,

... I went through with it, as I was urged to do, in the name of defending free speech. I knew it would be costly to me (although not how costly). Yet it seemed necessary. My problem since, as I began to express to you after the ceremony, is that I am not at all sure it was free speech I was defending. I commenced then to wonder, and I do so even more as time passes, whether—regardless of what anyone intended—what we ended up doing was something very different? Did we end up participating, all unwitting, in a monstrous and essentially political perversion of the idea of a university?

After the ceremonies, as you will recall, you said to me that you felt a distinction ought to be made between the way we respond to propositions we merely disagree with and propositions that are genuinely anathema. (I hope I paraphrase you accurately.) I entered a strong protest. I said that this was not the situation at all. No one was disagreeing with any views I had put forth. The disagreement (in its essentials) was with views I was falsely accused of holding. My accusers were and are liars. I recalled to you the Stalinist origin of this technique, which leaves the accused spluttering and mumbling that he never said any of those things, etc. ...

I have come to share Norman Podhoretz' view that liberal academia, faced with the neototalitarian assault on persons such as myself who might be described as liberal dissenters, has adopted a devastatingly effective device for avoiding having to deal with what it is we have to say. They do not acknowledge the fact that our views are systematically and viciously distorted by the Left. To the contrary, they let the lies stand unchallenged. What they do instead is to say we should nonetheless be allowed to speak. ...

I write because the whole experience has so put me off Academe, and I really do wonder whether I shall ever return. This raises the possibility of remaining a prisoner of the Waldorf Tower [official residence of the U.S. ambassador to the U.N.] the rest of my days, so you will understand the depth of my despond!

In response, Lyman wrote Moynihan on July 21, 1975, that he was "simply sorry that what was supposed to be a pleasant occasion turned out to be so disagreeable." But he added that it was not the university's place "to have smitten the critics hip and high" or grant "seals of approval" to speakers. Moynihan's reply:

JULY 28, 1975

Dear Dick:

Heavens. I would not dream that a university administration take a position on the accuracy or inaccuracy of attribution, et al. This would impose an impossible strain on the leadership of a university. In any event, it goes quite against my judgment, which is that the members of the community with a special competence in a given field have the responsibility to protest the misrepresentation of views. This kind of lying is not accidental; it is systemic. Within the academic world it comes almost exclusively, now, from the left. The cost is high to any individual who protests, but the cost to the community of not protesting in the end has been devastating.

Settled at the United Nations, Moynihan suggests to Secretary Kissinger that he make human rights a focus of his speech to the General Assembly session that fall.

SEPTEMBER 9, 1975

MEMORANDUM FOR THE SECRETARY:

... I do hope you will also take up the theme I outline here: that of human rights. ...

Everyone has been talking about a new international order, and as the United States has already indicated in your address of September 1, we stand ready to participate in the creation of such an order—a world from which starvation would be eliminated and in which everyone would be assured a basic minimum of economic sustenance. It must, however, be clear that the United States doesn't wish to do this because we accept responsibility for the economic condition of the Third & Fourth Worlds. We repudiate the charge that we have exploited or plundered other countries, or that our own prosperity has ever rested on any such relation. We are prosperous because we are an energetic and productive people who have lived under a system which has encouraged the development of our productive capacities and energies. We also consider that we have been reasonably helpful and generous in our economic dealings with other countries. We do not, then, wish to contribute toward the creation of a new international order out of guilt or as a matter of reparations. The idea of reparations implies a debt incurred as a result of past wrongs. The United States acknowledges no such debt. . . .

Not guilt, then, and not fear. We are moved as a matter of free choice and out of a growing willingness in our culture to broaden the boundaries of fellow feeling beyond those which define the territories of the nation-state. We elect to act because the plight of people in other countries increasingly presses itself upon us and we wish to take whatever effective measures we can to alleviate suffering that can be alleviated and to eliminate such causes of suffering as can be eliminated.

But it is important to stress that this willingness of ours has at its object the fate of <u>individuals</u>. Ours is a culture based on the primacy of the individual— the rights of the individual, the welfare of the individual, the claims of the individual against those of the state. We have no wish, therefore, to participate in any new economic arrangements whose beneficiaries will be the state rather than the individual. If there is to be an increased flow of wealth to the countries of the South, the United States will insist that it be channeled into the pockets of individuals and not into Swiss bank accounts, and we will insist that necessary precautions be taken to that effect.

The United States will also insist on another point. We will insist on broadening the definition of welfare to include not only the economic condition of the individual but his political condition as well. If there is to be a new international order, the United States will insist that the right to a minimum standard of political and civil liberty is no less fundamental than the right to a minimum standard of material welfare. President Ford affirmed our commitment to universal human rights at Helsinki, and we reaffirm it here. . . .

As this note to Moynihan's administrative officer suggests, he was having trouble adjusting to his new residence at the Waldorf Towers.

SEPTEMBER 22, 1975
(WRITTEN 9/21/75)
<u>MEMORANDUM</u>
TO: ADMIN: MR. MERESMAN
FROM: AMBASSADOR MOYNIHAN
SUBJECT: 42A WALDORF TOWERS

I am beginning to get the knack of living in the Towers. It is not all that easy, as this is the only United States Embassy in the world in which there are no household servants. Hotel maids come to clean and make beds, and suchlike, and they do this very nicely. But as for entertaining, which is what an Embassy is for, one had as well be in any other hotel room in New York City. Not any other, as a matter of fact. Some hotels are small, and rather efficient about getting things up from the kitchen, and suchlike. We are on the 42nd floor. The kitchen is on the 5th floor. A long way off. (Yesterday, for example, I brought two journalists home for lunch. I could have gone to a restaurant, but they wanted to take notes on our conversation. We arrived at one o'clock. Got lunch at three-thirty. In the meantime I was traipsing back and forth to the refrigerator for ice, looking for bottles of soda water, opening tin cans of peanuts. Nothing different from what I would be doing in my own home, save that in my own home the distances are less than half what they are here, and besides, I know where things are.)

What I would like to ask, under these circumstances, is that you try to <u>stock</u> the embassy in a way that I can manage to entertain people without too many long absences from the room as I go off to get this or that. This is the one thing I have found difficult. It means, for example, that asking a person in for a drink that should be over in half an hour, always takes 45 minutes. . . .

Please have the cigarette boxes filled. Marlboro, plus one or two with menthol cigarettes.

Please get me some matches with the American crest. Again this must be the only Embassy in the world that uses Hilton Hotel matches. . . . Would someone deliver the <u>Wall Street Journal</u> to the door, so I can read it on the way in.

Would you provide my study with a set of <u>Who's Who in America</u>, and a good dictionary. (Random House) I need some scotch tape, and a ruler. Otherwise am happy, and can get a lot of work done here.

A final note. A gratifying number of diplomats drink water. Could I have a supply of Evian routinely on hand. Also, many drink beer. Hence let us have some Guinness Stout and Bass Ale on hand, along with Budweiser.

The cause célebre of Moynihan's time at the United Nations was a resolution pressed by Arab countries, with support from many others, determining that Zionism was "a form of racism and racial discrimination." Despite Moynihan's highly visible campaign in opposition, it passed by a vote of 72 to 35 (with 32 abstentions) on November 10, 1975.

The Moynihan campaign was criticized by some diplomats, however, as needlessly blowing up an issue that could have been buried. A subsequent speech suggesting this view by the British ambassador, Ivor Richard, was seen by Moynihan as blessed by the State Department, and possibly Kissinger. The U.N. battle sealed Moynihan's friendship with the Israeli ambassador, Chaim Herzog, who denounced the resolution as "based on hatred, falsehood, and arrogance" and "devoid of any moral or legal value" and who then tore the document in half. In 1991, the resolution became the first ever to be repealed. Here Moynihan tells Averell Harriman that his tactics had been a success.

NOVEMBER 20, 1975

Dear Governor:

... I am beginning to get a certain amount of trouble up here not least from the Europeans who have been managing their affairs on a different principle than that which I think we should bring to multilateral forums. This is not a bilateral setting. I am personally capable of such diplomacy. I spent two years in India without a peep; my only press conference being given the day before I left and only for the purpose of saying goodbye. But here are a majority, or controlling elements within a majority, using a multilateral forum for ideological confrontations which <u>they initiate</u>. We have to fight back, I feel.

I did that on the Zionism issue and I am a little dismayed that in the face of what was a considerable success, it is being put about that somehow we failed. ...

The Israeli Ambassador was in to see me this morning and commented on the very same point. When the issue of Zionism and Racism first appeared in Mexico City in June there were two votes against it. In the key vote in the Committee here about a month ago we had 43 votes, plus many friendly abstentions. And in the key vote in the General Assembly there were 55 votes with us, and again many abstentions. For the first time ever, the combined vote made a majority for Israel. This is the view of Ambassador Herzog, who takes the event to be one of some significance. He and I both agree that the most notable fact was that, again for the first time in memory, <u>we won a majority of the black Africans</u>. Of the 30 non-Muslim African countries only 12 voted for the Zionism resolution on the key vote. (In the Committee we got more African support than Latin American support! Eventually we were able to bring around more Latin Americans, but never got Brazil and only partially won over Mexico, which worries me. As does the Japanese vote.) But there you are. A situation with which you are all too familiar. . . .

Moynihan's speeches were beginning to draw admiration from conservatives, among them supporters of former Governor Ronald Reagan's nascent campaign to challenge Ford for the 1976 Republican presidential nomination. Moynihan talked with Ford about his (Moynihan's) lack of influence but also his desire not to quit in a way that would help Reagan.

JANUARY 27, 1976

MEMORANDUM OF CONVERSATION

I met with the President at 4:30 p.m. on January 27, 1976, for some forty minutes. . . . I reported on the outcome of the Middle East debate in the Security Council, which, I said, was on balance quite positive, certainly civil. At the end of our meeting I said to the President that in my view it was now up to the Israelis to take some initiatives toward peace, and some resolution of the problem which the PLO now constituted for them. We had represented them well, even successfully, in the Security Council, but they could not let the matter drop there. It was their turn to show some movement. I would say so to [Prime Minister Itzhak] Rabin this week. The President agreed but asked that I be careful in the way I put it. . . .

I said to the President that my leave at Harvard expired this week, and that while it meant more to me than anything save my family and my dog, I would give up my professorship and stay on in the Administration through the primaries and the convention, as I did not want to do anything to hurt him. I said it may or may not be true as the <u>Wall Street Journal</u> put it that I was the most popular member of his administration, but I certainly didn't want to give any ammunition to Reagan who was constantly invoking my name. I suggested he might fire me as a warning to other members of the Cabinet not to get too close to Reagan. I noted that I had said I would stay on to Secretary Kissinger at a meeting we had on January 9. With [Brent] Scowcroft [the national security adviser] out of the room I said that there really wasn't any other point in my staying on, as I was completely cut out of policy, and would remain so. There was nothing I could do about it and nothing he could do about it. The President did not disagree. . . .

After Moynihan told Ford he would not resign, James Reston of the NEW YORK TIMES *wrote a column declaring that Ford and Kissinger "support him in public and deplore him in private." Moynihan saw the column as an authorized leak and concluded that he should resign after all. In his memoirs he told the story also that when he called the dean of the faculty of arts and science at Harvard to inform him of the letter of resignation to "the president," the dean at first thought he meant the president of Harvard. Following are excerpts of three letters of resignation: to Richard Cheney of the White House staff, to Ford, and to Kissinger.*

JANUARY 31, 1976

Dear Dick:

I resign now, or a month from now, or a month after that. It isn't working, and it won't work. I am scarcely without fault in this, but mine is not the preponderance of fault. See Reston this morning: "Now Messrs. Ford and Kissinger support him in public and deplore him in private." No Ambassador can survive that: one is useless or worse. (And, of course I know the President had nothing to do with what Reston wrote. But this only makes it harder.)

Sorry. God knows I tried. And we did not do badly. The American public is altogether supportive of the President's policy at the United Nations, and I shall waste no opportunity in the months ahead to make clear that it was indeed the <u>President's</u> policy, and that it continues....

Kissinger replied to the letter below praising Moynihan's "unique blend of perception and wit" and concluding: "There is, after all, only one Pat Moynihan."

JANUARY 31, 1976

Dear Henry,

After an agonizing reappraisal (!) I have decided to return to teaching, and this is my last day to do so. As I remark in a letter to the President, which I enclose, I have spent almost five of the last eight years in government, nine of the past fifteen, thirteen of the past nineteen. If I stay on longer, I shall never get back and that is a thought I can't deal with.

We've had a good run here. With something to show for it. Just today, for example, the Security Council adopted a resolution on Namibia by unanimous vote: and in a very different atmosphere from the confrontation of last June which brought on a triple veto by the United States, Britain, and France.

Tap Bennett [William Tapley Bennett] returns Monday from two weeks sailing and will be more than equal to such challenges as may arise in the Security Council. For the moment nothing seems in the offing save a complaint from the Comoros that a French proposal to have a referendum on the island of Mayotte is a threat to international peace and security.

It has been an honor to serve you, and I would hope you might think of me as still somewhat in your service. I worked for Harriman for four years in the 1950's, and he has treated me more or less as indentured ever since....

Ford accepted Moynihan's resignation "with the deepest regret and reluctance" and said he had "consistently elevated public discourse by puncturing pretense and by eloquently advocating the cause of reason."

JANUARY 31, 1976

Dear Mr. President.

Today is the last of my leave from the University. I must return now, or must give up for good my professorship there and, in effect, give up my profession as well. The effort to persuade myself that this is a kind of personal fate that must be accepted has not succeeded. I have spent almost five of the past eight years in government, nine of the past fifteen, thirteen of the past nineteen. It is time to return to teaching and such are the conditions of my tenure that I return now or not at all.

It has been, for me, a high honor to serve as your Ambassador to India during the latter part of my stay there, and more recently as your representative at the United Nations. Indeed I was scarcely back from the former post before you asked me to take up the new one. You have been unfailing in your encouragement and support and I have with the fullest commitment sought to carry out your general policies and your specific instructions. For that opportunity I am permanently in your debt, even if I must with a heavy and still divided heart, now depart your service.

CHAPTER NINE

"Dear Yorker . . . Dear New Yorker"

Despite his earlier disavowal of interest in running for the Senate—he had said it would be "dishonorable" for him to do so in the middle of the Zionism-is-racism fight—Moynihan changed his mind as 1976 unfolded. He ran as a delegate in the Democratic presidential primary in New York for Senator Henry M. Jackson of Washington, who was supported by cold war anti-Communist and pro-Israel Democrats. Jackson won in Pennsylvania and New York, and Moynihan won as a delegate from the Bronx. But Jackson eventually dropped out as former Governor Jimmy Carter of Georgia outpaced him in other states. Subsequently, prominent Democrats in New York—led by Richard Ravitch—recruited Moynihan to run to head off a victory by Representative Bella Abzug. Moynihan continually said he had only belatedly been persuaded to run because of these supporters and also because of his concern about budget and social issues and defending a tough anti-Communist foreign policy. While teaching at Harvard, Moynihan maintained his farm in upstate New York as his legal residence.

After defeating the Republican incumbent, James Buckley, Moynihan had no problems adjusting to life in the Senate. He had been dealing with Congress while serving under four presidents and was well acquainted with many of his new colleagues. But it did take a while for him to find his political voice, as evidenced by his official newsletters. They began with "Dear Yorker," an archaic salutation that the Senator said he wanted to revive, and later with "Dear New Yorker," apparently yielding to concerns that he was confusing his constituents. Moynihan began his Senate career as a champion of the anti-Communist, hawkish wing of the Democratic Party and indeed recruited some of his staff from the leader of that wing, Senator

Jackson. He tangled with President Jimmy Carter over issues like the importance of human rights and Jewish refuseniks in the Soviet Union, and told Secretary of State Cyrus Vance of his concern that his brand of Democratic Party politics was being sidelined. He also worked closely with Senator Jacob Javits, a Republican, whom he first got to know in Albany in the 1950s. Together, they pressed Congress to assist New York City, which had plunged into near-bankruptcy in 1975. But with the advent of President Reagan, Moynihan veered left in two important ways. First, he defended domestic spending and especially the Social Security program from Reagan's budget cuts and came to believe that Reagan's tax cuts, which he had voted for in 1981, had been a cynical device to force Congress to cut these budgets. Second, he opposed Reagan's uses of secrecy, especially keeping Congress and the Senate Intelligence Committee uninformed of covert activities in Central America. These stances brought him into conflict with some of his old conservative allies, though he continued to maintain friendship with many of them. Moynihan threw himself into his constituent work and easily won re-election in 1982. These letters trace Moynihan's first term in the Senate as he gains a footing as a somewhat conservative Democrat, especially in foreign policy, and defender of New York's interest, who evolved into a critic of President Reagan, particularly on the budget.

After his election to the Senate, PLAYBOY *magazine published an interview with Moynihan in March 1977, in which he repeated his long-held contention that Kissinger had undercut him in 1975 as he vociferously opposed the "Zionism is racism" resolution at the United Nations. Moynihan said again that he had understood that the criticism of his supposed confrontational and counterproductive style by the British U.N. envoy, Ivor Richard, had been tacitly encouraged by Kissinger and that he construed the column by Reston describing disapproval "in private" by Ford and Kissinger to be a signal from them.*

Kissinger denied these charges in a heated private letter to Moynihan, asserting that the PLAYBOY interview had caused him considerable pain. It was "absurd" and "outlandish" to think he would use Richard to telegraph a message, Kissinger said, adding: "Both Reston and I have told you several times that he and I were not in touch directly or through intermediaries" before Reston's column ran.

"If you choose to believe I conspired in such an uncharacteristically convoluted way against a friend who happened to be one of the few men of real strength in the government, I suppose there is little I can do about it," Kissinger wrote. "I cannot *let it go by without telling you how greatly mistaken you are, however, or without saying I am deeply hurt that if you really felt this way, you did not feel you could raise the matter directly with me at the time. Candor was never difficult for you and me before, and I am greatly disappointed that you now think it is." In his memoir of his years at the United Nations,* A DANGEROUS PLACE, *Moynihan noted that Kissinger had assured him he had nothing to do with Richard's criticism, but that the facts as he understood them at the time left him no choice but to believe Kissinger played a role in undercutting him. It was clear that he never really accepted Kissinger's explanation.*

Moynihan's response:

APRIL 7, 1977

Dear Henry:

Your letter, of course, settles the matter, and a measure of apology is due from me.

The Playboy interview (I recall you once saying of a not dissimilar concatenation of indiscretion "Why I did it. I will never know.") was taped in two parts. First, there were several long sessions in March of last year at which time I produced the passages to which you refer. I had just left the United Nations. A follow-up session took place in November. By then I had quite changed my view on the Richard affair but the interviewer never brought it up, and I did not think to do so.

I am writing a short book on the United Nations. It will give me the opportunity to say I was wrong in this matter, and I will certainly make the most of that opportunity.

I would indeed like sometime to talk about my sense that you felt the country was slipping badly. It has always been a matter of some importance to me that you seem to have come to the same conclusions as I did, as I take your judgment in these matters to be far superior to mine. Did you not see Holbrook in Foreign Policy last summer in which he asks how it could be that you, Schlesinger, and I fussed so when we all had virtually the same view of the decline of the West.

It being Holbrook's further judgment that we be the only three people to hold that view, and that we were/are quite mad.

Could you send me your Georgetown speech, it sounds splendid.

Letter to Senator Edward M. Kennedy, reflecting Moynihan's concern about using his papers to write books and earning extra income as a Senator. The letter also shows Moynihan's continuing identification with the Kennedys.

AUGUST 2, 1977

Dear Ted:

I have not wanted to write this letter, and do so only as I begin to see there is no alternative.

As you may know, I gave little thought to running for the Senate and finally did so on sheer impulse. (I got up one morning to learn that City College had been closed down.) Certainly I gave no thought to money matters. I have been pretty much on my own since age fifteen, but I have always been able to make all the money I needed, even as children and parents and life styles steadily raised the ante. When I needed more I was always able to make more. I saved nothing, but I owed nothing. Then came the Senate and the new code, and I suddenly find myself with a fixed income—salary plus $8,500 in lecture fees—that just doesn't come anywhere near my obligations.

The <u>only</u> way I can earn extra income under the new code is from writing books. This is not the most cheering thought. I have churned out, on my own or in collaboration, a dozen or so. But only the first one, <u>Beyond the Melting Pot</u>, has ever earned more than four or five thousand dollars, and most earn nothing, being published by the American Academy of Arts and Sciences, or whatever. (The Melting Pot was the best mind you. I sent President Kennedy a copy, which he took off for a weekend at Hyannisport and apparently read.) All this means I will have to try harder now. But my only real resource—as I can never do any serious research while I am down here—are the papers I have collected over the quarter century, and which I had planned to give to the Kennedy Library. They are mostly there now, on loan. Nothing made me prouder than to think they would always be there. But in the circumstances I just don't see any alternative but to ask the Library to send me the material that deals with events before and after the Kennedy Administration. I will of course leave my Kennedy papers in the Kennedy Library. The others I will probably deposit with the Library of Congress, where I can get to them and work on them weekends, as it were.

I need not note that I have never asked for or received any tax deduction or any other benefit from the gift of these papers, and will not do so now.

That this letter is so needlessly long will perhaps suggest to you the difficulty with which I send it.

Moynihan's letter to his daughter, Maura Moynihan, after her performance in George Bernard Shaw's "Pygmalion" at Harvard. He refers back to a review of one of her performances in a play in New Delhi.

NOVEMBER 14, 1977

Dear Maura:

Your Ms. Sherlock review was pretty good I thought. Even so, my favorite is still the one in the Commie magazine in New Delhi where they said, "Maura Moynihan is convincing as a nymphomanical alcoholic."

Of course, the review is marvelous and your mother was reduced to mistiness. I was fascinated by the first two paragraphs which discuss Shaw's meaning. I am, I suppose, a person whose accent was changed and for rather the purposes that Professor Higgins' would have recognized. I shall never forget the Pascal film. The best I had yet seen. I thought, without thinking, that I knew exactly what Shaw intended, and this was something wholly different from what Ms. Sherlock thinks. "False illusion of middle class splendor" indeed! Shaw knew that nothing was more important than having a warm house and enough to eat and that that is exactly what middle class splendor involved.

Again, it was a great evening.

After the election of both Carter and Moynihan, the two had a somewhat uneasy relationship. Moynihan continued to press the cause of human rights in the Soviet Union and in third world countries as he had at the United Nations.

DECEMBER 7, 1977

Dear Mr. President:

This is a most personal letter, and I ask your indulgence to presuming to write you in such terms.

I am just finishing a book entitled—perhaps with equal presumption—<u>The Politics of Human Rights, 1975–76</u>. It is part United Nations journal, part commonplace book. I try to describe the emergence of the issue, and, in an Afterword, set forth some general principles along the lines of the article I wrote for <u>Commentary</u> last summer, which I sent you. (It appears in this month's <u>Reader's Digest</u>. Jody Powell [Carter's press secretary] called to say how much he liked it, which was thoughtful of him.) I would like also to touch upon the drafting of the Democratic Platform, and finally, your espousal of human rights as a central theme of American foreign policy.

On Monday (at the time the United Nations General Assembly voted not to establish a High Commissioner for Human Rights) Ambassador Young commented:

> We in our Government got trapped into human rights. I don't think the President ever decided to sit down and make human rights a cardinal platform of this Administration. I think what happened was that the American people began to sense that they were being utilized through their tax dollars in the denial of human rights in other places in the world. You know them as well as I do. They seem to think that we were supporting group or individual denials of human rights. Everywhere the President went as a candidate he began to be asked about what is the United States going to do to divorce itself from the oppression that is going around the world. That is where human rights came from.

I recognize this as one of the ways things happen in government. But, of course, it is not the only way. And it may not be your recollection of the event.

I wonder if we could talk about this for twenty minutes some time. I fully understand that it is something for <u>your</u> memoirs, not mine. But I would be remiss not to ask you, even if it does not prove possible.

The Moynihans bought their family farm in Delaware County on February 15, 1964, still grieving over the Kennedy assassination. They later acquired two adjacent properties in the nearby town of Franklin. These properties were sold soon after Moynihan entered the Senate and were subsequently purchased by John Lennon, the rock singer, songwriter, and author, who paid off the mortgages held by the Moynihans. After Lennon's death in 1980, his widow, Yoko Ono, spent time there and kept in touch with the Moynihans.

DECEMBER 29, 1977

Dear Mr. Lennon:

My wife Elizabeth and I are so pleased that you and Mrs. Lennon have purchased the mortgage on our two farms in Franklin. I bought them years ago thinking perhaps one day to build a home on the crest of the hill. It has I believe one of the loveliest views in all of New York. The village of Franklin at the foot of the hill is an architectural treasure, and the whole area is a joy. Alas, I stayed in politics.

We live in the town of Davenport, not far away. Perhaps we will meet sometime.

After the funeral of former Vice President Hubert H. Humphrey, Moynihan rode back to Washington with President Carter and wanted to follow up their conversation about the 1968 antiwar campaign by Senator Eugene McCarthy, a Minnesota Democrat like Humphrey and Carter's vice president, Walter Mondale.

JANUARY 17, 1978

Dear Mr. President:

I do thank you for giving me a ride back yesterday afternoon. My wife is disappearing into Central Asia to finish a book and this was the last evening on which we could have dinner together before she leaves.

I am concerned that I did not make a sufficient case for Gene McCarthy. The point to be made is that he recognized the moral crisis which the country had come to in 1968 and acted to resolve it. This is precisely what Hubert

Humphrey had done, with respect to another moral crisis, twenty years earlier. It was to be the bitter irony of Humphrey's life that when the time came that the country was at last ready to reward what he had done in the earlier crisis, he was overwhelmed by the subsequent one. One can understand his feelings about McCarthy's role. And yet, is it not in the nature of moral crises that they leave but little room for friendship, even at times for civility?

It is the fact, I should think, that half the persons in your administration under age forty came into politics at the behest of Gene McCarthy. Literally he summoned them; and they came. And yet there now seems no place for <u>him</u> in our public life!

Reflecting on Soviet lawmakers to Senator Robert Byrd, Senate majority leader.

JANUARY 18, 1978

Dear Mr. Leader:

On Monday morning, the Soviet "parliamentarians" will come to the Capitol. I know of the origins of the upcoming visit and it is not an easy matter.

I wonder whether visits such as these do not lend too much credence to the false notions that the Supreme Soviet is a "counterpart" to the United States Congress. Surely we do ourselves and our colleagues in the other parliamentary democracies no honor to say that we will receive as colleagues these Soviets, who meet a few days each year to rubber stamp the proposals of the oligarchs who engineer their "election" by the admirable plurality of 99 percent! This is a small point.

A larger point is driven home by the blandness of the brief biographies of the visiting Soviets which our own State Department has been distributing. Take the case of one Boris Nikolayevic Ponomarov, described as having served in a post "in the executive committee" of the Communist International between 1936 and 1943. This is a needlessly polite way of saying that Ponomarov was involved in the liquidations and purges then in progress in Moscow. And what is Mr. Ponomarov doing today? He is the head of "International Department of the Central Committee." Which is to say that he is in charge of the Soviet effort to subvert the few remaining parliamentary democracies in the world—in West Europe especially—even as we now have the strong statement of the President about the political situation in Italy. There is also in the group a Mr. Chakovskiy described as a "critic" of dissident Soviet writers. Mr. Chakovskiy is the head of the Soviet writers union and he is no mere "critic." He is the censor, the oppressor of all Soviet writing not in conformity with prevailing orthodoxy. And the list goes on. I understand diplomatic niceties. I even practiced them. I even believe in them—so long as we are not deceiving ourselves by failing to inform ourselves of unpleasant facts. Sometimes I think that by doing this we define the political problem in the world in a way such that the definition of terms already concedes the victory to the totalitarians.

Moynihan had at first thought he borrowed the phrase "benign neglect" from British history but here tells David L. Kirp, professor of public policy at the University of California, Berkeley, that his research proved otherwise.

MARCH 8, 1978

Dear David:

I had always assumed the phrase was in the report of Lord Earl Durham on governance in Canada which was about 1842, as I recall. Briefly, and with a bad memory, there had been a minor disturbance in the Colony and Durham was sent over to ask what should be done about the governance in Canada. He came back and said a half century of benign neglect by the Britons had got conditions to the point where they were already governing themselves and nothing need be done save to legitimate the existing arrangements. However, I have had occasion to look at the report in another connection and did not find the term "benign neglect." I am left with the assumption that it may be my own.

Edmund Burke somewhere uses the term "a wise and salutary neglect."

A furor within the Carter administration erupted over disclosures that the Soviet Union was using its diplomatically protected properties in Washington, D.C., to

install equipment for interception of microwave telephone calls. Moynihan gives
his own agitated response in this memorandum after his meeting with President
Carter and Vice President Mondale.

MAY 18, 1977

MEMO OF CONVERSATION

The Select Committee on Intelligence met in the Cabinet Room with the
President and Vice President and the Attorney General at 10 o'clock on Friday, May 13th. As I requested him to do, the Chairman, in his presentation
to the President, raised the matter of the Soviet activity that had been reported
to me by Leo Cherne and Commander Lionel Olmer, on which I was later
briefed by Raymond Tate. In effect, the Chairman asked what are we going
to do about it.

The President responded to the general statement of Senator [Daniel] Inouye without touching on this matter, which took up at least half the time of
Inouye's introductory remarks. When it became clear the President would not
respond, I interrupted and asked if he would not wish to do so.

The President spoke of the great need which we had for the equivalent activities in the Soviet Union. The President turned to the Attorney General
and asked his advice. The Attorney General said that it was quite clear to him
that he could get an injunction. The President said we do not have their
sources of information and therefore must accept the present situation. He
said the Washington Post had shown "reticence" about the matter.

The Attorney General happened to be sitting next to me, and I passed him
a note which stated "It will be—what? Two months before this is known publically. What will the President have done?"

When the meeting broke up I said to the Vice President that I had been
in that room under five Presidents and had never heard anything that had
disturbed me more. With a touch, charitably, of impatience—more likely of
anger—the Vice President said a final decision had not been made.

Outside the White House I talked with Admiral [Stansfield] Turner
[C.I.A. director], Senator [Gary] Hart and Senator [William] Hathaway.
Hart must sense my political agenda much as I seem able to sense his, and
took the view that there was no end to the horrors one learns about. Hathaway
seemed to be getting genuinely interested. Turner asked what he could do. I
said he could blow the goddamn place up—that I wanted to restore his com-

bative spirit. Much talk all around of listening to [former Soviet leader Nikita] Khrushchev in his automobile, as if it mattered one damn.

Telegram to Robert A. Katzmann, Moynihan's former teaching assistant at Harvard and longtime confidant, wishing him well on the day of his Ph.D. defense with a line used by Fred Astaire in the movie THE GAY DIVORCÉE.

APRIL 21, 1978

Bob: Good luck. Remember: Chance is the fool's name for fate.

Moynihan favored federal aid to parochial schools, a controversial stance among liberals in New York. Here he shares frustrations over explaining his views to Arthur O. (Punch) Sulzberger, publisher of the NEW YORK TIMES, *who had supported his candidacy in 1976.*

JUNE 12, 1978

Dear Punch:

Further, as they say, to my letter of May 18 on the problem I seem to have getting ideas into the Times, and my need for advice and counsel.

You will have noticed that a bill to provide tuition tax credits for higher education and for elementary and secondary schools has been making its way through the Congress, having been introduced by Senator Packwood and me this last winter. The President has promised to veto the measure. Albert Shanker [teachers' union president] in his column in the Sunday Times has called it the most important (and dreadful) education bill in a century. The Times editorialists inveigh against it. The Letters to the Editor column is filled with charge and countercharge. . . .

A vast coalition has been formed to condemn the matter as illiberal and to consign it to defeat. Nonetheless, it has been reported out of the Senate Finance Committee on a 14–1 vote and recently passed the House.

What is going on here? I submit that part of the answer is that a year ago in a series of commencement addresses I introduced a new idea into the debate over aid to church related schools. For a generation this debate had turned on the question what forms of aid would meet the restrictions imposed by the Supreme Court commencing with the <u>Everson</u> decision of 1947. But last May at LeMoyne College I put forth the argument that the Supreme Court in <u>Everson</u> was wrong; that the decision was based on 19th century religious bigotry and that it was wrong in just the way <u>Plessy</u> was wrong. Given the opportunity the Court would say so, or in any event ought to.

Now clearly, no one need agree with me. But if I am right in my judgment that it was this new and quite radical argument which revived the dormant movement to provide some form of federal aid to nonpublic elementary and secondary schools, then it would seem to me what the <u>Times</u> ought to record that view. Otherwise your readers will have trouble understanding what is going on. But in a whole twelve months I have never once been interviewed by a New York <u>Times</u> reporter on this issue.

Friday a week ago the <u>Times</u>, as did the other papers around the country, reported the House action. The front page story carefully stated that Attorney General Griffin Bell felt that tuition tax credits "would be unconstitutional under the doctrine of separation of church and state." The story carefully reported Secretary Califano's statement that "'The parochial schools of this country will never see a dollar of the unconstitutional aid the House voted today because the courts will invalidate it.'" What the <u>Times</u> did not quote was my statement that, to the contrary, the bill which has been passed by the House is constitutional. As you will see from the enclosed, The Boston <u>Globe</u> story did balance Califano with a quote from me. So did most of the papers in New York State.

What is my problem? ...

The sociologist Christopher Lasch was starting to get much publicity over his essays on the future of capitalism and consumption. They later became part of his book, THE CULTURE OF NARCISSISM: AMERICAN LIFE IN AN AGE OF DIMINISHING EXPECTATIONS, *published in 1979.*

JUNE 19, 1978

Dear Professor Lasch:

. . . I quite take your point about capitalism and consumption, which as you surely recognize, is close to Schumpeter's. I have somewhere written—possibly in the enclosed, but I just don't have the time to search—that if there is any one instance of historical determinism that impresses me it is the way in which capitalism having evolved from an ethic of saving and the deferment of gratification, finally reached a level of investment, somewhere early in the twentieth century, such that it became necessary to transform that ethic into one of consumption. Otherwise there would be no final profit to be had from all that saving. Hence, presumably, the rise of advertising and the stimulation and discontent which Schumpeter identified as the condition of late capitalism.

I am quite moved that you might take my essay on Dollard seriously. It sank without a trace, largely I fear because the Rockefellers had lost interest in the Commission on Critical Choices by the time the volume <u>Qualities of Life</u> appeared. (He had gone on to become Vice President.)

Clearly the move from a utilitarian ethic to therapeutic ethic corresponds to the shift toward consumption under late capitalism and might be thought to reflect some external objective reality. But I wonder if that is all there is to it. I have the utmost regard for John Dollard, who was our first Freudian social scientist and is a wonderful person as well as a great scholar. (Has anything been done better than <u>Caste and Class in a Southern Town?</u>) Thus I have another level of concern. Quite apart from whether Dollard's frustration/aggression hypothesis is convenient, the larger question is whether it is time. <u>Is Dollard right?</u> The objective of my essay was simply to suggest that we are all going about with two models of behavior in our head which are not quite compatible.

B. Bruce-Briggs of the Hudson Institute is doing a huge "New Class Study." All manner of folk are writing papers, some of which are quite good. It occurs to me that you might want to be put on his mailing list as his concerns are obviously yours, although his contributors are "neo-conservatives." God save us from labels. . . .

A tribute to the New York Public Library in a letter to Richard Couper, its president.

JULY 26, 1978

Dear Mr. Couper:

In one of the more exotic developments in recent political history, I took part in a political campaign which, two years after the event, has managed to pay all its bills. Yet more extraordinary, we came up with a slight surplus. I have topped this off to a round $1,000 and, on behalf of my contributors and myself, have the honor to contribute it to the New York Public Library.

Of the institutions that have shaped my life, there is none for which I have a greater sense of personal gratitude than the New York Public Library. It introduced me to the idea of generosity, and to the dignity and graciousness of large public purposes.

I cannot but suppose there are ways I can be of help here in Washington. Perhaps we might talk about this sometime.

The novelist and historian Alexander Solzhenitsyn—who had served time in prison and exile in the Soviet Union, and who was deported in 1974—was a hero to Moynihan and many others. Some of Moynihan's views are in this letter to Mrs. Natalia Solzhenitsyn.

SEPTEMBER 21, 1978

Dear Mrs. Solzhenitsyn:

A thought has been with me during this week of promise for a settlement of the conflict in the Middle East, a thought that I would hope might provide some satisfaction and encouragement to you, your husband and your brave coworkers still in the Soviet Union.

You will recall that on October First, 1977, the United States and the Soviet Union issued a joint communique which purported to outline a settlement for the conflict in the Middle East. That document, clearly a Soviet draft, proposed an approach which would have relied heavily on Soviet co-operation and good will. The American public instantly recoiled against this proposal, much to the astonishment of our State Department. The public saw with admirable clarity that the Soviet Union would not be a responsible partner in the search for a genuine peace. The Carter Administration was persuaded to adopt a different approach—and it now appears that this approach has begun to bear fruit.

In my judgment, your struggle, the message you and your co-workers brought to the world about the character of the Soviet Union, was the decisive factor in persuading American opinion and world opinion of the need to proceed in these peace negotiations without the inevitably destructive involvement of the Soviet leaders.

Your work may now become somewhat more difficult. As you know so well, democracies sometimes yield to a reckless optimism when stirred by even the most fragile hopes. But I have no doubt that you will persevere, and that, as you do, the value of your efforts will over and over again bear precious fruit. I do hope that I can continue to be helpful.

During the Carter presidency, Moynihan continued to be concerned about the influence of what he called the anti-Communist and pro-McGovern peace negotiation oriented wings of the Democratic Party. His concerns are reflected in this memorandum of his conversation with Secretary of State Cyrus R. Vance. The "peace treaty" negotiations refer to the talks between Israel and Egypt.

DECEMBER 18, 1978

MEMORANDUM OF CONVERSATION

I met with Secretary [Cyrus] Vance for breakfast at the state department at eight thirty. This was at his invitation, extended some weeks ago. . . .

I said that no member of the cabinet was more respected or liked on the Hill and that because I shared that respect and admiration, indeed felt myself foremost in these matters, I wished to speak to him with great frankness about the situation of his Department of State.

I said I hoped he would take it as a measure of that respect and affection that I would first say that I was not at all certain that he would understand what I was about to say. I asked him to consider that I had not understood half of what he had told me about the peace treaty negotiations, or rather had not been able to keep one detail in mind as we went on to the next. He, by

contrast, was a master at constructing agreements, in seeing where one position was not the same as another. It was a role of limited use, but at times
necessary, and not least in recent times.

He would recognize that in foreign affairs there are in fact two Democratic
parties. I intended this in much more formal terms than would ordinarily ever
occur, which is to say one might use the image of two parties to describe two
tendencies, or two wings, but with us at this moment the more formal term
was not inappropriate. The party had in the late 1960s divided as it had never
done since the late 1850s prior to the civil war. At the 1968 convention the
leader of the established party center, Hubert Humphrey, was bitterly opposed
despite the great personal affection for him because the things he—which is
to say the older party—stood for were thought to be hateful in the extreme.
It was thought by many that the best thing to happen would be for Humphrey
to lose the election and the opponents of Humphrey at the convention to take
over the party. (I described my gradual involvement Negotiation Nov.
RFK/McCarthy/HHH. [Robert Kennedy, Eugene McCarthy, Hubert
Humphrey—the candidates for president in 1968.] Followed by growing and
deep concern with The [peace] Movement and its position about American
foreign policy, which led me into the Senate primary against Abzug and
[Ramsey] Clark). In a pronounced and unmistakable way the opponents of
the former policies—which presumedly had been Vance's policies also—took
over the Democratic Party in 1972, under the banner of Senator [George]
McGovern.

I described in brief the ideological conflict which then formed between the
McGovernites and those of us who, without having necessarily supported the
old positions, very much opposed the new ones. I explained that this was a
battle about real things. That each side felt the other to be hateful and wrong
and dangerous and divisive.

A certain coming together occurred in 1976. I put it to him that as a member of the drafting committee for the Democratic platform I had written most
of the foreign policy planks of the platform. He said he knew this. I recounted
my efforts to accommodate the McGovernites. Ms. Burke's resolution, devised
by Brown, to give no military aid to governments that do not observe human
rights. My proposal to add no economic aid either, their objection. My reply
that they wanted to give economic aid to countries that got their military aid
from Czechoslovakia. That if Brown would be against the dictators I didn't
like, I would be against the dictators he didn't like. This became known as the
Brown-Moynihan compromise.

Then the election, and our great shock. (I mentioned having had lunch with [Lane] Kirkland [president of the AFL-CIO] on Tuesday). Almost without exception he and the President had appointed to the Department of State persons of the opposite camp from us, persons who were not only different in their views but who regarded us as their enemies.

As [to] the Secretary's enemies. I said there were some persons who tried to keep open channels as good diplomats will do and mentioned [State Department counselor] Matt Nimetz, saying I knew he would think it odd if I did not. But thinking of CDM [Coalition for a Democratic Majority, founded by Senator Henry Jackson] as a general surrogate for our positions, out of all the diplomatic appointments made, the only post given someone from CDM was to Micronesia.

I would mention one more name, only to illustrate my point. Michael Janeway had been his speechwriter. I knew him somewhat, and liked him greatly. After he left Washington I learned of an account he had given at a Cambridge gathering of the meetings in State at which some document or other was being assembled when Janeway would suggest it might be passed by Jackson and Moynihan to get their reaction. [The response] would be shocked silence, followed by the assertion that we were enemies.

I will never know how much Vance understood this, or agreed. But he indicated that he did understand, and did realize it was a problem for him. Certainly he did not dispute any of my "facts." He said he surely did not think of me as an enemy: to the contrary, etc. He said that this was not as easy with Jackson. He mentioned [Richard] Perle [a Jackson protégé and fellow conservative]. He said he felt Jackson's attacks on the President and him were personal. He said he would have to do something about all this. . . .

Former Vice President and Governor Nelson Rockefeller, who had defeated Averell Harriman in 1958, was often criticized by Moynihan, but he obviously softened his views in this letter to Rockefeller's widow.

JANUARY 31, 1979

Dear Happy:

I was awakened early Saturday morning by a newspaperman calling to tell of the Vice President's death, and could only think to say, "There was not a more generous man in American politics, and yet we were never as good to him as he was to us. May God bless his soul." The Washington <u>Post</u> and some others used this, and you may have seen it, but I would want you to hear it from me directly for it came truly from the heart. You would know that we think of you, and pray for him.

As senator, Moynihan supported legislation providing for the federal government to pay more of the cost of welfare in New York and other states. The Carter administration opposed it, saying it would impede Carter's efforts to reform welfare, as Carter had long advocated. This is an excerpt of Moynihan's defense to President Carter.

FEBRUARY 8, 1979

Dear Mr. President:

It was most courteous of you to see us yesterday, and I am conscious that I risk imposing on your good nature to raise yet again the question of welfare reform, but we seem to have somewhat divergent understandings of what happened last year, and I would hope to do my part to clear this up, as there is nothing I want more than to be with you in these matters.

From the time you sent your welfare reform bill to Congress in August, 1977, <u>I was for the President's bill and none other</u>. I introduced it; held hearings; talked it up, as it were.

In June, 1978, it was made known that the Ways and Means Committee would not take up your bill which, in the manner of President Nixon's Family Assistance plan, included a comprehensive "negative income tax" type guarantee for all families.

At this point, in my judgment, which God knows is faulty and self-interested, yet I would plead fifteen long years at this enterprise, it seemed best to go ahead with a much more limited bill providing fiscal relief and certain modest but useful reforms. Senators [Russell] Long and [Alan] Cranston joined me in this measure. The total cost was to be $1.5 billion. <u>In no sense was New York to get an excessive share of the relief contemplated.</u> The entire state would have received 13.8 percent of the relief, significantly less than our proportion of welfare costs.

The Administration lobbied vigorously against our proposal. I dare to say vehemently. From first to last the charge was made that passage of our bill in the 95th Congress would jeopardize enactment of a truly comprehensive bill in the 96th, the explicit understanding being that the Administration would send up such a bill. . . .

I have to say to you now and—had anyone from the Administration talked to us—I would have said then that I did not think you were going to send up such a bill in the 96th Congress. I assumed you would judge the prospects too dismal and the cost too great.

I was not wrong, Mr. President. I hope and believe that our relations are candid enough, and close enough, for me to say straight out that I was right.

The bill Mr. [Stuart] Eizenstat [Carter's domestic affairs adviser] so courteously outlined to me is a sensible, modest, limited measure of the kind that has been routine to welfare policy since the 1930s.

The New Deal made the basic policy decision—some have bemoaned it, others not—to leave the administration of programs such as Aid to Dependent Children (as it then was) and Unemployment Insurance with the individual states, allowing them to set their own levels of payments in accordance with Federal matching formulas.

This meant, from the outset, that Southern states had low payment levels. It has also meant, from the outset that "Washington" has recurrently sought to raise those levels, by various devices.

The proposed Administration bill would raise minimum AFDC [Aid to Families with Dependent Children] payments in 15 Southern and Southwestern states. It would make the AFDC-U program mandatory in 24 Southern and Western states. Apart from some modest fiscal relief, there would be nothing for states such as my own. (In point of fact, as Governor [Hugh] Carey [of New York] noted, our AFDC-U payments from the Federal government would be reduced.)

In any event, there is little evidence that such measures will be accepted. As I understand it, Senator Long has told you he cannot accept a minimum AFDC payment.

My candid, and caring, advice is that this new proposal will not be enacted. Or if it is, it will merely force on these Southern and Southwestern states what manifestly they do not want. In the meantime you will have dropped the party's commitment to a negative income tax: a flawed idea no doubt; but surely a noble one. Come 1980 there will be no fiscal relief of the kind we have repeatedly promised.

Cannot I ask you to go over this with Stu just one more time? I am, of course, completely at your service in any help I might provide.

Excerpt of a letter to Peter Steinfels, a prominent Catholic intellectual and executive editor of COMMONWEAL *magazine, who had written an article in* ESQUIRE *about liberals and conservatives. He refers also to an article in* COMMONWEAL *by James Barry about the "New Class," a term used by Soviet scholars to describe the cadre of ruling bureaucrats but also used by conservatives to describe liberal bureaucrats in the United States.*

FEBRUARY 20, 1979
PERSONAL

Dear Peter Steinfels:

. . . I thought your article in <u>Esquire</u> sensitive, informed, and, more to the point, fair-minded. I have only one dissatisfaction, as it were. I take it that just now "neo-conservatism" is all the rage. This will be reassuringly alarming news to a great many persons of the sort you and I will tend to know. But would you consider that the far more significant effect is likely to be much less complicated. A good many persons of open mind and friendly mien will simply learn that the smartest people these days are something called Neo-conservatives, and adapt their own dispositions accordingly.

Is it a service to liberalism to encourage this? Irving and a few others apart, none of us is a conservative. We are liberals much as John F. Kennedy was liberal. A bit more so. The term "neo-conservative" was coined in epithet. One "fraction" of the socialist democrats having been expelled by another "fraction," the expelled "fraction" promptly labeled the new controlling group to be "neo-conservative." A familiar enough business. But why allow the arguments of the left—intended to discredit—to distort analysis of what is going on in the center. . . .

In the first issue of <u>The Public Interest</u> [James Barry, author of an article on "the New Class"] will find an article wholly supportive of the Great Society—of which I was then a part—but analytic about certain trends. He might also look at Sam Beer's Presidential Address to the Political Science meetings in New York last Fall.

But to repeat. Yours was a fine article, in a marvelously readable and interesting issue of <u>Esquire</u>, which, phoenix-like, rises all the more brilliantly.

Moynihan's advocacy of tuition tax credits and other help for Catholic schools was a consistent position all his career, but here it became a point of contention with the Reverend Donald S. Harrington, chairman of the Liberal Party, which endorsed Moynihan in 1976.

MARCH 23, 1979

Dear Reverend Harrington:

I have your letter of March 15, and am saddened by its tone.

Surely you must know that a United States Senator may not in any circumstance submit to such an ultimatum. Even had I changed my view on tuition tax credits, which I have not, I would now as a matter of principle be forced to continue to support them.

This is an issue of the integrity of a Senator, and there can be no compromise.

Having said that, may I also say that I can quite understand that you might have interpreted my statements to the Policy Committee in 1976 differently from me. But surely my desire to find some constitutionally acceptable means of supporting nongoverment schools was well-known at that time. This was central to the language which I negotiated in the 1964 Democratic National Platform, which led to the passage of the Elementary and Secondary Education Act of 1965, the first great breakthrough in our long campaign for Federal aid to education. I drafted similar language for the 1976 platform, and did all I could to draw attention to this issue in the campaign that followed.

Certainly I received a large and welcome vote from Liberal Party members in the November election.

This makes me wonder if the party leadership is really in touch with rank and file opinion in this matter. As you know from our recent luncheon conversation, I believe tuition tax credits to be quite within the American liberal tradition. A tradition of pluralism and of choice. . . .

Finally, may I say that it seems to me somehow inappropriate for the Liberal Party to make one single issue its overriding concern with respect to the performance of a United States Senator. There is so much we have to deal with. You will recall that I asked you and Mr. Harding at our lunch on February 17 was there any single vote which I cast in the 95th Congress, other than the vote on tuition tax credits, with which you disagreed. You could think of none. And indeed my record on civil rights, on labor legislation, on social welfare, on Israel are, I believe, wholly in consonance with the views of the Liberal Party.

And so perhaps you will arrange for me to meet with the Policy Committee. I must be candid and tell you that I do not feel quite comfortable confining my contacts with the Liberal Party only to the leadership.

Alex Rose [longtime Liberal Party leader who died in 1976] and I were friends for a quarter century. I fully expect to be your nominee in 1982. It is an honor I cherish and a duty in which I will not fail.

More than two years after taking office, Moynihan began sending newsletters to constituents. In this introductory letter, he defines his role as Senator and says he will report also on individual legislative measures. Moynihan spent considerable time composing his letters, often in his little schoolhouse office on his farm in upstate New York.

APRIL, 1979
FELLOW NEW YORKERS:

PART I

Two years ago I was sent to Washington to represent the people of New York in the Senate of the United States. The 1976 senatorial contest in New York was hard fought, and the choices were clear. The outcome, it would seem, showed some acceptance of the campaign proposition that "New Yorkers often seem to be fighting against the federal government. It is time we begin fighting to get the federal government on our side."

The following is a personal report to you on what we did—and, in some cases, did not—accomplish in the 95th Congress. It attempts a reasonably detailed account of the work of the Congress, and therefore must be sent to you in two parts. The first deals chiefly with the issues that came before the Senate Finance Committee, and includes a listing of Senate votes on major issues: the second deals with other matters, and mentions some things which have helped New Yorkers gain cooperation from the many agencies of the federal government.

First, the Senate's committees. There is little that makes a reader's eyes glaze over more quickly than a Senator or Congressman discussing his or her committee assignments. At least that is the natural reaction of an outsider to the Senate. One knows one is *supposed* to be interested, but one just can't be. This is probably a general response. And yet committees are life down here. One's day revolves around committee hearings; one's night around committee reports. There is a sense in which Senators think of one another mainly in terms of their respective committee assignments.

My two principal committee assignments in the 95th Congress were the Finance Committee and the Environment and Public Works Committee. These were the two committees, it seemed, that could mean the most to New York. One other assignment has been the Select Committee on Intelligence, which has oversight of the intelligence community. It is an immensely serious assignment about which, as you will understand, one has a responsibility *not* to speak.

Finally, a few months ago, as we organized for the work of the new session of Congress, I was appointed to the Budget Committee. In the last Congress it became clear that there had to be better liaison (for lack of a better word!) between the Finance Committee and the Budget Committee. Together they should shape Congressional economic policy; but too often they have been somewhat at odds. As a result, it was thought that someone should serve on both.

Now we New Yorkers need and deserve a close, cooperative relationship with the federal government. We contribute much to the Federal Treasury, as to other aspects of our nation's life. Indeed, in past years Washington has collected more money in taxes from New York's residents and businesses than it has returned to the state in federal expenditures. But we have recently begun to restore the balance: in Fiscal Year 1977, federal spending in New York increased by $7.7 billion, the largest increase obtained by any state.

Ours is a mature industrial economy, facing stiff competition from developing regions—in this country and abroad. We must, ultimately, meet this competition with our own skills, intelligence, and energy. But we have every right and obligation to ask Washington to help assure that the competition is conducted by rules which reward competency—not those which penalize decency.

In keeping with this conviction, I have supported federal welfare reform which would relieve New York of much of the cost of what is truly a national responsibility: labor law reform which would bring national standards in industrial relations close to those of our own state; changes in federal education policy which would ease the great burdens on both public and non-government schools; stronger federal guarantees of full civil rights for all racial, ethnic and linguistic minorities, and for women; fairer—and lower—federal taxes for individuals and businesses; and many other federal measures which would bring us back a better share of our tax dollars.

New York has been making its fight, and our entire Congressional delegation has conducted itself commendably. While some important victories have been won—some of them noted in these pages—our work has not been growing easier. The nation at large, the Congress and the executive branch are now much affected by a spirit of fiscal austerity. While we indeed do need a greater sense of fiscal responsibility in government, the present mood—sometimes so unthinking—could make matters worse, both for the nation and for New York. We must join ranks in the months ahead to ensure that government fiscal policy is not seized by a new recklessness which could do great and unjustified harm to states such as our own.

Besides fighting for New York, a Senator should speak for the principles that should guide our foreign policy: the principles of liberty and human rights, of loyalty to our democratic allies, of firmness toward our adversaries, and of candor in explaining our situation to our own people. The new Congress will have a long agenda of foreign policy and defense issues and of domestic issues with vast importance to the people of New York state. Your views on any matter that interests or affects you will be most welcome.

※

A history lesson on Vikings for Vice President Walter F. Mondale, who was proud of his Norwegian heritage.

DECEMBER 11, 1979
PERSONAL

Dear Mr. Vice President:

On our way back from Milwaukee in October we got to carousing and you, [Senators] Gaylord Nelson, and Scoop Jackson got to talking about Vikings. Perforce, I listened.

As a descendent of a race of scholars much victimized by these folk when they first appeared on the rim of the earth, I have had reason to learn their history with perhaps greater precision than some. In any event, at one point I broke into the conversation to tell of the Viking encirclement of Europe which at one point put them simultaneously in occupation of Kiev and at the gates of Constantinople. None of you had heard anything about any of this, and wearily (as one can spend only so much time trying to explain things to Norwegians), I undertook to get the details.

It turns out, however, that the available facts are not precise. The attack on Constantinople took place June 13, 860, involving a flotilla of some 200 ships. Some twenty years earlier (or thereabouts) the Russ (as the Scandinavian Varangians were known) had occupied Kiev. However, while Varnadsky in Ancient Russia (1940) has the attack coming from the West, across the Mediterranean from then established bases in Sicily, others hold that it came down from in the North. And so the pincer question is somewhat in dispute.

You are familiar, of course, with the aftermath. Exhausted by these adventures, and thoroughly befuddled by their brief encounter with civilization, the Norsemen withdrew to the wastelands whence they had come, and relapsed into the morose melancholia that has characterized them since.

Other than the sacking of Irish monasteries, they are best remembered for having contributed the name, and so many national characteristics, to modern day Russia.

Excerpt of a letter to James [Scotty] Reston of the NEW YORK TIMES, *on the stalemate in Washington.*

DECEMBER 24, 1979

Dear Scotty,

... The constitution is not working all that well. You, indeed, have described the stalemate between the Congress and the Presidency at the time of the assassination of President Kennedy as a "constitutional crisis." Something such has been going on for some time, and has been much in evidence under President Carter. Having served in the subcabinet or cabinet of each of the four administrations that preceded this one, and having been in the Senate since this one took office, I find myself increasingly concerned with this. (Do you by chance recall Dick Donahue's description of the relations between Kennedy and the Congress? "A mutuality of contempt.") The essence of it, clearly, is the constitutional decision to separate the executive from the legislative in a way not found in any other government, much less any other democracy.

This has led me to a study (of sorts) of conflict techniques, on which I discoursed in the Lehman lecture two years ago. (The Iron Law of Emulation: An Imperial Presidency leads to an Imperial Congress leads to an Imperial Judiciary.) If you would like a copy I will send one. The first principle is that organizations in conflict become like one another. (Think of newspapers, baseball teams, navies, television programming.) The constitution builds conflict into relations between the three branches. The migration of conflict techniques can be traced. Theodore Roosevelt got himself an office building, Presidents previously having worked at home, with their wives going on about papers being all over the living room. Presto the West Wing. Followed by the Cannon Building, followed by the Russell building, followed by the Supreme Court building. The Presidency and the Congress have three each now, and the Court wants to expand. Overwork is a conflict technique. Mr. Hoover started it; it is now established in all branches. Staff is a conflict technique. Mr. Roosevelt started it in the Presidency; by 1945 it has migrated to the Congress; and soon infested the Court. (Surely you have read Renata Adler's brilliant review of The Brethren in the Book Review of a week ago. She makes the elemental point that once the number of clerks per justice began to expand they became "a bureaucracy like any other—with confidences to violate....") Budgetary control is a conflict technique. Mr. Harding established the Bureau of the Budget; the Congressional Budget Office came a generation later. Two, actually. Mr. Eisenhower established a Science Advisor; Congress in short order had an Office of Technology Assessment. And so it goes.

The result is an enormous amount of entropy in the system. The initiative in making laws has passed to the President, owing largely to superior organization and the nature of modern government; but Congress does not respond effectively, neither submitting not substituting, as it were, and the Court increasingly breaks deadlocks in a manner never contemplated.

My thought is that the time is at hand to involve the legislative with the executive, and that this could be done by the practice of appointing members of the House and of the Senate to the Cabinet. The President would have the advantage of devising legislative proposals that would be seen by Congress as partly legislative in origin, <u>and</u> the President's proposals would have advocates in the Committees and on the Floor. . . .

Does this make any sense to you? If so, share the thought with whomever you like.

And a happy New Year to Sally and yourself,

Excerpt of a playful letter to Walter Cronkite, on discussing the possibility of running as vice president in 1980 with Representative John Anderson, a moderate Illinois Republican who ran as an independent presidential candidate (and came in third) against Reagan and Carter in 1980. For a time Anderson was considered a contender, and there were news reports that he had considered asking Cronkite, the widely respected CBS news anchor, to be his running mate. Moynihan's continuous troubles with back pain are also referred to here.

MAY 1, 1980

Dear Walter:

This is not an easy letter for me to write, and I cannot suppose it will be pleasant for you to read. Even so, knowing your devotion to TRUTH, and assuming that neither of our archives will be open until the next century, I feel it is in your best interests to know the facts concerning your recent foray into electoral politics.

The fact is that you were No. 2 for No. 2 on the Anderson ticket.

The enclosed news clipping from the <u>New York Post</u> proves this. As you will learn from it, on Monday, April 21, ABC evening news reported that I had already been offered the position. As you will imagine, this required a statement from me and an arranged telephone conversation with Congress-man Anderson the next evening. We opened with mutual assurances that we had not the least intention of embarrassing one another. John observed that this was surely a matter he would want to talk with me about one day. I did not demur, but went on to explain the unusual circumstances that led to my viewing [ABC News anchor] Frank Reynolds the previous evening. It seems I was in the New York Hospital, sent there by a friendly but stern doctor friend when of a sudden I came down with an affliction of some as yet undi-agnosed variety. I explained to John that I had just come back to my room from having a biopsy, filled with needles and pins, and awaiting a bone scan. The only diversion available was television news, drowsy as I was. (Normally the likes of us do not get home until the evening newses are quite past.)

For reasons I do not fully understand, the more I talked of biopsies the less John Anderson seemed to think it pressing that we got together. I need not follow that that is how you got on the list, but even so, you have a right to know.

We should have a drink one day and talk about what might have been.

Letter to Brooks Brothers, on holes in his socks.

NOVEMBER 24, 1980
SIRS:

As a customer of thirty-five years standing this spring (I bought my ensign's outfit from you!), I hope you won't mind this friendly "return." As I have got-ten older, with less time available for shopping, and somewhat more credit, I have taken to buying socks, shirts and sundries in rather large quantities. Such is your quality control that they tend to go on seemingly indestructible and then collapse in the manner of the one-horse shay.

In just such a manner a complete wardrobe purchased for India lasted four and one-half years and then disappeared in a fortnight. The point of the tale is that last spring before a trip to the Middle East, I stopped at your down-town store and stocked up on various items. I bought one dozen socks, one of which I enclose. <u>All</u> of them developed holes within a month. Of the kind you will see. This is something I know you would want to know about, and which I would like made up for in whatever manner you think best.

Walter Wriston, chairman of Citibank, was widely mentioned as a possible treasury secretary under President-elect Reagan.

PERSONAL AND CONFIDENTIAL
DECEMBER 3, 1980

Dear Walt:

I worry that I was not supportive enough when we talked Monday. Desperate is a strong term, and ought carefully to be used, but that is our situation in the world, and it has its origin in economic decline the origins of which in turn are in no small measure political. (See your fine letter of October 27.) Just at this moment, for example, we are trying to devise a position with which to confront the Soviets over Poland. If the sequence that led to the invasion of Czechoslovakia is any standard, they are moving toward a similar invasion of Poland. What are our options. We cannot threaten war, not least because if the conflict were kept to conventional weaponry it would be over in 72 hours with the Russians at the Channel. We cannot threaten economic ruin, because our allies do not respect us enough, or need us enough to cooperate in any such effort. And so we are moving to a threat of a military alliance with China, which is to say we are threatening a larger and more devastating war.

In a word, we are so weak we must resort to balance of power politics, choosing one totalitarian power as against another. An utter bankruptcy of policy. Utter failure. And unperceived. Brzezinski seems to think he has the Russians cornered at last.

And so you see we need you here. You will enjoy it, even if, as is likely, in the end you are not successful. Few succeed in politics; few even survive. It is simply that it must be done.

Letter to the outgoing and long-suffering president, Jimmy Carter.

DECEMBER 22, 1980

Dear Mr. President:

As the year comes to a close, may I take a few moments of your time to thank you for all you have done for our country and the world in your four years in office. I can imagine that you will think that such thanks were little enough in evidence in November, and my own difficulty is that I have not seen any of the Presidents I've known live to receive the appreciation they deserved. I believe, however, that you will do; and it will be good for our people that you should.

Nothing, to my mind, was so splendid as your effort during the last campaign to bring the issue of nuclear strategy into the realm of public discourse. The Republican Platform, it must be acknowledged, began the sequence, announcing their rejection of the "mutual-assured-destruction (MAD) strategy which limits the President during crises to a Hobson's choice between mass mutual suicide and surrender." (In a subsequent spat with General Rowny who was defending this proposition in the <u>Washington Post</u>, I pointed out that a Hobson's choice is in fact no choice at all!) I picked up the subject in my remarks to the opening session of the Democratic National Convention. But it was you who raised the issue to the level of Presidential politics in the finest sense of that honorable term. It is too early to know what impression you made on the public mind, but for sure the process has begun, and you began it.

It is, or so it seems to me, profoundly important that this be kept up, and I do hope that you will find it possible to do so. Nuclear strategy, like nuclear weapons, has for a generation now been the realm of a tiny scientific and academic elite. It has been shaped far more in faculty seminars in Cambridge than in any of the committees of Congress, or even I dare to think, the National Security Council. This arrangement served so long as American preeminence was secure, which is to say so long as the polity supported whatever was required to maintain that preeminence. But our preeminence is past—in this the Republican Platform was not wrong—and we face choices which must now be <u>public</u> choices, else the resources to sustain them will not be forthcoming. Nothing was so Presidential as to begin that public discourse. In this sense it is not only the nation, but truly the world that is in your debt.

I want you to know this because there are, of course, some matters in which I have differed with the Administration. I believe our policies at the United

Nations were wrong, and did great damage both to your administration and to our party. The March 1 vote [supporting a United Nations Security Council resolution criticizing Israel] was not, if I may be presumptuous, a "mistake." It was the logical and necessary consequence of the ideas which we brought to that forum. Ideas in such settings are destiny; outcomes almost Euclidean. I must tell you that so long as those ideas are in place in our party I do not believe we are fit to govern, and clearly the American people are of much the same view. But that is what debate is for; and we shall have the debate. I mention this only because I mean now to reply to the attacks that the U.S. Mission unceasingly made on me during your administration, but which I felt restrained from answering until the very last.

I happened onto Pat Cadell the other evening. He reports that you may be writing about Camp David [Middle East peace agreement]. May I urge you to do so, if only to keep <u>that</u> process going. Surely your greatest contribution to peace in the world! Consider: of how many men may it be said that they themselves added to the prospect of peace among men.

Excerpt of a letter to Martin Peretz, owner of the NEW REPUBLIC *magazine, complaining about his being labeled a neoconservative.*

DECEMBER 27, 1980

Dear Marty,

I have to tell you this. There is something inexplicable in the way I keep getting battered by your magazine. Because you are a friend let me speak in the most personal of terms. I don't need the praise of the New Republic. The censure—more like libel—is terribly hurtful and I have to assume is so intended.

The current [Morton] Kondracke. Democrats need a Heritage Foundation. The Conservative one has "neoconservatives (Irving Kristol's crowd, Pat Moynihan's, and Midge Decters'). For the Dems "What's needed is a research factory for the Kennedy-Mondale-Jackson-McGovern moderate liberals. . . ." Not Moynihan.

<u>Who</u> pray God make up my crowd? Which of them is to be found at the Heritage Foundation?

This is deadly, Marty, and you pay for it.

Best,

If this seems cranky, and it is, let me explain. I am in my office at mid-morning, Saturday. I got here at five fifteen to try to finish before the day is out a long paper on Welfare Reform. I have some new data showing that a third of all American children will receive AFDC payments before age 18. Am trying to make some case to the new administration that there are things it could try. (There has been no increase in AFDC payments in NYC since 1974.) I broke for a moment, glanced at your Dec 20 issue and there was that line. Hurtful, and intended to hurt, and published by you. (Pls don't tell me you were out of the country.) The people I need in NY will read the NR, not the Journal of the Institute for Socioeconomic Studies. . . .

Excerpt of a letter to Philip B. Heymann, assistant attorney general for criminal justice, about his name and that of Senator Jacob K. Javits figuring in the Abscam investigation, a sting operation led by the FBI that eventually led to the conviction of Senator Harrison Williams of New Jersey and other political leaders on corruption charges.

JANUARY 5, 1981

Dear Mr. Heymann:

As I have not heard from you since December 19 when you and Judge Webster were so kind as to come to my office to discuss the appearance, as it were, of my name and that of Senator Javits on one of the "Abscam tapes," it might be useful to recapitulate the two questions I put on that occasion.

As you will recall, I asked, first of all, how was I to be persuaded that I had not come upon a politically motivated conspiracy by the Federal Bureau of Investigation to engage Senator Javits and myself in illegal activities. All that I <u>knew</u> was that a convicted criminal, then working for the FBI, evidently encouraged another convicted criminal to offer large sums of money to the two of us in return for our introducing legislation, or some similar act. Mr. Weinberg, you will recall, told Mr. Rosenberg: "Javits we would definitely like and we'd like Moynihan."

Let me be clear—as perhaps I was not sufficiently so at our meeting—that I do not believe there was any such conspiracy. I know something of the sequence by which these events got under way; I have confidence in you and in Judge Webster; I have confidence in our system. But it is precisely because I am so confident that I <u>must</u> ask myself whether I am, in fact, merely complacent. As I remarked to you, in all save a half dozen or so societies on earth, the exchange between Messrs. Weinfeld and Rosenberg would constitute for anyone of minimal political sophistication <u>prima facie</u> evidence that the government was out to destroy two legislators. Eternal vigilance, we tell ourselves to the point where perhaps we no longer listen, is the price of liberty.

It seems to me that this subject should concern you as well. <u>You</u> know that you simply stumbled onto your connection with legislators. Nonetheless, it happened. What is to prevent some future administration from embarking on a <u>true</u> political conspiracy under the guise of rooting out corruption it happened upon at JFK airport, or whatever, and benefiting from a pervasive public assumption that this was routine procedure? Can you follow me on this point? How, for example, did it come about that your agent, Mr. Weinberg, encouraged a known criminal to bribe two United States Senators when there was not the slightest evidence that he knew them, or had been in touch with them, and there was, to the contrary, the somewhat improbable proposal that he would involve Senator Kerr as well. I know that the Department is frequently charged with failing to prosecute. Your task, in a word, is complex. But that is no excuse for not performing it. The Division of Civil Rights is supposed to be concerned with just that. I believe I have a civil right not to have the government attempting to induce me to commit a crime. But I leave that to the disputations of law professors. What I <u>do</u> know as a Senator and sometime professor of government is that you have established a precedent that could easily be abused by an unscrupulous Executive Branch and that a Senator has a responsibility to say so. You need to leave behind a record of how this all came about, including what, if any, controls you placed on the criminals who were acting as your agents. In this manner there will be some standard against which to test the probability of truth or falsehood in the representations of some future government.

In this manner, also, you will be faithful to the injunction of <u>The Federalist</u> No. LXXX that "for maintaining in practice the necessary partition of power among the several departments" of government it is necessary to contrive an "interior structure of the government as that its several constituent parts may, by their mutual relations, be the means of keeping each other in their proper places." It is your task to prosecute and prevent crime. It is ours, or so I would think, to ensure that you do so in a manner that does not lend itself to the aggrandizement, much less the abuse of executive power. . . .

My second question in our December 19 meeting was much simpler. I asked in what way would the Department of Justice make public the fact that Mr. Rosenberg had informed the United States Attorney's office here in the District of Columbia that he was lying when he told Mr. Weinberg that he had been in touch with Senator Javits, Representative Lent, and me. You will recall that you read from a Department memorandum you brought along with you, which evidently reported that the Department of Justice had told the judge hearing the trial at which these videotapes were shown, that Rosenberg was lying, and that the defense attorney had also been told this. My question is when is the public going to be told? I stated, you will recall, that I would quite understand that this might have to await the end of the trial.

But it is <u>not</u> in my view enough for a Department spokesman to tell a <u>New York Times</u> reporter that "there has been no suggestion whatsoever of any impropriety on the part of either Senator Javits, Senator Moynihan or Congressman Lent," as was done by Mr. Robert M. Smith on December 12. I don't want to be told that you are not investigating me. I want you to tell the public what you told the judge: that the man was lying.

I know these are busy days for you, and I can imagine that I appear something of a pest. I must tell you, however, that I am not a pest. I am a United States Senator concerned with use and potential abuse of executive police powers which could grievously impair the constitutional basis of American government.

Continuing his practice of constituent letters, Moynihan adopted the salutation, "Dear Yorkers," in 1981, explaining that the term was popular in the nineteenth century. In the excerpts here he celebrates the return of the fifty-two American hostages held in Iran following the seizure of the U.S. embassy in 1979, discusses New York's loss of congressional seats after the census, the new Senate leadership, his friendship with Senator Jacob K. Javits, and his welcome to Senator Alfonse D'Amato, who defeated Javits in 1980.

FEBRUARY, 1981

Dear Yorker,

That is not a familiar term any longer, is it? Still, I wouldn't like to see it lost. (Like the hyphen in the New-York State Historical Society.) Through much of the 19th Century, or such is my impression, people would speak of "York State" rather than "New York," and we were known, and knew ourselves as Yorkers. As late as 1940 Harold W. Thompson dedicated his incomparable collection of folk tales, <u>Body, Boots & Britches</u>, to two "Yorkers" and clearly preferred the term. (The title, incidentally, is a Dutchess County expression meaning "the whole thing.")

It will in any event serve as the salutation of this newsletter, which I hereby commence. I have been thinking about the subject for some time, and resolved at New Year's to try. Not much of a personal voice comes out of Washington. Our debates in the Senate tend to be formal, and ought. Our after dinner speeches, mercifully, go unreported in the main. If anyone sees us on television asking questions or offering comment, it is usually a twenty or thirty second "take," as the cameramen say. Something more personal is surely possible. My friend and colleague Barber B. Conable of Alexander in Genesee County regularly writes a newsletter to his constituents in the 35th Congressional District. By which I mean <u>he</u> writes it. So shall I write mine.

THE HOSTAGES

I have got to think more about the agreement with the Iranians that led to the release of the Americans they held prisoner. Was it an agreement made with the kidnappers, as it were? Most certainly. The government of Iran was in criminal possession of our Embassy, our two Consulates, and 52 Americans. Ought we have entered into such an agreement? Should we be bound by its terms? Clearly we do not have to be, but I think we need not rush to fixed conclusions until we know more. I will write about this subject next time.

For the moment they are back, and how proud we are of them. Bruce Laingen, the Charge d'Affaires in Iran at the time of the seizures of the Embassy by "student militants" (who really are Terrorists), is a personal friend also. He was India desk officer when I was Ambassador in New Delhi. He was calling at the Iranian Foreign Office at the time of the seizure, and was held there. Several times it would have been possible to get out of the country. He refused to leave until every American went with him.

For their Christmas card his wife Penny reproduced a painting of birds seen from the window of the room in which he was held prisoner. With it was this inscription:

> As you gather with your family at Christmas, ponder these three gifts of God—Love, Faith, and Freedom.

THE 1980 CENSUS

As you all will have noted, despite a plethora of lawsuits, many of them brought in New York State, notably that by Mayor Koch of New York City, the 1980 Census, pursuant to law, was delivered to the President on the last day of the year and transmitted to the House of Representatives where it will be made the basis for reapportionment in the 98th Congress that will assemble two years from now. The population of the Nation is recorded as 226,504,825, and New York as 17,557,288. This marks a decline of 684,103 in our population, the first recorded in our history. (Only one other state, Rhode Island, showed a decline, but proportionately much less.)

This is not good news, but neither is it calamitous. The Westward Movement continues: what do we suppose the Erie Canal was all about? The loss was concentrated, of course, in New York City. Manhattan is shown with a population of 1,411,743. But it is worth noting that the 1910 count was nearly twice that—2,762,522—and the count has declined in every census since. The population density in 1910 was something we could hardly imagine today, and would not live with.

There is, of course, the issue of "the undercount." That is to say, persons missed. There has always been an undercount: no Census is perfect. (Actually, sampling would give better answers than counting.) That is not the issue. The issue is whether the undercount is greater for some groups and some jurisdictions, such that the claim can be made that such groups and jurisdictions are underrepresented in Congress, and receive less than a fair share of Federal programs such as revenue sharing. In 1968, as director of the Joint Center for Urban Studies of M.I.T. and Harvard, I organized a small conference on this subject, addressing the particular question of the 1970 Census. The proceedings of the conference, published as The Census and the City, set the basis for much of the present dispute. Having until now taken the side of the mayors, as you might say, let me balance the record with some observations "on the other side."

First, this was undoubtedly the best census we have ever taken. Vincent Barabba of Rochester is the best census taker we've ever had. The undercount was discovered by the Bureau of the Census: they have never tried to cover up, but to the contrary have sought to tell us more.

Second, there is no question in my mind that Buffalo, Rochester, New York and other cities were not fully counted. (Mayor Erastus Corning in Albany felt his city was fully counted. But then he knows everybody in Albany anyway, and could have done the count himself.) But in <u>national</u> terms, the largest undercount is rural and Southern. In terms of Congressional apportionment, adjustments for our state would most likely be more than offset by adjustments elsewhere. There are those who will take the strongest issue with me on this score, but I must tell you what I feel to be the case.

Put plain, we will lose five Congressional seats in 1982; four in the New York City area, one in the Buffalo area. I can report, as if it were a secret (!), for no one to my knowledge has yet picked it up, that we almost lost six seats. Apportioning the Congress is not a simple calculation at all, because every state has to have at least one Representative. (There are six states that have only one.) Thomas Jefferson had a formula which was used for awhile; also Daniel Webster. The formula used at present was thought up by a Harvard Professor of Mathematics, E. V. Huntington, and adopted in 1941. In its final distribution of the 435 House seats, the Census statisticians always allocate a hypothetical 436th seat, to see which state would get it and by what margin it failed to get the 435th. This year Indiana lost out to New York for number 435 by 7200 persons.

New York will remain the second most populous state, with the second highest number of electoral votes.

One good thing. In December, when Congress finally got around to extending Revenue Sharing, the Senate, and then the House, accepted an amendment I offered which requires the Census to adjust for the undercount in future population estimates which are the basis for the distribution of funds under this program. This has never been done before. It means that soon now we will have a set of corrected figures to use for revenue sharing and, I cannot doubt, for other Federal programs based on population.

What to make of it all? Many things, no doubt. But surely one thing above all. Taxes in New York State, despite some recent cuts, remain by far the highest in the land. I give you Stein's First Law of Taxation, which I name after Professor Bruno Stein of New York University: To Tax 'em, You Got to Catch 'em. . . .

THE TRANSITION

I was on hand for the Inauguration which showed our Nation and our new President at their respective best.

But this was only one transition. For Senators, <u>the</u> transition took place on January 3rd, when for the first time in a quarter century the swearing in of new Senators made for a Republican majority. The last majority lasted a brief two years, and left no special record. It is likely to last a lot longer this time around. And so it matters that it be a capable and responsible majority.

The fact that Howard H. Baker, Jr. is now Majority Leader is an extraordinary stroke of fortune for the Senate. There is not a finer, or more responsible man in public life. It happens I wrote an introduction to his fine book <u>No Margin for Error</u> published last year. I saluted him from across the aisle and wished that he "long remain Minority Leader of the United States Senate." Cloudy crystal ball. But a fair judgment of character. As for the balance of the group, the issue to my mind is how soon they will come to accept the complexities they must now live with. I can imagine people growing weary, impatient, and on the edge, exasperated at Democrats, myself included, going about mumbling that things are complex. And often intractable. But they are, you see, and that is where you have to begin if you are going to get anywhere with issues in government.

ON A PERSONAL NOTE

I am now the senior Senator, Jacob K. Javits having left the Senate. Few save those who served with him will know how great is our loss. I revered him, and will say no more for he has put the matter behind him and is off on a mind boggling set of enterprises, including the publication of his autobiography, an event I for one look forward to. Had he been reelected, he would have become chairman of the Senate Committee on Foreign Relations, the culmination of a life's work. And what did he say in the aftermath? He said that, like Moses, he had been allowed to see the Promised Land, but not to enter.

I welcome my new colleague Alfonse D'Amato. He brings great energy to the Senate and he and I will work closely on the important issues we face as New Yorkers. Yorkers? . . .

Letter to Senator Robert Packwood, chairman of the Republican Senatorial Campaign Committee, charging that the Republican Party was violating the law in its polling in New York.

MARCH 10, 1981

Dear Bob:

I have the somewhat painful duty to inform you that the Republican Senatorial Campaign Committee, through the agency of Robert Teeter is, in my opinion, breaking the laws of the State of New York.

Our Fair Campaign Code (Section 6201.2) requires that a committee releasing public opinion poll information about a candidate must file the methodology, questions, and responses with the New York State Board of Elections within 48 hours.

It appears that just after the November election Mr. Teeter conducted a poll in New York for the Republican Senatorial Campaign Committee.

Early this year Mr. Teeter began to give out selective bits of his poll to journalists designed to suggest that I would have difficulty in a Democratic primary. Most journalists declined to publish such manifestly partisan and partial data. Some, however, did. I ignored the first instance on February 6. I ignored the second on March 5. But yesterday's use of the data in a nationally syndicated column is enough to make me feel I must ask you to stop.

You know of my warm and close regard for you. There is no reason in the world to expect that you would be familiar with the election laws of the State of New York. In no sense do I suggest that you are in any way culpable in this matter. But Mr. Teeter knows these laws, or ought to. And he is your agent, or else ought to stop representing himself as such.

Cease and desist, dear friend. You represent all that is fine and responsible in our political party tradition. We had thought the Republican Party had put Watergate behind it. You will not stay that ghost by flagrantly illegal conduct in pursuit of a narrow political purpose. In any event, as senior Senator from the State of New York, I must ask you to stop breaking our laws.

Letter to President Ronald Reagan, following the attempt on his life on March 30, less than three months into his presidency.

APRIL 3, 1981

Dear Mr. President:

I had of course intended to write to express my gratitude for your disarmingly gracious response to my remarks at the Gridiron dinner, and also to express my admiration for yours that followed. But the events Monday turned all our thoughts to your well being, about which we are profoundly reassured.

Yesterday afternoon the Majority Leader came on the floor to report to the Senate on his visit with you that morning and to tell how splendidly you are coming along. As it happened, I was the Democratic manager of the measure on the floor at that time and it fell to me to respond to Senator Baker. What I said, <u>extempore</u>, is perhaps a better expression of my feelings, and those of all of us here, than anything I might more carefully compose.

> MR. MOYNIHAN: Mr. President, if I could yield myself some time on the resolution, may I just express this Senator's appreciation to our Majority Leader for his report.
>
> I was glad to hear how well the President is recovering, but there is something larger at stake.
>
> Ernest Hemingway once described courage as grace under pressure. I do not know that in our time we have seen so great a display. It makes us proud of our President. It is perhaps no time to talk about the Nation, but it is the Nation that nurtured that quality in him, and we are all enhanced by it.
>
> MR. BAKER: Mr. President, I thank the Senator for that remark. I could not agree with him more. . . . He has expressed, I am sure, the sentiments of all of us.
>
> I may say that I told the President when I first entered the room that I thought the country was proud of him.
>
> I thank the Senator.

It is splendid to know you are up and about, but I hope you will restrain your natural high spirits just a bit until you are fully recovered.

Excerpt of a newsletter discussing the legal requirements for newsletters as well as his memories of the 1963 assassination of President John F. Kennedy.

MAY 19, 1981

Dear Yorker,

This April newsletter is being sent you in May and you are entitled to an explanation.

I wrote it in April (admittedly late in the month), and as is our custom submitted it to the staff of the Select Committee on Ethics to make certain I had not somehow breached the ever more complex <u>Regulations Governing the Use of the Mailing Frank</u>.

The legislative branch, you see, is growing ever more like the executive branch, and the judiciary is copying both. There is a kind of law operating here: Organizations in conflict become like one another. Football teams. Television networks. Navies. Automobile manufacturers. This is increasingly evident in American government.

Unlike most constitutions (which assume harmony) the American Constitution assumes there will be conflict between the different branches of government, and even builds in such conflict. This has meant that over the years, whenever one branch came up with a new "conflict technique" it pretty soon migrated to other branches. Thus in 1902 Teddy Roosevelt built himself the West Wing of the White House complete with the Oval Office where for all the world to see he sat behind a desk just like he was J.P. Morgan. Senators, who until that time, had made do with individual desks in the Senate Chamber as the whole of their administrative panoply, promptly built themselves an office building. The House followed suit. Next the Supreme Court moved out of the Capitol into its own Roman Temple.

Then came staff. First in the White House under FDR. Then in 1945 to the Congress. Next the Supreme Court began beefing up its corps of formerly confidential clerks (who now tell journalists just about anything they wish to hear). And of course regulations.

You would think a United States Senator would be a reasonable judge of the sort of issues he could properly discuss in a newsletter. In April I was thinking, as we all were, about the attempt on President Reagan's life. (Just as we are now thinking of the attempted assassination of Pope John Paul II.) And so I wrote about it, first in the large context of the stability of American government, and second on the specific subject of gun control.

You would suppose this a simple matter for a staff to pass on, would you not? Of course not. A staff counsel to the Ethics Committee promptly wrote Senator Wallop, the Chairman, and Senator Heflin, the Vice Chairman:

> Senator Moynihan has submitted another newsletter which we are hesitant to approve.

Don't blame the poor fellow. Hesitation is built into bureaucracy. As is absurdity. For a goodly part of 1979 my Senate staff devoted a fair proportion of its energies to negotiating with the staff of the Senate Ethics Committee over the question of whether I had used the word <u>I</u> more times per page in a proposed newsletter than <u>Regulations Governing the Use of the Mailing Frank</u> permitted. A 1975 change to Section 3210(a)(5)(C)—sic—decreed that "Personally phrased references . . . shall not appear more than five times on a page." The essence of the argument was whether the term "<u>we</u>, New Yorkers," implied the term I. A sample paragraph from the staff director of the Ethics Committee:

> We . . . advised that the Committee has not yet ruled upon what is meant by "or other personal references," such as, "we," and "this office." It was suggested that until such time as we are able to obtain guidance from the Committee, that references which, arguably, might be construed as a personal reference, be avoided in situations where if counted, the total of all personal references on a given page would exceed five."

That is when I gave up on newslettering,* only to try again last February.

Of course, once Senators Wallop and Heflin found time to review the case (they have serious things to do, after all) the newsletter was approved. It follows in abbreviated form. But not before a brief homily. If you create a bureaucracy do not be surprised if you become bureaucratic. On coming to the Senate the first proposal I made in the Budget Committee was to reduce the size of the Senate staff by 10 percent. I begin to think 50 percent would be wiser.

THE ASSASSINATION ATTEMPT ON PRESIDENT REAGAN

I was in the White House at the moment word reached us that President Kennedy was dead. Or, rather, at the moment the realization came. It was, by any objective assessment, a moment of the greatest peril. Only a very few per-

---

* Under assault I turned to the Oxford English Dictionary to settle this usage. Sure enough the first meaning given for "lettering" is: "The act of writing letters; letter-writing." For an example they cite Byron: "I hate lettering."

sons in the government were in Washington. The President and Vice President were, of course, in Dallas.

It is not generally remembered that much of the Cabinet was in a plane half way across the pacific, headed for Japan. As if to symbolize the event, the G.S.A. was using the occasion of the President's absence to take up the rug in the Oval Office. His furniture was piled up in the hallway outside, with his rocking chair on top. Was there ever a setting in which the possibility of conspiracy would more readily come to mind?

And yet I think the thought never occurred to us. We were sitting in a circle, hardly talking, in the large south west office that Ralph Dungan occupied. The only thing that could actually be said to have happened was the arrival of Hubert H. Humphrey, who surged into the room in shock. "What have they done to us?," he exclaimed as he hugged Dungan. But there was no they. None of us thought that. McGeorge Bundy rose quietly and went into Mrs. Lincoln's office, picked up the telephone, and said to the White House operator, "This is Mr. Bundy, would you please get me Mr. McNamara." Government never missed a beat.

Our only mistake was not getting custody of Oswald. It was all too clear that he would not survive that Dallas police station, and that conspiracy theories would follow ever after. (President Johnson, hearing of my arguments that a conspiracy would be alleged, concluded that I was alleging one. Thereafter my days in Washington were less happy!) Our judgment about Oswald was flawed perhaps, but the government never faltered. Far from shaken, it seemed almost to take strength from this demonstration of its stability.

It was not different this time. The shooting of President Reagan occurred before our eyes as we sat in the Cloakroom watching the television replay of the actual event, watching the struggle with the assassin, watching Jim Brady struggle to recover. The Secret Service agents were magnificent. So too were the doctors and emergency room staff, skilled beyond any understanding by the rest of us. The White House staff was almost practiced, summoning the Cabinet to the Situation Room in the basement of the West Wing should it be judged that the President was for the moment "unable to discharge the powers and duties of his office" (Amendment XXV). The Vice President was superbly responsive to his responsibility and of any line where he might have overstepped them.

Above all, President Reagan. In the history of the office has anyone ever so triumphed over danger and pain and near death? It is awful to quote oneself, but I was on the floor at the time when Majority Leader Howard Baker—no less masterful in crisis—gave an early report of the President's condition. There being no one else present (he was really informing the Press Gallery) at just that moment I responded.

> I was glad to hear how well the President is recovering, but there is something larger at stake. Ernest Hemingway once described courage as grace under pressure. I do not know that in our time we have seen so great a display. It makes us proud of our President. It is perhaps no time to talk about the Nation, but it is the Nation that nurtured that quality in him, and we are all enhanced by it.

And once again the Republic did not falter. There was not the least tremor. We should appreciate this more about ourselves, and others might usefully do so as well. There are today 154 members of the United Nations. Of these there are exactly seven that both existed in 1914 and have not had their form of government changed by force since then. (They are the U.S., Britain, Canada, Australia, New Zealand, South Africa, and Sweden. Switzerland is another, but not a UN member.) The stability of the American Republic is without equivalent in the experience of mankind, and only the continuity of the British monarchy (and democracy) compares with it.

This is not to say that President Reagan's administration has not been hurt. (That of President Kennedy was extinguished.) The President cannot for some time now have the strength he had before, and the President is the center of our system. This argues a certain holding back in the pounding we tend to give one another. (It fell to me to give the "Democratic" speech this year at the Gridiron Dinner, the great ritual truth telling that the Washington press corps puts on each spring, in this case the Saturday evening before the President was shot. I pounded pretty well, and he pounded back even better. If you think of him as a great performer, let me say he is an even greater audience, looking up, beaming and glinting, as you try to say things that are both wicked <u>and</u> true. Gridiron speeches are off the record, but if anyone would like a copy please write, as I think it captured a moment of good feeling and confidence and shared regard that we should not forget.) We are surely proud of him. . . .

⌗

Excerpt of a letter to the Reverend Paul Moore Jr., archbishop of the New York Episcopal Archdiocese, challenging his assertion that Moynihan had supported Reagan's budget.

MAY 22, 1981

My dear Paul:

If we are going to continue this correspondence, we really ought to set some ground rules.

Politics is not an exact science, any more I should think than theology. But it does benefit from a certain disciplined adherence to texts.

First you write me that you had read I was absent from a session of the Budget Committee in which nutrition matters were voted on. It was not I, but the Senator from Colorado who was absent. Next, April 15, you ask "Why did you vote for the Budget Bill." I assume you mean the reconciliation instruction of April 2 which called for some $36 billion in recisions from the overall proposed Carter budget of $739 billion. I did that because I felt there was plenty of room in a budget of $702 billion to decently apportion our resources. When this, in my view, was not done in the Budget Committee I voted against the budget resolution. (Technically, the First Concurrent Resolution on the Budget—Fiscal Year 1982.) I was, as I recall, one of the five votes in opposition. Next on May 12 I voted against the Resolution on the floor (77–20). Today I voted on the final conference report (76–20). I enclose the report of the Committee of Conference, should you like to glance at it. The overall total is $699.4 billion.

But really now. Would you not think it a bit bold for me, on the basis of something I had read or heard, to write to ask if you really still are a practicing Christian, or some such ultimate assertion? . . .

Letter to Anatoly F. Drobynin, ambassador of the Soviet Union, pleading for the case of Anatoly Scharansky, the human rights activist arrested on espionage charges. He was released in 1986 and emigrated to Israel, where he adopted the name Natan and became a prominent Israeli political figure.

JULY 22, 1981

Dear Mr. Ambassador:

I am writing to express my concern for the well-being of Anatoly Scharansky, who is presently imprisoned at Perm Labor Camp in Siberia. I am especially concerned with Mr. Scharansky's situation because of his deteriorating health. Recent reports indicate that, although Mr. Scharansky's health is failing, he is being punished more severely than in the past.

The vague charges against Anatoly Scharansky have never been substantiated. To many observers, it seems that Mr. Scharansky has been imprisoned for expressing his opinions.

Mr. Scharansky is a man of great courage and conviction. His belief in human rights and his devotion to his faith have drawn citizens of many countries to his cause. He is a symbol for those concerned with human rights everywhere. He will not be forgotten.

In the spirit of the Helsinki Accords I ask you to convey to the highest levels of your government my deep and continuing concern for Anatoly Scharansky's safety and my hopes for his release.

Letter to Sydney Schanberg, columnist for the NEW YORK TIMES, *on the difficulties encountered with American Express.*

PINDARS CORNERS, N.Y.
AUGUST 21, 1981

Dear Sydney,

That was a marvelous column (among many!) on your colleague's application for a credit card. Lest you think her experience marks yet another new and baneful development in American life, let me recount mine.

It would be sixteen years ago—fourteen, come to think—I was sitting here in the school house writing my letter of protest. A few months earlier I had run into one of those counter displays asking "Why pay cash? Why pay at all? Get an American Express Credit Card." Good idea, thought I. I took one home, filled it out, sent it in. I flunked. Not overly distressed—they were something of a novelty then—I nonetheless took advantage of summer idleness to write and ask why <u>did</u> I flunk. I was a reasonably sober, reasonably married man. I held a tenured chair at Harvard University. I had just been on the cover of Time. (Urbanologist.) I had no debts to speak of. And they had solicited my business.

There followed a four month correspondence. Back at Cambridge I xeroxed a copy of the Time cover and sent it to them. That did it. I think. Anyway, I have been in debt ever since.

Don't tell <u>that</u> to your colleague.

A favorite subject of Moynihan's constituent newsletters was his effort to calculate the flow of funds to and from New York State in connection with the federal government. Moynihan's annual studies of this balance in what he called the "Federal Fisc" were a hallmark of his time in the Senate.

SEPTEMBER 4, 1981
PINDARS CORNERS, NY

DEAR YORKER,

There is a rule of sports in government, or ought to be, that you never do anything about a problem until you learn to measure it. Paul F. Lazarsfeld, the great Columbia University professor who developed the art of polling, used to tell his classes that the moment you attach a number to an idea you have learned something. You know more than you knew before. The number seems too large, too small, about right. You are already thinking in a more precise way.

Heaven knows I've nothing against words. For the large purposes of government only words have the power to move and convince us. But for the secondary purposes of government, numbers help mightily.

In point of fact, the statutes of the United States commence with just this combination. The first law enacted by Congress established the form of the oath of office to be taken by those who would enter the service of the new republic. The second law imposed a duty of ten cents a gallon on imported rum. A tax, that is, designed to help the whiskey distillers on the frontier and the rum distillers in Massachusetts—a nice regional balance—and also, no doubt, to raise some revenue.

It was to such specifics that I turned after being elected to the Senate in 1976. The City of New York had barely escaped bankruptcy the previous year. The City of Yonkers was in similar straits. They were not alone. The State government itself was not without difficulties. All these matters derived basically from a weak economy, a weakness in part induced by extraordinarily high levels of state and local taxation (our taxes were, and are, roughly twice those of Texas), but also by low levels of Federal outlays compared to Federal taxes.

Governor Rockefeller first raised the proposition that our problems arose in part from this imbalance in our fiscal relations with the Federal government. We paid much more in Federal taxes than we received back in Federal outlays. (I state with confidence that Governor Rockefeller was the first to do this, as I was Assistant Secretary and for a time, Secretary, to Governor Harriman who preceded him. In those days the Federal government barely entered the consciousness of persons concerned with state matters.) But there was no response in Washington to Governor Rockefeller's assertion <u>because he had only stated the proposition. As yet no on in New York had attached numbers to it</u>.

Moreover, the Federal government <u>had</u> attached its own numbers to the proposition, and had come up with a very different conclusion. Each year, the Community Services Administration (which had originated in President Johnson's anti-poverty program, and was concerned with such issues) compiled a detailed report, <u>Federal Outlays in New York</u>, and of course for the other states as well. Outlays of the various Federal programs were broken down to the county level. The report for 1976, for example, indicated New York had a comfortable <u>surplus</u> in its fiscal relation with Washington, receiving more in Federal outlays than we paid in taxes. And so if any President, in the privacy of the Oval Office, were to ask his budget director whether the Governor of New York had a legitimate grievance, the budget director would reply that he did not. Thereafter, whatever the President <u>said</u>, you can be sure what he <u>thought</u>: New York had no case.

A puzzle. The first clue to solving it came in a letter from Erik Johnsen, formerly of the Technical Assistance Center at the State University College at Plattsburgh. He had taken the trouble to <u>read</u> the <u>Federal Outlays</u> report and noticed that New York was credited in 1976 with receiving some 49.1 percent of the interest paid on the Federal debt, some $13.3 billion that year. Now obviously this was not so: the money was simply deposited by the Treasury in New York banks, whence it made its way around the country and across the world. Searching through the document we came on a half dozen other such instances. For example, that year New York "received" 41 percent of the foreign aid payments of the United States. We set to work revising the Federal accounts, as you might say, and in June 1977 released our first report, NEW YORK STATE AND THE FEDERAL FISC: FISCAL YEAR 1976. We showed Federal taxes collected in New York at $33.7 billion, Federal outlays at $25.7 billion, making a deficit of $8 billion.

We have published a report each year now, five in all. The numbers are compelling.* While the fifty states, collectively, received $145 billion more in Federal outlays than they contributed in Federal taxes between 1976 and 1980, New York received $11.5 billion less than it sent to Washington.

Yet more striking, we learned (it was slow but we got there) that New York has the least ratio of imbalance of any of the great industrial states of the East, which Joel R. Garreau in a striking image has labeled "The Foundry." . . .

So we came to a further conclusion: any trend in the Federal budget to hold down or cut back spending on social programs will have a disproportionate effect on a state and region such as ours. So will any trend in the Federal budget to maintain or increase defense spending.

This is exactly what happened in the administration of President Carter. If you read the newspapers you will have learned that with the coming of the administration of President Reagan, we are in for a period in which "social spending" will be cut and defense spending increased, thus entering a "new era" in American life.

Nonsense. We are in that new era. It began with the inauguration of President Carter. This is not much noticed because President Carter was expected to do just the opposite. He campaigned promising to cut defense spending, and on a party platform that called for many new social programs. In the end, however, there was a real increase in defense spending for every year of his administration, reversing the decline of seven of the previous eight years. There was little real increase in anything else save mandated programs such as Social Security.

---

* This year's report uses tax payment figures of the Tax Foundation rather than those of the Internal Revenue Service. Economists think the IRS overstates New York taxes. The resulting deficit is lower, but still emphatically there. If you would like a copy of the report, entitled NEW YORK STATE AND THE FEDERAL FISC: V (Fiscal Year 1980), please write. I caution you, it is not light reading.

Now if President Carter had <u>wanted</u> it that way it would be one thing. But he didn't. That is why the event suggests large forces at work, apart from party, apart from Presidents. One elemental fact is that our defense position had become ominously weak relative to that of the Soviet Union. In the course of the 1976 campaign I repeatedly stated that the next President, no matter who he was, was going to increase defense spending and not decrease it. But I certainly looked for and hoped for some social legislation, especially welfare reform, which would take some of the burden off New York. But none came.

President Carter found himself standing before a Democratic Convention in 1980, upon receiving his party's renomination, as the first President since Calvin Coolidge with no major social program to his credit. (Or so I calculate.) Every administration since that of Herbert Hoover has left behind some large initiative for which it can be remembered. President Carter had surely hoped for important new reforms and initiatives in domestic matters, and proposed some welfare reform amendments. Yet nothing came of them, or any of his other proposals of that order, even though his party controlled both houses of Congress with large majorities. If you happen to be interested in when eras get going, <u>that</u> tells you something.

And so the imbalance remains, and is likely to grow worse. I voted for the new tax bill. Taxes are too high and personal rates have not been reduced for two decades. We had to lower them just to keep pace with inflation, but I would have preferred a modified plan, different from the bill eventually signed into law. We must recognize that the new tax bill just about wipes out any growth in Federal revenues in the years to come. (I felt we could well afford a $37 billion tax cut in 1982. But $267 billion in 1986!) We shall spend the coming years worrying about the deficit, arguing about military spending, and trying to cut domestic programs to ease the burden of both.

In the Oneonta <u>Daily Star</u> of August 17, my old friend William F. Buckley, Jr. set forth some proposals for dealing with such matters. One was that we limit Federal welfare benefits to states with a per capita income below the national average. Senator Moynihan, he writes,

> ... has become a positive encephalophone on the subject of how much money, net, is going out of New York compared with what's coming in. Some of us remarked this about a generation ago. So: Why not a party plank limiting social philanthropy to those states that need it?

By "encephalophone" I think he refers to what Mr. Dooley used to call "brain fever." (As is widely commented, Buckley is undoubtedly sesquipedalianistic.) But it is true that conservatives were well ahead of the rest of us in pointing out that the Federal budget of the great liberal decades was no bargain for New York.

I could accept his proposal. One of the striking numbers in our new report, NEW YORK STATE AND THE FEDERAL FISC: V, is that real per capita income in New York is now approximately 2.6 percent <u>below</u> the national average. Don't suppose these issues don't touch us all. It is sometimes painful to measure but it is sometimes necessary also.

I am writing from the school house on the farm in Delaware County that has been our home for something like seventeen years. We have <u>weather</u> here, as against climate—a distinction G. K. Chesterton made. Yesterday was the first day of our autumn, our best time. Morning started bleak black with hard, cold wind from the North. The swallows had departed overnight. Then it grew less dark, then bright. Finally the wind drove all before it and by late afternoon the sun shown cool and brilliant, picking the russet of the corn tassels out of the green fields, as if getting ready for the harvest. Walking back up from the house yesterday afternoon, the roadside of a sudden seemed engulfed by Canadian Goldenrod and Aster, the yellow and blue the most intense and yet serene combination of colors. They and the joe-pye mark autumn.

It will be a cold winter, as you shall learn when I write next about the economics of the new tax legislation.

Excerpt of a newsletter discussing President Reagan's budget and tax cuts, with which Moynihan disagreed.

WASHINGTON, DC
SEPTEMBER 25, 1981

DEAR YORKER,

The President's speech of September 24th calling for a new round of budget cuts in the Fiscal Year which starts October 1st seems to have caused some confusion. Didn't we just do that? At the same time we had the big tax cut? The answer, of course, is that yes, we did. But the tax cut was too big, and there is now no revenue growth left. And so the politics of the coming decade risk becoming an endless, joyless, pointless squabble about how big the budget cuts must be in order that the budget deficit not be even bigger. . . .

There is no question that we needed a tax cut. Nor, to my mind, any question that the first object of such a cut should be to offset the "bracket creep" that has increased the real rate of taxes for people who have had no real increase in income. A tax system must not only be fair, it must be seen to be fair. It is useful to keep in mind that our country was founded in a revolution that started over unfair taxation.

To my mind there was a second object to be pursued by Congress: an increase in savings. For a generation now, the United States has had the lowest rate of capital formation of any major industrial country in the world save Great Britain. That is why the United States, which a generation ago had far the greatest per capita income of any nation on earth, now ranks eighth. (Britain ranks nineteenth.)

We have been eating our seed corn. You cannot do that for long. Indeed last year American incomes, in real terms, dropped 5.5 percent, the largest decline since this statistical "series" began in 1947. . . .

Keynesian economics was a huge idea that swept through the universities of Britain and this country in the 1930s by purporting to explain how the Great Depression came about, how to get out of it and, most important of all, how to avoid another. At the time this was a great message of hope in a world on the verge of despair. (And of yet another World War largely brought on by the collapse of the old economic system.) It was brilliant, but it was flawed. Central to Keynesian thought was the idea that modern industrial economies <u>oversave</u> and that, as a result, large resources of capital and labor end up unused. The Keynesian answer was to <u>overspend</u>. For the government, that is, to overspend. Enter the deficit as public policy.

In a curious way, this message was reinforced by the <u>maturing of the industrial economy</u>. By this I mean nothing more complicated than that railroads and the steel mills and the assembly lines finally all got built. Until then saving—the forgoing of consumption—was absolutely necessary in order to make those investments. Now, the investments having been made, they could only return a profit if people commenced to <u>consume</u> their products. The advertising business began in earnest. Someone invented the installment plan.

The Federal government began to guarantee home mortgages. The logic of our economy, as of our reigning economics, also decreed: overspend. . . .

Letter to Arthur O. (Punch) Sulzberger, as part of a continuing series of complaints that the NEW YORK TIMES *keeps referring to Moynihan as a "neoconservative." Sulzberger writes Moynihan on November 18, 1981, that "I think you have a point on that neoconservative bit" and that he would take it up with his style editors. Moynihan's response:*

DECEMBER 4, 1981

Dear Punch:

I think I have a solution. Inasmuch as a neoconservative is a liberal who votes for the defense budget, it is possible to clarify the whole matter for your readers by describing such persons as patriots. Thus you could refer to "Senator Daniel Patrick Moynihan, a well known patriot." Alternatively, "Senator Daniel Patrick Moynihan, a member of the patriotic faction of his party."

As Secretary Watt opined in the San Joaquin Valley just the other day, "I never use the words Republicans and Democrats. It's liberals and Americans."

"Dear New Yorker": Excerpt of a newsletter to constituents with footnote indicating that his salutation of "Dear Yorker" was not especially well received, and he was reverting to the traditional form. This newsletter follows the recent Soviet-backed crackdown on the Solidarity movement in Poland.

WASHINGTON, DC
DECEMBER 26, 1981

DEAR NEW YORKER,*

The holidays are a time to reflect on the year past and to hope for peace and happiness in the year ahead. Christmas, as an official holiday, came late to the United States. The English Puritans detested it as a papist rite, and there were laws against its observance in the Commonwealth of Massachusetts. The Scots celebrated on New Year's. The Germans kept Christmas, as they say, but in those days also kept somewhat to themselves.

The first Christmas tree in the White House was the inspiration of one of those Presidents of the 1880s whose sequence I can never keep straight. This was imported behavior, Prince Albert having introduced the custom to Buckingham Palace a generation earlier. But it was not until 1894 that Grover Cleveland, perhaps responding to his political experiences among the German folk of Buffalo, gave the civil service the day off. The occasion has been, in that sense, sacred ever since. The Capitol shuts down, and becomes rather a private place. For once, all is calm. It is possible to think.

This year, all it has been possible to think about is Poland, and it has been heartbreaking.

Three years ago I published a book about my experience as ambassador to India and to the United Nations. I began with a bit of biography: I had first gone to Washington, I wrote, with John F. Kennedy and then stayed on with Lyndon Johnson. "There I learned as an adult what I had known as a child, which is that the world is a dangerous place—and learned also that not everyone knows this." My editor picked up the phrase—the theme, if you like—and the book was given the title A Dangerous Place.

Nothing has happened since to change this view. Looking back, that is, from the vantage of the day after Christmas, 1981. But in between something did happen. Solidarity. "Solidarność," in the Polish language with which we are all becoming familiar.

This is to say that, in the midst of a Communist state, on the very border of the Soviet Union and thanks to the Warsaw Pact, not only surrounded by So-

---

* You will note the new salutation, replacing "DEAR YORKER," which I have used since commencing this newsletter. Though "Yorker" is a term with a proud history, residents of our state have written to tell me they are equally proud to call themselves "New Yorkers." So am I.

viet armed forces but half occupied by them (there are two Soviet tank divisions stationed permanently on Polish soil, and "maneuvers" recurrently bring larger forces across the border), a free trade union movement was organized and seemingly moved from strength to strength. It grew incredibly in numbers. Two weeks ago Solidarity had some ten million members, perhaps half the adult population of Poland. Its leaders developed uncanny organizational skills, and its membership learned discipline. One-hour strikes would begin exactly at noon and end precisely at one o'clock and close down a whole city.

Solidarity's demands were elemental and just. It sought the right to free association. To free speech. To a somewhat better life for the working people of Poland. It brought down one set of Communist Party leaders. It forced that group's successors to the bargaining table. It obtained formal contractual agreements. It produced an extraordinary leader, Lech Walesa. A man of the people, he was a shipyard electrician.

For years, persons in government and universities (myself included) have made their living teaching that this was not possible. The 20th Century Marxist-Leninist state, first we learned, then we taught, was something wholly new in the history of man. It was all powerful and implacable. It would never share power; it would permit no opposition. It was <u>total</u>. No institutions were permitted to exist independent of the state. And it endured. No such state was ever transformed from within. . . .

At a Christmas lunch last week a friend from the Department of State was predicting (correctly) that our allies would resist any real economic sanctions against the Soviets and even political sanctions, such as taking the issue to the United Nations. He gave a good imitation of a career diplomat explaining away the need for Western action by assuring everyone that by crushing Solidarity the Soviets will only show the world that "Communism does not work." "To the contrary," said another friend present, "they show the world that Communism <u>does</u> work." The all powerful, pitiless, totalitarian state. . . .

When news of the military repression of Poland arrived in Washington, the United States ought instantly to have gone to the United Nations Security Council and declared that so massive a violation of human rights, so patent an intervention by one nation in the internal affairs of another, was a threat to international peace and security and must be condemned. As I write, the administration has decided not to do this, having first decided it would. The fear is that we would stand alone. Am I wrong in thinking that Madison, Hamilton, Jay stood alone? This is what our books are supposed to tell the world about <u>us</u>.

A dear friend, a lady born in Central Europe who was put in jail by the Nazis during World War II and by the Communists afterwards, remarked the other day: "Are we losing our capacity for moral behavior?" Let us hope not. Let us hope for a better year. While we pray for Poland. Pray for the men and women described by the Soviet news agency, TASS, as "counter-revolutionary scum," but who we know to be patriots for whom no praise can be too great.

Excerpt of a newsletter reporting on the Reagan budget deficits.

WASHINGTON, DC
FEBRUARY 8, 1982

DEAR NEW YORKER,

This is Budget Day in Washington. . . .

By the time this reaches you there will have been a torrent of commentary and outcry having mostly to do with the extraordinary deficits that are projected for the coming years, along with the further budgetary "cuts" that are to keep the deficits from being even greater. In a commentary in yesterday's New York Times the able young journalist Steven R. Weisman observed that the proposed budget "would lead to more than $270 billion in new debt in the next three years alone, and more than $500 billion if (the President) fails to get his spending cuts or tax revisions through Congress." Thus, Mr. Weisman continues, the President is forced to contemplate "a possible 50 percent increase in the national debt in a mere three years. . . ."

Just a year ago the President said that our then trillion-dollar debt was of a magnitude "literally beyond our comprehension." But it took near to two hundred years to accumulate. Now it will grow by a quarter to a half in three years.

To repeat, you will hear and read a great deal of comment on the specifics of the budget. Perhaps I can be most helpful by offering some background.

We are in a crisis; a word not to be used casually. It will be a crisis of some duration, and it will not go away unless we can bring ourselves to understand how it came about.

The crisis came about because of an economic theory that held there could be a wholesale reduction in tax rates without any loss in revenues, indeed, that a huge reduction would <u>increase</u> revenue. This belief—the so-called Laffer Curve—took hold in the formative stages of the present administration. The President himself summed it up best in a campaign address in Flint, Michigan on May 17, 1980. He said:

> *. . . We would use the increased revenue the Federal government would get from this [tax] decrease to rebuild our defense capabilities.*

. . . By charging too much, a merchant will find he or she earns less because people buy less. Just so with taxes. Sometimes cutting them increases revenues. In 1978, a proposal I made in the Senate was adopted which reduced capital gains taxes from 49 percent to 28 percent for individuals, from 30 percent to 28 percent for corporations. The next year the revenues from the capital gains tax <u>increased</u>. Which we had predicted they would. (The Treasury Department, of course, had disagreed.) But there is a limit to this, as to any such calculation. There was no evidence it would hold true for the whole of the revenue system. . . .

Excerpt of a letter to John C. Bierwirth, a member of Moynihan's fundraising committee and chairman of Grumman Corporation, then headquartered on Long Island, which ends with a rare discussion of fundraising as the 1982 campaign approaches.

FEBRUARY 12, 1982

Dear Jack:

. . . 1982 will be a year of transcendent political consequence. The issue, plain put, is whether the center will hold—in both parties. I am a born Democrat and a practicing one, but without the least hesitation I agreed to serve in the cabinet of the two previous Republican Presidents. In three decades of government and politics I have felt myself living in a comprehensible and creative political environment. Of a sudden, I am not certain. Of a sudden, both parties are under attack from extremes. (If you would measure the toll, the present Senate is the first since Reconstruction in which a majority of members are in their first term!)

You may not have learned this, but I am to have a challenger in the Democratic primary. He is Mel Klenetsky, "a Democrat," as he put it in his announcement of January 27, "and leading member of the National Democratic Policy Committee founded by Lyndon H. LaRouche, Jr...." This is a native fascist movement. An ugly, brownshirt brigade now invading the Democratic Party. All the stigmata are there: Beginnings on the far left. Conspiracy theories. Name changes. (They were formerly the U.S. Labor Party.) Codewords. (For British read Jewish.) A virulent anti-semitism. (The holocaust is a Zionist myth.) And a certain raving incoherence. (Thus from the January 27 announcement: "And it is no surprise when or how this intellectual fraud (DPM), this British-loving fop and moral abomination, became a eugenicist. He owes his career to Averill (sic: Harriman, the granddaddy of the eugenics movement against which our nation fought a war 40 years ago.") For reasons not wholly clear to me, there is also a pronounced animus against Felix Rohatyn [investment banker and head of the Municipal Assistance Corporation, who helped rescue New York City from bankruptcy in 1975]. In his recent campaign in the Democratic primary for Mayor of New York, Klenetsky declared that he would "target the 'Big Mac' [Municipal Assistance Corporation] policy of Felix Rohatyn as the chief culprit responsible [for bringing to New York] the 'planned shrinkage' policies for urban centers variously put forward in the Carter administration's Global 2000 Report and the New York Council on Foreign Relations 1980 Project...." And so forth, interminably.

I will beat Klenetsky handily. But the vote will not be unanimous. And the campaign will cost money, and most of all: <u>what am I doing running against a brownshirt in a Democratic primary?</u>

Then I shall encounter Mr. Bruce Caputo. He was once a centrist; in the Assembly he could be fairly described as a Rockefeller Republican. Clearly, he has made the judgment that the political future lies with the extremes, and has moved to the extreme right of the Republican spectrum. Evidently busing, abortion and the death penalty will be the substance of his campaign. (Again, code words; conspiracy.) This, too, could be dismissed, save that it has worked so. It is the "proven formula" of the National Conservative Political Action Committee, which will pour hundreds of thousands of dollars into his campaign. This seeming success formula has begun to affect the Republican center as well. I take no pleasure whatever in telling you of a letter from the Republican Senatorial Campaign Committee reporting that the Research Division has supplied Mr. Caputo with information on my votes on "affirmative action." Yes, I vote for affirmative action. I was an Assistant Secretary of Labor for Policy Planning under President Johnson and helped draft Executive Order No. 11246 which proclaimed that to be the policy of the United States government in matters of employment. (The Executive Order was directed in the first instance to the Department of Labor.) I thought we had settled that issue; that both parties accepted the principles of equal opportunity. Evidently not. . . .

I am deeply, deeply, grateful for your willingness to help. I am at your disposal for any purpose that will advance the goal at any time I am not bound to the Senate floor. We have a large and active finance committee which will also help.

It is turning out that ours is one of those generations of which, in President Roosevelt's words, much is expected. So be it.

Letter to Eve Zartman, daughter of Moynihan's friend Story Zartman, about his personal life.

MARCH 29, 1982

My dearest Eve,

What a grand thing to have your letter. But what searching questions you ask. I shall do my best to answer.

"1. How did you get to school?"

Now this is a sentence that can have more than one meaning. In one sense it asks how it is one went to school. Much as I might ask of you, "How did you get to be such an old good friend at such a young age." The answer to the question in that sense is that by the time I was age six, or whatever, the law required that all six year olds go to school. Another sense of your question would be "By what means did you travel to school." Much as I might ask you, "How did you get to the concert?" To that question the answer would be, mostly I walked. In one wicked phase of my youth I used to leap on the back of the 96th Street crosstown bus in Manhattan and, spread-eagled, ride free from Amsterdam Avenue on the west side to Second Avenue on the east side, whence I would make my way north to Benjamin Franklin High School.

"2. What did you do in your spare time?"

Mostly I read. Actually I did not have a lot of spare time after I was about eleven, because in my youth young people used to try to find ways of making money after school. From about age eleven on, I either shined shoes or did something such. Thus in my youth I had plenty of money. This led me to suppose that there was always plenty of money around; a supposition that has proved costly in my mature years. Eventually I got a job in Gimbels, sorting credit slips. Then I went to work on the docks. This made me decide to run away to sea. I did so. Where I met your father. Only we weren't at sea at all, we were at Middlebury College. It was, even so, a romantic adventure because all the girls there that summer had taken a pledge to speak only French.

"3. Did you a alowance to spend?"

I think you have left out a word as well as a letter. Yes, indeed, I had an allowance when I was very young, and I was very bad with it. Mostly I bought Dusky Dans at two for a penny. I suppose I ate, all together, about $20 worth of Dusky Dans. They have since cost me about $20,000 worth of dentistry.

"4. What kind of food did you like?"

I liked the "mickies" we would cook in vacant lots before dinner. This was a widespread practice in New York City during my youth. Your (one's, that is) mother would give you one "Irish" potato at about five in the afternoon. All the kids would get together and make a fire out of old crates or whatever, and once there were coals we would throw our potatoes on them. They came out wonderfully charred and steamy delicious. That, you might say, was our hors d'oeuvre. Hors d'oeuvre is a French word for a small course served before the main course of dinner. Your mother is super at hors d'oeuvres.

"5. What was your favorite toy?"

You know, I can't remember. I don't think I had toys after I was old enough to remember such things. What I did have was marbles. I had the best collection of marbles of anyone. Tiny little "peewees," wonderfully colored agates, great big fellows whose name I can't remember. We used to play marbles for keeps. If you lost, you lost. It is the same way with politics, but not everybody knows this.

"6. What kind of clothes did you wear?"

Any kind. Still do.

Much love to you my old friend and new pen pal. And to your wonderful mother and dad.

[handwritten] Uncle Pat

Newsletter around Memorial Day of 1982, reflecting on spring at his farm and a commencement address discussing nuclear arms negotiations with the Soviet Union.

PROSSER HOLLOW
PINDARS CORNERS, NY
MAY 31, 1982

DEAR NEW YORKER,

Memorial Day did not really begin in Prosser Hollow this year. It emerged, rather, from a deep grey at dawn that was not fog but mist, only now at mid-morning beginning to lift, as if to show how quietly it can be done. All is peace here, and as Yeats wrote,

> . . . peace comes dropping slow,
> Dropping from the veils of the morning . . .

In truth, all is tumult as well, for this is nesting time. The swallows arrived just as we did on Friday, and are swooping about the stable with abandon. A pair of martins are going about their project with nervous deliberation. Rare event, a pair of blackbirds. All welcome. A new survey shows that 61 percent of New York is covered with forest—up 8 percent in a decade. Let it halt there. My wife, Liz, and I are people of the fields, and prefer that the forest keep its distance.

The fields, too, are a tumult of wild flowers and herbs. In one evening walk: mouse-ear, speedwell, mad dog, pinkster, bastard pennyroyal, marsh violet. . . .

We have to recognize that a transition crisis has begun in the Soviet Union. General Secretary Brezhnev—the head of the Communist Party in the Soviet Union is now <u>de facto</u> the head of the government—has reigned for almost two decades but he is now old and sick and the struggle to succeed him has passed. . . .

How are the Soviets not to suspect a change in United States policy, even perhaps an elaborate, if as yet undeciphered, deception? Especially now that we have come along with the proposal for them to <u>give up</u> weapons they acquired at huge expense? . . .

There is not the least hope of getting through all this unless arms reduction becomes an issue <u>above party</u>. The 1972 Joint Resolution passed almost unanimously. The vote was 88 to 2 in the Senate, 308 to 4 in the House. By contrast, SALT II from the first was tangled up in party conflict, with the results we see. . . .

There is a message here for those in favor of arms reductions as well as for those suspicious of them. A kind of "domestic linkage" has developed with respect to the various "freeze" resolutions now in the Congress. If opponents of school busing will be for one "freeze," champions of the Alaskan timberwolf will be for another. This reckons to trivialize a transcendent issue. Much is at stake. The world is at stake. Either we do this together, or it will not be done. . . .

Letter to Rep. Jerome A. Ambro, a Long Island Democrat who suggested Moynihan should run for president after his reelection in 1982.

DECEMBER 15, 1982

Dear Jerry:

What a kind letter!

As you can imagine, I'm very pleased about the election results. I've just seen the final tally, which showed that I received 65.6 percent of the vote, with a majority of over 1.5 million votes. The largest percentage for a Senate candidate in our state's history and the largest margin of victory for a Senate candidate anywhere in a contested, off-year election.

I hope to use this strong showing as a base for being a national spokesman for the Democratic Party. The Democrats have to make the case for recapturing the White House in 1984, and I plan to play a major role in helping the party define its alternative. But not as a presidential contender.

With this in mind, I once again ask you to keep your eyes and ears open. As always, I'd be pleased to have any suggestions you feel might be helpful.

My great thanks.

Excerpt of a confidential letter to Jeane J. Kirkpatrick, President Reagan's envoy to the United Nations, explaining how he decided to go back on his pledge not to run for the United States Senate in 1976. During the "Zionism is racism" fight at

the UN, Moynihan had said he would consider it "dishonorable" to resign as UN
envoy and run for the Senate.

JANUARY 29, 1983

Dearest Jeane,

Your report of Henry Kissinger's conversations with you, as related in the course of our most recent rendezvous on the Eastern Shuttle, set me to thinking: Indeed, just how did I get caught up in this Senate business. I have now reconstructed the evidence and put it as much for my own records as for any marginal interest it might have to you other than to suggest that as a member of DCM you were, in fact, involved!

First, let me get rid of Henry's suggestion that my conduct at the United Nations was in some way in preparation for a Senate campaign. Nothing could be less true. . . .

Now what did happen?

Scoop Jackson is what happened, and I now reconstruct the events from the indispensable Economist Diary.

On Friday, January 30, all in the aftermath of a Reston column, I knew I had to go and sent in my resignation. It was accepted, without fuss or bad feelings. A week later, Sunday, February 8, at his request, I met at the Mission with Scoop Jackson who was running at full campaign speed and had come round to meet with me and praise what I had been doing there, and by implication to express his disapproval of the Administration that has "forced" me to go.

I just barely knew Scoop at the time but admired him, and when on the way out to Newark Airport, he asked me if I would help in his campaign, I said I would. . . .

One thing led to another. Next thing I knew, I was running as a Delegate for Jackson from the Bronx where I won and hence got deeper involved. Scoop dropped out of the race after the Pennsylvania primary. (Where again I had campaigned for him.) But soon a fair number of people who had supported him in New York began to ask me to get into a primary race in which Bella Abzug and Ramsey Clark had already entered. It was, in a sense, a continuation of the Jackson campaign.

I dithered for weeks on end. The very model of indecision until mid-June. One morning in Cambridge I got up early to finish grading seminar papers which were due, as it were, at the Registrar's at mid-day. The week before I had told Len Garment I definitely would not run, but Liz asked one last time what did I want to do. The choice was between taking a nap and commencing a long, lovely summer or getting on the shuttle for New York and announcing for the Senate.

It was, as the Duke said of the Battle of Waterloo, "a damn close run thing." By an internal vote of 51 to 49, I got on the shuttle and the rest is personal history.

To repeat, sorry to take you through all this, but it seemed worth settling in my own mind. I have never until now recognized how the Jackson campaign drew me into the electoral orbit. . . .

Excerpt of a newsletter about the response to one of his earlier newsletters about George Washington's Farewell Address.

WASHINGTON, DC
MAY 16, 1983

Dear New Yorker,

Among the joys of writing these newsletters, none is so fine as the letters that come back in response. I am not going to say that New Yorkers are smarter than other people—that risks spiritual pride—but there are an awful lot of us, and we <u>know</u> more than other people do. As you would have reason to believe if you were to read through the thousand or so letters that arrive faithfully after each of these mailings.

Last Washington's Birthday, I wrote about opium growing and heroin laboratories in Pakistan. Who but a New Yorker, in this case Bernhardt J. Hurwood of New York City, would write with the information that the term "heroin" was adopted as a trade name by the Bayer pharmaceutical company in Germany around the turn of the century because when tested on company employees it made them feel "heroische," which is to say heroic? The drug is technically *DIACETYLMORPHINE,* a distillation of morphine which is, in turn, a distillation of opium. It was originally a trade name just as the word "aspirin" was.

To say again, New Yorkers know more than other people. On the other hand, I could not say that we are necessarily more generous. For it is from Grand Rapids, Michigan, that I have received the most extraordinary response to anything I have ever written—newsletter, magazine article, book, or what you will.

You may recall the Washington's Birthday newsletter began with an account of our annual practice in the Senate of reading Washington's Farewell Address. (I had just come from the Senate Chamber and was thinking once again of the wonderfully subtle directness of Washington's thought.) I believe I mentioned that Washington never actually delivered the address. He simply wrote it out and one presumes, gave it to the <u>Daily American Advertiser</u> of Philadelphia, then the capital, where it appeared September 19, 1796.

But hark! That is not the only newspaper in which the Farewell Address was printed. The text also appeared in <u>The Times</u>—of London—on November 9, 1796. Alonzo Curtis of Grand Rapids, Michigan, having read the newsletter, learning of a fellow admirer of Washington's great text, and having in his possession a copy of said edition of <u>The Times</u>, simply put it in an envelope and sent it along with best wishes!

<u>The Times</u> of that date was a single fold, four sheet affair, surprisingly like <u>The Times</u> of today in what is reported and the manner thereof. What is surprising is the generosity of the editorial comment on Washington's having "concluded a life of honour and glory." As the reproduction on page one is not very clear, let me give the full text below. (In English, as then printed, the letter "s" in lower case looks like the letter "f." But you easily get the hang of it.)

We are forry to announce the RESIGNATION of GEORGE WASHINGTON, efq. of his fituation of PRESIDENT of the UNITED STATES of AMERICA.

This event was made known yefterday by the arrival of the Belvidere, from New York, with letters from thence of the 27th of September.

Notwithftanding the intention of General WASHINGTON had been long announced, it was expected that the folicitations of his friends would have prevailed upon him to continue in office, for the peace of America. He has however declined all further public bufinefs, and, in refigning his ftation, has concluded a life of honour and glory. His Addrefs in refigning his office, is a very mafterly performance; and we fhall give it at length.

It is expected that MR. ADAMS will be chofen his fucceffor.

It happens that the only holograph copy of the Farewell Address (which is to say written in Washington's own hand) is in The New York Public Library. They do not, however, have a copy of <u>The Times</u> version. (Somewhat at odds with the original.) Now they shall, thanks to the generosity of a noble Michigander. . . .

Letter to his mother, Mrs. Margaret Moynihan, on life in the Senate. Ellen is Moynihan's sister, Ellen Moynihan Parris. John McCloskey Moynihan is his son.

PINDARS CORNERS
JUNE 26, 1983

Dearest Mother,

Am here in the school house for two blessed days. Then back to Washington to raise everyone's taxes. What a wearisome job the Senate turns out to be. When you're in the minority, that is.

Ellen tells me you are back at Hillrest and feeling as well as to be expected. She has asked Dr. Ramos to look after you, and I am sure that will please you. I have written Dr. Myers to thank him for all that he did. (I hope I have these spellings right.) If you need anything you don't now have, please tell Ellen, and have her call me.

The big surprise of the season is that John McCloskey graduated from Wesleyan "With High Honors for General Scholarship." One of two such persons in the graduating class. The only higher distinction—reserved, one hears, for molecular biologists—is University Honors, which five persons received. So that however you figure it, John was no less than seventh in his class. And a very fancy class at that, as I am sure you know. He broke through with an absolutely absorbing novel—journal, what you will—recounting his voyage around the world on the Rose City, that tanker that shipped out of Camden New Jersey and paid off in Seattle. The language is a bit rough, but then so were his mates!

Much love, Pat

Letter to Jane Perlez of the NEW YORK TIMES, *explaining again why he objects to the label "neoconservative."*

PINDARS CORNERS
JULY 2, 1983

Dear Jane,

On reflection, I think it <u>would</u> be a good thing to try to clear up this "neo-conservative" matter, and would ask you to share this letter with your editors and the bureau chief.

I have an interest in your knowing something of my politics, and as the senior Senator from New York, I assume you all have something of the same interest.

(A problem here. I have had lunch with the editors of the Times on 43rd street more or less regularly since the time of Arthur Hays Sulzberger. By contrast, after a near quarter century in and out of Washington I have never got past the reception desk at the Washington Bureau.)

My point is that my "ideological roots" are not, and in truth could not be, in the "neo-conservative movement." I am a 56 year old man: my ideological roots are in the Democratic party of Franklin D. Roosevelt. (For years I taught students that the most important thing you could know about a person's politics is how old he or she was.)

If this be so, it follows that I cannot have been "distancing" myself "from them" in order to keep my options open for a Presidential "bid." That must be read as suggesting a lack of personal integrity, which I cannot find agreeable.

It is true that an article in National Journal found me to be the most "liberal" Senator in the 97th Congress. (A Republican Senate in the first two years of the Reagan administration: i.e. nothing notable.) You may as well know that Friday's mail brought the news that I had a 100 percent record with the League of Women Voters (or, as they say, Political Accountability Rating) and a 95 percent for 1982 with A.D.A.—of which I was for years a member of the national board.) But I do not think it fair to suggest that I was once someone who would have voted differently. People who suggest that must be asked to cite a vote.

I happen to believe this is important to my Party and to a body of ideas. The term "neo-conservative" was coined in epithet in Dissent circa 1974. It was directed against persons such as I who did not "see" that the country was moving left. Thus in the introduction to <u>Coping</u>, written in this school house in September 1972, I wrote of my views at the close of the 60s.

> For what it is worth, my judgment was that the rhetoric of violence—
> and the reality—had already overreached itself and that this had begun
> to move politics in a conservative direction that would take a decade or
> so to run <u>its</u> course. p. 48

Politics, being an argument about the future, inevitably divides those who have a different view of the future.

Apart from all else, the term is—for me—too resonant of the 1930's epithet "Social Fascist"—the period, as I say, from which I date. If the Washington Bureau really does believe I am a neo-conservative fine: but I would like to be assured that it is an informed belief, and not just something that somebody told somebody who heard it from somebody else.

Thanks for bearing with this.

Letter to William D. Ruckelshaus, director of the Environmental Protection Agency, insisting that acid rain was killing lakes upstate.

JULY 22, 1983

Dear Bill:

I gather the scientists are confusing you on acid rain. Which is their wont on most subjects, but a necessary part of the process.

I have an idea. We have a natural laboratory on this subject in the Adirondacks where much of the high altitude air flow runs into the mountains. Could I interest you in a tour?

The Environmental Conservation Department has a first-rate helicopter, and as you would imagine, they have some first-rate scientists. If you have never seen the Adirondacks, they are the closest thing we have in the East to the Western grandeur that you were becoming accustomed to. It is quite striking to see a "dead" lake from the sky. They are a beautiful Caribbean blue, indicating the absence of life!

Excerpt of a newsletter reflecting on the death of his closest friend, mentor, and role model in the Senate, Senator Henry "Scoop" Jackson of Washington.

PINDARS CORNERS, NY
SEPTEMBER 11, 1983

Dear New Yorker,

Senator Henry M. Jackson died at his home in Everett, Washington on September 1st. We had known each other almost a quarter century, from the time of the Democratic National Convention of 1960. He served his country longer, and many would say better, than any public man of his time. Fashions changed, he did not. This led to much misunderstanding in later years. But he was invincibly good natured about it.

He was my closest friend in the Senate, and without him the place will not be the same for me, as for so many others. Helen Jackson, herself a person of rare spirit and grace, asked me to speak at the funeral in Everett on September 7th. The Vice President was there, the Chief Justice, and two-thirds of the Senate. None but knew what we had lost.

I had not much to say, but it mattered so much to be asked. May I share with you just a few of my words, as I spoke them that day:

> *There is an old belief in the Judaic tradition that at any moment in history goodness in the world is preserved by the deeds of nine just men who do not know that this is the role the Lord has given them. It is a thought to which one has returned these last days. For if it be so, and of course in the large sense it is, Henry M. Jackson was one of those men. There could be no more telling evidence than that this would never have occurred to him.*
>
> *He lived in the worst of times, the age of the totalitarian state. It fell to him to tell this to his own people, and to the world, and he did so full well knowing that there is a cost for such truthtelling.*
>
> *But he was a Viking also, and knew the joy of battle. Of all things human, the only emotion he never knew was fear; the only weakness he could never comprehend was the love of ease.*
>
> *The poet Yeats wrote once of a man who was "blessed and had the power to bless." Scoop was such a person also.*

To know him and to love him as generations of men and women in American public life have done, is to have been touched by that abounding grace which he brought to the affairs of the Republic. He never took, he only gave; and he never stopped giving.

To Helen, to Anne Marie, to Peter, wishing in no way to intrude, we would even so say that, as we shared your love for him, we share your loss.

And yet, now that it is over, we may celebrate his life as much as we mourn his death.

The Senate goes back into session tomorrow, so this for me is the last day of summer. The goldenrod and the wild aster are making their appointed round, while high on the wooded hills there are flashes of scarlet and yellow. The oats are long since in the barn, and the feed corn in the far field is fully tassled. The Silver Queen, greatest of sweet corn, is over now, as are the Schoharie melons.

It has been a rare summer. The high moment was the appearance of bluebirds, which in twenty years we've never seen. We understand there is a special kind of nesting box which the local students have been setting out. We thank them, and commend the idea to others. We do not commend the catbird to anyone. Liz was planning to put up some elderberry sauce, but guess who got there first.

CHAPTER TEN

"Therefore They Will Decline"

As the 1984 presidential election approached, Moynihan was a figure of increasing influence in the Senate. He had won a comfortable reelection in 1982 and was mentioned, though not widely, as a possible vice presidential candidate for the leading presidential contenders: Vice President Mondale, the Reverend Jesse Jackson, and Senators John Glenn and Gary Hart. In this period he continued his interests in demanding accountability from the C.I.A. and asserting that the Soviet Union was militarily weaker than many experts believed, struggling under the weight of an outmoded economic system, unable to hold its fractious empire together, and headed toward decline. This was the beginning of his increasingly confident criticisms of the failure of the intelligence establishment for overestimating Soviet economic and political power. As Moynihan concentrated on this issue, he used his Senate position to press for historic preservation and helping New York. Events continually threw him back to his earlier years, and in his letters he continued to defend his earlier pronouncements on race, family, and poverty.

Anticipating a role at the 1984 Democratic National Convention, but not as a delegate for any particular candidate, Moynihan writes to Senate Majority Leader, Senator Robert Byrd of West Virginia.

JANUARY 26, 1984

Dear Mr. Leader:

As you asked that we do, I would like formally to request that I be designated as a delegate to the 1984 Democratic National Convention.

I have no greater claims for your preference in this matter than any other of our colleagues, save perhaps that I represent New York, which is the second largest of the states and one which with any fortune we will be able to carry this Presidential year. The Governor will want me with him on the delegation and so will the State Party.

My plurality in 1982 was 1,535,385 votes, the largest in the history of the United States Senate races in New York and the largest in off-year contested elections in the Senate. Mind, I will never get a Robert Byrd percentage of the vote, but I did get 65.5 percent which again was the largest margin in a United States Senate race in New York history.

Excerpt of a letter to Eve Zartman, daughter of his childhood friend Story Zartman, again discussing his own upbringing in response to her reply to his earlier letter.

FEBRUARY 28, 1984

Dear President-Potential Eve:

. . . What, you ask, are Dusky Dans. Alas, I wish I could tell you I had never heard of them. But this is anything but the case. Dusky Dans were small blocks of tan-colored toffee which sold two for a penny in the candy stores of the West Side of New York in the 1930s. At the time of the 1939 World's Fair, I got into the habit of going out to the fairgrounds most every afternoon. Alas, I have to tell you that this was not an expensive trip, as one could sneak under the turnstile of the IRT at Broadway and 96th and therefore avoid the meager fare. Arriving at the fairgrounds, there was a way to slip over the fence that had been established by enterprising youth in Queens.

There were many things to do at the fair, of which the most intriguing was the fact that Coca-Cola bottles when emptied were simply left in receptacles placed about the fairgrounds, which is to say the 2¢ return deposit was not paid and therefore not claimed. But by stuffing four of these bottles inside your trousers, you would bring home 8¢ worth of bottles. This could be cashed at the candy store and six Dusky Dans purchased, leaving 5¢ for the next day's journey. (At the fairgrounds entrance to the subway, there were many guards and no possibility of slipping under the turnstile.)

This is how I passed a brief year with my molars encased in sucrose-ridden toffee casings. The result was that by the time I was 50, I had no molars left. I would estimate that on the whole I have paid $100 worth of dental work for every penny's worth of Dusky Dans over a lifetime. Therefore, I advise you to avoid them as the cost and difficulty will interfere with the campaign plans, and the dentures might even become a campaign issue. They were not for George Washington, but then people were more tolerant in those days— especially before the invention of television.

I will see you often in the susquicentennial year.

Letter to Berl Bernhard, a civil rights official in the Kennedy and Johnson admin-
istrations, who had tried to clarify a painful episode in Moynihan's career—his not
being selected as cochairman of a panel on the Negro Family at a White House con-
ference on human rights. Bernhard wrote Moynihan on March 16, 1984, trying
to mend tensions with him from that episode. Bernhard explained that LBJ "took
an uncommon interest in this conference" but that when Bernhard mentioned his
intention to make Moynihan cochairman, Johnson "said to [Bernhard], about
[Moynihan], in the exact words as I best recall, 'you couldn't find your ass with both
hands.'" Bernhard realized that in responding to LBJ's wishes, his own subsequent
comments ("there was no such man named Daniel Patrick Moynihan") were "per-
haps not felicitous" but also not intended as criticism. "The lesson for me was that I
should have been more direct or circumspect or silent," Bernhard wrote Moynihan,
adding that history was proving Moynihan correct on the issue and that he wished
that "this boil of misunderstanding had been lanced much earlier." Moynihan's con-
ciliatory reply:

PERSONAL AND CONFIDENTIAL
MARCH 26, 1984

Dear Berl:

What a thoughtful, moving letter. There has been a huge misunderstanding here which I ought to have cleared up years ago. I never for a moment thought of your remark as anything more than an effort to relieve the tension at some point or other in the course of those tension-filled days. I never for a moment took it personally.

My view of the matter has scarcely changed in the near twenty years that have passed. The President found himself with a political problem he had not anticipated, and most emphatically did not need. This was a moment when, among other things, the civil rights protest was beginning to merge with the anti-Vietnam protest, and a genuine threat to the Administration was taking shape. The President made the elemental decision to get rid of as much of that particular political problem as was possible, and this meant there would be no discussion of social organization at his conference. And there was none. As a professor of government I would have expected nothing other and was never the least distraught on that score.

My animus, then and now, is directed to those members of the academic community who for political reasons of their own dissociated themselves from my research, or in many cases, viciously misrepresented it. This sort of thing was much too prevalent in that "slum of a decade," and only just beginning to wane. We have paid a fearful price for what American scholars in those years decided not to learn about.

In time this tendency reached the point of suppressing research findings. In the course of Finance Committee hearings on President Carter's welfare reform proposal, a young economist (in 1978, as I recall) of a sudden appeared in the Committee room with the information that the Seattle-Denver income maintenance experiments [SIME/DIME] had produced results wholly at variance with the outcomes that had been hypothesized. This was known in HEW, and by the reputable economists at Wisconsin who had done the work, but none of it had been made public. A letter from Jim Coleman arrived in today's mail discussing just that. In his view, the SIME/DIME results are among "the most profound that social research has provided in recent years," yet the profession and the government were prepared to suppress them.

To repeat, my problem was and remains with the academic not in the political system which has only the most limited tolerance for matters of this kind.

Please show this to Harry [McPherson].

Letter to former Secretary of State Dean Rusk, who also had written Moynihan that he felt LBJ had treated him badly, attaching his testimony to the Democratic Party platform hearings, at which he again appealed for a muscular anti-Communist foreign policy.

APRIL 15, 1984

Dear Dean:

How I agree! LBJ was a bit of a brute to me. Thought me a disloyal Kennedy sort. He was wrong in this, but it matters not. He was a great American President. Someone who was here then and here now will notice the difference. Jimmy Carter should not have allowed all the Scoop Jackson sorts to conclude there was no room in the Democratic Party for them—and so many have left—but he tried to be a great President.

I gave the enclosed at the first regional platform hearings last week. No one showed the least comprehension of what I was trying to say, which means I probably didn't say it right. But you will recall the LBJ tale.

Letter to Jeane J. Kirkpatrick, United Nations ambassador under Reagan, who along with other conservatives in the administration was growing concerned that Moynihan was too critical of the C.I.A. and covert activities in Central America.

PERSONAL AND CONFIDENTIAL
MAY 1, 1984

Dear Jeane:

I am sure you feel as I do that every effort be made to avoid misunderstandings between us, so allow me to review the events that led to my proposing to resign as vice chairman of the Intelligence Committee (although not from the Committee itself).

A bit of background. Following a vast series of Congressional hearings on the C.I.A. during the mid-1970s, it was decided that a "Charter" should be drafted for the intelligence community, stating what it may and may not do. (The existing statutory language is a 194-word passage in the National Security Act of 1947). I was a member of the subcommittee involved. At one point the draft Charter reached 300 pages. Sanity took hold, and in 1980 we passed the Intelligence Oversight Act, a two-page affair, which simply stated that with respect to "any significant anticipated intelligence activity" we be given prior notice, with a constitutional escape clause if the President thinks it too tender. (In which event we are to be told as soon as possible.)

The Senate Committee was not told about the harbor mining as authorized by the President at the NSPG meeting of February 17. (You were present.) On April 9 Senator Goldwater wrote the Director of Central Intelligence and said this. He then left on a trip to Asia. On April 12, in an address at the Naval Academy, the Assistant to the President for National Security Affairs said that the Committee <u>was</u> informed. This appeared in the Friday press of April 13, just as I was about to leave for a trip to Japan with Howard Baker. I was stunned. I cancelled the trip, and when a journalist from the Brinkley show came by to film a segment for Sunday, it seemed to me as good a time as any to state my view that Barry Goldwater is not a liar.

Ten days later Mr. Casey, following lunch with the Majority Leader, delivered a handwritten letter of apology to the Chairman, and called me asking me not to resign. The next day Mr. Casey appeared before the Committee and "profoundly apologize(d)." The Committee issued a statement which began:

> The Senate Select Committee on Intelligence met on April 26 to review the events that led to the mining of Nicaraguan harbors and attacks on Nicaraguan ports. At the conclusion of this review, the Committee agreed that it was not adequately informed in a timely

manner of certain significant intelligence activity in such a manner as
to permit the Committee to carry out its oversight function. The Director of Central Intelligence concurred in that assessment.

At the request of the Committee, and "in light of the Director's acknowledgement," I agreed to stay on as Vice Chairman.

This may have seemed to you as "a way of avoiding a lot of the toughest
questions, and the toughest problems...." But from a Senator's point of view
the toughest question was whether or not the Executive was going to obey
the law. We take an oath to uphold those laws, which we also enact.

You took part in the decision to mine. Fair enough, if you thought that
wise. However, you were, in my view, badly let down by those who failed to
abide by the Oversight Act and inform the Senate.

*Letter to Mario Cuomo, complaining about Philip Geyelin, a columnist (and former
editorial page editor) at the* WASHINGTON POST, *and discussing the need to renovate
the Kleinhans Music Hall in Buffalo, New York, an architectural landmark.*

PERSONAL
PINDARS CORNERS
JULY 3, 1984

Dear Mario,

I gather the chairman of the State Power Authority sees you as a somewhat
overcompensating son of Italian immigrants.

I can only counsel resignation.

I have known Philip Laussat Geyelin ("grad. Episcopal Acad., Overbook,
Pa., 1940; B.A. Yale, 1944") for, well, a quarter century now. In that time I
have been a member of the cabinet or subcabinet of four Presidents, several
times an ambassador, a professor of government at Harvard, a Senator, and,
gad Sir, a member of Henry L. Stimson's club!

No matter, I am still an "Irish pol" to Geyelin, even when he is trying to be
nice.

Thank you for your nice note about the tax bill. The secret clause preserves
a sale-leaseback option for the Kleinhans Music Hall in Buffalo. I am sure

you know it. It is a masterwork of Saarinen father and son. Trouble was that if you've never seen it, it <u>sounds</u> like a run down burlesque hall, and it took a huge effort, but we got it. Now we need a buyer. It is my understanding that the symphony is at stake. We have got to keep that orchestra, tear down that steel mill, maybe bring the university back down town—which it never should have left—do something, anything, to perk up Buffalo. I also got an IDB exemption for a marina they want to build, and will. The steel plant has good harbor facilities. The Niagara Frontier Transportation Authority is brainless. [James] Larocca [New York State commissioner of transportation] should have a look.

Finally, my great thanks to the Rockefeller Institute for their help on the FISC. Thanks to them, this was our best product. Not the cheeriest, however.

Letter to L. Bruce Laingen, career diplomat and former hostage held at the U.S. Embassy in Tehran, explaining why he favored moving the U.S. Embassy to Jerusalem from Tel Aviv, a position opposed by the State Department.

PERSONAL

PINDARS CORNERS

JULY 11, 1984

My dear Bruce,

It is unconscionable that I have taken so long to answer your plain and sensible note of March 27th. Put it down to the difficulty of finding an adequate reply.

Here is my problem. I was appalled at our vote in the Security Council in March 1980 in favor of a resolution declaring Jerusalem to be occupied Palestinian territory. Just in legal terms, what is Palestinian. What does that tell the Israelis about our expectations for their future? But when asked, Washington ambassadors would reply that of course they only meant East Jerusalem, or the Arab quarter of East Jerusalem, etc.

In February 1983 I was in New Delhi, and got hold of a copy of the Indian drafted Final Declaration for the Nonaligned Summit that was to meet the next month. This was a hurried arrangement: Baghdad had been the designated site. The Indians were most conservative in the draft, which they hadn't expected to be doing. The boiler plate of the NAM was simply restated. (I don't suppose you restate boiler plate, you simply re-use it.) A section stated that "Jerusalem" was occupied Palestinian territory. At the March meeting few changes were made in the draft. The Jerusalem section, however, was changed to read "West Jerusalem" was/is occupied Palestinian territory.

This seemed to me outrageous. If the United States has an interest in peace in the Middle East, the Indians and their friends surely did not advance it. I decided that in the circumstances we should move our Embassy to West Jerusalem. (Which had emptied out after the March 1980 resolution.) The present situation is anomalous. The State Dept telephone directory lists Jerusalem as a country, with its consulate in Jerusalem. On the same page with the Country Israel, where the consulate is in Tel Aviv. (We do not recognize East Berlin as the Capital of the G.D.R., but we have our embassy there.)

The proposal was no great novelty. The Democratic Platform called for the move in 1976 and 1980 (and does so again this year). People will swear President Reagan told a group in 1980 that he would do the same. In any event, I offered the move as an amendment to the State authorization bill last September, as I recall. Percy said there had been no hearings. I asked would he have such if I withdrew. He said yes, I did. The hearings waited till February, again as I recall. No hurry by me. Then the issue got caught up in the March Democratic primary in NYS.

I am fully sensible of your concerns. You of <u>all</u> persons. But I can't get anyone on State to talk to me in terms of how to solve our problem. I keep warning George [Secretary of State George Shultz] about accidents. A majority of the Senate has cosponsored the bill. Anyone can offer it on any measure. Who's being careless now?

Could you help? For heaven's sake don't get involved if you're not welcome or don't care to do. But just possibly. . . .

Letter to Bob Grady of the PLATTSBURGH PRESS-REPUBLICAN, *explaining why he speaks and writes for money as Senator—because he needs the money. His reference is to his article on nuclear arms negotiations for the* NEW YORKER *in 1979.*

PERSONAL

JULY 22, 1984

Dear Bob Grady,

Hey! Thanks! We take such an awful beating on those earnings reports. It is over now, as we are limited henceforth to something like $21,000. (Hence my scurrying to pay six years accumulated bills!) But somehow in all this umbrage the plain fact is overlooked that just about half the Senators today are millionaires. I do not suppose this can ever have been the case before—even in constant dollars. This is getting just a bit out of touch would you not agree? Yet all the fuss is directed at those of us who have no capital, must speak and write for money (as I would normally do; have done all my life) and pay half in taxes.

Three years ago I wrote a long article on SALT II for a journal—the journal—that pays well. They sent me—routinely—a check for $20,000. I had to explain that I could only accept $2,000. I then tried to arrange for the rest to be given to Syracuse University, but the Ethics Committee said no. <u>Now</u> were I to <u>own</u> that magazine they could send me a $20,000 check once a day, with no difficulties whatever.

This could become a problem for democracy. Your editorial was the only one I have yet seen—I see a lot of the other!—which suggests as much.

Excerpt of a letter to John Chancellor, the NBC news anchor and commentator, arguing presciently that the Soviet Union's military and economic capability was overestimated. Moynihan's former aide, Tim Russert, had also joined NBC.

SEPTEMBER 25, 1984

Dear Jack:

... For some years I have been arguing that what the United States lacks in dealing with the Soviet Union is a <u>strategy</u>. That strategy must begin with the central fact of Soviet failure. They cannot modernize their economy. They cannot expect to keep their empire together. Etc. Therefore, they will decline. Therefore our strategy should be to permit this decline to go forward without erupting into one last spasmodic effort to restore their fortunes by seizing the Gulf, or striking Western Europe, or even launching a first strike against the United States. It is in the context of <u>strategy</u> that you decide policy. Does a policy of selling them grain fit with a strategy of containing their decline? Probably yes. Does a policy of stirring up the Eastern satellites meet with such a strategy? Probably no. Central America. China. Angola. Positions on discrete issues flow from a general strategic position.

The problem of the Reagan Administration is that they started out asserting almost the opposite. Thus, the President started going on about the Soviets having achieved nuclear superiority. I would argue back on the occasional television show, but to no avail, whilst a good many Democrats didn't want to argue at all. Strobe Talbott writes in his new book <u>Deadly Gambits: The Reagan Administration and the Stalemate in Nuclear Arms Control</u> that never before "had a President made pessimism about the existing state of the military balance a basic and continuing tenet of his world view and program."

Of a sudden, however, there is a great reversal, of which the President's U.N. speech <u>may</u> be an example. For certain, something very close to this line of argument is being made in the higher circles of the government here. . . .

I enclose a copy of <u>The Washington Times</u> and of Evans and Novak, and also an article I wrote for <u>Newsweek</u> in 1979 suggesting that the big event of the then-approaching decade could well be the breakup of the Soviet Union.

Meyer's assessment is straightforward. We must, in effect, manage the Soviet decline, and particularly assure them that we have no intention of trying to hasten it. The sources of decline, in other words, are internal and inevitable. Easy does it is the obvious prescription. Alas, Evans and Novak turn this into "the days ahead 'will be the most dangerous that we have ever known.'"

We are all so proud of Tim Russert down here, and know you will enjoy his company as hugely as we miss it.

Letter to Secretary of State Shultz, arguing that the United States should use the International Criminal Court to defend its actions. Moynihan became increasingly convinced that the United States should defend its policies as aligned with international law.

NOVEMBER 30, 1984

Dear George:

There is no reason you should know this, but since coming to the Senate I have spoken with some frequency on the subject of international law. It has seemed to me that our sense of this subject has faded: a concern that was once near to the center of American foreign policy has somehow drifted off to the periphery.

As an instance, following the seizure of our embassy in Tehran, it was weeks before we finally went to the International Court of Justice. I believe the history is that it wasn't until I raised the question in the Senate that any action was taken. It seemed to me clear that the Court would promptly declare the rights and wrongs of the issue, which is exactly what a unanimous Court did, and did promptly.

Thus I was aghast last spring when Nicaragua took us to the Court over the mining of their harbors and the United States responded that it could not accept the jurisdiction of the Court. At minimum it was a doomed argument, the terms of the U.S. acceptance of the Court's jurisdiction being so explicit. Thereafter our people up at the United Nations developed a singularly bizarre theory that matters involving military confrontation are inadmissible per se in the Court. I said at the time that the proposition revealed a combination of ignorance and arrogance altogether, as lawyers might say, with precedent.

Now, this week, the Court has overwhelmingly rejected both arguments. Our contention with respect to jurisdiction was rejected 15–1 with only the American judge supporting us. The question of admissibility was rejected 16–0.

I think it is fair to say that the U.S. has never sustained so severe a setback in an international tribunal. I cannot see how the men who thought up those arguments in any way served our President or our country.

All this was absolutely predictable. Yet the Times reports

> State Department lawyers, who had recently said they had an "open and shut" legal case on jurisdiction, seemed stunned today by the lopsided vote of the Court, if not by the outcome.

I put it to you that no half-competent lawyer had any right to be surprised, much less "stunned."

There is now evidently talk that we might next simply walk away. It seems to me that would be profoundly ill-advised; it would break with one of the oldest commitments of American foreign policy.

At the time the case first arose, I argued that we would surely lose on the issue of jurisdiction and that it would be far better to welcome the opportunity to meet Nicaragua in Court to discuss what has been going on in Central America and to bring El Salvador into the case as well. That is still possible. I plead with you to consider that a matter of great importance is at stake here.

Letter to Graham Allison, dean of the John F. Kennedy School of Government at Harvard, urging more study of social science issues, including the achievements of the Great Society.

JANUARY 24, 1985

Dear Graham:

I have been thinking more about the subject for the Godkin Lectures and have come to the judgment that while I could make a good enough case that the Marxist-Leninist era is over, I don't think I could make the definitive case. Principally because I am not a Marxist-Leninist scholar, and in fact, know precious little about the internal workings of the Soviet Union. One way to put it simply is that too many people in the audience would ask afterwards whether I spoke Russian!

On the other hand, social science and social policy is something I do know, or did teach. I have been hard at work for the last couple of months on a set of propositions about the present impasse in social policy. I don't know quite what got me started, but there was nothing to do in December, and I suppose I was thinking that this coming spring will be the 20th anniversary of "The Moynihan Report." My proposition goes about as follows:

We have entered a deeply conservative period in our politics which is characterized not just by the fact that there are no social initiatives taking place, but more significantly that none are being proposed. In part this is the result of a long sequence of evaluation studies which gave rise to Rossi's "Iron Law" which he proposed in a paper given in 1968.

If there is any empirical law that is emerging from the past decade of
widespread evaluation research activities, it is that the expected value
for any measured effect of a social program is zero.

At the same time, this is misread as a generalized proposition that the programs of The Great Society "failed." This is nonsense and can be demonstrated. The programs that are directed to the aging have brought us to the
point where the per capita income of the elderly now exceeds that for the
population as a whole. A parallel problem is that in the aftermath of the response to my report, a twenty year silence commenced in which almost no
one worked on the subject. Your colleague Glenn Loury has recently written
this, as has Julius Wilson in Chicago. In any event, we look up at the twenty
years and find a situation far worse than even I anticipated, and very possibly
irreversible. In any event, there are no resources in the public Fisc to attempt
any efforts of that order. All of which has the makings of a permanent social
crisis. Loury writes, for example:

> If the new American dilemma is not dealt with soon, we may face the
> possibility of a permanent split in our political system along racial lines.

I would like to discuss what role social science can play in response to all
this and generally examine the entrails for clues to the future. I think such a
discourse would touch on a number of important issues in which interest is
just now reviving—with luck, not too late.

I can <u>do</u> this for you, and right or wrong, there will not be many people
taking issue with me. Can we agree on this course?

*Excerpt of a letter to Prime Minister Rajiv Gandhi of India, shortly after his elec-
tion victory, which occurred months after he succeeded to the post upon the assassination of his mother, Indira Gandhi. Elizabeth, with Maura, was at that moment
in India, documenting the archaeological excavation of a garden built by the first
Mogul emperor, Babur, at a site she had discovered in 1979.*

JANUARY 24, 1985

Dear Mr. Prime Minister:

. . . I wholly agree! How could there not be differences in our respective perceptions of world events from what are virtually opposite sides of the earth! And why oughtn't we differ? At times Canada and the United States seem hardly to agree on anything, save that we are brother democracies with the deepest interest in protecting our shared democratic values and institutions. And that gets us through the most confounding difficulties with barely a raised voice.

For nations blessed with such values and institutions, what other nation could matter more than India?

I much agree that India is so often misinterpreted or misunderstood. When I left New Delhi in 1975 I returned home by way of Beijing where the then-Foreign Minister (little did I realize a member of the Gang of Four!) had indicated he would like to exchange views on Indo-Chinese matters. On the way there I stopped over in Hong Kong and addressed the Press Club. I talked, naturally enough, about what a fine place India was, and these remarks duly appeared in the local newspapers. On my arrival home I found a letter waiting for me from your mother in which she remarked in the most moving way how rare it was to see a pleasant remark about India in the foreign press. How she could have come to see the "cuttings" I will never know, but nor will I ever forget her letter and its message.

My wife and daughter are just now in Rajasthan where they are measuring and photographing the garden palace of Babur which Liz discovered in 1979. The Archaeological Survey has been enormously helpful and generous in the whole, not uncomplicated undertaking, and I take the opportunity to express our thanks to you.

And finally, of course, great congratulations on your historic victory. The flourishing Gujarati and Bengali and Tamil citizenry of New York City are hugely admiring!

Letter to Mrs. Moynihan, while she travels in India, reporting on President Reagan's second inauguration.

JANUARY 24, 1985

NAMESTE!

It has taken an age to get your proper address, but hope this gets through, as I think you will enjoy having the Prime Minister's letter, and also news that the 1988 campaign is heating up. Thank heaven she doesn't speak Hindi, or at least not that I know of.

Inauguration was a bit of an anti-climax. After all that summery autumn the country fell into true freezing—hope it didn't make its way to Rajasthan—and the outdoor ceremony <u>and</u> the inaugural parade had to be cancelled. City quite empty. Thanks to Tim Russert (I cannot doubt) I started out the post inaugural address commentary with Roger Mudd. I got in one good line with respect to the Star Wars defense, to which the President gave great attention. The problem, I said, was that while the Senate continued to be concerned with missiles coming in from outer space the newest and most revolutionary innovation in weaponry was the cruise missile which would come in under the Brooklyn Bridge. (That <u>is</u> the problem with his space shield.) . . .

Rolling Stone just out with big Russert piece "A Man This Good Is Hard to Find." Lance Morgan hands me a note that Marty Peretz [owner of the *New Republic*] has had an attack of angina, but will not need bypass surgery (says member of New Republic staff.) Spent most of day on arms talks observer business. If not careful the ten of us will spend the next three years in Geneva [where arms talks were under way].

Must call Marty, get tomorrow's schedule and escape courtyard with jeep before eight o'clock.

Much love and sufficient warmth. . . .

Excerpt of a letter to Mrs. Moynihan in India, reporting on politics, parties, and dental problems. The 60 MINUTES *reference is to a televised feature about Arkady Shevchenko, a Soviet diplomat stationed at the United Nations when Moynihan was there and who later became one of the country's highest-level officials to defect or to "come in the from the cold."*

FEBRUARY 5, 1985

Dearest Liz,

... Much Hullabaloo over the 60 Minutes program Sunday. It was twenty minutes, just me and Shevchenko. Front page of the Times and Post Monday morning. Odd, people are responding as if no one noticed his coming in from the cold—what?—six years ago.

I went up to Norman's affair, as I told you. Nice letter from him, and commentary from Marty. (Who is obviously better.) Wish I were same. In Puerto Rico this weekend tooth trouble began. Unmistakable onset. Funny feeling, aspirin, worse feeling, more aspirin. Couldn't get to dentist today, but fear another round of root canals. ...

Letter to David Rockefeller, then former chairman of Chase Manhattan Bank and prominent businessman, philanthropist, and family patriarch. Moynihan regrets hitting Rockefeller up for campaign funds.

PERSONAL AND CONFIDENTIAL
MARCH 8, 1985

Dear David,

I fear I embarrassed you terribly by calling last week about fundraising. It was a dim idea of otherwise very bright people who help me with these things. Do not give it another thought. On the other hand, do not put it out of your mind that you might buy a ticket or two!

The President gave a most interesting breakfast at the White House this morning for the Senate observers going off to Geneva. Alas, I shall not be among them as the Budget Committee meets all next week, and I must be around to fight over the scraps that have fallen, as you might say, from the defense table. And increasingly, of course, the inexorable problem of debt service.

Bud McFarlane [national security advisor] tells me that [Soviet leader Konstantin] Chernenko is either dead or will be within the week. This to my mind argues a long negotiation on arms control, if only because the Soviet pattern of leaders coming in weak and only gradually consolidating their power. What was it—five years?—that it took Brezhnev before he felt secure enough to move into Stalin's office. On the other hand, the Russians do seem to be interested in an agreement and are making quite extraordinary proposals to us in private—by us I mean the Senate observers who really have nothing to do with negotiations but are really background sources.

Best to my farmer friend [Mrs. Rockefeller].

Letter to Moynihan's lawyer Joseph Kehoe, about setting up a trust to which he could contribute honoraria and other payments that exceeded Senate rules on gifts. The trust later became a source of small controversy for Moynihan when he was accused of operating a "slush fund," after which he shut it down.

SEPTEMBER 14, 1985

Dear Joe,

Some while ago I learned—after eight years!—that our $2000 limit on speech honoraria, and $22,000 or so limit on annual outside earned income (i.e. if you are not a millionaire collecting dividends) is not absolute in that amounts above the $2000 per speech and the annual limit can be given to charity. On the Income Tax return the money is reported as income and deducted as a charitable contribution: hence a wash.

A while back I formally applied to the Ethics Committee for "approval" of my setting up a charitable trust to which I might contribute such excess income as I can garner. The point is that there are no heavy demands on me in this regard. My one enterprise has been to establish an annual award at the Maxwell School at Syracuse for excellence in an untenured member of the faculty. This will require $20,000, and I shall have paid up by the end of the year. After that I would like to begin building up a small trust. The thought is that when I leave the Senate I will still be a quasi public person with some demands made on him, but I shall have no income save a Federal pension and some rapidly diminishing lecture fees. A trust would give me the wherewithal to maintain a certain shabby gentility.

Now then: Would you consider drawing up the necessary papers for purposes of incorporation and such? I assume that the legal costs involved are a legitimate deduction, or perhaps a legitimate expense of the trust itself. Check this out first, and let me know, for I wish to pay <u>full</u> legal fees, but would have to reconsider the whole enterprise if these are not "deductible."

Name? The Moynihan Trust. Something such. Purpose: general charitable activity. If something more specific is required—I should hope not—educational activity. I assume there are to be trustees. Would prefer that these be simply myself and Liz, but you let me know. We have three adult children.

Bob Peck [of Moynihan's staff] has my correspondence with the Ethics Committee, which you will want to get hold of, if this task commends itself to you, and if I can pay for it!

Excerpt of a letter to Governor Mario Cuomo, discussing whether former Representative Geraldine Ferraro, the New York Democrat who had run unsuccessfully for vice president with Walter Mondale in 1984, would be willing to challenge Senator Alfonse D'Amato in 1986. Much of her time running for the vice presidency was consumed rebutting charges of irregularities in her and her husband's finances. Ms. Ferraro did not run in 1986 but she did run (unsuccessfully) for the Democratic nomination for Senate in 1992 and 1998.

NOVEMBER 20, 1985

Dear Mario:

... Geraldine has just come by for a long talk. She is exhausted and troubled and quite incapable of making up her mind about anything. Apparently the Justice Department is still pursuing her and John about intra-family loans in the 1978 campaign. He was down here yesterday talking with his lawyers and Justice Department representatives for an awful ten- or twelve-hour stretch. She reports that the Philadelphia Inquirer assigned 26 investigative reporters to her case during her campaign. (Does the Philadelphia Inquirer have 26 reporters of any sort?) One of them is doing an "unauthorized biography." Full of Newburgh Mafia tales. All of which makes her feel she simply can't run. And yet when I say to her: "Geraldine, you aren't going to run, are you?" she comes back: "Yes, I might." Then allows that today she is against it, but that yesterday she was for it and likely [would] be again tomorrow. No, they will not make a decision by Thanksgiving. They are going off to St. Croix the first week in December and will make a decision then. We couldn't have had a more affectionate talk, but I cautioned that she mustn't give the impression of being unable to decide.

Barring one consideration (about which we might talk in private), it seems to me overwhelmingly likely that she will not run, and therefore we must find a candidate. She tells me that you and she talked about Felix Rohatyn but that his Liz won't have it. Time passes and the election will go by default if we don't organize ourselves. . . .

Letter to his friend Paul Horgan, the author, novelist, and poet.

DECEMBER 8, 1985

Dear Mr. Horgan,

I am an admirer of your poetry and aspire to becoming a poet myself. Last evening, returning from a restaurant where we dined on Beaujolais nouveau, I composed the following lyric:

> *Louis Quatorze*
> *Peed outdoors.*
> *He led the Nation*
> *In sanitation.*

My wife said first that this was not funny and second that I was drunk. If you do not agree what would you recommend? I have tried thumping her but she thumps back.

Excerpt of a letter to Secretary of State Shultz urging that the State Department keep better record of votes at the United Nations.

Dear George:

. . . One of my first surprises on going to the U.N. in 1975 was to learn that neither our Mission there nor the Bureau down here (I.O.) kept any voting records. As a sometime professor of government, this struck me as odd—Americans <u>invented</u> voting records—and led to the general thought that as an <u>old</u> country with an extraordinary continuity of institutions—I count seven members of the U.N. that both existed in 1914 and have not had their government changed by violence since 1914—we have had difficulty learning new ways. (I recall when going off to India being called in by one of the senior career officers to be told in great confidence that the Department quite understood that I was not someone with personal resources and that I was going to a big place, and that if I found I just couldn't manage on the representation allowance, Benjamin Franklin had left a bequest that was available to help in such circumstances.) I came to feel that we had difficulty connecting bilateral relations with multilateral ones. No one in Washington cared how countries voted, or generally speaking, behaved in New York.

This can have consequences. Early in my stay up there I had dinner with the Egyptian Ambassador. We talked about the 1973 war with Israel. He remarked that it might not have happened if the United States had not vetoed the Indian resolution in the Security Council. I left shaking. I had never <u>heard</u> of any Indian resolution, and I had been in New Delhi at the time. With war in the offing, and still to come the oil embargo and all that, could it be I was vacationing in Kashmir or simply napping in Roosevelt House and paid no attention when I could easily have rushed over to the Foreign Secretary and pleaded with him to stay out of the Middle East if they expected us to stay out of the Indian Ocean, etc. Discreet, nay timorous enquiries in Washington gradually led to a considerable surprise. The Department, while deeply concerned with the Indian proposal and gearing up to veto when we rarely did that, had never once asked if the New Delhi embassy could help out with the government <u>in</u> India, where their U.N. instructions were coming from.

In time I discovered a professor at the Naval Academy who had twenty years or so of voting records on a computer which he used in a course on international relations. We got a terminal in New York. (He got tenure!) A three person operation was started up in I.O. to keep embassies posted on how countries were voting, and to try to pick up some votes here and there. (We could show that so far as half the countries in the world are concerned, our only significant relations are <u>at</u> the U.N. and suchlike places. It gives our poor man in Ougadougou something to do! Which is where I left it.)

The scene shifts to Beijing last August. Bob Dole had taken a delegation of seven Senators on a trade-oriented trip to the Far East. On the next to last day came the Big Meeting with Deng Xiaoping. Early in the trip Dole had worked out an arrangement by which one of us, each in turn, would take the lead in our successive meetings. With Deng there were a number of issues to be raised, and a number of us spoke by this prearrangement.

Deng opened the meeting by declaring that the relations between the United States and the People's Republic were such that there would be "no need to use diplomatic language." Our bilateral relationship had "entered a new stage" of friendship and nobody could "obstruct this."

When my turn to speak came I referred to what he had said about our bilateral relations, adding that our delegation surely hoped this was the case. However, when we looked at our relations at the United Nations we saw a very different picture. It was as if the People's Republic had a Two United States Policy. (Two America Policy is a better term.) Thus at the 1984 General Assembly the P.R.C. had voted against the United States, as we saw it, and in favor of the Soviet Union 87 percent of the time. This was a higher figure even than that for the Non-Aligned Nations which for practical purposes were mostly aligned with the Russians. Yet more worrisome was the record of the P.R.C. on what we call "name calling votes." These are votes in the General Assembly or the Security Council where the United States asks that some quite gratuitous insult to the United States be excised from some resolution or whatever. In 1984 we chose 20 such incidents and kept count of how nations voted. To our great disappointment, barring three absences, on every such occasion the P.R.C. voted against the United States and with the Russians who invariably were the source of the insult. One such vote condemned the United States for "continued nuclear cooperation" with South Africa. This we found difficult to understand and in the circumstances unwelcome. . . .

If you're still with me, this won't take much longer.

The point of the episode in Beijing is this. At no point in our journey, from the briefing books handed us on the plane, to the staff conference at the embassy, was any mention made of the Chinese behavior at the U.N. (Nor of Korean or Japanese, for that matter.) The thought to raise the subject with Deng came to me once we had arrived, and I got to thinking things were a mite too cozy. I cabled Washington and the information I asked for was immediately provided. First-rate work. Ambassador Harvey J. Feldman at U.S.U.N. had all the information at his fingertips. <u>But I had to ask for it.</u> It still isn't provided routinely as information a CODEL [i.e. Congressional Delegation] would find of interest. And so I ask. Do our ambassadors and negotiators know? Which is only to say that in my view we are never going to break out of the present U.N. patterns until we press home in capitals that it matters how they vote in New York and Geneva. . . .

Have a great Christmas. And slow down.

Excerpt of a letter to Chancellor Joseph Murphy of the City University of New York, explaining why his wife, Elizabeth Moynihan, deserves an honorary degree. The CUNY Graduate Center awarded her a doctor of letters degree in 1986.

PERSONAL
DECEMBER 27, 1985

Dear Joe:

. . . You know, you're right. I have been thinking about it, and by God you are right. I have fifty-two honorary degrees, and have perhaps become just a little insensitive to how much they can mean to someone who has none of any kind.

And so, for the first time in our thirty years of marriage, it has occurred, thanks to you, to this ingrate to compose a <u>vitae</u> for Liz. Something she would never do herself.

I have known all these bits and pieces <u>as</u> bits and pieces. Assembling them in some order produces a very different picture.

First, Liz is a scholar, specifically an archaeologist, of signal and widely acknowledged achievement. The Regius professor of something or other pronounced <u>Paradise as a Garden</u> to be the "definitive work" in the <u>Times Literary Supplement</u>. To write the book she made her way through valleys in Afghanistan that a Soviet armored brigade could not traverse. (Secret? Took daughter with her. Grey-haired mother in kurta, unmarried daughter: Allah protects.) She has been to parts of Iran we may never again see in this century; to chunks of Soviet Asia that may yet be off bounds, and to regions of India which are, well to be frank, getting dangerous.

Her discovery of Babur's "lotus garden" was the most important archaeological find in India in half a century, and the <u>Indians</u> said so. They asked her back to survey the site on behalf of the Archaeological Survey of India. I believe she is the <u>only</u> Westerner granted such a privilege.

Second, she has become an academic administrator of genuine achievement, or at least heroic effort. You have probably never heard of the American Schools of Oriental Research, but it is the network, or what you will, of biblical archaeology in this country. (There is a general distinction between biblical and classical, but everything gets mixed up in the Middle East, a fact which you <u>do</u> know!) The centers, Albright in Jerusalem (where the Dead Sea scrolls were authenticated), Amman, Damascus, and suchlike were there generations before the present countries were established. There would be no chance of setting up an American institution in most of these places today, accepting scholars and students from 500 or so American institutions. (And I mean American. Every member of the Ivy League, every Bible School in Arkansas.) Political conditions in the Middle East have caused various crises, which is why Liz, a diplomat and a politician as well as a scholar, was asked to become the organization's first-ever Chairman of the Board.

And then she went and organized CAORC which brings the classical academies—Rome, Athens—in with the Biblical ones and after nursing it for the Smithsonian for a few years, got it named in statute a few weeks ago. She feels, and with reason, that these institutes give more local prestige to the United States than a dozen USIA transmitters. Among other things, they are creating histories for nations that on their own have none.

She is more than just a scholar or administrator. A human rights issue such as the fate of Raoul Wallenberg can absorb her. She <u>sees</u> what it can teach others. Incidentally, thanks to her and her committee there is to be a Wallenberg Collection at the New York Public Library, which will provide travelling exhibits for other places.

But I go on, and you have got the point. Do you suppose Hunter might be interested? I know that [Hunter College president] Donna [Shalala] thinks that careers such as Liz's should be recognized more.

At all events, thank you for even thinking of the matter.

Walter B. Wriston, former chairman of Citicorp, also served on the board at New York Hospital, which was opposing Moynihan's legislation to do an inventory of

the work of the great nineteenth-century landscape architect (and designer of Central Park), Frederick Law Olmsted.

JANUARY 29, 1986

Dear Walter:

I really do think you owe yourselves an explanation of the behavior of the attorneys representing New York Hospital in this zoning dispute in Westchester.

As you know, over two years ago I introduced in the company of Rep. Seiberling in the House a simple bill that called for nothing more than that the National Park Service compile an inventory of the work of Frederick Law Olmsted and his associates. . . .

This simple measure was making its way through the legislative process when on June 13 I received calls from you and John Weinberg telling me that this would complicate a problem New York Hospital was having in White Plains where it hoped to develop some property it owned there. In a familiar enough pattern some local residents opposed this. Part of the objections included the claim that this was an Olmsted landscape and needed to be preserved. This argument had been going on for a very long while—well before our legislation was introduced. Even so, I said that I would surely not want to have anything happen down here that would seem to have an adverse effect on the hospital, and said I would promptly look into the matter.

That was a perfectly good faith response on my part. I do not believe there was a comparable response on the part of your lawyer, Mr. Chauncey L. Walker. To the contrary, the man commenced a veritable campaign directed at me and our legislation. He went about the country rousing alarm that H.R. 37 was going to close down Massachusetts General Hospital, Princeton, Harvard, Cornell, what you will. Believe me, the tales are atrocious, and I do not find them amusing. Observe the enclosed three-page letter from Harvard University which included the dreadful accusation that if you start listing the Olmsted parks in the country, "will other bills follow for the work of Louis Sullivan, Frank Lloyd Wright, and other designers? . . ." (In an interview in The New York Times of January 27, not coincidentally, Mr. Walker states, "It's a dangerous precedent to have a special bill, even for Olmsted. If this bill passes, will the next bill be for Frank Lloyd Wright?") Heaven forfend! . . . That this fellow Walker could reduce Harvard to the philistine level of the enclosed letter is a matter for Harvard's concern, I suppose. But I take very serious objection to your man having lobbied that university as he has lobbied other universities to encourage my colleagues to take an action against legislation I have offered. He has done this without speaking to me or informing me. I have been shown memoranda he has written to the government affairs committee, or whatever exactly is the name, of the Hospital which I find offensive in the extreme. I do not think it right that I should be treated so. . . .

Letter to Alan Bullock, the British historian, asking for inclusion of an essay on ethnicity in THE FONTANA DICTIONARY OF MODERN THOUGHT, *a favorite Moynihan reference book. He was proud that the dictionary agreed to run his small contribution.*

JULY 7, 1986

Dear Sir(?) Alan:

I have for some years now kept the Fontana Dictionary of Modern Thought in my school house here in upstate New York where, at intervals, I have been scribbling away for a quarter-century. It is a delight; and an overwhelming achievement.

This morning, however, I set out about organizing what perforce must pass for thoughts in a lecture I am to give this fall, in return for which the Encyclopaedia Britannica folk are to give me a gold medal. (They started this up just his year: the Astronomer Royal of Scotland is a fellow medalist.) I had in mind to pursue the general subject of social science: does it have any predictive qualities, that sort of thing. I have in mind a "model" of the American political economy which I set forth a decade ago, and which seems to be proving out. (To use an oil field image.) I am stumbling about trying to describe how I got there and why I think I'm on to something. Here my best case history is a book Nathan Glazer (now at Harvard) and I wrote a quarter-century ago (<u>Beyond the Melting Pot: The Negroes, Puerto Ricans, Jews, Italians, and Irish of New York City</u>; M.I.T. Press, 1963) which argued that ethnicity far from being a premodern holdover, was in fact quite a viable social form, and likely to become more prominent in post-industrial societies. (To which I would now add post-colonial.) In the early 1970s the two of us cobbled together a seminar at the American Academy of Arts and Sciences, out of which came a big collection: Ethnicity: Theory and Experience (Harvard, 1975. A dear friend, Dan Bell, one of your Consultant Editors was also one of our contributors.) Typically, he contributed the most compelling formulation: that ethnic groups combine "affect with interest."

Right or wrong, and as I saw we have been at this for a quarter-century, we have been testing the Marxist thesis that industrialism "has stripped him [the proletarian] of every trace of national character. Law, morality, religions, are to him some many bourgeois prejudices, etc."

And of course I think we have been right: that Marx and Engels were wrong, and once you're wrong about that, you're wrong about a lot more things.

Well. My point is simply to ask why there is no entry in the Dictionary for "Ethnicity." As I learn this morning. You would be more within your rights to reply, "Sheer ignorance," as did Dr. Johnson. But it is just possible that you thought about an entry and dropped it. Which is either to say that our work (and that of many others) has not been accepted, or possibly that it has not been noticed. (In which event it still might be accepted!)

It is almost rude to write a letter of this length. But then you wrote a dictionary. And the briefest post card reply would be hugely appreciated.

Letter to John Cardinal O'Connor of New York, again expressing the view that the Soviet Union was experiencing difficulties, citing his wife's studies of the growing Muslim population.

FEBRUARY 19, 1987

Dear Cardinal O'Connor:

. . . It happens that my wife Elizabeth is an archaeologist who had wandered over most of Central Asia in search of Moghul ruins and antecedents. In point of fact, she was once named "Tourist of the Month" in Pravda Vostoka. (When the knock came on the hotel door instructing her to come immediately to the lobby, she thought the end had come. But only a photographer was waiting, not the KGB!) She returned fascinated by the intensity of Soviet anti-Muslim efforts. This would have been about seven years ago. At the Tashkent Airport they genuinely search for copies of the Koran being smuggled into Soviet Asia. Tashkent, Samarkand, and Bukhara are ancient cities which once had magnificent mosques. Wherever Liz went, however, it turned out there had been an earthquake which had leveled the ancient edifices. She wondered that 600-year-old brick towers were still standing, but the mosques had disappeared!

I would hold with the general assessment that Gorbachev is trying to get the rewards of a liberal economy without incurring the penalties—from his point of view—of a liberal polity. Theory says it can't be done, but on va voir, as the French say. My personal view is that the Soviet empire is in any event heading for an extended period of ethnic tensions and disorders. The recent riots in Alma-Ata are only the latest in a series of dramatic events which in the past four years have been sweeping through the five Soviet Central Asian Republics. One ethnic Russian party leader after another has been either fired, or, in one case, clearly committed suicide. The divergence in birthrates is extraordinary. The average family size is 3.3 compared with 6.0 or thereabouts in Central Asia. Most of the people speak Turkic (the five Republics are artificial affairs drawn in Moscow in 1924). And they are Sunnis. If Liz's observations are still valid, the attendance at mosque and prayer meetings is very considerable and considerably frowned upon.

Letter to Professor Uwe E. Reinhardt of Princeton, explaining his agreement with the view that the Reagan administration had cut taxes in order to create large budget deficits. David Stockman, Reagan's first budget director, had been an acquaintance of the Moynihans and a babysitter for their children while he was at Harvard Divinity School in the 1970s. His reference to the Washingtonians is to those who had served in previous administrations.

APRIL 10, 1987

Dear Professor Reinhardt:

I greatly enjoyed and hugely agreed with your article on Reaganomics and take the liberty of asking if you could not help me just a little more. You write:

It has been suggested that the administration deliberately triggered the large deficits to pressure Congress into overall spending cuts.

Here is my difficulty. Early in the Reagan administration [David] Stockman, who is an old acquaintance, or perhaps I should say an old young acquaintance, told me of his strategy. It seemed evident enough to me that that is what they had in mind, and when I pressed him, he agreed. I began writing about it. I enclose an article from The New Republic and a lecture at NYU. Some Washingtonians such as [Brent] Scowcroft, [John] Deutch, and [James] Woolsey (see enclosure), accept the proposition as being self-evident. Stockman's legal advisor at the time has said to me that he cannot understand why I go about claiming there is a conspiracy to bring about a deficit when it should have been as plain to anyone with eyes to see. i.e. they were doing just that and were a little surprised that no one seemed to notice.

Here is my question. Assuming the facts are right, and Stockman has since in his book stated explicitly that this was his purpose, why is it still a matter of conjecture and for that matter faint conjecture. My theory is that as a political culture Washington has almost no capacity for recognizing true <u>ideological</u> motivation. It is simply not possible for your average Member of Congress or editorial writer or lobbyist to believe that someone would actually create a crisis by inducing an enormous structural deficit. The President obviously does not think he did any such thing, and continues to ask for a Constitutional Convention to adopt a balanced budget amendment. What do you think, a professor of political economy?

Letter to Meg Greenfield, editor of the WASHINGTON POST *editorial page, proclaiming success at last in completing the construction plans for Pennsylvania Avenue, particularly a new international cultural and trade center. The center, eventually built and named the Ronald Reagan International Trade Center, housed in one of its wings the Woodrow Wilson International Center for Scholars, where Moynihan moved his office after leaving the Senate in 2001.*

MAY 2, 1987

Dear Heart,

I know, I know. You've heard it before. In the course of some twenty-six years, as I count. But this time, we've got it! KEY to Pennsylvania Avenue. U.S. International Cultural and Trade Center. Largest (not highest) building in town. Public corporation, finances construction on basis of thirty-year lease from GSA, after which building reverts to government. Zero cost. Vast efficiencies. Treasury goes from 38 locations in town to 4 . . . State to 3. Giant indoor mall, all purpose passport and visa services; trading in arms, armours, armadillos.

Largely thanks to Harry McPherson and an associate from the Federal City Council who has evidently made such a fortune renting to GSA over the past quarter century (since LBJ stopped building Federal buildings) that he feels he should give a little back. You never got yourself one of those babies on K Street, did you? Well, neither did I. Anyway, big point is that the Federal Triangle will be finished, Justice and Commerce finally back in a single build-ing complex and Andrew Mellon vindicated at last. Super GSA administrator Golden is all for it. Only OMB is surly: can't understand anything that doesn't cost money.

All that is lost is the world's oldest parking lot.

Check it out. Hard to believe, I know. Everybody on board. Held hearing yesterday. Bill to floor soon. Will wear Pearly Grey Trilby at dedication. (Open in five years.) Close out Pa. Ave. in thirty. Honest: this, with the things PADC has underway now, will wrap it up. And make you want to move into the Star Building.

CHAPTER ELEVEN

"We Have a Prospect of Peace on Earth"

Moynihan's service in the final years of the Reagan administration and the beginning of the administration of his friend, President George H. W. Bush, was marked by his intense joy and sense of vindication over the collapse of the Soviet Union. He took many opportunities to note his early and lifelong anti-Communism and his latter day conviction that ethnic and economic difficulties would doom the Soviet empire before long. In 1987–1988, Moynihan worried about his own reelection, in part because of his difficulty raising funds. He even thought about retiring from the Senate. As he pressed the cause for redevelopment of Pennsylvania Avenue and lower Manhattan he was bothered that the news media and others seemed to be ignoring his accomplishments. The many personal concerns in these letters include his unhappiness over having to deal with accusations that he had a drinking habit and his worry about lack of financial resources.

Letter to President Reagan, expressing thanks for his support of the Federal Triangle Development Act, again recounting the history of his involvement in the project to renovate Pennsylvania Avenue. Moynihan subsequently supported naming the international trade center on the avenue after Reagan. Jacqueline Kennedy Onassis wrote to Moynihan later in the year: "Twenty-five years is a long time to not give up on something. . . . You are right about my asking President Johnson to not let it fade away. . . . I think that the completed Pennsylvania Avenue will be a monument to your dedication. I hope that Americans realize that. I will be forever grateful,

*dear Pat, for your messages to me all along the way, for the spirit you brought to
something Jack cared about so deeply, and for this happy ending."*

AUGUST 24, 1987

Dear Mr. President:

May I express my great gratitude for your approving the Federal Triangle
Development Act.

This brings to a close a quarter century's effort on my part. On June 1,
1962, President Kennedy signed an order, which I had drafted, calling for the
redevelopment of Pennsylvania Avenue. Our plan was ready a year later, and,
as it happened, the last instruction the President gave before leaving for Dallas
was that on his return a coffee hour be arranged with the Congressional leadership where he could introduce the new plan. Well, of course, he never did
return and so the task devolved on me. Block by block, project by project, if I
may say, President by President, we have put it together and now it is finished,
thanks to you.

May I make one final point? In this age of what has been called the architecture of coercion, we set out to make Pennsylvania Avenue "lively, friendly
and inviting as well as dignified and impressive." The result is cluttered and
eclectic but very much American, and Americans should feel at home on the
Avenue of the Presidents. This looks accidental. It was nothing such.

Again, my great thanks.

*Letter to Senator Howard H. Baker, White House chief of staff under Reagan, sug-
gesting the political and diplomatic benefits of a presidential invitation to Moynihan's friend, the Irish-born Chaim "Vivian" Herzog, the president of Israel, for a
state visit. Herzog was Moynihan's colleague at the U.N. in battling the Zionism-
is-racism resolution.*

SEPTEMBER 17, 1987

Dear Howard:

Would you have ten minutes sometime for me to make the case for inviting Chaim Herzog to pay a State Visit? It is the curious and anomalous fact that while for thirty years Prime Ministers of Israel have practically camped out in Blair House, the President of Israel has never been invited to visit the United States. I believe this causes us more difficulties than perhaps we realize. In any event, Herzog is such an exceptional person. He was there at the United Nations when I was, and we have remained good friends withal at a distance.

I think it would be a master stroke for the President to invite him to visit sometime next year. At the risk of introducing ethnic considerations, you should know that Vivian is a genuine Belfast-born Irishman.

I can make this case in ten minutes, but it is something that needs to be done in person.

Having read of your indisposition, may I add that I will consider myself honor bound to get out within ten minutes and not ever to mention welfare!

Letter to Walter Shorenstein, the California real estate developer and Democratic Party contributor, expressing concern about campaign fundraising, gloomy thoughts about the upcoming presidential race, and his own reelection in 1988. He suggests that without funds he may not run for reelection, and this would jeopardize the Democratic nominee's chances in New York. He also shows chagrin that he is not himself being discussed as a presidential candidate, though he did not make any efforts himself to press such a candidacy. The reference to Senator Howard Metzenbaum, an Ohio Democrat, is to the campaign of savage attacks on him as he was preparing to run for reelection in 1988.

SEPTEMBER 29, 1987

Dear Walter:

[California Senator] Alan Cranston has passed on your note and your check. I write in awed appreciation. This sort of thing rarely happens—at all events, to this New Yorker.

I find myself baffled by my fundraising situation and wonder what to do. In the last campaign, after fighting off a sudden LaRouchite challenge [i.e. from a supporter of the cult leader and conspiracy theorist Lyndon LaRouche] in the primary, I had just $600,000 for the general election campaign. Thinking I had learned a lesson, I set to work early this time. Five years later I have a little more than $1 million. (Two weeks ago Bob Dole raised as much in one hour at a Manhattan cocktail party!)

This may mean I will not run [i.e. for reelection]. However, unless I run in 1988, it is almost certain that none of the present Democratic Presidential candidates can carry New York, which is to say we will not elect a Democratic President, and we will begin genuinely to recede as a competitive national party.

I don't suppose you are any more happy about the Presidential campaign than I am. With Gary [Hart] and Joe [Biden] shot down we look accident prone. I begin to think it is getting too late for my Governor [Mario Cuomo] to get in. The more then ought I to run. The more then ought New Yorkers who want to see a Democratic administration, to be part of one, to be useful to one—the more ought they to want to see me in a position to run. But they don't seem to put the two things together. They will raise money for just about any Senate candidate save their own.

The last time we won the Presidency, in 1976, I ran miles ahead of Carter. In 1982 I had a margin of 1,535,385, the largest in an off-year election in the history of the Senate. This was done by carrying 50 of the state's 62 counties, something no New York Democrat had ever previously come near. 1982 also marked the first time a Democratic Senator was re-elected having served a full term since Robert F. Wagner in 1944.

As your sainted uncle would attest, New York is not nearly so Democratic as people tend to think. We have controlled the state legislature for only four years in the 20th century. Owing mostly to personal history, I run as well "upstate" as in the City, which for nearly a century and a half has been the only reliable Democratic base. Herbert Lehman, for example, was elected with 5 counties—which is to say the City.

Nor have we New York Democrats helped our Presidential candidates all that much. We carried the state for Hubert by .01 percent, and have lost ever since save for Carter.

The Republicans know they will have a problem with me on the ticket. (I know this.) They will throw at least $10 million at me and probably have prepared an assassination manual as well—a la [Ohio Senator] Howard Metzenbaum.

Letter to John Darnton, metropolitan news editor of the NEW YORK TIMES, *recounting the "horrific experience" of erroneous reporting about the charitable foundation he had established to receive some of his speaking fees.*

OCTOBER 20, 1987

Dear John Darnton:

I have been thinking of our conversation about the scrutiny of public people, and it occurs to me that you might like to know of an occasion when the Times acquitted itself with great distinction, albeit negatively and albeit this is a personal view of mine.

Last May I had a truly horrific experience. Liz and I had gone up to the farm for the weekend and were opening up the house peacefully unaware that the phone wasn't working. Meanwhile, here in Washington, Doug Turner of the Buffalo News had got hugely excited on learning that we had set up a small charitable foundation using speaking fees that are in excess of the amount I can keep in the Senate. I had written the Ethics Committee about it to find out if it could be done and had a written response that it could be. Legal papers were approved by the IRS, and we received an official number, or something such. The Office of Charitable Trust of the Attorney General of the State of New York was duly notified, and all seemed peaceable and inconsequential until Turner learned that I had left it off a list of organizations to which I belong (Delhi Post #190 of the American Legion, Council on Foreign Relations, American Academy of Public Administration, etc.) and decided that I was absconding with the money or something such. The phones eventually started working, but I was unable to dissuade the reporter. I enclose the story that appeared on the front page the following morning as the lead story. Also a column by Murray Light offering a "public apology" for the headline.

The next day, having learned that a story had moved on the AP wire out of Buffalo, we called a number of papers to ask if we could give our version of the event.

Most, frankly, weren't much interested, and just ran the wire copy. The exception was the Times. We reached the wire desk and asked the editor if he planned to use it, and received the simple answer: "No, it's not true."

May I say that was important to me. The story wasn't true, of course. As Murray Light reconstructed, nobody in his newsroom realized that when money is contributed to a charity, title passes and is in no sense available for personal use. He told me he was going to have someone from the University Law School come over to explain it all. In any event, it didn't need explaining to the Times.

Letter to Nathan S. Ancell, cofounder of the Ethan Allen furniture company, with a fundraising plea and an apology for the fundraising plea.

PERSONAL AND CONFIDENTIAL
NOVEMBER 4, 1987

Dear Nat:

What a grand thing to have you a member of our Finance Committee! That and yesterday's sweep—Montauk to Niagara—make it a year to look forward to.

Well, almost. There is the fundraising! . . .

There is no thing more painful than raising money. At most one can wish that it not be degrading. That is why it makes all the difference that some such as you would join me. It is evidence that I may not after all be eternally damned; so much that eternity is not time enough to expiate my sins and that punishment must begin here and now on earth!

It is not made easier by the fact that I have now turned sixty, and after a lifetime in one or another form of government service I have no estate of any kind, and virtually no retirement benefits save the standard Federal pension. This begins at age 62, so that in my third term I will be working for half pay, as well as giving up any realistic chance to cobble together a modest estate.

Still, it has to be done. And do it I shall. We have entered a time of troubles. This will require new men. But also it will require some of the continuity that is the good fortune of parliamentary, but regimes lacking in the American arrangement. Thus I can claim to be the only person in American history to have served in the cabinet or subcabinet of four successive Presidents. But this occurred in a span of only twelve years!

I am now in my twelfth year in the Senate where the turmoil has if anything been greater. I am already the 35th ranking member (20th ranking Democrat). In a third term I would assume a position New York has not had since the early 1940s: a senior member of the Senate majority who will have worked in the closest terms with almost any of the men most likely to be the next President.

I have already done more than people know. In part because the things that have to be done . . . and not done . . . are difficult to understand. (Were it otherwise the City would not have been on the point of bankruptcy, fiscal and political, when I was elected the first time.)

You be of cheer; there will be no more letters of this length. But somehow I had to say thank you in a coin I do have at hand.

Moynihan's campaigns were often accompanied by accusations and suggestions in news reports that he had a drinking problem. In response, the columnist George F. Will wrote on December 7, 1987: "Does Pat Moynihan drink? My answer is: yes, thank God. He is my friend and I do not like to drink alone." But he added that it was not accurate to say that Moynihan drank "too much," and he attributed stories about the Senator's drinking to Irish ethnic stereotypes and the "odd cadences" of Moynihan's speech. Here Moynihan thanks Will and notes that his own speaking style has given some the impression of insobriety. The reference to "something that was excruciatingly present all those years" is evidently to the alcoholism of his father and perhaps other members of his family.

DECEMBER 2, 1987

Dear George:

How am I to tell you? How much it mattered. Meant. I know I have a speech impediment. (My brother is near to disabled by the same, I assume genetic trauma. Yet our youths were sufficient for nurture to have done its work.) Yet, I deny it. For it is close in the impression it makes to something that was excruciatingly present all those years. To what?—age about eleven, as I recall. In truth as I reconstruct; I recall almost nothing. Great thanks.

Letter to Yoko Ono, widow of John Lennon, agreeing to meet with young Sean Lennon to talk about Northern Ireland. The Lennons acquired property the Moynihans' had once owned near their farm.

NEW YORK, NEW YORK
JANUARY 18, 1988

Dear Ms. Ono,

I ought long since have answered your moving letter about your son Sean. I can imagine—only that, but still—his troubled concern about a still bleeding land which bred his father. (And farther back, my forbears and those of my wife Elizabeth.)

The specific situation in Ulster has engaged me continuously since going to the Senate, and I expect will do so as long as I am there. You would scarce imagine how difficult it is to persuade entirely peaceable and law abiding New Yorkers not to support violence in a world of which they have at most a muddled folk memory.

If you think it might be useful I would be delighted to have a talk with young Sean. We are staying at the Carlyle which, I believe is just across the Park from you. Between bouts at trying to learn to work this new typewriter I have plenty of free time this week. Perhaps you would write or telephone here. . . .

Letter to Woody Allen, discussing his views of ethnicity, apparently after the comic and director expressed bafflement over the persistence of ethnic conflict.

FEBRUARY 1, 1988

Dear Mr. Allen:

I wonder if this helps. Thirty years ago, it would be, Nat Glazer and I began work on a book we would call <u>Beyond the Melting Pot: The Negroes, Puerto Ricans, Jews, Italians, and Irish of New York City</u>. It is still around. Indeed, the Japanese Edition has just appeared. Me, I was mostly going on about the old neighborhood, but Nat had something much larger in mind. We were writing about the emergence of ethnicity as a post-modern social form. Tame enough stuff you might think, save as follows. If we were right, Marx was wrong. I expect you have to have gone to City College when we did to absorb the enormity of that proposition. The initial reception was, well, reserved. But we kept at it, and some fifteen years ago cobbled together a sort of general theory. (Ethnicity: Theory and Experience. I am sending you a copy with this letter.)

What we wrote may just slightly have helped others follow events of the years since, for surely they have been dominated by just this phenomenon. A small thing, the sort of detail you obviously like, occurred a year ago. There is a British volume entitled, The Fontana Dictionary of Modern Thought, a compendium of polymaths assumed under the auspices of my Lord Bullock of St. Catherine's. What they know not is not knowledge, as was said of that old Master of Balliol. I keep it in the school house along with a Webster's and a Who's Who, which is all anyone needs, at least in my experience. At all events, I happened one morning to note that there was no entry on Ethnicity. I wrote Bullock who invited me to contribute one. I then, of course, turned to Glazer. We produced a succinct entry (also enclosed) which declares in passing that the "Workers of the World belief, central to Marxism, is increasingly presented as central to the falsification of Marxist prediction." This was accepted without comment, and somewhere at home I have a fuss of papers which if filled out would net us five quid. Now then. Thirty years ago it would have been rejected out of hand. Falsification of Marxism, indeed. Fifteen years ago a genteel row of sorts would have broken out among the editors, and we would have been asked to revise. No longer. The great expectation of the 20th century declared to have been disproved by a pair of CCNY men, and Oxford agrees. (Or so I think. We will await publication of the 2nd Edition.)

My point is this. Do not be baffled. It is everywhere. I was once our Ambassador to India and returned for the funeral of Indira Gandhi. Shot dead in her garden by her own bodyguards. Sikhs loyal unto death now doing their ruler to death. That evening Howard Baker and I accompanied George Shultz on a sequence of bilaterals, as they are known in the trade. Other heads of government or foreign ministers in town also. At length we met with J.R. Jayewardene, President of Sri Lanka. Do you know that place? As near to the peaceable kingdom as ever existed. The Sri Lankese a Buddhist folk: gentle, humourous, accepting. Jayewardene, a man of transparent goodness and gentleness. He plain cried—tears—as he described mobs in Columbo dragging Tamils—who are Hindu and of a different ethnic stock—dragging Tamils from buses and throwing them alive into bonfires.

That is our world. Not the one we expected. The more then to try to understand it and cope.

I hope this is not tedious. I write out of great respect.

Letter to Dr. Leonardo Ramos, who took care of his mother, about her death.

APRIL 27, 1988

Dear Dr. Ramos:

As you know, we buried our mother Saturday morning. It was a small but warm occasion, first at the Coots Funeral Home where her father was laid out (as the term goes), and then at Walnut Ridge Cemetery, where she lies a few feet from her father and mother. In all an extraordinary sequence. Mother died about two hundred yards from where she was born, and was buried about a half mile from where she died.

She had a long life, full of adventure and at least a normal share of happiness. Never great in any life, I don't suppose. For us, and I am sure for mother, it was a great blessing to have your generous and loving care in those final days.

Our family is deeply grateful to you for your professional skill and great humanity and, of course, at the end, your reassurance and calm.

Letter to his lawyer, Joseph Kehoe, discussing matters related to his upstate farm and to the Derrymore Foundation, set up by Kehoe and Moynihan to receive some of his honoraria that ethics laws barred him from receiving directly.

JUNE 4, 1988

Dear Joe,

Two domestic matters.

First, would you address all Derrymore Foundation matters to me—not to Liz, who has much else on her mind—and none to me until after the election. Unless of course something urgent arises. Please also note that we are under no obligation to consider or yet to acknowledge unsolicited requests.

Second, I find the process of collecting rents on these two farms increasingly troublesome. A decade ago the two farmers would come to the school house some weekend in late June and just give me a check. Now it takes three to four months, lawyers, letters, whatever. All for the pittance I am paid compared with the taxes, much less any return on equity. This year will you get me my rent on July 1 and no later. Please let them know ahead of time that this is what you expect. Send a taxi to collect. Or Whatever. Please no elaborate new leases. Just an agreement that the rent is the same next year as this year and the terms also.

Off campaigning!

Letter to Gary McCulley, Davenport highway superintendent, expressing impatience over highway construction encroaching on his property and destroying a 150-year-old memorial erected there.

PINDARS CORNERS, NY
JUNE 5, 1988

Dear Mr. McCulley:

My wife and I have lived here in Prosser Hollow for just a quarter century now. We have paid our taxes, and asked little of the Town. Indeed, to my recollection the only thing we have ever asked is that the highway department stop its relentless acquisition of the school yard at the juncture of McDougall and Prosser Hollow Roads. The one room schoolhouse there, built in 1857, is an historic structure of true importance. I have restored it and maintained it. Each spring, however, for a quarter century, I come back to the Hollow to find another foot of road having taken over another foot of school yard. This year it is a full four feet. Desecration. Outrage. What is the matter with your crews? Can't you undo this?

I want to put up a small but lovely memorial to a youth who died in "Dedenport" in 1829 that was standing by the roadside just 100 feet from here when I arrived. Two trucks knocked it down, and a friend has it in safe keeping. It belongs in the school yard. It would enhance the hollow and keep true to the purposes of the people who erected it as a memorial a century and a half ago. But I dare not. <u>Because</u> of the Town.

Can you not help me? Would you at least respond to me?

"I guess at heart I am a city planner." This letter is a part of a series to NEW YORK TIMES *writers and editors—this one to Max Frankel, executive editor—lamenting the lack of coverage of plans for a courthouse and other buildings at Foley Square, near City Hall.*

JUNE 22, 1988

Dear Max:

Oh, Lord. Of course, you had Cliff May's fine story of our getting (my getting, if I may say) the Foley Square authorization in the Continuing Resolution down here. But your coverage stopped there.

Subsequently, on December 30, 1987 I met with the Mayor at City Hall and laid out the proposal. We had, I said, a vast opportunity. One-half billion dollars worth of buildings and a chance to design a great urban space at Foley Square. (Which is a wreck at present.) Our situation, however, was urgent. The deal turned on a technique, lease to own, which had been thought up by the best GSA administrator in a generation, Terence Golden, <u>who was leaving</u>. (He left March 18th.) He and I had teamed up to build the Federal Triangle building on Pennsylvania Avenue, two-thirds the floor space of the Pentagon, and brilliantly conceived, all without a nickel of public money. . . .

On March 11 we had a big signing ceremony at City Hall. The deal done. Save, as I say, the deal is never done unless the <u>Times</u> reports it. (In fairness, the <u>News</u> and <u>Post</u> gave us good stories. But this kind of thing either is in the <u>Times</u> or the City does not feel committed.)

I spent the spring trying to interest [*Times* architecture critic] Paul Gold-berger. No luck yet. Then I raised it at lunch with you all on May 4.

My point is this. The City doesn't give a damn about these things. Not really. The one exception is [Deputy Mayor Robert] Esnard (who, it turns out, is an architect). Therefore, the City needs to know that other people <u>do</u> care. Especially about the redesign of Foley Square. That is wholly an oral under-standing that I reached in the Mayor's office just before the signing of the memorandum of understanding.

So there it is. I will not be happy until I see something like this morning's front page. Granted, we have no model. Well, let Goldberger show his stuff. Or I would settle for a street plan. I enclose a brochure put together by the local GSA, whose head, Bill Diamond, is a peach. Foley Square. (Do you re-member the old fella? When he died it was said they'd buried the brains of Tammany Hall.) Federal Court House. Justice. Decorum. Design!!

I guess at heart I am a City planner. Like Glazer I had hoped that after Pennsylvania Avenue I would finish my years seeing the Westway through to a triumphant conclusion. That obviously is not to be. And so, the only thing I will ever do for the City—the only architecture—is this. And so I plead!

Excerpt of a letter to William F. Buckley Jr., the conservative editor of the NA-TIONAL REVIEW, who disagreed with Moynihan's criticism of the Reagan admin-istration's actions in Nicaragua.

JUNE 27, 1988

Dear Bill:

. . . On the mining of the harbors. I would ask you in particular to remem-ber that I was defending the word of Barry Goldwater. In a public letter to Casey he stated that our committee had not been informed of an elementally important event. He left for Taiwan. I look up and Bud McFarlane has told an audience at the Naval Academy that contrary to Senator Goldwater's as-sertion, the committee had been fully briefed. I said if you're going to call Barry Goldwater a liar, you're going to have to get yourself another vice chairman.

Casey apologized. McFarlane—who, I think, had been misled—has since testified that we should have been informed and <u>were not</u>.

Trust—not propriety—is the coin of this realm.

*Letter to John Cardinal O'Connor, suggesting that the annual St. Patrick's Day
parade be used to bring Protestant and Catholic children together from Ulster
(Northern Ireland). The parade, as Moynihan notes, had become controversial because of invitations to Catholic militants to participate. Moynihan was part of a
group of four Irish American political figures (Senator Ted Kennedy, House Speaker
"Tip" O'Neill, and former Governor Hugh Carey of New York) denouncing the
Irish Republican Army's tactics. His mention of wearing "body armor" was a reference to threats some had received for their criticism.*

JULY 28, 1988

Dear Cardinal O'Connor:

Reading accounts of your visit to Ireland emboldens me to make a suggestion about the St. Patrick's Day parade here at home. Ours, which is to say
the City's, is the oldest continuously-observed public occasion in North
America. It has been the model for an increasing number of ethnic parades
in the City itself, and St. Patrick's Day parades elsewhere. Of the latter, the
most recent had begun in Syracuse and for the purpose of raising money to
bring Protestant and Catholic children from Ulster to spend the summer with
families in Onandaga County. It is a lovely affair which I try to attend every
year. On my first visit there was an ecumenical service at St. Patrick's, which
happens to be the Episcopal cathedral. This year we were at Immaculate Con-
ception, the Catholic cathedral—a stygian, fearful place 30 years ago when
our youngest was christened there, but which has been wonderfully redone,
full of color and light.

I think of this not least because Joe O'Keefe officiated (do I have that
right?), and prior to the service we talked a bit about the 1983 parade in
New York when Cardinal Cooke closed the doors of the cathedral until the
Grand Marshal had passed. He then asked Bishop O'Keefe to join him on
the steps, where he was obscenely jeered by the mob that had been assembled
for that purpose. According to Joe, however, the Cardinal remarked that it

was not as bad as he expected. That it was not as bad as he expected. <u>That</u> was a man. In any event, I dare to say after half a century of watching and marching, our parade has not been the same since. The mass has not quite been the same. (On 1983, Liz and I sat alone in the front pew, none other would sit with us as I had announced I would not march. The next day, one tabloid suggested that the seats we occupied should henceforth be known as the "Gypo Nolan Memorial Pew," after O'Flaherty's informer.) I, for one, am now required to march in body armor, which takes some of the spring out of one's step!

Hence, this thought. Might we not start a project such as they have undertaken in Syracuse? Which is to say, use the parade as an occasion to raise monies to bring children over here. In Syracuse, there is a series of dinners the night before. We could do it any number of ways. I would be happy to join in, although it may well be my involvement would not be helpful. This is not why I write. I write mostly to say that something is owed the memory of Cardinal Cooke and his witness on that occasion.

Excerpt of a letter to John O. Marsh, secretary of the army, assailing the performance of the Army Corps of Engineers in construction projects in New York.

AUGUST 5, 1988

Dear Jack:

It occurs to me that I have not properly thanked you for that fine breakfast. Nor yet have I followed up with regard to my concerns about the Corps of Engineers.

Let me straight out, and as something very much more than politeness, state that I have hugely enjoyed my relationship with the Corps over the past twelve years, especially since becoming chairman of the Subcommittee on Water Resources in 1979. It is in every sense a noble institution, with a singular history.

My concern is that it may have lost its sense of mission.

What do I mean? I don't know really. Hamilton's formula for good government: energy in the Executive. I think I know it when I see it. And I do not see it in the Corps. . . .

By definition Corps projects are "local" and a Senator will pay a good amount of attention to Corps activities in his own state. In my state, the record of the past decade has been, well, disastrous. Alternately, profoundly disappointing. The great blow was the loss of Westway. It was planned under President Ford. The last thing William Coleman did as Secretary of Transportation was to call Jack Javits and me down to look at the model. I was hugely interested. It clearly would be the most important undertaking of its kind since New York City built Olmsted's Central Park in the 19th Century, and would set the same standard of design, with the addition of a return-to-the water theme, which much interests me in American urban planning. But we lost it because the Corps could not figure out what a Federal judge required of an Environmental Impact Statement. (The local EPA man tried to tell them.) Organizations that lose cases lose wars. Something like that. It was what ecologists call Failure to Adapt. (I fair to begged for an After Action Report. What happened? Why did we lose? None came. No interest.)

Then Coney Island. A tiny project with vast potential. Not only for the city but for the Corps itself, and in Brooklyn, where the Corps began. The shoreline of 1794, which the Corps surveyed. I got the legislation years ago. Maybe the 21st Century will see the beach. I don't know. The Corps doesn't seem interested.

After touring Coney Island, a year or so ago, I asked the District Engineer to come take a look at the Gowanus Canal. Typical derelict landscape. One thousand yards from Wall Street. A natural for clearing and developing. Poor man had no street map. Never go into the field without a map. Right? Never go to sea without charts. Well, not with the Corps any longer. How in the name of heaven did they locate the headwaters of the Missouri! Anyway, we found the canal, and looked it over. I asked the Colonel to stay to a bang-up lunch at a good Italian restaurant almost on the banks of the Gowanus. He couldn't. It was Saturday. I have not heard a word of the matter since.

Then there is the Erie Canal. I have never wanted much for the Canal. Just enough Federal participation to make certain that the State maintains its end of things until it is recognized as an irreplaceable artifact. (There are four canals, actually. You can paddle from the Cornell University boathouse to Quebec, Saulte Sainte Marie, Key West. All points in between. I have had nothing but resistance and sabotage for ten years. Bob Page has cleared it all up, but it took the Assistant Secretary himself to do it. Even after OMB put up the money, the Corps had so damned many conditions that the State was despairing of ever entering into a Memorandum of Understanding.) Which raises a worrisome point. The Corps lavishes attention on the Intracoastal Waterway, a public convenience for the rich and super rich between Sea Island and Palm Beach. Somehow Coney Island and the Oswego Canal can't compete for its attention.

These issues will seem parochial. Perhaps they are. But they are symptomatic. Back in the 1970s, President Carter asked me (as chairman of water resources) if I could somehow get the Corps interested in developing at least two 60-foot harbors to accommodate the super colliers which are now appearing on the seas. Europe has half a dozen such ports. I believe the Japanese have one or two. At issue is whether the coal for these countries will come from Australia, South Africa, or the United States. The former two have already dug their harbors. We have not. Seeming cannot. And the Corps seemingly doesn't care.

I wonder. Ought we to get the Corps out of the civilian construction business and keep it a war fighting outfit? It doesn't seem to have its heart in the pedestrian, but surely urgent, business of infrastructure. I remarked to you that I once suggested to President Nixon that he establish a Department of Public Works, run by the Corps. (He liked the idea.) Increasingly, I think that we do need such a department, not as an addition to the cabinet, but as a merger. I would take Transportation, Energy, the Environmental Protection Agency, and the General Services Administration and put them together as the agency responsible for capital planning and construction.

There is a great new era of infrastructure ahead. I think we need a new organization. What do you think?

Letter to William H. Webster, newly reappointed as director of the Central Intelligence Agency by President-elect George H. W. Bush, urging him to review what he regarded as a dismal record of failing to consult the Senate Intelligence Committee.

DECEMBER 9, 1988

Dear Judge Webster:

I do so much welcome President-elect Bush's offer for you to stay at your present post and your decision to accept. You seem to have steadied things over there, and heaven knows they needed it. I say this as a recipient of the

Agency's Seal Medallion. As an ambassador I have worked with the Agency in the field, and for eight years I served on the Select Committee on Intelligence here in the Senate. I don't know that you would find anyone more admiring or supportive of the intelligence community in the large. Yet I remain profoundly concerned about the events that led to the Iran-contra affair, and am, well, determined that they not simply be sent to the archives.

By "events that led," I refer to the mining of the Nicaraguan harbors beginning in January 1984. There are two possibilities here. The first is that the President knew about the mining and approved it in advance. John McMahon so indicated to our staff director, Rob Simmons, in a telephone conversation in April or thereabouts. In that event, the relevant statutes and the by-then established practice clearly required that Senator Goldwater and I be notified of the plans in advance. It was a "significant anticipated intelligence activity." We were not briefed. In his new book Goldwater, Barry describes his disbelief, hurt, and alarm when he finally learned what had gone on. . . .

But that is the least of it. In the aftermath of the discovery that the Agency had itself carried out the mining operations, Senator Goldwater, as Chairman of the SSCI, wrote a vigorous protest to Mr. Casey. This letter leaked to the press. There followed a sequence of ominous events. Mr. Casey, as I understand, posted notices at the Agency's headquarters stating that the Committee had indeed been briefed no matter what Barry Goldwater said. Bud McFarlane repeated this assertion to an audience at the Naval Academy. I stated that I would resign if this position were maintained; Mr. Casey apologized, and so forth.

But this was not the end of it. To the contrary, this was the beginning. On March 3, 1988, in the course of the debate on the Intelligence Oversight Act of 1988, I remarked that at this point,

> a practice of deception mutated into a policy of deceit.

. . . It all began there. Before it was over we had a brush—just the tiniest, but even so a brush—with Constitutional crisis. Writing of the entire event, Theodore Draper states the proposition as follows:

> If ever the constitutional democracy of the United States is overthrown, we now have a better idea of how this is likely to be done.

Why do I trouble you with all this? Obviously out of my concern with Legislative-Executive relations. (You may recall our conversation in my office in December 1980 about Abscam, as it was called. That was under a previous administration. To my mind this concern has nothing to do with political parties. Something far more fundamental is at work.) Also because in a new administration, you might feel free to undertake a review of the mining episode.

Someone might even offer to make amends to Barry Goldwater. As you do know, he and I tried to make some good come out of the events in the winter of 1983–84. Perhaps, we thought, there just wasn't enough mutual understanding as to what was meant by "significant anticipated intelligence activity." Having served as a Counselor to the President I came up with the thought that anything actually signed by the President would be considered significant and reported. (Only so much paper gets to the President's desk. There are things you would never do without his approval. Things you would never do without his order.) This was incorporated into an "accord," signed by the DCI, Senator Goldwater and me on June 6, 1984. It called for a review one year later. The time slipped, but two years later a second accord was signed by Mr. Casey and our successors on the Committee. It was solemnly agreed that the early agreement had been working fine.

This was of course a solemn lie.

I really do think that the intelligence community should ponder this fact. Can it possibly be that <u>only</u> Mr. Casey knew of the lie. I would doubt that. Then if not, who else?

Newsletter conveying emotions and thoughts over the end of Marxist-Leninist ideology with the advent of Mikhail Gorbachev in the Soviet Union. "Rejoice!" Moynihan concludes.

DECEMBER 20, 1988
WASHINGTON, DC

Dear New Yorker,

END OF AN EPOCH?

The editorial writers at *The New York Times* are a careful lot, certainly not given to gushing. And so it was no small event to turn to their page of December 8 and read:

> Perhaps, not since Woodrow Wilson presented his Fourteen Points in
> 1918 or since Franklin Roosevelt and Winston Churchill promulgated
> the Atlantic Charter in 1941 has a world figure demonstrated the vision
> Mikhail Gorbachev displayed yesterday at the United Nations.

I agree, but with a particular reading of the term "vision." It was a kind of
rear vision. Gorbachev declared the end of the Marxist epoch, a century or
more in which great nations, great movements the world over were seized by
the absolute conviction that the future was foretold, and that that future was
theirs. The "scientific" work of Marx and Lenin was said to have discovered
the laws of history, much as Newton discovered the laws of gravity. As for the
Soviet Union, as one writer put it, their claim was not so much to be a com-
petitor with the western nations but rather to be a step forward in history.
They were what was coming next. The laws of history so decreed.

Hence, the stunning moment when the General Secretary of the Communist Party of the Soviet Union stood before the General Assembly of the
United Nations and told the world:

> We are, of course, far from claiming to be in the possession of the ulti-
> mate truth.

Yet that is exactly what Communists had claimed for a century!

And now it is all over and the General Secretary of the Communist Party
of the Soviet Union so states. That is an event!

I am now a man in his 60s: my first political memories are of New York City
in the thirties. One almost has to have had a personal history such as that to
take the measure of that Wednesday's event. And so I am going to ask those
of you, those who never went to City College, listened to speeches in Union
Square, attended lectures at the Rand School (I still have a book Bertrand
Russell autographed for me there)—I am going to ask you to be patient with
me and let me walk you through some of those times and places.

We were in the Depression, of course, in the 1930s and in the course of
that decade a vast number of both ordinary and extraordinary people came to
the conclusion that Marx and Lenin were indeed correct, that capitalism was
in its final, doomed stage, and that Communism was the fore-ordained next
step forward in history. It was already in place in Russia: it would soon spread.

Altogether, as many as a million Americans belonged to the Communist Party at one time or another. (There was much turnover.) The center of all this was New York City, which was the center of political writing and thinking, much as London was when Marx scribbled away at the British Museum, the counterpart of the New York Public Library. Robert Warshow, writing in Commentary, in December 1947, summed up the 1930s in New York:

> For American intellectuals, the Communist movement of the 1930s was a crucial experience. . . . There was a time when virtually all intellectual vitality was derived in one way or another from the communist party. If you were not somewhere within the party's wide orbit, then you were likely to be in the opposition, which meant that much of your thought and energy had to be devoted to maintaining yourself in opposition.

And this was true the world over. There might not have been much of a Communist party in, say, Peru. But you may be sure there was one. And there were mass political parties in all of continental Europe. A half century ago the "future" seemed at hand.

What saved us?

I have no greater claim than the next person to have figured this out. And, of course, it is by no means over. But I have some thoughts. First of all, above all, is the fact that the Communist state in Russia almost immediately became a totalitarian state. The first totalitarian state. No such system of total government control had ever before existed. Hitler merely copied it. Sooner or later, people came to see how hideous it was. And there were men and women who would not submit. These have been the martyrs of the 20th century; and their grace has touched us. (I once observed to Alexander Solzhenitsyn how remarkable it was that some of the greatest literature of our time had been written in and smuggled out of Stalin's Russia. Where would such writing next appear, I asked. Easy, he replied. In China, when they begin to write about Mao's reign.)

And then there was the United States. The Great Republic, as John F. Kennedy like to say. As the conflict grew ominous at mid-century, led by the likes of Truman, Acheson, Marshall, we armed ourselves and armed allies and decreed that we would not go quietly into the "dustbin of history." (A favored Communist phrase.)

Yet, there was more. The basic fact is that Marxism did not predict the future even though it claimed to do so. Take one proposition from the *Communist Manifesto* of 1848. "Working men of the World unite. . . . The proletarians have nothing to lose but their chains." Marx predicted that under the new mode of industrial production a simple world-wide hierarchy of classes would emerge in which ethnic differences disappeared, as workers submerged their personalities, as you might say, into a uniform, international mass. . . .

In his UN address, Mr. Gorbachev spoke pointedly and openly of the urgency of "harmonizing inter-ethnic relations" in the Soviet Union. The Baltic Republics are in orderly, if not open rebellion. The Caucasus is riotous. And, of course, in the 1950s the Chinese made clear they were not about to have Russians tell them how to run a revolution. And so the Russian Communists fell in with the Vietnamese Communists because they hated the Chinese Communists who hated the Russian Communists, and so it goes. Ethnic conflict as usual!

But the greatest failure was precisely where there was going to be the greatest success. Economics. It is now hard to remember, but a central tenet of Marxist-Leninist belief was that "socialist" production would be more efficient that capitalist production. This was to prove momentously mistaken.

I invite the thought that there is a certain symmetry to these events. The rest of the world catches on: then the Soviets catch on.

By mid-century no one in the West had any illusions about the nature of Soviet Society: there was no equality, no justice, merely horror. Then in 1956, three years after Stalin's death, in a <u>secret</u> speech to the Supreme Soviet, Nikita Khrushchev told of the crimes of Stalin. End the illusion of justice. Next came the break with Red China. End the illusion of proletarian unity. Next came the revelation that they couldn't even feed themselves. End the illusion of efficiency.

When you consider how fiercely they believed they would win out, you have a sense of what they must now feel. In 1961, Khrushchev declared that by 1970 the U.S.S.R. would "overtake and surpass" the United States in economic production. He wasn't faking. That is what they <u>believed</u>. Lars-Erik Nelson of the *Daily News,* whose commentary on that week's events was unequalled in my view, suggested I go back and read the editorial in *Pravda* (the Communist party paper) following the ouster of Khrushchev in October 1964.

The text is triumphant. The Soviet economy is about to soar!

... Undeviatingly pursuing this Leninist line, the Party and the Soviet people are gaining victories in accomplishing the chief economic task—creating the material and technical base of communism.

... [T]here is a swelling torrent of joyous tidings of new enterprises being opened, of the mastering of production of progressive types of goods, of glorious labor achievements by our working class, collective farm peasantry, state farm workers and specialists in all branches of the national economy. Millions of Soviet people by their creative labor in plants and factories, at construction projects, on collective farm and state farm fields, in scientific institutes and laboratories and in cultural, educational and public health institutions are implementing in practice the Program of the C.P.S.U., advancing the great cause of communist construction, which has become the dear cause of the millions, of the entire Soviet people.

At just that moment, the new leader, Leonid I. Brezhnev, began 18 years in power which Pravda now refers to as "the period of stagnation." American wheat began arriving. The Pacific Rim took off. In 1987 in Moscow, officials would speak of the "widening gulf between the Soviet Union and the advanced capitalist countries." But they were not talking of Holland. Peter the Great figured out Holland. They were talking of Korea—South Korea that is—Taiwan, Hong Kong, Singapore. The proverbial toiling Asian masses suddenly sweeping world markets with electronic circuitry, whilst all the Soviets could sell abroad was fish eggs and furs, trading goods of a hunter-gatherer economy.

It seems to me that in the 1980s a good many people here in Washington missed all this. Much talk of Soviet military superiority; Soviet expansion. Grant, their military force was and is formidable; albeit Gorbachev on Wednesday suggested they can no longer afford it. But expansion? Apart from Afghanistan, an old involvement—I could not see anything new in the Marxist-Leninist regimes that popped up here and there in the Third World. There was once an international Communist movement with great expectations. Remember New York in the 1930s. But by the 1980s this had been over for years. Over in New York, in Paris, in Rome, good lord, over in Moscow. But how were the Sandinistas to know? It takes a long time for word to reach a place like Managua, or La Paz, or Maputo. . . .

We are not at the end of our problems with the Soviets. If that society commences to break up, it could be a hugely dangerous moment. But the notion of Soviet conquest is surely behind us. We have to watch that the rest of the world doesn't conclude that we, too, exhausted ourselves in the "long twilight struggle" of which President Kennedy spoke in his Inaugural Address. (Will the next superpower competition be the drive to replace the United States as the world's largest debtor?) But, still, freedom prevailed.

Be clear. Soviet antagonism is real. Soviet missiles are real. They have hardly surrendered. But they <u>have</u> given up on the notion that they can live as a closed society and eventually triumph. Our defense budget has been declining for four straight years. Theirs continues to rise. But we have allies who could do much more than they are doing. The Soviet allies are economic basket cases. Paul Kennedy of Yale notes that Britain, Japan, France, and West Germany <u>each</u> spend more on defense than the non-Russian Warsaw pact countries together. And then there are those thriving overseas protectorates, Cuba and Vietnam!

Remember, it remains Russia. Don't expect democracy. Have no fear that the "I" word will catch hold. Even so, the vision of world ideological dominion is past.

Which is the end of an epoch.

It seems to me that Jerry Hough of Duke University has it about right. "It is the end of the post-war world," he states. "We're not going to invade them and they're not going to invade us. The challenge now is that economic strength is a more important chip and what we need is a President with an economic interest, not just a military-security interest." I might add, a Congress.

But that will keep 'til January. For the moment, we have a prospect of peace on earth such as we've not known for most of a century. Rejoice!

Letter to Louis Henkin, law professor at Columbia University, reflecting on his own status as a liberal in the Senate. The "massive change" on welfare to which he refers is the passage of the Family Support Act in 1988, which Moynihan cosponsored. It strengthened child-support enforcement and provided for education, job training, work incentives, payments to two-parent families, and medical and child-care benefits to families that leave welfare for work.

PERSONAL

JANUARY 25, 1989

Dear Lou:

Of the thousands of persons who read the stirring "A Reaffirmation of Principle" which you and others published shortly before the last election, there can only have been a limited number who were running for the United States Senate at the time. I was one, and read it with close attention. It occurs to me that the outcome of the Presidential election may seem to have confirmed your fears. I write, uninvited to be sure, but not without a sense of family, to encourage instead your hopes.

For specifics, I would simply call attention to my own race in New York. I don't think you could count many persons running for the Senate last fall who had a more "liberal" record that I. (I learn today that ADA has scored me at 90 percent for the 100th Congress. My colleague, Senator D'Amato, weighs in at 15 percent. Only two Senators running last year had a higher score.) This voting record comes in the aftermath of a particularly trying twelve years in the Senate where an active minority successfully sought opportunity after opportunity to force liberals to vote on issues where "our" views were thought to be such at variance with those of our constituents.

I went through those years cheerfully enough. Even to the point where the "liberal" vote on a particularly nasty homophobic amendment was down to Lowell Weicker and me. Two. (Bear in mind that I represent the whole of New York State, not just selective districts. New York, incidentally, has had a Democratic legislature for only four years of the twentieth century.) I was cheerful about it all because I had never represented myself as anything other than a liberal Democrat. Accordingly, my votes didn't take any explaining. What would have taken explaining was to have started voting differently. In New York, as in the nation, only about a quarter of the voters will describe themselves as liberal. But it is a legitimate tradition, an accepted one, and non-liberals can be persuaded to vote for you. (Just as any of us would be open to voting for a self-described conservative given the time, the place, and the issues.)

In the end we won overwhelmingly. Broke every record. 68.3 percent of the vote. More than any other candidate for U.S. Senate in New York history. A plurality of 2,172,865. The largest in a contested Senate race in American history. Sixty-one of sixty-two counties. (In New York, Democratic Senate candidates would win, when they did win, with seven or eight counties at the most. Bob Kennedy, in the 1964 convulsion, carried twenty.) But most importantly, we seemed to have carried the greatest possible range of voter groups. . . .

Back to your concerns. Which I share, but with perhaps some differences. The conservatism of the 1980s came as no surprise to me. I had expected it and had predicted it. Let me cite the Stearns lecture given at Andover in January 1973. It was entitled "Peace." It asserted that the era of campus turbulence was all over, and that the unprecedentedly swollen cohort of "radical" youth would turn quite conservative when the time came that the task at hand was not that of locking up the Dean, but rather choosing his or her successor, two or three times removed, from a swarm of qualified candidates. I offered the advice that if the young of the time wanted to know what their future would be like they should read Balzac. There were many more reasons that I felt as I did, but I'll leave it there. The current environment was foreseeable, and some of us foresaw it and said so. This was, of course, unwelcome to some others. So much so, that three months after "Peace" appeared in The Public Interest (Summer 1973), I found myself (along with many solid liberal friends) labeled a "neoconservative" in Dissent. The celebrated prudential rule, pas d'enemis a gauche, was soon at work. So much that a fair number of my friends said to hell with it and switched. Those of us who did not are still suspect, and we know it.

Which is hardly a plea for sympathy. I won the absolutely critical newspaper endorsement of the 1976 Democratic primary principally because the editors concerned were inclined to accept the label as reassuring! However, the whole episode and the atmosphere, before and after, in which it took place was discouraging. . . .

That the Bush administration will be very different from that of President Reagan's is cold comfort for liberals. Good for the country, mind. But for liberals it could well prove their general superfluousness as an opposition. A Republican President might well prove just as caring and considerably more competent.

I am fixated on this matter of competence. Those of us who began writing on these matters in the 1960's were fully in agreement with all that liberalism was attempting. But we began to worry as to whether we would bring it off. This kind of critique was much too often greeted as a renunciation of goals rather than an inquiry as to means. A quarter century later I find that too little has changed. I will put it thus.

Last fall, after a quarter century's [effort], I brought off a major, I like to think massive change in the welfare system. I could only do this because there was a Republican President. A Democratic White House would have been paralyzed by the insistence of "liberal" constituencies that the bill wasn't generous enough. It being ever the case that nothing is better than not enough. It might be said for the Leninists that their "the-worse-the-better" approach at least had the intellectual rigor of a strategy. But what is to be said for the liberal posture? It is utterly dysfunctional. So much of late, that one would dare to suggest that the causes liberals advocate are likely as not to fare better when they are out of office.

If we are somehow to keep our tradition alive for the next century, we are going to have to return to Trilling. Or so I believe. So far, however, all I have in the newspapers are accounts of conferences at which the losers of an eminently winnable Presidential election get together to blame the American people. I didn't for a moment think we were fated to lose the Presidency again this time. But my hopes vanished on the day a news director of one of the television networks told me of an editorial meeting with a top Dukakis manager. The news people had asked about the Pledge of Allegiance controversy. They were assured that there was nothing to worry about; "any second-year law student would understand" the issues involved. . . .

Letter to the Century Association urging that it not admit Pamela Harriman, Democratic Party doyenne and third wife (and widow at this point) of Averell Harriman, to the Century Club, the prestigious literary salon in midtown Manhattan. The "slander" Moynihan cites evidently relates to her charges in the 1976 campaign that he had a drinking habit. Harriman was nevertheless admitted to the Century in 1990.

MOST CONFIDENTIAL
FEBRUARY 8, 1989

Dear Gentlemen:

I am asked to support the nomination of Pamela Harriman. I regret that I write with the opposite purpose.

It happens I was an aide to Governor Harriman during his four years in Albany, and we remained reasonably close thereafter. Hence the hurt when, at a crucial moment in the 1976 Democratic primary in New York, his new wife, supporting another candidate, slandered me in the most vicious and hurtful terms. A hurt which persists. At that time, I had met her once only, at an occasion on which the Governor was honored at a meeting of the American Academy of Arts and Sciences in Boston, where I had resumed my role as aide-de-camp. The more, then, was I appalled at the personal nature of her remarks.

I am now in my thirteenth year in the Senate. In that time in Washington, I have never entered her house. It is depressing to say this, but I would find it difficult to enter the Century were there any prospect of this person being there.

I believe the Committee will find that this is the first letter in opposition I have ever sent.

Letter to Lawrence Kirwan, chairman of the New York State Democratic Committee, praising Moynihan's wife's work in his reelection the year before.

MARCH 23, 1989

Dear Larry:

Here is a summary of the '88 election returns, along with the exit polls I mentioned the other evening.

* Highest plurality—2,172,865 votes—in the history of contested U.S. Senate elections.
* Highest percentage—68.3 percent—in the history of New York Senate elections.
* Highest number of counties—61 of 62—won by a Democrat in the history of New York Senate elections. (There are only 910 Democrats in Hamilton County, and for that matter only 4,009 voters. You can't win 'em all!)

We did very well among the various groups pollsters poll. In the NBC/Wall Street Journal exit poll, we had a clear majority in thirty of some thirty-two categories. ("Reagan Democrats," 90–10.) We lost out only with Republicans (37–63) and ideological Conservatives (a close 47–53).

The ticket splitting was unprecedented. President-elect Bush carried Staten Island by a 61.8 percent margin. We had 63.1 percent. He got 57.8 percent of the vote in Nassau County; we got 57.6 percent. In Monroe County: Bush 50.3 percent, Moynihan 69.6 percent.

George Bush carried the village of New Square in Rockland County by a margin of 773 to 9, whilst we came in at 756 to 21. A friend who follows these things writes: "I am not sure if this qualifies as the most lopsided example of ticket splitting in the history of western democracy, but it certainly ranks among the finalists."

In the end, as you know we had an easy race. You, of course, know better. It is very hard to make a race in a state as large and complex as New York look easy!

Liz went up to New York in March of 1987 and commenced a campaign that went on, without a break, for 537 days. On August 1, 1987, we opened our campaign headquarters at 500 Fifth Avenue where we remained through election day. She assembled a staff—never more than seven persons on the payroll—and set to work. We planned for a half dozen serious candidates, including one of the richest men in the world. We raised such money as we could. Never a lot, but enough. A year ago November, we decided to go on television in January 1988 as a kind of pre-emptive strike. We were ready. The research was done. The money was in the bank. The polls were taken. The TV spots produced. Ready, aim, fire. Another candidacy sunk. All told we went through 29 potential opponents. Each in turn looked at the situation and found that <u>Liz was ready for him</u>. Research done. Strategy in place. Money in the bank. Finally, a 30th potential opponent stayed in.

And so it went day in day out, week in week out, month in month out, 1987 then 1988.

It wasn't in the least bit easy. It is simply that when things got tough we were ready. Liz was ready.

Letter to former Speaker of the House Jim Wright, of Texas, expressing support following Wright's resignation in the wake of a controversy over ethics charges,

including his alleged profiting improperly from sales of his book. Moynihan thanks Wright for his help in passing the 1988 Family Support Act, which provided education, job training, health and childcare benefits, and other services to help welfare recipients find work. The Act was a major Moynihan achievement.

PINDARS CORNERS
JUNE 26, 1989

Dear Jim,

I am writing from the one room school house (1859) on the edge of the "farm" in upstate New York which we bought just after John F. Kennedy was assassinated and we had in mind to leave Washington and the world pretty much. I have been thinking of his remark that "life is not fair" and thinking especially that just now it is not being fair to you. Our country owes you so much. From the day you climbed into the B-24 in the South Pacific to the great 100th Congress which saw the first significant social legislation enacted since the 88th and 89th when Lyndon Johnson was able to move a shocked nation and Congress. You had nothing of that order to work with. Just your own sense that it was time we got back to basics.

I was much involved with the welfare legislation and the drug legislation. I had been after a redefinition of welfare for a quarter century. I'd seen just about every President since Lyndon try. All failed until you came along. As you know something like one child in three will live on welfare before reaching 18. If we can get "them" to make the legislation work, you will have touched the lives of a generation. Something like a third may well be struck by the current drug epidemic. Again you made it possible to respond in trying to treat what is in fact a disease of the brain. Something the medical profession is finally beginning to accept. And for which we now have research money. I for one will never forget your walking into that room on the morning of the last day of the 100th Congress and announcing quietly that you just "found" half a billion dollars! Style.

Speaking of which I treasure that Stetson your friends gave me when I went down to Fort Worth to speak. You asked if it fitted. It does. And I wear it around here with pride!

⊗

Newsletter with thoughts of the "terrible beauty" born from the uprising of Chinese students in Tiananmen Square in Beijing the previous month.

PINDARS CORNERS
JULY 4, 1989

Dear New Yorker:

"A TERRIBLE BEAUTY IS BORN"

At Easter 1916 a band of nationalists, as they were termed, seized the Post Office in Dublin and proclaimed an Irish Republic. They were soon over-powered, and the leaders executed by order of a British general who was probably mad, but the event was irreversible. William Butler Yeats, the greatest poet of our century, came as close to the heart of the matter as anyone could do. He was himself a nationalist, but had been indignant with the insurrectionaries, many of whom were friends, for needlessly sacrificing their lives, as he felt. But gradually, his biographer writes, "their death became ennobled in his mind." In "Easter, 1916" he wrote their eulogy, wrote of a world

changed, changed utterly:
A terrible beauty is born.

The near insurrection of Chinese students in Tiananmen Square in Beijing, culminating in the Army massacre of June 4 had just this transforming quality. And more. For the whole world was watching. And what it was watching was not what at first appeared. But much more. The death, as George Will writes, of "the Totalitarian Pretense," the claim to have spoken for history.

I wrote of this subject in a newsletter last December headed "End of an Epoch?" Note the question mark. But just the possibility that this might be so seemed in and of itself momentous. Nothing of the kind had been promised us. To the contrary. And now, of a sudden it seemed possible! I could see this. But I surely could not see the crash of events that were just upon us. There would follow what Will has termed "the most momentous months in mankind's history." And not just the shaking and crashing of regimes, but the clarity with which the great arguments of this century are being resolved.

Bear with me on this, won't you! I <u>swear</u> I will get back to acid rain, and mass transit, and global warming, and capital gains <u>soon</u>. But this is a Fourth of July like none I have ever known and I have to write about it.

What do I mean? Fair question. Especially for younger persons. What I mean is that for those of us who came of age during World War II and its Cold War aftermath, the conflict with totalitarianism seemed certain to be not merely protracted but permanent. This was especially so after China fell in 1948 and the Euro-Asian landmass was under Communist rule. Nothing it seems could ever bring down these regimes. Save that which would bring us all down. Listen to Hannah Arendt, that most brilliant of refugees from Hitler's Germany. In 1950 she opened her classic study, <u>The Origins of Totalitarianism,</u> with this passage.

> *Two world wars in one generation, separated by an uninterrupted chain of local wars and revolutions, followed by no peace treaty for the vanquished and no respite for the victor, has ended in the anticipation of a third World War between the two remaining world powers. This moment of anticipation is like the calm that settles after all hopes have died.*

These, mind, were the words of a cheerful enough soul. I knew her slightly. She was married to a professor of philosophy at Bard College, with its sublime campus at Annandale-on-Hudson. She was simply describing what she saw. Totalitarian states built upon "mass organizations of atomized, isolated individuals." The leaders "thought in continents and felt in centuries." It would go on without end unless or until that war came. George Orwell's <u>Nineteen Eighty-Four,</u> which had appeared the previous year, told of the world awaiting us <u>after</u> that "third World War."

Yeats had foretold this in his poem "The Second Coming," written in the aftermath of World War I.

> *Turning and turning in the widening gyre*
> *The falcon cannot hear the falconer;*
> *Things fall apart; the centre cannot hold;*
> *Mere anarchy is loosed upon the world,*
> *The blood-dimmed tide is loosed, and everywhere*
> *The ceremony of innocence is drowned;*
> *The best lack all conviction, while the worst*
> *Are full of passionate intensity.*

More than once, many more times than once, I have heard those last two lines invoked by American statesmen of the last forty years as they struggled with near despair. . . .

The world is going to continue to be a difficult and dangerous place. But dangerous in profoundly different ways. Some years ago John Dollard wrote that "one of the ideas man tolerates least well is the notion that a large number of hard-to-control forces and circumstances dominate human and social life. Somebody or something he feels must be to <u>blame</u>." In his view, "one of the great reasons for the invention and rapid spread of Marxism is that it permitted men to claim that they were robbed." Ethnic differences are just as powerful a device for alleging guilt. And not just in Central Europe! Try mainstream America. Still the nightmare years are passing.

I gave the commencement address at Syracuse University May 14 which began:

> *Commencements are happy times for young people, moving on to a new and hopeful stage of life. It is your special fortune that the moment comes to you at the same time the world itself moves towards a new and hopeful stage of history. . . .*
>
> *The age of totalitarianism is ending. This has the most elemental meaning to the Class of 1989. It means you aren't going to go to war; you aren't going to die before ever having lived; civilization is not going to die; the planet is not going to die.*
>
> *I would hope you might just hug yourself for the sheer luck of it all! And find a few moments in the years ahead to think of those who made that luck for you, lest you lose the sense of it, and even, indeed, lose it.*

Letter to Joseph Papp, the director and impresario of the New York Shakespeare Festival, supporting government backing of the arts and praising Papp for his contribution.

Dear Joe,

I dare to think the NEA [National Endowment for the Arts] will get through the present troubles with its budget and mandate more or less intact. The new chairman designate sounds just right. (Do you not think?) This ensures more than normal solicitousness from the two Oregon Senators who are in any event exemplary supporters. [Budget director Richard] Darman can be depended upon at the doctrinal level; but for the rest of the century count no budget director your friend!

Do not underestimate the constituency of artists themselves.

Come the three corners of the world in arms,

And we shall shock them:

Shock 'em all right. As you note, piss on each other and assorted objects. Nothing else holds fashion.

But how, now, Fellow! What is the business of "our . . . revered National Endowment for the Arts." The NEA is a government agency. In the U.S. Government Manual it comes immediately after the National Credit Union Administration and immediately before the National Labor Relations Board. It was created in 1965 to show that Texans got kulcher too. Enhanced 1969–74 for much the same reason. Take the money and run. Do not linger to revere graven images. Remember what your mother taught you!

I am sort of serious. I was once asked by a (justifiably) irritated witness something to the effect "Very well Senator, what would you do to have Government encourage the arts." Without much thinking I said that I supposed the only thing government can do to encourage the arts is to forbid them. That seems to work. As in the Soviet Union. Now if you mean supporting the arts, that is different. You support the arts by giving them money. Giving artists money that is. Like you.

There was a price when it came from the Medicis or the Morgans. There is a price when it comes from Congress. Soon or late there is a price. I sense we are beginning to pay it. But Nothing ever stops the real artists. Save actual starvation. And that is rare in the era of food stamps. Of course the audiences can be deprived without knowing. That is what you know, and you, Sir, really are revered.

Excerpt of a letter to James Q. Wilson, his friend and former colleague at Harvard, lamenting again his lack of money and his inability to find a publisher for his latest book. Wilson served on the President's Foreign Intelligence Advisory Board (PFIAB) from 1985 to 1991.

PINDARS CORNERS
AUGUST 27, 1989

Dear Jim,

In some 30 years we've talked of just about everything except money. A matter of no concern to persons of high academic degree. Still, there is bound to be <u>something</u> you don't know, and I may be on to it. TIAA/CREF. [Teachers Insurance and Annuity Association/College Retirement Equities Fund, the retirement fund for university faculty.]

I have just retired. Not a moment too soon. In the course of my fitful professorial years it turned out I accumulated something like $150 grand. We have this pay thing now, and with one thing and another I am short. Mind I have been short for all these years, but considered it man's fate or capitalism or some such fixed condition. No! I checked in with hq. They sent me a packet—written so I could understand. You can "retire" any time you chose. You can get 10 percent up front for the condo in Arizona. You can assign your monthly payment to heirs should you and spouse depart across a twenty year period. You and spouse go on in any event if you stay about. Result: I paid off two bank loans and some goddam credit card accumulated in last year's fracas. I now have $2,000 a month indefinitely, Liz just a little less. I have given this to the Delhi bank. <u>All</u> the mortgages on this place will be gone within four years, which is to say I could leave the Senate with nothing to bother with here save school and property taxes which the rents about cover.

Charles Blitzer was here for a few days. I raised it with him. He is always fussing with a few stocks and such. But has half a million in TIAA etc. I suggested to him that he could be drawing fifty thousand or more a year, none of which he would need. Endow a chair at Smith or something such. He was a trustee for years. Buy a yacht. Give champagne breakfasts <u>regularly.</u> Weekly. Well, he can do that anyway on the expense account of the Wilson Center.

But you get the idea. I suggest you might get the packet. There comes a time when one lecture less might be in order!

Speaking of money. I have just about finished a "book" entitled, God save us, On the Law of Nations. Art. I, Sect. 8. It is not that bad. Jovanovich turned it (and me) down in advance. They are into theme parks and novels. This may be more fictional that I would like to think, but won't have many readers. On the other hand it is time a member of the Senate Foreign Relations did try to lay out what it was we once thought about this subject and ask what is it we think now and suggest what we ought. I would like an advance. I only asked ten thou for Came the Revolution which was certainly well reviewed. But did not sell. They seem to agree they didn't try. Gave [Donald] Regan one million. Which I'm happy to say he had to give to charity. All I really need is a publisher. Any thoughts? Basic? . . .

P.S. Where [is] pfiab [President's Foreign Intelligence Advisory Board] now?

In the wake of yet another college outburst, Moynihan writes to President Frances Fergusson of Vassar and returns the stipend he received for speaking there. The Vassar protesters had claimed that Moynihan had made a racial remark after his lecture on January 29, a charge Moynihan denied.

FEBRUARY 14, 1990

Dear Frances:

Heavens, what hath one lecture wrought! Everyone was so kind and welcoming on the occasion of my visit January 29 that I can scarce believe the present ruckus, but would not want to prolong it.

I gather the students have asked that I return—whatever that means—the Eleanor Roosevelt Professorship and the stipend that went with it. I know you won't approve of this, and I'm sure Eleanor Roosevelt would not have done, but let me do so anyway. The times, unhappily, have changed.

One point, however. I am being quoted as describing the United States as "a model of ethnic cooperation." The text of my lecture (p. 14) reads:

The United States of America provides a model of a reasonably successful multi-ethnic society. . . .

The lecture, of course, concerned ethnic dissonance in the Soviet Union and multi-ethnic societies generally.

Letter to Dr. Robert Krasner of the Attending Physician's Office at the Capitol, asking for help with his leg and apologizing for having forgotten about a prescription.

FEBRUARY 20, 1990

Dear Bob:

Last year every time I saw a doctor, I got a new disease. Accordingly, I decided not to see any doctors this year.

It seems I got the causality direction wrong. I have seen no doctors but, even so, have a new disease. My left leg won't work. Below the knee. Absent a surgical saw and a bottle of rum, I guess I had best turn myself into sickbay. I will call.

Also, anent our last conversation. I returned home that evening, and as I dropped my keys in a wicker basket provided for that purpose in the hallway, I noticed a plain brown wrapper inside which was the prescription. And so, I guess I need a new course of the wonderful Memory Pill you have devised.

Letter to George Kennan of Princeton, the Cold War diplomat and scholar, celebrating the fall of Communism.

APRIL 10, 1990

Excellency!

I have been much aware of your letter of last summer, setting forth your thoughts on a Presidential Council. And more than a little nagged by not having replied. I suppose my thoughts tugged me in opposite directions; a formula for indecision and procrastination. However, just a while ago, I happened on a review in the American Political Science Review in which a professor of government at Smith proposes something just so. Here is a copy, which I think you will find interesting. He is not afraid of ideas, I will say that.

In the meantime, I have asked the Congressional Research Service to do me up a paper on the Governor's Councils, which were such frequent fixtures of colonial government, and continued on into the 19th century as I best recollect.

You must be so enjoying the spectacle of the world turning your way. Well, it only took half a century!

CHAPTER TWELVE

"I Propose that Kuwait Be Liberated . . ."

Moynihan was emotionally and intellectually caught up in the fate of President George H. W. Bush, a political leader with whom he was friends but with whom he disagreed on his approach to the Iraqi invasion of Kuwait in 1990. In this period Moynihan grew increasingly convinced that the end of the cold war called for new thinking both in how the U.S. government was organized and how the U.S. related to the rest of the world. His new cause was international law, and he wanted to make the response to Saddam Hussein's seizure of Kuwait an example of the revival of the international system created after World War II, especially the United Nations. Critics wondered why someone who had been so critical of the U.N. had become so confident of its effectiveness, but Moynihan struck back saying that American institutions, especially the C.I.A., had so misjudged the character and strength of the Soviet Union that it was time for a break with the past. Moynihan seemed to pour his passions on the subject into his personal letter to President Bush, calling on him to master the first post-cold war crisis and achieve a historic first. It was not to be, though both sought to maintain their friendship.

In the 1990s, Moynihan seized on the integrity of Social Security as a major political issue. He argued that deficit-spending in the Reagan and Bush administrations, which he charged was a result of the Reagan-era tax cuts, were siphoning revenues generated by the Social Security tax system. His successive proposals included a law barring the use of these funds, and later he proposed that payroll taxes that fund Social Security should be cut. Although neither of these steps had any chance of passage, he was making a point that would later become clearer: that the financial integrity of Social Security was in jeopardy because of overall federal deficit-spending. The military invasion of Kuwait by Iraq reinforced Moynihan's conviction that after the collapse of Communism and the Soviet empire, the United States should lead in establishing a new order based on international law. His book ON THE LAW OF NATIONS *was published in September 1990.*

Letter to Secretary of State James A. Baker III, again reminding him that the C.I.A. had overestimated the size of the Soviet economy.

APRIL 26, 1990

Dear Jim:

You may recall appearing before the Finance Committee last October and suggesting that the Soviet economy was nothing like the size we had been estimating. In your testimony you thought they ranked third. On the way out of the hearing you suggested that they might even be as low as seventh.

On Tuesday I met with a group of Soviet economists over here for a meeting on this subject sponsored by the American Enterprise Institute and run by an old young friend, Nick Eberstadt. They would appear to be the best of the lot, notably Grigorii Khanin of the Academy of Sciences in Novosibirsk, and Vladimir Tikhonov of the Academy of National Economics of the USSR Academy of Agricultural Science. They offered the view that the Soviet economy is, in fact, as small as one-seventh that of the U.S. economy (i.e., about 14 percent of GNP, as against the CIA estimate of 52 percent). As it happens a Soviet economy of $694 billion, rather than $253.5 billion as the CIA now estimates, would place them seventh in the world just behind Italy.

Maybe you didn't know how much you knew!

Letter to Senator Lloyd Bentsen, chairman of the Senate Finance Committee, complaining again about tapping funds from the Social Security system.

MAY 10, 1990

Dear Lloyd:

At the forthcoming summit, I would hope that the Democratic representatives might insist that the size of the deficit to be dealt with be the true amount, defined as current expenditures minus current general revenues.

There is now a large and growing surplus in the Social Security trust fund. This will come to $74 billion in FY 1991, rising to $128 billion in FY 1995 (CBO). These surpluses are disguising the size of the true deficit. An argument can be made that the government has no alternative but to use the surplus in this manner. I would plead that if this has to be done, there has to be a <u>decision</u> to do it. The F.I.C.A. rate increases of 1977 created this surplus. It was never contemplated that the surplus would be spent as if it were general revenue. I could understand a decision to do so in any event—I would not agree, but I could understand. But I hold it would be contemptible for our government to use trust funds in this manner without openly acknowledging that this represents a change in policy.

Letter to Governor Mario Cuomo of New York, thanking him for his help on the Social Security issue.

MAY 18, 1990

Dear Mario:

A few weeks ago Ron Brown [chairman of the Democratic National Committee, later Commerce Secretary] asked me to speak to a D.N.C. Trustees meeting in New York on the Social Security issue. I ended up something of a common scold, but no one seemed to mind much. To the contrary, the group seemed much impressed that almost no one there knew that median family income, taking into account Social Security payments, is <u>lower</u> today than it was fifteen years ago. Concerning which I remarked:

> If your family income has not increased in fifteen years, there is likely to be one thing you will know about the Democratic Party, and that is that the party does not know about you.

Anyway, I sent it off to <u>The New Republic</u> and it appears in this week's issue.

I have some poll numbers. A preeminently respectable poll taker has established that as of May 17th:

> A 68 percent majority are opposed to the use of Social Security payroll taxes to help cut the federal deficit.

As of April 25th, the same poll found the President with a 57 percent negative rating for "his handling of Social Security." However, Gallup finds the public still does not quite connect the misuse of trust funds with a cut in the payroll levy. As reported by the Employee Benefit Research Institute this morning, "An overwhelming majority (81 percent) of all respondents said that it is inappropriate that part of the Social Security trust funds are loaned to the government to pay for defense, education, and other programs." However, "A majority of Americans (57 percent) are opposed to cutting the Social Security payroll tax. . . ."

I thank you for your great and unwavering support.

Letter to State Senator John B. Daly of Buffalo, urging that tolls be lifted on the New York State Thruway, reflecting Moynihan's lifelong interest in transportation issues and the construction of the New York State Thruway, which was built in the 1950s when he was working in Albany.

MAY 18, 1990

Dear Senator Daly:

I do thank you for your letter on Thruway tolls. Respectfully, I must continue to disagree.

The interstate system was intended to be financed by dedicated revenue: the federal gasoline tax. Yet the New York State Thruway—the largest and grandest segment of this great project—continues to be burdened by tolls.

Long have I argued against this. The people of New York have paid their share toward the construction and maintenance of the federal system. They should not pay twice for the Thruway.

I must emphasize further that the State will <u>not</u> bear alone the costs of operating and maintaining the Thruway if the tolls are removed. In 1978, I got a law passed that made the Thruway immediately eligible for full federal maintenance money if—and only if—the State agreed to remove the tolls in 1996, when the bonds are due. The State agreed to this in 1982.

But if we keep the tolls come 1996, we will owe Washington the $500 million in federal money that will have been spent on maintenance since. A half a billion dollars. What then? Another bond issue?

Even without this arrangement, the Thruway should be toll-free. New Yorkers have paid too much for their own road. And can the costs of travelling this road be viewed as anything but a disincentive for industrial development in the State?

It's not just that we have tolls. It's that others don't.

Letter to John N. Nordstrom of the Nordstrom department store, thanking him for the service at a store in Pentagon City.

MAY 22, 1990

Dear Mr. Nordstrom:

A few weeks ago my wife insisted on taking me to your new store in Pentagon City to buy some clothes. Something I am typically loath to do, but cannot indefinitely avoid. There I met Bill Baer, the manager of your men's clothing section. He could not have been more helpful.

Last Friday we were back for a final fitting and were told if we could wait an hour over lunch, the whole thing would be done on the spot. Something unheard of. But in the end I had to get back to the Senate and we decided to wait for another weekend.

I got home that evening only to find Mr. Baer on my doorstep, having crossed the Potomac and found our house on Capitol Hill. He waited long enough for me to make certain the pants were the right length and left with the greatest good cheer.

Extraordinary.

Thank him. And thank you.

⊗

Letter to Mayor David N. Dinkins of New York, laying out the terms for the Museum of the American Indian to move to Washington from the old U.S. Custom House in Lower Manhattan. The building, a beaux arts masterpiece by the architect Cass Gilbert, now houses the New York branch of the National Museum of the American Indian as well as the Bankruptcy Court for the Southern District of New York.

MAY 22, 1990

Dear Mr. Mayor:

I have just concluded a meeting here at the Senate with Robert McC. Adams, Secretary of the Smithsonian Institution, David Rockefeller, and William Diamond, Regional Director of the General Services Administration, concerning the George Gustav Heye Center of the National Museum of the American Indian, which is to be located in the old U.S. Custom House at Bowling Green.

We have now agreed in principle on all essential matters. The Museum will, of course, move from New York to Washington, but a permanent branch will remain at the Custom House. (By way of comparison, the exhibition space will be roughly that of the Whitney.) It was further agreed that an all-out effort would be made to mount an exhibition in 1992, in time for the 500th anniversary of the European discovery of North America, with materials representing the various Indian cultures in place at that time. The Heye collection is, of course, gathered from the whole of the Western Hemisphere.

With this agreement, my role in the affairs of the Museum of the American Indian comes to a close. It has been going on for some 14 years, many of them bleak indeed. But in the end things have worked out well enough. I suppose.

In the mid-70s, a group of downtown businessmen had grown concerned with the seeming abandonment of the Custom House, a masterwork of Cass Gilbert; the finest structure the Federal government has ever built outside the Washington area. You could not put a price on it, but surely it would have been a great addition to the City's inventory.

Enter the Museum of the American Indian, which at about this time announced that unless a suitable building was found for it, it would leave the City. We rushed money to the Custom House to fix the roof and do first order maintenance. There now commenced a ten-year negotiation during which the City was asked to accept the Custom House and the Museum to move in. In 1986, President Reagan himself offered us the building. But nothing availed. The City would not take it. It was pure disaster, compounded by bad faith and deceit. And so Congress came along and invited the Museum to Washington, and in fairly short order the deal was done. May I state, as a Regent, that the Smithsonian did not grab our treasure. (This is the most important ethnographic collection in the world.) In point of fact, the proposal to take over was first broached by a New York member of the Board of Regents some fifteen years ago.

However, there is a saving remnant of large value. There will be a George Gustav Heye Center. If the Museum itself has moved to Washington, well, that is New York's loss and Washington's gain. Nothing new these days!

In closing, may I express what I believe should be our greatest gratitude to James D. Wolfensohn, who headed the group put together by the Downtown Association which identified the importance of the Custom House, to Barber Conable, now head of the World Bank but then chairman of the board of the Museum, who was heroic in his concern for the collection, and no less desirous to see it remain in New York; and finally, to David Rockefeller, who, as in so many things, was unwavering in his support for the City and his appreciation of its treasures.

Letter congratulating Chancellor Joseph S. Murphy of City University.

PINDARS CORNERS
JUNE 1, 1990

Dear Joe,

Bravo! Will we never stop running down our most precious institutions. In the summer of 1943 I left Pier 48 on the North River at about six in the evening, went uptown, longshoreman's hook in my rear right pocket (the prescribed mode on West Street) and took entrance exams for City College. I had only one year—there was a war on—but it changed my life. As it has done thousands on thousands of others before and since.

Letter to Governor L. Douglas Wilder of Virginia, lamenting the decline in the growth of wages for Americans.

JUNE 19, 1990

Dear Governor Wilder:

I have just been reading of your admirable remarks at the Humphrey Institute for Public Affairs at the University of Minnesota. In this regard, you might be interested in an article I recently wrote for <u>The New Republic</u> concerning the astounding indifference, or so it seems to me, of Democratic leaders to the virtual freeze on income that working Americans have experienced during the past generation.

Taking into account Social Security taxes, median family income was $458 <u>lower</u> in 1988 than 16 years earlier in 1973. More strikingly, average family earnings in 1989 were, in these terms, lower than three decades earlier in 1959.

I spoke about this to our State convention in Albany awhile back. My wife and I met in Averell Harriman's campaign in 1954, joined his administration and were married the following spring. It was a decade of phenomenal success. Average weekly income rose by almost one-third. I put it to the delegates that Liz and I began the decade with subway money and ended up with a station wagon. (I could add three children and a dog.)

Nothing was clearer than the fact that as we moved from single individuals to married couple with a family, our standard of living just about doubled. I can't imagine what it would be like if during the last three decades nothing whatever had happened to our earnings. This, however, has been the experience of the average worker. I wrote in <u>The New Republic</u>, "If your family income has not increased in fifteen years, there is likely to be one thing you will know about the Democratic Party, and that is that the party does not know about you."

You, sir, are a notable exception.

Letter to the columnist Murray Kempton, lobbying for Social Security payroll tax relief.

PINDARS CORNERS
JULY 7, 1990

Dear Murray,

What a hugely generous and warming passage in your column "New Taxes." I know you have not always felt that way, and on that account matters all the more. Liz much agrees and sends love.

Did I ever send you the paperback of the Godkin lectures? In it I expand a bit on the notion of The Great Divide. For those you and I would call working people economic growth stopped in 1973. Median family income has only just now got back to the level of that year. Wives working. Average weekly wages are <u>below</u> 1959. Hourly earnings in mfg are 2¢ below 1967. We have no vocabulary for this phenomenon. Nothing like it has happened in the history of the European settlement of North America. Perhaps you will find time for the passage at p. 201. Jim Miller was a hugely conservative budget director, but implacably honest. He really did think, in 1986, that family income was at an all time high. He was startled to find it was near a post war low. More startled that it's all there in a plain table in the Economic Report and not one of the half dozen senior types in the E.O.B. even noticed his mistake. For the phenomenon has not been noticed.

This is my plaint on Social Security. How can we not see that "our" people need a break.

It would give many two earner households an extra $1000 and finally get them above 1973 incomes. Yet it makes no claim—no gut claim—on any but the supply siders. Jack Kemp would be for it. Lane Kirkland? Not really. The Congress? In theory, but not, to say again, in the gut. I wrote of this for the New Republic a while back, saying that if you are one of the persons this has happened to the only thing you're likely to know about the Democrats is that they don't know about you. . . .

Letter to Richard Darman, director of the Office of Management and Budget, joking about both being cited as "farsighted" politicians in U.S. NEWS & WORLD REPORT.

PINDARS CORNERS
JULY 9, 1990

Dear Mr. Darman,

I see from the July 9 issue of U.S. News & World Report that I have won the "Most farsighted politician" contest by a slim lead over you and Mayor Hudnut.

I offer the consoling thought that you have many years ahead of you and many taxes to raise. And I ask this question. If I am so foresighted, why am I broke?

P.S. Have I ever thrust upon you a lecture I gave years ago entitled The Iron Law of Emulation? It proceeds from the proposition that organizations in conflict become like one another. I trace conflict techniques such as the West Wing of the White House and the Russell Office Building through the 20th century. It is an instructive perspective, or so I believe. I now note that the President has created an <u>Office of Management and Administration</u> in his immediate preserve, clearly suiting up to take on the <u>Office of Management and Budget</u> in yours. Hmm.

Letter to Senator George Mitchell, the senate majority leader, again complaining about the failures of the C.I.A.

JULY 11, 1990

Dear George:

After that discussion at our last Policy Committee meeting of the Directorate of Intelligence estimates of per capita GNP in East and West Germany, I got to thinking of the subject generally. I am at that point in life where I have trouble remembering the names of nephews, but have total recall of luncheon conversations thirty years ago.

Anyway, of a sudden I recalled Walt Rostow, in 1962, then head of the policy planning staff at State avowing, "I am not one of those six percent forever types." The Agency was then estimating Soviet growth at a sustained 5.9 percent. That number almost defined the foreign policy of the Kennedy administration! It was wrong. Hugely, now irretrievably wrong.

I spelled some of this out in the Washington Post this morning. It appeared with an article by Robert J. Samuelson about NSA's plans to turn from spying on the Russians to spying on the Japanese. This, of course, is dementia. The Soviets spent half a century trying to steal our economic secrets. Only just now are they realizing that the secret is that there are no secrets. There is a market, instead. So, now we begin acting like commissars. Real smart.

Letter to Lee Krenis-More of the Rochester DEMOCRAT AND CHRONICLE, *who had written an editorial praising Moynihan but citing the* ECONOMIST *magazine as saying that Moynihan's "eyes are bloodshot for exactly the reason you think they are." The apparent reference to a symptom of drinking is described here as caused by glaucoma, for which he used eyedrops every day.*

JULY 18, 1990

Dear Lee:

You are a peach. And Liz loved it.

I have to expect I will pay for those blood-shot eyes one day. The truth, alas, is worse. Glaucoma, which doesn't go away. Every time I saw a doctor last year I got a new disease. First that. Then spinal stenosis (operable, but not worth the bother; at least, not yet). I resolved not to see any doctors this year, but inadvertently looked in at the Attending Physician here at the Capitol and, don't you know, came out with a rheumatoid condition in my left knee!

So you will understand that it was with some considerable enthusiasm that I voted for the Americans with Disabilities Act.

Letter to Senate Majority Leader George Mitchell, on reorganizing the U.S. government after the cold war.

AUGUST 15, 1990

MEMORANDUM FOR THE MAJORITY LEADER

A while back I dropped by to say that I was thinking whether you might want to form a select committee, or some such arrangement, to consider the organization of American government in the aftermath of the cold war. You asked if I would put something on paper.

Forgive me if I go on a bit, telling you things you already know. I am trying to sort out the argument.

The proposition is about as follows. In the course of a half century of confrontation with a totalitarian Marxist power, American government changed. This was foreseen. In his <u>Constitutional Government in the United States</u> (1908) [Woodrow] Wilson wrote that the assertion of American power abroad (which he himself would take to unprecedented levels) had "changed the balance of constitutional parts," projecting the President "at the front of the government." . . . It was advocated. Thus Clinton Rossiter in 1948 argued that constitutional revision was necessary in the context of the cold war.

> In time of crisis, a democratic, constitutional government must be temporarily altered to whatever degree is necessary to overcome the peril. . . . The government is going to be powerful or we are going to be obliterated.

And, you might say, it was written. Political scientists have a rule: organizations in conflict become like one another.

I

Three institutional changes are most conspicuous.

First, the President as Commander in Chief.

This was never previously so. A President as head of a National Security Council (1947), a military aide carrying the "football" (circa 1950); a vast Secret Service (Budget under Wilson, $21,220; currently $367,000,000); Generals everywhere, Marines at the entrance of the West Wing; Air Force One. A profoundly changed institutional presidency.

Like all huge events, this has many origins, but there is one date in particular. On February 21, 1947 the British government announced it would suspend military and economic aid to Greece and Turkey. Breaking with a century and a half of American peacetime diplomacy Harry S Truman propounded the doctrine that took American arms and aid first to the eastern Mediterranean and in time the farthest reaches of the world. There are four aspects of this decision worth noting. First, the apocalyptic terms. By all accounts (O'Neil, 1986) Marshall's briefing of congressional leaders was too matter of fact to stir them. This required Acheson: "like apples in a barrel infected by one rotten one, the corruption of Greece would infect Iran and all to the east. It would also carry the infection through Asia Minor and Egypt and to Europe through Italy and France . . ." Enter the domino theory. Second, our analysis of Soviet intentions was probably off. By this time there was a communist party in every country on earth, or as near as makes no matter. In Greece, as in other European nations, notably Italy and France, the Communists had taken up arms against Nazis, and were now contesting the post war settlement. As for outside support, it seems mostly to have come from Tito and stopped the next year when he broke with Moscow. Third, it did the hawks no good at home. We no more started containing Communism than the architects of the policy began to be accused of subversion. Fourth, the commitment never stops. Getting on to a half century later we are sending over one third of a billion dollars per year worth of economic and military aid to Greece; more than half a billion to Turkey.

Two, the secrecy system.

With the advent of the cold war the principle decisions made by the Presidency and to a related degree the Congress have been based on secret information, available only to the actors within the system. (Some 3,000,000!) Some of these secrets were of domestic deception. I can recall in 1962 an old New Dealer referring to Vietnam as the "Top Secret War." Then the "incursion" into Cambodia. On to Iran-Contra, of which you are the resident expert. Of the latter, Theodore Draper has written: "If ever the constitutional government of the United States is overthrown, we now have a better idea of how this is likely to be done."

The central and enduring problem of the secrecy system is that while the principle actors typically feel that they have no choice but to rely on the secrets as a guide to national policy, the secrets are frequently wrong. When I came by to see you about all this I had just finished a hearing on the C.I.A. estimates of the size of the Soviet economy over the past forty years. It turns out they have been hugely wrong; vastly overstating both the size of Soviet GNP and the rate of growth. I would predict that this issue will not go away. Indeed, it has the makings of a conspiracy theory. I don't see it as such, but I do see such calamities as inherent in the secrecy system itself. Analogies will be found in the economic literature about the market value of information and the costs associated with missing information. ("Asymmetric information"; when one party withholds information from the other.)

A formative event was the report of the 1957 Gaither Committee, "Deterrence & Survival in the Nuclear Age" which reached President Eisenhower a few weeks after the launching of Sputnik, the first artificial earth satellite. The committee warned of a "missile gap"; concluded that the Soviets had surpassed the U.S. in terms of military effort; and projected a rate of growth of the Soviet economy which would have them passing the U.S. two years from now. (Soviet machine tool production was asserted to be <u>twice</u> that of the U.S.) This document, replete with profound error, remained classified until 1973. This is what Presidents in the grimmest years of the cold war "knew." What they knew was largely wrong but there was no way to correct the errors as the errors were secret.

In the end, the system failed utterly to foretell the collapse of the Soviet empire. We couldn't even recognize the event as it was happening, what Brumberg (1990) calls "essentially the eclipse of the despotic one-party state and the emergence of a functioning parliamentary democracy." Instead we drove ourselves into fiscal exhaustion as we watched what we took to be the empire expanding to within miles of Harlingen, Texas. Thus the Comptroller General: "The military budget doubled between 1980 and 1985 . . . a build-up that was much, too fast." "Six short years ago we were the world's leading creditor nation. Today, we are the world's largest debtor." (Bowsher, 1988)

<u>Three, permanent crisis.</u> This is a pattern of the modern age in arms. We associate it with totalitarianism of the fascist variety, but Communist regimes have similarly sought to maintain an indefinitely mobilized society, fighting internal or external enemies, or both. Orwell is our mentor in this.

The United States went through a period of near panic about subversion. The Internal Security Act of 1950 authorized the President to detain all persons whom the government had a "reasonable ground" to believe "probably" would commit acts of sabotage and the like. Hubert Humphrey among others voted for an appropriation in 1952 to build detention camps just in case. By the 1970s some 470 such statutes existed "delegating power to the executive over virtually every facet of American life." (Lobel, 1989). The Iran Contra period was replete with such fantasized peril. (There had been, of course, a real Communist presence in the United States. By the time these reactions began, however, it had all but disappeared.)

II

One of the consequences of the structural changes and preoccupations wrought by the cold war is that the rest of the government doesn't work very well. "The United States came to define itself in terms of its opposition to the Soviet Union." (Pfaff, 1990). Anticommunism became the "central organizing principle" of American politics. (Ornstein and Schmitt, 1990). Let us not wonder then if we have as a matter of fact paid just about "any price" to deal with this external threat. (Sometimes, of course, internalizing it. As in the discovery that General George Marshall was "a front man for traitors" (Jenner, 1950).

We have become the first society in history in which the poorest group in the population are the children, the supreme indicator of a protracted period of national life preoccupied with the perpetual crisis of the moment. Obviously this exaggerates, but how much? We have close to 700,000 Americans in West Germany and a third world infant mortality rate in our inner cities. Our inner cities; not theirs, you may be damn well sure. In the meantime, average weekly earnings in the Unites States are lower than they were when Dwight D. Eisenhower was President.

This approaches special pleading, but it does appear to me that a once vibrant concept of public administration as a definable profession is in eclipse if not ruin. In the American democratic structure, the "basic organization structure is to provide legal authority to officers and accountability by those officers to politically responsible officials." (Moe, 1990). Or, rather, was. Consider the Financial Institutions Reform, Recovery, and Enforcement Act of 1989 (FIRREA) more commonly known as the "S & L Bailout Bill." Has there ever been an equivalent phantasmagoria of evasion, avoidance, incompetence, muddle, and panic, all with a nice overlay of swindle? From a Treasury Department once headed by Alexander Hamilton! The largest scandal in the history of the national government; for which no one is responsible. That being the first sign of a government whose true energies and talents are directed elsewhere. Chalk it up to the cold war.

A nice combination of domestic crisis arising from foreign entanglements and the secrecy system is to be found in the environmental disaster areas the nuclear weapons program seems to have left in its wake.

Economists like to look at issues such as this in terms of "opportunity costs." The subject is easily approached in terms of gross aggregates. How much GNP do the Soviets forego when they draft an extra million 18 year olds? Or what other opportunities do we forego when we send the Iowa class battleships back to sea. Other calculations are more elusive. What do you give up when your best brains and most ardent energies are directed to cold war priorities, as against others? (You probably have noticed that I have spent some years now trying to get the government involved with the development of magnetic levitation. This is an American invention which will arguable be the defining transportation mode of the next century. That or high speed rail. The Germans and Japanese are roaring ahead on Maglev; the French on TGV. We dropped the subject fifteen years ago. This year, as a sort of personal favor, Darman put up $9.7 million in the budget. When same budget routinely proposed $4 billion or whatever for Star Wars.)

III

Is there any systematic way we might set about thinking through this subject? If the Cold War is over, if we are no longer to define ourselves in terms of opposition to the Soviet Union, what institutional arrangements need to be revised? I am not sure. I toyed with the idea of a kind of Hoover Commission On Organization of the Executive Branch of the Government. This was a congressional initiative. Acheson, who was Vice Chairman, had the assignment of going up to the Waldorf to ask on behalf of President Truman whether former President Hoover would take on the chairmanship. He once described to me stopping in a bar off the lobby to have three martinis to prepare himself for the encounter. (Hoover awaited him in the Towers with a bowl of same!) The point is they were to plan the Republican administration that would be elected in 1948. When that failed to come off, the Commission report had but a small effect. There is no comparable, energizing expectation around just now. Nor do I sense much feeling that anything needs doing that won't happen anyway. (The Defense Budget will more or less decline on its own, etc.) Republicans in 1947 wanted to tighten up a government they felt had grown gigantic in size during the New Deal and the Second War. If there is any equivalent sense of a cold war aftermath to be dealt with, which is to say the concentration and abuse of power, I haven't picked it up.

To the contrary. Consider that chilling business of Iran Contra. A new book by Harold Koh of the Yale Law School observes: "At this writing, not one of the Iran Contra committees' legislative recommendations has been enacted into law." You helped me get an amendment through last year on soliciting and diverting. It was vetoed without any stir in the Congress, or among the public. The executive departments will not change. Three years ago and then a year ago I enacted a temporary then permanent repeal of the visa provisions of the McCarran Walter Act. A national embarrassment for forty years since Truman's veto was overridden and we began barring subversive visitors. You would think the State Department would feel free at last from a know nothing law that over the years probably helped the Soviet cause by discrediting ours. But you would be wrong. They are still keeping the "watch list" up to date, denying a visa to a Canadian union leader whose parents enrolled him in a left wing little league forty years ago, etc. Even the C.I.A. where you usually find a high order of seriousness and professionalism simply can't bring itself to admit to me that in the mid-70's they were estimating Soviet GNP at 62 percent of U.S. They send me the revised figures. They know that I know that they know that I know. But "sources and methods" are involved, and these are secret.

Consider the Defense Budget. Last January the Administration sent us a budget that made sense only if nothing had happened in the world in 1989. The most momentous year of modern history. You will recall the figures Tim Wirth presented in one of our caucus'. The proposed Pentagon budget, and the reduced one we passed, does not even get back to the "norm" of the cold war. Eisenhower's military-industrial complex will go on indefinitely so long as the secrecy system makes responsible men feel they have no choice but to make what turn out to be awful mistakes. (In the debate on the Defense budget I wanted to have us go on record that the aggregate appropriation for the intelligence "community" should be made public. No chance.) In the meantime the cold war institutions scurry about for new assignments. Narcoterrorism. "Economic intelligence." Law enforcement. (Hardly more than two years ago the chief of staff of the Army fair to pleaded with me to not let his Army get involved in domestic law enforcement of the drug front. We had, he said and I agreed, the finest army in history. He never wanted to see his American soldiers pointing their guns at other Americans. Something very like that happened last week in California as the force of regulars and guards swept through some marijuana country. I assume the Chief of Staff has changed his mind.)

IV

If you are still with me. . . .

I conclude that a select committee is not possible, or at least not possible now. However, I think we can go ahead with a series of Foreign-Relations Committee hearings that will explore the three main themes of this memorandum. Claiborne is supportive. It will focus on three themes.

One.
The institutionalization of the policy of containment.
Two.
The domestic constraints imposed by the cold war.
Three.
The opportunity costs of protracted mobilization.

By the end of the year I hope to have a report which the Foreign Relations Committee may want to adopt.

After I set out some of these thoughts in an opening statement at our hearing on the CIA estimates, Haynes Johnson wrote: "nothing could be more timely, or important." (I sent you the clip.)

I agree. And what else is a six year term for!

Letter to Senate Majority Leader Mitchell, on the situation in the Persian Gulf following Iraqi President Saddam Hussein's invasion of Kuwait, which had begun August 2. The invasion prompted immediate talk of the U.S. leading an allied military action to push Iraq back. Moynihan suggests that this be made a case study of international law, requiring sanctions and not a military response.

PINDARS CORNERS
AUGUST 26, 1990

MEMORANDUM FOR THE MAJORITY LEADER

You asked if, as chairman of the subcommittee on Near Eastern and South Asian Affairs of the Committee on Foreign Relations, I would prepare a memorandum on the situation in the Gulf, especially as it involves the United Nations. You had in mind sending it around to other Democratic members.

I.

THE UNITED NATIONS

Nearly one half century after it was established, the UN has been given a chance to perform as it was intended to do. There is every present indication that it might succeed. No small matter. This is our first post cold war crisis. (It didn't take long. Literally 17 days after Soviet agreement to the reunification of Germany.) It is precisely the kind of crisis the Security Council was designed to deal with, which is to say armies crossing borders. This is how the second World War began, and the first World War before that. But then nations stopped behaving in this way. Internal borders were crossed, as in Korea, later Vietnam. Disputed borders were crossed, as with the case of China and India. But invasion for the purpose of conquest and annihilation, as with the case of the German-Russian invasion of Poland in 1939 pretty much ceased.

The characteristic form of aggression during the half century of cold war was an internal uprising supported from the outside, but indigenous even so. (If Khrushchev could boast that our grandchildren would "play under Red Flags," he did not mean they would be planted here by the Soviet army.) The UN could not handle conflict of this kind. The facts were never clear, events never concise, but above all the two great powers of the world were at odds, whereas in order for the system to work the Charter required them to cooperate.

By contrast, the Iraqi invasion of Kuwait is the clearest possible violation of the Charter, and is accompanied by grievous breaches of other treaties. The great powers are, for the moment at least, united in opposition. The smaller nations are in no less accord, and have as much or more at stake. If events now in train work out, we may well set a pattern for world order which has been the continuous but defeated quest of the twentieth century.

II.

INTERNATIONAL LAW

A compelling aspect of the current crisis is the reappearance of international law in the pronouncements of the American presidency. The disappearance of international law from our decisions and our statements, lost in the fog of the cold war, was one of the defining developments of the past half century. It was a huge break with our past, a past which, for one thing, created the UN system. Its sudden reappearance marks, in effect, the re-emergence of the UN in our statecraft. On August 3, the day after the invasion, President Bush declared, "What Iraq has done violates every norm of international law." This theme continues unbroken. In his press conference of August 22, the President cited "international law" or the "rule of law" no fewer than seven times.

There has been a parallel Soviet response. In a televised address on August 17, President Gorbachev declared:

We have witnessed an act of perfidy and a blatant violation of international law and the U.N. Charter—in short, a violation of everything the world community now pins its hopes on as it seeks to put civilization on the tracks of peaceful development.

He went on to state, "It is essential to restore respect for international law."

Gorbachev first set out this position in an address at the UN in December, 1988. Few in Washington noticed—we were pretty tone deaf on these matters—but he went before the General Assembly in New York and invoked "the political, juridical and moral importance of the ancient Roman maxim: Pacta sunt servanda!—agreements must be honoured!" He called for "a uniform understanding of the principles and norms of international law" and concluded:

As the awareness of our common fate grows, every state would be genuinely interested in confining itself within the limits of international law.

III.

THE PARTICULARS

Iraq is in actual or imminent violation of three fundamental statutes.

First, the invasion and occupation of Kuwait. Article 2, section 4 of the Charter of the UN, of which Iraq is a member, provides:

All Members shall refrain in their international relations from the threat or use of force against the territorial integrity or political independence of any state. . . .

Under Chapter VII of the Charter, ACTION WITH RESPECT TO THREATS TO THE PEACE, BREACHES OF THE PEACE, AND ACTS OF AGGRESSION, the Security Council has adopted five resolutions in response to Iraqi actions.

Resolution 660. Condemned the invasion and demanded that Iraq withdraw immediately (14–0, with one abstention).

Resolution 661. Imposed economic sanction against Iraq pursuant to Article 41 of the Charter ("measures not involving the use of armed force") (13–0, with two abstentions).

Resolution 662. Rejected the annexation of Kuwait by Iraq (15–0).

Resolution 664. Demanded "that Iraq permit and facilitate the immediate departure from Kuwait and Iraq of the nationals of third countries" (15–0).

Resolution 665. Called upon "those member states cooperating with the Government of Kuwait . . . to use such measures commensurate to the specific circumstances as may be necessary under the authority of the Security Council to halt all inward and outward maritime shipping. . . ."

In his televised meeting with British hostages in Baghdad, President Saddam Hussein claimed that Kuwait rightfully belongs to Iraq.

> . . . the Arab nation is one nation. It's a single nation. British colonial rule scissored away—cut away—the Arab nation. All that happened was for this spot, this particular part, called Kuwait, has now come back to its motherland.

This is nonsense. The countries of this region are in the main products of the Paris Peace Conference which ended World War I, specifically the Treaty of Sevres (1920) between the Allies and the sultan of Turkey under which the Ottomans renounced claims to all non-Turkish territory. Syria became a French Mandate; Mesopotamia and Palestine became British Mandates. In 1932 Iraq was granted formal independence. Mesopotamia, obviously, goes back a long while. Kuwait begins in the 18th century when a Bedouin tribe settled on the coast. For a time the sheik paid tribute to the Ottomans and Kuwait was nominally part of the province of Basra. But by the end of the 19th century Kuwait had independent treaty relations with Great Britain, and by 1914 it had become a British protectorate. (Kaiser Wilhelm had announced the Berlin to Baghdad railroad would be extended to Basra and the Gulf.) In any event, any conceivable Iraqi claim was extinguished in 1963 when Kuwait became a member of the UN.

Second, Iraq by various harassments and pronouncements is in actual or imminent violation of the immunity of foreign embassies and envoys. The Preamble to the Vienna Convention on Diplomatic Relations (1961), to which Iraq is a party, states that "People of all nations from ancient times have recognized the status of diplomatic agents." The situation in Kuwait is somewhat complicated in that the missions there are accredited to a government which is not in control, but there is no doubt on the larger issues. During the Iran hostage crisis the International Court of Justice ruled overwhelmingly in favor of the United States and held that Iran was violating its duties. The Security Council was only prevented from imposing sanctions by a Soviet veto—an event not likely to be repeated today.

Third, Iraq, through the internment and removal of foreign nationals, is in actual or imminent violation of human rights guaranteed by the Geneva Convention Relative to the Protection of Civilian Persons in Time of War of 1949, known as the Fourth Geneva Convention. This treaty, to which Iraq is a party, sets forth in explicit detail the rights of "protected persons" not to be taken hostage, to be interned under these circumstances, or to be treated as members of proscribed groups. As is known, a principle purpose of the 1949 Geneva conventions was to give formal international standing to the judgments of the Nuremburg tribunals. If a single American, Briton, Egyptian, Pakistani, whatever, is executed at the order of Saddam Hussein, he and his commandants are personally responsible and can be—and should be—hung.

IV.
"THE IRAQ INTERNATIONAL LAW COMPLIANCE ACT OF 1990"

As we have seen, a formidable regime of international law is now arrayed against Iraq. This is unambiguous treaty law, to which the United States is then a party. (Making such conventions "the supreme Law of the Land" under Article VI of our Constitution.) What are the prospects of proceeding on this basis, in the manner the President has so clearly indicated?

It is necessary to state that the State Department in recent years—decades—has shown little disposition to define Untied States policies in terms of such treaties, albeit the same State Department negotiated them, and without exception urged them upon the Senate.

Iraq provides an ominous instance. Its long war against Iran was as much as act of aggression as its war against Kuwait, but neither the United States nor any other UN member attempted any sanction. Its use of poison gas was a hideous act, clearly in violation of the 1925 Geneva Protocol. (The Protocol for the Prohibition of the Use in War of Asphyxiating, Poisonous or Other Gases, and of Bacteriological Methods of Warfare, of which Iraq is a signatory.) The international community paid little heed and did nothing, albeit this was the first systematic violation of a standard that survived even the second World War. . . .

V.
NOW WHAT?

If indeed after nearly half a century the UN has been given a chance to operate as it was intended to do, so equally after nearly half a century the Congress must face up to some of the assumptions implicit in those UN arrangements.

Specifically, can the President commit American forces to combat on the basis of a Security Council resolution without reference to Congress' power to declare war?

This subject was specifically and extensively considered in 1944–45. (See On the Law of Nations, pp. 73–79; 111–15.) In 1944 President Roosevelt and the Senate leadership of both parties explicitly supported the Dumbarton Oaks provision that the "executive council" of the new international organization should be "authorized to provide for the use of armed force" and that member states would provide it. The President would have the power to commit American forces. Congress would be consulted, as Congress was—most meticulously—being consulted at that time. In 1945 the United Nations Participation Act provided:

> The President is authorized to negotiate a special agreement or agreements with the Security Council which shall be subject to the approval of the Congress by appropriate Act or joint resolution, providing for the numbers and types of armed forces, the degrees of readiness and general locations, and the nature of facilities and assistance, including rights of passage, to be made available to the Security Council on its call for the purpose of maintaining international peace and security in accordance with article 43 of said Charter. The President shall not be deemed to require the authorization of the Congress to make available to the Security Council on its call in order to take action under article 42 of said Charter and pursuant to such special agreement or agreements the armed forces, facilities, or assistance provided for therein. . . .

Note, however, that no such special agreement was ever negotiated. The Truman administration tried; but the cold war intervened. And so we find ourselves back with the provisions of the Constitution and enactments such as the War Powers Resolution. Thus, President Bush's letter of August 9 to the President Pro Tempore was ambiguous in the now familiar way. He began by declaring the Iraqi invasion a "flagrant violation of the Charter," but ended by describing U.S. action as an exercise of our "inherent right of individual and collective self-defense." That phrase (complete with the hyphen) is from Article 51 of the Charter, the last of Chapter VII, which in effect gives members the right to act independently of the UN.

VI.
A NOTE ON LOGISTICS

Iraq imports three quarters of its food, and pays for it with a single export which is in adequate world supply. If ever economic sanctions <u>could</u> work, this is the ideal case. (Armed conflict could still break out and that would be another matter.) If a protracted land and sea blockade is to be put in place, it may be worth noting that during a number of years of the 1980s the Corps of Engineers carried out more construction in Saudi Arabia than in the United States. We have a proven capacity to provide the infrastructure for our forces in that region.

VII.
A NOTE ON OUR OBLIGATIONS

The United States has duties under the Charter, but as for Kuwait, we have few obligations discernable to this Senator. During the hearing on the Iraq International Law Compliance Act it was brought out that Kuwait almost never supports <u>us</u> at the UN. (Well, in 1989, twice out of sixteen key votes.) During the worst of the cold war days it was forever receiving Soviet arms, much as Iraq did. As regards U.S. interests in the Gulf, early in the 1980s the Kuwaiti minister of state for foreign affairs declared that "the people of this region are perfectly capable of preserving their own security and stability." Shortly thereafter, Erich Honecker of the German Democratic Republic was given a gala state visit by his worship the Emir.

I propose that Kuwait be liberated by the United Nations and donated to UNICEF.

Letter to Erwin N. Griswold, the former dean of Harvard Law School and former Solicitor General, thanking him for his support of Moynihan's invocation of international law.

PINDARS CORNERS
SEPTEMBER 8, 1990

Dear Mr. Dean,

I have read and re-read you letter. I have treasured it; clung to it as you might say through the rapids of the past five weeks. It was the first indication that the book would be taken seriously by persons who are, well, <u>serieux</u>. And then to see the UN come alive. Next our President invoking "international law" six times in one press conference! Then to find myself seated in King Fahd's throne room and listening to <u>him</u> go on about "international law"! I don't know that it will last, but it did happen. I had coffee with the President Wednesday morning. He seems to understand that he has set in motion a set of policies much distant from what Louis Henkin calls the "Bush-Reagan doctrine" having regard to Panama. Yet you never quite know with George Bush whether he is <u>thinking</u>. He does think, but not always. Reagan of course never did.

I have one purpose left in life; or at least in the Senate. It is to try to sort out what would be involved in reconstituting the American government in the aftermath of the cold war. Huge changes took place, some of which we hardly notice. Item. I would estimate that about $100 billion is appropriated annually for purposes that are kept secret from the public, and indeed are compartmentalized within both the executive and legislative branches. Half a century ago this would have seemed monstrous, much less unconstitutional. (Art I, Sect 9, Clause 7). Now even to suggest, as I did on the floor in July, that an aggregate number be published as regards the intelligence community, is to invite incomprehension and alarm! But I meander. I write to tell you of my great gratitude and reassurance.

Letter to Jacqueline Kennedy Onassis, reporting on the Pennsylvania Avenue renovation.

SEPTEMBER 24, 1990

Dearest Jackie,

Come to think, do read the book. It is not long and evidently quite good. I am getting mail from the professoriate, if you can believe!

In which category I can also report that Pennsylvania Avenue is now finally, at long last, almost certainly, quite probably, unquestionably on its way to completion. The one—vast—missing piece was the Federal Triangle site. A parking lot for exactly sixty years now, since the Depression halted Andrew Mellon's great enterprise. We got the statute three years ago, but the General Services Administration just wouldn't sign the contract. Big meeting Tuesday. War dance by senior Senator NY. Head of GSA agrees to sign contract. Now nothing should stop us. The design is as close as you would wish to spectacular: I.M. Pei's firm, the site without equivalent, and enterprise modestly munificent. Throw in half a billion dollars of real estate, and you have a $1.2 billion enterprise here, the largest in the history of the Federal government, and yet all to the Avenue scale. Twenty-nine years!

Excerpt of a letter to Governor Mario Cuomo, putting in perspective the hatred of Americans for their government and highlighting Moynihan's faith in Social Security.

NOVEMBER 9, 1990

Dear Mario:

We are evidently fated not to reach each other by telephone. Let me then jot down a few thoughts. First of all, I caught your call-in show last evening, and thought you were in great voice. In the large sense of the word. I don't know what Harry had in mind, and I suppose we never will, but every body else got straight, direct answers, necessarily to the effect that things alas <u>are</u> complex.

The Times this morning reports your remarks at campaign headquarters yesterday. (I would have been there if anyone had let me know.) You are right. People <u>are</u> "screaming at the government that we don't trust you anymore." But this is nothing new. It is only that at times it seems more intense. Two

thoughts. First of all, government in a place such as New York City is manifestly less effective and functional than it was even a generation ago, much
less three generations (as they are now counted) when I grew up alternately
on the East and West Side of Manhattan. This has to do primarily with social
regression. That, and the fact that we don't know what to do about it. I know
as much as most about these matters, have been at it longer than most, but I
simply don't know what is to be done.

Yesterday the 25th Anniversary issue of <u>The Public Interest</u> arrived. Our
first issue appeared in the Fall of 1965. I wrote the lead article. It was suffused
with social ambition, but argued for a little more measurement and a little less
promising. . . . There simply are limits to what can be achieved by large hierarchical government organizations. For this we were labeled neo-conservative,
and a lot of good men ended up leaving the Democratic party. But there are
limits ever so, as you well know.

I think of Albany Before Rockefeller. A far more effective government.
The Executive Chamber held fifteen or so people and we wouldn't have
known what to do with more. Ditto the staff of the legislature, which routinely
passed a budget in April and went home in May. Then came Gigantism, the
Mall ("the architecture of Coercion" as Hughes has it) and the protracted
stalemate with which you struggle.

Washington is no different. The Hundred Days of Franklin D. Roosevelt
are so denominated because that is how long Congress was in Session his first
year in office. They arrived in March, enacted first phase of the New Deal,
and went home in June when it got hot. We of course just finished up the
longest session since World War II; the stalemate only really stopped when
time ran out.

Is this the condition of postmodern government? I don't know. But, I sense
that it is, and that if we work with its tendencies rather than against them
we might come out better. Thus my perennial preoccupation with Social Security, <u>the</u> great success of big Government in our time. Fifty years of benefits
now: never a day late or a dollar short. Yet a majority of nonretired adults do
not believe benefits will be there when they retire. It does no good to "tell"
them. But I have arranged that beginning in 1995 people will receive annual
statements, recording their contributions, estimating their benefits. We know
you're there. We <u>are</u> connected. More of that, don't you think?

No matter. You have a great heart, are a great public person. You have enlarged us, even when we at times appear to have diminished you. We know
not what we do!

Letter to Sam Roberts of the NEW YORK TIMES, *arguing in favor of legal restrictions on ammunition rather than guns.*

NOVEMBER 12, 1990

Dear Sam:

It has taken a bit to get back to you on the subject of ammunition, but I have been learning up on the subject. Or rather Amy Barrett, the soon to be fabled head of our New York office, has been doing so. Here goes, then.

The basic proposition is that there are already so many handguns in existence that it is not possible to affect the problem by restricting the entry of new handguns into the existing stock. That is no reason not to try; measures such as the Brady bill are basically ethical statements, and greatly to be admired. But they won't reduce the number of handguns out there. There are an estimated 70 million handguns in the country. Craig Wolff's splendid two part article estimates that there are 2 million in New York City alone. "Every Other 14-Year Old, Armed" as Saturday's editorial put it.

Second proposition. Guns don't kill people, bullets do. If we have, say, a century's supply of handguns, we have only about a four year supply of ammunition. As we will see, we don't know nearly as much as we need to know in this area, but it is all pretty much knowable.

Third proposition. This issue isn't marginal or symbolic any more. A societal breakdown has been accompanied by a technological breakthrough on the part of what once were called the criminal classes. As for the first part of said sentence, I offer you my forecast of 1966 in <u>America</u> magazine.

> [T]here is one unmistakable lesson in American history: a community that allows large numbers of young men to grow up in broken families, dominated by women, never acquiring any stable relationship to male authority, never acquiring any set of rational expectations about the future—that community asks for and gets chaos. Crime, violence, unrest, disorder . . . are not only to be expected, they are very near to inevitable. <u>And they are richly deserved.</u>

As for the second, I refer you to the <u>Times</u> two part article. To wit: criminals now have automatic weapons. Forget all those Edward G. Robinson movies; the number of machine guns in the 1920's was insignificant, and tightly controlled by the syndicates. Now 14-year olds have Uzis. <u>But note!</u> Automatic weapons consume huge amounts of ammunition. The clip for the TEC-9 (shown in Wolff's article without clip) contains twenty 9mm. rounds. (I went down to the Police Academy to fire it.) These can be fired in about ten seconds if you're good at it. Meaning mostly having the slight strength needed to cock the thing.

THEREFORE. <u>Make it as near as possible impossible to get hold of 9mm. ammunition</u>.

Look at those old movies. What is the worst thing that can happen to the wagon train? <u>To run out of ammunition!</u> Let us make that national policy.

Right now there <u>is</u> no policy. Neither one way or the other. A Federal license to manufacture ammunition costs $10 per year. License good for three years. There are some 7,900 licenses extant. However—note well—the Bureau of Alcohol, Tobacco and Firearms keeps no record of how much ammunition is actually manufactured. Obviously this could be learned, but it is of no institutional interest until we rename it the Bureau of Alcohol, Tobacco, Firearms, <u>and</u> Ammunition.

What to do? Several thoughts come to mind. Back in 1986 (at the behest of Phil Caruso of the PBA [the Patrolmen's Benevolent Association] here in town) I introduced and passed the legislation banning the manufacture or import or sales of cop-killer bullets. P.L. 99-408. This was the first law ever to outlaw a round of ammunition. Next I introduced a bill (S. 25 in the 99th Congress) to outlaw .25 and .32 caliber rounds. At that time about one quarter of the rounds fired at New York City police officers were of this caliber. The Saturday night special, as the weapons are called. The round is not used in rifles or, generally speaking, for hunting or target practice.

I could not interest anyone in S. 25 or its successor, S. 229. In part I think the gun control groups were disinclined to have attention turned to "another" subject. Which is understandable. Also I find myself once again in that pitiable role of the meliorist. I wanted to try to cut back on the number of functioning weapons around, not to eliminate them altogether.

The fact that it is not possible to do that has nothing to do with what makes the best banner. Not for nothing did the old Marxists scorn the "trade union mentality." This however may change with the advent of the 9 mm. automatic or semiautomatic weapon. The police are literally outgunned. They are down there in the street with .38 caliber revolvers. The others are up on the roof tops—the high ground of Marine Corps doctrine—with a truly ferocious firepower. . . .

Newsletter with thoughts going back to Pearl Harbor and World War II, reflecting on President George H. W. Bush's preparations for war with Iraq following its invasion of Kuwait. Moynihan continued to advocate sanctions as a preferred approach.

NOVEMBER 15, 1990
WASHINGTON, DC

Dear New Yorker,

WAR?

I learned about Pearl Harbor from a man whose shoes I was shining at the corner of 79th Street and Central Park West in Manhattan. I was fourteen; war meant little to me, and I went on working until I had accumulated the usual one dollar, and then went home. My mother had the radio on, there were occasional announcements, but mostly military music interspersed with football songs. I distinctly remember:

> *Hail! Men of Fordham, Hail!*
> *On to the fray!*
> *Once more our foes assail in strong array.*

The West Side piers began working seven days a week. This meant I could go to City College three days a week, work three days, and have plenty of time and money left over. In March of 1944, I walked into the lobby the Baruch Center on 23rd Street and saw an announcement that officer training tests would be given the following week. On July 1, I entered upon an association with the United States Navy which lasted until I was discharged from the Reserves 22 years later.

It was never an intense relation, in the sense that my life was never at risk. I missed the Pacific thanks to the atom bomb. But soon the Iron Curtain came down and the Reserves were up and running. Crises large and small came and went. Then Korea. I was called back briefly to what was to have been an American North Atlantic Command based in Bremerhaven, the German Naval base. (Churchill, as it turned out, blocked the plan. No American admirals in the Home Waters!) And so I returned to the London School of Economics but not before visiting Berlin. In Berlin you saw what war was all about. The last one, the next one.

And so, fast forward to the morning of December 2, 1989, when I stood at the Brandenburg Gate and watched the Berlin Wall coming down. The forty years had passed quickly with a certain numb sameness to it. Constantly waiting for the war I had returned to Berlin in 1953 after the anti-Soviet riots of that year and I had driven through the same Brandenburg Gate with the late Paul Niven of CBS News and a British journalist. The wall was not up yet and you could move freely from sector to sector. As we drove down the Stahlmallee, the great sterile boulevard festooned with banners proclaiming the triumph of the Red revolution, the Briton remarked: "There's nothing here but the handwriting on the wall." The war would come.

But then of a sudden, scarcely a year ago, it became clear that <u>that</u> war would not. It <u>hadn't happened</u>. After what, seventy years? We could begin to think of peace again.

What I wondered was whether we any longer knew how. To think, that is, in terms of a nation essentially at peace with the rest of the world. Readers of the April issue of this newsletter may recall the excerpt from Woodrow Wilson's 1919 speech in St. Louis where he prophesied the changes that would take place in American government.

> *You have got to think of the President of the United States, not as the chief counselor of the Nation, elected for a little while, but as the man meant constantly and everyday to be the commander in chief of the armies and navy of the United States, ready to order us to any part of the world where the threat of war is a menace to his own people. And you can't do that under free debate. You can't do that under public counsel. Plans must be kept secret. Knowledge must be accumulated by a system which we have condemned, because we have called it a spying system. The more polite call it a system of intelligence. . . .*
>
> *And you know what the effect of a military nation is upon social questions. You know how impossible it is to effect social reform if everybody must be under orders from the government. You know how impossible it is, in short, to have a free nation if it is a military nation.*

There are three principle features of the American government which changed in the course of the cold war. First, as Wilson foresaw, the emergence of The President as Commander-in-Chief, a person primarily concerned with his role as head of the military. (Little things. It was not until 1981 that a Presidential Assistant was designated "Chief of Staff," but the inevitable did come to pass. There is now, incidentally, a Deputy Chief of Staff.) Next, The Secrecy System of which Wilson wrote. Finally, The Permanent Crisis that he could be said to have anticipated.

All this was accompanied by a huge increase in the power of government, especially the executive branch. It was foreseen; it was advocated. In 1948 Clinton Rossiter of Cornell University put it this way:

> *In time of crisis, a democratic, constitutional government must be temporarily altered to whatever degree is necessary to overcome the peril. . . . The government is going to be powerful or we are going to be obliterated.*

It should be clear that such a government will be disinclined to ease up, to divest power, to admit mistakes. God knows ours was.

The first sign of how much the cold war had changed us was that our government seemed wholly disinclined to think it was over, much less to wonder what had happened. Democracy had prevailed. Fair enough. But just as importantly, the Soviet economy had collapsed, something no President had been prepared for. To the contrary, our Presidents had been kept in a constant state of, well, fear of growing Soviet strength. Last spring I pursued the subject of those hugely exaggerated estimates of Soviet economic growth. They go back to 1957 when a Presidential commission chaired by Rowan Gaither, head of the Ford Foundation and one of the founders of the Rand Corporation, produced a report entitled *Deterrence & Survival in the Nuclear Age* which reached President Eisenhower a few weeks after the launching of Sputnik, the first artificial earth satellite. The commission warned of a "missile gap," concluded that the Soviets had surpassed the U.S. in terms of military effort, and projected a rate of growth for the Soviet economy which would have them passing the U.S. two years from now. (Soviet machine tool production was asserted to be twice that of the U.S.) This document, replete with profound error, remained classified until 1973. This is what Presidents in the grimmest years of the cold war "knew." What they knew was largely wrong but there was no way to correct the errors as the errors were secret.

As a result, Comptroller General Charles Bowsher stated in 1988: "The military budget doubled between 1980 and 1985 . . . a build-up that was much too fast. . . . Six short years ago we were the world's leading creditor nation. Today, we are the world's largest debtor."

Just yesterday in the *New York Times* Flora Lewis, writing of the revelations taking pace in Europe, reported how everyone is just now finding out just how awful the eastern bloc economies actually were. She adds: "An American with senior government experience remarked recently that it was a massive intelligence failure by the West."

But we can't admit it. I held hearings on the subject; made enquiries. Silence. For example, I <u>know</u> that the C.I.A. once estimated that in 1975 the Soviet economy was 62 percent the size of the American economy. They know that I know this. They know that I know that they know I know. But they can't bring themselves to admit it. No breaking ranks with the past.

In midsummer the test came. On August 2, Iraq invaded Kuwait. American officials would proclaim that this was the first crisis of the post-cold war world. At first it seemed to develop in just such terms. Within hours the United Nations Security Council condemned the invasion and demanded that Iraq withdraw immediately and unconditionally. The next day, August 3, President Bush stated that "What Iraq has done violates every norm of international law." A new theme for us. Further, we would turn to the United Nations in response. "We're also talking at the United Nations about Chapter VII actions." Chapter VII of the UN Charter is entitled, ACTION WITH RESPECT TO THREATS TO THE PEACE, BREACHES OF THE PEACE, AND ACTS OF AGGRESSION. Article 41 provides that the Council may impose economic sanctions. Article 42 provides that if such measures "have proved to be inadequate," it can direct the use of force. In my time as U.N. Ambassador (1975–76), Chapter VII was a dead letter. Any action the United States might propose would automatically be vetoed by the Soviet Union or China. Now the five permanent members were unanimous.

On August 7 the President began sending military forces to the Gulf. It was an incredible display of our strength. In an instant there were 210,000 troops in Saudi Arabia. (The F-16's arriving after 17 hours in the air, eleven in flight refueling.) A fleet assembled in the Persian Gulf, including the battleship Wisconsin.

Our mission was to "deter and defend." That is to say to convince the Iraqis that they dare not invade Saudi Arabia and to fight them if they did. It was called Operation Desert Shield. Two weeks later with members of the Foreign Relations Committee I flew out to take a look.*

My entire instinct was to support the President. Speaking to a Joint Session on September 11, he told us he foresaw a New World Order coming out of the Gulf crisis. Fair enough. This is what Franklin D. Roosevelt had hoped for. It is what the United Nations Participation Act of 1945 specifically provided for. This would not be an <u>American</u> war about access to raw materials in the Third World. Instead, the world community would act to confront aggression. And if ever there was a test case for worldwide economic sanctions, this was it. Iraq, an unquestioned aggressor, living off one export, oil, of which there was a sufficient quantity elsewhere, and importing two-thirds of its food supply. It even imports its currency which is printed in London.

Back in Washington I urged that the Congress adopt a resolution supporting the President's actions at the United Nations. Somehow, however, nothing happened. It gradually became clear that the White House didn't <u>want</u> any such resolution. It had all the authority it needed, thank you very much. This seemed dim to me. This was the cold war mentality. The President as Commander-in-Chief with secret information that Congress and the rest would just have to put up with. We talked of international law and collective security, but somehow didn't really believe it. In the end it would be "us against them," whoever the "them" was.

I tried. Sanctions would take a lot of stomach, a lot of time. I began giving speeches on the Senate floor outlining the history of economic sanctions, trying to make the point that these were not a kinder, gentler form of diplomacy, an alternative to violence. How many people were we prepared to see starve? On the TV. Iraqi Republican Guard would not be the first to go. I cited a Twentieth Century Fund study of 1932:

> *Food embargoes will be extremely efficacious in some cases, and useless in others; again, the problem must be studied with reference to the particular country under punishment. But in considering them at all, we must in all honesty*

---

* And to meet some great New Yorkers. Tanya Miller of the Bronx, Jimmy Velazquez of Brooklyn, Kevin Brady from Rochester, Mike Rosenblatt from Albany. And sure enough from Trout Creek, in Delaware County about ten miles from Pindars Corners, Lance Corporal Strat Van Valkenburg. How is that for a Catskill name! The temperature was 128 degrees in the shade of the Marine camouflage tents. There was no trout stream in sight.

admit that food embargoes, placed against a country which really needs the
food, are not persuasive measures, but the most savage of war measures. They
are particularly difficult to uphold on merely moral grounds, since they bear
more heavily on the civilian population than on the army, and more heavily
on women and children than on the men. For effectiveness, and for moral
standing, a really successful food embargo ranks well in advance of torpedoing
hospital ships and is somewhere near the class of gassing maternity hospitals.

I was not opposed; I was simply saying that we had to get ready for something new.

After a point I began to worry. On the day before the 101st Congress adjourned, I took to the Senate floor to plead that the President speak to us,
quoting from Reston's *New York Times* column of the previous Sunday:

One of [the President's] major foreign policy objectives was to persuade
Mikhail Gorbachev not to use military force to achieve political objectives in
the Baltic states and Eastern Europe, but he invaded Panama against his
treaty commitments to the United Nations in order to capture a two-bit dic-
tator, and did not know what to do with him when he caught him. Having
defied the U.N. in Panama he then relied on it in Iraq.

(This last detail has not escaped the world's attention. On September 2,
the press reported the story of an American lawyer captured by Iraqi troops
while trying to cross the desert out of Iraq. The American stated, "they treated
us very nicely, gave us soda, water and tea, and the soldiers talked politics with
us. They said: 'You invaded Panama, you invaded Grenada. So we invaded
Kuwait.'") Had the President changed his mind about international law? In
my Senate speech I noted:

The President has proclaimed a New World Order which he has not defined.
The President has of a sudden invoked standards of international law by
which we have not, within this very year, abided ourselves. The President
has set in motion a set of actions, to wit, economic sanctions in the Gulf, with-
out any effort to explain to the American people how long it will take to make
them successful; how painful will be the consequences; and above all, he has
not sought to obtain from this Congress, this Senate, a statement of coopera-
tion, consultation and support with definitions, limits, terms. They have de-
cided to go it alone.

Congress adjourned. Elections took another week. Only <u>two days later,</u> on November 8, the President announced that he was doubling our troop strength in the Gulf, sending another 150,000 troops. Soon the battleship Missouri would be joining the Wisconsin. There would be no troop rotations. You were to go to the desert and stay there until . . . Operation Desert Shield had become Operation Desert Sword. Two thousand Marines would hit the beaches ten miles south of the Kuwaiti border in a "training exercise" called Operation Imminent Thunder. The White House spokesman kept talking about the possibility of provocations, without saying just what that meant.

Wednesday morning, November 14, the President told Congressional leaders that in this regard he was already provoked by the Iraqi attempt to starve out our Embassy in Kuwait. In the afternoon at a Senate briefing, I asked Secretary of State Baker whether we had put in place a formal effort to track the effect of sanctions; to estimate how long it would take to affect Iraqi behavior; to look for signs that it was beginning to hurt. I asked, had we tried to think through just how long it would take? Say, two years? The Secretary replied that two "major" countries had earlier suggested that two to three months would do it, implying that we had waited long enough.

The "augmentation" of troops will take about two months to complete. Ramadan, the Islamic month of fasting begins March 17, which raises problems for any Moslem troops on "our" side. That is followed in June by the <u>hajj</u>, the annual pilgrimage to Mecca. Next it is summer and too hot and a year has gone by. We would have begun to lose the "edge" of our "credible offensive military capability."

The briefing over, a Senator whose military judgment is respected as perhaps none other in the body, came up to two of us, took a $5 bill out of his wallet and pronounced: "My bet is January 5." [Editor's Note: Aerial bombardment started January 17.]

It doesn't have to be war. Certainly not an American war. Nor yet a United Nations war in which the others send us off to fight. There is still time to agree that our policy and the world's policy is that of economic sanctions. In the meantime, so long as our troops are sleeping on sand, it would be nice if those Kuwaiti billionaires would get the hell out of the Presidential suite of the Sheraton Hotel in the Saudi resort town of Taif in favor of a more battle-ready position.

Letter to former President Jimmy Carter.

NOVEMBER 26, 1990

Dear President Carter:

How gracious of you to send me a copy of Professor Berman's absorbing and generous commentary on my little book. He is, of course, quite right to point out that I neglect the fact that "at levels below that of political confrontation" American foreign policy, and that of almost all nations, is routinely and unselfconsciously dictated or informed by existing international law. Some of this is customary, the equivalent of common law, but the greatest portion is treaty law, the direct counterpart of statutory law within nations. But it is, of course, the level of political confrontation that is most relevant, as you and he would agree.

And yet, consider all that has come from your administration's emphasis on human rights as an international norm!

How in the hell are we going to get out of that desert once we have 450,000 troops there? Just when we could commence to think what kind of place we would like to be <u>after</u> the cold war! I started a series of hearings this morning. Have been planning them for six months. But few are interested. In Washington, that is.

Excerpt of a letter to President George H. W. Bush, arguing in favor of sanctions against Iraq.

DECEMBER 1, 1990

MEMORANDUM FOR THE PRESIDENT

Your secretary Patty called yesterday to say that you really would like to have some thoughts from me to take on your trip to South America. She left instructions as to how to get this through to the Usher's Office. Herewith, then, a few pages worth, which I do hope reach you.

If you were going by sea, this would be longer. Indeed I would send you a book I published in September <u>On the Law of Nations</u> (Harvard, $22.50). I have already sent you one, but could easily afford another as the book is doing very well, is already in a second printing, and this in large measure is thanks to you. (You used the term "international law" three times yesterday!) You are coping, as you repeatedly state, with the first crisis of the post–cold war period. From the first hours of this crisis you have defined it in terms of Iraqi violation of international law. You have repeatedly stated that the way in which this crisis is resolved will do much to determine the nature of the new world order. You have been in my view absolutely correct on both scores. Our problem however is that while we are using post–cold war terms we continue with cold war techniques and cold war perspectives. During the cold war the United States came to define itself in terms of its opposition to the Soviet Union. Anticommunism became the central organizing principle of American politics. The President became Commander in Chief presiding over a more or less permanent crisis. We were locked in a zero-sum game; anything we lost they gained and vice versa. There was no room for error, or at least not much room, and an enormous premium on reaction time. (That football that follows you around.) The idea of international law was pretty much lost in the fog of the cold war; they didn't play by the rules, how could we afford to? Nothing less than civilization was at stake; the issues were such that the United States would pay "*any price*" to prevail. (My italics, of course, but your fellow naval officer of World War II.)

The issues of world order now that the cold war is over are of a wholly different nature. They are, as you have brilliantly perceived, essentially just that. World order. The nature of legal entitlements, legal obligations, legal authority. There is a structure in place in the United Nations Charter. A structure almost wholly of our design. You automatically and instantly turned to that structure, and have stayed with it ever since.

It could turn out that history will record your Presidency as the one which finally, at the end of the twentieth century, put in place something like the world order that Theodore Roosevelt and Woodrow Wilson had so hoped for at the outset of the century.

The problem is this. Can we ease our way out of cold war ways? I think of that great remark of Acheson's after World War II when he said that Britain had lost an empire and not yet found a role. Before they could find that role, (and maybe they are yet to do; such changes do not come easily) they tried Suez. They have never been the same since; never will be. My hope is that we will not attempt the equivalent.

What do I mean? Two things basically. First of all, our rush of forces to the Gulf had too much of crisis about it to begin with and thereafter became much too large and too nearly unilateral. What was the hurry? Iraq is a regional power, nothing more. Semi-stable internally; surrounded by enemies. Saddam would seem to be marginally more brutal than his counterparts, say, Assad. But nothing notable for the region. (Wait 'til we get to know [Pakistan President] Nawaz Sharif better. He with our F-16's and his bomb.) Kuwait is an oil emirate, with borders drawn 1922–23. The whole region is an artifact of the Treaty of Sèvres. These two particular "countries" have oil fields but neither would withhold its oil from world markets voluntarily. Iraq is just now the "strongest" regime in the region; but if it goes down another goes up. Syria most likely. The world will then be dealing with the aggressions of Syria.

The only large risk to the United States that I can see in the Gulf is that the world will lose sight of your insistence that what is involved here is the world community upholding international law and instead come to see that this is a conflict between the United States and a third world country over access to raw materials. That later "model" is one the Soviets and Marxists generally have tirelessly proselytized for three generations and is readily enough believed in many countries of the world, not least our own.

That is why I had hoped we would take sanctions with great seriousness. This requires first of all that we realize sanctions take time. . . .

I hope I am not naive. I know something of the history of sanctions. But if ever there was a chance that Article 41 could be made to work, we have it here. The place has one export, of which the world has in any event a sufficient supply. It imports most of its food and almost all its technology. (It even imports its currency. I attach a five dinar note printed in London. This is an old arrangement. Under the Mandate the rupee was the official monetary unit in Iraq. Currency like this wears out in twelve months.) Moreover, as the leader of a minority regime, Saddam has shown himself hugely sensitive to matters such as consumer goods. No shortages were allowed during the war with Iran; hence in part the post war debt.

During September I went to the floor a number of times to talk about sanctions. I began to ask why the administration wasn't preparing the nation for the fact that sanctions, obviously, would take a long time to have any effect, and that they would not be pretty. They would in fact be brutal. Brutal, but better than war from our point of view. And as for Saddam, he was free to choose. I was particularly puzzled that there was no discussion of whether we

were going to include food. A rational strategy could be to confine the blockade to manufactured goods. There used to be a huge literature on this subject
in the United States. Thus, the 1932 report of The Committee on Economic
Sanctions set up by the Twentieth Century Fund. John Foster Dulles was a
member; Nicholas Murray Butler was chairman. In an opening statement
Butler explained that as a result of the Kellogg-Briand Pact: "War is no longer
either necessary or even respectable; it is illegal." But some miscreant might
come along and would have to be dealt with. How, if other nations such as
ours had renounced war as an instrument of national policy? By sanctions, of
course. These however could be rough. Here is the passage on food:

> Food embargoes will be extremely efficacious in some cases, and useless
> in others; again, the problem must be studied with reference to the par-
> ticular country under punishment. But in considering them at all, we
> must in all honesty admit that food embargoes, placed against a country
> which really needs the food, are not persuasive measures, but the most
> savage of war measures. They are particularly difficult to uphold on
> merely moral grounds, since they bear more heavily on the civilian pop-
> ulation than on the army, and more heavily on women and children
> than on the men. For effectiveness, and for moral standing, a really suc-
> cessful food embargo ranks well in advance of torpedoing hospital ships
> and is somewhere near the class of gassing maternity hospitals.

One may agree or disagree. The essential point is that they were trying to
think about the subject. We haven't been doing that for a long while, albeit
for perfectly understandable reasons.

The executive branch has done no real planning for economic sanctions as
a serious instrument of foreign policy. Cold war policy, that is. (Carter em-
bargoed wheat to Russia after the invasion of Afghanistan; Reagan promptly
dropped the measure.) The world was never united; all one did was impose
costs on oneself. Nothing changed with the end of the cold war. On November
14, after the announcement that additional forces would be sent to the Gulf,
Secretaries [of State and Defense] Baker and Cheney briefed us on events to
date. I got the second or third question, asking how long it was felt it would
take before sanctions began to bite. Jim replied that "two major countries" had
told us that sanctions would do the job in "two to three months." I responded
that if that represented their grasp of economics, they wouldn't be major countries long. The room took the point to be that sanctions had been tried and

had not worked and that war was now necessary. I came away with a slightly different view, simply that we had never thought through this subject, it having no place in cold war plans. Hence we asked the opinion of others; just as you talked with President Ozal who offered the truly astonishing thought that three weeks might suffice.

Well, you will have got my point. The cold war construct does not work very well in shaping a new world order <u>after</u> the cold war. A legal world order will surely be boring, if not tedious. So are domestic legal regimes. But the alternative to violence is thought worth it. (One legal nitpick? The United Nations is under no legal obligation to restore the Sabahs. Nor are you under any political obligation to endure Hill & Knowlton.)

A final thought. You have written the My Turn column in the current *Newsweek*. It happens that I have written the next one which will appear Monday. It is not irrelevant to what you are now dealing with. Back in 1979 *Newsweek* had a symposium on what Big Events would take place in the 1980s. In a brief entry I predicted that by the end of the 1980s the Soviet Union would break up and that this could lead to some dicey moments as they parceled out those ten thousand nuclear warheads. I argued that the break up would come about because their economy was in ruins and ethnic hostilities were reaching a prerevolutionary phase. (A nice Marxist term!) Inasmuch as Marxism-Leninism could not account for either event, indeed depended doctrinally on just the opposite happening, there would be a crisis of belief and the U.S.S.R. would blow up or collapse or whatever. The purpose of Monday's My Turn is to ask why U.S. foreign policy could not grasp, could not even entertain this possibility. I wasn't guessing. I was proceeding from method; I proved to be right. I offer two suggestions. The first is that the advent of nuclear weapons gave great comparative advantage to strategic analysts who had little if any interest in political ideas. They never bothered with the Marxist analysis of the necessary disappearance of ethnic/nationalist attachments, for instance. Second, the vast secrecy system that grew up during the cold war hid from us our own mistakes. Thus the CIA estimated that in 1975 Soviet GNP reached 62 percent of U.S. product. Which is to say twice, maybe three times greater than we now know it to have been. (We know it because the Russians have told us!) Nobody was to blame, as such. The system was to blame. Our mistakes, you see, were secret. Hence we could not correct them. I make this point because I have been trying to get hold of various estimates now being made within the government of the effect of the embargo. I am told they are secret.

In sum. Get us out of a war fighting posture. A war to be fought by the U.S. and Britain, that is. Insist that others send troops, phase down ours as others arrive. Get a United Nations commander. Get a UN flag. Send Perez de Cuellar to Baghdad. Hunker down, as LBJ would say, like a jack rabbit in a hail storm. When it is all over declare victory, for you will have earned one.

Excerpt of a letter to William F. Buckley Jr., characterized by Moynihan here as "a conservative, not a right winger." The phrase "the Constitution is not a suicide pact," evoking the belief that national security should not be compromised by constitutional concerns, was evidently invoked by Buckley.

DECEMBER 20, 1990

Dear Bill:

That was a most mellifluous column, for which I thank you. And even more, of course, for the chance to appear on "Firing Line." I do believe this was my 20th year, which is a gerontological note which we can both let pass.

In my reply to Kinsley's [Michael Kinsley, a frequent guest on "Firing Line"] question (an excellent question, indeed), if I seemed a little evasive it was simply because in those heady years 1944 and 1945, the Congress did indeed contemplate turning over to the Security Council quite extraordinary powers. See page 112, with the excerpt from the United Nations Participation Act of 1945. It was contemplated that, by previous agreement, the President would, through the Security Council, be able to send American armed forces into battle and "shall not be deemed to require the authorization of the Congress" to do so. That bill passed. The Bricker Amendment didn't. If the bill came before us today, I most certainly would vote against it. But that was an earlier time.

Now, knock off the suicide pact nonsense. As your excellent Mr. Michael Lind states:

> On this point at least Senator Moynihan is correct: At present in the United States, there is a liberal theory of international law and a right-wing theory of its nonexistence, but no *conservative* theory of interna-

tional law. If there is to be a principled conservative approach to public international law, the work of reconstruction will have to begin from scratch.

Someone has to tell you, and it might as well be me. You, Bill Buckley, are a conservative, not a right-winger. . . .

Excerpts of a Memorandum of conversation following a meeting with President Bush and aides to discuss Moynihan's reservations about a military action against Iraq.

JANUARY 11, 1991

MEMORANDUM OF CONVERSATION

I met with the President in the oval office at ten o'clock exactly, our meeting lasted a little more than twenty minutes. Scowcroft and Sununu were there to welcome me. Scowcroft remained, took notes.

President said, I know you are committed the other way but wanted to talk with you anyway. I felt my letter in response to yours was inadequate. I said I would make a general point and two suggestions. The general point was that he had the fullest support in Congress for his sanctions policy. A Senate Concurrent Resolution which I helped draft passed 96–3. He had not made any decisions beyond sanctions and so that support would continue. . . .

I said that in my view we could leave the forces we had there in October, and turn to other questions. We were a great power. We could afford to be patient. Biggest issue the breakup of the Soviet Union. Who gets those warheads. If the Azeris get a deterrent, heaven help Georgia. There is Gorbachev four weeks from the Nobel Peace Price sending paratroopers to Lithuania.

We talked of Saddam. He still hoped Perez [United Nations Secretary General Javier Perez de Cuellar] with his quiet Peruvian manner might get through. We agreed that we did not know what reality testing he had. I mentioned [Israeli President Chaim] Herzog and the profile. Which suggested in the end he might suddenly switch if convinced he was trapped. Suggested I send it to Scowcroft. President says, I read everything, send it to me. Gave me note card [of his assistant]: Patty Presock, White House.

President talked of the economic cost. To [President Abdou] Drouf of Senegal. To [President Vaclav] Havel at Czechoslovakia. I agreed, but said that even so we could wait.

President spoke of those who concerned with loss of life. So was he. Even one life. I said that he would not hear from me on that subject. Marines do not sign up for summer camp. Scowcroft approved.

As we left I mentioned that the little girl he and Barbara were so nice to in Beijing those years ago—Moira, he said [Editor's Note: mispronouncing Maura]—was now big-bellied with brat. He asked was this the first. Old fellow like me ought to have more. No, you're younger than me.

I had opened our conversation saying how good he looked. He said he was at peace with himself. As I left I mentioned there might be reporters. Say what you like, free country. Tell them Scowcroft looks good. I said Scowcroft is where Broder got his notion that the President was down. Scowcroft did in fact look ghastly.

Earlier I mentioned my relapse to cold war theme of yesterday's speech. . . .

Letter to fellow Senator Alfonse D'Amato, recommending nomination of Sonia Sotomayor for a federal judgeship. By mutual agreement with D'Amato, Moynihan was entitled to recommend one of every four federal judgeships under a Republican president, and D'Amato would have the same privilege under a Democratic president. Moynihan told aides at the time that he believed Sotomayor would eventually be named to the Supreme Court, which she was by President Obama in 2009.

MARCH 4, 1991

Dear Al:

It is my honor to forward to you my recommendation of Sonia Sotomayor to fill a vacancy in the Federal District Court for the Southern District of New York. Ms. Sotomayor comes highly recommended to me by my Judicial Selection Committee. She is a former Assistant District Attorney with the New York County District Attorney's office, and currently a member of the law firm of Pavia & Harcourt.

Ms. Sotomayor has considerable expertise in criminal law from her work as a prosecutor, as well as commercial litigation, in which she currently specializes in private practice. Her academic achievements are truly outstanding. She graduated <u>summa cum laude</u> from Princeton University in 1976, where she was elected Phi Beta Kappa and was a co-winner of the M. Taylor Pyne Honor Prize, awarded to the graduating senior who has most clearly manifested excellent scholarship and effective support of the best interests of the University. She received her law degree from Yale University, where she was an editor of the <u>Yale Law Journal</u>. Ms. Sotomayor has also found time to make substantial contributions to community affairs. She presently serves on the Board of Directors of the Puerto Rican Legal Defense and Education Fund, the State of New York Mortgage Agency and the New York City Campaign Finance Board.

I enclose for your review Ms. Sotomayor's response to the Candidate's Questionnaire of my Judicial Selection Committee.

I believe that Sonia Sotomayor's considerable accomplishments merit an appointment to the Federal District Court and I am confident that, upon confirmation, she will serve with the highest distinction.

Excerpt of a letter to Anthony Lewis, the NEW YORK TIMES *columnist, to the effect that Nixon was more liberal (on the Family Assistance Plan [FAP], revenue sharing, the environment, etc.) than liberals gave him credit for.*

JUNE 10, 1991

Dear Tony:

. . . It is now twenty-two years and some since I went to work in the Nixon White House. I had not known what to expect, but quickly found myself in an entirely workable environment. No one would ask for better company—or, as on occasion, adversaries—than, say, Arthur Burns or Paul McCracken or Herb Stein. George Shultz, Bob Finch, George Romney, Elliot Richardson. And such like. Thus, in seven months time—August, 1969—the new President sent to Congress a message proposing a guaranteed income (FAP), revenue sharing, and a reworking of manpower programs. Nothing quite like it had ever happened.

There was more of the same for the next two years. Things of which you write. It may have been the most progressive administration on domestic issues that had ever been formed.

Then something else happened that had never happened. Liberals commenced to denounce the proposals as reactionary, racist, lord knows what. From the outside this might not have seemed much harassment or rejection. From the inside it seemed a continuous, relentless barrage. I watched the high spirits of the cabinet gradually subside. It was no use. They would never be accepted as reformers. And so? And so, why bother.

At the time, and since, I saw this as a fairly simple misreading on the part of liberals, as the term is generally understood. The phrase went, if you recall, that "the center is no longer where the center was." This was intended to mean that what had seemed "left" at the beginning of the New Frontier or whatever, was no longer left but center. All this was much in play in the 1968 convention. I would argue that the proposition was correct, but that the movement of the center had been to the—right. I argued for seizing the moment of this extraordinary administration to make what might be the last such gains for a long while. If anyone heard this counsel, it was surely rejected. The Nixon domestic program was taken as proof positive that the maxim was correct. The center had moved left. Even Republicans were proposing measures that a Kennedy or Johnson would never touch. Just wait 'til 1972.

I have described some of this in my book on FAP. In 1970, for example, I told a meeting of the Urban Coalition here in Washington that if we did not get a guaranteed income in that Congress, we would not get it in that decade. This was duly reported in the Post and briefly became the object of some derision. In those days, I used to journey up to Capitol Hill to lobby a bit for the bill. Making my way down the corridors of the Longworth building or whatever, looking for the office of a sympathetic Republican or Democratic Representative, I had an easy time finding my way. Look for the office where the sit-in was taking place, denouncing the fellow for supporting slavefare.

In that setting it did not take much wit to figure out that, by contrast, those who were absolutely opposed to income floors and such like measures were left in peace. In 1970 George Bush, who voted for FAP, was said in consequence to have lost a Senate election. If you follow me.

The miscalculation was large. But it was no more than that. A tactical error. Mind, so was Gettysburg, I suppose.

Letter to William Safire of the NEW YORK TIMES, *about his aspirations as a "language maven." Moynihan refers to a playful rebuke by a* TIMES *editorial on his failed attempt to gain coinage of the word "floccinaucinihilipilificationism" as the longest word in the dictionary.*

JULY 1, 1991

Dear Bill:

You will remember me, I hope. We had some good times in the old days and when I had dough to treat the gang, my hand was never slow. Well, things haven't worked so good of late and I have been attacked by The New York Times for pretending to be a language maven when all I ever really wanted was to get one word—just one word—in the O.E.D. I have three solid citings so far. One more, in a publication by you, would surely do the trick. I don't have much to leave my grandchild, but he maybe could grow up to learn that his old granddad amounted to something after all.

Letter to the columnist E. J. Dionne.

PINDARS CORNERS
AUGUST 11, 1991

Dear Mr. Dionne,

I have grown so much in your debt, notably since your recent book appeared, that I have wondered what I might do this side of sending roses. Next best from a fellow <u>jongleur</u>, I suppose, is a booklet. Herewith, then, the 15th of a series I put out on what New York gets for what New York pays in terms of national politics.

This year I explore a possibility: that it's not worth it. Much of the liberal project, as you so nicely put it, comes out of my state. It was never a unified or even especially coherent affair. More a matter of assorted tribes breaking out of Central Asia. But there was one common technique. We would pay the rest of the country to be like us. It never succeeded completely, but now it almost completely fails. As I put it in this year's FISC, we send a dollar to Washington, and get back 77¢ with a Helms amendment. In the process, one generation, New York's share of the Federal income tax—has been cut in half. Moreover—p. xxiii—it may be the case that all federal aid does is to freeze relations, as any good Weberian would predict. I am still looking for an editorial writer who can get interested in a rank order correlation. But there it is. 77! Jesus, you used to be able to get a Ph.D. for something like that.

I will try this out for its shock value. It happens to fit with a larger theme. The liberal project began to fail when it began to lie. That was the mid sixties when a range of social science appeared—Think Coleman [i.e. the 1966 report by James Coleman on equality of education]—which said it was going to be a bitch. The response was that said social scientists and their craven lackeys were objective right wing deviationists. Whereupon the rot set in and has continued since. Of course we will not reduce social security rates. The surplus— pretty soon it will be $2 bill a week—is our only hope for new programs. Which won't work but there used to be jobs for the boys in them. We are so rotted out by now that we no longer notice that they are no longer even our boys.

On making government work, you might like chap IV: Public Sector Disease.

Letter to Bea (Mrs. Irving) Kristol, also known as Gertrude Himmelfarb, discussing his evolution as a liberal and a conservative, and expressing gratitude for her influence.

PINDARS CORNERS
AUGUST 30, 1991

Dearest Bea,

I have kept your wonderful letter about in the school room, school house rather, these past three weeks as I have been working, fitfully, at a lecture I must give at Oxford in November. A Victorian confectioner left a considerable sum to endow a lecture by a "sincere person" on ways to bring about world peace. I am calling it "Pandaemonium" after that wonderful essay by

Solomon F. Bloom in Commentary, 1947, "The Peoples of My Home Town."
Nat tells me he was a teacher of yours. How I should have liked to know <u>that</u>
man.

But then I have done, haven't I? And so many others I should never have
known save for that "hotbed of ex-Trotskyite, Jewish, European-oriented, self-
made intellectuals." It changed my life completely. Which is scarcely to be remarked, given how much you all have changed the century! Seriously. I do
want to write about it, and may just do, although I doubt my powers in such
matters. What I got from you all apart from love which is what matters most
was another way of looking at things, that slight shift on the compass that allows you to fix objects in the distance, and I have been fairly good at that.
This is not necessarily helpful in politics. (And bless you for knowing that
that was my vocation. I went to a university when Harriman lost the 1958
election.) Thus I went through the past dozen years or so saying the Soviet
Union was about to break up. Watch where the warheads go. No one in Washington could fathom a word of it.

Which is no great matter for it ends well. Less encouraging is the racial
violence now turned openly anti-Semitic. In Brooklyn two weeks ago a sem-
inarian was stabbed to death in the middle of a crowd screaming "Kill the
Jew." When has this happened before in our nation? I saw it coming, tried to
say it in a way that could be heard. No luck there either. But no consolation
either. . . .

Excerpt of a letter to Arnold Kupferman of the New York State Department of
Transportation, asking that the department use the name Erie Canal for the canal,
which Moynihan was helping to renovate with government funds.

SEPTEMBER 9, 1991

Dear Mr. Kupferman:
　. . . What a very nice thought to put Pindars Corners on the map. It is not
more than that, a typical Upstate "corners." The most prominent feature is
the Pindars Corners Volunteer Fire Department which, logically enough, is
located there. It used to be the first stop on the express bus line from New
York to Oneonta, but those days have vanished. On the other hand, it is the

principle turn-off from Route 23 onto I-88 as you come in from the East, and is indeed getting much too busy for my tastes.

On a related matter, what would it take to get the Department of Transportation to stop labeling the Erie Canal as the Barge Canal? It breaks your heart that we have so little sense of our past. Not you, but we generally. I was travelling around the Mohawk Valley last Thursday and every time I came to one of your nice green and white signs that simply said "Barge Canal," I wanted to weep a little. I am sure you will find that technically it was the Erie Canal. The whole thing was renamed by someone unknown around 1910.

No one would think of sending you to jail for calling the Erie Canal by its right name.

Letter to President George H. W. Bush, urging him to take the lead in repealing the notorious "Zionism is racism" resolution at the United Nations. With administration backing the U.N. General Assembly voted to revoke the resolution the following December.

SEPTEMBER 16, 1991

Dear Mr. President:

This past week Elie Wiesel was in Kiev marking the 50th anniversary of the massacre at Babi Yar. As you know, after years of delay, the Soviets put up a monument there but with no mention of Jews. This for the reason that official Soviet held that Babi Yar was a collaboration of the Gestapo and "their accomplices and followers—the Zionists."

This assertion (Pravda, 1971) led directly to General Assembly Resolution 3379 of 1975 declaring "Zionism to be a form of racism." The Ukraine was the Soviet sponsor. But last week Ukrainian President Leonid Kravchuk pledged to Wiesel that the Ukraine would vote to rescind 3379, there being a considerable international movement to do just that. Tom Pickering can give you details.

This is the moment. If you were to propose repeal in your address to the General Assembly next Monday (the 50th Anniversary is September 29), it would surely happen. Do that, get a treaty on tactical nuclear weapons, and you will have pretty much wrapped up the 20th century!

Letter to Laurence Tisch—wealthy businessman, philanthropist, head of CBS, and ardent supporter of Israel—and his wife, reflecting on efforts to repeal the "Zionism is racism" resolution at the United Nations.

OCTOBER 3, 1991

Dear Larry and Billie:

It's true. I never came near to understanding the Holocaust until I encountered the Zionism resolution. It was October, 1975. I was our U.N. ambassador, sent by President Ford to keep the peace. We seemed to be doing nicely. A Special Session of the General Assembly had ended on September 15th with unanimous agreement on a vast resolution on North-South economic relations. All seemed well. Then this. This . . . obscenity. This . . . outrage. That Zionism should be a form of racism! Were these delegates mad?

They were not in the least mad. The Soviet delegates, that is. Four years earlier Pravda had begun the campaign. The specific charge: Babi Yar was a collaboration of the Gestapo and the Zionists.

There was no secret about the Soviet charge. To the contrary, the Soviet propaganda machine had been going at full blast. There was another secret, however. It was the secret behind the Holocaust. The charge was too hideous to believe. The mind goes blank; denial sets in; avoidance.

I thought of the voyage of the St. Louis in 1939. Outward bound from Hamburg with 930 German Jews. Twenty-two allowed to land in Havana. Then up the Atlantic coast of the United States. Lights ablaze at night. Refused entry. Back to Antwerp and the death camps. We had denied the possibility of death camps.

We were equally unprepared for the Zionism attack. Chaim Herzog fought; I fought at his side. But practically alone. And as soon as it was over everyone wanted to forget about it. Two weeks after the vote, Liz was sitting at dinner next to the French ambassador. (Louis de Guiringuad, I can tell you.) Ma chere, said the Ambassadeur de France (a title reserved for five men at any one time), we would never have lost the vote save for your husband's intemperate speech. Even though I had spoken after the vote. In Jerusalem there was silence. It wasn't until 1984 when Herzog had become President that a conference was finally held on the subject. But not at one of the universities.

In the President's <u>house</u>. I arrived with a paper; the Israeli scholars, if they came at all, came with notes.

It has been this way in Washington. I have now been fifteen years in the Senate. I have worked at this issue from the day I got here. I have argued that it was the last great horror of the Hitler-Stalin era and had to be exorcised. We passed four laws; but nothing happened.

The break came when Elie Wiesel went to Kiev September 12 and visited Babi Yar. This time there was a new Ukrainian regime. Ukrainian President Leonid Kravchuk knew perfectly well what the original propaganda charge had been. He volunteered that the Ukraine would vote to repeal the Zionism resolution. In 11 days time President Bush went to the United Nations and said Now. The Soviet foreign minister and the Ukrainian President have followed him to the podium and repeated: Now. (In Kravchuk's speech, he explicitly linked Babi Yar with the Zionim resolution. I made that point last night in a Senate resolution adopted 97 to 0, with an unprecedented 97 cosponsors.)

And, indeed, the time is: Now. In the immediate aftermath of the President's speech, the press accounts generally described the resolution as having been an Arab initiative. Such is the blinding force of that Big Red Lie. I wrote the piece in the Washington Post to set the record straight, lest the Arabs begin to feel proprietary.

We have the votes in the General Assembly. The moment is: Now. A moment of truth and of deliverance. . . .

Letter to Max Frankel, executive editor of the NEW YORK TIMES, *pleading for coverage of his success in passing the Intermodal Surface Transportation Efficiency Act (ISTEA), a major legislative measure that transformed what had previously been a road-building program into a broader transportation effort. He regarded the measure as one of his proudest if perhaps least appreciated legislative accomplishments, because it secured $5 billion to reimburse New York for the construction of the State Thruway in the 1950s, when he was in Albany. Hence his reference to it taking thirty-five years to get the funding. The payments did indeed get disbursed over the next fifteen years.*

DECEMBER 7, 1991

Dear Max:

There must be days when you wish the Times was <u>not</u> the Newspaper of Record. But it is, thank heaven, and I need your help.

The Transportation bill passed last week (which the President will probably sign the week after next) provides for New York to receive $5 billion as reimbursement for having contributed the Thruway to the Interstate System back in 1956. Specifically, $337 million per year for fifteen years starting in FY 1996. The first two annual installments are in the current bill.

It has taken me thirty five years to bring this off. I was in the Governor's office in Albany in 1956 when the Interstate got started. I thought it was madness of New York not to insist on payment then and there; settling instead for a vague undertaking in the 1956 legislation that levied the gas tax and established the Trust Fund. (A tax we would pay to build freeways elsewhere. We have since lost one third of our Congressional delegation.) Anyway, my moment came this year, and I shall soon have it in statute. But for obvious reasons I didn't make a great deal of it on the floor. And neither did the Times. At least I have not been able to find any reference, and believe me I have searched.

This means there is no "record" of the event. This is real money. Trust Fund money. But New Yorkers will never get it if New Yorkers don't know about it. (Nor those in New Jersey and Connecticut who are also included.) Think what we could do with an annuity of a third of a billion dollars a year for fifteen years. One of our two wonderful undertakings. To startle the world. As did the Futurama exhibit at the 1939 World's Fair where the Interstate idea was born! But there needs to be a record!

CHAPTER THIRTEEN

"What Is to Be Done?"

The 1992 election year drew Moynihan close to Bill and Hillary Clinton, but also planted the seeds of their difficult relationship. In this interval Moynihan continued to try to hold the intelligence establishment accountable for its failures during the cold war. His hopes for the Clinton presidency rested on his anticipation that the new president would at last pick up the cause of expanding welfare reforms. Instead the Clintons chose a health care overhaul—expanding coverage for the uninsured and installing cost controls—as their main priority. Moynihan was also concerned as Clinton ran that he would not recognize the role of ethnic conflict in the post–cold war world, and he sent a long memorandum to the president-elect on his trip to the Balkans, where he saw little solution as the region sank into an all-out war among Serbs, Croats, and Bosnian Muslims. Moynihan became chairman of the Senate Finance Committee when Senator Lloyd Bentsen of Texas was appointed by Clinton as his Treasury Secretary. But Moynihan's relationship with Clinton was damaged at the beginning of the new president's term, in 1993, by a magazine article that quoted an unnamed Clinton aide as asserting that the incoming White House would, if necessary, "roll over" Moynihan at the finance panel. Although Clinton apologized to Moynihan and promised to dismiss the aide, Moynihan noted in his letters that no one was ousted, and distrust between the Clintons and the Moynihans was always a factor in their dealings.

Separate limericks written for two friends but sent here to Robert Conquest, the
British historian of the Soviet Union. The first was in honor of a friend's fortieth
birthday. (Cos d'Estournel is the name of a fine Bordeaux wine.) The second was
written for Moynihan's friend, Father Andrew Greeley—the priest, columnist, au-
thor, novelist, and frequent critic of the Catholic hierarchy.

FEBRUARY 18, 1992

> *A story too shocking to tell!*
> *In an hallucinogenic spell,*
> *A blue stocking Miss,*
> *Transported by bliss,*
> *Put ice in the* Cos d'Estournel.

> *With countenance awesome and steely,*
> *The Cardinal Archbishop said, "Really.*
> *In the name of proportion,*
> *I'll go for abortion.*
> *But must I endure Father Greeley?"*

Excerpt of a letter to Herbert Block, the cartoonist better known as Herblock, re-
counting the history of mentally ill patients being given drugs to let them live out-
side mental institutions. In the letter Moynihan laments that this policy has led to
homelessness.

FEBRUARY 20, 1992

Dear Herb:

    . . . Part of the problem I have had is getting us to face up to the present
misuse of the trust fund is that down deep, groups such as the American Association of Retired Persons and the AFL-CIO and others really would like

to spend the surplus on health insurance and similar benefits, and accordingly, do not object to the looting which you so brilliantly depicted in your cartoon of January 25, 1990.

Not long before he died, John Heinz and I were together on a morning television program. I had quoted an upstate New York editorial which described what was going on with the Social Security trust funds as "thievery." John was then asked, "Senator Heinz, do you agree that what is going on is thievery?" "Certainly not," replied my dear friend. "It's not thievery. It's embezzlement."

Perhaps I could interest you in a related subject. As I have been remarking in hearings of late, surely the most conspicuous problem of health care in our country today is that of the homeless mentally ill. For some reason, we simply cannot bring ourselves to understand that 30 years ago the people who are now sleeping on sidewalk grates were sleeping in hospital beds. Which is to say, mental institutions. Then, as a matter of government <u>policy</u>, we put them out on the streets. It was called deinstitutionalization.

I happen to have been present at the creation of this policy. In the spring of 1955, Averell Harriman, then newly-elected Governor of New York, met with his newly-appointed Commissioner for Mental Hygiene Paul Hoch. Jack Bingham, the Governor's secretary had sponsored him and was there at the meeting, as was Paul Appleby, the budget director for Harriman. I was note taker. Hoch described the extraordinary work of Nathan Kline at Rockland State Hospital in the lower Hudson Valley. Kline had developed reserpine, what we would come to think of as the first tranquilizer. It had been tested clinically and Hoch had been satisfied that it should be used systemwide. Appleby said he could find the money and Harriman agreed. The next year, after a century of steady inexorable upward movement, for the first time ever the population of the New York mental hospitals dropped. Today it is down to 15 percent of the 1955 level.

I came down to Washington with this experience behind me and ended up representing Arthur Goldberg on a cabinet committee to carry out the recommendations of the Joint Commission on Mental Illness and Health, which had also been established in 1955, and ended up writing the report. I enclose a newsletter on this subject. I was naive. I believed what the doctors told us about those wonder drugs. So did everyone else. The last bill-signing ceremony President Kennedy had was on October 31, 1963, when he signed Public Law Number 88-164, The Mental Retardation Facilities and Community Health Centers Construction Act. (He gave me a pen which I still have.) We were going to build 2,000 mental health centers by 1980. We got started well enough, but soon other things came along and the program was pretty much forgotten. In the meantime, the hospitals were emptied out everywhere. Whereupon, 20 or so years later the strangest thing happened—the former mental patients, and their confined schizophrenic successors were living on the streets. Everyone asked how could this be?

I think it is a scandal amounting to malpractice. The professionals did not know enough about the treatment of schizophrenia as they thought they did and have not been willing to 'fess up and to help the public understand what has happened.

Sorry to raise a seemingly unrelated issue, but for my money, the health scandal is that the mentally ill are sleeping under bridges.

Letter to Robert Laird, columnist and editor at the NEW YORK DAILY NEWS, *reflecting on his forty years as a former young person.*

FEBRUARY 24, 1992

Dear Bob:

What a grand column. You are a most patient listener! I was surprised to see myself described as a "loner" but come to think, I can see how that impression could be got. And I think I can explain. I am of the political generation that came back from World War II simply assuming that New York Democrats would resume the leadership of the state, the nation, and the world that had come to seem so natural during those years, and the 1930s that preceded them. You should have seen us at meetings of the New York Young Democrats. You be Secretary of State, you be Governor, I'll be President, you run Treasury. Franklin D. Roosevelt, Junior. Robert F. Wagner, Junior. *Et al.* My first campaign was Wagner for Mayor. Then Roosevelt for Governor. Went to Albany with Harriman as Bingham's assistant. Liz with me all the way. I was not up for cabinet rank, mind. Was mostly useful for knowing papal encyclicals which seemed to endorse the New Deal. But somehow I stayed at it longer—I was younger to begin with—and am now the only one left. I assure you that forty years ago I ran with a gang as youth will do!

*Letter to Senator Lloyd Bentsen, chairman of the Senate Finance Committee, op-
posing legislation that would require "mark-to-market" accounting for securities
firms. The practice of marking securities at their "market value" as opposed to
their "book value" was adopted by the accounting profession in the 1990s and it
helped precipitate the drastic write-downs that aggravated the financial crisis of
2007–2008.*

FEBRUARY 27, 1992

Dear Lloyd:

We may be having trouble getting through to the Committee staff that I
simply could not vote for a bill that includes the mark-to-market provision
for securities firms that the administration has proposed. The entire burden
would fall on the securities industry in New York, which has lost 50,000 jobs
since 1987.

*Letter to Admiral Stansfield Turner, former director of the Central Intelligence
Agency, congratulating him for acknowledging a point Moynihan had made for
years—that during the cold war the agency overestimated the strength of the Soviet
Union. Here, as on many occasions, Moynihan tweaks former Secretary of State
Kissinger for asserting that no one had predicted the fall of the U.S.S.R. Moynihan
subsequently saved a letter from Kissinger dated April 2, 1992: "Dear Pat: I stand
corrected. Your crystal ball was better than mine."*

APRIL 1, 1992

Dear Stan:

In what appears to be an alarming pattern, your spies withheld some critical
information. On the morning of the Nixon seminar, I said you were a great
man for the acknowledgement in your <u>Foreign Affairs</u> article. In the afternoon, Kissinger dismissed it as self-interested revisionism. In fact, I have been

citing you with stupefying regularity. As, for example, the enclosed from the current issue of The National Interest.

Starting in the late '70s, I became convinced the Soviet Union was going to break up in the '80s; the Cold War was over; the arms control issue had to do with the danger of civil war in the former USSR. None of this made the least impression on anyone in the intelligence community, not even to the point of bothering to say it was wrong. This seems to me an interesting question to discuss but that possibility is now denied by the revisionists to which you referred. But which Henry and company refer to as revisionism in its own right.

Letter to Bryant Gumbel, host of the TODAY *show on NBC, again arguing that Social Security is not a regular government program but a "contributory insurance system." As before, he warns against spending the "surplus" generated by the program, though Congress and presidents ignored this advice.*

APRIL 7, 1992

Dear Bryant:

I was so pleased to learn on "The Today Show" this morning that you regard me as your Senator and even more pleased to find that the notion that a flat tax might destroy Social Security "scares" you.

This whole episode baffles me. I wonder if there is not something large to be learned here. The facts are simple enough. Social Security was devised as a contributory insurance system, with individuals paying into their individual accounts, matched by their employers. There is not an inconsiderable "literature" in this field which is more or less unanimous on the point that the only way to keep a program such as this going from generation-to-generation is to see that people not only have a claim on benefits, but a specific, concrete claim. No one was clearer on this point than Franklin D. Roosevelt, as we know from a wonderful little note jotted down by Luther Gulick after calling on the President in the summer of '41. Gulick taught public administration at Columbia for years and years, and is generally regarded as the man who created the modern Executive Office of the President during the Roosevelt years as a member of the President's Committee on Administrative Management. It was his belief that it was not good management to have all these individual accounts which were being kept by hand in a pre-computer age. Here is his aide-memoir:

> FDR replied: "I guess you are right on the economics, but those taxes were never a problem of economics. . . . We put those payroll contributions there so as to give the contributors a legal, moral, and political right to collect their pension and their unemployment benefits. With those taxes in there, no damn politician can ever scrap my Social Security program."

What worries me about the Brown position paper is that it would have been and still would be so easy to fix as regards Social Security. There is nothing wrong with advocating a flat tax, so long as you continue payroll deductions for Social Security. These are commonly referred to as "payroll taxes" but aren't really. If you look at your pay check, you will see the initials F.I.C.A. which stand for Federal Insurance Contributions Act. These are insurance contributions which go into a Trust Fund. They are not meant to be used for anything but benefits.

Here, perhaps, is the problem. The system is in <u>huge surplus</u>. I say again, <u>huge</u> surplus. $1.5 billion a week, rising to about $4 billion a week by the end of this decade. By 2015 this surplus would buy you the New York Stock Exchange. We are not saving that money as a trust fund ought, but rather spending it as if it were tax revenue. This comes at a time when half of the non-retired adults don't think they are going to get their Social Security anyway. The combination of these two things may mean that what would once have been an explosive proposal goes relatively unnoticed.

Which scares <u>me</u>.

You might think of doing a segment sometime in which you lay out the facts of the surplus, and show people how they can write in and get a statement from the Social Security Administration of their contributions and expected benefits. I enclose mine. Very few people know they can do this. I have spent 10 years trying to get the administration to send them out annually and this will start later in this decade. But we need bucking up here. If half the non-retired adults think their government is taking their money from them under false pretenses, what else do they think?

P.S. (It might interest you to know that Luther Halsy Gulick, age 100, lives at 15 Spring Street, Potsdam, New York, up on the St. Lawrence River.

I spoke with him just last Thursday, his mind as clear as Easter bells. According to <u>Who's Who</u>, his birthday is January 17. *Deo volente,* he will be 101 on that date next year, a point your colleague, Willard Scott, might want to pencil in.)

Letter to Senator George Mitchell with an early disquisition on "Baumol's disease," offered by William J. Baumol, a professor at the NYU Stern School of Business. Moynihan was fascinated by Baumol's explanation for why health care costs keep rising despite the lack of gains in productivity in the health care field. But his insistence on promoting the theory led to his confrontation in following years with President and Mrs. Clinton, who contended—contrary to Baumol's thesis—that they could cut health care costs as part of their health care program. Moynihan came to regard the Clinton cost-cutting proposals as harmful to the New York hospital and health care system.

APRIL 10, 1992

Dear George:

Yesterday's luncheon of the Democratic Policy Committee set me to thinking about our future as a party. You will recall that our guest (according to the Committee notice) was "Stuart Altman, Dean of the Heller Graduate School for Social Policy at Brandeis University." There is no such place, but let it pass. My question concerns our having described him as "A renowned health care expert. . . ."

In the general discussion I offered the view that health care was a preeminent example of an economic sector suffering from "Baumol's disease." Or "cost disease," as Baumol prefers to call the phenomenon which he first described. This refers to a class of services plagued by cumulative and persistent rises in costs at a rate which normally exceeds to a significant degree the corresponding rate of increase for commodities generally. (I am paraphrasing Baumol here.) These services tend to have a "handicraft" quality. You may recall my mentioning that Baumol started out by asking himself why the cost of the performing arts always seemed to be rising. I remarked that if you want a Dixieland band for a campaign rally today, you will need the same five players you would have needed in Storyville at the beginning of the century. Productivity just hasn't changed much. And when it does—e.g., playing the Minute Waltz in 50 seconds—it doesn't seem to work right.

Whereupon, I turned to the Dean and asked if he wouldn't agree that health care had Baumol's disease. For example, a visit to the doctor took half an hour today, just as it did a hundred years ago. The Dean demurred. He said that a visit to the doctor today would be shorter and that the doctor would probably order "96 tests" before the patient got to see him. <u>He obviously could not grasp that what he was saying was that patient care that once took 30 minutes per unit of output now requires 96 or 96.5 times that</u>. Productivity (in gross, not qualitative terms) is regressing!

Now then. It is a characteristic of "stagnant services" to drift into the public sector. Why? Because there's little or no money to be made. Other examples: education high and low, welfare, the arts, legal services, police. (Law enforcement was once in the private sector. See Banfield.) This means that the public sector will continue to grow. Baumol estimates that by 2040, education and health will require 55 percent of GNP. He insists there is no guilty party here. The cause is to be found in the nature of the technology of these services. Thus, in the past 39 years, the price of a physician visit has increased 750 percent in absolute terms, 150 percent in relation to the general price level. But for much of this period the real earnings of doctors in the U.S. have been virtually constant.

It happens that this morning (Friday) I chaired a hearing in the Finance Committee on managed health care. The Deputy Secretary of HHS testified that Medicaid costs had risen 250 percent in the period 1989–92 (sic). That the Medical CPI was rising at <u>twice</u> the rate of the overall CPI. Again, a change in relative costs typical of Baumol's disease.

Now then. I also remarked yesterday that unfortunately for us, the Democratic party is identified with this very public sector in which relative costs are rising. By contrast, the Republican party is identified with the private sector where relative costs are declining. (Owing to continued productivity increases. Consider how the FAX and the cellular telephone have crept into our lives in the last few years, quite unannounced, but instantly welcomed and soon to be taken for granted.)

One last Now Then. I don't see that we have any choice as a party as regards the public sector. We care about health and education and welfare. <u>But</u> is it possible that we can absorb—internalize—the realization that this means we are going to be constantly on the defensive as Big Spenders. This could sensitize us to approaches to public sector spending that are seen as good faith efforts to keep relative costs from rising more than necessary. My first big leg-islative adventure in the Senate—some 14 years ago—was on behalf of tuition tax credits. Which would have helped preserve, among others, "private" Catholic schools in inner cities. Which functioned beautifully as schools, and at half or one-third the cost of "public schools." A Democratic administration opposed the bill and a Democratic Senate defeated it. Which, I believe, was a mistake. In any event, ought we not, for example, to try to think our way through the inevitable, ineluctable rise in the cost of public schools that will not be associated with any improvement in public schooling? Sorry about that. None.

Incidentally, Baumol estimates that the cost per pupil day of elementary schooling is rising steadily at a rate intermediate between that of a physician visit and that of a hospital stay. Title One anyone?

Letter to Monsignor C. Sepe of the Vatican Secretariat, explaining that in de-nouncing "liberalism," the Pope and the Vatican were using a term in a way that was being misinterpreted by American audiences as an attack on liberal Democrats. Liberalism, as the Vatican uses it, and as Moynihan tries to explain, refers in Vat-ican pronouncements to the nineteenth-century laissez-faire philosophy and not to government social programs as advocated by liberals in the United States. Moyni-han complains that his queries have not been considered, and in a letter to Thomas L. Friedman, the NEW YORK TIMES *writer (later columnist), Moynihan com-plained that the answers he got back from the Vatican were "either uncomprehending or dismissive."*

JUNE 9, 1992

Dear Monsignor Sepe:

I am writing, after some reflection and a longish interval, to ask your help. You may recall that I wrote His Holiness last February concerning the use of the term "liberalism" in *Centesimus Annus*. I said that in my understanding, the Papal usage dates back to economic debate in 19th century Europe, notably in the United Kingdom. With the passing of time, the term has acquired quite a different meaning in "American English," as it is sometimes called. Such that

Catholic congregations in the 1930s were baffled by Episcopal denunciations of "liberalism" by decidedly liberal Bishops. More recently, the term has entered the political vocabulary of American conservatism as a term of all-purpose dismissal and disdain. All perfectly fair political knock-about. What concerned me, however, is that the Papacy not be seen to be taking sides.

And so I wrote. I did so on the advice of a number of priests, some of whom teach in Catholic universities. They felt confident that such a letter would be taken seriously. But was it? ". . . I would assure you that your observations have been carefully noted." Again, this may be a matter of usage, but in American letters, this is a mode of dismissal.

I did not write to have my observation noted. I wrote to tell you that, in my view, the Church has a problem and ought to consider what might be done about it. If you do not think it a problem, why not say so? If you do think it a problem, why not do something?

An undated letter to the Senate majority leader, George Mitchell, assailing the mistakes of the C.I.A. during the cold war.

Dear George,

In considering the future of the "intelligence community," could I suggest a thought experiment?

Imagine the cold war never happened. World War II had ended with the destruction of Nazism and the emergence of a status quo government in Moscow.

Therefore, there never was a C.I.A.

Now, a half-century later, the United States finds itself thinking about assorted subjects, some new, some old. Trade. Rain forests. Sporadic terrorism. Drug trafficking in the Caribbean.

Would we decide to create a vast, new <u>secret</u> agency to deal with these old subjects, which had for so long been the province of the Departments of State and of Treasury, or, in the case of new subjects, new organizations such as the Environmental Protection Agency, or established international groups such as Interpol?

Or supposing the subject had to do with Pakistani tank crews. Would we turn this question over to a civilian agency? And not let the future Pattons in the Pentagon think it through?

Again, of course, we would not.

Now, if all we were dealing with here was institutional maintenance, I would not much mind. (See Herbert Kaufman, <u>Are Government Organizations Immortal?</u>, Brookings Institution, 1976.) (Answer: Yes.) I have a deeper concern.

The Central Intelligence Agency began as an institution helping to wage the ideological war that broke out in Europe in the first-half of the 20th century and which by mid-century had spread to almost the whole of the globe. In its early years the Agency was characterized by persons intensely committed to the outcome of that armageddonic conflict.

However, with time and routinization, this engagement and understanding faded. My eight years on the Intelligence Committee were hell. The plainest thing in the world was that Marxism was dead as a political force. This fulfilled the major premise of containment. Kennan had laid it out that we must deal with post-war Russia "by an adequate balance of opposing power, primarily political (because that was where the threat was) but also, in a defensive sense, military." Thus, by the 1980s, the cold war was over, containment had succeeded.

No one at the C.I.A. could grasp this. Instead they took us into Central America. They saw the Marxists there as a new wave. When they were a last gasp. When an idea dies in Madrid it takes two generations for word to get to Managua. But to say again, by now the people in charge had never known Marxism alive.

A man for whom I have the greatest respect retired from the Agency in 1987. He told me recently that there was not then a single person in the whole system who had the least inkling that the wall would be coming down in two years time. "Had I said any such thing they would have sent me to St. Elizabeth's [a Washington psychiatric hospital]." Those people are still in charge.

Angelo Codevilla, who was Malcolm Wallop's staffer on the Intelligence Committee, has written a powerful and devastating account of American intelligence over the past thirty years. Perhaps you will find a moment to read the review in the current <u>Economist</u>.

Can it be that we are going to leave this disaster in place?

Letter to Hillary Rodham Clinton. Governor Bill Clinton, the Democratic presidential nominee, had joined with his wife and Senator Al Gore and Mrs. Gore in a campaign appearance in Chautauqua, in upstate New York. Moynihan was just beginning to forge a relationship with her on family and health issues.

PINDARS CORNERS
AUGUST 24, 1992

Dear Mrs. Clinton,

Liz and I want you to know how moved we were by your address yesterday at Chautauqua. It must surely have been the first occasion in American history that candidates for President and Vice President, joined by their spouses, devoted an entire campaign event to the subject of family stability. (Or as near as makes no matter.) And did so with sensitivity, information and a clear aversion to understandable untruth. Some while ago Samuel Preston in a presidential address to the Population Association of America spoke of "the earthquake that shuddered through the American family" since the early 1960s. It continues. It will be the most important issue of social policy in the generation to come, and thanks to such as you may now be addressed. I picked up the early tremors, and have followed the subject for thirty years now. But haven't the faintest notion as to what, realistically, can be done.

Letter to Alfred S. Berne, a prominent radiologist and professor of medicine at the State University of New York in Syracuse, about his taste for bow ties—and Bill Clinton's request that Moynihan teach him how to tie one.

PINDARS CORNERS
AUGUST 26, 1992

Dear Dr. Berne,

My bowties? Well I get them here and there. But the ones I most admire, and I suspect have caught your eye, are from Lock & Co. on the Burlington

Arcade in London. I was over there on a Fulbright Fellowship and the G.I. Bill some forty odd years ago and having a pocket full of money bought a few then. Ever since, when I get to London, I buy a half dozen which keeps me in ample supply. You will be cheered to know that at the Chautauqua Institute last Sunday Bill Clinton asked if I would teach him how to tie one. I told him his mother had done that when she taught him to tie his shoe laces. He seemed a bit skeptical. I went on to say that what with Velcro (sp?) coming in mothers probably weren't doing that any longer and the art of bow tie tying was very likely dying out. That when he is elected President I will apply for a folklore grant to keep it up. Poor man at this point wished he hadn't raised the subject. But if I get the grant perhaps you will partake.

We used to live around the corner from you on Harrison Street. I taught at Maxwell.

Letter to the novelist John Updike.

PINDARS CORNERS

AUGUST 31, 1992

Dear John,

Your letter about the Blashfield lecture was wonderfully complex and consoling. I was enabled to see that I was onto something, but hadn't got it yet. Possibly never will. But I resolved to try again. Perhaps you will find a moment for the enclosed. You will get no further variations and need not fear an indefinite correspondence!

A bit of a downer, yes. Let me go on a bit, as this might interest you. For getting on to forty years I have been involved with a group of persons who in the 1970s got labeled—from the left—neo-conservatives. All had thought themselves liberals (if not Trotskyites) up to that point, and much confusion has followed. Our problem—it got to be a crypto-collaborationist anti-people deviation—was to have been involved with the social science of the 1960s that established what weak hold social science would have on social change.

To a man (some women) we did not expect such findings and did not welcome them but did accept them. The leading exemplar is James S. Coleman whose 1967 report on Equality of Educational Opportunity said in effect that if families are going to hell, forget it. The report had been commissioned by the Civil Rights Act of 1964. See the enclosed from Ronald Berman <u>America in the Sixties, An Intellectual History</u> for my work. There is much else. It all came together in about three years in the mid-60s. We got no thanks for our efforts, of course. But that did not change the data, if you follow. As I am sure you do.

There is some evidence that we are beginning to be accepted. Coleman was president of the American Sociological Association this year. I am not sure he would have been allowed to speak twenty years ago. But again, that does not change the data either.

It might cheer you up to know that this same perspective made it possible to predict the collapse of the Soviet Union with some precision. I know because I did. The Agency hadn't a clue. The realpolitikers said Moscow would be The Threat forever. I said it would all be gone by the end of the 1980s. Typically, the only person who has so far noticed is Seymour Martin Lipset, one of the gang of ten or fifteen. In a paper at this year's ASA meeting. <u>He</u> will be the next president.

This is so long as to be presumptuous. Please know of my great admiration and special thanks for your letter. I am stretched to the breaking point most of the time, and thus may appear taller!

Excerpt of a Memorandum to President-elect Bill Clinton, on Moynihan's trip with Peter Galbraith (son of Moynihan's friend John Kenneth Galbraith and staff member of the Senate Foreign Relations Committee) to the Balkans as civil war was breaking up the country of Yugoslavia. The refusal of the military to let him visit Sarajevo was especially irritating to him for years. Galbraith later served as United States ambassador to Croatia.

ZAGREB, CROATIA

NOVEMBER 28, 1992

MEMORANDUM FOR THE PRESIDENT-ELECT

You will recall our conversation of November 13 in which I mentioned that I would be visiting this region. You asked if I would share my impressions with you. . . .

First some atmospherics. We arrived at Frankfurt at dawn on Monday, and made our way to the air base. Galbraith had been sending cables and making telephone calls from New Delhi saying we would need a plane, adding that I was travelling as a member of the Foreign Relations Committee, but that I also planned to send a report to you. However, the base commander at Rhine-Main, as it is called, had heard nothing of this. Nothing daunted even so, he set out to find us a C-12. As we were sitting about, waiting for news, he mentioned that they were sending three relief flights a day into Sarajevo. That's where I want to go, said I. He leapt to the phone with instructions that UN Two Zero Three was not to move, piled us into his car, and out to the runway. We were airborne in five minutes. Good man.

About the time we were leaving Austrian air space (all rules suspended in this massive, fifteen-nation exercise) our pilot received a radio message that U.S. Senators were not allowed into Sarajevo. I told him to signal back that if the West Virginia Air National Guard, our crew, could take the risk, so could I and that I had no intention of being diverted. This appeared to settle the matter. But another half hour later we received word that the airport in Sarajevo was closed in, and that we would have to land at Zagreb.

This was a lie.

Our chargé here in Zagreb, the admirable Ron Neitske, was on hand when we landed. I apologized for disrupting his day, but explained about the weather in Sarajevo. What weather? he asked. Five minutes ago two C-130s had taken off for Sarajevo. The airport was indeed open. Which it isn't always, and when it is, you know. Great.

I will spare you the details, but Tuesday morning we were aboard a Canadian C-130 bound for Sarajevo. We stayed the night and flew back Wednesday on a U.K. Hercules. EUCOM was furious and CODEL MOYNIHAN was denied any further logistic support; in particular no plane was provided for our planned trip to Kosovo and Macedonia, two as yet uninvolved entities where there is no fear of flying whatever.

That is a lot by way of atmospherics, but I can think of no better way to impress upon you, as it was impressed upon me, that the outgoing administration is beginning to realize the magnitude of the foreign policy disaster they are bequeathing to you here in the Balkans. At minimum it will be a human disaster. The International Rescue Committee representative suggests in a best case scenario—peace in Bosnia-Herzegovina—50,000 people will starve to death by spring. In the worst case half a million. Others scale the worst case back toward a quarter million deaths. But then, of course, the seasons go round and winter comes again. It is entirely possible that in time the Muslim population of Bosnia-Herzegovina will be systematically extirpated. Genocide.

It is also possible that before that happens there will be something like a European war in this region.

So much for the New World Order.

The order to keep me out of Sarajevo, and the subsequent tantrum, came directly from Cheney. Scowcroft knew of it. Men I have known for a quarter century and think of as friends. I can't blame them. They depart leaving behind an awful crisis, for which a share of the blame is clearly theirs. Or at least that would be my judgment.

SARAJEVO. The most intense urban warfare environment in the world just now. Disembark, AK-47s chattering. Dash for the sand bags, insinuated into a Ukrainian armored personnel carrier, set out across no man's land to the city proper. UNPROFOR (United Nations Protective Forces) headquarters. An Egyptian APC, considerably more user-friendly, to the presidency. Television as you are greeted by President Izetbegovic. Back to HQ. Briefing. Artillery getting heavy now. Whiskey. A good meal in the mess. (Morillon, the commander, is a Legionnaire. They have a thing about dining well under fire.) To bed, shells landing 300 yards away.

I was first in Sarajevo forty years ago. Undamaged by World War II, a Muslim/Viennese city of considerable charm. It is damaged now, but not yet destroyed. That is only partially the object of the Serbian forces in the surrounding mountain tops. Their object is to destroy the population. We are driven around by a former captain in the Gurkha Regiment, now with the British Foreign Office and seconded to the UN High Commissioner for Refugees. With a staff of two, he is responsible for feeding a third of a million persons. The siege began May 2nd. There are no longer any food stores in the city. What arrives by plane or truck one day, is eaten the next day. If the planes can't land, or the convoys can't get through, starvation comes quickly. The Brit is uncomplaining but disheartened beyond what would be explained by exhaustion. He says two things. First, you can never believe anything told you. Second, for seven months there has been a steady decline, which continues.

The military are much in evidence, but it is not clear how much they do. The main forces are French, Ukrainian, and Egyptian. This is meant to enable Roman Catholics to talk to Croatians, Orthodox christians to talk to Serbians, and Muslims to talk to Muslims. How well this works is another question, for their only mandate is to support the relief effort, but to do so without using force. This presents no great problem for the Serbs, who are content that some supplies get through, so long as they are not sufficient. There is no prospect whatever of breaking the siege.

HOW DID ALL THIS HAPPEN? There is a sense, I suppose, in which nothing very much has happened. The twentieth century began in August, 1914 when a Serb nationalist assassinated the Austrian Archduke in—Sarajevo. The cause was that of Greater Serbia. War followed, a sort of peace, then another war, then a protracted Cold War. Greater Serbia was kept on hold, but then all that came to an end, and the conflict resumed. In the interval, however, largely at the behest of the United States, the international order had proclaimed the principle of self-determination, such that the conquest of a place such as Bosnia-Herzegovina, by a state such as Serbia is expressly forbidden by the United Nations Charter. (In the event it was Stalin who insisted that "self-determination" be included in Article I. But Woodrow Wilson, and the United States, first insisted that this must be the international norm.) A place such as Serbia, however, argues that it is only seeking to provide that self-determination for Serbs living in Bosnia-Herzegovina. Hitler said the same thing when he invaded Czechoslovakia, citing Wilson chapter and verse. A year ago the Serbs were seeking to annex portions of Croatia, citing the same principles.

The fact is that most of the conflicts of the 20th century have been basically ethnic or nationalist in character. (Same words, really. One Greek, the other Latin.) However, the reigning ideologies, world views, what you will, have obscured this reality, perhaps especially for Americans. At the outset of the century there were two such dominant views. On the one hand the liberal expectancy, which held that ethnic attachments were pre-modern modes of thought, not very attractive, and would soon go away with the progress of the enlightenment. On the other hand, there was the Marxist prediction, which held that ethnic attachments were epiphenomena of pre-modern modes of production, and would soon go away with the progress of socialism. Both were wrong. Ethnicity is in fact post-modern.

The foreign policy and intelligence institutions you are about to take over have never been able to see this. You are entitled to know that this is a bit of grievance of mine, and my views may need some balancing. In brief, in 1979, when I was a member of the Intelligence Committee, I began to argue, in public and private, that in the 1980s that the Soviet Union would break up along ethnic lines, and that this could conceivably lead to catastrophic nuclear exchanges between the successor nations, in the first fusion of ethnic hatred with nuclear power. No one at the CIA could grasp the concept. The USSR was seen as a permanent antagonist. After all, it worked, didn't it? (The same Agency which in 1987 formally estimated per capita GDP in East Germany to be higher than West Germany.) During the 1980s I was an Observer to the START talks in Geneva. I would go over from time to time and ask the company at the ambassador's table did they ever consider the possibility that by the time they finished with the mind-numbing details of their treaty with the USSR that there might no longer be a USSR? Blank looks, no comment. (When the treaty did arrive in the Senate I asked the negotiators when did that possibility occur to them? Mid-1991.)

As the Cold War ended, and the Soviet Union began to break up, American analysts by and large said it wasn't happening. Then we began to say it oughtn't to be happening. We were clinging to our bi-polar certainties. In August, 1991 President Bush went to Kiev to warn the parliament there against the dangers of "suicidal nationalism." This after it had become inevitable that the Ukraine would separate from Russia. Bill Safire called it the "Chicken Kiev speech." In the same manner, two months earlier, June 21, 1991, Secretary of State Baker went to Belgrade to warn against the break-up of Yugoslavia, noting the separatists could expect no help from the United States. This just four days before long-planned Slovene and Croatian declarations of independence were to take effect.

Here in Croatia, over in Bosnia, those remarks are held to have been a signal to the Serbs that the United States would not object to a drive to annex territories with Serb populations, consolidating a Greater Serbia.

WHAT IS TO BE DONE? Probably not a great deal. The administration has left you with few options. Had we got over our Cold War rigidity sooner, we might have understood that Yugoslavia was going to break up whether we liked it or not, the Serbs might have got the message to accept this reality. Instead we gave the impression that we would not that much object to their seizing the opportunity to start expanding again. Had we seen to it that the sanctions voted by the Security Council on May 30th were instantly enforced—Serbia imports at least three-quarters of its oil—the Serbs might have got the message to stop. Instead we dithered for five months, and only two weeks ago said we really mean it. Had we brought the Security Council around to voting "demonstrations" under Article 42 of Chapter VII—taking out every bridge in Belgrade in one bombing raid—we might have sent a message to the Serbs that "ethnic cleansing" wasn't going to be worth it to them. But now we have some 1600 UN troops spread out all over Bosnia. To start bombing Belgrade is to commence the massacre of our peacekeeping forces. Thus Morillon, no stranger to combat, made clear to us that if we were going to ship arms to the Bosnians, he would only ask 48 hours notice so that he could get all his men out of the region.

All that we can do at this point is to see that the food gets in. It is possible that the administration will use the intervention in Somalia, also an ethnic conflict, as precedent for Bosnia, in which event, there will be some additional forces on the ground by the time you take office. If not, you can do more on your own. I would caution, however, that American troops are not needed. What will be needed in January is a clear message to Belgrade that there is a new President who has no history of seeing things from Belgrade's point of view and who, among other things, has instructed the United States embassies in the region to provide the fullest support to the War Crimes Commission announced by Secretary General Boutros-Ghali on October 26. The Commission will operate under the 1949 Geneva Conventions, which grew out of the Nuremberg Tribunal. This was very much an Anglo-American initiative. There are a dozen detailed measures that might make sense. Thus, Croatia is currently supporting 800,000 refugees; the comparable ratio of refugees to population in the U.S. would mean the equivalent of 50 million refugees. Inflation runs at 3000 percent a year, unemployment upwards of 60 percent. But the main thing is to send the message that a new President has brought a wholly new point of view to this situation.

BEYOND THE BALKANS. If I were asked to pick a symbolic date on which our present crisis may be said to have begun, it would be back in June of 1965. The United Nations, very tentatively, had decided to convene a Seminar—nothing so grand as a conference—on the Multi-National State. Yugoslavia had offered to play host, and had offered the site of Ljubljana, capital of Slovenia. (Which would be the first secessionist state.) The "Minorities" issue was thought to have been the undoing of the League of Nations, and so it had taken a long time for the U.N. to get around to touching on the subject once again. You would have thought that this would be reason enough to hurry, but the Cold War was judged to have put all that nonsense behind us. And so nobody in the Department of State wanted to bother with such a marginal matter. I was then Assistant Secretary of Labor for Policy Planning.

I had recently published, with Nathan Glazer, a book on the ethnic groups of New York City. (Still in print, mind!) A call came from State. Would I be willing to represent the United States at Ljubljana? Sure, said I. Off I went, enjoyed it—one good cable line, "AM IN LJUBLJANA. I HAVE SEEN THE AUSTRO-HUNGARIAN EMPIRE AND IT WORKS"—came back and told everyone who would listen that Yugoslavia clearly was going to come apart and was fair to begging us for help and advice. As I suggested earlier, persons listened but did not hear.

There are going to be, what? fifty new states in the next fifty years. A number during your administration. Most will come into being through violent ethnic upheaval. The world needs rules for these upheavals which do not now exist. The old rules of sovereignty, the Westphalian state, just don't fit with this new reality. We have to ask ourselves just what "self-determination" means. And under what circumstances the world community, through the United Nations usually, but not necessarily, has the right to intervene. Without setting ourselves up for an inquest by some future Non-Aligned Conference.

These are not the kind of questions the United States government has been asking within its own councils. The subject has seemed irrelevant, and somehow soft. International law was seen as saying what cannot be done, a device for restraining and controlling national actions. Which is to say, ours, inasmuch as those other bastards could care less. But that was then, now is now. I repeat that in discussions in Geneva with our START negotiators—our Ambassador Max Kampelman will attest to this—I would ask why we seemed to take it for granted that the Soviet Union would exist by the time the Treaty was finished. Utter incomprehension. But now you, poor man, are going to have to deal with the fact that one of the successor States, the Ukraine, is suddenly not so sure that it wants to be a non-nuclear nation. All predictable, but not predicted.

It would not, for example, be too great a task to instruct your Secretary of State to work up a scenario for ethnic conflicts between now and the year 2000 that would concern the United States and which might or might not be avoided or diverted. (I beseech you not to ask the CIA. It is brain dead and should be honorably interred.) Let us reward persons who find patterns, and anticipate Somalias. As for example, a pattern of conflict the world over is for a "backward" group to attack an "advanced" group. This is what is going on in Bosnia, where the Muslims are the people of the towns, the professional classes and the intelligentsia, while the Serbians are the peasants. Mind we are not used to thinking of Muslims as more advanced than Europeans. Albeit, these <u>are</u> Europeans (Muslims are not accustomed to thinking of Europeans as more advanced than they.) But all this is lost on official Washington.

My closing thought would be to hope that the people you bring into government try to absorb and to come to terms with the forces of hate in the world. Glazer and I have been writing about ethnicity for a third of a century. (I have a book out in January based on last year's Cyril Foster lecture at Oxford.) but we have never celebrated it. To the contrary, if anything we have been warning about it. You could do worse than to send every new Assistant Secretary over to the coastal town of Slano, say 15 km north of Dubrovnik. It was occupied for about six months by Montenegrin territorials. (Or so I would gather.) There is nothing left there but the handwriting on the wall. In roman letters, so that the Croatians would be sure to understand, the graffiti declares that there will be more to come. One soldier named Marko was concerned that his message go beyond the boarders of Croatia, and so scrawled in English letters to wit: YOU ASK FOR IT. I find the slight inaccuracy in the English wonderfully evocative. Not "you asked for it" and now you have got it. Past tense. But rather, your very existence constitutes grounds for retaliation against you. Unto the end of time.

I will be happy to talk with you further, if you like, or with anyone you ask to call. Perhaps, however, you could hold this memorandum more or less closely.

Memorandum of the conversation with President Clinton in which Moynihan records Clinton's profuse apology to a quotation from an unnamed aide in an article by Michael Kramer in Time *magazine. (In the article, an anonymous aide is quoted as disparaging Moynihan and declaring that the administration will "roll over" him if necessary. Clinton promises that when he finds out the aide's identity, he will be dismissed, but it never happened. Their disagreement on this issue was to produce bitterness on both sides. Many years later, in 1996, Moynihan recorded in a private memorandum that Kramer told him that the person he quoted was Rahm Emanuel, of the White House staff. In 2000, however, Kramer wrote a column for the* New York Daily News *identifying his source as Clinton's Treasury secretary, Lloyd Bentsen, who died in 2006.) Aware that Clinton needs his help to get health care legislation enacted, Moynihan persists in believing that the administration should enact welfare reform as a more urgent priority than health care.*

JANUARY 25, 1993

MEMORANDUM OF CONVERSATION

I returned the President's call at 3:45 p.m. He came on. I said I appreciated his calling as I was just baffled by the quote in Kramer's article. He had arrived for his interview with me having come from the White House <u>with</u> the quote. It was not a response to anything I said on that occasion.

The President said, "Thank you for what you said yesterday." He was "horrified." He had no idea who did it. He was "livid." He said if they catch the bastard, he will be "fired." If it ever happens again, that person will be fired as well.

I said, "If you are bothered, I am not." He said, "I am more than bothered. You helped me a lot. You helped me bring down Jerry Brown. I remember exactly what happened in New York. That was a dead giveaway. That's why we knew it was someone who didn't know us. Some smart ass."

He said the health care issue was coming along. They had an economic meeting this morning. He asked, "What are your thoughts" in terms of a consultative proposal. I said he would want to include myself, of course, and Senator Kennedy and Congressmen Waxman and Dingell.

He wants to set up a working group in the next 100 days. I said, good. You wouldn't know any more in 150 days. In terms of consulting arrangements, he should work with the Majority Leader and the Speaker.

I said why didn't he start something on welfare as well? I told him of the PSID studies Paul Offner and I had done. Black children in 1967, 72 percent of whom were on welfare before age 18. Today the percentage is probably over 80. It is not rocket science but these are the ranges.

He said, "Horrible."

I said the commitment was so visible. He should read the lead editorial in this morning's New York Times. The proposal is spelled out in <u>Mandate for Change</u>, the Democratic platform, and in his acceptance speech. I recalled his cite of Franklin D. Roosevelt in his inaugural address, "Bold persistent experimentation."

He said, "That was a great day." There is one such in a lifetime like that, I said, and it was yours. . . .

Memorandum of a conversation with Hillary Clinton, discussing welfare and referring to Donna Shalala, the Health and Human Services secretary.

JANUARY 27, 1993

MEMORANDUM OF CONVERSATION

Mrs. Clinton called at 9:20 a.m. We talked about P.S. 115 and welfare and illegitimacy. I raised the issue that our commitment on welfare is a defining
one. That it had moved the electorate. She said, "I agree. We have to keep it."
Carol Rasko would concentrate on this. She had worked with the President
on the Family Support Act.

She said, "This is such a tangled subject. As, for example, the divorce laws.
We must restore some sense of what is acceptable now." She agreed that this
ought to be put in writing so the Donna Shalala's would get the idea. . . .

*Excerpt of a Memorandum to Senate Majority Leader Mitchell, complaining that
the new Secretary of Health and Human Services, Donna Shalala, referred to Social
Security as an "entitlement" program. Though the usage was fairly widespread,
Moynihan argued that it undermined support for a program he maintained was a
"social insurance" program.*

JANUARY 29, 1993

MEMORANDUM FOR THE MAJORITY LEADER

I must get this to you by 11:45 and so am rushed.

The administration is asking for it. Yesterday Rivlin. This morning, on
"The Today Show," Shalala. To wit "No final decisions have been made, and
as you know, if you want to make a serious move on the deficit you have to
look at *entitlement programs.*" (My italics.) Meaning Social Security retirement.
This ought to be considered an outrage coming from a Democratic Secretary
of H.H.S. The term entitlement means something for nothing. Exactly what
the enemies of social insurance would wish you to believe. In diplomacy it is
called "semantic infiltration," i.e., getting your adversary to start using your
terms in a negotiation.

Social Security is a contributory retirement system; designed as such by
FDR. Benefits are legitimately seen as owned. . . .

Memorandum to Robert Rubin, economic counselor at the White House (before he later became treasury secretary) on proposals to raise the retirement age in Social Security.

FEBRUARY 5, 1993

MEMORANDUM FOR ROBERT RUBIN

I have been busy with the actuaries concerning the matter the President asked you to bring up with me. I assume the Progressive Policy Institute proposal to raise the retirement age by 2 months per year beginning with those who reach age 62 in 1994. This would produce $800 million in savings during the President's first term. Another $8.1 billion in his second.

I cannot know this, but would state with some confidence that it will raise holy hell. 1.7 million people retire each year; the majority at age 62. For many, perhaps most of these folk, retirement involves lots of planning and no small amount of pleasant anticipation.

Then, of a sudden, the President says I am breaking the deal. You had planned on X amount of money per month. I am making it X minus. (All of the savings in the first term will come from lowering the 80 percent rate at which persons now retire at age 62.)

I hate to sound so negative. But these are quasi-fiduciary undertakings. If we want to raise real bucks, why not announce that the maturity date of 30-year Treasury Bonds will be put off two months a year starting in 1994 with no interest to be paid for the extra waiting period?

Letter to Hillary Clinton on Baumol's analysis of the inevitability of cost escalation in the health care sector. Moynihan and his wife invited Hillary Clinton to lunch with Baumol at the Moynihan apartment on Pennsylvania Avenue. But Mrs. Clinton persisted in believing that health care costs could be curbed. Moynihan got a health care bill sent to the Senate floor but criticized the administration's cost-cutting as a threat to hospitals. His earlier comment that no health care crisis existed also upset the White House.

MARCH 26, 1993

Dear Mrs. Clinton:

You may recall my mentioning Bill Baumol's hope that he might be some help to your health group. He has not yet heard from anyone, and still hopes he might. As do I, for he has a rare feeling for the economics that underlay so many baffling questions. You may recall my mentioning "Baumol's disease"— a term of his colleagues' choosing, not his own.

He and his wife Hilda have just produced a wonderful paper, "On the Economics of Musical Composition in Mozart's Vienna." Sheer joy. One detail. At the end of the great Tudor inflation real wages reached the lowest point between the 13th and the 19th century. Today it takes well over a year for a non-musical play to recoup the expenses of production. Before World War I less than two months to break even. But at the time of the Globe Theater, "if a play ran for two weeks, it was a great and profitable success." Hence, the great demand for new plays, with an average of seven or eight performances per play. Thus, Shakespeare turned out 37 plays over a period of 23 years. A successful modern playwright might produce six or eight.

He can be reached at his New York University office. . . .

Letter to Mayor David Dinkins of New York City, expressing concern about possible cooperation of Islamic and I.R.A. (Irish Republican Army) terrorists, following the first attack on the World Trade Center in 1993.

MARCH 29, 1993

Dear Dave:

. . . With one thing and another, I have been involved with counter-terrorism for a quarter century. Two weeks after my arrival in New Delhi, my colleague in the Sudan was assassinated by an Islamic terrorist network which had more than ample connections in India. And so, I spent my time there under considerable pressure, more or less. It was not all that different at the U.N. where a terrorist group blew the front off our mission on Fifth Avenue just a few moments before I arrived. Thank God, a few minutes late. . . .

Saturday morning I went down to the World Trade Center to take a look about. Much impressed by our clean-up operation and by the structural strength of the Towers. Obviously, not much impressed by the security that let the bomb get indoors. However, it appears to have been a homemade bomb. Standing there it came to me that the <u>bombing</u> of the tallest skyscraper in New York had to be a clone of the IRA bombing at Canary Wharf in London the day after our elections, November 4.

As you know, the Islamic terrorists and the IRA terrorists are in close contact and have been for decades. Collaboration I don't think we could prove but we could certainly surmise. When I was last in Egypt, Mubarak had just returned from a meeting in Tripoli. I asked how his visit with Quadafi had gone. He replied that Quadafi had suggested that he was changing his ways. For example, he had stopped sending any further help to the Irish, meaning the Provisional IRA. However, the British know and the government in Dublin knows of five shiploads of Libyan, which is to say, Czech semtex dispatched to Ireland. Four got through; the French intercepted the fifth. But this means there's semtex all over Ireland and Britain. Semtex was the explosive used at Canary Wharf.

My concern is that the IRA will now get involved with providing semtex to Islamic terrorists or on some deranged impulse will decide to try their own hand at a New York site. You can never tell with such people, but you must always expect the worst.

Note how casually they have been killing children in Britain. You, perhaps, have seen the response in the Irish Republic itself.

Memorandum of his conversation with President Clinton, in which Moynihan recommends the nomination of Ruth Bader Ginsberg to the Supreme Court, despite Clinton's concerns that some women's groups were uncertain of her support for abortion rights.

MAY 24, 1993

MEMORANDUM OF CONVERSATION

On the way up to New York on May 12, the President asked, "If you wanted to appoint someone to the Supreme Court, who would it be?" I said, "It is not for me to say." The President said, "I asked." I said, "Ruth Bader Ginsberg." "The women are against her," the President said. "That is your problem, Mr. President. You have too many friends. You cannot govern without enemies." . . .

Harold Ickes travelled with us. He said, "Your Marist [i.e., recent polls from the Maris Institute for Public Opinion] is astounding." I said, "Compared to Cuomo." The President asked, "Can he run again?" Ickes said, "Maybe. Big decline. Partly due to rhetoric, partly longevity." The President said longevity.

In this letter, Moynihan is lobbying Meg Greenfield, editor of the WASHINGTON POST *editorial page, on the Clinton cost-containment proposals in health care.*

PINDARS CORNERS
JUNE 1, 1993

Dearest Meg,

Here is my essay on Baumol's disease. I hope you like it. Someone needs to yell it at the White House before they take us over the cliff on health care. Thinking, that is, that they can cut back or at least hold down. The equivalent of slashing waste fraud and abuse under President Reagan. I also enclose a bar chart of Baumol's showing health care at 35 percent of GDP and education at 29 percent a half century hence. Might be useful illustration.

Memorandum of a conversation about the gathering controversy over the budget process in Congress, focused on the "reconciliation bill," which needed to be passed to enforce budget restraint supported by the administration. Moynihan assails the C.I.A.—and the budget for it—as "corrupt," angry that he was expected to vote for a budget that would withdraw funding from hospitals in New York while funding the C.I.A. as well as scholarships in honor of Senator David L. Boren, chairman of the Intelligence Committee. Again Moynihan brings up the failure of the C.I.A. to foresee the collapse of the Soviet Union.

JUNE 21, 1993

MEMORANDUM OF CONVERSATION

The President called Friday afternoon to thank me for getting the reconciliation bill through the Finance Committee. I said that it had to be done but that it wasn't easy to take $1 billion out of teaching hospitals in New York City in order to increase the budget for the Central Intelligence Agency. I said the agency has become corrupt as I watch [C.I.A. director Robert] Gates corrupt Senator Boren. I always expected to hear Gates was in Oklahoma to announce a grant. Instead I learn that he has given $150 million for the David L. Boren scholarships. That is corruption.

The President mumbled. (The next day Sidney Blumenthal allowed as how he just doesn't know enough about such matters to feel comfortable enough to say yes or no.) . . .

I also asked the President if he ever had a session in which he discussed how we had missed the collapse of the Soviet Union. I said the real problem would not come from expansion of the U.S.S.R. but its dissolution. In the meantime, we are $3 trillion in debt. The President said he had asked a few questions but never got an answer. . . .

Memorandum of a conversation with President Clinton, as the White House tries to round up votes for its budget in the Senate after it was approved in the House. With health care legislation foundering, the administration was in danger of a major defeat on the budget because Senator Bob Kerrey, the Nebraska Democrat who had run against Clinton and was planning to vote no. Asked to help with Kerrey, Moynihan expresses to Clinton his own continuing feeling of betrayal over funding for the C.I.A., and asks Clinton to remember his complaints.

AUGUST 5, 1993

MEMORANDUM OF CONVERSATION

The President called at 9:45 this morning to tell me that Bob Kerrey had got out of bed in a bad mood and was planning to vote no. The President said he didn't seem to understand what that would do "to me and to the cause." He said Kerrey does not like the House leadership and thinks they will jack him around. Leon Panetta is working out a $10 billion recision bill with him but he doesn't think that will happen. The House Committee chairmen would not go along. The President said a "cut session" is entirely doable, but Kerrey thinks that would have to involve people like Chafee, which is "a dream world." He thinks the Democratic leadership will slam-dunk him.

I said to the President that if he did not trust the leadership, he had every reason not to. I for my part felt terribly betrayed that he had secretly proposed an increase in the CIA budget. I asked him if he knew how I felt about the CIA. He said he did. I asked if he knew of the damage it had done to the national interest in the last two decades with its wildly inaccurate estimates of Soviet strength and intentions. He said yes. And yet I was asked to cut the budget for hospitals in Harlem so the CIA could maintain its bloated budget. The President said it was a one-year increase in order for them to consolidate their satellites and thereafter would be cut over five years. I said that's what they say now and only because the material was leaked. He asked if I had been told. I said, of course I was not told. I was lied to. I said I have written to you about the Ukrainian nuclear weapons. I was an observer to the START talks. Max Kampelman will tell you. I would go to Geneva in 1985. I would be invited to lunch. I would ask the negotiators what made them think that after they had completed their mind-numbing negotiations with the U.S.S.R. that there would <u>be</u> a U.S.S.R.? They did not say to me that was a good question, that they had considered it and decided there would be. They simply dismissed the question. Then, of course, the treaty arrived with the U.S.S.R. that no longer existed.

The treaty was not with four countries. I asked how did they know. They said they had letters. This is the same outfit that supported the David Boren International Fellowship. The President said, "That is not going to happen." I said there still was a secret CIA budget. I said it was inconceivable to me that his administration would still be keeping a secret CIA budget. It is unconstitutional. And if that's so, I certainly don't blame Bob Kerrey.

I asked the President if perhaps he would remember this conversation. He said he certainly would.

Memorandum of a conversation later in the day, as Clinton asks whether he was able to lobby Kerrey. Moynihan says not yet but is keeping in mind that his wife Elizabeth will do so.

AUGUST 5, 1993

MEMORANDUM OF CONVERSATION

The President called at 1:00 p.m. to ask how I had done with Kerrey. I said I hadn't done anything. Kerrey was simply calling on me to tell me what he decided to do, which was vote no. I said there would be some other efforts made later in the day, but did not want to talk about them right now. Meaning Liz. I said the final event for Kerrey was the additional billion dollars which was given to Harkin in the flood relief bill, after Byrd and he had held out against Dole's efforts to double spending. Etc. Etc. No one around here was serious about cutting spending or holding down spending.

The President said [Senators Tom] Harkin and [Paul] Wellstone had called him in the afternoon. Wellstone said, "If you kill us, I'm off your bill." Howard Pastor [chief congressional lobbyist for the White House] argued that Wellstone was serious, "You know how he is." The President said, "In retrospect it was a bad decision. A decision made in two minutes."

I continued my complaint about the CIA.

Memorandum of a conversation still later, in which Moynihan reports that Liz Moynihan had pleaded with Kerrey not to reject the budget and doom the Clinton administration and his own career. Her intervention helped persuade Kerrey to change his mind at the last minute.

AUGUST 5, 1993

MEMORANDUM OF CONVERSATION

Liz spoke to Kerrey at six o'clock. She said she was very upset. "God, your future as a national Democrat is at risk. Did Pat tell you this? You guys, I just don't understand." She asked if it was all right if I [i.e. Liz] called you and I said yes. Kerrey said, did I think this? Yes. Liz said, "I wish you were President. I want to live to see you President. You are a person of character and commitment. You are not against this bill because you didn't get something you wanted, but because you think it's a bad bill. Pat thinks the same. But he feels we cannot have another President fail. We cannot have the United States at the end of the cold war as dilapidated as the Soviets. It is necessary to stay alive and be a player. . . . Kerrey said, they don't seem to know what they are up to on health. Liz said, "They don't seem to know what they are up to on anything. You be the alternative and stay alive. Don't let those people do you in."

Letter to President Clinton, as Moynihan circles back to his prediction of the breakup of the Soviet Union (and the uselessness of the C.I.A.). "Self-congratulation is not the most appealing epistolary style," Moynihan acknowledges.

PINDARS CORNERS
SUNDAY, AUGUST 8, 1993

Dear Mr. President:

. . . Friday morning I had a good talk (from the cloakroom, mind) with [national security advisor] Anthony Lake. He agreed that the discussion of budget cuts now scheduled for September should extend to the intelligence community, and specifically, the C.I.A. He specifically did not agree that this discussion would be public, nor yet did he rule that out. (I am firmly of the view that secrecy is unconstitutional. And does great disservice to the Presidency, be that as it may.) I drafted a statement to this effect which I inserted in the Record of the day's debate.

We also discussed a troubling telephone call my office had received the previous day, Thursday, from George Tenet of the N.S.C. staff. Mr. Tenet, who was formerly Senator Boren's staff director on the Intelligence Committee, is now in charge of intelligence matters under Mr. Lake. Evidently, you had passed on our conversation in which I told you how dispirited I had been to learn in the New York Times of April 15 that even as I was trying to negotiate the Medicare "cuts" and such like through the Finance Committee, the Administration was planning to increase the budget of the C.I.A. Mr. Tenet offered sincere apologies to Mr. Stephen Rickard of my office for not having kept us informed. He told Mr. Rickard that they had "kept Howard [Metzenbaum] in the loop. Clearly Senator Moynihan has thought a lot about this and cares about it and should have been consulted." . . .

In the thought that you might have a moment before we come back to town, and myself wishing very much to think of something other than the gasoline tax, let me lay out this subject as I see it. If it interests you, we can continue. . . .

Let me make this fearless prediction. For the next half century, western social scientists and intellectuals will be debating just how the collapse of the Soviet Union could have been so altogether unforeseen by those who professed to understand such matters. The National Interest has just devoted an entire issue to the subject. (With a wonderful review of Pandaemonium by Fred C. Ikle.) Seymour Martin Lipset has written a long paper, "Anticipations of the Failure of Communism," which was delivered at the 1992 meeting of the American Sociological Association in Pittsburgh. It is not easy going but well worth the effort. (Give up the NID for a week!) Barone will not have seen Lipset's essay but the analyses are much alike. To wit: most of the Sovietologists and analysts, in and out of government, were liberals. Barone: "Most doves believed that the Soviet Union was dangerous but not evil, dangerous because it was militarily powerful and on the rise in the world because of the attractiveness of socialism; not evil because our system and theirs were converging." Lipset, like Barone, says there were two exceptions: Reagan on the right, me on the left.

It is important to be clear that whatever President Reagan may have thought, the people he appointed thought very differently. Hawks, their views were even so very much those of doves. The Soviet Union was growing in strength and attractiveness. They could imagine red hordes sweeping up Central America heading for the Rio Grande.

I have a letter from Max Kampelman, a Humphrey Democrat who served as President Reagan's ambassador to the START talks in Geneva. I was one of a dozen Senate "observers" to the talks. I would go over there from time to time. Meet with the negotiators and ask: What makes you think that by the time you have negotiated the mind-numbing details of this treaty with the U.S.S.R. that there will still be a U.S.S.R.? Never once did anyone reply that this contingency had indeed been considered, but dismissed as improbable. They simply could not "access" such a thought, as the youth would say. And so now your deal with a nuclear Ukraine. Of that period Kampelman writes:

> . . . [W]henever I am asked whether I had predicted the break up of the Soviet Union or knew anybody who did, I have uniformly stated that the one person who had fully understood and made the correct analysis was you. (MMK to DPM, December 3, 1991)

I hope I still have you. Self-congratulation is not the most appealing epistolary style. Here now is my concern. The system that altogether failed to foresee the collapse of communism and the end of the cold war and the onset of ethnic violence is still in place and untouched. You have not sent to us for confirmation a single person who had any inkling during the 1980s that the end was at hand, <u>or who has any inkling that any argument was put forward to that effect</u>. None. The standard conservatives have been replaced by the standard liberals. Shouldn't that bother you? Shouldn't there be one person, possibly two, in the administration who asks on your behalf: Good Christ, if we missed that, what else are we missing?

Instead, we are seeing the institutional equivalent of a cover up. Never good news for the Presidency.

Constituent newsletter on how he was instrumental in the establishment of a museum, memorial, and Women's Rights National Historical Park at Seneca Falls, where the first women's rights declaration was signed in 1848.

AUGUST 16, 1993
PINDARS CORNERS, NY

Dear New Yorker:

THE LADIES OF SENECA FALLS

Most anyone who has read *The Adventures of Huckleberry Finn* will remember those opening lines: "You don't know about me, without you have read a book by the name of 'The Adventures of Tom Sawyer'. . . . That book was made by Mr. Mark Twain, and he told the truth, mainly." Herb Cables, Deputy Director of the National Park Service, introduced me at the dedication of the Wesleyan Chapel Block of the Women's Rights National Historical Park in Seneca Falls on July 31, and mainly he did the same:

"Many consider Senator Moynihan as the father of Women's Rights National Historical Park. . . . A little less than 20 years ago, local resident and town father George Souhan was hosting a good friend, and told him how sad it was that only a plaque marked the place where one of the most important events in history took place, the signing of the Declaration of Sentiments, [which] was on a par with the signing of the Declaration of Independence."

I <u>was</u> in Seneca Falls in the mid-1970s visiting George Souhan. We were walking around that wondrously lovely village in the Finger Lakes region. I was going on about the architecture—Greek temples, Italian villas, Mansard mansions—when George said he'd like to show me something different. An old brick building on Fall Street, then a laundromat.

He pointed—otherwise you wouldn't notice—to a bronze plaque that told you these were the remains of the Wesleyan Chapel where in 1848 a group of women and men adopted a Declaration of Sentiments that called for women to have equal rights in education, property, voting and other matters such as access to better job opportunities and the ministry. Taking the Declaration of Independence for a model, the Declaration of Sentiments states: "We hold these truths to be self-evident: that all men and women are created equal. . . ."

The convention was organized by Elizabeth Cady Stanton and Lucretia Mott. Mott was a founder of the American Anti-Slavery Society. In 1840 she had gone as a delegate to the World Anti-Slavery Convention in London. The men who ran the convention refused to seat her and other women delegates on the convention floor, consigning them instead to the gallery. While in London she met Stanton; the two resolved to work for women's rights.

[The year] 1848 was about the busiest year of the 19th century in Europe. Everywhere kings were abdicating, ministers fleeing, mobs roving. In London, Karl Marx and Friedrich Engels composed a pamphlet entitled *Manifesto of the Communist Party*. Revolution was all the rage. But the real revolution was taking place in a small brick chapel in a village in upstate New York where people had begun to think of a revolution unlike anything known to man—equal rights for women. . . .

But back to Seneca Falls. I knew about the Declaration of Sentiments in a general way when George Souhan showed me where it had been adopted, and I was vaguely aware that Susan B. Anthony had linked up with Stanton a few years later, out of which the National Woman Suffrage Association emerged. But it was not until sometime later when I came upon *The Ladies of Seneca Falls: The Birth of the Women's Rights Movement* by Miriam Gurko that the largeness of the event began to sink in. As Ms. Gurko writes:

> *Most histories contain, if anything, only the briefest allusion to the woman's rights movement in the nineteenth century—perhaps no more than a sentence*

> *to include it in the general upsurge of reform. Here and there the name of a*
> *woman's rights leader might be mentioned, generally that of Susan B. An-*
> *thony, sometimes Elizabeth Cady Stanton. The rest might never have existed*
> *so far as the general run of historical sources is concerned.*

But now the others, Lucretia Mott, Mary Ann McClintock, Jane Hunt, Martha Wright, Amelia Bloomer, came to life for me. This was hallowed ground and needed to be celebrated. It happened that Judy Hart of the National Park Service was looking at something just such.

In 1980 I introduced the legislation that created the park. We took as our model the Lowell National Historical Park in Massachusetts where they bought and restored an old textile mill. We commenced to buy up the houses of women who attended the convention. Almost all were there, waiting, perhaps a little impatiently. We have most of them by now; and there is a wonderful tour. The Chapel site will be a conference center and a center for women's studies. . . .

Letter to President Clinton, urging him to discuss ethnic factors in the breakup of nations at an upcoming speech to the United Nations.

SEPTEMBER 23, 1993

Dear Mr. President,

At the White House meeting of September 10th where you laid out for us the rudiments of the Israeli-PLO agreement, you asked if we would send along any suggestions we might have as to your speech at the U.N. next Monday. I would not have presumed this on my own, but I have been there and you did ask!

The first thing to know is that you will be heard. Mostly, in the past three decades, we have not been. We were on one side; "they" were on the other. Then, of a sudden, there was no they there. I can still feel the shock of meeting Andrei Kozyrev in the Mansfield Room on the morning of June 19, 1991. [Russian president Boris] Yeltsin was coming for coffee with the Foreign Relations Committee. The Soviet Ambassador accompanied him into the room. A gaggle of aides followed. Some of us formed a receiving line of sorts.

Kozyrev came up to me with the greeting familiar to all politicians: "You don't remember me, do you?" "Why, yes . . . ," I replied doubtfully. "I was at the U.N. when you were there." "Of course!" I answered and asked what he was doing now, thinking a second secretary, of sorts. He handed me his card: "Minister for Foreign Affairs of the Russian Soviet Federative Socialist Republic." Then added: "You didn't think any of us were listening, did you?" The point being that President Ford had instructed us to speak as much of the truth as we could divine about what the Soviet Union was really like. They recognized our description.

I wonder if this might be the occasion to describe—in the sensitive terms you employ so well—what the rest of the world is like. The world other than the O.E.C.D. With few exceptions they bet wrong in the cold war, and know it. With few exceptions they are now caught up with fierce internal ethnic conflict; some of it washing over borders. Many, I think especially of India, are now deeply depressed, if you can speak of a sub-continent in such terms. Certainly, their educated elite is baffled and despairing. The sociologist Edward O. Wilson recently wrote me that these ethnic trends "were not fully revealed until the overwhelmingly suppressive force of supranational ideology was lifted." Whereupon, "a coiled and ready ethnicity" was awaiting. You could acknowledge this and say that we must do the best we can, not perhaps expecting too much. Which is to say, don't depend on the rest of the world to save you from yourselves.

The U.N. Charter is sheer wickedness in this respect. Article I guarantees the right of "self-determination of peoples." This was put there at Stalin's insistence, he having in mind the break up of the "colonial" empires. In time, it broke up his own. But the disintegration goes on.

CHAPTER FOURTEEN

"Thus Ends the Progressive Era"

Following the defeat of the Clinton health care proposals in 1994 and the subsequent Republican victory in the midterm elections that year, Moynihan ceded his chairmanship of the Senate Finance Committee and played defense as the Republicans pressed their conservative agenda on issues of budget, welfare, and social policy. Reelected in 1994 in the face of the Republican congressional sweep, he found that his relationship with Clinton continued to be hobbled by the earlier health care battles. Another major breach with the Clintons then opened when Clinton angered many fellow Democrats by signing a Republican-backed law ending welfare as an entitlement, prompting Moynihan to warn that the measure would lead to a vast increase in homelessness among poor families, especially children. Moynihan focused his attention in his last term on poverty, welfare, health care, budgets, ethnic conflicts around the world, and securing aid for New York. He seized on a new issue of what he felt had been overweening secrecy in the government during the cold war, and he continued to criticize the intelligence establishment for its exaggerated estimate of the Soviet threat. Many of his letters also show his keen interest in the campaign to convert the old beaux arts Post Office building in New York City into a new Pennsylvania Station. Moynihan was later pained by Clinton's behavior in the Monica Lewinsky scandal, but he supported the president in the impeachment trial in the Senate. In the end, he backed Mrs. Clinton as his successor in the Senate, and she told him that if she had listened to him on health care, both the country and she would be better off.

Letter to John Dalton, Secretary of the Navy, requesting that he be interred in Arlington Cemetery. Moynihan was buried there with full military honors following his death in 2003.

APRIL 20, 1994

Dear Secretary Dalton:

Fifty years ago come July 1st I enlisted in the United States Navy, a fact which puts me in mind of mortality. I would like to be buried in Arlington Cemetery and I assume this requires some form of prior notice or application, or both. I have had a number of conversations with Navy Liaison officers over here but nothing ever happens. Could I trouble you to let me know how one goes about what I should have thought is a not especially complicated process?

Letter to the columnist Murray Kempton, passing the word from Lloyd Cutler, the White House counsel, that he agrees with Kempton on "almost everything."

APRIL 29, 1994

Dear Murray:

I was one of those asked out to the Nixon funeral and went along, aboard Air Force One, if you will! On the way out, on the way back, there was a certain amount of discussion about Alger Hiss and Whitaker Chambers and all that. I remarked on the difficulty many in Washington have had grasping what Lionel Trilling once called "the powerful attraction to Communism felt by a considerable part of the American intellectual class during the Thirties and Forties." Not everybody understood me. It is one of those gulfs between Washington as the political capital and New York as the intellectual capital which has always seemed to me a hugely important fact of American life.

As it happened, Lloyd Cutler had brought with him a copy of the current issue of <u>The New York Times Review of Books</u>. On the way back, I picked it

up from his table and began reading Garry Wills's wonderful review of <u>Re-</u>
<u>bellions</u>. . . . There I came upon this paragraph about your affinity with Alger
Hiss, in which both you and Wills take for granted that there were people in
the '30s who were, yes, communists. I marked this and passed it over to Lloyd
with the imprecation, "Read & Ponder." He wrote back,

> Pat:
> I agree with Kempton on almost everything.
> Lloyd

You will note that he does not necessarily commit to agreeing with this
paragraph. Not for nothing is he White House Counsel! But this information
could be of use to you if you are, as I believe, still not too old to get into trouble.
I enclose the original.

Letter to Representative David Obey, asking for help in moving Pennsylvania Sta-
tion to the old Post Office building in New York City, which he says is "hugely im-
portant to me" with an election that year.

JUNE 9, 1994

Dear Dave:

I need your help. As you surely know, some 30 years ago New York City
allowed Pennsylvania Station to be torn down by the then-private owners.
Some good of it came, namely the preservation movement. But New Yorkers
were left with a subway station when there had once been the Baths of Caracalla. Vincent Scully at Yale put it, "You used to enter New York City as a
king; now you slither in like a rat."

However, in a miracle of sorts it turns out that the Post Office is leaving
the Farley Building which is directly across 8th Avenue, built to the same proportions, by the same architects (McKim, Mead & White) and sitting atop
the exact same tracks. Amtrak has come up with a plan to turn the Post Office
into a new Penn Station. First Mayor Dinkins, now Mayor Giuliani backed
the proposal. Governor Cuomo backs the proposal. President Clinton backed
the proposal and put the Federal share, $100 million, in next year's budget. We

managed to get $10 million in the supplemental bill so the project is already underway. Alack, on Tuesday the Transportation Subcommittee recommended no further funding. The Federal Railroad Administration tells us that the project needs $40 million to keep going, but that the remaining $50 million can come next year.

May I plead for your help? Almost one-half the Amtrak passengers in the country arrive or depart from Penn Station, so it is important to the future of rail transportation. It is also hugely important to me in this election season. . . .

Newsletter recalling Memorial Day in Oneonta.

WASHINGTON, D.C.
JUNE 17, 1994

Dear New Yorker:

DELIVERANCE

Fifty years ago come July 1, I joined the Navy. This was much on my mind this Memorial Day. It was a grand moment in Neahwa Park in Oneonta on the banks of the Susquehanna. The ceremony of placing flowers on the graves of Civil War soldiers began May 5, 1866 in Waterloo, New York, over in Seneca County. It has not much changed in all these years. The color guard advances, a bugler plays taps. In the distance a drummer boy in Civil War uniform responds with a soft, hesitant tattoo. Children assemble with wreaths to be placed on the war memorials—more than one by now. A hundred or so citizens listen quietly as the program begins. This year Grant Coates, a Vietnam veteran, was master of ceremonies, a healing event in itself. In years past the Vietnam vets would stand apart, in fatigues, present but not participating. I spoke without notes, but the *Oneonta Star* printed passages the next day and I repeat some of them here. The first thing I said was that I got out of the war alive because of the atom bomb. That is not a pleasant thing to say: "Very few of us of that generation had any real expectation of standing at a Memorial Day parade—observance—50 years later," but it happens to be the truth.

Absent the bomb, President Clinton would be visiting American graves in the Japanese islands next autumn.

But that deliverance was brief. Soon after the end of World War II the Soviets had the bomb also, and we began a near half-century of nuclear terror. Ever more destructive weapons mounted on missiles buried in North Dakota, floating under the polar icecap aboard nuclear submarines, airborne from places such as Griffiss Air Force base in Rome. (Our Rome, that is.)

In 1951, I was in London on a Fulbright scholarship, still in the Reserves. The Korean War had broken out in the East. Obviously, something would happen in the West. I was called up. (Briefly, as it turned out.) We mustered at the American Embassy in Grosvenor Square. By late afternoon we were crossing Holland, headed for the former German submarine base at Bremerhaven. I had brought along a copy of Hannah Arendt's recently published masterwork, *The Origins of Totalitarianism.* (A wondrous woman—I would get to know her years later. German, Jewish, she had escaped to the United States in 1941, bringing with her the devastating insights of someone who had seen totalitarianism up close.) I settled into my compartment and read the opening paragraph.

> *Two world wars in one generation, separated by an uninterrupted chain of local wars and revolutions, followed by no peace for the victor, have ended in the anticipation of a third World War between the two remaining world powers. This moment of anticipation is like the calm that settles after all hopes have died.*

I read it aloud to my companions in the compartment. There were six of us in all, including two much-decorated veterans of the carrier wars in the Pacific. No one demurred. Calm had descended.

But here we were in Neahwa Park years later and it hadn't happened. To the contrary, on that very day, May 30, 1994, for the first time since they were created, the ballistic missile warheads of the United States and Russia (along with those in Ukraine, Belarus and Kazakhstan still controlled from Moscow) were no longer targeted on each other's people. They were now retargeted to land in the North Atlantic or Arctic Ocean if accidentally launched, an agreement to this effect having been reached by President Clinton and President Yeltsin last January 14. A similar agreement was reached between Russia and the United Kingdom. And so I found myself saying:

Now peace is coming to the world—not the end of violence, not the end of anger and conflict, but the end of the prospect of the annihilation of the race. We have been delivered. . . .

Memorandum of a conversation recounting a comment about Hillary Clinton from Paul Ellwood, a health policy expert.

JUNE 21, 1994

MEMCON

. . . A few days ago Paul Ellwood dropped into see Lawrence [O'Donnell, chief of staff of the Senate Finance Committee]. He told of his first meeting with Mrs. Clinton. He said to her that many of the changes that she was hoping for are already happening. She said, no they are not. He said that costs are already going down. She said, no they are not. He commented to Lawrence that where he had studied the subject all his life, she had studied the subject three weeks and already knows more than he.

Letter to Representative John D. Dingell, also asking for help in the Pennsylvania Station project.

SEPTEMBER 20, 1994

Dear John:

On an intensely personal note, could I ask you to withdraw your objections to the $40 million appropriation for the Pennsylvania Station project which the House Appropriations Committee will be taking up tomorrow? This is a huge undertaking with only a tiny Federal component. A $100 million out of almost a billion. $10 million has already been appropriated. $40 million in this bill would allow construction to begin in the fall. $50 million next year will be the end of it.

The present Pennsylvania Station, a hole-in-the-ground built in 1963, is deplorable and unsafe. A fire Sunday two weeks ago could have been a disaster, save that it took place in an off hour. In the meantime, across the street the great Farley Post Office, is sitting on top of the same tracks and soon to be vacated by the Postal Service.

President Clinton, of course, has endorsed the project and put the money in his budget.

Up in New York, the Governor, the Mayor, and the heads of half a dozen commissions have signed agreements. This really is a formidably important project to which I have made a strong personal commitment. New York City has never quite got over the destruction of the original Pennsylvania Station. As one architectural critic has put it, you used to enter New York City like a king; now you slither in like a rat.

This is our chance to get back an ancient glory. The Post Office was designed at the same time by the same architects. It is a chance to get Amtrak heading toward profitability. Forty percent of Amtrak passengers go through Penn Station. And it is a chance to get your devoted friend here re-elected so we can get health care together in the next Congress.

Letter to Representative Charles E. Schumer, asking for his support, noting that he was "hugely disturbed" by the Clinton health bill and that Schumer would one day succeed him as senator. Schumer was elected senator, defeating D'Amato in 1998, joining Moynihan in the Senate. Fred Siegel, cited here as disenchanted with the Clinton administration, was, and is, a prominent conservative scholar and author.

SEPTEMBER 22, 1994

Dear Chuck:

Oh, Lord. I said it for certain, although [Fred] Siegel may have taken my meaning a little differently from that intended. I was talking not just of our delegation—myself included—but what I consider to be the generally dysfunctional liberation of the Northeast.

I was just then hugely disturbed by the Clinton health bill which would have devastated New York City's hospitals. Devastated. The principal cost control strategy was to reduce the number of doctors. It would have cut the residents in New York by as much as 40 percent in some places. A quarter system-wide. This formula was repeated in the House Ways and Means bill, the House Education and Labor, Senate Labor and Human Resources, and now, finally, the Mitchell bill. All save Finance. You will get a better sense of what I mean from the enclosed Work Group XII document which we have retrieved from the archives.

Fred Siegel is a thoughtful academic and a Democrat. He was hugely enthusiastic about Clinton, hoping he would govern as he campaigned. But then, that did not happen, did it? Hence, his concluding paragraph:

> The shame of it is that Clinton the New Democrat, Clinton the campaigner, promised policies like welfare reform and decentralization that might have helped pull the city out of the pathologies of its own political culture. Instead he has, as president, governed on the big-government principles of New York's old believers. It is a measure of their faith that nothing, not even a health care plan that would have been disastrous for New York, has shaken their beliefs.

One of these days you are going to succeed me over here and we must talk at length about this issue. I could surely be wrong, but I have to say, my convictions grow with the passing of time. You might recall this passage from my 1990 Fisc. I asked New Yorkers whether it was . . . time we began to ask just how much a bargain Federal programs are for a state such as New York? I know. This is heresy. Since the time of Theodore Roosevelt, at the very least, New Yorkers have consistently supported an expansion of the programs of the Federal government. . . . New Yorkers can be counted on to support Federal programs that redistribute resources away from New York. We manage to get back a share of Federal outlays proportionate to our population. But with a higher nominal income we continuously, systematically send resources elsewhere.

Fundraising letter to Walter Shorenstein, asking for a contribution to the Liberal Party. Democrats traditionally ran on the Liberal as well as the Democratic line.

OCTOBER 6, 1994

Dear Walter:

You mentioned that you are sending $50,000 for Cuomo in connection with the October 19 Presidential visit. Without having any claim, I would ask if you could possibly help me <u>and</u> the Governor with a gift to the Liberal Party. Both he and I have the Liberal line and it may make the difference for him. However, things are so glum just now that they are fearful of dropping below the 50,000 mark which keeps them on the ballot. I have agreed to try to raise money for them that will go into the general Democratic campaign.

Alas, I have none of my own. A fairly well kept secret is that I am never able to raise any money in politics. We have $1.5 million for the rest of the whole New York campaign, and very little will come in between now and November 8.

If you could write a check for the Liberal Party, I would be hugely, personally appreciative.

Letter to Governor George Pataki, appealing for help to build a new Penn Station.

DECEMBER 15, 1994

Dear Governor-Elect Pataki:

In the Times of November 28, Ada Louise Huxtable wrote a wonderful op-ed, "On the Right Track," describing our progress on Penn Station. This brought on an exchange between me and a citizen who would prefer we fix the subway station at 72nd Street and Broadway. Not a bad idea by any means, but why not do both? Also, a fine letter from Martin Gill, a New Jersey resident, who remarked, "the fact that almost all of the city's outstanding man-made features . . . date from before WWII suggests that New York's best days are behind it."

Are they? I believe the two of <u>us</u> think they are ahead of us, and we are in a position to prove it. A new Penn Station is within our grasp. Congress has appropriated $50 million, half the Federal commitment, although we still need a Congressional authorization, normally a routine matter. More importantly, we

still need a binding agreement between City and State and the various authorities. In short, we must work together or indeed resign ourselves to nostalgia.

There is a looming recision movement in the coming Congress which can
bring us all down unless we show more energy than is presently evident. We
have in our power a new landmark for the City and region, but it is our choice
to succeed or fail. If we were to lose Penn Station, we would not only lose a
sorely needed public work, but we also would gain a symbol of our own decline.

Letter to Mr. and Mrs. Andre Emmerich, eminent New York City art dealers.

DECEMBER 16, 1994

Dear Suzanne and Andre:

The 103rd Congress adjourned at midnight last Thursday, and finally I
have a moment to thank you for your help and support in the November election. As you know, the Congress had to come back for a lame-duck session
on the Uruguay Round trade agreement. As the (lame duck!) chairman of the
Finance Committee, I was to be floor manager of the legislation, and so returned here on the morning after the election. That was November 8th. We
counted 26 yeas. By Thursday we were up to 76, and so gave President Clinton
a somewhat anti-climactic, but no less real triumph at the close of his first
Congress.

And so now to thank you. This was my fourth Senate campaign—only two
other New Yorkers in our history have served four terms—and there was peril
aplenty. Even so, we decided once again to do it our way. We would have a
small, some would say tiny, headquarters. A small budget. No negative advertising—none.

All of which seems frugal enough, and indeed it was. But even so it cost
money. Which had to be raised, agonizing as it is. The more then am I in
your debt for your generosity—or should that be mercy!—in hosting that
event on April 30, 1990. You could not have been more gracious, nor I more
grateful.

It worked. In the end, we had a margin of 610,182 votes over our Republican challenger. This was the highest margin of victory among the thirty-five

Democrats who ran for the Senate in 1994. We got the most number of votes of anyone running for office in New York, and four times the margin of the Governor-elect, a rare event.

And so we begin again. I would ask us all to be of good cheer. We are the oldest political party on earth, and we have had to pick ourselves up off the deck more than once. And have done. I had a bit part in the 1992 Democratic convention in New York City, a few words before the lights went out and television came on. But looking back, I dare to think I said something worth hearing, which few could have done on that Monday afternoon.

> Our party has known good times and bad. Sometimes we have merely endured. But more often we have prevailed, triumphed even, because at heart we have embodied a great idea, which is that an elected government can be the instrument of the common purpose of a free people; that government can embrace great causes and do great things, providing only that it not be set to work for which it is not qualified under the conditions of time and place.

I was only allowed four minutes, which suggests it won't be a long read and so I take the liberty of enclosing a copy. Again, with my great gratitude and Liz's also. Along with our warm holiday greetings.

Letter to Governor Pataki, again reflecting on architecture.

JANUARY 12, 1995

Dear Governor Pataki:

It was grand of you to visit and you must have sensed how much we appreciated it. I had a good talk with [Representative] Susan Molinari about Penn Station and with luck we should keep the $50 million already appropriated. This is as much a national project as Union Station was. That the Federal government is to put up one-third the cost, as the President has proposed, is entirely appropriate. I am also told that on Tuesday, the Mayor will announce $25 million for the station in his Financial Plan—the first $8.3 million could be available as early as July.

We have it from Ada Louise Huxtable that Penn Station was modeled on the Tepidarium of the Baths of Caracalla. Hence, Vincent Scully, from *Architecture: The National and the Manmade.*

> The generosity of Roman public space in comparison with the squalor that has overtaken our own during the later twentieth century was underscored by the destruction of Pennsylvania Station's high vaults in favor of low tunnels, like the burrows of rats through which we proletarians now sniff our way while the homeless, refuse of our barbarous tribe, lie huddled against the walls.

I am, with you, a great admirer of Richardson's Albany City Hall, but my heart really goes out to the Albany Academy designed by Philip Hooker, built 1815–17. Possibly because I courted my wife in that snippet of park, lo these 40 years ago when we were both newly arrived in the Governor's office. Hooker designed the first State Capitol on the present site and was, in my view at all events, the first great New York architect.

Letter to Joseph Lelyveld, executive editor of the NEW YORK TIMES, *disputing a story in the* TIMES. *Moynihan was defensive about his severe criticisms of the Clinton health care plan. He also was upset about being portrayed as opposed to the measure. The subject had become moot: the Republican Party swept the elections the previous November, relegating Moynihan to the role of ranking Democrat on the Senate Finance Committee.*

FEBRUARY 24, 1995

Dear Joe:

Let me see if I can't straighten out the problem with Elisabeth Rosenthal's article of February 13, "ELITE HOSPITALS IN NEW YORK CITY FACING A CRUNCH." It treats many subjects, but the most important, in my view, is the statement that the hospital presidents "persuaded legislators like Senator Daniel Patrick Moynihan to revoke their support of the Clinton plan." I have to tell you that in my view this is libel. The presidents made no such attempt, and I made no such revocation.

As you know, Dr. Rosenthal never called any of us. We have now talked with her and think we see the problem, which is that the legislative process can be confusing from a distance.

Let me provide the details in brief. As you may recall, the President's plan took much longer in the drafting than they had expected. The first session of the 103rd Congress was about to close and we still did not have a bill. Finally, I got a text, one day before we adjourned *sine die* and introduced it, 1,342 pages and counting. (Actually, it was still not finished.) Three weeks earlier, on September 30, 1993, Hillary Rodham Clinton appeared before us in the first of 31 hearings. On June 29, 1994, I put before the Finance Committee what is known as a "Chairman's Mark." This essentially is the Chairman's view of what should pass and something of a judgment of what can pass. The Committee then begins to vote. The "mark" was written in close cooperation with the administration, which by then had dropped a number of the original proposals, most importantly, the mandated health alliances. Leon Panetta was in my office for a long session on June 27, just two days before.

By this time, the employer mandate was much out of favor and on June 30th the Committee voted 14 to 6 strike the provision from the Chairman's Mark. It also turned down some other provisions. I, however, voted against all such actions. Finally, on July 2nd, the bill was reported out of the Committee by a vote of 12 to 8.

I don't say the administration was pleased with our product. This was July. They had settled—this, of course, is my view—into a huge delusion that they could "have it all." More, for example, than our commitment to universal coverage, with a 95 percent coverage goal by January 1, 2002. In the end, as you know, they got nothing.

It was a devastating defeat that led to the further ruin of the November elections. One of the President's chief counsellors remarked to me a few weeks ago that it was the worst Democratic disaster since Vietnam and likely to have as long-lasting effects. Part of it was inexperience. Early in the spring of 1994 during a meeting at the White House, Bob Dole passed me a note, "Time for Moynihan-Dole?" I pleaded with the White House that in the Senate a measure of this importance either has 80 votes or 40 votes. No one there could follow this. Hadn't we passed the deficit reduction bill the previous year with 50 votes, plus the Vice President?

But I go on. The point to assert, with insistence, is that at no time did the heads of "New York's elite medical centers" seek to persuade me to "revoke" my support for the Clinton plan. This is a terrible charge to have on record in a lead story of The New York Times that I must tell you I am confounded. The one thing I will treasure from that otherwise grim year was the experience of getting to know these extraordinary men at the height of their powers and New York's pre-eminence in the world of medicine. I can tell you those with whom I have talked are equally dismayed.

Letter to Philip R. Lee, senior health policy official at the Department of Health and Human Services, expressing concern about the Clinton health care bill as "coercive."

MAY 19, 1995

Dear Phil:

. . . Here is my thesis. The health care proposal by the Clinton administration envisioned a huge change in the medical profession. The number of physicians entering the profession was to be reduced by about a quarter. The ratio of specialists to general practitioners was to be more or less reversed. It seems to me that a case could be made for such changes; a case could be made against them. In no way is it an issue that should be banned from public scrutiny or debate. However, it is my contention that the administration for all practical purposes kept this proposal SECRET. I first got an inkling when New York hospitals came to me saying that putting a near embargo on foreign medical graduates would be devastating to their hospitals. I began rooting around in the various bills and, sure enough, the measure was to be found in almost every committee draft. With the specific exception of the Finance Committee where I would have nothing to do with it for the simple reason that it was quite unacceptable to tell a university what it could teach or not teach and possibly quite damaging to limit the number of Indian, Pakistani, Philippine doctors and the like.

All of this is by the by. What concerns me is to learn just how much the proposals were kept intentionally obscure, even, as I say, secret. Mention is not to be found in any of the far too many White House documents on the subject. Notably, the 1239 pages entitled, "The President's Health Security Plan" released September 7, 1993. (See the enclosed table.)

I don't want to seem antagonistic, but I have to tell you I very much share Martha Derthick's comment that in a lifetime of reading government proposals for social security, she had never come upon one so coercive as that of the Clinton health care plan.

I agree with the President's pollster that it was a principle of the 1994 elections disaster. Which clearly has brought an end to the period of progressive legislation that began with the New Deal and is symbolized by the Social Security Act. For what it is worth, at yesterday's meeting of the Senate Democratic Policy Committee attended by Leon Panetta and Alice Rivlin to discuss our priorities in the budget debate, I asked the following question: We spent much of 1993 discussing the President's proposal to enact one of the largest and most expensive entitlements in our history, which is to secure universal health care coverage. That failed. Now the Republicans have proposed to abolish one of the most important entitlements in our existing welfare policy, which is to say, Title IV-a in the Social Security Act, Aid to Families with Dependent Children, which provides some level of benefits to dependent children, and it is not one of our priorities to preserve it? I was told by the Minority Leader that there was no consensus among Democrats that the entitlement for children should be preserved, and added that if everything is a priority, nothing is a priority. Panetta and Rivlin, in effect, nodded agreement.

So we have gone from proposing a unacceptably bloated White House health care plan in one Congress to abandoning a 60-year old entitlement for children in the next. The Democratic Party may survive but it will not be recognized.

Can you help me on this? Was it intentional to keep the medical profession provisions secret? Or at least undisclosed? Can it be that such a mindset had settled on the Democratic Left, or whatever one calls it? It is a subject the historians will address and I would like to straighten it out in my own mind for now. I might add that not only did the administration documents conceal the medical profession provisions but journalism failed completely to report them. From all I know, neither The New York Times nor The Washington Post wrote a line about this subject. If there was, it was way down deep in the story. I know there is a case for doing what the administration proposed. I enclose a letter from Alain Enthoven and a young colleague of his. I have no reason why it was sent to me since all the Democrats seem to be doing is cutting programs. And again, although I acknowledge the case for doing what the administration wanted, but why in secret?

With the Republicans in control of the House and Senate, a move to end the status of welfare as an entitlement gained ground. In this letter Moynihan describes his intervention at a meeting of top aides to President Clinton and senators in the Democratic Policy Committee, decrying the possibility that welfare "reform" would cut children off from welfare assistance.

MAY 19, 1995

MEMCON

Yesterday, at the Democratic Policy Committee meeting, Leon Panetta and Alice Rivlin came to explain our budget strategy. Once again, they passed out the four priorities, these having been agreed to on Tuesday at a Cabinet Room meeting with the President and the leadership. By arrangement with Reid, I asked the first question. I said, we had spent last year in that room . . . discussing the administration's proposal to create perhaps the largest and most expensive entitlement in history. This had not come about. Now it appears the administration is ready to abandon children under AFDC.

Could it be preventing this will not be a priority for us? Panetta said something about one of our priorities is helping young Americans and their families by restoring Republican cuts in student loan and education programs. I said I was not talking about students, I am talking about children. No response. "Babies!" Hollings leaned over to O'Donnell and remarked, "He's got him now."

[Senate Democratic leader Tom] Daschle said, if everything is a priority, nothing is a priority. He said there is no consensus among Democrats on our priorities, so we will stay with the four priorities decided.

Thus ends the progressive era.

In a note written from his upstate farm to his recently-widowed real estate lawyer, Paul F. Eaton, Moynihan refers to the Republican majority that took over Congress. John Burns was a Democratic Party figure in New York. Eaton's son, Richard K. (Dick) Eaton, was the senator's chief of staff and later a judge of the United States Court of International Trade.

JUNE 3, 1995

Dear Paul,

We have just had a week at home for the first time since the election last fall. I seem to have spent most of it sleeping off the New Republican Majority. No travel save for a trip to Binghamton to help John Burns with a campaign debt. We had wondered if Dick and the Ladies might come up, so that we might see you. But that is for the summer now to come.

Affectionately,

Gloomy memorandum about possible cuts in social programs pressed by the Republicans. To counter a Republican measure that would turn welfare payments to states into a block grant, three Democratic leaders (Tom Daschle of South Dakota, John Breaux of Louisiana, and Barbara Mikulski of Maryland) offered a counter-proposal to provide states with financial help to move welfare recipients into the work force. Moynihan here tells a White House meeting that the bill would be costly. His reference to "Adelman" endorsing the measure may refer to either Marian Wright Edelman or Peter Edelman, longtime advocates of assistance programs for poor children who later parted company with President Clinton over the issue of welfare "reform."

JUNE 15, 1995

MEMO

We met in the Oval Office yesterday at about 12:30 p.m. President, Vice President, [Senate Majority Leader Tom] Daschle, [Senator Barbara] Mikulski, [Senator John] Breaux, Moynihan and Governor [Buddy] Roemer. When it was my turn to speak about the welfare proposal I said that I had always supported entitlements as the basic social policy for children. President Kennedy had supported benefits with a family allowance of the Canadian sort. President Nixon had supported a guaranteed family income. I found in the Daschle, Breaux, Mikulski bill a major new entitlement for the working poor, which is to say, a guarantee of child care. This would cost about $24 billion a year but would be worth it, in my view.

The Vice President's jaw dropped, as if a caricature, when he realized what I said. No one else seemed to get it. Daschle said the entitlement was capped. I left it at that.

I did mention to the President that I did not think the Governors knew what they were getting in the way of block grants. The President said the new Governors were ignored in that they didn't have enough experience to follow it. The President said he would veto the present welfare bill.

Daschle said Adelman will endorse his bill. The President said, "My God," or something to that effect.

While making our way down the hall to the Oval Office, [Health and Human Services Secretary] Donna Shalala turned to me and said, "Have you ever walked down this hall at such a bad time for social policy?" I said, "Never."

Excerpt of a letter to John Gardner, former Health, Education, and Welfare secretary under President Johnson, hoping that congressional gridlock will derail plans to dismantle social programs.

PINDARS CORNERS
JULY 9, 1995

Dear John,

. . . I am not so much discouraged—that is a White House Whisper explaining their retreat on all these issues—as resigned. If Marx turned Hegel on his head, the new conservatives—neopopulists, really—have done that to the arguments of the past sixty years. The Republican Governor of Virginia asks for a Federal waiver to cut off AFDC benefits after two years. Period. Says it is "most compassionate" proposal yet. Proposal that would in short order, nationwide, leave some three to six million pauper children on the streets and on their own. President goes on nationwide Saturday radio to say it is a swell idea and waiver granted! Just so he let us down on <u>habeas corpus</u>—we ended up with <u>eight</u> votes on the Senate floor. Now it looks as if the Fourth Amendment is in for radical revision.

It may be we have to go through this. In any event we are, and there is more intelligence on the other side (if you like) than is yet recognized. They have quite silenced all those "advocacy" groups and protest crowds you dealt with for so long. No liberal guilt there. This might clear up a fair number of things over a decade or so. In the meantime I have somewhat helped get the Senate Republicans squabbling over the welfare spoils and there is still hope of GRIDLOCK!

Letter to Senator Edward M. Kennedy, expressing gratitude for joining him in a small minority that voted against ending welfare as an entitlement.

SEPTEMBER 25, 1995

Dear Ted:

You may have seen the enclosed from *Time*. It surely was "a moment worth marking—a clear signal that when it comes to protecting the poor, the party of the New Deal and the Great Society can't and won't do much anymore except trim the rough edges from G.O.P. plans."

You were one of eleven and I shall not ever forget this. Nor, I expect will you. For we will be remembered. The Congressional Budget Office has just let us know that we can expect that within five years a minimum of 2,500,000 dependent children will be completely without support. The Democratic party did not have to go along with this but sure as hell did. Save for eleven.

Letter to Governor Pataki, lamenting the slow pace of building big things.

NOVEMBER 16, 1995

Dear Governor Pataki:

I have a copy of The Encyclopedia of New York City and just looked up the Empire State Building. Demolition of the old Waldorf-Astoria began 1 October 1929. (Their usage as to dates.) First structural steel columns were set 7 April 1930. Opening ceremonies were held 1 May 1931. That would come to about thirteen months.

Governor Dewey built the Thruway from a standing start in just eight years. I believe the Erie Canal was dug in about six.

Have we lost the touch for famous things?

Letter expressing shock at the cost of dental surgery.

MARCH 29, 1996

Dear Drs. Stiglitz and Gadaire:

I write as a patient somewhat presumptively to offer advice and, in a more traditional role, to ask for help.

Last winter, Dr. Stiglitz advised that I ought to undergo an obviously complex procedure involving tooth implants. I had no idea what a tooth implant was, but agreed in the passive way persons of my generation deal with medical advice. I then had an appointment with Dr. Gadaire, who, after checking me out, took me into his conference room, explained what he would be doing, and said the cost of the procedure would be $18,500. This is more than I had ever paid for a medical bill before, but I resigned myself that it would be paid somehow, and, of course, agreed. I was a little surprised that after my first session with Dr. Gadaire on January 15, his secretary gave me a written bill for $21,386. However, Sue Wright of my office, who handles such matters here, verified that Dr. Gadaire's bill would be $18,500 and no more.

Alas, I had understood Dr. Gadaire to indicate that the bill would be for both [himself] and Dr. Stiglitz. He did <u>not</u> say this to me; I simply took him to mean it, such is my innocence in such matters. More recently, Mrs. Wright mentioned to my wife that Dr. Stiglitz's bill was $12,500. This was a shock but nothing compared to what I learned today that it is the bill so far. That, indeed, it was the bill for one morning in Dr. Stiglitz's surgery on January 24. Thus, I have no idea what the final cost will be. Nor do I have any immediate sense of how I am going to pay it. I have no insurance, or rather the insurance I do have pays no dental bills. I have spent most of my life in public employ, and have almost nothing by way of savings or investments.

And so I need to ask, can anyone estimate what will be the total bill? Is there any possibility of stopping the procedure at this point? I feel quite comfortable and I would assume my present "teeth" would last a good while.

Finally, may I presume to suggest that I needed a lot more information about these procedures before I agreed to them. My first session with Dr. Gadaire on January 15 was difficult but not overly so. It was arranged for the Martin Luther King, Jr. holiday such that I had a day to recover. By contrast, the January 24th session with Dr. Stiglitz was traumatic in the extreme and took place in the middle of a difficult week in the Senate. I would never have scheduled it if I had known how long it would take to recover. It was more than a month before I was myself again. Still don't think I am.

Letter to John Hilley, director of Congressional liaison under Clinton, showing the depth of Moynihan's estrangement from the Clinton White House.

NOVEMBER 19, 1996

Dear John:

The first Clinton administration began with a White House aide telling *Time* Magazine, "Moynihan supported Bob Kerrey during the primaries. He's not one of us, and he can't control Finance like Bentsen did. He's cantankerous, but he couldn't obstruct us even if he wanted to. The gridlock is broken. It's all Democratic now. We'll roll right over him if we have to." Everyone knew who said it. I knew. The statement was much disavowed but the "son of a bitch" kept his job.

What I would ask is that you tell Mr. Galvin what you have now told me. The idea of my inviting myself to a State Dinner is vulgar and I don't like it the least little bit.

Letter to Dr. Lloyd John Ogilvie, chaplain of the Senate, expressing thanks for a condolence note on the death of his younger brother, Michael Moynihan, who had worked as spokesman for the President's Special Trade Representative in the 1960s. Senator Moynihan says his brother was the "initial drafter" of the phrase "a rising tide lifts all boats," used by President Kennedy to suggest that economic growth helps the poor as well as the rich.

NOVEMBER 21, 1996

Dear Chaplain Ogilvie:

We said good-bye to brother Mike, an old sailor, at a wonderful ceremony at Arlington yesterday morning. As The Washington Post obituary noted, he "was the first spokesman for the White House Office of the President's Special Trade Representative during the Kennedy administration. He was the initial drafter of the phrase 'a rising tide lifts all boats,' for a presidential message on trade policy." He lived to see so many of those policies come about; but then, as it must, his own tide ebbed. Your note helped so very much, and I shall ever be grateful.

Letter to William F. Buckley Jr. recalling with amusement that as a favor to Buckley he spoke at Buckley's alma matter, the Millbrook School in the Hudson Valley, in the freezing rain, causing him to give up making the speech he planned.

DECEMBER 3, 1996

Dear Bill:

Your memory does not serve, and you might want to have it checked out. In 1981, you asked me a considerable favor, which was to journey all the way to the Millbrook School in Washington, New York, to give an address on the occasion of their 50th anniversary. I prepared an extensive paper, appropriate to the occasion. (Note, Mike McCurry was Press Secretary.) When I got there, I found dinner was in a tent and everyone was freezing. This made it impossible to give my address and I was reduced to standing up, saying how honored I was to have been invited, that I would put the speech in the Congressional Record and would send copies to any who wished. With that, I sat down. This brought the students to their feet applauding. I never did understand WASPS. . . .

Another letter to Buckley, who had written Moynihan for help in Buckley's preparing to write his latest espionage thriller, THE RED HUNTER: A NOVEL BASED ON THE

LIFE OF SENATOR JOE MCCARTHY, *published in 1999, in which his hero encounters the British spy Kim Philby. Buckley had asked in a February 19 letter about the Venona project files, a U.S.-British code-breaking effort to uncover Soviet espionage in the West. As chairman of the Bipartisan Commission on Protecting and Reducing Government Secrecy, Moynihan was instrumental in making the project public, including its conclusion that Julius and Ethel Rosenberg were spies long before they were charged. FDR and Truman were not told of the findings, however—according to Moynihan, because the F.B.I. suspected the Truman administration was itself compromised by Communist infiltration. Moynihan confides to Buckley that Truman was, in his view, inexperienced about Communists in the government.*

FEBRUARY 25, 1997

Dear Bill:

Here is the first copy of <u>Secrecy</u>, the report of a commission I got started a couple years ago which led to the release of the VENONA decryptions. This may be all we accomplish but that will be a better showing than the only other such commission which 40 years ago in 800 pages proposed press censorship and wire-tapping. I have a foreword which discusses your subject, starting at page xl. In effect, Hoover had custody of the files. The NSA broke the code. Specifically, Meredith Gardner on December 20, 1946 broke a cable in which the KGB named most of the physicists working at Los Alamos. Then there were code words for the Soviet agents. Julius Rosenberg, I regret to say was LIBERAL. It was up to the FBI, notably a splendid agent named Robert Lamphere, to break the code names, as it were. At this point, Hoover had evidently decided that the Truman administration was filled with Soviet agents. See two pages of his letter on xlii and xliii. Acheson, McCloy, Appleby. But also Hiss and Silvermaster. It is clear that he never told Truman, may not have told Attorney General Tom Clark. Leaving the President wholly open on the matter of Hiss and the others.

Truman probably never met a Communist until he got to Potsdam and so it was easy for him to think all the talk as the work of right-wing cranks. A great national agony followed. If only he had been a New Yorker!

Do you know that wonderful apocryphal but true story of British Foreign Secretary Ernest Bevin, sometime head of the Transport and General Workers Union, on his return from Potsdam? Asked what the Soviets were like, he replied, "They're just like the bloody Communists."

Letter to Jonathan Brent, editorial director of the Yale University Press and director of its studies of the history of Communism, discussing plans for his book SECRECY: THE AMERICAN EXPERIENCE, *published by Yale in 1998, about the history of government's needless suppression of secrets during and after the cold war. The book was Moynihan's last.*

PINDARS CORNERS, NY
JUNE 22, 1997

Dear Mr. Brent:

I am here in the one-room school house which will be found on Jay Gould's map of Delaware County, 1856. It was in use until the school bus appeared in 1946, whereupon it reverted to the farm and has been ours for some 37 years. I have written a dozen or so books here, but after last week's "mark up" of the tax bill in the Finance Committee, me thinks 'twere well that I get on with the next, if I am to live to see it finished!

Now then: what have you in mind? Is this to be a collaboration of some kind with Professor [Richard Gid] Powers [a historian]? Could you lay this out for me? If indeed this is what you do have in mind.

For my part, I really don't have a larger purpose than to elaborate somewhat on the Brief History I wrote for the Secrecy Commission. There will be some new material of note. By August, I should be free to settle once and for all the matter, which I suppose I raised, as to whether Truman was told of the VENONA decryptions. (He was not. Nor his State Department. The information was, in effect, withheld from the President. Had it not, I can imagine our politics being quite different in the half century since.) There is Hans Bethe's recent letter to the President urging that we stop working on all new types of nuclear weapons, especially pure-fusion weapons. "Secrets that will eventually leak," he writes. Just as he knew and stated that the Soviets would get the earlier weapons on their own, albeit in the first round helped a bit by espionage.

I would also like to comment a bit on the marginalization of the State Department with the rise of the IC (for Intelligence Community) and the "iron triangle" sequence in Congress and the associated industries. Finally, I have a long letter from the Society of Archivists which deserves an answer, as it were. (They are hugely supportive, but know the territory all too well.)

Harry Evans at Random House called to say they would be most interested in a book, but I explained my conversations with you. Lastly, if we are to go ahead, I will have to be in touch with Aida Donald at Harvard, who generously published my current blockbuster.

Memorandum of a conversation with President Clinton, describing Clinton's gratitude for help on trade legislation and Moynihan's desire for more of a boost to the Pennsylvania Station project.

OCTOBER 6, 1997

MEMCON

President Clinton called Friday afternoon to thank me for helping get the fast track bill through. I told him of the ILO provisions and the possibility of using the ILO as a way of responding to Labor concerns. I mentioned the view of [Economist Jagdish] Bhagwati and others that environment and labor provisions ought not to be in trade legislation. He asked me if I would help with Members of the House and I said, of course. He then asked me what I felt about climate change. I said I was skeptical. He said it is real.

I then asked if I could turn to another subject and reminded him that just four years ago he made that splendid promise to move Pennsylvania Station to the Old Farley Post Office. I said all the necessary work has begun; the problem is no one in the administration has been assigned this task. I said that I had given John Podesta a letter for him, the President, asking if this could not be done. He seemed not to recall any of this.

Letter to Leonard Downie Jr., executive editor of the WASHINGTON POST, *expressing dismay at the* POST's *coverage of Moynihan's role in the Pennsylvania Avenue redevelopment project.*

DECEMBER 2, 1997

Dear Len:

I have spent the better part of a fortnight wondering whether to send you this letter, lest it steal Christmas. I will get it off and be done with it. (You are free to stop reading right now!)

It concerns the two-part series on Pennsylvania Avenue—"Grand Designs: the Making and Unmaking of the Ronald Reagan Building" (November 16 and 17, 1997)—written by Lorraine Adams and Maryann Haggerty. Some while ago I received a request from Ms. Adams to discuss the Ronald Reagan Building. I was happy to do. *The Post* has been a great supporter of the Pennsylvania Avenue project from the time it began in 1962. Early on. Nat Owings and I came by to describe the proposal in general. Mrs. Graham said something to the effect, "Nat, we're all with you." . . . Ms. Adams and her colleague came to see me at 4:00 p.m. on Tuesday, September 23. I expected to be interviewed. Instead, I found myself being interrogated. All manner of questions about contractors, of which I knew nothing, and a fair amount of insinuation. Thus: Mr. Zeckendorf is a power in Democratic politics in New York, is he not? (If he is, it is news to me.) But in the published story there was this: "The four-way partnership included two companies—Zeckendorf Co. and Silverstein Properties Inc.—from Moynihan's New York." Does that suggest criminality? . . .

I would hate to see this fine enterprise end up with a squabble about construction costs. I do not doubt the Reagan Building might have been better managed. But Ben Forgey approves of the result. And it does wrap up a century's planning. . . .

Memorandum, as part of a series of notes to himself relating to the Monica Lewinsky scandal that enveloped President Clinton, in which he tells his press secretary to stop spreading the idea that Moynihan favored impeachment.

FROM: DANIEL PATRICK MOYNIHAN

DATE: AUGUST 27, 1998

MEMCON

Yesterday Nick Katzenbach called from Martha's Vineyard to say he had been told I was about to issue a call for impeachment and hoped I wouldn't do that. I said I had no such thought.

Later I talked with [Manhattan district attorney] Bob Morgenthau who is in Martha's Vineyard. He wanted to talk about [prosecutor Kenneth] Starr, saying he had distanced himself from all parties. "Plague on both your houses" but thinks Starr is a menace to the Presidency. He said first rule is you do not call a "target" before a grand jury and try to get him to commit perjury. This is in the U.S. Attorney Guidelines.

This morning I called Mike McCurry [White House press spokesman and former press secretary of Moynihan] and asked if he would be good enough to have them knock it off. He much agreed.

This afternoon Mike McCurry left me a message through Vicki [Moynihan's secretary]: "I got the message through, and it was gratefully received."

Memorandum of a conversation with Senator Bob Kerrey, who reported to Moynihan that Clinton was not going to call him about whether he would vote for impeachment.

FROM: DANIEL PATRICK MOYNIHAN

DATE: AUGUST 28, 1998

MEMCON

Spoke with Bob Kerrey this morning in Idaho. He called yesterday to tell me of a conversation with the President, who had called him. Went on at great length about this and that and finally got to the point, which was that Moynihan was going to call for his resignation. Would Kerrey call me. Kerrey asked why don't you call him? POTUS said, "I couldn't do that."

Memorandum of a conversation with President Clinton, who tells Moynihan that he is not calling senators for help but talking to those who call him. Moynihan concludes that Clinton is hoping for censure as opposed to removal from office. Subsequent memoranda describe conversations with Senators Tom Daschle (the majority leader), Slade Gorton, Joseph Lieberman, and Trent Lott, and that Moynihan agreed to a censure motion as long as it would be signed by the president. In the end, following impeachment by the House, Clinton was tried and acquitted by the Senate but not censured.

DECEMBER 28, 1998

MEMCOM

the president called, make that white house, at 320 saturday afternoon, leaving message on phone. liz found it, i called next day, pres out, called again sunday early evening; pres in.

he was calling to thank me quote for the new york time piece. no mention meet the press, but i mention mccurry, pres says two things. he is not calling senators but talks to those who call him. adds that dodd came by for a visit. (front page foto wash post) he then says if we can just get six or seven republicans we can work this out, indicating, i should think, that he is open to censure.

Dec 28 monday memcon

12:30 talked with Daschle who is returning my call from his office. he has just learned that slade gorton has called joe lieberman with a proposal. lott depends on Gorton quite a bit and it is that sort of proffer.

Jan 11 start trial. house presents case

Jan 12 white house presents case

jan 13 senators ask questions

jan 14 lott and Daschle present question: do facts warrant removal. vote loses

jan 16 adjourn

jan 17 vote censure.

dpm says this is a fine sequence with one exception. the president must have agreed to sign the censure resolution. and it must be adequate. therefore we should be in a position to reconsider the removal vote if he doesn't.

Daschle agreed, commenting that all censure motions are not alike.

i had called howell raines. now called tim russert. much excited about response to meet the press. one caller said i was the political laureate. a Rock Pasatono joe dimaggio's godson called to say dimaggio watched and so approved. he has perhaps two weeks to live.

The following letters between Moynihan and the NEW YORK TIMES *were prompted by a 7,500-word* TIMES *magazine cover story on November 5 about Moynihan by Jacob Weisberg, which declared that his Senate career had accomplished little. In this initial letter to Arthur O. Sulzberger Jr. (dated Nov. 3, 2000, before the article was distributed), Moynihan disputes the trivial (that he wore a monocle while living in London in the early 1950s) and the major substance (that he did not hold hearings on the Clinton health care legislation).*

NOVEMBER 3, 2000

Dear Arthur:

Why would the *Times Magazine* publish such a nasty cover story? "Who Was Pat Moynihan?" Here I am, three years shy of a half-century of government and politics, leaving quietly and peaceably. I have begged off all manner of interview requests. Yet I felt an obligation to the *Times*. And look what it got me.

It is no great matter to be called a "Shakespearean fool" or to be described going about London as an "English dandy" sporting a monocle. But it's not true. A monocle? Any fact checker could have called me. Still, no matter. But to read that I "declined to hold Finance Committee hearings" on the Clinton health care bill is outrageous (p. 51). I held seven months of hearings. One of which is described in the very next paragraph (p. 52).

A further letter to Sulzberger, repeating not only that the facts were wrong in the article but that the correction was itself disingenuous.

NOVEMBER 15, 2000

Dear Arthur:

That Weisberg article is ruining my leave taking of the Senate! People stop me on the streets, send me copies of letters. Two days ago, meaning to say farewell and thanks, I walked into an editorial board upstate to be met by disappointment and hurt. Why had I never done anything for New York? Why had I "declined" to hold hearings on the Clinton health care bill? . . .

Your correction this Sunday was even more troubling. "While chairman of the Finance Committee, he at first declined to hold hearings on the bill, but he held them in 1994." Someone has caused you to publish a lie. . . . Where do you get such misinformation? Do you really suppose a student at L.S.E. in 1950 went about in a bowler hat carrying an umbrella?

Moynihan thereupon cancels lunch plans at the NEW YORK TIMES.

NOVEMBER 27, 2000

Dear Arthur:

Perhaps you saw the enclosed from yesterday's Letters page in the magazine.

> Jacob Weisberg's cover article on Daniel Patrick Moynihan prompted a storm of protest.
> If this was our idea of a farewell salute to a great statesman, some suggested, then thanks for nothing. But many said that we got it right, and that our writer said what had long seemed to be unspeakable.

That last sentence seems to me gratuitous. In any event, we would make wretched luncheon guests come Thursday, and I beg for us to be excused. Our sole purpose was to thank you one and all for so much over so long. And we do!

Letter from Elizabeth Moynihan to Arthur Sulzberger, following up on her husband's cancellation of lunch.

TO: ARTHUR O. SULZBERGER, JR.

Dear Arthur,

I just learned that Pat faxed a letter canceling lunch on Thursday. He was accurate in saying that our purpose of calling on newspapers has been to say thank you—to them and through them to the citizens of New York for having him serve as Senator for twenty-four years.

However, I cannot allow him the liberty of speaking for both of us as he does at the end of his note to you. "Our sole purpose was to thank you one and all for so much over so long. And we do!" I do not!

It has not been Pat's habit as Senator to call publishers, editors or reporters to complain about stories—what bothers him is being *misquoted*—and Times reporters usually get it straight. To him words matter—that is why he may be the last politician who prefers the print media. True, he was surprised by the inaccuracies, errors and the mean tone, but said that's the price one pays today for public life.

But I don't feel that way—not for a second—it is evident that the rot that Weisberg wrote was intended to injure and the captions to reinforce it, and the photo was appalling. . . .

For that farewell tour of the papers I asked Pat's staff to check his legislation (that he wrote or introduced—not the grants, etc.) And total how much money he brought to New York—it's in the neighborhood of $87,000,000,000.00. For things few people even know about like West Valley!

I totaled what we raised for the four campaigns—under $20,000,000.—not each but for the four. We never ran a negative ad and didn't use soft money.

Pat's interest is government—not politics—and I am proud of him and feel he has been a good example of a life in public service. I am ashamed of the Times for kicking him as he leaves.

I do not feel grateful and would not break bread there.

Liz

Letter to Gerald Marzorati, editor of the NEW YORK TIMES *magazine, again correcting the Weisberg article's assertions on whether Moynihan held hearings on the Clinton health legislation.*

DECEMBER 5, 2000

Dear Mr. Marzorati:

Last letter!

You refer to Mr. Weisberg's "perhaps less-than-precise sentence," concerning the Clinton health care bill. To wit: "Worst of all, he declined to hold Finance hearings on the bill."

The President proposed his plan to a Joint Session on September 22, 1993. On September 30 I held the first of what would be twenty-nine hearings; leading off with Mrs. Clinton. I enclose my opening statement; wholly supportive. On November 20, when the 1,342 page bill was finally ready, I introduced it along with Mr. [Daniel] Rostenkowski [chairman of the House Ways and Means Committee]. The following July 2, the Finance Committee approved the only bipartisan measure to emerge from any committee.

Perhaps this will help explain how it was we learned of the magazine article in a disbelieving call from your Washington bureau. . . .

As Moynihan's term in the Senate came to an end, the TIMES *ran a laudatory editorial. Moynihan thanked Sulzberger for it:*

JANUARY 11, 2001

Dear Arthur:

That was a fine farewell (December 31), of which I am most sensible. Do thank Howell [Raines, editorial page editor] and all concerned.

But, oh, that magazine article! It fair to follows me down the street, people asking how could I have refused to hold hearings on the Clinton health care plan? Of course, the facts are just the opposite. I started hearings, with the

First Lady, early in the fall of 1993, before the administration bill was sent to us, and continued into the following summer.

My object, self-evident to a legislator, was to build a consensus. We were coming along fine. On the morning of May 12 Bob Dole, Minority Leader, passed me a note. "Pat. Are we ready for the Moynihan-Dole Bill??" I literally put down the gavel and rushed into the back room to call the White House. In his splendid new memoir <u>Eyewitness to Power</u>, David Gergen described what followed. He, Bentsen, Shalala all had hoped for something such. But of a Sunday evening meeting, shortly after my bulletin arrived, the new President grew agitated and declared, "We won't compromise!" Gergen: "Looking at my watch, I wrote a note to myself: 'At 10:22 p.m. tonight, health care died.'"

What followed was a calamity for social policy. It will take a decade to get back to where we were. <u>If</u> we come to understand what happened.

Still, we may get a new Penn Station!

CHAPTER FIFTEEN

"I Write to Say Farewell and Thanks"

Final epistolary thoughts of Daniel Patrick Moynihan as he wound down his Sen-ate career and prepared to resume writing and teaching in his retirement.

Undated reflections by Moynihan on weeping as a boy over Lou Gehrig's failure (in two games) to get a hit, and hating Joe DiMaggio because he hit a home run (in both games), and Moynihan's willingness to forgive DiMaggio upon meeting him in a restaurant.

BY DANIEL PATRICK MOYNIHAN

I am too old for fantasy. This is the truth.

In the late 1930's I had a hero. I quite understood that the relationship was to be for life, and I have never had a hero since.

He was, of course, Lou Gehrig. As a man says of himself in one of Yeats's stanzas, Gehrig "was blessed and could bless." I did not understand that then, but I knew it.

Then something awful happened.

I had never seen him. All I really knew of him was from pictures in the Daily News and the daily story of yesterday's game.

My mother understood what it meant, my never having seen him play. One day she gave my 60 cents—50 cents for the Yankee Stadium bleachers, a nickel for the subway each way—and said, go on, it's something you have to do.

And so I went as to a great and solemn consummation. This was no game; this was the meaning of life. And then Gehrig, his disease coming on now I suppose, didn't get a single hit. And Jo DiMaggio, rising now, hit a home run. And then it started to rain. And they played on anyway until the game was official and called it at seven and a half innings so I didn't even get my mother's 50 cents worth.

I went home to my room and cried.

The next day my mother gave me another 60 cents. I went back and the same thing happened. Gehrig did not get a single hit; DiMaggio homered.

Then the awful thing happened. Out of love, I came home hating DiMaggio. I hated him. Hated his youth, his grace, the fact that he was a champion.

I went on hating him. Decades would pass and still, every so often, I found myself thinking how I hated Joe DiMaggio and how awful that was.

Years went by and I was having dinner at La Scala on 54th Street. Joe DiMaggio came in with a friend and sat down by the wall opposite. I had seen him enough on television over the years. But this was the first time I had seen him in person since the 12 year old had seen him, and I was now Ambassador to the United Nations.

I got up and went over to him. He nodded (he had seen me on television) and then stood up and shook hands, and in the way he smiled let me know that he knew, and that he understood and that it was all right.

I walked out onto 54th Street delivered. I mean just that. I was possessed by grace, I was forgiven. Gehrig <u>was</u> blessed and <u>could</u> bless, and had.

Letter to John F. Kennedy Jr., publisher of GEORGE *magazine.*

NOVEMBER 13, 1997

Dear Mr. Kennedy:

Last spring, I took Daughter to a State Dinner. We went through the usual barriers; were pinched, prodded, sniffed. Finally passed on to the East Entrance where a bright young Secret Service man with a clipboard looked in the car window and exclaimed, "Good evening, Senator Thurmond!" And so I felt in elevated, even deserved company for which you have my great thanks, and also for the fine photograph by Herb Ritts.

On the other hand, I cannot be equally grateful for being named one of Washington's ten "best-dressed." I was wearing my only blue suit for the occasion of the photograph session. But in the aftermath, Liz dragged me off to J. Press for two more of the same and assorted elegant accessories. And so, it is to be another year of deficit financing!

Letter to President Clinton, recommending a visit to India.

JANUARY 19, 1998

Dear Mr. President,

I am just returned from a periodic visit to India where I was Ambassador in a hard time. It is clearly understood that good manners, if nothing else, require you to put off your planned visit now that yet another election is underway. However, I do hope you will find time later this year. The cold war is over and so, it would appear, is the era of the Congress Party. And yet, the habits of our estranged democracies, in Dennis Kux's phrase, continue. I saw little to counter his concern that India might decide "almost viscerally that opposing the United States is the natural state of affairs for Indian foreign policy." A visit from you as a new government forms might well change that.

*Letter to the author Godfrey Hodgson, whose biography of Moynihan (*THE GEN-
TLEMAN FROM NEW YORK*) was published two years later.*

APRIL 25, 1998

Dear Godfrey:

What a fine and thoughtful message. All, of course, is well.

I am of a sudden busy. My lecture at the JFK School did indeed start a Social Security debate which proceeds with but little rancor. This surprises journalists and such, the subject having been decreed the third rail of politics. I may just be getting through to the libs that the privatization movement is real and anything but right wing quackery. I have been sending around copies of the Fiftieth Anniversary Edition of Hayek's *The Road to Serfdom*, which Chicago published over here, after it appeared in the U.K. in 1944. Introduction by Milton Friedman. The point is that conservatives are discovering a history they didn't know they had. Which liberals seem incapable of imagining even. Conservatives with ideas. Really. Note Paul Gigot from yesterday's *Wall Street Journal*. And a column by a most conservative Texan.

The NATO debate begins Monday, will last the week, I expect. This is something of a success in itself. It was being treated like a Joint Resolution congratulating Kansas on its 150th anniversary, or whatever. Something for the end of the day which we call "wrap up." Unanimous consent. I was asked down to Dallas to speak to the AP on <u>their</u> 150th anniversary. They had expected Social Security. But were, I believe, genuinely interested once I got them to think of linking the nuclear dimension. Yesterday a fine letter arrived from Paul Nitze. Trouble is that there are so few of us left in the Senate who can recall the founding of NATO and what it meant at the time. We shall see. I don't see us defeating the Resolution, but we will have got the administration's attention.

On that subject, the White House was suddenly inspired to celebrate the 1993 Budget agreement which, as you will recall, passed the Senate with the Vice President twice casting a tie-breaking vote. The first and crucial one came after Liz called Bob Kerrey from the farm to urge him to vote for the President lest it be thought he was taking his revenge for New Hampshire. The next day the President called Liz to say she had saved his administration. But came 1995 and he was telling Texans and others that he agreed he had raised taxes too much. Now they commence to see that the deficit reduction—in the end something like $1 trillion—led us to the present surplus. And decided to take credit for it after all. Danny Rostenkowski was back in Washington for the first time since getting out of prison. POTUS, he, and I had a good photo op.

Finally, I raised a huge amount of money—for me that is—at a cocktail party at the St. Regis and don't you know the Mayor showed up! Was most generous, but no one equals Robert C. Byrd, Jr.

Love to Hilary. And to San Francisco!

At the White House ceremony on August 9, 2000, in which he received the presidential Medal of Freedom, Moynihan encounters fellow medalist Gardner Taylor, the African-American pastor and civil rights leader. He notes in this memorandum that Taylor had once denounced him on race issues but told him at the ceremony that he now recognized that Moynihan was right.

FROM: DANIEL PATRICK MOYNIHAN
DATE: AUGUST 16, 2000

MEMORANDUM OF CONVERSATION

At the Presidential Medal of Freedom ceremony August 9th we were kept standing in the West Room to a point where my back began to trouble me. I slipped out to find a place to sit down. There was Gardner Taylor and a friend on a bench. I shook hands and sat down beside him. You know, he said, I owe you an apology. Years ago when you issued your report on the Negro family— not sure he used that term—I was one of those who denounced you. I now realize you were right. He repeated this several times that afternoon. . . .

Moynihan's last constituent newsletter, thanking New Yorkers for supporting him in four Senate terms and reporting on his receiving the Presidential Medal of Freedom from President Clinton, the very award he helped establish in the Kennedy administration. He received the medal along with two friends, former Senator George McGovern and John Kenneth Galbraith.

Dear New Yorker:

FAREWELL!

This will be our last newsletter in a series that began some twenty-four years ago. Under Senate rules it must be printed and mailed by early September and so I am writing it now from the schoolhouse at the farm.

I write first to say farewell and thanks. New Yorkers have been surpassingly generous to us, which is to say Liz and me. Assuming I make it to January 3, 2001, I will be the 120th person to have served four terms in the United States Senate. Only one other New Yorker has done so, my beloved Jacob Javits. In 1988 you gave us a victory margin of some 2,172,865 votes, which I reckon the largest for a legislative seat in, well, history. No doubt some Californian will someday do better, but for now the record is ours. And so, again, great thanks.

This has been a nostalgic month, which I hope to snap out of, but for the moment perhaps you will bear with me. On August 9th I received the Presidential Medal of Freedom from President Clinton, in a fine ceremony, some 15 of us at the White House. The Presidential Medal of Freedom is the highest civil honor conferred by the United States Government. Yet to receive it was almost melancholic. For it happens I was among those who thought it up for President Kennedy.

It is a tale of those times, when so much seemed possible. And was. Early in his administration the President mentioned to Secretary of Labor Arthur J. Goldberg that the United States ought to have a system of civil honors. The subject was around at the time. President Eisenhower had set up a commission which proposed a somewhat elaborate system to be created by statute. All went well until it reached the Senate where it was denounced as smacking of monarchy.

Goldberg set me to work on the subject. There was no point thinking up yet another bill. Finally it came to us, and we put it to the President just so. If he wanted a system of civil honors, he simply had to announce that he had one. There was a Medal of Freedom created in 1945 by President Truman to recognize persons who had served overseas during the war, though not in uniform. From time to time, succeeding Presidents had handed out a few. We proposed that come Washington's Birthday Kennedy announce that henceforth it would be known as the Presidential Medal of Freedom, would be conferred <u>only</u> once each year, and as an award for contributions to "cultural or other significant public or private endeavors" as well as national security.

A then more trusting press asked no questions. The front page of <u>The Washington Post</u> reported simply: "Presidential Order Adds Luster and Scope to Medal of Freedom." The list was announced on July 4th. The President would confer them as his schedule allowed. Some while later it was announced he would do so on December 6 when he returned from his trip to Dallas. Of course, he did not return. After some hesitation the ceremony went forward. President Kennedy was awarded the medal posthumously. It fell to me to write the citation, which is the last entry in his <u>Public Papers</u>. While it was being read, Jacqueline Kennedy listened from behind a screen in the West Room. For those of us who knew she was there, it was a moment never to be forgotten.

I had been in the White House on November 22. The realization set in; the President was dead. One of the last instructions he left before leaving for Dallas was that on his return there also be a coffee hour at which he could show the Congressional leaders the model of a revived Pennsylvania Avenue which was now ready for display. The President's close friend, the artist Bill Walton, had invited me to lunch at his house to discuss the arrangements. The phone rang. The White House for Walton. We sped downtown.

It was an eerie moment. Official Washington was deserted. The President, Vice President, their staffs were in Dallas. Half the Cabinet was in a plane crossing the Pacific to meet with their Japanese counterparts. The House had adjourned. The few of us in town gathered silently in Ralph Dungan's southwest office, a few doors down from the Oval Office. (Where they were changing the rug. The President's furniture had been moved to the hall outside. His rocking chair on top of the pile. As I say, eerie.) McGeorge Bundy went to a phone and asked for the Secretary of Defense. The silence returned, to be broken when Hubert H. Humphrey burst into the room, embraced Dutton, and with streaming tears exclaimed: "What have they done to us!"

By they, of course, he meant Texan reactionaries who hated the President. We broke up, on the way out I pointed Walton to the White House flag being lowered. It was more than he could take. Later in the afternoon the radio reported that the Dallas police had arrested a man associated with Fair Play for Cuba, a pro-Castro group. My God, I said to myself, he will be killed. I met the Cabinet plane that arrived back at Andrews Air Force Base late that evening, pleading with the Treasury officials on board to have the Secret Service—their agency—get custody of Oswald, get him out of that jail.

I don't know how I knew that. But I knew. A day or so later I was on television. How were we all taking it all? I replied that I didn't suppose there was any point in being Irish if you didn't know the world was going to break your heart eventually. It is just that we thought we had a little more time. Then from nowhere came Prospero's passage from Act IV of <u>The Tempest</u>. "Our revels now are ended." I did not know that line. I had never read the play; seen it perhaps twice. But there were the words, somehow rising to the moment. In just this way, I have to suppose, I knew that Kennedy's assassination would create a conspiracy theory that would live on and on.

In the days and weeks that followed I pleaded with who would listen that our investigation had to look into the jaws of hell, lest it be dismissed as a cover up of the plot. I took to carrying about a recently published memoir, <u>Fifty Years of the Church of Rome</u>, which revealed that Jesuits had plotted the assassination of Lincoln. The Warren Commission did its work, sort of. Then proceeded to seal some of its documents until 2039. <u>Why</u>? Why to cover up the fact that there had been more assassins than Oswald. In 1979 the House Select Committee on Assassinations agreed. By 1998, thirty-five years later, nearly three-quarters of Americans believed that a conspiracy was either definitely or probably behind the assassination. Just the other night I watched on the History Channel a segment of a five-part documentary series, "The Men Who Killed Kennedy." All fantasy—but believed.

It happens that the day before the assassination Richard Hofstadter, professor of history at Columbia and a dear friend, delivered at Oxford his incomparable lecture, later book, "The Paranoid Style in American Politics." He begins:

> Although American political life has rarely been touched by the most acute varieties of class conflict, it has served again and again as an arena for uncommonly angry minds.

People who see a hostile and conspiratorial world directed not at them so much as the nation, the culture, the way of life. It is in that sense a rationalizing mode. Facts are everything—and facts are <u>never</u> accidental. "For every error or act of incompetence one can substitute an act of treason." And always, of course, this is proof of "the existence of a vast, insidious, preternaturally effective international conspiratorial network designed to perpetrate acts of the most fiendish character."

As I've said, I am writing from the schoolhouse where we have a <u>History of Delaware County, 1797–1880</u>. It includes a brief but informative history of our town of Davenport. Including:

SOCIETIES

There have been three secret societies in the township.

The Fugine Society was organized in 1843. It was anti-church and free-love.

During the rage for an American party there was a dark-lantern lodge that claimed to Know Nothing about it.

The Free Masons were also represented.

I don't know about the Fugines. Free Masons are fine citizens—then and now. The Know Nothings, however, were the genuine article. They flourished in the 1850s, carrying Massachusetts in the 1854 elections, polling large votes in New York and Pennsylvania as well. They were opposed to immigration (read Irish), opposed to the election or appointment of Catholics, and to the Roman Catholic church. When asked any question regarding the party's policy, the member would answer, "I don't know." Hence the popular name. Had they not split over slavery in 1856 they had the makings of a national force. And note, it would be a century before a Catholic would be elected president.

Much of that group prejudice is behind us. Colin Powell of City College could have had the vice presidency for the asking this time around, and Joe Lieberman does. But the paranoid style persists, and we have got to take care.

As I close out near on to half a century of government and politics, the great fear I have for our democracy is the enveloping culture of government secrecy and the corresponding distrust of government that follows. Since the end of the Cold War—which, incidentally, all those secret agencies quite missed— our armed forces have declined considerably, but the secret side of government just keeps growing. In 1994 I passed a bill creating a Commission on Protecting and Reducing Government Secrecy. We came up with a unanimous report calling for a number of simple measures designed to slow the accumulation of classified documents. Thus the person doing the original classification must sign his/her name and state the duration of the classification. (In

1975 President Ford had in mind to name me Librarian of Congress. An historian writing about the subject learned of this and inquired at the Ford Library. Yes there was a file, but it could not be released as the material was classified. It consisted of cables to and from New Delhi where I had been ambassador. Such "traffic" is routinely classified. But forever?) Our proposals were unanimously approved by the Senate Committee on Governmental Affairs, but slowly the permanent government did them in.

Look out they don't do us in. Secrecy is a form of regulation and can be stifling. In the course of our Commission's work we were able to release—thanks to John M. Deutch—the so-called VENONA decryptions. Starting in 1946 the Army Security Agency was deciphering cable traffic of the Soviet K.G.B. Soon we had the identities of a limited but still formidable espionage operation. In time, as always happens, the Soviets got on to this. Soon the moment came when they knew what we knew and we knew they knew. The one person in the United States government who absolutely ought also to have known was President Truman. But he did not. On orders from his friend Omar N. Bradley whom he had appointed the first Chairman of the Joint Chiefs of Staff. And why? All I can figure is bureaucracy: Army property. And so a generation of American politics and government was tormented by reciprocal charges of "red baiting," "comsymp" and such. Wittaker Chambers, you see, was telling the truth.

Near hysterical fear of revealing the "secrets" of the Pentagon Papers—there were none, really—led step by step to the destruction of Richard M. Nixon. Concealing from Congress "secret" arms sales to Iran—the Iranians knew!—very nearly spoiled the presidency of Ronald W. Reagan. And it won't stop.

I hope that in a new century we get a hold on this and open up our government. Alfred Marshall, the great English economist, wrote more than a century ago: "Government is the most precious of human institutions, and no care can be too great to be spent enabling it to do its work in the best way." To which I would add, the best way is not in the dark.

So there it is. Outside the goldenrod mixed with blue aster is gleaming. And signaling time to go. And so again, Liz and I are ever grateful.

Celebrating the election victory of Hillary Clinton to his Senate seat on November 7, Moynihan records in a memorandum for his files that President Clinton was appreciative of his endorsement of his wife's Senate candidacy. He was fond of noting

that in the closing weeks of her Senate campaign, when the TIMES *ran a piece that recalled some of Mrs. Clinton's quotes from the 1993–1994 health care battle, she sent him a conciliatory handwritten note. In it she said she found it "jarring" to read her six-year-old comments and that "if I had listened to you about health care in 1994, I would be far better off today—but more importantly—so would the nation's health care system."*

TO: FILES

DATE: NOVEMBER 15, 2000

MEMCON

Election night (Tuesday, November 7), in a freight elevator on the way down to the ballroom of the Grand Hyatt, POTUS said, "If it had not been for your endorsement, Hillary would never have won."

Letter to the "Lexington" columnist of the ECONOMIST, *expressing thanks for its tribute, but clarifying that one of his famous phrases—"boob bait for the Bubbas"— was a regrettable wisecrack referring to the Clinton administration's welfare plans, not health care legislation.*

JANUARY 23, 2001

Dear Lexington:

That was a wonderful farewell, of which I am more than sensible. My only regret is that business about "boob bait for the bubbas." It was a wisecrack— instantly regretted, but mine own doing—about an early Clinton proposal on welfare. It turned up not long ago in a *New York Times Magazine* article as having been directed to the health care proposal. On the contrary, I was all in favor of a general health measure. The planners of Social Security in '34- '35 were all in favor of such a measure, but put it off at the last minute. I got to know Frances Perkins in the Kennedy years, and she kept asking when we would get on with that agenda. Actually Truman had tried and failed. Then Nixon. Now Clinton. My thought was to build a center coalition. Bob Dole was in favor. See enclosed. But the White House would have nothing of compromise. See David Gergen's fine memoir with its laconic conclusion: "I looked at my watch and wrote down 'Health care died at 10:22.'"

We will get back to it someday, but not soon. British governments make their own mistakes, but none so total as ours can be.

Letter to Alberto R. Gonzales, counsel to President George W. Bush, on why he thought it a waste of time to fill out all the forms in order to serve as co-chair of the President's Commission to Strengthen Social Security.

MAY 15, 2001
ALBERTO R. GONZALES, ESQ.
COUNSEL TO THE PRESIDENT
THE WHITE HOUSE
WASHINGTON, DC 20500

Dear Mr. Gonzales:

The enclosed arrived by Fed Ex just the other day. As a member of the Presidential Appointee Initiative, which the Brookings Institution sponsored, as Co-Chair of the President's Commission to Strengthen Social Security, I would respectfully ask whether you really want to put our Commission members through this ordeal by document.

At Brookings, Nancy Kassebaum Baker and Franklin D. Raines heard their share of horror stories, but nothing to equal the PERSONAL DATA STATE-MENT and TAX CHECK WAIVER you have asked be answered in five days.

I couldn't do it in five months. And certainly would not get any of the Commission's work done whilst trawling through my tax records.

I am sure this is not your doing. But surely you can undo it. Have we lost our senses? I served in the cabinet or subcabinet of four successive Presidents. Evidently I am the only person in American history to have done so. In those years I do not believe I ever filled out a form, much less a life history.

Whilst still in the Senate I ran into this sort of thing in the case of nominees for the Department of State's Cultural Property Advisory Committee. It is any wonder citizens hesitate to volunteer their services to our government?

As for full-time appointments, I recommend the PAI publication <u>A Survivor's Guide for Presidential Nominees</u>.

As for me, I will provide name, rank, and serial number as prescribed by the Geneva Convention. I have a commission signed by Forrestal somewhere in a closet at home and will dig it out to get my serial number. Otherwise I fear I must invoke my right to remain silent.

Letter to William J. vanden Heuvel, thanking him for his proposal of a portrait of Moynihan to be painted by Everett Raymond Kinstler for Moynihan's beloved Century Club. It hangs there on the second floor today.

DECEMBER 18, 2001

Dear Bill:

I am altogether astonished. Not by your generosity—to which I am long accustomed—but by your proposal. A Kinstler portrait! For the Century! I must hurry to agree lest I expire with the very thought.

Of course I know his work, having spent the better part of forty years getting the National Portrait Gallery into a proper setting in the Patent Office. (Where 'Enfant located the National Cathedral!) I should be honored to accommodate his schedule, as I have so little [to do] just now. Perhaps he maintains a studio at Gramercy Park?

Bewildered!

Letter to Senator Edward M. Kennedy, thanking him for his note about Moynihan's speech earlier in the year at Harvard, which was drowned out by rain.

SEPTEMBER 5, 2002

Dear Ted:

What a wonderful note! And more appreciated than you might imagine. As you will recall from the graduation in 1979, the Harvard Yard is filled on that occasion. Alas, this year the monsoon got mixed up and landed on 20,000 sons and daughters of Harvard at mid-morning. By mid-afternoon when they got around to me, there were about 70 folk left in the audience. And nobody behind me in the Tercentenary Theater could hear a word. So the audience was not what one might have hoped for. I gather they put it on the web, and this somehow got to you. You cheer me beyond words.

I watch you all with wonder and admiration. Steady on.

Memorandum lamenting his fall at a ceremony saluting plans for a new Pennsylvania Station.

OCTOBER 9, 2002

ON THE USES OF OSTEOARTHRITIS

October 8 was Bad Knee Day. And so with some apprehension I joined in the small company announcing that at last there would be a new and splendid Pennsylvania Station. I slipped up the stairs of the Post Office to a small platform with, alas, no chairs. The Governor [George Pataki] spoke; the Mayor [Michael Bloomberg] spoke; I spoke. And as quickly slipped down to street level and sat on the edge of the stage. Next, the photographers asked for a group picture. I demurred; I could not get back up. Whereupon the Governor jumped down to join me. The others followed. And the *Times* had a picture it could hardly not print.

Memorandum dated March 2003 (the month of his death), summing up his central belief about society and culture.

In some 40 years of government work I have learned one thing for certain. As I have put it, the central conservative truth is that it is culture, not politics, that determines the success of a society. The central liberal truth is that politics can change a culture and save it from itself. Thanks to this interaction, we're a better society in nearly all respects than we were.

Daniel Patrick Moynihan
March 2003

MY FATHER THE WRITER
BY MAURA MOYNIHAN

When I was five years old, I asked my mother, what does Dad do? She replied, he's a writer. And he was: he wrote every day—even at Christmas—articles, books, speeches, and in great abundance, letters.

Throughout my childhood we moved many times, following my father's career as a diplomat, academic, and politician. Mom packed and unpacked three children and two fox terriers, Whiskey and Mr. Dooley, in succession, the Shaker furniture that traveled with us, Christmas ornaments, special books, and blankets. She was a gifted hostess, cook, painter, seamstress, gardener, author, and my father's most valued confidant and advisor. Our home, wherever it was, became a nexus of friends and colleagues that linked Washington and New York and England and India.

In February 1964, Mom and I drove from Washington to upstate New York in search of a farm. It was deep winter, the land was frozen and still. We were taken to look at a property for sale in Pindars Corners. We drove up a dirt road, where a one-room schoolhouse stood above a valley. We saw a barn, two stables, and a white farm house. I seized my mother's hand; I felt it was ours. And so we bought the farm on Prosser Hollow Road for ten dollars an acre.

Over the years Mom added layers of beauty to the land around the farm. She created herb and flower gardens, did battle with woodchucks, moved rocks, planted trees, and dug a pond, all to create a sanctuary that was our home for four decades.

The farm had a pasture, an apple orchard, streams—one a tributary to the Susquehanna River—and an ox lot, thick with trees, where a great oak stood. Dad named the farm Derrymore, Gaelic for "Great Oak." The one-room schoolhouse became his study. Inside there were an old wood stove, two blackboards, two long Shaker chests, and a large canvas campaign poster that read "Al Smith for President." On the desk were a Smith Corona electric typewriter, books and paperclips neatly and precisely arranged, an antique Pennsylvania Dutch crock filled with pens, and a gigantic Webster's Dictionary. But no telephone.

In the summer, every morning after breakfast, Dad walked up the hill to the schoolhouse to write. At 10:30 A.M., one of the three children would bring him a thermos of coffee and a muffin. From the doorway I would watch, enchanted, as he would pace in circles, speaking aloud in a rapture of thought, then sit before the typewriter and pound away. I would deliver his coffee and muffins, but I did not linger too long. He did not like to be interrupted, hence no telephone, radio, or television ever entered the schoolhouse.

At lunch he returned to the house for a meal on the back porch. Then a nap, and more writing, and a walk though the woods and pasture. Our neighbor, Bub Briggs, kept his dairy cows in our barns. In the summer they etched trails upon the hillside, and we would follow them to the Indian Spring that stood in a glade at the top of the pasture, Dad swinging a wooden stick. Then he'd walk home for an evening swim and dinner on the back porch—with wine, corn, and fresh bread from Oneonta, the town in the nearest valley. Friends often came to stay, and we would invent plays and musicals, frequently set to the songs of Dad's favorite stars, Fred Astaire and Ginger Rogers.

The farm had a vast library, gathered from Dad's collection of history books and Penguin Classics from his London years. There were shelves for poetry, mythology, literature, encyclopedias, and dictionaries of many languages. Collections of Dickens, Jane Austen, William Butler Yeats, Dylan Thomas, T.S. Elliot, e.e. cummings, Greek and Roman history, biographies of Disraeli, Gladstone, Pitt the Elder and Younger. Collections of letters, the diaries of Samuel Pepys, Dr. Johnson, Evelyn Waugh, Winston Churchill. A special shelf for books written by friends, and special places for gifts Dad brought from his many travels—a Yugoslavian yak horn, a Bhutanese sword, Peruvian blankets, a Japanese doll from Tokyo, and an etching, from his London years, of a parliamentary debate on the Corn Laws.

The farm was a refuge from the traumatic years of my father's early Washington career. Dad had been in the Oval Office the day Kennedy was assassinated. Hubert Humphrey ran in, crying: "What have they done to us?" Dad tried to get Oswald into federal custody. When he heard that Oswald was shot, he cried out and pounded his fists on the wall.

I watched my mother dress for the president's funeral in a black veil and gloves. (Five years later, I would also watch her dress for Senator Robert Kennedy's funeral.) I could see, in the faces of my parents and their friends, that something more than the president had been killed. Many of the young men and women who had come to Washington with Kennedy were driven out of

Washington and out of government as the war in Vietnam escalated. Dad grieved for the fallen president and witnessed many of his friends abandon politics, but he pressed on, still believing in the power of government to do good. He always kept a special portrait of John F. Kennedy in his office. As the years passed, he would become the last New Frontiersman to remain in electoral politics.

In 1965, as undersecretary of labor in the Johnson administration, Dad wrote *The Negro Family: A Case for National Action.* The report was initially well-received, but in the fractious political climate of the mid-6os, my Dad was vilified by the New Left for blaming the victim. I worried terribly for my father. He endured jeers and attacks for years afterward, but he held himself with stoic grace and he never spoke of it at the dinner table.

Dad's first campaign for public office took us to New York City, where he failed to be elected as president of the City Council, to our great relief. We missed the farm and the woods of Tregaron, our home in Washington. We spent a happy year at Wesleyan in Middletown, Connecticut, and finally moved to Cambridge, where Dad became director of the Joint Center for Urban Affairs at Harvard and MIT. Our home on Francis Avenue filled with friends and students—Dad held seminars and office hours at home.

When, in 1969, President Nixon asked Professor Moynihan to lead his new Urban Affairs Council (which shocked Democrats and Republicans alike), schoolmates were ordered not to play with us. A journalist later asked him why he'd joined Nixon's White House staff, and Dad replied, "The cities were in flames and the president asked for my help. Under those circumstances, if you don't serve your country, what kind of a person are you?" Two years later Dad had returned to Cambridge, but the president called again, and after a twenty-minute phone call Dad emerged from his study, scratching his head, and told us, "The president just asked me to be his ambassador to India, and I said yes."

In January 1973 we moved to New Delhi to commence a great adventure that would transform our lives. U.S-India relations were at a low ebb; Dad decided to fix this by negotiating a settlement of the PL 480 debt. This was an age of cables and aerograms; international telephone calls had to be booked a week in advance. Senator J. William Fulbright of Arkansas was furious to learn that Dad had given a USAID building in Delhi back to India, and sent an enraged telegram to New Delhi. Dad cabled back: "I gave the keys over yesterday got your telegram too late." A certain state department official who had a reputation for harassing embassy staff all over Asia castigated Ambassador Moynihan over a debt repayment deal. Dad replied: "In response to your latest missive, Fuck You. Sincerely, Ambassador Daniel P. Moynihan." Years later, in Bangkok, I met a consular officer who had kept this cable framed on his office wall.

We were in India in 1974 when Mrs. Gandhi tested India's first nuclear device. A cable arrived from the state department, which read: "You spend tax payers' money while the Indians explode the A-Bomb; we know what you are doing." Dad framed this cable and hung it on his office wall.

In 1975, we returned again to Cambridge. Dad resumed teaching at Harvard until President Ford asked him to serve as ambassador to the United Nations—and we briefly occupied the official residence at the top of the Waldorf Astoria. I will never forget the speeches Dad gave at the UN. On November 10, 1975, after he denounced the Zionism is racism resolution—"the terrible lie will have terrible consequences"—Dad walked over to Israel's ambassador, Chiam Herzog, an old friend whose father was the chief cantor of Dublin, to say "Fuck 'em." Dad then wrapped his arm around Herzog and led him out of the UN, to The Four Provinces, a now-defunct Irish bar, where they drank Guinness for many hours while the fevered press corps swarmed the Waldorf lobby in pursuit.

In the eight months Ambassador Moynihan served at the UN, he received thousands of letters of support from across the nation and the world. Of the many accolades he received, one that baffled us—he was named to Mr. Blackwell's 1976 "Best Dressed" list. Dad had a distinctive style of dress, but it could not be construed as fashion. He loved English suits and silk bow ties—but his shirts had holes and he often wore baggy tweed jackets with leather elbow patches. When he left the UN, he received a medal from the Irish Hatmakers' Association for popularizing the tweed hat in which he was photographed daily.

In 1976 Dad left the UN and returned to Harvard. There was a Senate race in New York State and friends encouraged Dad to run, but he considered the task and decided he couldn't do it. Dick Ravitch heard of this and dragged him to the Madison Pub in the East 70s. Dick recalls: "He said he couldn't give up Harvard. I told him Harvard can go to hell, he had to do it, because if he didn't, Bella would win and Buckley would beat Bella, and that would be bad for New York." Dad wandered back to the family and announced his candidacy the following day. The 1976 primary election night was agony. The returns came in at 4:00 A.M.: Moynihan beat Abzug by 1 percent of the vote. The next day, in a haze of exhaustion, I wandered into the living room of our campaign flat. Dad sat there in silence with a faint smile, as if peering into the future.

The general election against incumbent James Buckley was conducted in a style that has long since vanished from politics. When Buckley called him a "professor," Dad replied, "Ah, ha, the mudslinging has begun!" In the week after the general election, however, Dad and Senator Buckley met for lunch in New York. They remained friends over the years.

And so, once more our worlds united—Pindars Corners and Washington, D.C. Every summer during the August recess we went to the farm; Dad to the schoolhouse to write a new book. He continued his social science research, and corresponded with academics, doctors, and scholars. One of his favorite projects was his quarterly newsletter to his constituents. It was a diary and history lesson, complete with illustrations and graphs. Another favorite project was composing letters to friends—pensive, curious, hilarious, often with limericks or rhymes. I admired his great capacity for friendship, his affection and concern for all the people in his life. He wrote hundreds of letters of recommendation. He loved to see his friends, colleagues, staff, and students succeed. He would argue vigorously about ideas and laws, but he disliked gossip and was fierce in his loyalties. He was devoted to his staff and students, and they to him. Sadly, few letters remain from these relationships. They were mostly carried out via conversation and debate, often on the back porch at Derrymore. Always a teacher, he pushed his staff like students in a graduate seminar. Ross Frommer, Moynihan New York State director, recalls: "He was very demanding, and your work had to be done well and done on time. But you learned so much, and he believed it was his mission to teach you things."

In the Senate, Dad had found the perfect world for his gifts as a writer, teacher, and orator. He loved the history, the architecture, the "laws of comity," and the great national rostrum, the Senate chamber. "It was not unusual for senators from both sides of the aisle to come to the Senate floor to hear Pat speak," Ted Kennedy once said. "Senators sitting like students in class, trying to understand a complex issue we were struggling with."

The Moynihan Senate campaigns were unique in the annals of American electoral politics. My mother was the campaign manager. I served as a surrogate speaker and fundraiser. The staff and campaign committee comprised a small band of friends—an extended family. The campaigns were great fun. From Derrymore, Dad traveled across New York State, where he learned the history of every town and valley. Traveling from Niagara Falls to Montauk, Dad loved attending local theaters and concerts, wandering through towns and villages in search of imperiled landmarks, dining in a local tavern, and conversing with his constituents. We did not hire expensive consultants. Dad preferred to write his own campaign ads. My parents took pride in being the worst fundraisers in the Senate: winning eight elections (four primaries and four generals) over twenty-four years at a cost of a mere $18 million.

I once asked Dad why he didn't run for president. "Oh my dear, I wouldn't be good at that." Said Mom: "He thought being senator from New York was the best job in the world." I am deeply grateful to the people of New York State for sending my father to the Senate for four terms. It was the happiest time of his life.

In 2001, at the end of his fourth and final term, Dad decided we would have to sell the farm. He joined the Woodrow Wilson Center in Washington and taught at the Maxwell School in Syracuse. But he missed the Senate, and without the schoolhouse he never wrote another book.

In January 2003, Dad's health started to fail. He died in March, ten days after his seventy-sixth birthday. We laughed and wept when Monsignor Vaghi said in his eulogy, "We will all remember Senator Moynihan. How could we ever forget him? On Sundays he would come to service, passing the collection basket among his neighbors. It was hard to believe he really was chairman of the Senate Finance Committee."

I often close my eyes and see Derrymore, our farm—the cows in the pasture, the corn crib by the pond, the hill with the Indian spring. I see my father walking up the road to the schoolhouse, tapping his walking stick, with Mr. Dooley at his heels. I wonder what he is thinking, what troubles him, as he paces round the schoolhouse, pounding his typewriter, searching for answers, trying, always trying, to make the world a better place. He left us his letters, throughout which he shares the story of his ideals, travails, and convictions, and his bonds of friendship and love. I hope these will keep him with us.

After my father's death, I wanted to create a book to chronicle his life and his great and many interests. I went to the Library of Congress to visit his papers, the largest collection the Library has ever received—three times higher than the Washington Monument according to John Haynes, the curator of the Moynihan collection in the manuscript division at the Library. The Moynihan stacks loomed like canyons. The categories were immense: family policy, transportation, architecture, the MX Missile, teaching hospitals, India, Tibet, welfare. I wanted to cry. Where to begin?

In New York I met with my agent, David Kuhn, who suggested an anthology of letters. David brought me to Peter Osnos, Susan Weinberg, and Clive Priddle at PublicAffairs, who labored with energy and dedication to develop the project. We needed someone special to conjure a book from the vast and complex Moynihan archive. It was our great fortune that a beloved friend, Steve Weisman, offered to do it. Steve knew my father, New York, Washington, and India—no one else possessed such singular insights into Pat Moynihan's life and times. Steve guided a brilliant team of researchers from the Maxwell School in Syracuse. For two years they patiently toiled in the stacks of the Library of Congress with the support of John Haynes and his generous staff. This remarkable constellation of individuals gave so much time, talent, and skill to this endeavor to bring this book to life, and to all of them I am profoundly grateful.

ACKNOWLEDGMENTS

FROM MAURA MOYNIHAN

In the years following my father's death, I strove to complete his legacy with two projects, this book and Moynihan Station. So many people gave so much time, advice, and moral support, which I appreciate beyond measure. First and foremost, I thank my guiding star, my mother Liz, and our family—my brothers, Tim and John, my sister-in-law, Tracey, my niece, Zora, and my devoted and wonderful son, Michael Patrick Avedon.

I owe a special debt to Doug Schoen, Dad's student at Harvard, an indispensible member of the Moynihan campaign team and Dad's first biographer. Doug buoyed my spirits and pushed me onward as I searched for a home for this project, then cheered it over the finish line. And I am grateful to Bob Katzmann, another Harvard student who would come every week to Francis Avenue to study with Professor Moynihan in the green library with the old fireplace. Bob edited and updated *Daniel Patrick Moynihan: The Intellectual in Public Life* and advised on this volume. I must also thank Steve Hess and Dick Eaton for the time and effort they gave to reading the manuscript and sharing their meticulous knowledge of Dad's life and work. We miss having the input of Tim Russert, who was a part of Dad's early years in the Senate.

Shelby White has given so much to the Moynihan legacy with unfailing generosity, endowing the Moynihan Chair of Public Policy at Syracuse University, advancing the noble quest to build Moynihan Station, and supporting the exhibition "New York's Moynihan" at the Museum of the City of New York. Susan Jones, the museum's director, created the show with elegance and acuity. And special thanks to Lady Lynn de Rothschild, a volunteer in the 1976 Senate race and a pillar of the many campaigns that followed.

I am grateful to all the generous and steadfast friends who knew Dad; Marty Segal, Steve and Sharyn Mann, Dick Ravitch, Don and Vera Blinken, David and Annie Childs, Tom Smith, Dan and Joanna Rose, Tom and Margot Pritzker, Sara Miller McCune, Peter and Isabel Malkin, Loretta Brennan-Glucksman, Theresa

Heinz, Richard Kurin, Lawrence O'Donnell, George Will, Tony Bullock, Paul Browne, David Luchins, Steve Rickard, Ray Price, John Brademus, Richard Moe, Joel Motley, Mike McCurry, Chris Finn, Patty Clark, Bob Peck, David Podoff, Vicky Bear Dodson, Dan French, Mark Patterson, David McCallum, Gray Maxwell, Matt Lusins, Sylvia and Christopher Addison, Peter Burleigh, Mary Graham, Alex Washburn, Tom Ryan, Barbara Rainville, Lance Morgan, Pete Friscia, Ross Frommer, Dan Crane, Eric Biel, Rob Shapiro, Shelia Dwyer, Joe Gale, Ken Gross, Brian Connolly, Scott MacConomy, Polly Trottenberg, Tom Malinowski, Adam Levine, Tom Melia, Katie Callahan, Jim Kane, Billy Cunningham, and John Zagame.

And special thanks to those I have known and loved since childhood; my cousins Michael, Molly, and Eamon Moynihan, Frank Fenton, Jan and Dante Campaillia, Margaret Bright, Sandy Vanocur, Cynthia Grenier, Nat and Lochi Glazer, Carol and Lee Rainwater, Kit and Joe Reed, Jim and Roberta Wilson, Dan and Pearl Bell, Judy Weinraub, Jeffrey LaRiche, Rajeev Sethi, Bim Bissell, Ruth and Cyrus Jhabvala, Jamie and Peter Galbraith, and forever in memory, Paul Horgan, Charles Blitzer, Ismail Merchant, James Ivory, and Ken and Kitty Galbraith.

Above all, I thank my father for the love, wisdom, and joy he gave to me throughout my life.

FROM STEVEN R. WEISMAN

The one overriding regret I have as editor of this volume is that I was never able to talk about it with the author. But I did have the crucial help of the late Daniel Patrick Moynihan's remarkable wife and political partner, Elizabeth, and their daughter, Maura, who together conceived of this book of Pat's letters, diaries, and memoranda and endeavored to bring it into being after he died in 2003. Maura and Liz believed from the start that these papers would illuminate Pat's life and times—based on the letters they had been familiar with and the fact that Pat put so much time into his correspondence. But neither had ever read anything more than a fraction of the letters, which were scattered through hundreds of boxes at the Library of Congress. The ensuing process of discovery and affirmation that I shared with them was one of the most rewarding aspects of editing this book. I thank Liz and Maura for their vision, thoughtfulness, sense of humor, and confidence in me as editor and treasure-hunter-in-chief on this enterprise, and for their help in understanding the context and history of the letters.

As I described in the introduction, this book came into my life when Peter Osnos of PublicAffairs reached out to me for suggestions on who might be able and willing to edit a volume of Moynihan's letters. His query came at a fortuitous moment of transition in my career, and Peter has continued as the indispensable force for this venture. But many others at PublicAffairs have been superb partners. I am especially grateful to my brilliant editor, Clive Priddle, and to Susan Weinberg, the terrific publisher of PublicAffairs, for their support, advice, encouragement and judgment. Thanks also to Melissa Raymond, Niki Papadopoulos, Lisa Kaufman, Jaime Leifer, Timm Bryson, Shena Redmond, Doug Easton, and K.O. Campbell at PublicAffairs for their help, and to Christine Davis for efficiently accomplishing the enormous task of transcribing the letters into word documents.

Syracuse University was Pat Moynihan's first and last academic home. He joined the faculty after his time in Albany under Governor Averell Harriman in 1959, and again after his retirement from the Senate in 2001. I can well understand his affection for this fine institution, for without the help of the Maxwell School at Syracuse this book would not have happened. Logistically, it was going to take the work of several people to excavate the letters from the Library of Congress's boxes of papers. Mitchel Wallerstein, dean at the Maxwell School, who has since become president of Baruch College at the City University of New York, enthusiastically supported this project by tapping funds at the school and also assisting in the recruitment of students and recent graduates to retrieve the letters and then photograph, organize, and file them. The outstanding team of students was led by Haley Swedlund, a graduate student in international relations, and Justin Deyo, a recent graduate and veteran of the Peace Corps. They have great careers ahead and I have valued their friendship and advice as well as their hard work. I also thank Mia Adamowsky, Chad Brooker, Thibaud Delourme, Rachel Eldridge, Matthew Hagerty, Greg Hershberger, Dayanna Torres, Jichong Wu, and Minyin Yin. Pat Moynihan himself would have been touched and inspired by the way this generation of gifted students, including one from France and two from China, embraced the challenge of learning about the issues and history of his times. In addition, these students helped me navigate the daunting technical difficulties of this project. Several other members of the Syracuse community helped see this undertaking through. I am especially grateful to Michael Schneider, Washington director of the Maxwell School, whose friendship and advice helped solve many a problem. In Syracuse, I appreciated the help of Michael Wasylenko and Mary Pat Cornish for their assistance in organizing the students.

It was a privilege to work as well with the fine staff at the Library of Congress, one of the crown jewels of American government. Connie L. Cartledge had earlier overseen the indexing and organizing of the Moynihan papers, without which it would have been impossible to find the letters. She was an enthusiastic supporter of this project, with nearly encyclopedic knowledge of the papers themselves. I thank her and Patrick Kerwin for their unfailing readiness to answer questions and help the Syracuse students. Karen Stuart provided helpful technical advice, and John E. Haynes, specialist in twentieth-century U.S. history and curator of the Moynihan papers, unraveled the mysteries of the library for me. Readers should know that an enormous amount of work by the dedicated staff at the Manuscript Room in the

Madison Building—too numerous to mention here—contributed to the collection of the Moynihan papers and ultimately to this book. I am also grateful to Timothy Naftali, director of the Richard Nixon Presidential Library and Museum in Yorba Linda, California, and Sahr Conway-Lanz, supervisory archivist of the Nixon Tapes Project at the Nixon Library in College Park, Maryland.

It was my great good fortune to join the Peterson Institute for International Economics as editorial director and public policy fellow in 2008, after many years at the *New York Times*. I am enormously grateful to C. Fred Bergsten, the institute director, for his friendship, support, and enthusiasm as I made my adjustment from journalism to the world of policy institutes. Both Fred and Adam Posen, deputy director of the institute until 2009, have been extraordinary mentors and inspiring leaders in the worldwide debate over global economic issues. Among the colleagues who have shared especially in my off-hour labors on this project, I thank Ted Truman, Morris Goldstein, Arvind Subramanian, Simon Johnson, Howard Rosen, Randy Henning, Anders Aslund, Bill Cline, Mike Mussa, Ed Tureen, Helen Hillebrand, and Jeremey Tripp. I also thank Katherine Stewart, Elizabeth Wilner, Katharine Keenan, Pete Peterson, and David Walker for their friendship.

An enthusiastic group of Moynihan friends encouraged me and served as a collective sounding board. I especially thank U.S. Appeals Court Judge Robert A. Katzmann—who edited the valuable collection of essays, *Daniel Patrick Moynihan: The Intellectual in Public Life*—and Richard K. Eaton, judge of the United States Court of International Trade. Both Bob and Dick generously read the entire manuscript and provided essential information and suggestions. Bob's support and counsel were indispensable to the whole enterprise. I also thank Stephen Hess for his advice on the manuscript and on Moynihan's life generally. Daniel French, in Syracuse, was also a great friend of this book. Among the many whom I consulted on these letters, I especially thank Elliott Abrams, Kevin Cahill, Mark Patterson, Charles Horner, Nathan Glazer, James Q. Wilson, David Childs, George Will (and his assistant Greg Reed), Sidney Blumenthal, Strobe Talbott, Ken Adelman, the late William Safire, Christopher Buckley (for help in interpreting his father's correspondence), and Eric Lax (for his help on Woody Allen). I also thank former Representative Lee H. Hamilton, president of the Woodrow Wilson International Center for Scholars, and Michael Van Dusen, the center's deputy director, for their early support of this effort.

My gratitude to my friend and agent Amanda (Binky) Urban and her colleagues at ICM, especially John Delaney, is tremendous because this turned out to be an unusually complex project to organize. In addition, from the start of this project, a number of close friends have helped with advice or simply by listening to my stories about its ups and downs. Daniel Yergin, always my toughest and most sympathetic editor since our high school days, pushed and prodded me every step and helped make my own writing better. Walter Isaacson, with his matchless understanding of modern political history, was a fabulous source of ideas, analysis, and encouragement. Ellen Chesler and Matt Mallow have been great supporters of all I have tried to do as a writer and editor. At the *New York Times,* I also thank Dean Baquet, Jill Abramson, Bill Keller, Arthur Sulzberger Jr., Maureen Dowd, Steve Labaton, Mark Mazzetti, Linda Greenhouse, David Johnston, Phil Taubman, Helene Cooper, Paula Dwyer, Warren Hoge, and Nick Lewis for their encouragement.

Finally, perhaps like all those who are lucky enough to go down the sometimes lonely road of producing a book, I thank my family for making the path less solitary and for helping me understand what an adventure it was. My children, Madeleine and Teddy, were willing to learn more than they expected about U.S. politics of the second half of the twentieth century and always thought, or seemed to think, that this book was cool to do. My mother only asked me every month or so when it would be done. Above all I am grateful to my wife, Elisabeth Bumiller, for her wisdom, advice, perspective, humor, love, and strength in helping me reinvent myself in 2008 and set out on a new and rewarding path with her at my side.

INDEX

Steven R. Weisman is editorial director and public policy fellow at the Peterson Institute for International Economics, which he joined in 2008 after serving as a correspondent, editor, and editorial writer at the *New York Times* based in New York, Washington, India, and Japan. He won the Edward Weintal Prize from Georgetown University for his diplomatic reporting in 2004. His book *The Great Tax Wars: How the Income Tax Transformed the Nation* received the Sidney Hillman Award in 2003.

PublicAffairs is a publishing house founded in 1997. It is a tribute to the standards, values, and flair of three persons who have served as mentors to countless reporters, writers, editors, and book people of all kinds, including me.

I. F. STONE, proprietor of *I. F. Stone's Weekly*, combined a commitment to the First Amendment with entrepreneurial zeal and reporting skill and became one of the great independent journalists in American history. At the age of eighty, Izzy published *The Trial of Socrates*, which was a national bestseller. He wrote the book after he taught himself ancient Greek.

BENJAMIN C. BRADLEE was for nearly thirty years the charismatic editorial leader of *The Washington Post*. It was Ben who gave the *Post* the range and courage to pursue such historic issues as Watergate. He supported his reporters with a tenacity that made them fearless and it is no accident that so many became authors of influential, best-selling books.

ROBERT L. BERNSTEIN, the chief executive of Random House for more than a quarter century, guided one of the nation's premier publishing houses. Bob was personally responsible for many books of political dissent and argument that challenged tyranny around the globe. He is also the founder and longtime chair of Human Rights Watch, one of the most respected human rights organizations in the world.

·   ·   ·

For fifty years, the banner of Public Affairs Press was carried by its owner Morris B. Schnapper, who published Gandhi, Nasser, Toynbee, Truman, and about 1,500 other authors. In 1983, Schnapper was described by *The Washington Post* as "a redoubtable gadfly." His legacy will endure in the books to come.

Peter Osnos, *Founder and Editor-at-Large*